Penguin Handbooks
The Wines of Bordeaux

D0530447

Edmund Penning-Rowsell was educated at
Marlborough College and in Fleet Street, where he
had his first job on the *Morning Post*. Then, for nearly
thirty years, his career was in book publishing, first
with Frederick Muller, of which he was a director,
then with Batsford, and finally with Edward Hulton/
Studio Vista, which he directed. He first became
interested in wine just before the last war, becoming a
modest customer of a number of wine merchants in
London and Bristol, who helped his vinous education
and enabled him to start a wine cellar; as did the
International Exhibition Co-operative Wine Society,
which he joined in the first months of that war. From
1950 to 1963 he was the first honorary secretary of the
Society's Dining Club, and in 1959 was elected to the
Committee of Management of the parent body. In
1964 he was elected Chairman of the Society. In 1971
he was made a Chevalier de l'Ordre du Mérite Agricole
for his services to French wines, and in 1972 was elected
a member of the Académie du Vin de Bordeaux. He is
the Wine Correspondent of the *Financial Times* and of
Country Life and has contributed articles on wine topics
to many newspapers and periodicals. He has paid
frequent visits to the main European wine districts,
particularly to Bordeaux, which he first visited in 1939.

His other books include *Red, White and Rosé* and
(with Denys Sutton) *The Wine and Art of Mouton-
Rothschild* (1979).

Edmund Penning-Rowsell

The Wines
of Bordeaux

FOURTH EDITION

Penguin Books

To my wife Meg who has shared more bottles
of Bordeaux with me than anyone else

Penguin Books Ltd, Harmondsworth,
Middlesex, England
Penguin Books, 625 Madison Avenue, New York,
New York 10022, U.S.A.
Penguin Books Australia Ltd, Ringwood,
Victoria, Australia
Penguin Books Canada Ltd, 2801 John Street,
Markham, Ontario, Canada L3R 1B4
Penguin Books (N.Z.) Ltd,
182–190 Wairau Road, Auckland 10, New Zealand

First published by
The International Wine and Food Publishing Company 1969
Third, revised, edition published in Penguin Handbooks 1973
Reprinted with further revisions 1976
Fourth edition 1979

Made and printed in Great Britain by
Richard Clay (The Chaucer Press) Ltd,
Bungay, Suffolk
Set in Monotype Bembo

Contents

Foreword

Oddly enough this appears to be the first book written in English to be devoted to a reasonably comprehensive account of the wines of Bordeaux. Odd because by and large there has been a closer wine connection between Bordeaux and Britain over the past six hundred years than between the Gascon city and any other of its foreign customers. Claret, from *clairet*, a clear and light rather than a dark wine, is the English term by which red bordeaux is known throughout much of the world. Of course there have been books on claret, and no lack of English writing on Bordeaux wines; and on these I have gratefully drawn when necessary to provide a rounded account of the wines of a region which in my view produces the finest red wines in the world and at least some of the best whites. This is not to deny the appeal of the rival in Burgundy, particularly the incomparable white wines, or the charm of the Moselles and Rhine wines. But among beverage wines no other region can touch Bordeaux for range of quality, style and price. To paraphrase – and correct – Dr Samuel Johnson, he who aspires to be a serious wine drinker must drink claret.

However, this book does not set out to be a professional bible of Bordeaux. Even were it possible to write a 'complete' book on the subject, I would not be the one to attempt such a task; and the result would be very dull. The pages of the invaluable Cocks et Féret's *Bordeaux et ses vins* are not exactly easy reading. Like most other books on wine this one has been written by an interested amateur for others who care to look beyond the bottle and the label. Inevitably, therefore, errors as well as gaps will be found, and I hope that they may be dealt with charitably. In defence of amateurs it can be said that they may feel more free to state their opinions in print than those professionally engaged in wine.

Moreover exact information is not always easy to secure in Bordeaux. The detailed statistics of vineyard area and output vary, as they may do in any agricultural community made up of a great many comparatively small units. I cannot always vouch for their accuracy any more than I can for the figures of the composition of the vineyards in terms of grape varieties. For the latter I have had to rely upon information given me by proprietors, *régisseurs* and *maîtres de chai*; I sought these facts only when the opportunity presented itself and have included them only where they seem of interest. At least all such statistics should be sound enough to afford bases of comparison.

I have not attempted completeness for another reason. Although my publisher accepted uncomplainingly a manuscript more than twice as long as the length stipulated, basically I have written the book with wine drinkers in Britain and America in mind. While trying to provide a general account of Bordeaux wines, I have given much more attention to the wines of those districts and growths that they are likely to meet than to the lesser communes and minor growths whose wines are less seen outside France. A list of the châteaux producing *appellation contrôlée* wines in the commune of Ste-Foy might be impressive, but it would be of little practical value to those who may read this book.

For similar reasons I have paid much more attention to the red wines than to the white. Although Bordeaux usually produces more white wine than red,★ it is generally of far less interest, with the exception of the fine Sauternes and a handful of Graves.

For wine drinking is a highly personal and subjective matter, and to a great extent this book is founded on personal experience and judgements. I hope that the long chapter on

★ This was true until recently. (E.P.R., 1979)

vintages will prove useful and give readers an opportunity to compare their own views, but it cannot be definitive in so elusive and changing a wine as claret; and that variation is one of the great charms and attractions of Bordeaux.

I have made a point of visiting every one of the Médoc châteaux that were classified in 1855 and which exist today, as well as all the Sauternais estates similarly honoured. I have covered so far as I have been able the leading red wine growths of the Graves, St-Émilion and Pomerol. As others who have spent a day or two *chai*-visiting may agree, this is a formidable task, especially for a non-resident of the region. It is one thing to pass through the almost always open doors of the great châteaux with world-wide reputations and quite another to enter the small back-country farms, where the proprietor is out, and his child-girt wife does not venture to unlock the *chai* and allow one to taste. It took three persistent visits even to penetrate the cellars of one of the smaller *crus classés*.

Also where possible I have made some critical assessment of the châteaux and their various vintages. It has always seemed to me a failing of many books on wine that the authors through kindness, diffidence or unwillingness to risk giving offence, have been insufficiently critical of various estates' wines. Their comments have been diluted (or swee- tened) by unjustified addition of sugariness; and criticism has not gone much beyond such remarks as 'one of the first growths [un-named] has not in recent years been producing wines up to its glorious reputation'. My comments have been based purely on personal experience and are entirely without malice; for all of us surely want every grower to produce wine superlative in its class. So if my comments, commen- datory or otherwise, have obviously been influenced and limited by the extent of my experience, in neither direction have they owed their origin to anything else than my own taste; which may well be different from others', as well as deficient.

I have tried to give some historical perspective to the wines of an area whose vinous history is probably richer than that of any other wine region in the world; as well as having a particular association with the English-speaking world. Indeed there is a wealth of material to be drawn on, except in the case of the individual châteaux where it is often unexpectedly sparse; and I have had to resist the temptation to fill the bottle with too much historical sediment.

Although this is a book written by an amateur, it would be churlish as well as dishonest to deny or depreciate the amount of professional help that I have enjoyed, not merely in the compilation of this book but over long years of wine drinking. There can be no calling more generous with its products, articles of commerce, information and time than the professional wine world. In England my knowledge of Bordeaux and in particular of claret owes much to Mr Ronald Avery of the distinguished Bristol firm and to Mr Harry Waugh, formerly of Harvey's of Bristol in its independent days. Among wine drinkers of my generation both have done a great deal to encourage an appreciation of fine claret. Harry Waugh has also done me the additional service of reading my manuscript.

I owe equal and even more widespread thanks to proprietors and merchants in Bordeaux. First I must acknowledge the help I have had from Christian Cruse, doyen today of those Chartrons merchants who historically have put Bordeaux wines on the world map. M. Cruse's experience, extending over sixty years, and his exceptional memory have been immensely valuable; directly and through his wide contacts he has supplied many items of information and checked various facts. He has also read the manuscript and made many suggestions. With him I must bracket his son Édouard who for many years has been a constant guide on my visits to Bordeaux and the surrounding châteaux, not least in Pomerol and St-Émilion. He also has read much of the manuscript. The special love of him and his father for old claret has opened many rare and interesting bottles for me.

It is also a pleasure to acknowledge in print the help given me by that wine prince among the nobility, Baron Philippe de Rothschild and his wife Pauline, who have made me as welcome in their unequalled wine cellar at Mouton as in their comfortably equipped library, which several times has provided a base for some of my researches and expeditions. To one long associated professionally with books, to be able, as I have at Mouton-Rothschild, to dine and drink exceptional wines amid the unusually designed, book-filled presses of this charming room, has been a special experience.

Another very hospitable host and source of information who has also read part of my manuscript, has been Mr Ronald Barton of Langoa. Not only have I had the benefit of his wine and wine knowledge, but with my family I have more than once camped in his garden, occasions enriched by a steady flow of bottles from the joint private cellar of Langoa and Léoville-Barton.

So many other people in Bordeaux have helped me with information that it is impossible to mention all, but I must single out M. Henri Binaud of Cantemerle; M. Pierre Ginestet of Château Margaux; M. Philippe Cottin of La Bergerie; M. Jacques Théo of Alexis Lichine & Co.; Mr Peter Sichel of Sichel & Co.; M. Henri Woltner of La Mission-Haut-Brion; M. Jean Delmas of Haut-Brion; M. Guy Schÿler of Lafite; M. Fourcaud-Laussac of Cheval-Blanc; M. Roger Danglade of Libourne; M. Gaston Marchou of Bordeaux; M. Yves Fourault of Eschenauer who arranged accommodation at Rausan-Ségla; International Distillers and Vintners, who have afforded me hospitality at Loudenne and access to the Gilbey diaries there; and all those wine merchants in Bordeaux who enabled me to write the chapter on The Wine Merchants of Bordeaux. I must also acknowledge the help of the *Conseil Interprofessionnel du Vin de Bordeaux* in Bordeaux and the *Institut National des Appellations d'Origine des Vins et Eaux-de-Vie* in Paris.

In Britain I have had assistance on points of detail from a number of people including one or two already mentioned. I must also express my thanks to Mr Cyril Ray for allowing me to read the manuscript of his *Lafite* in advance of publication, and to Mrs Pamela Vandyke Price, whose reading of the completed manuscript for the publishers was also of considerable help to me; also to Mr Norman Alexander who read the proofs with concentration suitable to the subject, and to the staff of Rainbird Reference Books Ltd for their punctilious attention to detail. I am also grateful to Christie's and to Mr Michael Broadbent of their wine department, in particular, for access to their catalogue archives. Finally I must thank my wife for compiling the extensive index.

Wootton   Edmund Penning-Rowsell
Woodstock   July 1969
Oxford

Preface to the Fourth Edition

A change of publisher for the hardback edition, out of print for some time, and a resetting of the text for that and for the third printing of the paperback edition has provided a much-needed opportunity to extend, revise and bring up-to-date what in essence was written ten years ago. For, as I wrote in the first Penguin edition, like its wine, Bordeaux changes and develops. Indeed that is why it is the most fascinating and stimulating fine wine region in the world.

Before embarking on perusal – perhaps even further perusal – of a work even longer now than it was originally, readers are entitled to ask what is new. The answer is that additions and changes have been made to every chapter, minimally in those devoted to the minor areas and the sweet wine districts, where there is little to add or to amend, but considerably in some of the rest. For the additions to the history of the Bordeaux estates and trade I am greatly indebted to *La Seigneurie et le vignoble de Château Latour* (1974), based on the extraordinary discovery of the estate's documents shortly after its acquisition by the family interests of Viscount Cowdray. Edited by Professor Charles Higounet of the University of Bordeaux and contributed to by other members of the university, the two volumes, running to about half-a-million words, are treasure-trove for all interested not only in the history of Latour itself but in that of the Médoc and of the Bordeaux wine world in general. For the history one must be particularly beholden to the contributions by M. René Pijassou, to whose yet unpublished *Lafite: trois siècles d'histoire viticole* (part of his work on the Médoc) I also had access, thanks to him and to Baron Éric de Rothschild, who supplied me with a copy. These works have helped to fill out the story of the Bordeaux wine world.

Then for the contemporary period, I have taken account of the changes in the estates, alterations in their *cépages* and, often, increases in their production. Changing events in Bordeaux have also been recorded, including the extraordinary boom-and-bust period in the present decade and its consequences. As far as possible I have added to and up-dated the long chapter on the vintages, and this applies also to the appendixes, particularly those giving opening prices.

Revising a book, basically written a decade ago, on Bordeaux and its wines presents certain difficulties. First, the personalities change as well as the wines. Some of those whose help I acknowledged in my original foreword are no longer with us, properties and firms have changed hands and all the individual wines mentioned then or in more recent editions are that much older, more mature or perhaps now past their best. One's appreciation of certain wines and vintages may have changed too. How much should one alter?

Faute de mieux, what set out, as far as the wines themselves were concerned, to be largely a personal record has been taken to a great extent as a work of reference. Accordingly, to those who use it as such one has some responsibility, so I have tried to increase the amount of information and the degree of accuracy. Yet this does not set out to be an encyclopaedia or a drinker's guide and must retain its individual approach and preferences; as indeed almost everything connected with wine, and particularly fine wine, must. So if occasionally a 'period' flavour emerges, part of the blame must lie with wines that do change and do not last for ever. Yet I believe that many people who may never have a chance to drink the great 1920s, 1929s – certainly not at their best – or even the finer 1945s will be interested to read about them. For I was fortunate to be able to drink fine claret, and to a lesser extent, fine white Bordeaux, whose original ex-château prices had been far less fortunate for their producers. Many of such wines now have a world-wide demand and are subject to investment and speculation by those who will never see a bottle, let alone draw a cork. The problems of expensive finance make it impossible for wine merchants to hold stock for as long as they used to. So it is more difficult for newly fledged *amateurs* of the wines of Bordeaux; and the best advice is to buy early and keep.

Finally, as wine drinking is to some extent subjective in the expression of preferences, the opinions of readers may differ widely from mine. Some vintages and wines they may like better than I appear to have done; in other cases it may be the other way round, and they have been disappointed in certain wines. To the first group I can only reiterate *de gustibus* . . . To the latter I must say, as I ended the preface to the last edition, it was all right on the night.

March 1979

1. The Setting and the Wine

Bordeaux, set upon the last great curve of the Garonne before that broad river joins the Dordogne at Bec d'Ambès and both become the Gironde, is one of the most agreeable cities of France. Although its cathedral and churches are medieval, the chief imprint from the past is of the eighteenth century: Victor Louis's splendid colonnaded Grand Théâtre (1773–80); the Allées de Tourny, named after the intendant who helped to plan the heart of the city but failed to restrict the growing Bordeaux *vignoble*; the Jardin Public; and the merchants' tall houses on the Chartrons and the Cours Xavier Arnozan, formerly known as the Pavé des Chartrons. Thrust among them is the Place des Quinconces with its columns to the reforming, rejected Girondins. Even after 150 years the huge square still seems not quite at ease among its elders; a little *arriviste*. Wine, at least in the historic areas, seems to exert a conservative influence, and although Bordeaux has had its moments of revolt and counter-revolt, this is a conservative, bourgeois city, albeit, except in the centre, well blended with those whose political views are scarcely less red than the wines they naturally prefer.

The wine on which the city still principally lives is largely produced some way away, and much comes from flat and, except to *amateurs* of level country, rather dull surroundings. Broadly speaking the better the wine, the duller the Bordeaux countryside. The most attractive country is certainly that known under its modest wine classification as the Premières Côtes. This lies upstream from the city, opposite the white wine areas of Graves, Cérons and Sauternes, and edging the Entre-Deux-Mers. It is charming, hilly country, with hedges, small fields and curving roads, together giving an impression of England, perhaps of Devon. From its crests overlooking the Garonne, there are delightful views of the river, of the vineyards opposite and the dark shadow of the Landes on the horizon. Yet the wine is not very distinguished.

Just inland from the Premières Côtes, on the south-east of the department of the Gironde, which includes all the Bordeaux vineyards, is the white wine country of the Entre-Deux-Mers where the vine shares the fields with other crops. The country looks rich and contains some splendid châteaux and *manoirs*. On the northern edge it adjoins and almost surrounds the small Graves de Vayres district, through which runs the main road from Bordeaux to Libourne. This is not, as many people believe, a source of Graves wine, but takes its name from the gravelly soil.

North and east of the sprawling Entre-Deux-Mers – it runs far enough north to be traversed by the main Bordeaux–Paris road (*RN.10*) – there is across the Dordogne some agreeable country, particularly in and around St-Émilion, which describes itself as 'the pearl of the Gironde'. With few rivals in the region, it may fairly claim this title. Along by the Dordogne the land is flat and marshy – the *palus* – but rises with the valley sides to the town of St-Émilion and to the plateau which lies beyond, merging into Pomerol to the west and north-west, Montagne to the north, and on the other sides with the other outlying St-Émilion communes, mostly sanctified in name if not specially blessed in the quality of their wines. Montagne is a relative term of description but it is lofty for Bordeaux. Whereas the average height above sea level in the Médoc is a mere fifty-five feet, in St-Émilion it is around 230 feet, and about the same in the Entre-Deux-Mers.

Fronsac, downstream from Libourne, the port of St-Émilion and Pomerol and the centre of that part of the Bordeaux wine trade, is in part hillier still. The prominent Tertre de Fronsac is the high point of the Côtes de Fronsac, with a splendid view from the summit. Towards the sea and beside the Dordogne and nearing the Gironde there runs the gently rolling country of Fronsac, with plenty of trees in the valleys and a general air of modest agricultural prosperity. Both Bourg and Blaye afford excellent views of river and estuary, and both towns have the air as if history, of which they had their fair share in the past, has now passed them by. The rolling country behind them is an agreeable contrast to the flat, persistent Médoc opposite, and many Médocain château families in summer cross by the ferry from Lamarque to Blaye to picnic in the arcadian valleys of the twin districts. The soil is clearly much richer and heavier on this side of the river than on the left bank, and this alone accounts for the fuller, less elegant wines, which can rise to near-Burgundian richness in Pomerol and St-Émilion.

As the mean altitude demonstrates, the Haut-Médoc is by no means high. It is, of course, flattest near the river, and it rises slightly to the 'back' villages like St-Laurent, Listrac and Moulis. It undulates slightly by St-Estèphe, descends appropriately into the Bas-Médoc, as it used officially to be called, and the country then becomes Lincolnshire-like in its near-flatness, dykes and the feeling of being far away from the busy world. Indeed Lesparre, the main centre, is forty miles from Bordeaux, while St-Vivien, on the edge of the vineyard area and not far from the Pointe de Grave and the Atlantic, is over fifty miles away from the Girondin capital; as far as Oxford is from London. The Bas-Médoc has the slightly sad, forgotten air of a district that has seen better days; and so it has.

The Graves area, which strictly speaking includes the city of Bordeaux, is either flat and suburban or flat and forested. The soil, as the name implies, is gravelly and the sandy Landes encroach on it. The vineyards of the more remote parts look as if they have been carved out of the tree-belts. The sweeter white wine areas further up the Garonne have similar soil, but in the vineyard area there the country is generally less tree-enclosed.

So much, very briefly, for the lie of the Bordeaux vineyard land. The latitude of Bordeaux is 44·5° north, and the 45th parallel runs almost directly through Margaux.

GRAPE VARIETIES

Now must be mentioned the kinds of grapes which grow on it, producing wines of great but often subtle variety in the biggest fine wine area in France, and indeed in the world. Two to three thousand vines in full production are needed to produce one *tonneau* of wine; more in the leading vineyards.

No grape names are on record in Bordeaux until the sixteenth century when *La Bidure* was named as the common plant. Curiously enough the *cépage* of even the first-growth estates in the Médoc remains unclear until the nineteenth century. Certainly the Carmenère was an early variety, and this was likely to have been similar to the Cabernet-Sauvignon; but apparently neither was planted in the Médoc until the second quarter of the last century. Under the name of Carmenère it has almost if not entirely died out, for although it produced good wine it was difficult to grow and flourished only in a successful season. The Merlot too only arrived in the Médoc in the last century. No doubt in the early days there was a *mélange* of various varieties, only some of which would now be described as 'noble'. The *encépagement* in the more prominent estates then probably largely consisted of Malbec, Petit- and Grand-Verdot and what is now called Cabernet-Franc. Armailhacq in his authoritative *De la culture des vignes, la vinification et les vins dans le Médoc* (1855) stated that the main Médoc varieties were Gros Cabernet (or Carmenat), Cabernet-Sauvignon, Cabarnelle (or Carmenère), Merlau (*sic*), Malbec and Verdot. The Gros Cabernet was the same as Cabernet-Franc and was the most vigorous of all the varieties planted in the district. It had the most body and the wine lasted a very long time, but required three to four years in cask and at least two in bottle. It would improve in bouquet and delicacy for up to twelve or fifteen years and keep without losing its quality for twenty, but then became a little dry, losing some of its roundness though not breaking up. 'The most renowned *crus*', he wrote, 'are largely composed of this variety.' On the other hand the Cabernet-Sauvignon was the most esteemed and was greatly on the increase in recent years, particularly in Pauillac and St-Julien, 'where it is almost exclusively culti-vated', with a great proportion in the vineyards of Lafite, Mouton, Latour, Léoville and Pichon-Longueville. It was a little less vigorous than the Gros Cabernet, and perhaps the wine kept even longer but needed an extra year in cask. It was said not to do well in Margaux and Cantenac, where the soil is less productive. This is certainly true today as the *cépages* of each estate show. The Carmenère, said Armailhacq, gave roundness to the wine, but this does not indicate any associa-tion with the Cabernet-Sauvignon, as others have suggested. He confirmed the recent arrival of the Merlot in the Médoc; it could be bottled in the third year and one year in bottle would suffice, for the wine lacked body and did not last. The Malbec, a member of the Cot family of grapes but called Malbec in the Médoc as it had been introduced by a grower of that name, was only grown because it was very prolific, but was rejected by all concerned for quality. There was little in Margaux and Cantenac. The Verdot was a common grape of the *palus* adjoining the river. It was not long introduced to the Médoc and was planted more in Margaux and Cantenac than in Pauillac. Although it could produce a rather green wine, all the leading *vignobles* had it, as it gave fullness, round-ness and vinosity and blended excellently with Cabernet. As will be seen it is little planted today.

To complete the historical picture, of 1855, the Latour vine-yard was composed of 56·8 per cent Cabernet-Sauvignon, 22·7 per cent Cabernet-Sauvignon and Cabernet-Franc mixed,

13·9 per cent Malbec, 5 per cent Merlot, a tiny amount of Verdot and a relic of Syrah.

Today the leading red wine grape variety of Bordeaux is the Cabernet-Sauvignon: the grape on which claret's reputation is founded. In the Graves it is sometimes called the *Vidure*, which in patois can easily be rendered as *Bidure*, and this is claimed to be the same as the Latin *Biturica*, named by Pliny; but this is speculation only. It is the Cabernet-Sauvignon which produces much of the deep colour, the 'bloom' of the aroma, the finesse and the 'cut' in the flavour of a fine Médoc; the 'backbone' of an elegant claret. Its influence can be best noted in the fairly young wine of growths like Latour and Mouton-Rothschild. In the vineyards of both these leading Pauillacs at least 80 per cent of the grapes are Cabernet-Sauvignon. Like the leading grape of Germany, the Riesling, it flourishes in not too easy conditions, and is more resistant to rot than Bordeaux's second grape, the Merlot. It normally ripens later than the latter, and in the vineyard is picked afterwards.

The Cabernet-Franc variety is usually to be found in most Médoc vineyards, and is counted in as part of the Cabernet proportion of the *cépage*. It is however more disease-subject, irregular and produces a less coloured, less distinguished wine with rather less body. Some say it is half-way towards the Merlot but that is an exaggeration. Across the river in St-Émilion there is the Bouchet, a variety of Cabernet identical with the Cabernet-Franc.

The Merlot, the second most important red wine grape of Bordeaux, is particularly associated with St-Émilion and Pomerol. In the Médoc it was only known after the end of the eighteenth century. It produces much softer wines than the Cabernet-Sauvignon, as can be seen *par excellence* in Pétrus, where the Merlot is dominant in the vineyard (95 per cent); although of course the relatively rich soil of Pomerol is another factor in the flavour. The Merlot is also fairly prominent at Lafite and Palmer and contributes to the delicacy of these wines. It has the advantage of being productive, but, with a tendency to bud early, it is subject to spring frosts, which the Cabernets may escape. In 1970 the Merlot was particularly successful and prolific; and attractive, forward wines resulted. In 1971 the Merlot largely failed, and the wines turned out harder. In a poor season it is liable to rot. A vineyard with a heavy proportion of Merlot may suffer particularly badly from wet weather at vintage-time. The wine from the Merlot matures more rapidly, and in these commercial times this is a temptation to the growers. Unkind proprietors in the Médoc may whisper, with a pleasurable shake of the head, that their neighbours have unfortunately planted too high a proportion of Merlot; almost as bad as if the neighbours' daughters had taken to the streets! In St-Émilion Merlot is more acceptable, but then no Médocain will admit these wines to equality with a Médoc.

The other well-known red wine grape is the Malbec. It produces a big quantity of fairly large grapes, matures early, and the wine is inclined to be soft like the Merlot. It is, however, subject to the disease of *coulure*, when the flowers fall off without forming grapes. The least used of the four main varieties, it probably does not represent more than 10 per cent of a vineyard, and less in the fine growths. In St-Émilion it is called the Pressac. Generally it is in decline in the Gironde.

There are two other red wine grapes worth mentioning. One is the Verdot, of which there are two sub-varieties, the Gros and the Petit. The former makes rather ordinary red wine and is grown in the riverside *palus*. The Petit-Verdot, a late ripener, may be found in more distinguished surroundings, for it can give body to a wine. On one occasion Ronald Barton opened for me at Langoa two bottles of his Léoville–Barton of that light and not very renowned year, 1938. One was made from the normal blend of grapes: it was drinkable but rather faded. The second had been made exclusively from Petit-

Verdot; this had much more fruit and flavour than the first. However, it is only grown marginally, being subject to *coulure* and to rot in a late harvest.

A typical fine Médoc vineyard may be planted with 55 per cent Cabernet-Sauvignon, 20 per cent Cabernet-Franc, 20 per cent Merlot and 5 per cent Malbec; whereas a common 'blend' in St-Émilion might be 60 per cent Merlot, 30 per cent Bouchet and 10 per cent Pressac (Malbec). More exact proportions will be found in the chapters devoted to the various districts.

It will be appreciated that the secret of success in planting a vineyard is to secure a balance of the most appropriate and successful varieties for the situation and soil. In the leading vineyards of the Médoc too high a proportion of Cabernet-Sauvignon may mean a small crop and a big, slow-maturing wine. One of the reasons given for the traditional backwardness of Latour is said to be the high proportion of Cabernet-Sauvignon. Another reason is that until recent years the Cabernet was picked fairly early there, resulting in rather a hard wine. Yet Mouton-Rothschild claims an even higher proportion of Cabernet-Sauvignon and the wines are usually more forward. Here the soil is playing its decisive role. Too much Merlot or Malbec will mean a large production of rather soft-centred wines. At Haut-Brion their proportion is 55 per cent Cabernet-Sauvignon, 22 per cent Cabernet-Franc and 23 per cent Merlot. The lower proportion of Cabernet-Sauvignon compared with the two Pauillac leaders may be one reason for the rather soft texture of many Haut-Brions; but there is the Graves soil to be considered too.

Certain soils and situations may demand a different amalgam of varieties. In the statistical survey of the Gironde published in 1874 by Féret and quoted by Germain Lafforgue in *Le Vignoble Girondin* (1947), the commune of Pauillac was shown as being planted with 75 per cent Cabernet and 25 per cent Merlot and Malbec, whereas in Pessac in the Graves it was 50 per cent Cabernet and 50 per cent Merlot and Malbec; and in St-Émilion, Pomerol and Fronsac, it was one-third of each of these three grapes. As today, the further away from the Médoc, the more the productive Merlot and Malbec were grown.

To alter the balance of a vineyard is a long-term matter. To root up productive vines at the height of their quality – perhaps from ten to twenty-five years old – is uneconomic, as they have to be replaced by vines that will not be productive for three years and not fully extended for several more. Unless a vineyard can be territorially increased, it takes time to plant enough vines of another type to make a difference to the final blend of the wine. Too great a proportion of young vines of any variety will result in a green, stalky wine. This was the case, it seemed to me, with La Lagune, whose vineyard had been allowed to run down. In 1957 and the following years almost the whole of it had to be replanted. Not only must a balance of suitable varieties be maintained, but also a fair proportion of old and new vines.

In the white wine areas there are only two important grapes: the Sauvignon and the Sémillon. The former, also known as the Petit-Sauvignon, produces a big quantity of fruit, but not so much as the Sémillon, less subject to disease. The Sauvignon produces the finer quality wine but its flavour is too pronounced unless blended with a good proportion of Sémillon. On the other hand the latter is particularly prone to the *pourriture noble*, essential for fine Sauternes; quantitatively the Sémillon predominates.

Another white wine grape is the Muscadelle. This is never used on its own, for – like all Muscat-style grapes – it has too penetrating an aroma and flavour, but makes a valuable contribution as a small proportion of the blend in the sweeter wine areas; but not in such outstanding estates as Yquem.

There are other white wine grapes grown for wine in the Gironde, and as one goes further from the leading areas, so their use, although controlled, is less discriminate. They include varieties such as the Merlot-Blanc, the Folle-Blanche (best known in the Charente) and the Colombar. They are to be found in Blaye and in the lesser areas whose *appellation contrôlée* is only Bordeaux. In the sweet white wine districts the Ugni-Blanc is grown, and the Riesling can occasionally be met in the Graves. Occasionally, too, minor vines appear.

DISEASES AND PESTS OF THE VINE

While discussing the grape varieties it is appropriate to mention the diseases and pests to which now they are or in the past have been subject. The most famous, the oidium and the phylloxera, are frequently mentioned later, so it is as well to deal with them right away.

The three most serious attacks of disease and parasites suffered in the Gironde area followed in historical sequence; so it is easiest to describe them thus.

The first was the oidium. This is a small mushroom growth which attacks young wood, young leaves and young grapes. Small, whitish spots are formed and soon cover the whole branch, leaf or berry. The leaves curl up and drop off; the grapes darken in colour, split and dry up. It was first discovered in England in 1845 on some plants imported from the tropics in a greenhouse in Margate, by a gardener named Tucker and a naturalist called Berkeley. As a result it was named *Oidium tuckerii*. It then spread to Belgium and in France it was noticed in 1848, ironically enough in Baron James de Rothschild's greenhouse at Suresnes, near Paris. It was first observed in the Gironde in September 1851, first at Podensac in the Bas-Médoc and shortly afterwards at Preignac in Sauternes, but it really struck the Bordeaux vineyards in 1852–3. Initially it was most prevalent in the white wine areas of the left bank of the Garonne and spread rapidly through the Graves, attacking particularly the best grape varieties which were apparently less resistant. The leading white Sauternes were especially badly hit as the drop in production at Yquem showed. In the fine vintage of 1847 it had made 140 *tonneaux*; in 1853 only 18 were produced. By the following year production generally was down to only a quarter of the previous year. The three *premiers crus* of the Médoc produced only 52 *tonneaux* in the good vintage of 1854, compared with 254 two years earlier. Between 1854 and 1856 all the Médocain *crus classés* made only 3,400 *tonneaux*, estimated at not much more than half the crop of a single prolific year.

As usual in such crises many remedies were proposed. Some favoured using more manure, while others thought it was just a matter of the weather conditions; for a damp, humid climate seemed to encourage the mushroom. Although the disease was quickly and successfully treated by some growers by an application of sulphur, others were sceptical. For in some cases the wine stank of sulphur and in others it seemed to make the wine flat (as excessive sulphur undoubtedly does). Guestier refused to buy the 1855 wine of the Comte Duchâtel at Lagrange, one of the most enthusiastic pro-sulphurers. Perhaps initially the sulphuring was done inefficiently, but this bogy soon disappeared, and henceforth the estates did not wait until the oidium appeared but sprayed preventively in advance. Not all the estate owners, however, were anxious to adopt this sulphuring and at both Latour and Lafite it was done on a very experimental basis until about 1861.

Nevertheless, by 1858 the position was restored and there was a very large crop, with the *premiers crus* producing 333 *tonneaux* between them. One lasting effect of the oidium was a steep rise in prices; and they never went back to their previous levels. In 1854 Latour managed to sell its meagre crop to Barton & Guestier for the record price of 5,000 frs. a *tonneau*; Lafite and Mouton-Rothschild were sold at the same price and Margaux at 5,500 frs. a year later. The seconds rose to 4,000 frs., the thirds to 3,000 frs., though Palmer achieved

4,000 frs. from Johnston. Lafite secured 4,000 frs. for the ordinary 1857. The end of the oidium period marked for growers and merchants the beginning of the era of great prosperity which closed with the onslaught of Bordeaux's second and most serious enemy – the phylloxera louse.

The phylloxera is an aphid, about one millimetre in size and stout in shape. It feeds on the sap of plants, from the leaves down to the roots. No fewer than twelve generations can be produced in one year. Native to the eastern part of the U.S.A., where apparently it lives chiefly on the leaves, forming galls, in Europe the creature is more addicted to the roots, producing nodules on the young roots which eventually die. The insects then come to the surface in search of nourishment and proceed to spread the disease further.

An English greenhouse was again the setting for the first discovery in Europe of this largely subterranean invader. It was found in a Hammersmith greenhouse in 1863 and studied at Oxford by Professor I. O. Westwood, who did not name it as he could find no males; at one stage it is parthenogenetic. Later it was suitably named *Phylloxera vastatrix*. About the same time it was discovered on the Rhône in three communes near Avignon, including Villeneuve-les-Avignon. It spread very rapidly in the Midi, particularly after 1869. It is said that the disturbance caused by the Franco-Prussian War in 1870–71 was partly responsible for neglect in dealing with this invader, which in the end cost France more than the Prussian one. A contemporary estimate was £400 million.

In the Gironde it was first observed in 1866 and 1867 in the *palus* at Floirac a few miles across the river from Bordeaux. Initially the advance was slow but it began to spread into the Entre-Deux-Mers, and then along the right bank of the Dordogne, attacking Blaye, Libourne and St-Émilion. The Médoc was not seriously affected until after 1878, and there were those who claimed that this mysterious disease was an effect rather than a cause. Some thought it was a malady of the vine owing to impoverishment of the soil and lack of fertilizer in the outlying areas. Others, led by M. Laliman, a grower, as early as 1869 believed that replanting with resistant vines was the only cure.

By the end of the 1870s between a half and a third of the vineyards of St-Émilion and Fronsac had been devastated. A visitor at this time to Ch. des Tours, a large property in Montagne-St-Émilion, referred to the debilitated branches almost bare of leaves, and even those were yellow and impoverished. The grapes were scanty and dried up. The proprietor pulled at a forty-year-old vine and it came out of the ground without any resistance; the roots were mutilated and reduced to a spongy state. The Gironde area was one of the worst hit in France, and by 1882 no less than 138,000 hectares out of 141,420 were affected.

It will be understood that Laliman's radical solution first to plant resistant vines and then, in 1871, to graft French vines on resistant American stock, was far from popular. It was well known that the American vines produced a foxy-tasting wine (*un goût de renard*), and who was to know whether the splendid, unique flavour of the Bordeaux wines would be lost for ever? In 1874 M. Théophile Malvezin, a distinguished historian of Bordeaux, published a 56-page pamphlet in the form of a letter to the Bordeaux Chamber of Commerce, in which he suggested alternatives to replanting.

One suggestion made was that *la chasse* should be prohibited in all the viticultural departments of France (nearly all then), except for shooting, as it was thought that the snaring of small birds, who ate the insects, was a cause. Secondly flooding the vineyards, as had been practised successfully in Vaucluse, was advocated, but this was scarcely practicable in most other vineyard areas. All sorts of insecticides were advised and tried, from coal tar and phenolic acid to ammonia, sulphuric acid, carbon-bisulphide and potassium sulpho-carbonate. The last two were probably most extensively used, but they were very expensive to apply over wide areas. In 1883 at Loudenne, which had been bought only eight years previously by the Gilbeys, no less than £600 was spent on treating the vines.

The diaries of the visits of the Gilbeys still preserved at Loudenne give a picture of the long and uncertain struggle against the phylloxera, which in the Gironde alone did not, as is sometimes imagined, cease abruptly, in the same way as the oidium was conquered. It was 1879 when the Gilbeys first noted the presence of the phylloxera in the Médoc, although it was already established in the adjoining Charente. By 1882 potassium sulpho-carbonate was being used in their vineyard, and there was a reference to American vines being planted. 'This method will probably be adopted.' But in 1886 over £300 was spent on the chemical treatment which was thought to fumigate the soil, and up to £700 in later years. The problem was, of course, to avoid killing the vines as well as the attacker. This treatment was certainly temporarily success-ful, so was carbon-bisulphide as used at the Ch. des Tours.

The Bas-Médoc was thought to be more vulnerable than the Haut-Médoc, as the standard of cultivation was lower in the former. In the 1892 diary there is a reference to the planting of American stocks, but even in 1894 some French ungrafted Cabernet-Sauvignon vines were being planted, although a further note that year states that they were satisfied that American stocks were essential, as the phylloxera was still present in the Loudenne vineyard. Gilbeys were probably not backward in coming to this decision, but in the Loudenne diary for 1889 there is a reference to the fact that chemical treatment was still being used at Pontet-Canet.

Even as late as 1890 nearly half the Gironde *vignoble* was still planted or replanted with old French vines, mostly in the Médoc, Graves and Sauternes, where the sandy soil was less favourable to the phylloxera louse. In the 1893 edition of Cocks et Féret's *St-Émilion*, it is stated that nearly all the vines there were French vines. Moreover mass replanting was extremely expensive. In 1895 the Gilbeys reckoned that to replant 12 acres would cost £720, a figure which probably has to be multiplied more than ten times to correspond with present-day values. As late as 1898, treatment was necessary in that part of the vineyard not yet replanted.

The disaster was increased by the appearance of Bordeaux's third plague – the mildew. This was first reported widely in 1883 in the south-west of France. Mildew affects the leaves only, leaving white spots on the under side and yellowy-brown patches on the top. This occurs at the flowering. The result is an imbalance in the plant reflected in the wine itself. The means of combating this was discovered as quickly as the cure for the oidium; it was the spraying with copper sulphate – *bouillie bordelaise,* or Bordeaux mixture – which also destroys other vine diseases and parasites. As a result recovery began in 1887 and was complete by 1888.

There was some controversy as to who deserved the credit for the treatment. Apparently it was customary for the Médoc proprietors to have the lines of their vines nearest the roads or paths sprayed with copper sulphate to discourage amateur grape pickers. It seems certain that M. David, the *régisseur* (manager) of the two properties of Nathaniel Johnston, Ducru-Beaucaillou and Dauzac, had a hand in this, but the scientific basis for the counter-measures in the mid-1880s was certainly laid by M. Millardet, Professor of Botany at Bordeaux University.

In a way mildew had a more immediately disastrous effect than the phylloxera, for the latter affected quantity rather than quality whereas the former spoiled the wines. Otherwise, for example, it seems almost certain that 1884 would have been a fine vintage. Consequently Ch. Margaux '84 sold for 5,000 frs. a *tonneau,* of four *barriques* of 225 litres each, as it had not been touched by the disease, whereas Lafite which suffered badly was only able to secure the derisory price of 1,400 frs. a *tonneau,* or £15 a *barrique.* The wine was so poor that it was rejected by the Bordeaux trade. By 1887 Lafite was recovering and produced 120 *tonneaux*, and in the following year 300 *tonneaux*, including its subsidiary vineyard on the Carruades plateau.

Spraying against mildew was henceforth the most expensive vineyard operation of the year though for a long period it was insufficiently effective owing to lack of knowledge and equipment. One of the most disastrous mildew years was 1910 (another was 1915), when Latour did not offer any *grand vin* and some other classed growths almost went out of cultivation. In those days it was customary to go through the vineyards with copper sulphate only three or four times a year, and often too late. Now eight to ten times is more common, but in a very wet summer like 1977 leading châteaux will almost double this number of treatments, made easier and quicker by modern equipment.

One result of the combined phylloxera–mildew period was that a few vineyards at the lower end of the Bordeaux social scale went out of production; but an equally contributory factor to this was the slump in France during the 1880s. The Gilbeys in their 1884 diary wrote: 'The complete stagnation on the Bordeaux market had compelled proprietors to submit to prices that had not been known for *very* many years.'

Contrary to common belief, however, while output fell in the Gironde as a result of phylloxera and mildew, the acreage under vines did not substantially decline. In 1875 the total was a record 145,000 hectares, and 144,000 in 1889. In the succeeding period up to the First World War it varied between 129,000 and 142,000 hectares, and in 1911 was 136,000. This was owing to poor economic conditions rather than to the effects of disease. Indeed, surprisingly enough the Médocain *vignoble*, increased by planting in the *palus* in the Gironde estuary, was about 50 per cent larger when mapped in 1913 than in the middle of the nineteenth century: almost 24,000 hectares compared with 16,000 to 17,000. It was never to be so extensive again until our days. Nevertheless during the 1880s property values dropped sharply and the Gilbeys mention in 1886 one property in the Bas-Médoc valued at 200,000 frs. in 1878 and now worth below 150,000 frs.

For later generations of wine drinkers the big question about the phylloxera and the consequent grafting of French vines of the variety *Vitis vinifera* on to American stocks of *Vitis riparia* and *Vitis rupestris*, is whether the wines are so fine as they were. Wine drinking is to some extent an occupation which involves looking over one's shoulder and nostalgia deepens as the second and third bottles are reached. It was therefore natural for a certain generation of wine drinkers to believe that wines 'would never be so good again'; not altogether discomforting either, as these gentlemen often had enough of the pre-phylloxera wines below stairs to see them out!

But I see no reason to believe the wines less good since the 1880s. I believe that the great pair of 1899 and 1900 proved the pessimism unfounded, although one should be wary of deducing too much from the success of the last two vintages of the nineteenth century as it is not clear how many of the vineyards had by then been replanted with grafted stocks. It is sometimes imagined that, once it was obvious that this was the only sure way of securing immunity from the phylloxera, immediate replanting took place throughout the Gironde and elsewhere. As the Gilbey diaries show, this was not the case, for the very good reasons that it was a very expensive business and total replanting would have bankrupted the growers, left without visible means of income for several years. Moreover suspicion still continued as to the effects of the newly grafted wines on quality. As late as 1907 a five-year contract signed by Latour for exclusive supply to five Chartrons merchants had a marginal note excluding wines made from *les cépages américains*. Ten years later this prohibition had disappeared. However, even the first growths were cautious about replanting. Latour, for example, did not begin seriously until 1901 and it took twenty years entirely to replace the old *vignes françaises*. The first completely 'post-phylloxera vintage' was 1918.

It was pointed out by René Pijassou in *Latour* that the effects of the phylloxera became a sort of legend, wrongly attributing to the devastating insect a decline in the productivity, quality and reputation of Bordeaux wines. In fact the methods used to combat the disease increased the quantity of many leading wines, and the decline in quality and reputation was owing less to phylloxera than to mildew, fraudulent blending with inferior wines from the Midi and Algeria, the economic crisis and a number of poor vintages.

On the other hand the extraordinary longevity of the great pre-phylloxera clarets does suggest that perhaps the wines do not last as long now as they did; and this without taking into consideration contemporary methods of vinification developed since the last war to make the wines ready to drink earlier. There has not been yet sufficient time to judge the results of this, but it might be that they have had a more decisive effect on the life-span of claret than the adoption of American stocks.

It is also possible that the vines do not last so long; yet earlier uprooting may be owing to the need for higher yields; as the vines age, so their crop falls. It is said too that the grafted vines yield more grapes and have to be pruned more severely to maintain quality.

Here it should be pointed out that these three major plagues have been contained but not cured. To replant non-resistant French vines would be an invitation to the lurking phylloxera, and only the repeated applications of sulphur and copper sulphate keep at bay oidium, or powdery mildew, and the downy mildew or peronospora.

There are, of course, other diseases with which the Gironde growers have to contend. There is *millerandage*, which results in a proliferation of small grapes that fall off and never swell.

There is black rot, which attacked the French vineyards towards the end of the last century and had a disastrous effect on the 1897 vintage, but has not otherwise been a great problem in the Gironde. Allied to *millerandage* is *coulure*, which is the dropping of the flowers or of the newly produced berries, owing to bad weather at the time of the flowering. This occurs to some extent nearly every year. The rot which affects the grapes in wet years is *pourriture grise*. In more favourable years this rot results in *pourriture noble*, noble rot.

There are a number of somewhat specialized diseases which modern methods of treatment have rendered no great risk. These include anthracnose, which forms stains on leaves, grapes and young shoots; cochylis, which produces grubs feeding on grapes, and which was a danger soon after the phylloxera; altise, a beetle feeding on leaves; and red spider. However these and other disorders are normally under control, and while they may occupy the *vigneron* by day they do not keep him awake at night as the three plagues of the last century certainly did.

WINE MAKING

This book is in no sense a technical work, but after describing the grapes and their diseases, some account is needed of the vineyard year and the making and ageing of wine in the Gironde. In practice there are variations not only from district to district but from château to château. At Lascombes in Margaux they plough the vineyard four times a year, at Palmer in adjacent Cantenac three times; others plough twice and then remove the weeds by harrowing. When it comes to the making of the wine the differences are widespread. However the general principles are much the same, with the aim being to make as much good wine as is either consonant with the vineyard's reputation and prospects of sale or within the limit allowed under the regulations of *appellation contrôlée*. The two alternatives do not, of course, always produce the same results.

The vineyard year begins after the grapes have been picked. Except in Sauternes this will be over by the end of October at the latest, but in the sweet wine areas the final picking may go on into November. Then the vineyard is cleared of any debris and a preliminary ploughing may take place to earth up the vines as a protection against winter frosts.

In December pruning begins and continues through the winter; it should be completed before the sap begins to rise in the spring, although there are advocates of late pruning to protect the vines against spring frosts. Vine pruning is a technical affair and very important. Basically in the Médoc each vine is allowed two widely spaced branches, which are tied to the three rows of wire that run along the lines of vines. These vines are usually planted one metre apart, and there will be at least one metre between each row. It is usually more in the Sauternes, in St-Émilion and the lesser districts; and the needs of mechanization are tending to increase this distance. The two permitted branches – it is three in the *palus* – will have sprung out in the previous spring and summer; for the grapes are borne on last year's wood. In the old days these branches were supported on stakes, as they still are in some vineyards, but in Bordeaux wire is almost universal. Each of these branches is allowed to keep two or three buds apiece. In St-Émilion and Sauternes one fruit-bearing branch only is permitted, with seven to ten buds per branch. Great care is taken in the pruning to remove all unnecessary wood.

In January the vineyard may be manured. This is not done too frequently as it would encourage too much foliage; usually once every five years. Any defective staves are replaced, and some growers have a winter spraying against various diseases, notably red spider.

The important ploughing begins after the winter frosts, normally about 20 February. This 'opens up' the vine, by uncovering the ridge in which the foot of the vine lies, and transferring the earth to the ground between the vine lines; the earth which cannot be removed by the plough is hoed away from the vines. Ploughing is finished by the end of March; in the following month a new ploughing takes place, with a different type of plough, the object now being to replace the earth round the foot of the vine. At the beginning of May a further opening up of the vine may be done by plough, followed immediately by a final operation to cover the base of the vine trunk, as a protection against hot weather.

Planting and grafting continues until April. Any suckers that have emerged from the American root-stock below the graft are removed, the young leaves being sprayed against mildew and oidium, and surplus buds removed. There is a danger of late frosts in May, which are more damaging than those earlier in the year, for with the sap risen, once the vine is in leaf a very slight frost can devastate the vineyard. The most disastrous frosts in recent history were those in February 1956, when some vineyards were practically wiped out at temperatures as low as —24 degrees C., but this was also partly caused by a very mild January which had encouraged the sap to rise prematurely. Another year in which very severe frosts were experienced was 1977. At the end of March and ten days later at Easter the vines were damaged by unexpectedly heavy frosts. As a result, the red wine crop was the smallest since the poor year of 1969, the white the least for thirty years. In St-Émilion and Pomerol the crop was cut in some properties to a third or quarter of normal. Indeed after the diseases, particularly rot, frost has always been the chief hazard of Bordeaux. It was recorded in 1354 that the vineyards were frozen in St-Genès near Bordeaux, and in 1406 nearly all the vineyards of Guyenne were ruined by frost. The terrible winter of 1766 devastated the Bordeaux vineyards; and when Lafite was sold in 1797 after the Revolutionary confiscation, the sale notice prominently mentioned that the vineyard was free from the danger of frost. Today perhaps the low-lying Graves area is most subject to it.

At the beginning of June comes the flowering or *floraison*, when fine warm weather is needed to set the flowers without delay. The flowering should be over within three weeks, and the rule-of-thumb estimate is that the vintage will take place one hundred days after completion of flowering. Bad weather at this time will produce *coulure*, when the flowers or tiny berries fall off; and *millerandage* when the grape clusters may be composed of a mass of tiny grapes that will not develop. There is spraying in June and trimming of excessive vegetation.

Spraying continues in July and August, particularly after rain; the vine lines are kept trimmed and the ground below freed of weeds by ploughing or harrowing. Viticulturally there is no finer sight than a well-kept Bordeaux vineyard. Otherwise, August and the beginning of September is a quiet time in the vineyard, and the workers in the vineyards and cellars (*chais*) as well as the working proprietors usually take their holidays at this time.

Ideally the vintage begins about 15 September, although it normally begins later. The earliest vintage on record since 1795 was 1893, when it started on 15 August, with excellent results. The only other such summer vintage known was in 1822 when it began on 27 August; the vintage was not exceptional. Of the great years in Bordeaux's modern history, the starting dates were as follows:

1798 – 13 September	1900 – 24 September
1802 – 23 September	1920 – 22 September
1811 – 14 September	1921 – 15 September
1815 – 25 September	1928 – 25 September
1828 – 15 September	1929 – 26 September
1858 – 20 September	1945 – 13 September
1864 – 17 September	1961 – 22 September
1870 – 10 September	1970 – 27 September
1899 – 24 September	1975 – 22 September

It will be noted that few of the outstanding years had vintages beginning before 15 September. It is too early to assess the quality of the 1976 vintage, but it began earlier than any vintage since 1945 and on the same date: 13 September. Few leading years, however, started as late as October, although 1926 (4 October) and 1953 (1 October) succeeded. The latest modern vintages on record were 1816 (27 October), described in Tastet & Lawton's records, to which I am indebted for these details, as 'detestable', 1932 (15 October), 'execrable', and the notorious 1956 (14 October). It would be too soon to describe 1975 as a great year, but it began comparatively early on 22 September. On the other hand after the poor summer but splendid autumn of 1977 the vintage did not start until 10 October; but whereas this could not be considered a good year, in 1978, after a summer equally bad up to mid-August, picking that began about the same date produced excellent results.

It is a fact that nowadays the vintage takes place later than it did in the last century. Prior to the development of modern instruments to test the sugar and acid content of the grapes before picking begins, there was a natural tendency not to risk bad autumnal weather, and therefore to pick early rather than late. This meant that the grapes were often not completely ripe and the wine tended to be harder and slow-developing. Nowadays owing to modern methods the grapes in a good year should be *à point* when picked, and the resulting softer wines will develop more quickly.

Not all the vineyards will start picking simultaneously; and St-Émilion and Pomerol normally begin a few days before the Médoc. Much depends on the weather and the forecasts put out by the meteorological office in Bordeaux, as well as on the maturity of the grapes in the vineyards. These are usually tested for sugar and acid content. Some proprietors hope to squeeze the last drop of *surmaturité* out of their grapes before picking, but this can be risky, as was shown in 1964 when rain spoiled the latter half of a vintage that began only on 28 September. At Mouton-Rothschild during the vintage something like a council of war, armed with weather and vineyard reports, is held regularly, to decide when to pick and when to stop. Before picking in the fine wine areas, the sugar content of the grapes should be a minimum of 11 per cent degrees of alcohol and a maximum of seven grammes of tartaric acid. To pick or not to pick is the most momentous decision in the wine-making year in Bordeaux.

Harvesting is done in the big estates by teams of imported labour, often Spanish, who are accommodated and fed for the two or three weeks necessary to complete the picking; more in the Sauternes where the vintage may last for four to six weeks. The vintage probably occupied a longer period until quite recent times than it does today. For example, in the 1920s it took about three weeks at Latour, whereas today it will be be over in a fortnight or less, although the vineyard area and the average crop are now considerably larger. Very large *troupes* of 150 or more may be employed; previously the picking force was largely recruited from the regular employees and their wives, the latter being partly impressed to provide the meals of the *vendangeurs*. In the 1920s Latour had about 45 regular employees, but at a big (if poor) vintage, like 1925, they took on an extra 85 temporary workers and in the following moderate-sized *récolte* only 56. Less important, less prosperous *domaines* could afford fewer and this is true today, when in the smaller vineyards the harvesting is largely a family affair, reinforced perhaps by some neighbours. Some growers will employ local labour, particularly in the Sauternes, for obvious reasons, to ensure that the grapes are ripe to the point of 'noble rottenness', discussed in the chapter on sweet white wines. At the end of the picking, which is arduous, particularly in bad weather, there is usually a party, and on some estates it is still the custom to present the wife of the proprietor with a large bouquet of flowers – the *gerbaude*. I remember once at Mouton-Rothschild a bouquet, splendid enough to have gladdened any first-night *prima donna*, presented to the Baroness by the *vendangeurs*.

After the picking, the paths of red and white wine making diverge. Black grapes go through the process of *égrappage*, in which the stalks are removed; the white rarely except at a few Sauternes châteaux including Yquem, after the first pressing. This is usually done by a revolving cylindrical machine, which also breaks the skins lightly, and is known as a *fouloir-égrappoir*. The operation can also be carried out by hand on a kind of table with a grill top (*table d'égrappage*), as practised at Palmer and Cantemerle, but is not now common. If the stalks were not removed there would be an excess of acidity and tannin in the wine. At Yquem, one is assured, the grapes are never in contact with metal.

For red wine the grapes, skins and juice are at once pumped into large vats which have been scoured and put in sound, clean condition in the weeks prior to the vintage. Most fermentation vats (*cuves*) in Bordeaux are of oak, but some are of concrete and even of steel. Some châteaux such as Pontet-Canet and Mouton-Rothschild have an upper floor in their press-houses (*cuviers*), and the grapes are taken up from outside and poured into the tops of the vats; elsewhere they are tipped in from ladders placed against the sides of the vats. The fermentation usually begins within 24 hours, but in cold weather it can be delayed up to three days, and the *cuviers* may have to be heated. The period of fermentation varies from three to four days to a fortnight. In good conditions this may be over within four to six days, and the wine stays thereafter in the vats for varying lengths of time.

The object of the fermentation is, of course, to transform the sugar into alcohol by means of the natural yeasts on the grape skins; it is seldom necessary to add yeast during the fermentation, although it is said to be more common with modern sterile vats. The great risk is of the must becoming overheated to such an extent that the yeasts are killed and fermentation ceases; to re-start the process is very difficult, and the wine with unconverted free sugar may turn to vinegar. This happened at Lafite in 1921, and occurred very widely in the excessively hot vintage of 1895.

Accordingly it is desirable to keep the temperature below 30 degrees C., although it often goes up to 33 degrees; the top limit is 35 degrees, and at 37 degrees the fermentation begins to slow down. To keep the temperature low two methods are used. Ice is lowered in canvas sacks into the *cuves* – and at Mouton-Rothschild they bring in a ton a day during the fermentation period. The wine is pumped out of the bottom of the vat, through a piece of equipment consisting of a serpentine series of pipes cooled by ice or water, and then back into the top of the vat. This has another purpose. The skins float to the top of the fermenting must and form a hard crust known as the *chapeau*. This can be a foot or more thick and prevents essential air reaching the must as well as reducing the contact of juice with the skins. This is broken up by men with poles, and the wine released from the bottom of the vat is poured into the top. This process is known as *remontage*. Another way the *chapeau* is prevented from forming is by the laying of planks across the vat, a few inches below the top, as is done at Branaire, following the practice in Algeria.

At La Mission-Haut-Brion Henri Woltner installed vitrified steel vats, which keep the must relatively cool, and not over 30 degrees C. This is what he called *fermentation froide*.

During the fermentation period, attached to every vat in the press house is a chart, showing the arc-like rise and fall of temperature and the drop in sugar content expressed on the Baumé scale.

This raises the question of chaptalization or the addition of sugar to the must in order to raise the alcoholic strength. The term comes from Jean André Chaptal (1756–1832), a chemist who became Minister of the Interior and Comte de Chanteloup under Napoleon. He wrote a book on wine-making *L'Art de faire, de gouverner et de perfectionner le vin* (1801) and was a pioneer in France of beet sugar production. As the sugar should all be converted into alcohol the wine's degree of sweetness ought not to be altered, but with a claret which has had to be chaptalized heavily, a sweetish, glycerinery taste can often be detected; alcohol from cane sugar is likely to taste different from that produced from grape sugar. Moderate sugaring is unlikely to be noticed. There is a legal limit to the amount of sugar that may be added: 3 kilograms per hectolitre of must. Also no more than 200 kilos of sugar may be added per hectare of vineyard under production. As 1·8 kilograms of sugar will raise the alcoholic content by 1 degree, this means that it may only be increased by just over 1½ degrees. Chaptalization is only allowed when the wine already has the minimum alcoholic strength permitted for its *appellation*. The various minima of strengths are given later, under the districts, but the minimum for a wine to qualify for the lowest red wine *appellation contrôlée* of Bordeaux is 10 degrees, although a fine château wine will not be less than 11·5 degrees and normally nearly 12. So chaptalization may be resorted to not only in a bad year but also when the wine is a little below the desirable strength. This occurred in 1966 when many proprietors wanted to bring the wine up by half a degree; about one degree is lost in the fermentation process.

Common in Burgundy and elsewhere for many years, chaptalization was only legalized in Bordeaux in 1938, for that year only, and then not again until 1951, although on occasion it was certainly practised there long before this. In the difficult vintage of 1816 the *régisseur* of Latour, Lamothe, on finding the must in the vats excessively acid, bought 300 pounds of sugar and added it to three of the four vats in the proportion of five pounds per *barrique*. In the event, however, he was disappointed by the result, as he found the grapes tasted tainted and concluded that nature could not be improved on. Nevertheless this trial at Latour would seem to show that Chaptal's experiments were common knowledge. It may be added here that another traditional way of improving a claret was by the addition of brandy, sometimes armagnac. Added during a slow fermentation it would hasten its conclusion which might otherwise be dangerously prolonged.

Since 1951 chaptalization has only been allowed on an annual basis by the Minister of Agriculture at the request of the *Institut National des Appellations d'Origine* (*I.N.A.O.*), through the Prefect of the Gironde, on the representations of the growers and the advice of experts. As permission usually is given only a day or two before the vintage – or even after it has begun – one wonders how the growers manage to secure the necessary sugar so promptly! Sugar used for chaptalization is taxed at ·80 frs. a kilo. Some people consider that Bordeaux sold out its birthright of natural wine when this sugaring was permitted, but certainly it has saved a great deal of wine otherwise unsaleable or unpalatable. Permission is given with great frequency these days, even in successful years like '64, '66 and '70; indeed every year after '61. The addition of sugar to a wine after the fermentation is strictly illegal. Chaptalization applies only to red wine.

There has been much talk in recent years of wine being made differently, with a view to producing quick-maturing wines. In so far as this is true, it arises from the length of time the newly fermented wine is left with the skins in the vats before being drawn off into casks. The purpose is to give further colour and tannin to the wine, thus increasing its body and power of development; the skins, pips, etc., which contain the tannin, macerate in the wine. In the old days the wine lay on the skins for three or four weeks, before the latter were taken out and pressed. Nowadays the normal period among the *crus classés* is more like ten to fourteen days, while elsewhere as at La Mission-Haut-Brion the wine is taken off the skins once the fermentation is completed. Short fermentation with the wine being promptly taken off the skins is not, however, a modern invention as sometimes suggested. In the exceptionally fine 1811 vintage Lamothe removed the wine from the vats at Latour after five days to avoid bitterness arising from contact with the *marc*. At some châteaux, including Haut-Brion, the wine is often left in the vats for a couple of months after the skins are removed. Others leave it there until the first racking at the turn of the year or even longer. This keeps the wine fresh, but it develops more slowly than in wood, and takes longer to fall bright. In some small growths the wine is kept permanently in vats until bottled; this is of course a cheaper method of storage, and there will not be the same loss from evaporation, but the development will not be as good. Certainly longer contact with the skins will increase tannin content.

Whether the shorter period of maceration will adversely affect the quality and above all the longevity of the wine is still in question. There is little doubt it has done so in Burgundy, but the wines there naturally have less tannin. Until such vintages as 1959, 1961 and 1966 demonstrate whether they can or cannot last the twenty to thirty years of their pre-last-world-war predecessors we shall not know the answer; and only a few then may care. (The preceding sentence appeared in the first edition of this book when the 1959s were less than ten years old. It can now be shown that they are capable of staying the course for twenty years, but few would give them an extended life, and even some of the prized '61s show signs of decline. Whether, however, that is anything to do with the time of maceration in the *cuves* is not clear. In the first case, it may be the result of a very hot summer and a slight lack of acidity in the wine.)

Another reason for leaving the wines in vats for a certain

period is to try to have part at least of the second or malo-lactic fermentation over by the time the wine goes into cask. This fermentation transforms malic acid into lactic acid, and is an essential stage in a red wine's development. Only in fairly recent times has this been understood. It cannot be speeded up, and it may not take place until the spring after the vintage, or even later. A wine that ferments in bottle may well have not completed the malo-lactic fermentation before bottling. So if the growth is lucky this fermentation will follow hard on, or even occur almost simultaneously with the alcoholic fermentation. A wine that ferments in bottle seldom, if ever, completely recovers.

It should be mentioned also that a second wine, the *vin de presse*, is made by pressing the skins after the vats are emptied. This can be good wine, and a proportion is normally added to the first wine even in the leading growths. After that the grapes are distilled for *marc*, but by specialists in that process rather than by the growers. It is compulsory for the growers to produce some distillate, and this is how they do it. Before the development of the *fouloir-égrappoir* a *vin de queue* was made by pressing the stalks, but was generally added to the workers' *piquette*.

Ideally the young red wine should go into new Limousin oak casks. (New oak has been used for the young wine in the Médoc for 200 years. It used to come from the Baltic.) The casks make a splendid sight in those châteaux that can afford a complete new range every year. They are hardly worth it in off-years like 1963 and 1965. The new oak certainly adds something to the wine's flavour, and the wine is said to clear and fall bright more quickly in new oak. Most proprietors even of the classed growths buy only a proportion of new casks each year, for they now cost over £50 apiece, compared with less than £1 at the beginning of this century. When the wine is bottled at the château the hogsheads may be sold to second-hand dealers.

The capacity of the *barrique bordelaise* is strictly controlled. In earlier times it varied from 215 to 230 litres, but it was officially designated in 1866 at 225 litres (49·5 imperial gallons, 59·4 U.S. gallons), with four *barriques* making a *tonneau* of 900 litres. A tolerance of 2 per cent is allowed on either side. The shape, circumference and number of iron bands, etc., are also specified. This should provide 300 bottles of ·75 litres apiece, but in practice only 288 bottles or 24 dozen were allowed for until c. 1973, and when a customer had his wine château-bottled this was the quantity he expected from each *barrique*. Nowadays he will receive 25 dozen.

For the first ten months or so of its life the claret is in a cask with the bung on the top. Since there is loss by evaporation, it is necessary to top up the cask once or twice a week to replace the ullage (*ouillage*). At the end of December or early in January the wine is racked (*soutirage*) off the accumulated lees into a clean cask, and this is repeated quarterly for the first year, and probably three times in the second. The wine from the lees is collected, and also racked off, fined and later bottled as *vin de lie*, which can be excellent but is never marketed, and is consumed in the château. It is laid down that racking should take place in dry, still weather, as then the lees will more readily lie at the bottom of the cask, but this is not always followed today.

Early in the New Year will take place the *égalisage* or *assemblage* of the wines made from the different grapes in the vineyard, and hitherto kept separate. This is the moment of truth for the proprietor, the *régisseur* or the *maître de chai* (cellar master). The wine from each vat is carefully tasted to decide which is good enough to be included in the *ensemble* and sold under the château label, in bottle or cask as may be; and which will be rejected. The rejection may be owing to the grapes from a particular vat being too young, or they may have been picked under unfavourable conditions; fine sunny weather throughout the vintage cannot be expected.

The temptation to include too much in the *ensemble* must be considerable, since the difference in price between the château wine and the commune wine, or even a wine sold at lower *appellations*, is great indeed. Each vat rejected involves the owner in substantial financial loss, and the wine therein may have to be sold at less than the cost of production. On the other hand there is the château's reputation to be protected; too high a proportion of wine from young vines or indifferent wine may affect adversely the good name and perhaps the sale prospects of the estate. At Palmer in the very poor year of 1963 all the vats were rejected, in 1964 about one-third were not accepted, with over half rejected in 1965, but none at all in 1966. Along with the decision when to pick, this is the greatest problem each year for the proprietor or his deputy; and whereas the former decision is to some extent a collective one, for others are making up their minds publicly by sending the pickers out to collect the grapes, the *assemblage* is made in the isolation and privacy of the *chai*.

In the second year the casks will lie with their bungs halfway over on the side of the cask (*bonde à côté*) to reduce ullage. Accordingly samples will be drawn not by removing the bung, but via little spigots inserted in the cask ends. Usually the wine will undergo one fining (*collage* – once known as '*fouettage*'), to clear away the impurities, which are carried to the bottom by white of egg, blood, isinglass or patent chemicals. If a wine is very tough a second fining may be given it, to reduce the tannin. Fining is normally carried out shortly before the cask is dispatched or bottled off. Incidentally, what are known as keeping charges and fining for all wine sold are paid for by the customer. The former work out at $\frac{3}{4}$ per cent per month of the purchase price, and 3 per cent per fining. When Bordeaux wines were generally inexpensive this was no great addition, but it is no small matter these days when the customer has to pay 15 to 20 per cent on the purchase price of £250 or more per *barrique*. Today, with ever higher prices more and more growers and merchants quote prices including these charges. The prices of the *premiers crus* always include keeping charges but not the compulsory château-bottling. All *crus classés* now include these charges in their price, described as *rendu mise*.

The time of bottling or shipping in cask varies considerably. It depends to some extent on the vintage and the state of the wine, but dispatch of wine in cask is not undertaken either in the cold winter months or in mid-summer. The lesser wines probably will be shipped in cask in the late spring or early summer of the second year after the vintage. Bottling at source is likely to take place in the summer of the second year or before the second vintage, but should not be carried out in hot weather; although it often is. The finest red Bordeaux is usually bottled when the wine is over two years old, either in the third autumn or in the third spring; clear, dry weather is advised. After bottling or shipping in bottle all wine may be out of condition or 'bottle-sick' for a matter of months. Earlier bottling will take place sooner in light years, and also in St-Émilion and Pomerol.

Red Bordeaux should be bottled in green bottles, and white Bordeaux in white bottles.

The principal difference in the fermentation of white Bordeaux is that the grapes are pressed up to three times and for the finest wine the fermentation then takes place in the casks into which the expressed juice is immediately run. For lesser wines and for many well-known Sauternes the fermentation is carried out in vats. The third pressing should not be used in the best quality wine. In the Sauternes district before picking, a sugar content that will produce 20 per cent of alcohol is desirable. The fermentation will stop at about 15 per cent, thus leaving 5 per cent of free sugar to give the wine its special lusciousness. The high alcoholic content will prevent the wine turning to vinegar. At Yquem the *égrappage* is done only after the first pressing, and each pressing takes about an hour. The fermentation in cask may last anything from fifteen days to three months, but the most satisfactory period is one month. In the Sauternais where the picking may take place over an extended time there are likely to be bigger variations from cask to cask than with the red wines; so an *égalisage* has to take place to ensure a consistent wine. This is usually done when the wine is a year old. Bottling of these sweet wines may be carried out anything from two to three and a half years after the vintage, but the dry wines are put in bottle after fifteen to eighteen months, though these days some are bottled after only six months.

Rosé wine or 'Bordeaux clairet' is made in Bordeaux by taking the must off the skins in the vats almost at once; then the grapes are pressed and the juice is fermented out on its own in hogsheads, as with white wine. The bottling is usually done as with dry white Bordeaux. As mentioned later, this *rosé* used to be known as *vin de goutte*.

There are many variations in wine making in Bordeaux, and some of these are described in succeeding chapters. I have come upon small growths in Bourg and Blaye where a red wine is still in vat after two years. This may be because the grower thinks it will develop best that way, or he may be short of money to buy casks. Most growers have their own methods and even secrets of viticulture and wine-making. It is a hazardous and highly individual occupation, and so long as we have good Bordeaux, long may the individuality of Bordeaux – its chief glory – remain.

2. Bordeaux and Wine

It seems likely that Bordeaux was a wine trading centre before it was a wine growing region. The argument against it first being a wine growing area is that it is not mentioned as such by the geographer Strabo, who wrote about 63 B.C. Burdigala is indeed included but as an *emporium*, and it is thought that if there had been vine growing on any scale he would have said so. Broadly speaking the vine in France spread north and west from Provence and the Rhône Valley. One of the oldest wine areas of France was Gaillac, which continued to be important until the nineteenth century. From this town the wine could be shipped down the Tarn and Garonne and thence to Bordeaux. There is an inscription of the first or second centuries A.D. which mentions the presence at Bordeaux of a *negotiator britannicus*. What else was this English merchant doing in Bordeaux if not buying wine? Surely he was one of the pioneers of the Anglo-Bordeaux wine trade, whose successors in good times and bad, in peace and often in war, have visited Bordeaux in order to buy wine for the British market. Our British negotiator was not concerned with wine grown in and around Bordeaux, but with the young wine brought down from what later was known as the Haut-Pays. He would have been in character if he remarked to the Bordeaux merchant, 'A little lacking in body this year's Gaillac, don't you think?'

Moreover although the Edict of Domitian in A.D. 92, by which vineyards outside Italy had to be pulled up, was never fully implemented, it would have discouraged the planting of vines in an area which was not at that time considered so suitable for wine making as the country further east and south. For the soil was poor and the climate uncertain in a district subject to Atlantic weather. Much of the area was little above water level, and Dion (*Histoire de la vigne et du vin en France dès origines au XIXième siècle*, 1959) suggests that it took very hard work to establish the Bordeaux *vignoble*, by cutting down the forests and draining the land, and this was only possible out of the profits of the export trade.

When Probus became Emperor in A.D. 276 he took a much more enlightened view of vineyard planting throughout his empire, and Domitian's restrictions were officially relaxed in 280. Ausonius the poet owned vineyards in the Bordeaux area in the fourth century, and his is one of the earliest testimonials to their presence. His quite considerable vineyard probably overlooked the Garonne and it would seem likely that it was in what is now the Premières Côtes area of the Entre-Deux-Mers, or in the Graves or possibly opposite Bordeaux near Cenon, where the Paris road climbs the hill towards Carbon-Blanc.

The Bordeaux trade was certainly adversely affected as a result of the decrees of the Roman Emperors forbidding trade with the barbarians, and in the fifth century the Saxon pirates harassed its maritime commerce.

In 412 the Visigoths invaded the region and brought their usual devastation. They were succeeded by the Franks under Clovis but, as elsewhere when the Romans withdrew, history is very sparse. In the Merovingian period (sixth to eighth centuries) Plassac on the Gironde south of Blaye was a vineyard centre. Charlemagne passed through the area on his way to Spain; later the Norman long-boats reached up the Garonne and Dordogne, pillaging the surrounding country. It is thought that the vineyard area slowly increased, but there are no documents giving facts about the trade in wine until the arrival of the English following the marriage of Henry Plantagenet and Eleanor of Aquitaine in 1152. The period of the English association is dealt with in the next chapter. Here we are concerned with the general methods of viticulture and wine commerce in the Middle Ages, when Bordeaux became an important wine centre.

In the Middle Ages the grapes were either planted in closely spaced lines, as today, or widely, so that other crops could be cultivated between the vine rows. The vineyards were small, for they were worked by hand, an exception in the fourteenth century being the one in Pessac, belonging to the archbishop, which was worked by ox-drawn ploughs.

Diseases of the vine were regarded as being sent from the Devil and they were accordingly exorcized. There was no limitation on production per hectare as there is now, and output was probably fairly large. It should be borne in mind that in normal times, grape cultivation has always been among the most profitable of cash crops. Hence the tendency of the vineyards to spread at the expense of other and more necessary agricultural products, such as wheat.

In the Middle Ages and indeed until the end of the *Ancien Régime*, the crop could not be picked until the authorization was given by the landlord to his tenant. This *Ban de Vendange* was suppressed at the Revolution, as it inflicted severe loss on the peasants. Today the *Ban* is still proclaimed in the Médoc, but in fact it is no more than an occasion for jollification: the election of members to the order of the *Bontemps du Médoc et des Graves*, followed by an excellent luncheon or dinner. This is held in one or other of the leading châteaux. In the Middle Ages anyone who picked early was liable to prosecution, although sometimes special permission was given. In St-Émilion the start of the vintage was signalled by the ringing of the town bells. The date varied from the end of August to early in October.

It is to be remembered that until our reform of the calendar in the eighteenth century the dates do not correspond with our own. In the archbishop's vineyards the vintage in the fourteenth century started from the third week of August to the fourth week of September, according to conditions; at that time the calendar was about eight days behind. Therefore 12–15 September was the equivalent of 20–23 September. In the late vintage of 1410 they started picking the grapes in Pessac on 23–24 September (old style). By 1500 the old Julian calendar was about nine days in arrears.

Unlike Burgundy, where old presses may be seen in the *Musée du Vin* in Beaune and at Clos de Vougeot, there are no ancient presses extant in Bordeaux, but they must have been similar contraptions of huge beams and counterweights. The pressing (*foulage*) was done by feet, although afterwards there was a second pressing by a hand-operated press. This was not considered to produce as good wine, any more than the *vin de presse* is regarded today. The 'cake' of grapes, or the *marc*, was then liquefied with water and pressed again; the result was a thin wine, the *vin lymphaté* mentioned below, short-lived even by the standards of the time.

The fermentation usually took about ten days, and it should be noted that white wine was made in exactly the same way as red, with the fermentation taking place in large fermenting vats and not in casks. This did not begin for white wines until the seventeenth and eighteenth centuries. Even in bad years there was no sweetening of the must. Sugar was as rare as spices in the Middle Ages and the earliest known example of sugaring was at Ste-Foy-la-Grande in the eighteenth century; clearly it was a novelty.

Four types of wine were commonly produced: red, white, *clairet* and *vin lymphaté*. Much more red than white wine was produced in Bordeaux until about three hundred years ago; in the Middle Ages the proportion of white wine was very small. *Clairet*, from which our own word claret is derived, was made from a mixture of red and white grapes put together into the fermenting vat, thus producing a *vin gris* or *rosé*. The *vin lymphaté* was watered wine. The new wine was racked off its lees a few months after the vintage, but there is no evidence that fining (*collage*) was used to clear the wine, although this process had been used by the Romans with white wine.

After fermentation the wine was put into casks of oak from the upper Garonne, Périgord, the Saintonge or the Angoulême region. The *barrique bordelaise* was a kind of trade mark for the wines of the area. Not only were its dimensions carefully specified and supervised, but neighbouring wine areas were not permitted to use a cask of the same size. As is well known, the Bordelais reckon their output in *tonneaux*, although these 900-litre casks no longer exist, any more than do Bordeaux pipes, which contained 450 litres. They did exist, however, in the Middle Ages, and not only for wine; corn and honey were kept in these large casks. They were in use until the sixteenth century, when their unwieldy size for transporting by road caused their gradual disappearance. By 1789 the *barrique* was the norm. The coopers (*tonneliers*) formed an important skilled trade in Bordeaux, and in medieval times they tended to congregate in the St-Michel quarter of the city.

Certainly normally the new wine was blended, sometimes to give more colour to a light one. In the days when the wine was drunk immediately – the archbishop was recorded as having drunk his 1361 new wine in September – it was light in colour and alcohol, and doubtless was appreciated like that. Blending the wine of one year with another was, however, strictly forbidden, not only in Bordeaux but in London also. The wine was often shipped on its lees, i.e. un-racked.

It is difficult for us, accustomed to the fine gradations of vintage wines, to appreciate the conditions under which the trade operated and their customers drank wine. Both lived from-cask-to-mouth until the arrival of the bottle in the seventeenth century. There was no means of keeping wine to mature, so it had to be consumed as speedily as possible. For last year's wine was likely to be a dead loss. In 1342 the *vin* *nouveau* sold at an average price of 21 livres* per *tonneau*; the *vin ancien* for only 12 livres. In 1226 Henry III ordered that his stock of wines of the previous year held in Bristol be sold, and new wine bought with the proceeds. The Bordelais to protect themselves from loss did their best to ensure that their wine was sold promptly and that they secured every advantage to this end.

The burghers' wine was free of all taxes, both the *Petite Coutume* which applied to all wines sold retail in Bordeaux, and the *Grande Coutume* on exports; and could circulate freely anywhere. Their wines, along with those of the archbishop, two chapters and of the nobles resident in the city, alone could be sold retail from the end of September until early June. Even neighbouring but 'foreign' wines from the Haut-Pays (of which more below), whose arrival in Bordeaux was delayed until the feast of St Martin (11 November) or even until Christmas, had to be sold by a citizen of Bordeaux; and of course the imported wines were taxed. Bordeaux certainly looked after its own and had a reputation for commercial shrewdness which it has by no means lost today.

As elsewhere, the Bordeaux innkeepers were always suspect and were subject to strict supervision. They were particularly firmly forbidden to indulge in blending. In 1342 London innkeepers were not allowed to keep a Gascon wine in the same cellar as one from the Rhine; and the purchaser must be able to see the wine drawn from the cask.

The expansion of the Bordeaux vineyard area probably began in the eleventh century, as the forests surrounding the town were cut down. The Church was a powerful influence in the extension of the vineyards, first because wine was necessary for the holy offices, secondly for hospitality, and

*The livre tournois was the approximate equivalent of the franc. In 1795 the modern franc was instituted, and 80 francs = 81 livres. At 25 frs. to the £, the franc remained the equivalent of 10d. in English money and 19 cents in American money until 1919.

thirdly for the excellent revenue return from their estates that wine usually provided. Later on wine growing became very profitable. In the fourteenth and fifteenth centuries the revenue in a good year of a Bordeaux vineyard in full production might be as much as four times the outgoings; for the largely serf labour was very poorly remunerated. Vines were also planted on the right bank of the Garonne, increasingly as the marshes were reclaimed in the *palus* near the river. These riverside vineyards spread considerably in the twelfth and thirteenth centuries, upstream as far as Cadaujac, near Léognan. Until 1200 the Bordeaux *vignoble* was largely composed of the vineyards of the Côtes – Blaye, Bourg, the lower Dordogne and Garonne valleys – and the Graves area around Bordeaux. Until the fourteenth century, vineyards were numerous inside the city's boundaries. Where the Allées de Tourny now stand there were once vines. Across the unbridged river, Cenon and Lormont were centres of wine growing.

By the fifteenth century all the cultivable land within easy access from Bordeaux was under vines. Indeed the history of the Bordeaux *vignoble* is one of advance as the forest retreated in face of the vines, and then of decline in the nearer suburbs, as the town itself spread; but this came later, in the nineteenth and twentieth centuries.

The principal and most prolific medieval wine-growing district was the Graves. It was predominantly a red wine area, as indeed was the whole region now entitled to the *appellation* Bordeaux. The chief wine villages were Pessac, Talence, Mérignac, Gradignan and, further out, Cérons. In Pessac by the fourteenth century was probably the now oldest named vineyard of the region: Ch. Pape-Clément, as it is now known, although it was no château in those days, but rather part of the estate of the archbishops of Bordeaux. It had been presented to the See in 1305 by the Archbishop Bertrand de Goth, who had succeeded to the papacy as Pope Clement V. From here probably came the finest wine of the archiepiscopal estates, for although these included a good deal of vineyard property, the other main vineyards were on the right bank at Lormont and Queyries, now part of the Premières Côtes. These vineyards across the river remained archiepiscopal property until the Revolution. Lormont lies slightly downstream from Bordeaux, and Queyries is on the flat land. It was opposite what was then the village of Bacalan, which stood beyond the suburb of the Chartrons, named after the Carthusian monks who, in 1383, built their *chartreuse* in the marshy land by the river. Now Queyries is occupied by factories and somewhat decrepit suburbs, through which runs *Route Nationale 10*, prior to climbing the hill in the direction of St-André-de-Cubzac. On this slope were produced the *vins de côtes* of Lormont and Cenon, which were superior to those of the Queyries *palus* which nevertheless had a special reputation up to the eighteenth century. In the fourteenth century this *palus* area was owned by the de Grailly family, one of the first identifiable secular vineyard-proprietor families of Bordeaux. Another medieval family with large vineyards in Queyries was that of Puy-Paulin. In the late eighteenth century the deep-coloured wines of Queyries (*vin fort noir*) were much appreciated in America where they apparently matured well.

Further inland on the right bank there was always a good deal of wine made in the Entre-Deux-Mers, and the English kings held vineyards there. Even before this, vines were recorded as existing in the eleventh century in Vayres and St-Sulpice-d'Izon. There were also vineyards at Carbon-Blanc, Beychac, Langoiran, Cadillac, as well as further south at Loupiac and St-Macaire on the edge of the province of Bordeaux. In the twelfth century the Entre-Deux-Mers was the most widespread and developed vineyard area.

Upstream also, but on the left bank, were vineyards in Sauternes, Barsac, Pujols, Podensac and Cérons. Wine was certainly grown in the Sauternes and Cérons districts in the thirteenth century, and in the church of the latter village is a carving on a capital of a Bordeaux *barrique* placed under a human head. In this southern section the wines were white, but although probably fairly sweet, they did not at all resemble the luscious wines we associate with Sauternes and Cérons today; for this was long before the discovery of the properties and possibilities of *pourriture noble*.

In the Médoc, named after a Celtic tribe, the vineyards were few and scattered, except in the vicinity of Bordeaux. This was owing to their inaccessibility and to the marshy, waterlogged nature of the ground. So there were few vineyards in the Bas-Médoc to the north of St-Estèphe although in the thirteenth century there were church properties up in Soulac near the Atlantic. Where they existed they were sparse and insignificant. The vineyards of the Haut-Médoc (the name is modern) were naturally concentrated in the villages nearest to the city or near the main road to Lesparre. The chapter of the cathedral of St-André, which by the fourteenth century was nearly as substantial a vineyard owner as the archbishop, had properties in Blanquefort, Solesse and Le Taillan north of the Jalle de Blanquefort, and further afield at Listrac, Moulis and Avensan. Among the place names associated today with Médocain wine growing where there are records of medieval vineyards are Castelnau, Avensan, Bégorce near Soussans, Cantenac and Issan. The wines from the remoter villages, such as Moulis and Castelnau, probably came to Bordeaux by boat. Macau, then bounded by streams and considered an island, was full of vines by the thirteenth century. Its watery past is recalled today by the lake in the grounds of Cantemerle, which takes its name from the noble family who held the estate in the century following the English expulsion. Corn was also grown in quantity in the Médoc, and in the Middle Ages it cannot be regarded as essentially wine country; this did not come about until the seventeenth century.

However a part of the Graves area was sometimes included

in the Médoc, particularly Pessac (Pessac-de-Médoc). The cathedral authorities owned property here, and also in Léognan and Villenave-d'Ornon. The Pessac vineyard was considered unusual in the fourteenth century for being ploughed with an ox-plough, but the furrow was commonly drawn by hand with a *marre*, a special tool, between a hoe and a spade, which was certainly in use as late as the beginning of this century.

If the Médoc was largely undeveloped in vineyards, St-Émilion was a well-established wine area in the days of the English kings. The town of St-Émilion was accorded the rights of a commune in 1199, and Libourne in 1270. Edward III extended the commercial privileges of Bordeaux to the latter. After some disturbances near the end of the thirteenth century, the burghers of St-Émilion only regained in 1312 the right to elect their mayor and to maintain other privileges by promising to deliver to the English king 50 *tonneaux* of *vin clair pur et bon* before Easter. No doubt the provision as to the latest date each year was because thereafter it would be less good. There was also a fair-sized vineyard area in Fronsac by the thirteenth century, but if one existed in Pomerol it had no separate identity.

In the Middle Ages both Bourg and Blaye were important wine areas, with the convenience of having ports some way down the Gironde towards the sea. They were often viewed somewhat uneasily by the Bordelais. Bourg wines in particular had a high reputation, greater than they have enjoyed since.

Broadly speaking, and excluding the Médoc, the whole Bordeaux *vignoble* at its peak of expansion in the fourteenth and fifteenth centuries was not very different in extent from its appearance on the eve of the phylloxera in the nineteenth century. By the time the English were expelled Bordeaux relied on wine for its prosperity, while corn had to be imported from outside the region to feed the population; it was paid for by the sale and export of wine.

The export trade was much more important than the sale within Bordeaux. Each year there were two shippings of the young wine: the autumn shipping, known as the vintage shipping; and the spring or rack shipping, after the wine had been racked off its lees into fresh casks. The latter was the better. As already mentioned, the Bordelais took good care that their own wine had priority over that of the Haut-Pays, which was more consistent and less affected by Atlantic climatic conditions than Bordeaux. The Haut-Pays wines had to be kept outside the city walls, and this is why the Chartrons suburb grew up to the north of the town. This area in the fifteenth century was divided from the city by the Château Trompette, built by Charles VII (1403–61) after the expulsion of the English in 1453 as the new 'seat of government', in place of the English-built Château de l'Ombrière, which was turned into the law courts. The Haut-Pays wines, contained in casks distinct from the Bordelais type, and subject to tax which made them 10 to 20 per cent dearer than the burghers' wines, had to be removed from the area by 8 September each year if unsold, i.e. before the next vintage wine became available.

The Haut-Pays wine producers carried on a fight for over 300 years against the discrimination suffered by their wines. In 1500 they managed to secure some improvement by permission for Languedoc wines (which chiefly meant Gaillac) to reach Bordeaux by St Martin's Day (11 November), provided they were not put on sale before the Feast of St André (30 November), nor – showing the importance of the English trade to the Bordelais – sold to the English before Christmas.

The Haut-Pays growers, no less fly than their successors today in the south, and adept at blending and 'assisting' the wines of other areas, adopted several stratagems to send their wines down the river Garonne. Wine was shipped to the Bordeaux 'frontier' town of St-Macaire and taken overland to Bergerac, which maintained its ancient liberty of trade, first granted by the English kings. Thence it was shipped down the Dordogne to the Gironde and the open sea. How often must the Bordelais have bewailed the geographical fact that their city was placed above rather than below the confluence of the two rivers at the Bec d'Ambès!

Nevertheless the Bordelais merchants wished to control rather than exclude the Haut-Pays wines, to secure priority for their own wines but also to trade in the wines of their neighbours. For the Haut-Pays wines were not inferior. They included Gaillac, Quercy, Nérac and Bergerac, and normally they were drunk both at the English and French courts. Later on, in the middle of the seventeenth century, the wines of Quercy were considered superior to those of Bordeaux. Moreover the Haut-Pays wines provided important business for the merchants and shipping interests, as well as for blending. The Bordelais wished to sell their merchandise to the adjacent territories as well as to buy corn therefrom. Further, the Bordeaux wine and shipping trades could not subsist on the burghers' wines. The Haut-Pays was also a valuable source of trade for the Bordeaux shipping interests. They were great producers of woad (*pastel*) which, until superseded by indigo, was the source of blue dye throughout Europe, and particularly used in the Iberian peninsula.

From the sixteenth century onwards, the alternative to returning the unsold wine to source after 8 September was to sell it for *eau-de-vie*. In the Middle Ages there is no evidence of wine or *marc* being distilled, but in 1559 the *jurats* of the city forbade the distillation of wine within the walls for fear of fire. In the following century distillation became more common, and in the eighteenth century the *eaux-de-vie* of Bordeaux were classed along with those of La Rochelle, i.e., from the Cognac area. But the superiority of the more northerly brandy, along with the greater commercial acumen of the Charente traders in marketing their product, put cognac firmly ahead; and today the chief distillation for normal sale in Bordeaux is of liqueurs. The well-known firm of Marie Brizard et Roger was formed in 1755, and by 1791 employed 29 *distillateurs liquoristes*. Today the Vieille Cure and Cordial Médoc liqueurs are made at Cenon. There are also other distilleries.

Some of the Haut-Pays wine areas gave up the protracted, unequal struggle with the Bordelais, who controlled the normal exit way of their wines. Agen, for example, took to prunes instead of wine, and orchards displaced vineyards here and elsewhere on the Garonne. Yet the Bordelais never relaxed their vigilance and right into the eighteenth century inspectors were stationed at the Dordogne 'frontier post' of Castillon to make sure that no 'mislabelled' wine entered the Bordeaux region. It is fair to add that they were concerned with the quality of the wines of Bordeaux as well as with their own narrower commercial interests.

Even after the Revolution finally swept away the ancient privileges of Bordeaux in 1790, efforts were made to retrieve them. When Bordeaux made a last attempt in 1803, the town council of Cahors denounced the Bordelais, saying that they could not face fair competition from the Haut-Pays wines, which were more consistent. They alleged that the costs of viticulture in the Gironde were exorbitant, while their own were very low. However, although Bordeaux never recovered its legal privileges, what centuries of policing and discouragement had failed to do was largely achieved by the phylloxera and economic slump of the late nineteenth century. Thereafter the Haut-Pays vineyards, like those elsewhere in France including parts of the Gironde department, were never again so extensive.

The second potential rival to Bordeaux reads oddly in modern times: the Médoc. It was not so much the rather scattered wine producers of whom the burghers were afraid; they feared to lose the trade in those parts of the Médoc remote from Bordeaux, and particularly the carrying trade. Far too much wine went through the ports of Libourne, Bourg and Blaye for the liking of the Bordelais merchants, although it was only a fraction of what was handled in the Gascon capital; and they feared the development of ports on the Médoc bank of the Garonne and Gironde. The virtues of commercial competition are usually more readily appreciated in theory than in practice by those in the business. Accordingly the burghers contrived to secure from Edward III (1327–77) and later from Henry V (1413–22) a ban on wine being loaded anywhere from Crébat, on the city outskirts, to Castillon-de-Médoc in the commune of St-Christoly far up towards the Atlantic. No doubt this contributed substantially towards retarding the development of the Médocain *vignoble*, but the problems of clearing the forests, establishing vineyards, securing the necessary labour and above all the provision of transport by road along the fairly narrow strip of cultivable land were even more important obstacles. Étienne de la Boétie, friend of Montaigne, in the middle of the sixteenth century wrote a work entitled *Historique description du sauvage et solitaire pays du Médoc.*

Although until the sixteenth century, trade with England was much the most important for Bordeaux, and is discussed in the chapter on The English in Bordeaux, there was always a brisk trade with Brittany, northern France and with Flanders. At the beginning of the thirteenth century, only fifty years after the marriage of Henry Plantagenet and Eleanor of Aquitaine, the Gascon merchants were given by Marguerite, Countess of Flanders, the same protection granted to those of La Rochelle and other Atlantic ports. This was a reciprocal gesture, for the Flemings were prominent in the carrying trade, taking wine to England, Scotland and to northern European ports. They were particularly useful to the Scots, for in times of Anglo-Scottish warfare, the English merchants could not deliver the Gascon wines themselves. So it was shipped through 'neutral' Flanders. All attempts by the

English authorities to prevent wines destined for England from being carried in other than English ships failed; there were not enough of the latter, and the Netherlanders were the chief beneficiaries.

However, they did not only carry Gascon wine, and when once the special relationship between Bordeaux and England ceased in the mid-fifteenth century, the Bordelais had to compete not only with German and Spanish wines, but with those from further north in France. These included wines made right up to Normandy, which produced wine in quantity until the nineteenth century. No doubt this was far less good wine than from Bordeaux, but it was conveniently placed for transport across the narrow sleeve of the English Channel.

The account of Bordeaux wines and their sale is continued in later chapters. Meanwhile it is timely here to consider the role of the English in Bordeaux.

3. The English in Bordeaux

Having surveyed briefly the story of Bordeaux in its early days and in the Middle Ages, it is necessary to go back slightly to outline a very special and significant enclave in the history of Gascony.

Although the first part of this chapter is not immediately connected with wine, I believe it to be an essential part of any but a superficial account of Bordeaux and its wines. Most of us are broadly aware that for three centuries Bordeaux came under the English Crown; few of us remember many details of this connection. That one of our English kings was born in Bordeaux, and two others who ruled over it are buried in France is not all that widely known, nor that one positive feature of the luckless King John's reign (1199–1216) was the encouragement of Bordeaux wine growing and trading. No one can doubt that inevitably a great wine district would have developed in what is now the Gironde department, but if Henry Plantagenet had married a Burgundian princess, or if a successor had found himself possessor of a great strip of northern and eastern France instead of the bulk of the south west of the country, might we not have become a nation of (still) champagne and burgundy drinkers instead of leading consumers of Bordeaux? True the wine from the Gascon capital came easily by sea, subject to the hazards of piracy, but under favourable political conditions, the Marne, the Seine and the short sea crossing might have provided comfortable routes for the rivals of Bordeaux wine.

However, it was from the English tenure of territories in Gascony that stemmed a commercial connection between Bordeaux and Britain which has never been broken except in time of war, and often not even then. It was Gascon wine that was called for in the medieval taverns of England; and although some of it may have come from what is now the Charente area and been shipped from La Rochelle, most of it certainly derived from Bordeaux; particularly in the latter part of the period.

It is worth noting here that the terms Gascon and Gascony have often been used loosely, and with good reason: the region called Gascony varied considerably. At its greatest extent in the early Middle Ages it ran from the Pyrenees to the Gironde, and from the Bay of Biscay to the Garonne. But the more southerly part was hived off and Gascony became roughly the country around Bordeaux south of the Gironde. Guyenne, which usually included Gascony, roughly covered the present Gironde department, as well as areas to the east associated with the Dordogne, Tarn and Lot rivers. The Gers region, where armagnac is now distilled, was once part of Gascony.

The association with Bordeaux began when Henry Plantagenet, aged nineteen, married in May 1152 Eleanor of Aquitaine, then about thirty years old. She may fairly be described as being the most eligible young woman of her time, with a dowry that included most of the western part of France up to Brittany. Poitou, Gascony, the Auvergne, the Limousin, Périgord, as well as parts of Touraine and the Berry were all hers; while Henry filled in with the rest of Touraine, Anjou, Maine and Normandy. Eleanor had already been married in 1137, reputedly at the age of seventeen, to the French King, Louis VII (1137–80) at Bordeaux, but an annulment was arranged on the convenient grounds of consanguinity. Henry and Eleanor were married in Poitiers. Two years later on the death of King Stephen (1135–54), they became King and Queen of England with enormous territories in France. In 1156 Henry II visited Bordeaux for the first time.

From the beginning, the English possessions in France were a source of trouble, as the French kings naturally regarded the

English presence as an affront, as well as a sore loss of revenue, trade and military manpower. It has to be remembered that the French Crown did not then control the source of that other great centre of French wines, Burgundy. This was ruled by its own Dukes and, although they usually collaborated with the French monarchs, Burgundy only finally came to the French kings in 1477, twenty-four years after the final expulsion of the English from Bordeaux.

An intermittent series of wars was conducted against the English-ruled provinces, and in these the French were helped by having interior lines of communication, while English aid had to come by sea. Various English attempts were made by means of skilful marriages to divide and rule the French opposition; the other weapon was the appointment of English rulers of Guyenne, Poitou or Gascony, as the situation warranted and the breadth of territories permitted. The first of these was the future Richard Coeur-de-Lion, who at the age of twelve was installed in Poitiers with his mother Eleanor. By this time Henry's relationship with Eleanor was highly unsatisfactory and she abetted struggles against her husband's rule for much of his life. Their tombs lying side by side today in the great church of Fontevrault near Saumur give a false picture of uxoriousness.

However Queen Eleanor was very popular in her own country, and she and her son Richard, who was made Duke of Aquitaine and Count of Poitou, ruled their territories from 1169 to 1173. Then a revolt of the French nobles instigated by Eleanor broke out, but was easily crushed by Henry; in 1174 he sent his wife back to England to semi-imprisonment, but forgave his young son. Richard continued to spend much of his time in France, and held courts in Bordeaux in 1174 and again in 1176. Shortly before his father's death in 1189, Richard liberated his mother and they both returned to Bordeaux where they were warmly welcomed. He left the Gascon capital in 1190 to go on his Crusade, and only revisited it once more in 1199, just before his death. He too is buried in Fontevrault, although his heart is in Rouen Cathedral.

During their reigns neither Richard nor his brother John were very much interested in Bordeaux politically, as it presented no military problems. John, however, was by no means unconcerned with its commercial significance. Not long after his accession he arrived to visit his mother who lived at the Château de l'Ombrière, which overlooked the Garonne and was sited not far from the present city end of the fine Pont de Pierre. The present-day Rue du Palais de l'Ombrière marks its position. During the entire English occupation Ombrière was the headquarters of the English administration – a kind of Dublin Castle. Edward I (1272–1307) later rebuilt most of it, including a Tour du Roi which was reserved for the English kings on their somewhat rare visits to Bordeaux. It was at this château that John, having managed to divest himself of his marriage to Isabella (Avice) of Gloucester, who had been his wife for eleven years, married in 1206 another wife with the same Christian name, Isabella of Angoulême. She being only twelve had little choice in the matter, although already betrothed to a French noble named Adhémar.

Whatever John's shortcomings in other fields, he did a great deal to establish firmly Anglo-Bordelais commercial relations. Although the origins of the Bordeaux wine trade with England are obscure, this certainly began as early as 1203 in John's reign. It was he who, in order to secure the support of Bordeaux, Bayonne (which supplied most of the ships for carrying the wine to England) and Dax against the French king, gave their burgesses considerable commercial privileges and tax exemptions. In particular John exempted the Bordeaux burghers from paying the unpopular export tax known as the Great Custom (*Grande Coutume*), levied on all outgoing ships. This was the Crown's direct revenue, and no other town's citizen-merchants obtained Bordeaux's privilege. The Haut-Pays merchants who exported their wine were subject to this levy. He also made free grants of land mostly covered with wood or marsh near Bordeaux on condition that the land was redeemed and planted with vineyards. Henry III (1216–72) and Edward I (1272–1307) made similar grants, so the original planting of a part of the inner Bordeaux *vignoble* owes something to the English connection. In 1214 John exempted the nobles and burghers of Bordeaux from all taxes on the wines emanating from their vineyards, and these privileges were confirmed by the succeeding English kings.

Yet when John died two years later he owed the large sum of £720 to Bordeaux merchants, who after five years' negotiation never recovered more than £400. However he had been a good customer for Gascon wines. In 1212 out of 348 casks bought for the royal household, 267 came from Gascony. Most of the rest came from the Orléanais and the Île de France. That they were Gascon wines did not mean that they were all grown in the Bordeaux region. A considerable proportion came from Gaillac and Moissac, whose wines at that time were more esteemed and highly-priced than the red Bordeaux. They were probably more powerful and full-bodied.

However to keep Gascon goodwill the monarchs extended to their merchants privileges in London similar to the citizens', often to the disgust of the latter. Unlike most other foreign traders they were allowed to stay long in the capital, were not obliged to live in a specified quarter, and often settled in England. If they were citizens of both Bordeaux and London they escaped the import tax that non-citizen foreigners had to pay in England, as well as the *Grande Coutume*. Under the charter of Edward I Gascon citizens of London were also exempt from the municipal taxes. Later on English merchants began to settle in and around Bordeaux, a practice which has survived to this day. There was great competition between the Gascons and the English, each party accusing the other of securing unfair advantages in the disposal of their wine in England. The king had the right of 'prisage', which meant that he could take without charge one or more tuns of wine from the ship before it was unloaded near London Bridge and purchase further quantities at favourable terms, not only for his household use but for that of the army. In 1327 the English merchants managed to secure exemption from the 'prisage' tax, and this gave them a clear start over the Gascons.

A side-effect of the development of the Anglo-Gascon wine trade was the gradual decline of domestic viticulture in England.

In 1225 Henry III sent his younger brother Richard, Earl of Cornwall and Count of Poitou, to Bordeaux. He at first repelled the French, capturing St-Macaire and Bazas on the 'frontier', but in the following year he nearly lost Bordeaux, for the French troops arrived before its walls and only the timely death of Louis VIII (1223–6) and the accession of Louis IX (1226–70) led the French to make a truce, saving the city. Richard stayed until 1227 but the king himself did not pay his first short visit to Gascony until 1230, when he had been on the throne fourteen years. Twelve years later he came again to meet the threat of French advances. Landing at Royan in May 1242, he was heavily defeated at Saintes and retreated with difficulty to Blaye, a town of considerable strategic importance on the Gironde, which long held out for the English connection.

King Henry spent the winter of 1242–3 in Bordeaux and did his best to win the support of the nobles. He also bought largely of the fine 1242 vintage, making substantial purchases from the archbishop, whose spiritual duties did not preclude him from dabbling in the wine trade. In September 1243 he left France, but Gascony remained unsettled and in 1248 Simon de Montfort, Earl of Leicester and son of the savage leader of the Albigensian 'crusade', was sent over to establish order in Gascony with a seven-year appointment of office as Seneschal in his pocket. Bordeaux was divided between two rival factions: the Coloms, the head of the wine traders, and the

Delsolers, representing the nobles and feudal power rather than the trading class. Simon de Montfort supported the Coloms and imprisoned some of the Delsoler faction, thus directly or indirectly supporting the trading faction. Unfortunately in the process he made himself extremely unpopular, and by 1252 his rule was over; in the following year Henry III paid his last visit to Gascony, lasting 15 months. He did his best to appease the Delsolers, but the Coloms still remained dominant in Bordeaux. A royal viceroy seemed to be expedient and in 1254 Prince Edward, later King Edward I, married Eleanor of Castille and spent more than a year in Gascony, much of it in Bordeaux.

Of the ten English kings who numbered Bordeaux among their possessions, Edward I was probably the most successful in dealing with his Gascon subjects, who were more inclined to regard their rulers as Dukes of Gascony than Kings of England. When Edward first arrived he conciliated the Bordelais, still angry after Simon de Montfort's severe rule. For example the burghers of Bourg and St-Émilion were exempted from taxes on their vines for five years. The quarrels between the Coloms and the Delsolers were probably not entirely unwelcome to Edward, who was able to take the nomination of the important post of mayor into his own hands, and so diminish the independent political power of Bordeaux.

Edward spent a further year in and around Bordeaux in 1260–61, and after he became king in 1272 he made two more visits: from August 1273 to May 1274; and it was his chief residence from August 1286 to August 1289. Considering his preoccupations at home, not least in Scotland and Wales, Edward paid much attention to his French possessions. As Eleanor C. Lodge remarks in her valuable *Gascony under English Rule* (1926), 'The connection of Gascony with England was closer than ever before, and perhaps for the first time it could be considered an English possession rather than merely an outlying bit of royal property.'

Edward had his reward, for he received not only monetary taxes but Gascon soldiers to help him in his campaigns at home. Yet he had to tread warily. Even in 1261 when he had secured the right to nominate the mayor, he and the Seneschal had to swear to observe the customs of Bordeaux before the leading citizens swore fealty to him. He conciliated the nobles but relied on the townspeople. Later he also had the nomination of the mayoralty of St-Émilion in his hands, and in 1268 he ordered Jean de Grailly, the Seneschal of Gascony, to build a *bastide* on the Dordogne at an important spot which was to become a centre of the wine trade, and remains today the headquarters of merchants who specialize in the wines of St-Émilion, Pomerol and Fronsac. This was Libourne, said to be named after the English Seneschal of Guyenne, Roger de Leyburn, who is alleged to have been responsible for the erection of the town and its fortifications.

These fortified towns or *bastides* are a feature of south-west France, and were strong points created by the English or the French in their long struggle in this frontier country. The best-preserved of them today, such as Domme and Monpazier, still retain their fortifications and their gridiron pattern of streets which is the admiration and source of pilgrimage of modern town planners. Their other readily recognizable feature are squares surrounded by arcades, an example of which may be seen today in the Place Abel Surchamp in Libourne. Another relic is the fine Tour du Grand Port on the river-front. The English kings used to stay nearby at the castle of Condat. The Captain of Fronsac was usually an Englishman. One of these, Sir William Faringdon, later became Constable of Bordeaux.

Relations with the French Crown were always uneasy, and it must be remembered that Edward I held Gascony as a fief of the French Crown. He and the other kings who accepted this situation did not try to claim the French throne; indeed they swore loyalty to the kings of France, who took care to assert their dominance even when they were not actually engaged in fighting a war or planning the renewal of hostilities against their reluctant English subordinates.

In 1294 Philip the Fair (1268–1314) actually sent troops to occupy Bordeaux and the surrounding places. Although an English expedition later that year succeeded in recapturing Castillon and Macau in the Médoc as well as Bourg and Blaye, the French held the Gascon capital until peace was signed in Paris in 1303. The French occupation did not endear itself to the Bordelais, and the last years of Edward's reign were spent in repairing the damage, including the payment of large sums in compensation.

The close connection between England and Bordeaux in Edward's time may be shown by the fact that Henry de Waleys, Lord Mayor of London in 1274, was Mayor of Bordeaux in the following year. In the succeeding reign of Edward II the Bordeaux merchants in the English trade formed a trade association: The Merchant Wine Tonners of Gascony. It is not always realized that the Vintners' Company of London, one of the twelve great City livery companies, owed its original role entirely to its association with the wine trade with Bordeaux. Although the 'Mistery of Vintners' probably originated at the beginning of the thirteenth century, it became important only through the accession of Gascony to the English Crown which resulted, during the reign of King John, in Gascon wines being imported to the increasing exclusion of others, and the Vintners had the sole right of sale. For although their members were importing merchants to some extent, their chief role was as retailers or taverners, and their privileges were confined to the sale of Gascon wines. This was confirmed in their first charter of 1364, but not until 1437 were they finally incorporated as 'The Company and Mistery of Vintners of London'.

Edward II, born in 1284 and reigning from 1307 to 1327, who married Isabella of France and paid homage in person to

Philip the Fair in 1308, did not leave much impression on Bordeaux, but near the close of his reign there was a war, unsuccessful from the English standpoint. When Edward III (1327–77) ascended the throne he possessed only a strip of land from Saintes to Bayonne. Aggrieved by the failure of the French kings to observe the terms of the treaties or to treat them fairly as vassals, Edward laid open claim to the French throne. This, in 1337, precipitated the Hundred Years War which eventually led to the loss of Bordeaux in 1453. The maintenance of English rule in Gascony was a focal point of the war throughout its intermittent course.

This is not the place for a detailed history of this struggle, which began with the French seizure of Blaye by the stratagem of blocking the gateway with a provision waggon. Libourne and other places fell, but were recaptured in 1345 by Henry of Lancaster, Earl of Derby, who led a very successful two-year campaign right up into Poitou. After a truce in 1347 the war was renewed in 1355 and this time the Black Prince was in command. He played a considerable part in the history of Bordeaux during the period, and on his first arrival he presented his letters of patent to the notables of the city in the cathedral of St-André. The following year he led the campaign which culminated in the Battle of Poitiers which, it should be remembered, was not just an English victory, but an Anglo-Gascon one, for the Black Prince's army contained Gascon troops.

King John (1350–64) of France was captured and taken to Bordeaux, being civilly treated there before being sent over to England whence he was ransomed in 1360, but returned to London in 1364 and died there. Meanwhile following the Treaty of Bretigny in 1360, in which the English claim to the French throne was given up in return for full sovereignty in much of south-west France, there was another interval of peace, and the Black Prince was given the Principality of Aquitaine and Gascony. On 9 July 1363 Bordeaux witnessed a ceremony of oath of fealty made to the Black Prince by the nobles, mayor and *jurats* of Bordeaux, and the municipal leaders of such wine towns as Bourg, Blaye, St-Émilion and Langon. For seven years he ruled the country, often residing in Bordeaux where he organized lavish entertainments – perhaps on the principle of wine and circuses – which cost the principality a great deal in taxes. He also gave the top posts to the English. When war was resumed in 1369, the Prince was failing in health and he departed from France finally in 1371, leaving his brother John, Duke of Lancaster, in command. But John was no match for Bertrand du Guesclin, and by 1375 the English/Gascon side was in poor shape. Only Bordeaux, Bayonne and Dax remained to them.

Richard II who succeeded Edward III in 1377 was born at Bordeaux on Twelfth Night 1367, the son of the Black Prince and his wife Joan the Fair Maid of Kent. He has been popularly known as Richard of Bordeaux. Although he left Bordeaux when a small child and never revisited it after becoming king, this unfortunate monarch managed to establish a favourable local impression. During his reign truces persisted, and in 1390 he sent his uncle John of Gaunt to Bordeaux and appointed him Prince of Aquitaine. This title was extremely unpopular with the Bordelais who, without direct access to the English Crown, feared isolation, to be followed by a French take-over. It was then agreed that the new Prince should be received only as a representative of the King. When Richard was dethroned in 1399 by Henry IV, the Bordelais for some time refused to accept the new king and sent strong protests to England; although the nobles were quietened by an envoy of Henry, the common people were not and in 1403 started an insurrection and attacked the Ombrière, but without success. In 1406 the French under the Duke of Orleans, brother of Charles VI (1368–1422), took the field again and assailed Bourg and Blaye, 'the keys to Bordeaux and Gascony on the north', as they were described. Bourg was besieged from October 1406 to January 1407. However, ships from Bordeaux sailed down the Gironde and destroyed a French squadron, with the result that Blaye held out until the customary truce in 1407.

But the sands of English rule in Gascony were beginning to run out. Neither Henry IV (1399–1413) nor Henry V (1413–22) ever entered Bordeaux during their reigns. The latter was more interested in securing the French throne than in his Gascon territories. The Bordelais had to rely increasingly on their own efforts to keep the French at bay, for they were deeply concerned to maintain the English connections, which gave them a considerable measure of independence, while the towns under the French Crown were steadily losing their powers to the centralizing control of the royal administration. To clear the 'enemy' from her neighbourhood and to secure the freedom of trade on the Garonne and Gironde, Bordeaux began her own war in 1420 and captured St-Macaire and La Réole upstream.

However, Joan of Arc came to the fore and in 1429 Charles VII (1422–61) was crowned at Rheims. He was determined to clear the English from France, but it was not until 1442 that he felt able to attack and invest Bordeaux itself.

By now the chief defender of Bordeaux against the French and the leader of the pro-English party was the remarkable archbishop of Bordeaux, Pey Berland, the son of a peasant, who had been born in the Médoc. He was made archbishop in 1430, and became the chief founder of the university in 1442. When Charles attacked and captured Dax, so long an English stronghold, Pey Berland organized the defence of Bordeaux and set off for England to secure help from Henry VI (1422–61). He procured some aid, and in 1444 there was a truce which lasted for five years. However, in 1451 a much more serious investment took place and at last Blaye fell, followed by Bourg, Libourne and St-Émilion. Only Fronsac held out for a time but that too surrendered. Henry VI was far too occupied

with the domestic Wars of the Roses to send any help to the
Gascons. Archbishop Pey Berland treated with the French
commander, Dunois, and secured favourable terms from him.
The French were more concerned to conciliate rather than to
humiliate this important city. On 30 June 1451 Dunois clad all
in white and on horseback led a victory march into the city via
the Chartrons, where so many Bordeaux wine merchants
today have their offices and cellars. The only English stronghold left was Lesparre far up the Médoc.

Soon however the Bordelais had second thoughts. They
lived by trade, principally by selling their wine to England.
How and where were they going to sell their 1451s? When in
1452 they were asked to pay a tax for the defence of France,
and their objections that it was contrary to the capitulation
terms were waved aside by Charles VII, they began secret
talks with the English. Henry, better placed now to send an
expedition to Gascony, dispatched John Talbot, Earl of
Shrewsbury, in command of a fleet up the Gironde in October
1452. He landed in the Médoc and during the night of 22
October the gates of Bordeaux were opened to him by the
welcoming citizens. There was another triumphal entry and
the English commander, whose name is commemorated in the
name of the St-Julien château, was hailed as 'Le Roi Talbot'.
He went on to secure Libourne, Cadillac and Castillon. Again
only Fronsac held out, this time for its new French rulers, but
was captured during the winter.

However the next campaign was the last. Although the
English king sent more reinforcements from England, Charles
VII personally took over the French forces. His general was
Jean Bureau, still today a well-known name in the Bordeaux
district and borne by the former *maître de chai* of Yquem. On
15 July Talbot sallied out of Bordeaux, paused at Libourne and
then surprised the French advance guard at Castillon a short
way up the Dordogne. He made the mistake of not awaiting
the arrival of his main force, and on 17 July 1453 his troops

were routed at the Battle of Castillon; he and his son the Earl of Lisle were both mortally wounded. It is said that as the result of a promise given to the French king upon his release from captivity on a previous occasion, not to bear arms against the French, he went unarmed into the Battle of Castillon. His exact age is a matter of conjecture, but he was an old man, probably over seventy, and possibly as much as eighty. Talbot is a prominent, noble figure in Shakespeare's *Henry VI, Part One*, where his defeat is attributed more to the fraud of a delaying fellow-Englishman than to the French forces. According to Shakespeare, Talbot appears before the walls of Bordeaux but does not capture the city, and then there is a scene actually at Castillon, described merely as 'A Field of Battle'. Talbot's son John is killed first, and his body placed in his father's arms who dies with the words:

> Soldiers, adieu! I have what I would have,
> Now my old arms are young John Talbot's grave.

St-Émilion, Libourne and Fronsac immediately fell, and Bordeaux was encircled. The French king's soldiers invaded the Médoc in pursuit of the fleeing English, and the song ran:

> *Tous les jours, les Francoys courroient*
> *En l'isle et pays de Médot,*
> *Où Angloys et leurs biens prennoient*
> *Sans ce que aucun leur dist mot.*

In Bordeaux they held out until October, but then even Archbishop Pey Berland recognized that the end had come. The French troops entered the city on 19 October. Although the lenient terms of two years previously were cancelled, the Bordelais were not badly treated. If the French behaved comparatively moderately towards the Bordelais, with only one or two executions and some imprisonments, there was savage devastation of much of the previously English territory. Places such as Castillon, Libourne, St-Émilion, Cadillac,

Bourg and Blaye were ravaged, and the countryside devastated. The Médoc was particularly severely treated, with vineyards destroyed by soldiers and animals. Macau is mentioned as a substantial sufferer; and, as throughout this sporadic but savage Hundred Years War, the common people paid dearly for their doubtless often enforced loyalties to one side or the other. The English were allowed to depart in their ships, even being permitted to take with them cargoes of wine, a gesture which must be considered to have been a clever publicity move for the wines of Bordeaux. It is said that before leaving the shrewd English merchants hastily purchased the 1453s.

It cannot be said that the Gascons were soon reconciled to French rule. In 1457 the French king wrote to the Scottish king, James II (1437–60), saying 'as for the county of Guyenne, everyone knows it has been English for 300 years, and the people of the district are at heart entirely inclined to the English party'. Even thirty years later a chronicler wrote: 'the majority were so strongly for the English (and still are) that they did not know how to like the French, since for three centuries without a break they had been English.'

The basis of this support of the English connection had been commercial and economic rather than sentimental, and for reasons closely connected with the vital wine trade. Where could the Bordelais sell the wine not only from their immediate surroundings but also that which came down the Dordogne and the Garonne from the Haut-Pays?

Moreover the three hundred years of English rule in Bordeaux should not be thought of as English 'occupation' of French territory. Bordeaux and its surrounding region was indubitably no part of England, but no more was it French; it was Gascony. More than a century after the French take-over of Bordeaux, the *jurats* of Bordeaux declared in 1585, '*nous sommes en pays de conqueste*'. One of the attractions of the English connection was its remoteness. The distance of Bordeaux from England had been the best guarantee of its liberty, while the French kings, with their centralizing policy, were now all too near at hand. Even two hundred years later this antipathy existed. The autocratic, ambitious Louis XIV (1643–1715) was by no means popular in Gascony, and until the end of his reign the Bordelais retained a somewhat idyllic picture of the *époque anglaise*. In addition to economic considerations, the memories of the savage re-conquest, particularly in the Médoc and in the Graves near the capital, remained as vivid as the brutalities of Cromwell in Ireland did among the Irish.

THE WINE TRADE WITH ENGLAND

The beginnings of the Bordeaux wine trade with England can be firmly dated as not being substantial until the thirteenth century. In an edict of King John of 1199, the regions from which came the wines chiefly drunk in England were enumerated, and Gascony was not even mentioned; the leading supplies came from further north in the Poitou. It was in the thirteenth century that the Bordeaux vineyards really began to be extended, and then expanded rapidly in the fourteenth century – a period of great prosperity for medieval Bordeaux – and further still in the fifteenth century. All other forms of agriculture became of minor importance. In the thirteenth century the most prolific area was the Graves, pressing in on Bordeaux itself, where several of the parishes contained vineyards. There was even one in the garden of the archbishop, who was one of the largest vineyard owners, a prominence he shared with the dean and chapter of the cathedral of St-André. The former owned vineyards in Pessac and Mérignac; the latter possessed vineyard properties in the main Graves communes, including Pessac, Léognan and Villenave d'Ornon, as well as others in Listrac, Moulis, Avensan, Blanquefort and Le Taillan in the Médoc. But neither archbishop nor chapter seem to have spread their vine properties so far afield as those communes in the Médoc most famous today, such as Pauillac, St-Julien or Margaux.

The reason for this expansion of wine growing must have been based on the trade with England, and later to some extent with the Low Countries. There was no great market for Bordeaux wines in Paris or in other French centres of population. For one reason, overland transport was too arduous, and for another, regions as far north as Normandy produced their own wine, while Paris relied on the wine from districts relatively easy of access, including Burgundy, whose produce came down the Seine, and Champagne whence still wine was transported down the Marne. The Bordeaux trade was seaborne and its natural outlets were maritime, non-wine-producing countries, including England, Scotland, Ireland, the Low Countries and the Baltic States. Of these England was the most accessible, with its convenient ports at Bristol and Southampton, the chief English landing places for wine imports from Bordeaux in the Middle Ages.

Wine was indeed the leading French export of this period, and Bordeaux was almost certainly the chief exporter. It remained so for many hundreds of years, for until internal transport improved in the eighteenth and nineteenth centuries, Bordeaux could not depend on a substantial domestic demand outside the region. For much the same reason the English had to rely on Bordeaux for their table wines until the struggles with France that began at the end of the seventeenth century and continued intermittently until the defeat of Napoleon. This may explain the comparative rarity of burgundy in England right up to the end of the last century; it was difficult and expensive to transport to England and a ready market could be found nearer at hand.

Throughout the English connection, the Bordelais, well aware on which side their bread was buttered, set out particularly to win the support of the English kings in the thirteenth century. They had three possible competitors: La Rochelle;

the wine growers of the Haut-Pays; and, as the Bordeaux vineyards began to be developed, the more distant part of the Médoc, with its ease of access to the sea.

La Rochelle was a thriving rival wine port long before Bordeaux became important for wine, and had the advantage of being right on the sea, whereas to reach the Girondin port, ships had to make the difficult sixty-mile passage up the estuary – a disadvantage with which the Bordelais have to reckon even today. Fortunately for Bordeaux its rival was much more open to attack and capture by the French king. When in 1224 the latter's troops struck south and captured several Atlantic ports, the Bordelais were quick to write to Hubert de Burgh, the King's Justiciar, the head of the royal administration, reaffirming their loyalty to the English Crown and contrasting this with the infidelity and frailty of those towns further north which had surrendered. Therefore, as the French gradually encroached over the years on to the English king's possessions, the commercial standing of Bordeaux was improved.

Although demand from the Low Countries and others beyond the English Channel could take up the greater part of Bordeaux's wine exports, these markets could only be reached with the approval of the English king and his fleet. Accordingly the Bordelais were enthusiastic for the English connection for 200 years after the rest of the English territories in France had largely been taken over by the French kings. From the fall of La Rochelle in 1224 can be dated the supremacy of Bordeaux as a wine trading centre and port.

Meanwhile it appears as if the Bordelais decided that to have the English king on their side was not only a matter of politics and business, but also for the sake of what now would be called publicity. We all know these days that for some curious reason if a well-known personality, be it king, queen, president or film star, is known to be partial to a particular wine or brand of drink, this is a valuable commendation for other consumers. As the expertise of such personalities lies in other fields, this might seem a doubtful recommendation, but in view of the successful association of cognac with Napoleon and a Scotch whisky with a British Commander-in-Chief in the First World War, there is no doubt this works even in the twentieth century. Certainly it did with Bordeaux in the thirteenth century.

There was in England then a taste for the wines of Anjou and of the Rhine, but were it known that the king drank the red wines of Bordeaux, this should assure their success. So it did. Whereas in 1199, the Gascon wines were not even mentioned among the leading wines consumed in England, from 1206 onwards they appear among those bought for the royal table or offered as presents by the king. In 1214 John was thanking the Governor of Bristol for apprising him of the arrival there of a consignment of Bordeaux wines; and in 1215 he had bought 120 *tonneaux* of Gascon wines for his personal use.

Such was the royal interest in Bordeaux wine that by 1219 Henry III was writing to the Mayor of Bordeaux, complaining that a check had shown a shortfall in the amount of wine gauged in the *tonneaux*, and denouncing this fraud. By 1224 three-quarters of the wine drunk in the royal palaces came from Bordeaux, and by the middle of the century it was the customary wine to celebrate any solemn or festive occasion, as champagne is today. Sixty years later so much gold was being sent out of England to pay for the royal wines that Parliament protested (Simon, *History of the Wine Trade in England*, 1906-9).

The Bordelais did not confine their attentions to the king. They made suitable presents to the English notabilities and entertained the British merchants who made their annual trip to Bordeaux to buy the young wine. In the accounts of the archbishops of Bordeaux for 1382 and 1386, there are entries relating to the entertainment of 'the merchants of England

and Britain'. The English wine fleet left the English shores late in September, arriving in the Gironde in the first half of October, when the young wine was just about made. They spent eight to ten weeks in Bordeaux, tasting and bargaining, and then returned to England in time for Christmas. The voyage from Bordeaux to the English Channel ports took about ten days. The royal butler had first choice of their purchases. The wine, of course, was drunk at once – *le vin de l'année*, as this would now be called. It had to be drunk young, as before the development of the wine bottle and the cork no wine could be kept sound for any length of time.

Another problem for the Bordelais was to enlist the support of the English kings against the wines of the Haut-Pays. The wine that the English kings, and no doubt private citizens also, secured from Bordeaux did not come only from the area of the present Bordeaux *vignoble*, as confined by the modern boundaries of the department of the Gironde. King John bought wine in 1206 and 1207 from the vineyards of the Abbey of Moissac, situated some way up the Garonne and renowned now for its splendid romanesque cloister. Moissac wine is also recorded as being sold to England late in the thirteenth century. In 1225 the wines of Cahors and Gaillac were imported into England. These wines were sold and shipped by the Bordeaux merchants, except for the Dordogne wines from centres like Bergerac; these were often handled in the latter part of the Middle Ages by Libourne, the leading wine-shipping rival of Bordeaux.

However as the Bordeaux vineyards spread rapidly in the thirteenth and succeeding centuries, so did the Bordelais try to ensure that their wine was first on the market each year. They petitioned the English kings to this effect. As long as part at least of the Haut-Pays was English the kings were not anxious to practise discrimination against wine from such centres as Agen on the Garonne and Bergerac on the Dordogne, but once they had fallen to the French, they were in 'enemy territory', and might be punished to help the loyal Bordelais. Thus the latter were permitted to keep out 'foreign' wines until the feast of St Martin and even until Christmas. By this time their own new wine was on the high seas or even being consumed in the taverns of the City of London, as the *beaujolais de l'année* is today drunk in the Paris restaurants by the Christmas following the vintage. As the vineyards spread in the Bordeaux region, so did the other crops contract. Accordingly, in 1401 King Henry IV imposed the condition on the merchants in 'enemy-held territories' that they must send one *tonneau* of corn for every two *tonneaux* of wine. As the merchants had nowhere else to dispose of their wine, they had no option but to comply.

If wine was France's chief medieval export, it was also England's largest import, and although separate statistics for Gascon wine imports are rare, most French wine to be found in England then was from Gascony. At its height in the fourteenth century it represented 31 per cent of our imports, compared with 1 per cent today. Indeed on *per capita* basis the amount of Gascon wine imported into England in the early fourteenth century has never been equalled. According to the estimate of Marjory K. James 'The Fluctuations of the Anglo-Gascon Wine Trade During the Fourteenth Century', *Economic History Review*, 1951), over 20,000 tuns came in annually, representing between a quarter and a fifth of Bordeaux exports. Translated into hectolitres this amounted to 180,000. Yet in so recent a year as 1978 the total quantity of Bordeaux wines exported to Britain was no more than 176,000 hl. Early in the fourteenth century the Bordelais were exporting from Bordeaux, Libourne and the smaller Gironde ports as much as 90,000–100,000 *tonneaux* a year.

It must be added that these exports included large amounts of wine – up to 50 per cent of the total – that had originally come from the Haut-Pays, beyond Castillon on the Dordogne and St-Macaire on the Garonne. Although restrictions were placed on their sale in Bordeaux, for export purposes these wines were privileged. While the citizens, nobles and clerics did not pay to the English king the Great Custom on exports, the other Bordelais did pay it in full, but the Haut-Pays wines secured a reduction. The wine from the tax-exempt vineyards of the privileged classes of Bordeaux only amounted to between one-eighth and one-fifth of the whole. Incidentally there was no exemption from the Custom of Royan, which the wine-laden ships paid as they passed into the open sea.

What good customers the English kings were to their wine merchants is shown by the fact that in the early fourteenth century the normal 'annual order' given by the royal butler for the use of the court varied from 1,000–2,000 *tonneaux*; and to celebrate his marriage with Isabella of France in January 1308, Edward II ordered 1,000 *tonneaux*. By modern reckoning this would have produced something like 1,152,000 bottles. Quite a wedding!

The first half of the fourteenth century was the time of greatest economic prosperity, but this began to decline as the Hundred Years War got under way. As the fighting affected the hinterland on which the great trading centre depended for much of its supplies, and to some extent its markets, so exports declined. The Haut-Pays largely passed into French hands, and henceforth only a trickle of wine from the privileged districts that had enjoyed customs preference reached Bordeaux.

When the Earl of Derby's successful campaign of 1345–6 freed the nearer territories, notably St-Émilion and Libourne, trade improved. Yet the fighting had caused terrible devastation to the vineyards all the way from Blaye up to St-Émilion on the Dordogne and St-Macaire on the Garonne. Moreover the English kings had to organize convoys of ships to collect the wine, harassed by French and Spanish alike. Already before the war English shipping was taking an increasing share of this carrying trade, and by 1330 it was estimated that more Gascon wine was brought to London by English merchants than by Gascons.

Then in 1348 the Black Death reached Bordeaux, and recurred intermittently throughout the century. By mid-century half the greatly reduced quantity of Bordeaux wine exports came to England. As the war became increasingly unsuccessful for the English, so did the fortunes of Bordeaux run down. In 1348–9 Bordeaux shipped only 6,800 *tonneaux*.

Moreover prices rose sharply in mid-century. The king's wine, which had cost him only £3 or less a *tonneau* at the beginning of the century reached £7 to £8 in 1348. Total Bordeaux exports dropped from about 30,000 *tonneaux* to seven or eight thousand. Only the record crop of 1376 raised the total in that year to nearly 29,000 *tonneaux*: the last substantial total of the century. But in 1372 the English king had to pay up to £8 10s. a *tonneau*, and although prices dropped at the end of the century, they were still twice as high as at the beginning. By this time England virtually monopolized the Bordeaux export wine trade, accounting for three-quarters or four-fifths. They were taking probably between 15,000 and 20,000 *tonneaux*, a figure which dropped in the next century after England finally lost Bordeaux. Even by 1428–31 when Bordeaux exports were down to an average of 13,000 *tonneaux*, the English took the great majority. Moreover, they still remained loyal to Gascon wine, and at the beginning of the fifteenth century only about 300–400 tuns of Rhine wine reached England each year, while the wine from Spain, Portugal and the Mediterranean producers was only a fraction of the total imports. The last decade of the English 'ascendancy' included years with the highest imports of French wine into England in the fifteenth century; from 1444 to 1449 imports averaged about 13,000 tuns each year.

The value to Bordeaux of the English connection has been made clear. But what did the English and particularly the English kings receive in return? First and obviously, they re-

ceived wine which was a basic essential at a time when water
was usually undrinkable and ale had not taken over as the
drink of the better-off classes. If it had not been for the recurrent conflicts with the French kings, no doubt more wine
would have reached England from the then extensive wine
area in northern France and from Burgundy, via the prosperous port of Rouen. However, as it happened, Gascon wine
became the English staple.

The English kings not only needed wine in enormous quantities for the consumption of the royal household, but they
also expected a good deal of credit. At times they were very
bad payers, but no doubt the Bordeaux merchants, who
certainly flourished according to the standards of their period,
made up for this in the prices they charged their other customers. The Bordeaux merchants even lent money to the kings,
and Edward I was a borrower in 1280. Furthermore the king
took a 'prise' of two casks of wine per shipload entering an
English port, although the Cinque Ports were exempted from
this tax owing to their services against the adjacent French.
Some of this wine would have been used in the royal household, but the monarchy was not above a little state trading on
its own.

This was not the only form of wine taxation benefit received by the English kings. Wine from the Haut-Pays had
to pay a tax of 15s. a cask if from the English dominions, but
two or three times that amount if from French territories.
Only Bordeaux and Libourne were exempt from this tax, a
valuable relief afforded them by Eleanor of Aquitaine in 1188
and confirmed by Edward I in 1302. The English kings had
other benefits. They secured the help of Gascon soldiers not
only for their domestic campaigns against the Scots and Welsh
but also against the French king.

There were also commercial rewards. The English sent to
Bordeaux consignments of herrings, beans, corn, dairy produce and above all cloth. From Cornish ports dried fish was

dispatched to the Gironde. Bristol was the main port for the Gascon trade, and much of the cloth needed by the Gascons passed through the port of Bristol. In fourteenth-century records one reads of the Archbishop of Bordeaux buying his dried fish from Cornwall and cheese from England. In view of the excellent partnership between the milder English cheeses and claret, it is high time this medieval trade was renewed, and mature English Cheddar, Wensleydale, Double Gloucester and Scottish Dunlop be found in the circular Bordeaux market just off the Allées de Tourny; many of the French cheeses are too powerful for the delicate red Bordeaux.

The other, and in the long run perhaps the most beneficial result of the English ascendancy in Gascony, was the development of our shipping. As already indicated, over the 300 years of English rule, the proportion of English shipping used in the trade with the Gascon ports increased at the expense of the native shipping. This was helped in Edward III's reign by a ban on the export of capital, as it would now be described. One recorded exception was in 1364 when a group of English merchants were allowed to take the large sum of £2,000 to buy Gascon wines. The development of the English shipping also assisted the Bordeaux wine merchants. After the venturesome voyage from England and the anticipated dangers on the return trip from ships of the French Crown, pirates and the winter gales, the English shipmaster wanted a full load of wine aboard to repay him for his risks. Since there was only a relatively short period in which the new wine could be bought for current drinking, the Bordeaux merchants were often able to exact high prices for their newly vintaged wine. By the end of the fourteenth century a shipload might include 200–300 *tonneaux*.

The gradual passing of the carrying trade into English hands was to stand England in good stead, building up a tradition of seamanship which, in the centuries following their expulsion from Gascony, was to pay dividends in the wars against the

Spaniards, the Dutch and the French. In the formation of this tradition the Bordeaux wine-carrying trade played its part.

It is not clear, however, that from a balance of trade point of view the possession of Bordeaux and a gradually shrinking portion of Gascony was an asset to the English economy. These territories were not colonies, as the term was later understood. Accordingly, when the English lost Bordeaux in the same year that Constantinople fell to the Turks, there were no great lamentations. This was owing partly to domestic preoccupation with the Wars of the Roses, but also because the loss was not obviously detrimental to the English economy.

4. After the English

For the first few years of the French occupation, the Bordelais were politically and economically punished for their welcome of 'Le Roi Talbot' in 1452 and their obstinate adherence to the English connection.

According to Robert Boutruche in *Bordeaux de 1453 à 1715* (1966), perhaps 2,000 Bordelais emigrated to England, some of them nobles but also merchants. London, Southampton and Bristol were their places of refuge, and in the City of London many established themselves in the parish of St Martin Vintry. As with other refugees, this led to some bad feeling between the newcomers and the English merchants. When the French king pardoned them in the following decade, a number returned to Bordeaux. The pro-English Archbishop Pey Berland died in 1456.

The French king took the nomination of the mayor into his own hands. However, what the French kings wanted was possession of Gascony and its capital, not the prohibition of profitable trade.

So although Charles VII built the Château Trompette to overawe the citizens, his successor Louis XI (1461–83) immediately gave Bordeaux the Parlement (a legal court, not a proper assembly) which they had been promised ten years earlier. The famous Bordeaux privileges extorted from the English kings were confirmed. These by now included no taxes on burghers' wine on entry into the city or export, reduced taxes for wines from the *Sénéchaussée* (broadly speaking the present Gironde Department), full taxes on wines from neighbouring wine areas, and restrictions on the date of arrival and duration of such wines' stay in the city and its suburbs.

Louis XI also enforced the rule preventing the loading of any wine between Bordeaux and the Atlantic, save for wine intended for the city; and in 1462 he prolonged until Christmas the prohibition on Haut-Pays wines entering the Bordeaux region.

Anglo-Gascon trade went through a difficult time. At first it was quite possible for the English ships to maintain their trips to Bordeaux, except during the autumn of 1455, when access was barred to them. However, their ships were now controlled from the time they entered the Gironde. They were obliged to stop at Soulac to pick up their permits, and again at Blaye to deposit their arms. Residence for English merchants in Bordeaux was restricted to certain houses; they could only stay there for a maximum of a month and were subject to a 5 p.m. to 7 a.m. curfew. They were shadowed, and could only make purchases outside the city if accompanied by a Bordeaux merchant or official. During this period of economic warfare, which lasted from 1455 to 1463, trade dropped off. Whereas English wine imports from Bordeaux were as high as 10,000 *tonneaux* in 1447–8, and were as much as 6,000 *tonneaux* in the critical year of 1453–4, after a spurt to 9,500 *tonneaux* in 1454–5 they shrank to 3,000 *tonneaux* a year until economic peace was restored in 1463, and the kings of both countries once more issued trading licences to their subjects.

From Bordeaux's point of view this was high time, and it was the French king who initiated the truce. As quoted by Miss E. M. Carus-Wilson in an article in the 1947 *Bulletin of the Institute of Historical Research* on the effects on the wine trade of the English acquisition and loss of Gascony, Louis XI accepted the advice of a councillor 'that the whole basis of Bordeaux's wealth was the isle of England, that no other country could take England's place as purchaser of its wines and supplier of its needs, and that the English should therefore be allowed to trade once more as freely as they would'.

Allowed they were, but commercial relations were often

strained, and sometimes interrupted, until the Treaty of Picquigny in 1475, after which English merchants were no longer required to have safe conducts; they also secured a reduction in the *Grande Coutume* export tax. From 1482 restrictions on their stay and movements were removed. However, the visits of English merchants were personally hazardous; so much so that in 1483 the English king asked the French king for assurances as to the safety of English merchants visiting Bordeaux. These were given. Nevertheless the French Court always regarded a re-invasion as on the cards, and in 1485 Charles VIII (1483–98) assisted the repair of the fortifications of Bourg, for the town was 'in great danger of being taken by our old enemies – the English'.

After the English left Bordeaux, the wine merchants there certainly had to fight harder to maintain their trade. From now on the Bordelais had to compete in the English market with the wines of Spain, Portugal and even of Greece. It is possible that this competition led to an improvement in the quality of Bordeaux wines. They had little success in other parts of France, but they did begin to build up the important trade with Flanders, the Low Countries and the Hanseatic cities which was to be their mainstay later on.

In France economic conditions in the second half of the fifteenth century were poor, and the price of wine tended to drop. In England, however, according to André Simon in his invaluable *History of the Wine Trade in England* (1906–9), wine prices rose, and for a time imports fell. In the first twenty years of the fifteenth century they had averaged 15,000 tuns (a tun was 252 old gallons, a hogshead 62 old gallons). Then in the middle of the century they dropped as low as 8,000, since wine had become too expensive for the ordinary people; about the end of the century they rose to 20,000–25,000 tuns, and to 50,000 in the boom years of 1509–18. Thereafter they fell back to 20,000–30,000, except for a spurt in Queen Elizabeth's reign (1558–1603) to an average of 58,000. Yet by the end of the sixteenth century they were only 35,000–40,000 tuns for a population much larger than it had been a century or so earlier.

For wine prices in England continued to rise. In 1580 wine was 2s. a gallon in Oxford, and in 1598 Gascon wine cost 2s. 8d. a gallon in London. The gallon was the old gallon, five-sixths of the present one, and equivalent to the American gallon. The rise in wine prices was part of the general increase in the cost of living in the second half of the sixteenth century, following the discovery of gold in the New World.

Much of this wine continued to be Gascon wine. (It was not called claret in the modern sense until later. Simon quotes Edward Tremaine using the term as meaning a red Bordeaux in 1565.) After the loss of Gascony, the English kings continued to send an agent each year to buy the young wine, and until the end of the sixteenth century, the English wine fleet made its annual autumn voyage to Bordeaux, returning in mid-December each year. Henry VII (1485–1509) and others tried to enforce a decree that all wine from Gascony should come in English, Scottish or Welsh ships, but this was modified. Later on Charles I (1625–49) tried to do the same.

Bordeaux wines remained popular in England for much the same reason that they have been for the last hundred years: they were relatively cheap for their good quality, compared with other wines such as sack, Rhenish and those from further afield. Good relations were maintained between the traders of both nations. Simon quotes the French authorities as complaining in 1517 about the number of English merchants and sailors – seven to eight thousand of them at times – in the Bordeaux area. The merchants were on such friendly terms with the country people around Bordeaux and in the Médoc that in the event of war the English would have no difficulty in landing troops.

The wines that these English preferred above all were the Graves, followed by those of the Médoc fairly near Bordeaux and then the *palus* growths beside the river. Until the development of the big Médoc estates in the seventeenth and eighteenth centuries, it was the red Graves that won most esteem. It is for this reason that the first of the *premiers crus* to be mentioned in print, and in England to be praised by Pepys, was Haut-Brion. White wines were a minor consideration until a demand was created for them by the Dutch. The principal source of white wine was an estate owned by the Pontac family in Blanquefort, the nearest Médoc commune to Bordeaux. This, therefore, strictly was a Médoc not a Graves, although the boundaries then were not rigidly fixed as they are today. As mentioned earlier, Pessac was partly at least described as being in the Médoc.

At the beginning of the sixteenth century the Chartrons was only an *entrepôt* and that great arc of the Garonne was known as the *Port de la Lune*. It was not even a parish, and was full of cellars rather than dwelling houses. The products of the Haut-Pays caused the rapid development of the Chartrons in the sixteenth century; not only for wine but for corn and other up-country commodities.

During this century annual Bordeaux wine exports varied from 20,000–30,000 *tonneaux* a year to 80,000–100,000 in exceptional years. But the English connection was no longer dominant.

As the trade with England began to flag towards the end of the sixteenth century that of the newly formed Netherlands took its place. The Dutch and the Hanseatic traders had first made a noteworthy appearance in Bordeaux in the middle of that century. Then the declared independence of the Dutch states in 1579 led to a great increase in the commerce in French wines. For the next hundred years the Dutch Republic was at the height of its economic power. How powerful it was in the carrying trade may be gauged from the fact that in 1669 the French Minister of Marine, Colbert, estimated the French fleet at 500–600 vessels, the English at 3,000–4,000 and the Dutch at 15,000–16,000. So it was they who carried the wine up the continental coast and round to the Baltic, notably to the Hanseatic towns which established a reputation as wine trade centres which they have never entirely lost. Dutch merchants took up residence in Bordeaux as the English had done before them. Indeed the oldest existing firm of merchants in Bordeaux today is Beyerman, a Dutch firm founded in 1620.

But it was a different trade from that of the English, for the economically-minded Dutch and their Flemish neighbours preferred cheap white wines, particularly sweet Sauternes, and this caused an enormous increase in the production of white wine in the Graves area and further up the Garonne; but also in most other areas outside the stubbornly red wine areas, as the Médoc and St-Émilion seem to have remained. The white wine area included Ste-Foy as well as Bergerac, outside the Bordeaux region as we know it today.

Moreover while the English always maintained a preference for what were then the 'quality wines', the Dutch were interested in buying, drinking or re-selling cheap wines to other northern countries. It was reckoned by Colbert that they drank only a third of what they bought each year, and re-exported two-thirds. For this purpose they did a great deal of blending of what we would call *vin de consommation*. This 'mass production' blending was unpopular with the producers and merchants having interests in the fine wine districts. By the early eighteenth century there was more white wine produced in Bordeaux than red. As an example Dion states that 26,800 *tonneaux* of white wine and only 2,700 *tonneaux* of red were exported in 1738–40 to Scandinavia, Pomerania, Danzig, Lübeck, Riga and Hamburg. On the other hand in 1725 the Bordeaux Parlement complained that the English had maintained their tradition of buying *grand vin* at an 'excessive price', originating from only a dozen or fifteen sources, and representing only 2 per cent of the output. Today, perhaps, this complaint might be transferred to the other side of the Atlantic.

Nevertheless the Dutch certainly helped to develop the Bordeaux vineyards at a time when English interest was reduced and later was actively hostile to French wines – initially under the influence of Dutch William. And for all their preference for inexpensive white wines, it was, ironically, the Dutch who laid the foundation of the great red wines by their assistance with draining the Médoc marshes. A Dutchman, Conrad Gaussen, led the work. As for the English trade, at the beginning of the seventeenth century James I (1603–25) was partial to Bordeaux wines, partly perhaps owing to the traditional popularity of claret in Scotland, but also because he was economically careful; Bordeaux wines were fairly cheap. He sent a buying envoy to Bordeaux each vintage. At one point he issued an order forbidding the purchase of new wine in Bordeaux before 1 December each year, owing to the number of complaints about the poor quality. That the wine was not all that cheap can be demonstrated by the fact, quoted by Simon, that the price per hogshead then was £5 10s., yet 300 years later, in the inter-war years of the twentieth century, classed-growth clarets of good vintages could be bought for £12 and less a *barrique*. Owing to his arbitrary government, Charles I's reign (1625–49) was not encouraging either for wine traders or wine drinkers. In 1637 he clapped a tax of £2 per tun on all wine. This was abolished by the Long Parliament in 1640. Moreover like other taxes the duty on wine was farmed out. The Vintners' Company, which had attempted to monopolize the wine trade, in 1640 was denounced in Parliament by John Pym. The Company had paid Charles £30,000, had taken £80,000 themselves and by retailing had recovered £232,000. Charles himself was very abstemious and Simon says he was 'probably the soberest monarch who ever ruled over England and the one who spent less for wine'. Just before his execution, it is recorded, he 'drank a small glassful of claret wine'.

During this period it is interesting to have a record of Henry Thompson, perhaps the first 'modern' English wine merchant resident in Bordeaux, buying wine from the Graves, Médoc, Blaye, Ste-Foy, St-Émilion and Langon. There is no evidence that all this wine was destined for England and perhaps the cheaper qualities went to the Low Countries who were by then dominant in the Bordeaux wine trade.

The prices that Thompson paid, and the relative standing of the wines of the various districts can be estimated from the statistics given by Malvezin in his *Histoire du commerce de Bordeaux* (1892). In 1647 they averaged as follows:

Graves and Médoc	78–100 livres (per *tonneau*)
Côtes	72–84
Bourg	66
Entre-Deux-Mers	60–75
Blaye	54
Barsac, Bommes, Sauternes	84–100

As converted by Malvezin into the franc value of his own time, Blaye wines cost 430 frs. (£17) and the top Graves, Médoc and Sauternes were 800 frs. (£31).

Under the Commonwealth the Anglo-Gascon wine trade improved, for the Roundheads though Puritans were not, as some might imagine, teetotallers. Cromwell himself drank French and Spanish wine. However like some of his predecessors he made an attempt to confine the carrying trade, but in a different form. By the 1651 Navigation Act foreign shipping could bring in only the produce of its own country; a heavy blow at the Dutch who went to war over it, not very successfully. It also hit the French wine trade, for neither they nor the English had sufficient ships, as the earlier reference to Colbert's estimate indicates.

Inside Bordeaux during this period there were some political difficulties. In 1675, following the imposition of bitterly resented taxes from which the burghers had been traditionally free, there were riots. The city was occupied by the military, some walls and gates were demolished, and a number of the ringleaders were put to death.

Ten years later the Revocation of the Edict of Nantes, which had given tolerance to the Protestants, had a very bad effect on the Bordeaux wine trade. For its foreign markets largely lay in the Protestant countries, particularly in Holland and England, which did not care to buy from the persecutors of the Huguenots. Also in 1684 the expulsion from Bordeaux of 93 Portuguese Jewish families had been ordered, but was cancelled in 1686, as they had influential friends abroad, particularly in the Low Countries. Not many English merchants chose at this time to remain in the city; non-Catholics were not made very welcome.

As the conflict began with France, to last intermittently until Waterloo, so did the Anglo-French wine trade run into increasing difficulties; and of all areas Bordeaux, the source of most French wine, was worst hit. In 1667 the imports into England of French and Canary wine were briefly prohibited. Later, from 1679 to 1685, French wines were again forbidden entry. There were loopholes in this embargo, but trade was certainly discouraged, and if the French growers had not found other markets, including, later on, America, they would have been in a bad way.

It must be added that the English discrimination against the French was not unilateral. It was Colbert who in 1677 inflicted a steep tariff on English cloth goods, and a few years later the import of English cloth into France was forbidden; the English retaliated on wines. The Bordeaux merchants repeatedly tried to have the cloth embargo lifted and to secure special privileges and exemptions for themselves, but they failed. The English merchants on their side complained during Charles II's reign (1660–85) of excessive French taxes on wine, and that they were not allowed to buy their wine outside Bordeaux itself. They also alleged that Haut-Pays wines were sold as Médoc, and that the Bordeaux merchants blended their wines. Familiar complaints!

No doubt blending was practised but in fact Colbert

reiterated its illegality, and his ban assisted the development of 'quality' Bordeaux production, as well as a reduction in the amount of Haut-Pays wine passing through Bordeaux.

In 1693 William III (1689–1702) started the long-drawn-out discrimination against French wines that was not finally dropped until W. E. Gladstone's Budget in 1860. William raised the duty against French wines to £22 2s. 10d. a tun, or 2s. 1d. a gallon. The duty, high enough indeed, on Portuguese and Spanish wines was £17 13s. 3d. But within a few years worse was to follow. While the Iberian wines had to pay £21 12s. 5d., the duty on French wines shot up to £47, and in 1698 to £51 2s. or over 1s. a bottle. The cost of claret itself averaged only £16 a cask.

The effect on French wine imports was of course catastrophic. Simon quotes the English imports for 1700 as 13,649 tuns from Spain, 7,757 from Portugal, 1,430 Rhenish and only 664 from France. The situation was slightly relieved by a certain amount of smuggling and by the import of French wines in Portuguese and Spanish casks. The Bordeaux merchants carried out this little operation quite openly. Yet with Britain the French wine trade, which meant above all the Bordeaux trade, dwindled almost to nothing; in spite of protests, claret became readily obtainable only by the rich. The English Whigs took to port and only the Scots and some Tories, in protest against the Hanoverian monarchs, maintained precariously the French wine connection and the tradition of claret drinking.

5. The Rise and Development of the Estates

It is often thought that the famous château estates and the named growths that we know today are of considerable antiquity. Generally, this is not so. There is nothing in Bordeaux to match the old monastic *clos* of the Côte d'Or, unless we except the archiepiscopal vineyard in Pessac, part of which is now Ch. Pape-Clément. As has been pointed out by William Younger in *Gods, Men and Wine* (1966), the role of the Church in the development of viticulture has been exaggerated. Certainly it was not a prominent feature of Bordeaux, although the two chief chapters in the city as well as the archbishop owned considerable vineyards, which were cultivated by tenants on the basis of a share of the crop. This share generally varied from one-quarter to one-tenth, irrespective of whether the landlord was ecclesiastical or lay; but the archbishop took half the crop of his Pessac vineyards (there were two). These rents were known as *agrières*. In 1558 Jacques de Bécoiran, *seigneur* of Lafite, sold to Simon de la Bégorce the *agrières* due to the noble house of Lafite in Milon, Pauillac, St-Laurent, etc.

Until the seventeenth century there were no large compact estates as we know them today, and the vineyards were worked by peasants or small tenant farmers. How small they were may be judged from the *récolte* of the Pape-Clément estate in the middle of the sixteenth century. Allowing for the fact that the archbishop received half the crop, the total output was only 24 *barriques* in 1562; 40 in 1563; 48 in 1564 and 13½ in 1575. Judging by the very small output in 1575, it looks as if the vines were stricken by frost or hail, to which they are subject even today, notably in the Graves. In this period the vintage began between 12 and 23 September. Ten days must be added to these dates for modern comparison, as this was just before the Gregorian Calendar was adopted in France in 1582. From that year the dates in the annual calendar are the same as today, except it must be remembered that England was very slow to adopt this papal-inspired reform, and not until September 1752 did we fall into line with most of Europe.

As the Graves was the original heart of the Bordeaux *vignoble*, it is not surprising that the first secular estate that we know of was Haut-Brion in Pessac not far outside the city walls. As already mentioned, it was known to Pepys in 1663, but as 'Ho Bryen'. The name was a difficult one for the English to master, and it appears in curious forms right down to the nineteenth century. In *Bottlescrew Days* (1926) André Simon, quoting from the diary and expenses of John Hervey, first Earl of Bristol, mentions a purchase in 1705 of Obrian. Much later in the same century it appears, rather charmingly, in a Christie's auction catalogue as Oberon. We may discount the late Maurice Healy's ingenious suggestion that it was really O'Brien. The Irish arrived later on the scene in Bordeaux. Then John Evelyn in his Diary (16 July 1683) refers to Pontac and Haut-Brion 'whence the best Bordeaux wine comes'.

The development of the big estates largely coincided with the extensive plantation of the Médoc, which began in the sixteenth century, was accelerated by drainage of the marshes in the seventeenth century, and by the enrichment of the new *noblesse de robe* and of the merchant classes in the eighteenth century. With the seventeenth century came the decay of the old aristocracy, the *noblesse d'épée*, and the rise of the new families, the Montesquieus, d'Alesmes and Pontacs among them. The Léoville estate was created in 1638 by M. Moytié, a Bordeaux merchant, who called it Mont Moytié. These families acquired much of their rank originally from positions in the legal hierarchy of the Bordeaux Parlement.

This played an important part indirectly in the development

of the Bordeaux *vignoble*. Created by Louis XI in 1462 (though it is also suggested that it existed in 1451 before the English were expelled), it was one of a number throughout France. Situated in the former seat of the English government, the decrepit and inadequate Ombrière, it was mainly an appeal court for civil and criminal cases, but also issued legal decrees. It had the power too to consider and protest against decrees issued by the king and the central government. These local parlements became centres of opposition to the monarchy, and the Bordeaux Parlement, which opposed new taxes imposed by Louis XV in 1750, was often at loggerheads with the intendant Tourny (1743–57), the representative of the crown.

By the eighteenth century the Parlement had grown, and had a staff of 115 officers, including a first president and a procurator-general, both crown appointments. There were nine vice-presidents, known as *présidents à mortier*, owing to their mortarboard head-gear, and six presidents of the three courts. One way of acquiring nobility in France was to become a member of a Parlement, this ensuing on the ground, or excuse, that nobles were entitled to be tried by their peers, and the Parlementaires might have to judge them. Ennoblement could take place either by service by two generations of the same family or by twenty years in office. Although election was by a somewhat perfunctory examination and a rather more exacting election after extensive canvassing, the only prerequisites, as William Doyle points out in *The Parlement of Bordeaux and the End of the Old Regime* (1974), were money and being a Roman Catholic (though that did not hinder many of the Parlementaires from being freemasons).

Joining this elect body was rather like becoming a member of a very select club, and the rewards were social rather than pecuniary, as the fees were low; but one third of the Bordeaux aristocracy was of the *noblesse de robe*. By the time of Louis XVI there were five marquesses, four counts, four viscounts and twenty-eight barons in the Bordeaux Parlement. The cost of joining was heavy. In 1735 an incoming first president had to pay 150,000 livres to his predecessor's heirs, in the mid eighteenth century a vice-presidency cost 123,000 livres and by the 1770s even the junior rank of counsellor involved payment of 50,000 livres to someone who was retiring or who held the reversion. The impoverished de Gascq, owner of what later became the vineyard of Palmer, in 1778 sold his office as *président à mortier* for 126,000 livres.

The means to obtain entry to this aristocratic legal club normally came from land, including vineyards, many of whose proprietors were very rich. Arnaud de Pontac, first president, had his revenues officially estimated in 1663 at 25,000 livres a year. The de la Tresne family, later associated with Haut-Brion, were one of the Parlement dynasties, and Jean-Baptiste de la Tresne was Président in the middle of the seventeenth century. Another dignatory who gave his name to a vineyard was Président Pichard, who died in 1634. A surprising number of the châteaux and local names that we know today derive from the Parlementaires. They include Pontac, Pichon, Lascombes, Larose, Lalande, Brane, Sigalas and Bacalan. Another was Brivazac from the now vanished Pessac vineyard of Laburthe-Brivazac. Président Pichard owned six châteaux, including Lafite and Coutet, later selling the latter to Councillor J. de Filhot de Chimbaud. Lesser Parlementaires included M. Brossier, who owned Beychevelle as well as properties in Lamarque and Moulis, and others with less well-known estates. In the Sauternes seventeen properties were owned by Parlementaire proprietors, including the Président de Gascq at Barsac, the Councillor Filhot, already mentioned, and the Marquis de Lur Saluces in Preignac, Fargues and, of course, Yquem. The Parlement, exiled to Libourne for a short period in 1785, was closed down in 1790.

It is often thought that the leading wine estates of Bordeaux had a history extending back into the sixteenth or seventeenth centuries, if not further back still. As landed properties or *seigneuries* they did, as Pijassou and some of his colleagues in the University of Bordeaux have shown in their monumental studies on the Médoc and Latour, but not as vineyards. The fine château of Haut-Brion dates from 1550 and the turreted *manoir* of Lafite is certainly not much later. It seems likely that the first *vignoble* of what were later to be the *premiers crus* was Haut-Brion, and this is confirmed by the fact that it was mentioned by Pepys in 1663, whereas the others did not appear on the English market, the vital one, until the beginning of the following century. Pijassou in his *Lafite: trois siècles d'histoire viticole* is able to pinpoint very closely the date of the creation of the Lafite vineyard from contemporary documents which refer in 1680 to a 'newly planted' vineyard. The *seigneur* then was Jacques de Ségur, grandfather of the Marquis Nicolas-Alexandre de Ségur, and father of Alexandre, who in 1695 married the heiress of Latour, Marie-Thérèse de Clausel. It would appear probable that the Latour estate was already planted by then, for to produce wine fine enough to command high prices a vineyard must have been twelve to twenty years old. Yet both Lafite and Latour were offered on the London market at least as early as 1707, as advertised in the *London Gazette*. Ch. Margaux was certainly no younger, for, as quoted by Pijassou, in June 1705 '230 hogsheads of new Pontac and Margoose wine' were offered for sale. The proprietor of Haut-Brion then was François Auguste de Pontac, while Ch. Margaux was owned by his brother-in-law Jean Denis d'Aulède. These wines were described in the announcements as 'New French Clarets', which meant that they were of the preceding vintage 'and lately landed'. They had been shipped on their lees, unracked. In 1707 the wine was announced as coming from 'the growths of Lafite, Margaux and Latour'. In the same year 200 hogsheads of 'New French Obrion Claret' were offered at 'Lloyd's Coffee-House, in Lombard Street'.

That these wines were already something special may be

gauged from their prices as compared with ordinary clarets. In 1705 the Haut-Brion was offered at £60 the tun, whereas later in the same year some ordinary red Bordeaux was sold for only £18. Even earlier than these London sales, John Hervey, first Earl of Bristol (after whom so many Continental hotels were named), was buying four hogsheads of 'Obrion wine' which cost him £101 10s. That these wines attracted such high prices argues not only that they were of high quality, but that they were already established in reputation; and that could not have happened overnight.

Another testimony to the established status of the first growths occurs in a letter written in October 1723 by a merchant or agent in Bordeaux, J. Bruvenal, to Henry Powell, who looked after the wines of George Prince of Wales, afterwards George II. This letter from the Townshend (Raynham Hall) Mss. was kindly made available to me by Professor J. H. Plumb of Cambridge.

The 4 topping growths of La Tour, Lafite, Chateau Margaux and Pontac are exceeding good. No price made as yet, they are expecting to hear what Mr. Danluce shall ask for his Ch. Margaux, for he is their North Star; there are 175 tunns of La Tour & Lafite, 88 tuns at Ch. Margaux and 71 tunns at Pontac all perfect good, the quantity exceeds of 1/3 part that of the last year & for all that they pretend the same price, I paid but £2000 last vintage for the Pontacks & Mdm de Danluce has asked me the same price this year though she has 71 tunns when she had but 37 the last. I proferred £1600 & was refused as Mr. Bennett [a prominent wine merchant and Keeper of Wines at St James's Palace] can tell you. Never in my life have I tasted the Château d'Issan so good as this vintage. They are indeed charming wines. I wish I could send you some for the Prince.

'Topping' of course indicates that they were the top, i.e. first-growth wines. The vintage will have been the new 1723 one. At this time apparently, Ch. Margaux was the most esteemed of the 'topping' wines. Interesting too is this early reference to Issan, whose moated château is one of the oldest in the whole Médoc.

In the eighteenth century, according to Mr Robert Forster in the *Economic History Review* (August 1961), of the 68 families of the robe in Bordeaux, 73 per cent of their income came from the sale of wine. A mature vineyard yielded 8 per cent on its purchase price.

French colonial expansion early in the eighteenth century also brought wealth to the French trading classes and a big extension of the Bordeaux vineyards. What had been lost by way of trade with England had been compensated for by the demand for French wines in the colonies.

Boucher, intendant from 1720 to 1743, predecessor of Tourny and the first of the three great eighteenth-century Bordeaux intendants, described the 'fury of planting' as starting about 1709, following the devastating frosts and disastrous vintage of that year. Writing in 1724 to his chief in Paris to demand the pulling-up of all vines planted since that year except in the 'Graves de Médoc, the Graves de Bordeaux and the Côtes', he stated that since the beginning of the century, everything had been put under vines, and that for ten leagues (*c.* twenty-five miles) around Bordeaux one saw nothing but vineyards. Thus were revived the fears of the Emperor Domitian in the first century A.D.

The government was afraid of vineyards being planted at the expense of other crops, especially wheat. It was also believed that an extension of vineyards throughout France would lead to a drop in the price of wine and result in heavy losses to the proprietors. So from 1725 to 1766 all the efforts of the central government were in the direction of restraining wine output, of maintaining prices and preventing new plantations. From 1725 onwards strict laws were passed, forbidding the planting of new vineyards; and heavy penalties were imposed, including the ploughing-up of new plantations.

The important Gironde *vignoble* was particularly affected,

and the two intendants – carrying powers somewhat similar to the present-day *préfet*, and like him responsible to the central government – Claude Boucher (1720–43) and Louis-Urbain, Marquis de Tourny (1743–57), who did so much to embellish Bordeaux, were no friends to the growers wishing to expand their vineyards. Boucher earned the indignation of Montesquieu by refusing the latter permission to plant vines in land adjoining Haut-Brion, and Tourny in 1745 ordered an inquiry into the new plantations of vines in the Médoc since the beginning of the century. The results of this investigation came to light three years later when ten proprietors in Margaux, Cantenac, Soussans, Castelnau and elsewhere were heavily fined and their vines, some of them now very old, pulled up. Among those fined was the Président de Gascq at Cantenac, predecessor of General Palmer. He had to pull up about three hectares.

Certainly these measures had a retarding effect on the whole Gironde *vignoble*, especially at a time when Bordeaux was facing new competition from the expanding vineyards of Spain and Portugal, whose wines were cheap. However, in 1739 the total Bordeaux vineyard area was said to be double the size it had been twenty years previously, and just before Tourny retired in 1757 he admitted that in spite of all his efforts the area under vines was larger than twenty-five years earlier.

Nevertheless government policy changed in 1766, and new planting was encouraged. However, the terrible winter of that year resulted in a considerable temporary decline in the vineyards. Severe frost damage led to extensive replanting, and the restrictions lapsed; not to be renewed effectively until the 1930s when the law of *appellation contrôlée* came into being, with its consequent control over the vineyards and their output.

By the second half of the eighteenth century the pattern and extent of the Bordeaux *vignoble* was not all that different from that of the present day, although St-Émilion and Pomerol were not so heavily cultivated. This 'fury of planting' was part of Bordeaux's eighteenth-century renaissance, with the leading estates owned and extended by the nobles of the Parlement, the prosperous *noblesse de robe*. R. Pijassou in his chapter on the Bordeaux *vignoble* in *Bordeaux au XVIIIe siècle* (1968), on which I have drawn freely about the rise of the estates, shows how important this newly rich, mostly newly-ennobled bourgeoisie was in the development of the various districts. As the Parlementaires were all legal men, though some of the posts were hereditary, it can be said that the Médoc was first developed by the lawyers. Soon they bought out and overshadowed their peasant neighbours, and made considerable fortunes from their new estates, often worked by tenant farmers on a 50–50 share-cropping basis.

The Parliamentary Councillor d'Arche of Sauternes (who gave his name to Ch. d'Arche) received from his estate there between 20 and 65 *tonneaux* of wine, produced entirely by share-croppers. The average annual revenue was 9,928 livres, of which the share-croppers received 3,367 livres, and the proprietor, after deduction of expenses, 3,801 livres (38 per cent). In some years the share-croppers received nothing at all, as they had been obliged to borrow from the owners and were heavily in debt. Many under-privileged peasant owners and tenants had to sell out, and between 1755 and 1790 the size of the noble properties greatly increased. The Président Pichard paid over 1 million livres to Ségur for Lafite. There were great profits to be made, for the expenses on a mature 60-acre vineyard were only one third to one half of the gross receipts.

No wonder that the Bordeaux proprietors and the intendants were at loggerheads. No wonder, either, that the Médoc vineyard proprietors from 1730 to 1750 fought a plan of the Bordeaux merchants to have a road built from the city to the extremity of the Médoc. The merchants stated that this would be a better way of transporting the wine than by ships, as the latter often went aground. But the noble proprietors feared that the merchants would have access to the smaller *vignerons*. Among the successful opponents were Ségur, Pontac, Fumel and Villeneuve. The bitterness that was building up among the exploited 'little men' throughout the eighteenth century can be imagined from what happened in the Bordeaux region, and it is not surprising that the Président Pichard ended his days on the guillotine.

The *noblesse de robe* was often provokingly rich; also the Church. In Villenave d'Ornon at the Revolution 69 small proprietors owned only 34 hectares of vineyard; the Church, including the monks of Carbonnieux, and the emigrated proprietors, owned 384 hectares.

For example, the Président Nicolas-Alexandre, Marquis de Ségur, owned Latour, Lafite, Mouton and other properties in St-Laurent and the Graves, and was not exaggeratedly known as *le prince des vignes*. It was he certainly who established a wider reputation for Lafite and Latour. After his death, in 1755, it was officially estimated that the annual turnover of these two estates alone was 100,000 livres (c. £4,000 in the money of that day), of which 60 per cent was net profit. After a bad year in 1744 Ségur asked Tourny for a tax reduction owing to the sad state of his Lafite and Latour vineyards, but his gross income was estimated at 272,000 livres, with expenses at 34,400.

Ségur's only rival was the Marquis d'Aulède, who possessed Ch. Margaux, part of Haut-Brion, and the estate of Pez in St-Estèphe. From these his net annual revenue was about 25,000 livres (c. £1,000).

The Church also contributed to the development of the vineyards. In 1740 the Benedictines of the Abbey of Ste-Croix in Bordeaux bought Carbonnieux for 120,000 livres, and made a good profit out of this Graves estate. Some of the local priests too did very well out of wine. The *curé-prieur* of Cantenac in mid-century had a total revenue from wine of 25,000 livres a year.

Early in the eighteenth century all the first growths,* as they were later to become, must have had some entity, for we find them mentioned in the Earl of Bristol's records: 'Margoose' in 1703 at £27 10s. a hogshead; 6 dozen flasks of 'La Tour' for £14 8s. in 1720; 'Laffitte' at 50s. a dozen in 1721 and 'Chasteau Margoux' at £47 7s. a hogshead, including bottles, corks and carriage in 1723. Cyril Ray in his *Lafite* (1968) quotes an advertisement in the *London Gazette* of 1707, announcing the sale of 'an entire parcel of New French Claret . . . being of the Growth of Lafitt, Margouze, and La Tour'. Professor J. H. Plumb in his *Men and Places* (1961) mentions that in 1706 Robert Walpole imported wine in bottle, as it usually came in chests. In 1732–3 he bought four hogsheads of Ch. Margaux at a time and a hogshead of Lafite regularly every three months for his lavish entertaining at Houghton Hall, Norfolk, and in London. Pontac was the only other wine mentioned by name. Bottles then were not cheap at 2s. 6d. a dozen, although they were returnable at 2s. a dozen, and long French corks were 2s. 6d. a gross. The importance of the English 'quality' market may be gauged from the fact that in 1733 Walpole spent £1,118 a year on wine, much of it French. The way that some wine entered England is indicated by the example of Walpole who, when a high Admiralty official, smuggled champagne in by using an Admiralty barge!

If the fame of the individual first growths had penetrated to England by the first quarter of the eighteenth century, they must have been well established by then in France. Indeed the late P. Morton Shand in his *A Book of French Wines* (revised edition 1960) claimed that there were references to Haut-

---

*It is necessary in this and following chapters to refer to the classified growths prior to the full discussion on them in the chapter on the Classification of the Médoc. Readers unaware of the main facts and features of the classification codified in 1855 may turn to the relevant chapter on page 496.

Brion in chronicles prior to 1480. Certainly one of the oldest present-day estates with a firm vinous connection is La Mission-Haut-Brion, which had the unusual record of passing from secular into religious hands. For in 1630 it was left by the widow of a *président* of the Parlement of Guyenne to a clergy organization; and in the settlement there is mention of vines, a *grand chey cuvier garni d'une fouloire en pierre de taille*. Thence it passed to the Lazarist order of preachers, who built the still-existing chapel attached to the château and gave the vineyard its name.

In many cases, however, there were châteaux before there were vines, or any record of them. Ch. Margaux was Ch. Lamothe in the Middle Ages; Latour has associations with the Anglo-French Wars, and there is the splendid moated château of Issan. It is said that the English retreating after the Battle of Castillon in 1453 were able to embark at the harbour of Issan on the Gironde and to take their wine with them. But whether the wine was from this area is another matter. Much of the Médoc was undrained marshy land, until reclaimed by Colbert's orders in the middle of the seventeenth century. The Fort de Médoc on the estuary was built as late as 1689.

Not the least interesting references in the Earl of Bristol's records are to bottles and corks. For until the development of the bottle and the use of cork, probably about the turn of the seventeenth century, there was no serious possibility of keeping and maturing wine. Until then the young wine was drunk up quickly while still sound, as had been the custom for centuries. The new estates of the enriched and often ennobled proprietors could not develop and show the quality of their wines until towards the end of the eighteenth century when they could put them into bottles that might conveniently be laid down on their sides and the wine permitted to mature. There were bottles as such earlier than this, but designed for holding rather than maturing wine. Pijassou, who has examined the records of the Beychevelle cellar in 1748 in which there were only 24 glass bottles containing wine for immediate use, points out it was the *vin de l'année* that was drunk.

Latour probably accurately dates its wine-production records as a compact estate from 1670 when it was bought by a M. de Chavanas, who sold it in 1677 to the Clauzel family. Thence it passed by marriage to the Ségur family, who also owned Calon in St-Estèphe, to which estate the Vice-President of the Parlement gave his name. More details are given in the chapter on Pauillac and St-Estèphe.

Evidence of the firm establishment of the four *premiers crus* by the 1730s is given in official tax documents quoted by Franz Malvezin in his *Histoire de la vigne et du vin en Aquitaine* (1919). Not only were the production costs given, but also the size of the crops and the prices at which they were sold. In the decade from 1735 to 1744, the output of Lafite averaged 77 *tonneux* of *grand vin* and 30 of *second vin*. The comparable figures for Latour were 49 and 22. At this period Margaux was producing about 65 *tonneaux* of its first wine, and Haut-Brion about 50.

The opening prices, which were in fact the only important ones, for the whole crop was sold if possible *en primeur*, depended both on quality and quantity. For example, when in 1737 the combined crop of the Ségur-owned Lafite and Latour totalled 207 *tonneaux* of the *grand vin* the price was as low as 300 livres (roughly equivalent to frs.) per *tonneau*; but in the following year when production totalled only 97 *tonneaux* the price was 1,600 livres. In the decade of 1735–44, for which records exist, the highest price was 1,700 livres per *tonneau* for a crop of 106 *tonneaux* of *grand vin*. The second wine accounted for about 30 per cent of total output but sold for only 300–350 livres. These figures represented very large profits for the Marquis Nicolas-Alexandre de Ségur.

Thanks to the unique records of the wine-broking firm of Tastet & Lawton, established in 1740, it is possible to compare the prices of the first and other growths. In 1744 when

Lafite and Latour obtained 1,400 livres a *tonneau*, Brane-Mouton secured 530 and Pichon-Longueville 500, while Léo-ville fetched 850 livres, Beychevelle (then known as Brassier) 400, Giscours 380, 'Rozan' 350 and Malescot 285 livres. The supremacy of the first growths was complete, thanks probably to the English demand. Perhaps the only other classed growths well-known by name on this side of the English Channel were Léoville and Larose.

Many of the classed-growth names that we know today derive from eighteenth-century proprietors, for although the four first growths and Mouton are named topographically – La Fite means a height, and Mouton is similarly derived from *Motte de terre*, an eminence, and has no ovine associations – many of the others were named by and after their proprietors, a custom that still persists today, as may be evidenced by Mouton-Baron-Philippe and Prieuré-Lichine. It is true that a certain Jean de Lafite is said to be mentioned in a document of 1355 as living in Pauillac, but as likely as not he took his name from the locality. Among those châteaux which commemorate their former owners are Rausan, named after a seventeenth-century merchant, Léoville, previously named Mont-Moytié, but rechristened by Mme la Présidente de Léoville, who died in 1769, and Gruaud-Larose. This had been known as Fon-bedeau, but the rich, eccentric M. Gruaud bought it in 1757, and after his death in 1787 it was acquired by M. Larose, who added his name. Malescot takes its name from Simon Malescot, *procureur* in the *Cour du Parlement* in Bordeaux, who bought the property in 1697. The two Pichon estates were owned by branches of the Pichon-Longueville family, and St-Pierre took its name from the man who bought it in 1767. Grand-Puy-Lacoste was in the hands of the Lacoste family from the first half of the eighteenth century. The pattern of origin, name and period in the history of Bordeaux is clear from these examples. Mouton was known as Brane-Mouton (or Branne-Mouton), after the family who had owned it since the reign of Louis XV.

Whatever the reputation inside France of the Bordeaux growths, other than the *premiers crus*, it seems clear that in the eighteenth century they were little known in England, where in spite of duty discrimination many at least of the best Bordeaux wines continued to infiltrate; they were plentiful in noble households.

A good indication of the general anonymity of claret in Britain at this period can be obtained from the wines sold by Christie's, the London auctioneers, who conducted their first auction in 1766 and their first all-wine auction in 1769. Claret occupied a minor position, compared with madeira, then at the height of its esteem, port or sherry, and it was usually listed merely as 'fine claret'. Very often it was sold by the colour of the seal: red, black and green, but there does not seem to have been a recognized colour code; for sometimes the black seal fetched the best price, sometimes the red. This of course may have been accounted for by the quality of the wines themselves. Later on in the early nineteenth century, it appears as if the black seal was the better, but by then a great deal of claret was sold under the name of the merchants.

It has already been mentioned here that nearly all claret was shipped in cask until very recent times indeed. This applied even to the first growths until the second half of the last century. The estates themselves were only too anxious to dispose of their wine at the earliest possible moment, if possible when on its original lees, for this saved all the trouble of racking and fining. In the late eighteenth and early nineteenth centuries the estates liked best to sell and dispatch the first growths to the Bordeaux merchants by the Christmas following the vintage. Another reason for this was the very high price of hand-made bottles, often made by artisans, although in 1786 Latour is recorded as having bought 100 bottles from the glass factory at Pauillac. The largest number of bottles recorded as having been bought by Latour in this epoch was 600 in 1803 at no less than 30 livres the hundred, the equivalent 175 years later of about 3 frs. a bottle. Such purchases would have been for the proprietors' reserve, but even they had their wines sent to them in cask. In 1813 the manager of Latour sent to one of his employers who lived in Normandy two *barriques* of the 1807, recommending prompt bottling after the wine had had a few days to rest. Two years later some of the 1807 was still in cask in the cellars, though the manager stated that it needed bottling. There were of course no château labels either, and these were supplied by the merchant in Bordeaux or more probably by the importer and bottler.

The situation is clearly demonstrated from Christie's records of an exceptional sale of top-class clarets that took place in May 1877. The wine, which had come from a South-Wales mansion, had been selected over a period of twenty years by Harvey's of Bristol, instructed to 'accumulate gradually a selection of wines of the choicest vintages, bottled and laid down in the highest degree of perfection'. The nine vintages cellared ranged from 1847 to 1870 and included all the great years such as 1864 and 1865. The wines were all shipped by Barton & Guestier and Cruse and until the 1862 were all shipped in wood and bottled by Harvey's. From then on all were bottled by the two Bordeaux shippers and this included Yquem 1861. All were first growths except for two shipments of Léoville and one of Gruaud-Larose – then almost the only 'seconds' acceptable in the highest social circles. Lafite clearly predominated, Margaux appeared more often than Latour and Haut-Brion was not represented. The wines appear to have been bottled in the third spring after the vintage, though some shipped in bottle were laid down later.

The first Bordeaux bearing a name of any kind in the Christie sale catalogues was 'a hogshead of Canon claret' and another of 'Pontack', sold in 1778. Perhaps the first was a St-Émilion or even a Fronsac. If so it was the first to be mentioned by name for the better part of another century. Otherwise the first growths alone were singled out by name, but not always then. The first reference to them was in 1787 when 19 hogsheads of 'High Flavoured Claret of the First Growth' were offered. They fetched £34 in hogshead and 36s. a dozen in bottle. At the same sale a pipe of port (115 gallons, more than double the Bordeaux *barrique* in size) fetched £35.

In the following year four dozen 'Lafeete' fetched 66s. a dozen and 15 dozen of 'Ch. Margau' reached 49s. St-Julien and Médoc – unusually specific entries so early – went for 60s. and 43s. respectively. Pontac (which was probably Haut-Brion) made 45s. But this was an exceptional sale, for it was the stock of the retiring French Ambassador to the Court of St James, Count d'Adhémar, and no doubt he had rather more precise ways of identifying his Bordeaux than was usual in England. Whatever the cause, so far as I have been able to discover, this was the first time in which estate names were mentioned in Christie's catalogues. Slowly thereafter they became more frequent. In 1794, at the height of the French Revolution, 30 dozen Lafite, 24 dozen 'Château Margeau' and 50 dozen Latour were sold. The Lafite fetched 41s., the Latour 40s. and the Margaux 39s. a dozen. No vintage was given, but in 1797 six hogsheads of 1791 'first-growth claret' were offered, still in hogshead. The catalogue notes state that it was 'considered the best that France has produced for many years and similar is difficult at this time to be obtained and now in high order for Bottling'. Six years in wood!

In a trade sale in 1792, ten lots of 'the growth Latour' 1785 were sold in cases each containing '50 quart bottles'. They fetched from 41s. to 44s. a dozen.

By 1802 Ch. Margot (*sic*) and La Fitte (*sic*) were fetching 54s., but fine claret grew rare as the Napoleonic Wars dragged on and the prohibition of trade with France had its effect. In 1815 in the sale, held a month after Waterloo, for Count Merveldt, the retiring Austrian Ambassador, Ch. Margot fetched 112s. 6d. a case and Lafite and Latour 100s., while St-Julien reached 84s., and 'vin de Sauternes' 100s.

In the second half of the eighteenth century, there seems no doubt, Lafite was the leading first growth. During the Revolution it passed to a Dutch company and its later history is referred to in the chapter on the Médoc. By the end of the century many of the Médoc estates were producing large quantities of wine. The average production of Ch. Margaux was 110 *tonneaux*, and Brane-Mouton 130 *tonneaux*, while the large estates of Léoville and Canet were averaging 160 and 175 *tonneaux*. It must be realized, however, that for the leading châteaux at least there was usually a *grand vin* and a *second vin* with the proportion varying greatly according to the vintage and, no doubt, to the state of the vineyard. For example, in 1786 Latour made an exceptional amount of wine: almost 160 *tonneaux*, of which 102 *tonneaux* were designated as the *grand vin*. Usually the *second vin* accounted for about a fifth or sixth of the crop, but more in poor vintages like 1788 and 1789.

During the revolutionary years a number of the Médoc estates were confiscated and sold. This was not so much owing to the extermination or expropriation of the owners as to their emigration, as happened at Lafite. The Comte de Ségur was one of those who emigrated, and so his properties were confiscated, including the part of Latour which he owned. But the ownership of the rest of it, held by Ségur's daughter, the Countess of Miromesnil, was not disturbed, and she bequeathed it to her daughters. One of these married into the Beaumont family.

Haut-Brion was also partly confiscated at the Revolution, because the proprietor, Joseph Fumel, emigrated. The Brane family was not disturbed at Mouton. When the Marquis de Las-Cases-Beauvoice emigrated, the whole large Léoville estate was taken over by the state; but the three members of the family who owned three-quarters and who had not left the country demanded and secured restitution. The émigré's portion was eventually acquired by Mr Hugh Barton, partly in 1821 and the rest in 1826. Giscours was another estate confiscated, owing to the emigration of its owner, M. de Saint-Simon.

In the Graves both La Mission-Haut-Brion and Carbonnieux, which had been in Benedictine hands since 1740, were confiscated along with other ecclesiastical estates, and were bought by secular owners.

Since the purchase of Latour by the Cowdray family in 1962, a careful scrutiny of the château's archives has been made and now completed, so that a good deal of fascinating information as to the production and marketing of leading wines like Latour in the late eighteenth and early nineteenth centuries was made available to Pijassou for his chapter on the Bordeaux *vignoble* in *Bordeaux au XVIIIe siècle* (1968). *Égrappage*, removal of the stalks before the fermentation, was seldom practised and the wine was only left in the vats for eight days before being drawn off into new casks of Baltic oak, where the fermentation continued for about twenty days. The wine was racked twice a year and in the second year it was 'roused', or mixed up, to aid maturity. At the end of the eighteenth century the wine was no longer sold on its lees, but by the spring following the vintage, most of the *barriques* which had been sold were shipped via the little port of St-Mambert to the cellars of the Chartrons merchants who had bought them. These cellars were more suitable for keeping the wine than out in the Médoc, and there was less ullage in the cooler temperatures. The wine was racked every six months, in April and October, and was kept in cask for a minimum of four years, and even up to six or seven years. Not only was the wine generally sold in cask by the château; the merchants did the same. Neither kept any bottle stock beyond their own needs; it was too expensive a capital outlay. Consequently when in 1801 one of the Latour proprietors, the Comte de La Pallu, asked the *régisseur* to send him an assortment of the best wines of Bordeaux, the latter replied that the only way would be to buy a cask of old wine from each estate and either send it in bottle or in cask; and this would be a very expensive matter. Was it the quality or the cost of the wine to which this *régisseur* was referring when he said, 'The wines of Latour, they are like gold bars'?

The revolutionary epoch was an extremely bad period for the whole French wine trade, and particularly for Bordeaux, so dependent on export markets. From 1803 when war with England broke out, the French colonies were largely cut off, trade with England was at a standstill, and the markets in northern Europe were at the mercy of the British Navy. Moreover although the system of heavy indirect taxation on wine under the *Ancien Régime* had been abolished during the Revolution it was replaced by other taxes scarcely less onerous. Napoleon's later campaigns also fell heavily on the French taxpayer, so that the fall of Napoleon in 1814 and his exile to Elba were by no means unpopular among the wine-growing and trading sections of the Bordeaux region. For example Count Jean-Baptiste Lynch, born in 1749 of Irish extraction and proprietor of Dauzac from the end of the eighteenth century, was Mayor of Bordeaux in 1814 when Napoleon was exiled for the first time and the English army entered Bordeaux on 12 March. He told the English commander, General Beresford, that if the latter was an ally of Louis XVIII he would offer the general the keys of the city. He then proceeded to tear off his Napoleonic decorations, throw away his tricolour sash of office and put on a white one, white being the Bourbon colour. He then mounted the tower of St-Michel to cry: *Vive le Roi! Vive les Bourbons!* This Vicar-of-Bray tactic seems particularly unscrupulous in the 64-year-old count, for he had been mayor of Bordeaux since 1809, and in 1810 had headed the Bordeaux municipal delegation at the marriage of Napoleon and Marie-Louise, and had delivered an address extolling the Emperor and his great military victories. Not surprisingly, he had been made a Comte by Napoleon in the same year, so if the latter's return had been more protracted and successful, Count Lynch might have paid for his ostentatious loyalty to the Bourbons. As it was he fled temporarily to Plymouth aboard an English merchantman, but then returned, was made a peer by Louis XVIII (1815–24) and lived another twenty years, to die at Dauzac in 1835.

It is worth noting that at the beginning of the nineteenth century there were no notable estates in St-Émilion or Pomerol. That is not to say that there were no vineyards of repute. Both Ausone and Figeac were well established, but their wines had no very wide renown, and this remained true for more than another fifty years. No doubt, also, wine was made on great estates like that of the Ch. du Bouilh, whose immense, unfinished pile by Victor Louis, the famous eighteenth-century Bordeaux architect, still today dominates the Cubzaguais; but the wines were not well known.

A certain number of the classed-growth estates changed hands in the post-revolutionary period, but the next period of prosperity followed the Restoration in 1815 and, more particularly, in the reign of Louis-Philippe (1830–48), when the new French capitalist class really came to the fore. Bordeaux then was prosperous. Some of these new château buyers were also wine merchants, such as Mr Hugh Barton, whose firm of Barton & Guestier had been established in Bordeaux in 1725. In 1825 Haut-Brion was sold to a Paris stockbroker and to M. Beyerman, the Bordeaux wine merchant of Dutch origin, and he ran it until it was acquired by M. Eugène Larrieu. Brane-Mouton changed hands in 1830, and M. Vivens had bought Durfort in 1824 and added his own name; and in the following year Giscours, which had been partly owned after the revolutionary confiscation by two Americans, John Gray and Jonathan Davis, passed to a Bordeaux merchant, M. Marc Promis. Mr Brown, an English merchant in Bordeaux, gave his name to Cantenac-Brown.

Some of the estates well-known today were created at this period. For example Montrose was developed from woodland in St-Estèphe and acknowledged as a second growth in 1825. Château Palmer was named after the English general who bought the estate of Ch. de Gascq at the Restoration, and greatly extended it, winning recognition as a third growth. Details of these estates will be found in succeeding chapters.

The fifty years from 1830 to 1880 marked the peak of expansion among the Médoc châteaux. The 'new men' with new money moved into Bordeaux, buying up vineyards and building the often incongruous châteaux that lie heavily on the flat land, from the suburbs of Bordeaux to the extremities of the Haut-Médoc and even beyond. No comparable shift in ownership and development took place until the 1950s, when moneyed proprietors from Algeria and financial groups from elsewhere once more decided that vineyards were a profitable form of investment. But then they spent the money on the vineyards and the *chais*, not on new châteaux. In 1830 M. Thuret bought Mouton from the Baron de Brane (or Branne), and in 1836 the Franco-Spanish family of Aguado acquired Château Margaux. In 1835 Baron Nathaniel de Rothschild took over Mouton; and fifteen years later his cousin, Baron James de Rothschild, secured Lafite. Palmer had passed to the banking family of Pereire in 1853, and later on Beychevelle was to go to the Foulds, the financiers. How profitable these investments proved has not been publicized, but it is a fact that Lafite paid no dividend from 1868 to 1948. Yet perhaps the Rothschild owners preferred to plough the profits back into the soil and the *chais*; or to take them in kind.

As the nineteenth century progressed, the initiative and influence passed more and more from the growers and proprietors to the merchants of Bordeaux who had the capital, the accommodation and the sales organizations which the growers lacked. As will be seen later, many of these merchants bought châteaux out of their profits; but in no case of which I am aware did château owners buy merchant houses.

There were, of course, setbacks in this era of proprietorial prosperity. The 'spectre haunting Europe' in 1848 had an unsettling effect in Bordeaux, and the proprietors could not easily sell their wines, as is mentioned in the chapter on the Bordeaux wine trade. Then in 1852 the growers had a spectre of their own: the oidium. It was worse in the following year and crops were severely reduced until 1857. Probably that is the reason why M. Thuret lost money on his sale of Mouton to Baron Nathaniel de Rothschild in 1853. When he bought it in 1830 from the Baron de Brane he paid the then enormous sum of 1,200,000 frs. but twenty-three years later he recovered only 1,125,000 frs. It was a buyer's market in the stricken vineyards and Baron Nathaniel had to wait for five years until he secured much of a return on his investment.

However from 1858 to 1878 the leading growths did very well. For after the high prices of the '58s came the unequalled series of fine and plentiful vintages in the 1860s and 1870s. The attraction of the Médoc châteaux is demonstrated by the unusual number that changed ownership during the sixties. In 1860 M. Armand Lalande, a Bordeaux wine merchant, bought Cantenac-Brown and went on to buy the part of the Léoville vineyard belonging to the Baron Poyferré de Céres. This was in 1866 when the two Rausan vineyards, soon to be split, Ducru-Beaucaillou, Durfort-Vivens and Batailley also changed hands. Ducru cost Mr and Mrs Nathaniel Johnston, of the Bordeaux wine family, 1 million frs. Three years earlier they had acquired Dauzac. Another successful member of the Chartrons wine trade, M. Herman Cruse, paid 700,000 frs. for Pontet-Canet in 1865, and in the same year Lynch-Bages was purchased by another wine merchant, M. Cayrou. However the most notable sale of the decade was when Baron James de Rothschild bought Lafite in 1868 for the huge price of 4,140,000 frs.

These sales continued in the seventies. In 1870 the not very prominent growth of Le Tertre in Arsac was acquired by M.

Koenigswater for 530,000 frs. Cruse paid 1 million frs. for
Giscours in 1875, and M. Labar bought Carbonnieux for
400,000 frs. in 1878. At the very beginning of the phylloxera
devastation Ch. Margaux in 1879 passed to Comte Pillet-Will
for 5 million frs. Speculation ran a little mad, and unlikely-
looking châteaux were erected amid unprofitable vineyards.

Among the vineyard purchasers of this period should be
included the English firm of Gilbey who purchased Loudenne
in the Bas-Médoc in 1875 for 700,000 frs. or £28,000. Although acquired after a good deal of careful inquiry it was
not exactly a fortunate deal, for four years later the phylloxera
was upon them. However, publicly the Gilbeys never regretted their purchase, and Mr Alfred Gilbey senior, the
partner principally concerned with Loudenne, optimistically
compared its situation on a mild slope overlooking the
Gironde with that of Cliveden on its steep crest above the
Thames near Maidenhead. A palpable but pardonable exaggeration! However it has remained in the hands of the
Gilbeys and their successors to this day, and ships passing up
and down the Gironde will notice the Union Jack flying
from the terrace of the charming, turreted, pink-washed
château.

With the descent of the phylloxera on the vineyards, and the
mildew which followed it, there came a change in the affairs
of Bordeaux and the estates. The *vignoble* had reached its fullest
extent and was never to be quite so large again. Château construction was at an end, and the building in 1880 within the
precincts of the Mouton-Rothschild *chai* courtyard of the
Second-Empire-style villa, now called Petit-Mouton, must
have been about the last for many years.

Yet châteaux continued to change hands: Durfort was sold
again in 1882 for 450,000 frs. and La Lagune in 1886 for
340,000. In 1892 M. Dubos paid 770,000 frs. for Cantemerle,
as affairs were rather better then. From the 1890s until the
middle of the First World War the classed-growth estates

were not exactly baits for buyers, and relatively few changed hands. That there were probably many willing sellers may be gauged by the fact that in 1889 the family shareholders of Latour would probably have agreed to sell the estate that had been in their family for well over a century, if the anonymous buyer had not changed his mind. This is referred to on page 251, in the description of Latour.

However, the situation changed with the arrival of 'new men' during the 1914–18 war. Whether in France they resembled what Stanley Baldwin, surveying his fellow M.P.s in the first post-war House of Commons, described as 'hard-faced men who looked as if they had done very well out of the war', cannot be determined. But as Lenin remarked, 'war is terrible but it is also terribly profitable', and much outside capital, not least from the north of France, poured into Bordeaux. M. Désiré Cordier, a wine merchant from Toul, bought Gruaud-Larose-Sarget and Talbot in 1918, the same year that an outside group acquired Lagrange for 1·2 million frs. M. Cuvelier, wine merchant of Lille, acquired Léoville-Poyferré from the Lawton family for 1·3 million frs. Pijassou estimates that twenty *grands domaines* changed hands between 1918 and 1920. They included Giscours and Issan, each sold for 800,000 frs., Brane-Cantenac, sold for 675,000 frs., and Branaire-Ducru, which went for 1 million frs. During this period too M. Fernand Ginestet, who started as a wine merchant in 1899, bought Cos d'Estournel and Pomys in St-Estèphe. These sales reached a peak in June 1920 when a group from the department of the Hérault bought Ch. Margaux for 5·5 million frs.

But henceforth the châteaux on the whole had a very thin time until the post-war boom year of the 1950s. More details of the individual estates are given later in the appropriate chapters dealing with the districts.

The publication in 1974 of the great work on Latour (in particular the chapters contributed by Pijassou) has provided a much clearer, more detailed view of the development of the leading Médoc estates than previously was generally available. This is particularly true regarding the yield of the vineyards and the prices that the first growths and some others received for their *grand vin* over a long period. Of course there were ups and downs, physical and financial, depending on the one hand on conditions of cultivation and climate, and on the other of commerce, local and national.

In the last quarter of the eighteenth century and the first of the nineteenth century, Latour's two largest crops were in 1785 and 1786 with $154\frac{1}{2}$ *tonneaux* (1,390·5 hl) and $152\frac{1}{4}$ *tonneaux* (1,320·25 hl) respectively. However, it fell sharply in the Revolutionary period, partly no doubt through politico-economic causes, and only in 1808 regained a harvest of 141 *tonneaux* (1,269 hl). Only one vintage in five rose above 100 *tonneaux* in the fifty years, and though the yield in 1785 was 33 hl per hectare, the average over the period was only 15·8 hl. Average production was no more than 665 hl. Nor did yield and production vary in the next period that ended in 1853 with the oidium. Indeed average output actually fell slightly to 633 hl. In the following thirty years, the effects of improved methods of cultivation, replanting, expansion and general prosperity contributed to a sharp rise in average output to 825 hl and a smaller one in yield to 18·8 hl per hectare. Subsequent growth, together with average yield and the price per *tonneau* derived, can be seen in the accompanying table, compiled from the detailed tables in the work on Latour. In view of the dramatic and often rapid changes in economic conditions in the last century, the averages in the last two periods cover extraordinary variations. There was an exceptional rise in both production and yield around the turn of the century. In the celebrated vintage of 1900 Latour produced $198\frac{1}{2}$ *tonneaux* of *grand vin*, with a yield of 39·7 hl per hectare, but this was surpassed in the following (poor) year when 210 *tonneaux* and 42 hl per hectare were made. After that output, yield and prices all tended to fall in a period of depression, until shortly before the end of the First World War a brief period of prosperity and speculation began.

AVERAGE PRODUCTION OF GRAND VIN, YIELD PER HECTARE AND OPENING PRICE PER TONNEAU AT CH. LATOUR 1775-1973*

	Production	Yield	Opening Price
1775–1825	665 hl	15·8	1,617·5 frs.
1825–1853	633	15	1,775
1853–1883	825	18·8	3,353
1880–1921	1,095	30	2,080
1920–1973	1,186	33	400,000 (old frs.)

As will be seen from the table, the average price per *tonneau* of Latour reached a peak in the 'golden age' that began with the oidium and finished when the phylloxera had secured the semi-devastation of the vineyards. Latour and its peers were never to be so prosperous again until the 1960s. For the average price for the period from 1880 to 1921 masks a sharp fall

*These figures take account only of the *grand vin,* not the total production, much larger in recent years. In 1970 the total *récolte* was 416 *tonneaux* (3,753 hl), of which only 220 *tonneaux* (1,980 hl) were included in the *grand vin* and 81 *tonneaux* (729 hl) were bottled as Les Forts de Latour. The balance was sold off as Pauillac or without *appellation contrôlée.* The figures have been taken from the tables in *La Seigneurie et le vignoble de Château Latour,* which have been dated as above. The compression of almost the last hundred years into two tables obscures variations much sharper than in the preceding century. For example, the increase in yields has been much larger in the post-war epoch than earlier. In the 1920s they averaged 22 hl per hectare, in the 1930s 16 hl, in the 1940s 16·2 hl. Then in the 1950s they rose to 28·7 hl, in the 1960s to 36·3 hl and in the first four years of the 1970s the huge vintages of 1970 and 1973 produced an average of 60 hl, a figure above the normal yield permitted under the *AC* regulations, which were relaxed in these two vintages. Similar variations occurred in the opening prices, as will be seen in Appendix D.

in the immediate phylloxera period, a rally in the eighties and then a drop until temporary recovery from 1917. In this short boom most of the *premiers crus* failed to secure much recompense, as they were subject to contracts entered into just before prices revived.

Latour's growth in the second half of the nineteenth century was part of a general pattern. Ch. Margaux increased in production by two-and-a-half times within half a century, Lafite's rose from 85 to 152 *tonneaux* of *grand vin* between 1854 and 1902, Mouton-Rothschild's from 66 to 132. The second growths, such as Pichon-Longueville and Ducru-Beaucaillou, trebled their output, Cos d'Estournel and Rausan-Ségla even jumped by three-and-a-half times, while Palmer and Giscours registered a fourfold increase in this period. The big increases occurred in the renewed, post-phylloxera vineyards, planted with grafted stocks that gave large output. There was another reason: a far more liberal use of manure. A great deal too liberal, in fact, and production outstripped both quality and demand. This over-production was partly the cause of the sharp drop in prices that was noted from the 1900 vintage onwards. Neither the merchants nor the public wanted to pay excessive prices for often indifferent wines. In the decade 1898–1907, as recorded by Pijassou, the average price of Latour and Mouton-Rothschild fell by over 25 per cent, compared with the previous ten years; Lafite dropped by 15 per cent and Margaux (then the most esteemed *premier cru*) declined by just under 5 per cent. Yet some of the lesser classed growths suffered much worse: Léoville-Las-Cases, Giscours and Mouton-d'Armailhacq dropped by over 60 per cent. Some fifth growths only achieved 450 frs. a *tonneau*, compared with the depressed levels of the firsts at around 1,350–1,600 frs.

Before ending this chapter on the rise and development of the estates, it is appropriate to say something about their chronicler, Cocks et Féret's *Bordeaux et ses vins*. Fittingly in view of Bordeaux's long association with Britain, its first compiler was an Englishman, Charles Cocks, but unfortunately all too little is known about one whose name has remained ever since on each succeeding edition of the bulky 'bible of Bordeaux'. He was, it seems, a schoolmaster. That he also lived in Bordeaux is shown by the introduction to the first edition of his *Bordeaux: its Wines and the Claret Country*, published in English by Longmans of London in 1846. Herein he refers to 'a residence of several years in this delightful part of France'.

Before embarking on this work, essentially a guide-book to Bordeaux, he translated some works of distinguished French authors which were often highly controversial, not to say revolutionary. Most of them were anti-clerical books.

Fairly clearly Cocks was an anti-clerical freemason, for in his guide to Bordeaux are to be found, rather unexpectedly, the names, addresses and meeting days of no fewer than nine masonic lodges. Their names as well as their existence no doubt reflected the large number of foreigners or people of foreign origin, predominantly but not exclusively Protestant, living in Bordeaux. For one was called Anglaise, another was Française Élue Écossaise, a third Les Chevaliers de St André d'Écosse (Scotland's patron saint) and a fourth L'Amitié Réunie.

As already mentioned, the first edition of Cocks's book was essentially a guide-book, and this applied to a lesser extent to what may be considered the prototype of the work as we know it today. Issued in 1850 and presumably written in French by Cocks, it was entitled *Bordeaux et ses environs et ses vins classés par ordre de mérite*. A slim volume of 227 pages, the wines were reached only on page 130. Later the guide was separated, and its final edition which I have seen appeared in 1869. It was the second edition of the work that bore its present title and was issued in 1868. By that time Charles Cocks had left Bordeaux or was dead; unfortunately Féret, booksellers established in 1812 and still existing in the Rue Grassi, just off the Cours de l'Intendance, have no information about the creator of their celebrated work of reference.

The 1846 work is dedicated in polite, not to say sycophantic, terms to M. le Comte T. Duchâtel, Ministre de l'Intérieur and 'eminent proprietor of one of the most remarkable growths of this province', Ch. Lagrange in St-Julien. In the 1850 edition the wine regions are divided into six: Bordeaux, Lesparre, Libourne, La Réole, Bazas and Blaye – 'of which the two former are by far the most celebrated on account of the fame of their produce'. The Bordeaux section reaches into the Médoc up to Cussac; St-Julien northwards is included in Lesparre.

The 1868 edition included the classification of 1855; the third edition appeared in 1874 and was followed by another in 1881. Two years later this edition was translated into English 'owing to the demand we have received from England and America'. It was in the 1881 edition that first appeared the now-familiar engraved pictures of the châteaux, accompanied by paragraphs which combined information with praise in such a way as to suggest that if their insertion was not paid for they were at least written by or for the proprietor. To the confusion of the less sophisticated readers, this still applies.

Further editions appeared in 1886, 1893, 1898, 1908, 1922, 1929, 1949 and 1969. In 1893 a German edition was published by Verlag von Friedrich Naegel in Stettin. Such an apparently distant publishing point may be explained by the fact that the Bordeaux trade with Germany has always been centred around Hamburg, Bremen and the Baltic ports. The last English edition, based on the 1898 issue, came out in 1899. For a period the 1898 and 1908 editions were available in six different parts. The paper-covered 1908 section for the Graves has a typical *art nouveau* pink cover. It is fair to say that Cocks's work was preceded by a similar work, *Traité sur les vins du Médoc* by Wilhelm Franck, a German. It appeared first in 1824, and the last edition was issued in 1868, after which, no doubt, it was superseded by Cocks et Féret's more comprehensive work. References to both works are to be found throughout this book.

6. The Bordeaux Wine Trade from the Eighteenth Century

This chapter is about commerce, and that inevitably means many facts and figures. Those who wish to skip them can do so without much loss of wine information, but they are important for those interested in the background of Bordeaux.

To sketch in briefly the history of the wine trade in Bordeaux from the eighteenth century onwards it is necessary to retrace our steps. In an earlier chapter I have shown that during the seventeenth century the Dutch largely came in to take the place of the English; the Chartrons became the Quartier Hollandais. At the beginning of that century English imports of Bordeaux wine averaged about 8,000 *tonneaux* a year. By 1663, after the restoration of Charles II, they had risen to 11,000 *tonneaux*, but there were periods of Anglo-French economic warfare; in 1678 and 1689 temporary total prohibitions were imposed on the import of French wines; and as soon as William III's wars with France began they fell away more or less permanently. In 1699–1703 Portugal and Spain already provided 90 per cent of annual English wine imports, with the other 10 per cent equally divided between Germany and France. Even a generation later when trade between England and France was rather better and England was importing 5,000 *tonneaux* from Bordeaux, the emergent French North American colonies were shipping 7,000 *tonneaux*.

For punitive duties and the Methuen Treaty with Portugal in 1703 combined to turn the English away from the French, and above all from Bordeaux wines. By 1707 the English duty levied on a *tonneau* of Bordeaux wine was £55, thirteen times the price of a modest red Graves wine. The key formula had been devised in Article Two of the Methuen Treaty. In return for a Portuguese promise to admit in perpetuity British woollen goods, this Article in part says:

That is to say, that her sacred Majesty of Great Britain shall in her own name and that of her successors, be obliged for ever hereafter to admit the wines of the growths of Portugal into Great Britain; so that at no time, whether there shall be peace or war between the kingdoms of Great Britain and France, anything more shall be demanded for these wines, by the names of customs or duty . . . than shall be demanded for like quantity or measure of French wine, *deducting or abating a third part of the custom or duty.* (My italics.)

In other words the duty on French wines must always be 50 per cent higher than on Portuguese wines; and so it was for 128 years, and for 85 of them the duty on French wines was about 120 per cent higher. From 1707 to 1745 the impost was 5s. 3d. per (old) gallon, compared with 2s. 5d. for Portuguese (and Spanish) wines. For a further 37 years until 1782, it was 6s. (£63 per *tonneau*) compared with 2s. 9d. for the Iberian wines, and then for four years it jumped to 9s. 5d. (4s. 10d.). More liberal ideas temporarily prevailed from 1786 to 1794 and the duty was dropped to 4s. 10d. with a corresponding decrease in the duty on the favoured wines to 3s. 1d. The immediate result was a doubling of French wine imports into the United Kingdom for the three following years. But as the Napoleonic Wars got into their stride the duty rose to over 10 shillings per gallon, and higher still after 1803. A peak of no less than 19s. 8d. was reached in 1813, and not until 1825 did it sink to 7s. 3d. and then to 5s. 6d. in 1831 when the preference for Portuguese and other wines was abandoned. The next step had to await Messrs Cobden and Gladstone.

As described earlier, it was the Dutch who had saved the Bordeaux wine trade from the mid sixteenth century onwards, and particularly since the seventeenth century – not only in wine but also in *eau-de-vie*. In 1640 they were already importing 3,000 *barriques* from Bordeaux, whose reputation for

eau-de-vie up to the eighteenth century was on a par with the
eau-de-vie of La Rochelle or what is now called cognac. In
1677 a certain Jean Deschamp of Bordeaux was described as a
brusleur d'eau-de-vie. In the exceptionally prosperous year of
1700–1701 the Bordelais exported 90,000 hl of spirit, of which
60 per cent went to Holland. Not all of this came from the
Bordeaux area; much came from the former Gascon district
of Armagnac. Also unsold Haut-Pays wine was often distilled
in Bordeaux.

As to wine, in 1684 the Dutch bought 30,144 *tonneaux* of
Bordeaux, 33,127 in 1699–1700, and no less than 43,733 in the
following boom year. In these two latter years Dutch purchases were responsible for 65·6 per cent and 73·2 per cent of
total Bordeaux wine exports by quantity. By 1717 the Bordeaux Chamber of Commerce, founded in 1705, was reporting
an export to England of only 6,000 *tonneaux* of wine and *eau-de-
vie* (perhaps 10 per cent of the total), compared with 34,000 to
Holland, 6,500 to northern Europe, and 4,000 to the developing French colonies.

After the Revocation of the Edict of Nantes in 1685 many
Huguenots of Bordeaux and south-west France emigrated to
northern Europe and established commercial links with Bordeaux. In the same way Englishmen, Scotsmen and Irishmen
of Jacobite sympathies and/or Roman Catholic religion came
to Bordeaux to trade with their home countries. In return for
wine Ireland used to send salt beef to Bordeaux; England was
interested in the export of woollen goods.

The pattern of the export trade a little later was described in
a memorandum of 1739, quoted by Malvezin in his *Histoire
de la vigne et du vin en Aquitaine* (1919). The English consumption of Gascon wines was small, and then only the *grands vins*,
selling for between 400 and 2,000 livres per *tonneau*. The
second wines went to Scotland and Ireland. Holland drank
very little of these types. They were mostly interested in the
vins blancs de côtes, from the sweet wine areas, the Entre-Deux-

Mers, but above all from Bergerac (outside the region) and Ste-Foy. As for the Germans, they took the red *palus* wines and much the same whites as the Dutch. It was the Rhine wines that were fashionable in Germany, and only the common people drank Bordeaux.

Yet Bordeaux then as always had to live on exports; northern France drank other wines (the Paris region exported wines to Normandy and Picardy well into the eighteenth century), and the regional domestic market adjacent to Bordeaux was not nearly large enough to absorb the produce of a growing wine area. The surplus was one of the reasons for the distillation of *eau-de-vie*, until the Charentais took over most of the trade. Bordeaux's wine exports represented three-quarters of all French wine exports. Wine was the third most important item in the trade of Bordeaux after sugar and coffee, which were imported from the West Indies.

In fact, although the eighteenth century was an epoch of almost uninterrupted expansion for Bordeaux, the wine trade had its ups and downs. In addition to the continuing and increasing defection of the English there were the hazards of the vintage and the variations in the market. A notoriously bad vintage early in the century was the 1709. Then with the expansion of the *vignoble* there was overproduction in the first quarter of the century; and from 1720 to 1730 a slump in wine prices.

Furthermore, as the Dutch increasingly lost their prominent economic position in Europe, so Bordeaux's wine trade with the Low Countries declined. As the Dutch had largely replaced the English earlier on, so northern Europe and particularly the north German Hanseatic cities stepped in during the second half of the eighteenth century. The Germans who had previously bought through Holland now imported direct, and the Netherlands substantially lost its entrepôt role. By the Revolution the German colony in Bordeaux was larger than the Dutch; and henceforth until the First World War it was

Germany which supplied the mass demand for the cheaper and medium-priced Bordeaux, particularly the red wines which had not directly interested the Dutch.

Also towards the end of the century other Baltic markets became important for Bordeaux: Sweden, Denmark, Prussia and even Russia, which by 1789 was taking 5 per cent of Bordeaux's exports.

The other developing markets for Bordeaux wines were the French colonies, particularly the West Indies. In 1717 Bordeaux had exported 4,000 *tonneaux* to the French colonies; in 1788 the quantity had risen to 32,000 *tonneaux*, although by then French Canada had been lost.

Oddly enough the decline in trade with England helped the development of the leading estates in Bordeaux. As the duty was the same on a *premier cru* as on a *palus* wine, the rich English who could afford to drink claret naturally bought the finer wines, which relatively were better value for money. In Ireland and Scotland the duties against French wines were not so heavy, so they bought more but cheaper wines. For example, in 1740 Bordeaux sent 1,000 *tonneaux* to London, 2,500 *tonneaux* to Scotland and 4,000 *tonneaux* to Ireland, but according to F. Crouzet's estimates their respective values came to 1 million livres, 1·5 million livres, and 1·6 million livres. In spite of everything, the proprietors of Lafite, Haut-Brion and such second-rank wines as Léoville and Rausan could count on selling their wines to the English aristocracy. Thus even in 1787 when the total exports to the British Isles only accounted for about 7 per cent in volume, the value was as high as 26 per cent. The cheap white wines that satisfied many of Bordeaux's customers were not worth a tenth of the fine wines.

An extract from a table of F. Crouzet in his chapter on the commerce of Bordeaux in *Bordeaux au XVIIIe siècle* (1968) shows the changing pattern of the Gironde wine exports by percentage of volume.

PERCENTAGE TOTALS OF BORDEAUX WINE EXPORTS BY
VOLUME TO THE PRINCIPAL DESTINATIONS

	Netherlands	Northern Europe	British Isles	French Colonies
1717	67	13	12	8
1751–3	41	37	6	14
1775–7	35	36	4	23
1787	14	39	7	32
1789	10	46	5	34

The 1787 figures for Britain given above are a little misleading, as they reflected a jump in exports following the relaxa-
tion of duties in 1786. It is worth noting that the rise in exports
was not particularly vigorous in the eighteenth century. From
62,000 *tonneaux* in 1700–1701, they dropped to 50,000 *tonneaux*
in 1715, reached a 128,000 *tonneaux* peak in 1765, slumped
badly in the 1770s, and achieved a pre-Revolutionary maximum of 113,000 *tonneaux* in 1785; and this rise in exports
was entirely accounted for by the colonial trade. Yet the value
rose between 1728–34 and 1774–80 from 6 million livres to
20 million livres – far more than the rise in the domestic
French price of wine. This M. Crouzet attributes to the rise
in quality of Bordeaux wines, and in particular the birth of
the *grands crus*.

The French colonies not only helped to solve the Bordeaux
merchants' quests for new export markets; they also eased the
difficulties of the Haut-Pays wine growers, whose produce
was largely marketed and exported by the Gironde trade.
During the century the proportion of *vins de haut* exported
rose from 10 per cent of the total to 25 per cent in the 1770s.
Libourne was the great port for the wines of Monbazillac and
Bergerac.

After American Independence in 1776 Bordeaux's trade
with the former English colonies increased, but was not con-

siderable in wines and spirits for which there was little demand. In 1789 only 27,000 livres-worth of wine was included in total Bordeaux exports to the U.S.A. of 373,000 livres; but Bordeaux was the chief French port for the American trade.

Altogether wine became decreasingly important in the economy of Bordeaux. Whereas in the first third of the eighteenth century it was the major export in terms of money, as the general export trade with the French colonies increased – and it was this import–export colonial trade which was responsible for the city's great prosperity in this century and not wine – so did the share of wine drop. Between 1778 and 1786 there was another slump in wine prices, and on the eve of the Revolution wine accounted for not much more than 25 per cent of the total trade of the port, which from a comparatively modest size in 1715 had now become the largest in France. Nevertheless wine remained a vital part of the commerce. In 1760–68 wine exports averaged 76,000 *tonneaux*, and certainly less than half was drunk in the region. In the middle of the century when output had been about 130,000 *tonneaux* domestic consumption had accounted for only 55,000 *tonneaux*.

Although the Revolution in its early, anti-monarchical stages had the support of the middle-class Bordelais – hence the Girondins – trade suffered. This was basically owing to the wars with the English that broke out towards the close of the century and continued intermittently until the final fall of Napoleon in 1815. Also the merchants, who had clearly done very well for themselves in the pre-revolutionary epoch, were heavily taxed on their wines. The size of the Girondin *vignoble* contracted from 135,000 ha in 1789 to 99,000 ha in 1808, and did not recover its pre-revolutionary extent until 1835 when it reached 133,000 ha, with an average production of about 2,228,000 hl. Yet total production in 1808 was only slightly less than twenty years earlier. The average price of Bordeaux wines, excluding the classed growths, was almost halved in the post-revolutionary era and did not recover and surpass its 1789 level until the Elba exile of Napoleon in 1814. There was then a brief inter-war boom, including a flood of exports to Britain, which did not recur after the final defeat and exile of Napoleon a year later. Throughout the period of the Revolution, Directory and Empire wine exports fell away sharply, from a maximum of 100,000 *tonneaux* a year between 1783 and 1789 to 25,000.

Moreover although this period comprehended some very fine vintages (including 1795, the exceptional and plentiful 1798, followed by 1802, 1803, 1807 and the famous Comet Year of 1811), growers and merchants had great difficulties in selling their wines. This was partly owing to the drop in exports, partly to the problems of selling Bordeaux throughout France (Napoleon drank burgundy). A. d'Armailhacq in his book on the Médoc (mentioned in more detail in the description of Mouton-Baron-Philippe) wrote, 'The sufferings of the proprietors of vineyards of the Médoc were great at this period.' Not only was the British market closed by Napoleon's blockade, but the English fleet prohibited exports to the French colonies. Within France internal taxes and local tolls hindered the disposal of wines that previously had mostly been exported. When the short 1814 boom arrived many proprietors still had on their hands wines from the 1802 and 1811 vintages. However, demand for the leading wines improved towards the end of Napoleon's reign, and between 1811 and 1814 the price of first growths doubled; in 1814 buyers came in from Britain, Holland, Germany, Scandinavia and even from Russia.

Yet with the Bourbon Restoration, in spite of promises of reduced taxation, trade again declined. A strongly protectionist policy was followed, with consequent harm to the export trade. As shown above, the English duties on French wines were not reduced dramatically on the Bourbons' return; they remained largely political in intent and a weapon of economic warfare. Nevertheless when the English did equalize their duties on foreign wines in 1831, this was a liberalizing measure which was later followed by French trade agreements with other countries. In 1843, for example, a Franco-Belgian commercial treaty improved trade with one of Bordeaux's important customers. With the United States trade was increasing but difficult, owing to double duties: one on quality and a second *ad valorem*. There were stories of the American customs authorities, traditionally zealous, seizing shiploads of Bordeaux wines if the paperwork did not tally as to the value. However, over the years Bordeaux exports did improve, and between 1815 and 1850 the annual average for the world was 50,000 *tonneaux*.

In the 1850s the Second Empire prosperity was interrupted for the wine trade by the sudden incidence of the oidium disease, described in Chapter One. It came on very quickly in 1852–3, and was generally conquered by 1857, but in the intervening years the Bordeaux crop was heavily reduced. From over $2\frac{1}{4}$ million hl in 1850 it dropped to 726,000 hl in 1854 and 319,000 in 1855. Throughout France the vine crop slumped from over 55 million hl down to 10 million hl; it had the effect in Bordeaux of raising prices sharply and they never went back.

How sharply they rose is demonstrated by comparing the average prices of the classed growths as given in the 1853 and 1868 editions of Wilhelm Franck's manual, *Traité sur les vins du Médoc*. In the earlier year prices, which no doubt reflected the onset of the oidium, were little changed from the first edition (1824), as given in the chapter on the Classification (page 505–6).

	1853	1868
First growths	1,800–2,400 frs.	4,500–5,000 frs.
Second growths	2,000–2,100	3,500
Third growths	1,800	3,000
Fourth growths	1,500	2,000–2,500
Fifth growths	1,200	1,500–1,800

In 1854 Latour managed to sell 13 *tonneaux* of its meagre crop to Barton & Guestier at 5,000 frs. a *tonneau*, and even 2,500 frs for the second wine, an extraordinary increase since this firm had with the 1853 vintage just completed a ten-year contract by which they had paid only 1,750 frs. a *tonneau* since 1844. Lafite and Mouton-Rothschild were sold at the same price and Margaux even secured 5,500 frs. The seconds rose to 4,000 frs., the thirds to 3,000 frs., though Palmer secured 4,000 from Johnston. Such prices were more than 2,000 frs. a *tonneau* higher than ever before, and although the accepted 'class steps' of 300 frs. per class (referred to later in the chapter on the Classification of the Médoc) were abolished after about a century, the first growths moved ahead of the seconds (excluding Mouton-Rothschild) to a new pre-eminence in price that still exists today, while the lesser growths achieved a substantial if less permanent rise.

In the same period the prices of Sauternes went up from 450–1,200 frs. in 1853 to 1,000–3,000 frs. The wide range is explained by the high prices reached by the few top growths. By 1868 Yquem was much dearer than the others.

In this period of profit and plenty for the proprietors and merchants – Pijassou in the work on Latour describes the years 1854–85 as 'the second golden age of Latour' – it is worth remembering the *vignerons*. Until 1861 the general wage for men was one franc a day, and fifty centimes for women. Then in that year some of the proprietors, including those of Pichon-Longueville, Pichon-Lalande and Grand-Puy-Lacoste, raised the level to 1·50 frs. for men and also increased the annual perquisite of a *demi-barrique* of the *vin de presse* (the wine made from the skins pressed after the vats have been emptied of the first wine) to a whole *barrique*. This became the general level of payment. The women had an increase to one franc and the disagreeable jobs such as the vine-sulphuring were paid at two francs a day. Although the estate workers were housed free and leading estates like Latour looked after their staff's health and paid some pensions, the rewards of the workers in the *belle époque* were not exactly lavish. In 1866, after the twelve Latour *vignerons* had had their increase, their average annual pay totalled 691 frs. apiece and an unspecified number of female workers earned 2,579 frs. between them. In contrast, during Latour's 'golden age', from 1854 to 1883 the average annual dividends paid to the five absentee proprietary families totalled 151,000 frs., estimated by Pijassou to be the equivalent in current value terms of 751,000 frs. The net revenue in these years yielded the high percentage for an agricultural estate of 7·5 per cent to 8 per cent. No doubt the other *premiers crus* achieved much the same results, Lafite probably being even more profitable as it was larger than Latour. The other classed growths, Mouton always excepted, did less well as their over-heads per hectare were probably not all that less than for the firsts; but certainly the seconds and thirds did well enough. However, from the phylloxera onwards things were never to be the same again until the 1960s.

Dealings in the sought-after 1858 vintage, as recounted in Pijassou's study of Lafite, provide an illuminating picture of the rivalry between the leading proprietors and their running fight with the merchants of the Chartrons. Their conflict in the period of the oidium will be found in the chapter on the vintages (p. 536). Then the merchants certainly paid too much for poor years and so they approached the 1858s with caution. In those days the wines were sold by the growers as early as possible, and the practice was for the brokers to visit the properties as soon after the vintage as the wines were judged drinkable, probably in November. They might go armed with buying orders from the trade, in which case they would begin negotiations; otherwise they would report back their findings. Although the 1858 vintage was an early one, starting on 20 September, Goudal, the Lafite *régisseur*, reported to Scott on 11 November that the wines were still fermenting, but of very fine quality. Roux of Latour had the same opinion of his wine, while suggesting that the Lafite was not so good! Lawton, perhaps after the failure of the 1856 and 1857, was cautious. They seemed good, but one must wait, for sometimes 'the hopes of great quality are not always realized'. The merchants hoped to play a waiting game and buy late at low prices.

However, Sir Samuel Scott in London took an unusual hand in the business and by the middle of November had already sold his Lafite (the quantity is not given but presumably it was the entire crop) to a London merchant, Dobrée & Sons, for 4,000 frs. for the *grand vin*, 3,800 frs. for the Carruades and 2,000 frs. for the second wine; it was bought without tasting, for Mr Dobrée only had the chance to do this the following April, after the first racking. This coup, by-passing the Bordeaux merchants, caused a sensation in Bordeaux, although M. Lawton was honest enough to tell Goudal that it had been a very advantageous deal for Lafite. Nevertheless, he was unhappy at not receiving the brokerage of 2 per cent invariable on all deals; no doubt to keep him in good countenance Goudal gave him 1 per cent, though he had taken no part in the transaction. After all, Lafite had taken 726,000 frs. in the English deal. Dobrée must have done well too, for in October 1859 Cruse and Barton & Guestier repurchased in England the Lafite 1858 for 6,000 frs. a *tonneau*, a 50 per cent increase on the purchase price of less than a year earlier.

Moreover, in spite of the agitation this move of Lafite created on the Chartrons, Lafite's action certainly helped all the other growers, from the modest *crus bourgeois* of Moulis, Listrac and Cussac, who secured as much as 600 frs. a *tonneau* (and Citran at Avensan took 1,200 frs.), right up to the leaders. The fifth growths obtained 1,500 frs., the thirds up to 2,400 and the seconds from 2,800 to 3,800 frs., though Mouton of course managed to draw level with Lafite at 4,000 frs. The other two *premiers crus* stood firm and Latour went for 4,800 frs. and Margaux for 5,000 frs. Nineteen years later in the remarkable sale at Christie's of fine clarets bought from Harvey's of Bristol (referred to also on p. 117), over ten dozen of Latour 1858, shipped by Barton & Guestier, bottled by Harvey's and laid down in a South-Wales private cellar in 1861, were sold for the high price of 125s.–130s. a dozen. Originally it had cost the owner 84s. as against 60s. for the 1857 Lafite and 69s. for the 1862 Lafite and Ch. Margaux.

As this affair clearly demonstrates, commercially Bordeaux's chief target at this period was Britain, which in 1840 had actually increased slightly the duty on wine to 5s. 9¼d. a gallon, although without any discrimination against the French. In 1846 Frédéric Bastiat, who lived in the Landes and was a great agitator for free trade on the British model, organized in Bordeaux an Association for Free Trade, and in August of that year the association gave a banquet in Paris for Richard Cobden, the British apostle of free trade. The tenaciously tariff-minded French industry and administration had to be converted, and the successful 1855 International Exhibition in Paris, which was visited by Queen Victoria and for which the Médoc classification was prepared, was a step on the road. However the final adherence of the French Government, whose chief negotiator with Cobden was Michel Chevalier, was only secured by the agreement of the British Government to reduce the duties on French wines.

After long negotiations an Anglo-French Commercial Treaty was signed on 23 January 1860, and the duty on table wines was at once reduced to 3s. a gallon, and then to 1s. a gallon (2d. a bottle) the following January. W. E. Gladstone, the Chancellor of the Exchequer, is generally associated with this reduction in duty, and rightly so, for it was he who secured the agreement of the British Cabinet and Parliament to the terms of the treaty. 'Gladstone's Claret' and 'Chancellor's Claret' became known for many years, and British wine drinkers of left-wing sympathies do not forget that the next chancellor who made a substantial reduction in the duty on table wines was the Labour Chancellor, Sir Stafford Cripps, in 1949.

The President of the Bordeaux Chamber of Commerce described the treaty as 'a commercial action of the highest importance', and British wine imports from France rose from 700,000 gallons in 1859 to 2,227,000 gallons in 1861; the great majority came from Bordeaux.

To complete this happy and all too rare reduction in wine duties, some argument followed with the British wine trade, because the 1s. a gallon duty applied only to wines up to 18 degrees of proof spirit on the British scale, the equivalent of between 10 and 11 per cent of alcohol on the French (Gay-Lussac) scale. This was lower than any fine Bordeaux wines, and at the 1862 International Exhibition in London it was demonstrated that the average strength of the wines shown was over 18 degrees (British Sikes Scale). Higher duties obtained on stronger wines, with an overall rate of 2s. 5d. on all wines imported in bottle. Finally in April 1862 an amendment was made by which all table wines not exceeding 25 degrees (Sikes), or just over 14 per cent alcohol (Gay-Lussac) came in at 1s. a gallon, those not exceeding 42 degrees (24 per cent) paid 2s. 6d. and the wines in bottle incurred what became known as 'the bottle surcharge' of 2s. 6d. a gallon, i.e. the additional duty on château-bottled claret was 5d. Until entry into the E.E.C. British duty rates were still levied at these levels of strength, although in the 1880s the maximum for table wines was temporarily raised to 30 degrees (17 per cent). The Gladstonian duties remained unchanged until the close of the century; in 1899 the duty on table wines imported in cask was raised to 1s. 3d. a gallon, but the bottle surcharge was correspondingly reduced by 3d. to 2s. 3d. Since we in Britain consider ourselves fortunate if the duty is not increased almost annually, such stability for nearly forty years seems inconceivable.

These figures are given in some detail, because they had a

profound and immediate influence on the Bordeaux trade. Not only did sales to Britain soar; the position of the growers and merchants alike was strengthened. Moreover the changes led to a succession of commercial treaties reducing duties with other countries: another Franco-Belgian Treaty in 1861, a Franco-Prussian Treaty in 1862 and a Franco-Zollverein Treaty in 1865. For a few years in Europe there was a spirit of economic optimism and expansion. Yet during a short economic crisis in France in 1867 already there were manufacturing interests calling for the cancellation of the tariff concessions on British manufactured goods made by the French Government in the Anglo-French Treaty of 1860.

The purchase of classed-growth châteaux in the Médoc by the merchants, mentioned in the last chapter, demonstrated the prosperity of the Bordeaux trade in the 1860s, the second half of the Second Empire, and a period of economic expansion for France and of great wealth for the bankers, railway builders and other entrepreneurs; though not for their employees as the Paris Commune was to show in 1871. The cream of the wine trade was in the hands of a comparatively small number of firms – the commercial aristocracy of the Chartrons. Until 1860 about forty merchants dominated the export trade, each specializing in its own class of wine suited to the various markets. An example of the expansion of markets in the 1860s was Argentina. Her imports of Bordeaux wines rose from 35,000 hl in 1859 to 233,000 in 1869. U.S. imports were about 200,000 hl in the late 1860s.

Between 1846 and 1870 exports tripled, from an average of 445,000 hl in the decade ending in 1846 to 1,187,000 in the five years culminating in 1870. By 1875 they had risen even higher: to 1,500,000 hl.

Several firms well known today opened their doors between 1860 and 1870, as described in the chapter on the wine merchants. Moreover the growers were able to assert themselves. Previously, apart from the first growths and a few well-known 'names', a great deal of wine exported from Bordeaux was sold under the importing merchants' names rather than those of the châteaux or communes. Now these, particularly the better-known châteaux, began to publicize their names.

As indicated, the prosperity began before 1860. It was really the after-effects of the oidium in the mid-1850s which touched it off. The result was a tremendous increase in price for the diminished supplies available. Whereas in 1852 the average price of Bordeaux wine in cask was 30 frs. per hectolitre, by 1854 – in the middle of the oidium period – it was 145 frs., and even 120 frs. in the celebrated and plentiful vintage of 1858. The peak was reached in 1862, a moderate year for quality, with an average price of 221 frs. per hectolitre. For wine was still short overall; there had not been a harvest exceeding 2 million hl since 1850.

Indeed in the Bordeaux trade there developed a period of speculation that was not paralleled for another hundred years. The crop generally was small in 1861, owing to spring frosts, though they did not affect the classed growths near the estuary, but conditions were favourable at the vintage. Latour had no difficulty in selling its first wine for 5,000 frs. and the second wine for 2,500 frs. before the end of November, and Lafite secured the same price. The seconds fetched 4,000 frs. and the thirds 3,000 frs. According to the broker Lawton even the modest wines of the Premières Côtes were fetching between 1,200 and 1,500 frs. the *tonneau*. The German house of Finke, which had bought the whole Lafite crop, wrote in its circular to customers that the vintage could be 'classed among the greatest vintages of the century', though this turned out to be somewhat of an exaggeration as has been the case with subsequent 'vintages of the century'.

The 1862 vintage, rather smaller in quantity, was snapped up with no less alacrity, and the three Médoc firsts were quickly sold for 4,000 frs. a *tonneau*.

However a series of exceptionally plentiful years lay ahead, beginning with the indifferent vintage of 1863, when 2·2 million hl were produced. From then on until the last good pre-phylloxera vintage in 1878, only in two years were less than 2 million hl produced, with 4·5 million hl in 1869 and over 5 million apiece in 1874 and 1875. In these latter years this was partly owing to extensive planting in the later sixties, which bore fruit by 1873. The Gironde *vignoble* which hitherto had never exceeded 135,000 ha suddenly expanded to 145,000 ha. This growth was common throughout France, and in 1875 the fantastic national total of 83·8 million hl was produced, compared with an average of 60 million hl today. Naturally in this period of plenty the average price of Bordeaux wine dropped sharply, and by 1870 it was down to 80 frs. per hectolitre.

Speculation reached its height with the 1868 vintage. After the two leading years of 1864 and 1865, out of which both growers and merchants made large profits, 1866 and 1867 were very poor years. The summer of 1868 was torrid and the flowering was finished in the Médoc by 7 June, two or three weeks earlier than normal. A great deal of wine was sold *sur souche* (on the vine), and M. Lawton estimated that within a month of the vintage, which began in the Médoc on 6 September, only one sixth of the crop remained unsold. The first growths and some of the other classed estates sold at prices that in real terms they probably did not equal until the 1971s, more than a century later. Latour sold its whole crop to Finke for 6,250 frs. (payable, it is interesting to note in the Latour book, in five parts, from 15 February 1869 to 15 April 1870), Lafite obtained the same price, Margaux 6,000 frs. and Mouton 5,000; other seconds secured 4,000 frs. Even the *crus bourgeois* of the Médoc surpassed 1,100–1,200 frs. per *tonneau*. In fact, in spite of all the favourable prognostications, the 1868s, probably owing to unbalanced weather conditions, did not turn out successfully and the trade lost money. The reasonably good 1869s sold at about 3,000 frs. for the firsts, while the 1870s, upset by the Franco-Prussian War that autumn, had variable results financially and purchases were delayed. So Lafite fetched 4,500 frs., Latour and Mouton 3,000 frs. apiece, while some of the other classed growths received very low prices indeed. This of course was the vintage that took so many years to come round but thereafter survived most of the other years of its period.

The Anglo-French Treaty of 1860 also had a big effect on wine drinking in Britain. If 'Gladstone's claret' and 'grocer's claret' became terms of disdain in some circles, since it was now possible for licensed grocers to sell this inexpensive wine carrying only a duty of 2d. a bottle, the demand for claret greatly increased in Britain.

Nevertheless it must not be imagined that in Britain claret flowed like water. True, imports in 1860–62 were three times higher than in the three pre-treaty years, but they started at a very low ebb, at around 20,000 hl a year. André Simon pointed out in *Vintagewise* (1945) that in 1859 the little island of Mauritius was importing 40,000 hl, while in the U.S.A. the total of Gironde wine imported was just on 150,000 hl. Owing to the Civil War American imports suffered later in the 1860s, but recovered afterwards. The British market was still above all a 'quality' one, for only the well-off could afford to drink wine. Nevertheless of the wine drunk in England the percentage of French wine rose from 9·5 per cent in 1859 to 41·9 per cent in 1880. Thereafter it fell back slightly.

The popularity of claret was also linked with the improvement in the vintages of the sixties compared with the fifties. Christie's contemporary wine sales show the shortage of mature clarets until the later years. In 1862 the miserable '54s, with their flavour of oidium rot, were fetching over 60s. a dozen. The Lafite '54 made 73s. The pre-oidium Lafite '51, no great vintage, made 139s. per case of 6 magnums. Two years later Lafite '48, 'magnificent and almost matchless wine', sold for 130s. Thereafter prices appeared to decline for all but particular wines of outstanding vintages of the 1840s or of 1858. In 1867 magnums of Latour '41 from Lord Bath's cellar fetched the very high price of £16 a case, though bottles of Lafite '41 from Christophers made only 88s. At this sale Lafite 1848 'château seal, bought of M. Goudal' (manager of Lafite) went for 126s., and Lafite '58, 'bottled at the château bought of M. Goudal 1864', attained 105s. In the same year the celebrated Lafite '64 reached Christie's and sold at 68s. At this sale Yquem '47 went for 120s. and the '51 at 92s. The value of money was at least six times higher than it is today.

So far as Bordeaux was concerned the years up to 1878 were the sunshine before the storm; with the onslaught of the phylloxera, the area under vines diminished slightly and the output of wine sharply declined. Although Bordeaux suffered less than other French wine districts, there was not another 3 million hectolitre vintage until 1893. The Gironde *vignoble* did not decline substantially, unlike the rest of France, whose overall vineyard area by 1899 was only two-thirds of its peak in the mid-1870s. In 1889 total French wine output was only 23 million hl compared with 70 million ten years earlier. By the end of the century the total French vineyard area was less than 1·7 million ha; three-quarters of a million ha fewer than before the phylloxera.

This decline was not, as often attributed, solely owing to the phylloxera and the succeeding mildew. A general crisis in France in 1873 set off a slow decline in prices that continued for over twenty years. There was another crisis in 1882, which affected Britain, Germany and the U.S.A. as well as France. By 1896 when the drop in prices was arrested, they were down by 40 per cent compared with 1873. Thereafter they slowly rose, being 20 per cent up on the 1896 level by 1906 and 40 per cent by 1912. Yet in that latter year, according to A. Viallate in *L'Activité économique en France de la fin du XVIIIe siècle à nos jours* (1937), the price index was 118 compared with 144 in 1873.

The result of the recurrent economic difficulties in France led to the growth of a tariff lobby antagonistic to the free trade principles which had inspired the 1860 Anglo-French Treaty.

The lobby was not purely one-sided. An English pamphlet, *Our Trade with France Under the Cobden Treaty 1859–1880* (1881), the cover of which proclaimed Britain's adverse trade balance with France over the period as £480,463,630, produced statistics to show the way in which French wine imports into Britain had risen, from a mere £559,304 in 1859 to no less than £3,282,091 in 1880. In fact, after the initial post-treaty burst they did not exceed £1 million until 1866, but then advanced to £2 million in 1871, and £3 million in 1873, thereafter varying between about £2½ million and £3 million until the 1880 total quoted above. That is if these barbed statistics are reliable. Most of these imports will have come from Bordeaux.

After some hard bargaining the Anglo-French Treaty was renewed in 1873 but finally lapsed, when no further agreement could be reached, in 1882. However, by then so far as the British drinker of Bordeaux was concerned, the treaty had done its job, and until the outbreak of the Second World War the duties on French wines were no serious impediment to their consumption.

In the latter part of the last century it was the wine industry, dependent on exports, which had led all others in demanding the reduction of French tariffs; and Bordeaux had benefited particularly from the reduction of English duties on light wines, for those of some other French wine districts were often alcoholic enough to incur the higher rate of duty.

However the drop in wine production in the 1880s led to an insufficiency of wine for domestic consumption. As a result, for the first time in French history, wine was imported on a large scale. Whereas in the 1870s, before the phylloxera, no more than 50,000 hl of wine entered France annually, in the 1880s the totals surpassed first 1 million hl and then 2 million.

Even in the 1890s when the vineyards with their grafted vines had more or less recovered, imports still fluctuated between 1·2 million and 2·3 million hl. Although in the period leading up to the First World War they dropped to an average of three-quarters of a million hl, no return was achieved to the pre-phylloxera trickle. In 1972 France imported 8·5 million hl (7·5 million of them from Italy).

Much of the wine imported at the end of the last century came from the new vineyards in Algeria, whose abundant supplies of inexpensive, robust wines were for the next three-quarters of a century as welcome to the French wine merchants as they were hated by the growers of the extensive vineyards of the Midi, whose wines even lacked the body of those on the other side of the Mediterranean. Even after Algerian independence in 1960, its wine was allowed to be called French wine; a blend of Algerian and Bordeaux could legally be described as French – though not as Bordeaux. This situation lasted until 1967 when the protests of the southern French wine growers led to the admission of Algerian wine only under licence and the withdrawal of its status as 'produce of France'. Such restriction benefited Bordeaux, which could sell its lesser and off-vintage wines to the Midi producers, giving local wines quality if not body.

It was not only the Algerian wine growers who were stimulated by the drought of French wine in the 1880s. An impetus was given to wine growing and marketing in Italy, Spain, Portugal and other Mediterranean countries, who, at the cheaper end of the wine list, increasingly became France's competitors instead of her customers. Moreover Spanish and Italian wines were widely imported into Bordeaux for blending and supplementing its own thin wines in short supply.

From this period too stems the use of French wine-district names by growers in other countries competing in world markets. 'Graves', 'Sauternes', and even 'Claret-Type' appeared on wines originating far from France, let alone

Bordeaux. At the time the growers of Bordeaux and elsewhere were too poor, too unorganized and perhaps too indifferent to fight the misappropriation of what were later to be called their *appellations d'origine*. Since then they have had cause to regret their negligence.

Perhaps the French wine shortage also encouraged the development of wine growing in the United States too. For whereas in 1874 the total imports of French wines amounted to 218,000 hl, thirty years later they were down to 28,000, and dropped further thereafter, until Prohibition in 1919 gave them a knock-out blow from which they took many years to recover even after Repeal in 1933.

It should be mentioned, perhaps, that although the top ranks of Bordeaux wines were temporarily affected by natural disasters and economic difficulties, demand for them did not drop; it was the lesser wines, the *crus bourgeois*, *crus artisans* and *crus paysans* that suffered, for it was these which had to face competition from other wine-growing countries. As in the Côte d'Or, some marginal areas, particularly the *palus* vineyards, marginal in more than one sense, were not replanted, although in Bordeaux the decline in vineyard area really began in the present century; by 1911 it was down to 136,000 ha.

Meanwhile in the arduous eighties the Bordeaux merchants embarked on a lengthy agitation for the reduction in the number and value of the internal taxes on alcoholic drinks, whose yield had doubled from 223 million frs. in 1870 to 450 million frs. in 1880. They were also concerned over a minor economic war which had broken out between France and the United States of America, following the prohibition in France of American salt pork. As in the 'chicken war' of some years ago when the import of American 'broilers' into France was stopped, this led to American retaliation, which clapped extra duties on French wines, so that wines in bottles carried a duty of 14 cents (7d.) and champagne no less than 60 cents (2s. 6d.). Wines imported in cask were also penalized. The Bordeaux merchants, who suffered specially from this warfare, were quite willing at least in theory to eat humble salt pork pie, and urged their government to lift the ban and to make a commercial treaty with America, as they had done with Britain, to the great profit of both; but without any immediate effect.

The shortage and consequent high prices of wines in France resulted in falsification and sophistication which led to scandals. In particular these were exposed by the Paris municipal analysis laboratory. The consequence was a questioning of the quality of French wines in importing countries, including Britain, Germany and the United States, much in the same way as recent *appellation contrôlée* and 'non-beaujolais' disclosures in Britain shook public confidence. Then as now, voices were raised to protest that such scandals should not be made known publicly as they 'harmed the reputation' of French wines.

The flood of foreign wines, particularly from Spain and Italy, made the French wine trade in general go over to advocating tariffs against them, but the Bordeaux commerce was by now so deeply involved in the cheap, blended wine business, that it raised an outcry when the government introduced the Meline tariff in 1892. All the advanced countries were now becoming tariff-minded, not least the U.S.A., whose McKinley Tariff Act of 1890 helped to set the pace. Of course the countries on whose wines France levied duties proceeded to protect their own wine industry.

The French Government softened the blow to the Bordelais by establishing a local 'free port' area, supervised by the customs, in which imported wines intended for blending and re-export only were kept duty-free. This was satisfactory enough for the merchants, but much less so for the growers who claimed, with justification, that the shipment of blended, non-Bordeaux wines was harmful to the reputation of Bordeaux. So in 1897 these facilities were restricted to wines intended for countries outside Europe – on the grounds presumably that the 'natives' (including Australians and Americans) would never notice. In 1899 these 'free ports' were finally closed. The following year the government, moved partly by the wine trade's representations and partly because of the heavy spirit drinking in France, decided that wine consumption should be encouraged. Taxes were considerably reduced and then all were removed except a single tax, the *droit de circulation*, which was fixed at 1·50 frs. per hectolitre.

The general onset of the phylloxera devastation, usually reckoned as dating from 1879, marked the beginning of a crisis that lasted well into the First World War. This was not so apparent up to 1887 for, as Pijassou demonstrates in *Latour*, although the crops were reduced by the phylloxera and the succeeding mildew, prices kept surprisingly high – especially for vintages of moderate quality only. In these nine years Ch. Margaux came out best with an average price per *tonneau* of 3,211 frs., followed by 3,183 frs. for Latour, 2,633 frs. for Lafite and 2,445 frs. for Mouton-Rothschild. Next to Mouton among the seconds, Rausan-Ségla averaged 2,335 frs., and was succeeded by Palmer (1,889 frs.), Pichon-Longueville-Baron (1,889 frs.), Giscours (1,834 frs.), Ducru-Beaucaillou (1,800 frs.), Cos d'Estournel (1,483 frs.), Beychevelle (1,472 frs.), Cantemerle (1,450 frs.) and Pontet-Canet (1,350 frs.). These figures are given in detail as they display the rating of typical *crus classés* at this period. To translate them into current price terms they should probably be multiplied by at least ten. The best vintage was certainly 1887 and some typical prices are given in Appendix C.

It was in the next decade that the crisis became more evident, the fall in prices more decided, as can be seen from the average revenue per *tonneau* of the leading châteaux for the vintages from 1888 to 1897: Latour (1,809·50 frs.), Lafite (1,597·50 frs.), Ch. Margaux (1,689·50 frs.), Mouton-Rothschild (1,637·50 frs.). Many of the lesser growths suffered even more. The slide was most obvious in the second part of the decade, for the one good vintage, 1890, made good prices, as may be seen in Appendix C. But the final year, 1897, produced such poor wine that much of it was sold without the customary branded corks. Mouton-Rothschild did best at 1,100 frs., while Latour secured 700 frs., compared with 450 frs. for Lafite and Margaux. Curiously enough the Sauternes were doing well at this period; Yquem 1897 was sold for 4,000 frs.

Much of this abrupt drop was owing to lack of support from the export markets on which the classed growths so largely depended. The English were blamed (especially the journalists, as always on such occasions!) for holding off from the by no means poor 1893, but the real reason lay in the current economic depression.

Then, in spite of two vintages always regarded as of exceptional quality – 1899 and 1900 – the next ten years were even worse, as the comparative average prices show: Ch. Margaux (1,610 frs.), Lafite (1,435 frs.), Latour (1,355 frs.). Apart from Mouton, the second growths and others showed a drop of around 30 per cent on the previous decade. Few averaged more than 1,000 frs., and some typical returns were Palmer (780·50 frs.), Léoville-Las-Cases (765 frs.), Ducru-Beaucaillou (735 frs.), Pontet-Canet (730 frs.), and Giscours (642·50 frs.).

Even 1906, later well-considered though at the time viewed with mixed opinions, did not much redress the balance, as prices in the Appendix show.

One result of all this was the sudden growth of fixed-term contracts between the proprietors and groups of *négociants*. Although not unknown in the nineteenth century they were rare, but now they spread like wildfire. They were a form of speculation, with the merchants taking the risk on what the next five or ten years' crops would be like and the growers being assured of ready money every year. These contracts, known as *abonnements* (subscriptions) began in 1902. After the announcement that Schröder & Schÿler had secured a ten-year contract to buy the crop of Kirwan, which then belonged to the municipality of Bordeaux, a much more important contract of the same duration was made between Mouton-Rothschild and Calvet. It was unusual in that no fixed price was agreed, but one that took account of the prices of the three Médoc *premiers crus* along with such *deuxièmes* as the three Léovilles, Rausan-Ségla, Brane-Cantenac and Gruaud-Larose-Faure. Such variation stood Mouton in good stead when prices began to rise in the years preceding the First World War, when some first growths were tied by fixed-price contracts.

The next wave of these took place in 1907, comprehending the 1906 vintage that had not been sold *en primeur* – which in those days meant within a month or two of the vintage. These contracts were of course made in great secrecy, and when Margaux signed a ten-year *abonnement* early in 1907, the other firsts did their best to ascertain the terms, in order that they should secure no less favourable terms. However, Bordeaux has never been the place where commercial secrets are kept and it was soon known that the price was 1,650 frs. per *tonneau*; and at this rate both Lafite and Latour soon settled. However, Latour was wise enough to sign only for five years (covering the 1906–10 crops), which meant that when the 1911 was offered – sought-after more on account of rather better economic conditions than for its intrinsic quality – Latour was able to secure 2,500 frs., while the others were still bound to 1,650 frs. Haut-Brion did exceptionally well to secure 2,500 frs. for a ten-year contract.

The object of the merchants who made these contracts was to hedge their bets by re-selling part of their purchases at once. For example, within days of the contract with Latour being signed in 1907, the purchasers had re-sold 20 *tonneaux* of the 1906 at 3,200 frs. Then in 1911 half the crop of Ch. Margaux, contracted for at 1,650 frs., was re-sold a week before the vintage at 2,500 frs. and some of the Lafite at 2,300 frs. It should be noted that the merchants were careful not to commit themselves to purchasing an unspecified quantity of wine that might result from an unusually large vintage or overproduction on the part of the grower. The average production of Latour at this time was about 110 *tonneaux* and the 1907 contract stipulated a maximum amount of 120 *tonneaux*; higher quantities would be paid for at half-rate. Half-rate was the normal market price for a growth's second wine, normally not included in these *abonnements*. One point to be noted in these contracts was the early date of delivery from the château to the buyers: in the 1907 Latour contract it was 25 March, except of course for the quantity to be château-bottled at the instance of the purchasers.

These contracts were by no means confined to the first growths. In 1907 Beychevelle bound itself to Calvet and Barton & Guestier for five years at 800 frs., Palmer settled for 950 frs. to Rosenheim (and renewed it for another five years in 1911 for 1,200 frs.) and Dauzac sold to Nathaniel Johnston for 650 frs. All the leading Bordeaux merchants were engaged in this business, and in addition they owned ten of the classed growths. They almost certainly had the best of the bargain, particularly with the ten-year contracts. Owing to the drop in prices over many years, the growers were almost forced into such arrangements, but they probably did the quality and reputation of Bordeaux no more good than the 'exclusivities' that were so popular in the boom conditions of the early 1970s. For the growers had little incentive to improve their vineyards and their wines. They also encouraged the speculative side of the trade, never far below the surface in Bordeaux. An example was the extensive purchase *sur souche* (literally 'on the root', but perhaps best rendered as 'on the branch') of the 1913 vintage. Before the end of August much of the forthcoming Ch. Margaux crop had been re-sold at 650 frs. a *tonneau* above the contract price of 1,650 frs., Mouton-Rothschild had gone for 450 frs. above the original figure of 1,800 frs. and Haut-Brion for 2,900 frs., a profit of 400 frs. on the original purchasers' price. On this basis Latour was able to sell direct to seven firms at 2,300 frs. After all this the vintage turned out badly!

Although by and large Latour seems to have conducted its affairs better than most throughout this period, Pijassou in his contribution to *Latour* shows how its profits fell sharply from 1879 to 1917, and how the decade from 1898 to 1907, in spite of the great years of 1899 and 1900, saw its profits reduced almost to nothing. Between 1879 and 1917 a dividend was paid only one year in three. No wonder that as early as 1889 the proprietors almost agreed to sell the property for 3 million frs., and would have done so if the unknown purchaser had not changed his mind.

Moreover although prices rose somewhat in the next ten years, so did costs, including wages. For of course the *vignerons* and their families had suffered from the bad conditions of the post-phylloxera period. Wages had not risen since the 1880s, but the security of jobs enjoyed by the regular estate employees had led to an acceptance of low payment. However in 1913, to the horror of some of the Médoc proprietors, trades unionism suddenly appeared in their midst, with an eruption in St-Estèphe. (It was even said that the red flag was being paraded in its streets!) *Syndicalisme* became as dirty a word to the (often absentee) owners as Marxism to a more recent generation.

The Médoc *vignerons* were not alone in their demands, for this was a period of social tension in France, with the Socialist Party gaining adherents under the leadership of Jean Jaurès, who was to be murdered in Paris on the eve of the First World War. Two years previously there had occurred the celebrated 'revolt of the *vignerons*' in Champagne, when the dragoons were called in. All the Médocains were asking was an increase of fifty centimes a day on the existing two francs, for an eight-hour day, and twenty-five centimes for the women workers, to bring them up to one franc a day. Assuming a six-day week this meant a total weekly wage for male workers of 24 frs., at a time when there were 25 frs. to the pound sterling and *c*.5 to the U.S. dollar. Various higher rates were demanded for skilled workers and an increase in the amount of free wine given when the vines were being sprayed with copper sulphate. In addition, higher payment was to be given to those workers not lodged by the estates.

All this provoked a furious but not united reaction from the proprietors, for Mr Barton at Langoa and M. Faure at Gruaud-Larose-Faure acceded to the demands and so did the *régisseur* of Pontet-Canet, on the grounds that the *vignerons*' claims were just and humane. After several meetings and much inter-proprietorial correspondence the estates all seem to have given way, and at Latour at least more of the workers were given free lodging. The affair rumbled on and the freemasons of Pauillac as well as its trades unionists were accused of being behind it all. In the following year the conservative deputy for Lesparre was defeated at the parliamentary election in April by the Mayor of Soulac, with 'trade union support'. Whether social unrest would have continued in this somewhat isolated part of France cannot be estimated, as three months later the First World War was let loose and the *vignerons* began to be called to the colours. The names of those who never returned can be found on the war memorials of every village in the Médoc.

Nevertheless the period between 1900 and 1914 was a hard one for Bordeaux, particularly for the growers. Prices tended to drop over the years. According to figures given in the Chamber of Deputies, the average price of a *barrique* of Bordeaux wine fell from 142·5 frs. in 1905 to 105 frs. in 1910. While exports were quantitatively lower than in the 1880s (when the totals probably included foreign wines blended in), prices were even lower still. Whereas in 1890 Gironde wine exports to the United Kingdom totalled nearly 212,000 hl, from 1900 to 1914 they averaged 150,000 hl.

The pattern of Bordeaux exports and their relation to other French wine exports in the period before the First World War is illustrated by statistics for the year 1910 quoted by Jan Salavert in *Le Commerce des vins de Bordeaux* (1912):

| | Bordeaux exports | | Total other |
	cask	bottle	French wine exports
Great Britain	100,881 hl	9,096 hl	42,764 hl
Germany	221,159	1,810	193,407
Belgium	110,408	2,282	186,836
Holland	89,780	1,047	10,757
U.S.A.	5,798	4,962	1,271
Argentine	87,958	1,355	32,415

Value of Bordeaux exports in cask – 57,760 million frs.
Value of other French wine exports in cask – 51,716 million frs.
Value of Bordeaux exports in bottle – 7,872 million frs.
Value of other French wine in bottle – 4,959 million frs.

It will be observed that two out of every three bottles of French wine imported into Britain in 1910 came from the Gironde. These figures also show not only the predominance of Bordeaux in the French wine export trade, but also the vital importance of the German market, which bought the cheaper wines; when it collapsed after the First World War it meant the decline and disappearance of many of the *crus bourgeois*. Moreover the above export totals were a sad falling-off compared with the pre-phylloxera, pre-slump years. Whereas in 1875 the Gironde exported 1½ million hl the quantities dropped steadily, and by 1912 they had fallen by exactly 50 per cent – to ¾ million hl.

For although the Edwardian era is now looked back on in some quarters as a golden sunset before the carnage and social upheavals of the First World War, this was not a period of prosperity for any but the upper strata of society. It is significant that in these years the turnover of the International Exhibition Co-operative Wine Society, founded in London in

1874, and in 1900 composed of about 2,000 members drawn from the professional classes, scarcely advanced. It was about £16,000 in 1900 and £19,000 in 1913, although the membership had risen by a thousand. Wine prices remained unaltered over the years in a manner scarcely credible today, while British wages and salaries scarcely moved between 1896 and 1914.

In France economic conditions did not favour wine drinking, and there was a decline in consumption; indeed some doctors were suggesting publicly that wine was not all that good for the health. Salavert summed up the situation sorrowfully:

In *bourgeois* circles the number of drinkers of water and milk is growing; on the most lavish tables the good French wines are often replaced by bottles of insipid and disagreeable water, which is thought to be harmless; whereas formerly it was a luxury to have a well-furnished cellar, today one prefers to have an automobile, and rely by chance on the merchant when one wants to drink a good bottle. In working class circles wine is being replaced by spirits.

So the pre-1914 era was not quite the golden period of discriminating connoisseurs and splendid, inexpensive wines, as it is sometimes made out to be. The latter at least was to come later.

Nor, as already mentioned earlier, did the developing United States help much. The average annual imports of wine from the Gironde between 1900 and 1914 were only 11,400 hl.

Bordeaux was not as badly affected as some other areas, owing to its reputation for good quality wines, to the exertions of its merchants in overseas markets, and the fact that the red wines at least could be kept for a time. However, the growers could not hold stock for four or five years; they had to unload, thus accelerating the drop in prices. Often the money they received from the merchants was less than the cost of production, and bitter feeling developed between growers and traders, the former accusing the latter of being responsible for the low prices.

One cause at least of the crisis was over-production. Whereas in the five years ending in 1892 the average Bordeaux output was 2·13 million hl, it rose steadily, reached 3·7 million in the quinquennium ending in 1902 and 3·99 million in the following five years. There was no real delimitation of the Gironde *vignoble* and no control of production; much of the wine was inferior and badly made; this was made worse by the poor vintages. After three disastrous crops in the first three years of the century, 1901–3, there was not one outstanding year up to 1914, the best being 1906.

This over-production had been made worse by chaptalization, or sugaring of the must, to raise the alcoholic strength of the weak wine. In 1890 sugar used for vinification was detaxed, and this was not reversed until 1907, when it had become such an open scandal that a heavy tax was imposed, in order to drive the producers of 'artificial wine' out of business. However as this tax did not apply to purchases of small quantities of sugar under 25 kg, the wine 'manufacturers' were not very effectively deterred, although it is claimed that not much sugaring was practised in the Gironde after 1903. However it was not uncommon for producers to sell more wine than they had made by watering it, a highly illegal operation known as *mouillage*.

In such conditions recriminations were exchanged between growers and merchants. The growers blamed the merchants for selling 'imported' wine, to which the latter replied that if they did not do so, their foreign competitors would do so direct to Bordeaux's customers; another exculpatory argument heard since. The growers alleged that the high price of the wine to the consumer was because it passed through too many hands.

From this unsatisfactory state of affairs in the French wine area two developments stem: first the formation of growers' co-operatives, although in the Gironde they only started in the equally difficult inter-war years. There are now over 60 Gironde co-operatives and they produce 20 per cent of the total Bordeaux output. The other change was direct-selling to customers. This latter trend has not stopped, with the result that France has never had a body of good retail wine merchants as has existed in Britain, the Low Countries and even more recently in the United States. Not only the growers but also the merchants sell direct to private customers. One large Bordeaux firm once told me that they had 3,000 private clients inside France. Throughout the country direct grower–consumer sale expanded greatly in the seventies, partly owing to the trade's difficulties.

The misuse of French wine names in other countries spread further. At the Paris Exhibition of 1900 the jury judging the wine section found on display many foreign wines bearing French names. They refused to examine them. However that did not prevent the marketing of such items as Californian 'Mâcon', Crimean 'Lafitte', Bessarabian 'Médoc', Caucasian 'St-Émilion' or 'les Lur-Saluce, Le Château Yquem of the Crimea'. This last item was no doubt retrieved from the siege of Sebastopol!

Salavert, quoted above, also took a side-swipe at America and attacked Russia on similar lines. 'Everyone knows that in the United States one finds wines carrying French labels with no kind of authentic origin; one sees the "Bordeaux" and the "Mâcon" fabricated entirely in California or other parts of the United States; also in Russia one finds the Lur-Saluces, the Château Yquems, the Château Margaux of the Crimea, the word Crimean being dissimulated in a corner of the label; one finds Russian wines under the names of Sauternes, Haut Sauternes, Chablis; Bessarabian wines under the names of Saint Georges, Graves, Médoc; Crimean wines under the names of Bordeaux, Lafite, Muscat de Lunel, Sauternes and even in the restaurants bottles labelled "Saint Emilion of the Caucasus".'

After this who can deny progress over the years in the matter of *appellations d'origine*?

One result and positive gain from this unhappy period was the delimitation of the vineyard area of the Gironde department on 18 February 1911. Outlying districts such as Arcachon and parts of the Lesparre commune at one end, and sections of Castelnau, St-Symphorien and Bazas at the other end of the region, were no longer permitted to call their wines Bordeaux. This was the first step that was eventually to lead to the institution of *appellation contrôlée* in 1935.

In the war years, owing to the scarcity of labour – German prisoners-of-war and Spaniards were recruited – and to the steep rise in the cost of living in the later years, wages had to rise. That they were scarcely high can be judged by the raising of Latour's *maître de chai* from 3·50 frs. a day to 4 frs. For the 1918 vintage this château had to pay a visiting *troupe* 5 frs. a day for the men and 2·50 for the *coupeurs*, who presumably were women, plus of course food. Even if these figures are multiplied five or six times to equate them with current wage levels, they can be seen to compare unfavourably with today's levels. At the 1977 vintage the *coupeurs*, men and women alike, were paid 80 frs. for an eight-hour day.

Not only did labour costs rise in the four years of this terrible war; materials became dear and scarce. No doubt it was partly this that induced Latour to enter into another *abonnement* for five years from 1917; Lafite and Margaux did the same, and at an identical price: 2,650 frs. per *tonneau*. They were soon to regret this because, in spite of a poor summer, the 1917 was considered good and was heavily bought by the Bordeaux trade. Palmer sold for 2,000 frs., and the minor growth of St-Pierre-Sevaistre went for the same amount, while Duluc (Branaire-Ducru) rose to 2,300 frs. Haut-Brion, freed from its ten-year contract in time for the 1916 vintage, held it back and then sold to Eschenauer early in 1918 for 5,500 frs.; the latter re-sold it at 6,500 frs. – an unheard-of figure for over forty years. Then the newly-contracted Latour and Margaux were re-sold at 4,000 frs. and 4,500 frs. respectively.

Worse was to come with the 1918 vintage, scarcely made when the Armistice was signed on a day familiar in the Bordeaux of the Middle Ages: St Martin's Day (11th November). Haut-Brion secured 8,000 frs. for 78 *tonneaux*, while Yquem was re-sold for 10,000 frs. – in a poor year for the Sauternes. The first growths were not the only estates under contract – and seconds were mostly contracted at about 1,650 frs. – but those that were free secured very high prices. Rausan-Ségla went for 3,600 frs., Palmer for 100 frs. less. Ausone, under contract to Eschenauer at 4,000 frs., was sub-contracted to Latrille & Ginestet at 5,000 frs. Haut-Bailly, not then a very well-known red Graves, secured an *abonnement* with Schröder & Schÿler for 5,000 frs. Eschenauer re-sold 55 *tonneaux* of Latour 1918 for 4,500 frs. If the vintage was a good deal better than the last pre-war vintage of 1913, it never achieved much *réclame*.

Much the same happened with the 1919, another moderate though not bad year. The contracted first growths cannot have been very pleased to hear that Mouton-Rothschild had sold for 7,000 frs. and was re-sold at 8,000 frs.; nor, moreover, that 20 *tonneaux* apiece of Lafite and Margaux were re-sold at 6,000 frs. and then a further quantity at 7,000 frs. Among the seconds, Ducru-Beaucaillou achieved 4,300 frs., Rausan-Gassies 4,500 frs. and La Lagune went for the same price. The leading *crus bourgeois* could demand and secure 3,000 frs. – compared with 2,650 frs. for the contracted firsts.

Meanwhile costs were rising. *Vignerons'* wages were now 300 per cent higher than before the 1913 increases. If M. Jouet, *régisseur* of Latour, was horrified at having to pay 30 frs. apiece for new *barriques*, by 1918 he was paying 125 frs. and by 1920

210 frs. If the *premiers crus* were losing money, as they claimed, the position of other contracted *crus classés* must have been much worse. It was not surprising therefore that the three *abonné* firsts got together at the end of 1919 to approach their buyers to secure an amelioration of terms for the two remaining years of their contract: 1920 and 1921. Not surprisingly also, the merchants who were enjoying a new – though it turned out only a brief – period of prosperity returned a dusty answer.

Then in the following year the proprietors throughout the Gironde employing labour were faced with new wage demands. This time the *vignerons* were less isolated, for there were strikes in Bordeaux, including on the railway. Strikes took place in the Médoc, notably at Macau and Ludon. Wage increases were given, and later that year the proprietors got together and launched the idea of payment by the hour rather than the day and this took root. The basic pay was one franc an hour for the men.

One feature of the war years was large-scale requisitioning of wine for the army. This no doubt brought in a good deal of trade, and 810,000 litres of the 1917 vintage, nearly a quarter of the crop, were requisitioned. This must have increased the demand for what was left and encouraged speculation at the base, which was then carried up the hierarchy of quality to the *crus classés*. But the requisition business in itself was not very popular, for as soon as the war was over the senators and deputies representing the Gironde in January 1919 secured the end of it. The war years also marked a decline in the vineyard area, since the *bourgeois* growths were cut off from their principal market in Germany. By 1917 the area under vines was down to 130,000 ha.

This period ended not with the First World War, but at the end of 1920. The vintage, as is still well remembered today, was excellent both in quality and quantity. If slightly smaller than in the previous year, when over 5 million hl were made in the Gironde, the 4,870,000 hl of 1920 was the largest for any really fine year since the 5,738,000 hl of 1900. Prices initially continued their upward trend, with second growths such as Brane-Cantenac, Montrose and Gruaud-Larose-Faure selling for 4,500 frs. and Pontet-Canet making 4,000 frs. But a crisis set in owing to restriction of credit and a rise in interest rates. The long depression which was essentially to last for the next twenty years was at hand.

Immediately after the war, conditions temporarily improved with the expected post-war boom. This was backed up by a series of splendid vintages unparalleled since the seventies; and more wine was produced in the Gironde than at any time in its history. Unfortunately the boom petered out under the influence of the ensuing economic difficulties. The South-American market, of great importance in the second half of the nineteenth century, had dwindled to a trickle and in fact never recovered. The traditional trade with Britain especially of the *crus classés* and above all of the *premiers crus*, largely the preserve of the aristocracy and the established affluent, was no longer what it was. The new rich were more likely to be interested in champagne and whisky than fine claret; and there was an economic slump in Britain too. The war had interrupted the traditional trade with Germany, and this did not resume until about 1924, when it had a positive effect on the market. The Revolution had of course put an end to business with Russia. Prohibition had killed the trade with the U.S.A. and, in a nice phrase of P. Guillaume in *Latour*, 'reserved the sale of Bordeaux to the American doctors'. Nor did the fluctuations of the franc help, notably a sharp revaluation in 1926 which made that vintage impossibly expensive for foreign buyers.

As a result, relations between the growers and the merchants deteriorated, with the latter seeking to pay as little as possible for wines now not easy to re-sell. To avoid the stranglehold of the leading Bordeaux *négociants* Latour even went so far as to sell its 1923 crop to the great Paris wine firm of Nicolas, its 1924 wine to the grocery chain of Félix Potin (oddly enough to return to the Bordeaux market with its purchase in 1976 of Ch. Margaux) and the 1925 wine to a Dutch firm. At the end of 1924, on the initiative of Baron Philippe de Rothschild, the *premiers crus* formed an association of the first growths in order to protect their interests and the authenticity of their wines.

Trade was poor during the second half of the twenties and disastrously bad in the thirties, following the onset of the world slump in 1929. Germany, the source of much of Bordeaux's bread-and-butter business, was in a state of collapse, and when the Nazis took power in 1933, for political and autarchy reasons they almost prohibited the import of French wines. As a result the lesser *bourgeois* and other minor growths were even worse hit than they had been in the pre-First World War period. How small most of the growers were is shown by the fact that in 1923 there were 60,000 wine producers in the Gironde, and four-fifths of them owned less than 3 ha apiece; only 385 owned more than 30 ha. From the inter-war years, and particularly from the 1930s, dates the decline of the small estates and the contraction of the whole *vignoble*, which had once more expanded after the First World War. By 1939 it was only 131,000 ha.

As in the 1900s, difficulties in selling Bordeaux wines were accentuated by the huge production. It has been mentioned that in the five years ending in 1907 average annual output was 3·99 million hl. Yet from 1919 to 1929 the average was 4·8 million hl and from 1930 to 1939 it was 4 million in a world that could often not afford bread let alone wine.

Part of the trouble during this period was the poor standard of much Bordeaux wine, with quality sacrificed to quantity. In 1919 the system of named *appellations* was introduced throughout France, but no question of quality entered into it. This proved so inadequate that further legislation in 1927 did provide considerations of quality: no hybrid vines were allowed and only areas suitable for wine production could carry an *appellation*. Nationally this did nothing to stop the increase in production and little to stop the spread of vineyards, although this last did not apply to Bordeaux. So in 1929 a law was passed forbidding additional planting on any property over 10 ha; and growers producing more than 400 hl (roughly 44 *tonneaux*) were not permitted to sell more than a proportion of their crop with *appellation*.

The negative results of these three pieces of legislation on output can be seen from the figures. The total quantity of French wine declared with *appellation d'origine* rose from 5 million hl in 1923 to 9·95 million in 1931 and 15·7 million in 1934. Then in July 1935, largely as the result of long agitation by Jean Capus, former deputy and senator for the Gironde and one-time Minister of Agriculture, a law was passed setting up the *Comité National des Appellations d'Origine* to administer a strict system of *appellation contrôlée*. The result of the Loi Capus, as it is appropriately known, was the establishment of the *Institut National des Appellations d'Origine des Vins et Eaux-de-Vie*, which had the immense task of providing, in effect, a complete wine map of France, with strict delimitation. Also the correct *appellations* for every area entitled to them had to be fixed, along with permissible grape varieties, conditions of culture, minimum alcoholic strengths for all *appellations* and maximum permitted quantities that could be sold with these fixed *appellations d'origine*. It was an immense task that was not completed until after the Second World War.*

In Bordeaux the new control operated from 1936 and the amount of *appellation* wine fell off dramatically, although until 1942 the total was swollen by *appellation simple* wines, whose right to their names stemmed from the 1927 law. In 1947, the

*A list of Bordeaux *appellations contrôlées*, with their minimum strengths in degrees (Gay-Lussac), and basic maximum output per hectare is given in Appendix A (p. 653).

first peace-time year of relatively normal conditions, the Bordeaux *AC* wines amounted to 2·77 million hl out of a total French wine harvest of 39 million hl and an *AC* total of 5·5 million. In the seventies the amount of *AC* wine has tended to rise. In 1973, a record year, Bordeaux produced 3·75 million hl out of a national *AC* total of 13·63 million.

For Bordeaux the 1930s were a period of double misfortune: on top of the terrible world slump they were faced with a series of almost catastrophically bad vintages – 1930, 1931 and 1932. The next two were rather better, and indeed were initially assessed more favourably than they generally turned out; but 1935 and 1936 were very poor and among the final three vintages of the decade only 1937 received much acclaim. No doubt the growers and merchants would in any case have had considerable difficulty in selling even fine vintages, although trade did improve from 1937 onwards. But when for the most part they could only offer poor wines, the situation was well-nigh desperate. When even so important and solidly financed an estate as Latour made a loss in every year from 1931 to 1935 and lived solely on its unusually substantial cash reserves, the fortunes of lesser properties can be imagined. In the Médoc there was considerable abandonment of vineyards among the lesser *crus bourgeois* and the *crus paysans*. Stocks mounted in the growers' cellars. In 1935 Latour was driven to decide to sell its stocks of the 1931 vintage through retail outlets, and even thus they were not all cleared from the cellars by the outbreak of war in 1939.

The export markets were badly affected by currency devaluations, led by Britain going off the Gold Standard in September 1931, followed immediately by the Scandinavian countries. The pound fell from 110 frs. to 88 and by 1934 was down to 77. Then whatever good accrued from the repeal of the Prohibition 18th Amendment in December 1933 was sharply diminished by President Roosevelt's 40 per cent devaluation of the dollar a few months later; and in September

1936 the franc was devalued by the new Popular Front government. The extreme difficulties of Bordeaux are best illustrated by the enormous drop in prices of stocks already in merchants' cellars at the onset of the slump and of the vintages of the thirties as they came on the market. The already much-esteemed '28 and '29 first growths were re-sold at half their opening prices. The very fine Léoville-Las-Cases '29 that had opened at 9,000 frs. could not find a buyer towards the end of 1931 at 6,000 frs. The 1930s, which had been subject to severe mildew in a poor summer, sold for ridiculous prices: Gruaud-Larose at 2,250 frs., while most of the classed growths went for no more than 2,000 frs. a *tonneau*, the price of *vin ordinaire*, although that too dived as low as 1,500 to 1,600 frs. during this period. The 1931s fared no better and Lafite '32 was sold, a year after the vintage, for 2,000 frs., with the designation only of Pauillac; though the third-growth Lagrange managed to achieve 2,400 frs. Oddly enough Yquem '32 was actually sold for 16,000 frs. and other Sauternes fared well, though I never recollect seeing this vintage since.

With the '33s there was some recovery, for the vintage was the first one of reasonable quality for four years. There was some buying *sur souche* before the vintage, and Gruaud-Larose-Faure went for 5,000 frs and La Lagune and Lagrange for 4,000 frs. Then Berry Bros., the distinguished London wine merchants, made two remarkable purchases: the whole of the crop of Latour '33 at 11,500 frs. per *tonneau* and that of Beychevelle for 4,500 frs. They also bought a quantity of Mouton-Rothschild '33 at the same price – and lost a good deal when the Germans occupied Mouton in the following war. Cheval-Blanc which produced one of the better '33s sold for only 6,500 frs.

As can be seen in Appendix C the '34s, widely acclaimed, fetched less than the '33s. The next two vintages were very poor, but the '37s did a little better, as the opening prices in the Appendix show. The '38s were overshadowed by the Munich crisis, the '39s by the outbreak of war. The state of the market in these years can perhaps best be illustrated by the fact that the opening prices to the Bordeaux trade of the '34 first growths worked out, in terms of the exchange rates of the period, at about £1 5s. or $6·75 per case. The second growths sold for about one third of such prices.

Under such conditions it was, of course, a wonderfully cheap time for buying fine wines; for those who had the money and the taste – the latter being more prevalent than the former. English wine merchants could buy splendid wines at very low prices. Ronald Avery of Bristol once told me that he bought Latour 1920 at opening prices for 110s. a case duty paid and Latour 1929 at 76s. In the mid-1930s, the Wine Society paid £12 5s. a *barrique* for 50 *barriques* of Beychevelle 1934. Thirty years later the 1964 wine was offered at £150 a hogshead and the 1972 at £1,000! This price in the speculation boom was not equalled until the 1978 was offered at a similar figure.

Indeed in the 1930s claret and white bordeaux were cheaper than they had ever been, and in fairness to growers and merchants one must hope that relatively they will never be so cheap again. On the eve of the Second World War it was possible in Britain to buy fine 1920, 1924, 1928 and 1929 château-bottled clarets for between six and eight shillings a bottle. In 1940 I paid 7s. 10d. for Latour 1929. Now it would be difficult to find a bottle of this celebrated wine under £100; in 1978 at Christie's it reached £106, and £420 for a magnum.

In the Second World War, after the 'phoney war' period of 1939–40 when it was generally 'business as usual', the problems of Bordeaux were largely those of shortage of manpower to look after the vineyards and of chemicals to keep the vines free from disease. There was a steady black market in copper sulphate. The châteaux were occupied by German troops who had strict instructions not to loot the cellars, which on the whole they did not; the Nazi authorities wished to keep on good terms with the French *bourgeoisie*. They made an agreement with the Vichy Government by which they undertook to buy a certain quota of ordinary French wines, but would purchase the finer Bordeaux (and Burgundies) only from those merchants who had sold to Germany prior to the war. This certainly protected French-owned fine wine from confiscation and major pilfering, but in view of the way the Nazis behaved elsewhere in France, it is not surprising that after the war questions were asked about the trade, and punishment demanded. In the end all the Bordeaux firms that had made profits on these deals were required to refund them to the government.

Some 'enemy-owned' wine was confiscated by the Germans, but often was paid for, as at least one English wine merchant discovered after the war, when he found a tidy balance in his firm's name lying in a Paris bank; but by then he would rather have had the wine he had bought but not shipped before the fall of France.

The return to peace in 1945 did not bring immediately the expected restoration of trade. France was politically in a turmoil, and the franc was devalued three times in the twenty months between January 1948 and September 1949. Although the exceptional '45s and the plentiful '47s were judged very fine wines there was no great rush to buy them, and not until the 1949s were imminent was there much vitality in the trade. The important British market was controlled by quotas. Even Latour made a loss in each of the years 1946, 1947 and 1948, and was obliged to negotiate a bank loan. But with the '49s there was a sudden switch-round, and Bordeaux knew the first period of prosperity for many years. Latour made large profits and paid dividends to its approximately 150 shareholders on a scale unknown since the pre-phylloxera period. Not that the lesser estates would have done so well, although the *crus classés* began to benefit from an ever-increasing interest from abroad.

As in other fields, it was the best-known properties and the biggest merchants that fared best. Most significant was the great increase in the prices of the four *premiers crus*, as well as

Mouton-Rothschild, Cheval-Blanc and Pétrus. Their opening prices began to draw far ahead of the *deuxièmes* and lesser *crus classés*. For example, with the 1952s, largely sold very early owing to the good vintage reports, while the first growths ran from 375,000 frs. (Mouton-Rothschild and Latour) and 350,000 frs. (Lafite) to 300,000 frs. (Margaux), other leading châteaux such as Gruaud-Larose and Beychevelle secured only 130,000 frs., Palmer 125,000 frs. and Cos d'Estournel, Montrose and Pichon-Baron 120,000 frs. Many *sur souche* prices were paid by July 1952, and except for first growths, about 15 per cent had to be added for keeping charges, as was the case generally until about 1970. For the 1953s, sold after the vintage, the firsts all offered their wine at 300,000 frs., while Palmer topped the others at 125,000 frs., with Calon-Ségur and Beychevelle going for 120,000 frs., Lynch-Bages for 115,000 frs. and Pichon-Lalande for 110,000 frs.

1955 was another *sur souche* year (almost unknown thereafter for the next twenty years at least), with many wines being bought in the June of that year. The firsts ranged from 550,000 frs. (Mouton-Rothschild) down to 300,000 frs. (Margaux and Latour). The next level ran from 140,000 frs. (Beychevelle and Pichon-Lalande) to 120,000 frs. (Brane-Cantenac and Ducru-Beaucaillou), with Cos d'Estournel and Léoville-Las-Cases mid-way between the two prices. As can be deduced from Appendix D, the gap between the firsts and the rest was generally wider than in the pre-war period.

The principal reason for this was the substantial re-entry of the U.S.A. into the Bordeaux market. After the repeal of Prohibition in 1933, the average annual Gironde exports to the U.S.A. up to 1938 were only 8,700 hl, little more than a fifth of Britain's declining imports. From 1947 to 1959 the rate of U.S. Bordeaux imports was only double the pre-war one, but they began to rise sharply in the 1960s, with 25,600 hl in 1961 and 47,900 in 1967.

The Bordeaux trade was hit by the succession of bad-to-indifferent vintages from 1956 to 1958, partly arising from the devastating frosts in February 1956, but not so seriously affected as they would have been twenty years later, when much less stock of earlier years was carried. For the merchants' cellars then would have contained plenty of '52s, '53s and '55s, and so would the cellars of their clients at home and abroad. Then, with the much-heralded '59s, business improved and generally continued to advance throughout the sixties.

Nevertheless, if the merchants were experiencing better fortunes and new opportunities, they were also facing new problems, some of them arising from the growth of powerful purchasing groups and the increasing inflow of foreign capital into Bordeaux. Among these were the important British-owned brewery groups and other large amalgamations, which were looking for means of 'diversification' – a term used to describe the entry of one trade or industry into another of which it frequently has little knowledge besides the ability to read its balance sheets; of the latter it might be said that a little accountancy learning is a dangerous thing. This was not entirely true of these British groups for traditionally they had always sold wine in their public houses and through their wine divisions. They now believed that wine was too profitable a matter to be left to wine merchants, whom in Britain they began to buy up at an increasingly fast and expensive rate throughout the sixties and early seventies. Initially at least this was advantageous to Bordeaux, both to growers and merchants, for it brought immense new buying power into the market. However, these newcomers or old concerns greatly increased in size were less concerned with the accustomed methods of wine commerce than with buying as cheaply as possible, and as near to the growers' price as feasible. Traditionally the Anglo-Bordeaux trade had been conducted through agents, usually based in London and, until the German blitz destroyed it in 1940, concentrated in a few streets and alleys in the City. These agents, who usually also represented burgundy, champagne, cognac, port and sherry houses, largely did their work on samples supplied by their principals in France and elsewhere. Once a year, perhaps, they would be accompanied on their visits to retail wine merchants in London and the provinces by a partner in Calvet, Cruse, Eschenauer or one of the other Bordeaux houses with a trade in this country; and less frequently they would visit their American agents. There is an agreeable story of Jean Calvet, a constant visitor to his British clients between the two world wars. On visiting one such, during which the conversation ranged on matters remote from the business in hand, Calvet rose to leave, and as the door of the office was opened for his departure, he turned and, referring to the most recent Bordeaux vintage, said, 'Of course, it was the vintage of the century.' 'But', returned the perplexed wine merchant, 'you said that last year.' Not a whit put out, the distinguished shipper said, 'Of course, but one has to live.'

In this kind of gentlemanly commerce the big groups were little interested. In some cases they bought up these agency firms, in others they by-passed them, and in any case these declined sharply in importance. Moreover, whereas up to the fifties visits of foreign merchants were largely social jaunts devoted to generous entertaining interspersed with a few vineyard visits, the new generation of British wine merchants, many of them elected by arduous examination to the newly formed Institute of Masters of Wine, sponsored by the Vintners Company, had more commercial reasons for making the trip to the Gironde. They wished to see, to sample and to buy, often with the backing of the big groups who now employed them. This applied, rather later, to the Americans. Big groups there thought there was money to be made in wine. Alexis Lichine, at first independent, was responsible for introducing Bordeaux, as well as Burgundy and other French wines, to many Americans. Transatlantic business patterns, involving big names, marketing skills, publicity programmes and a penchant for novelty perhaps more dominant than a concern for quality – all these presented problems as well as new opportunities for Bordeaux. It must be said too that the growth of wine drinking in the United States produced a body of dedicated amateurs unequalled anywhere outside Britain – and often with the wherewithal to satisfy their interest which some of their opposite numbers elsewhere lacked.

Some of this foreign influx into Bordeaux resulted in châteaux changing hands, as recorded here elsewhere. They were acquired by American, British and returned colonists from Africa. Old-established firms were bought by the big groups: Alexis Lichine by Bass-Charrington, Barton & Guestier by Seagrams, Delor by Harvey's of Bristol (who themselves were absorbed by Allied Breweries and their wine subsidiary Grants of St James's), Eschenauer by Holt of Liverpool and de Luze by Bowaters, the big paper group.

Then an extraordinary change came over the Bordeaux trade at the end of the sixties and the beginning of the seventies. The poor quality of the '68s and the small quantity of the moderate '69s led to an increase in prices, already rising on account of inflation within France. The spectacular rise in first-growth prices can be seen in Appendix D on p. 667. However, the underlying causes of their increase – world demand for these prestige names, speculation and the rivalry between the two Rothschild proprietors as to which one should secure the higher price – were not present for the other classed growths, let alone for the more modest estates. Their turn came in 1970 and 1971. For the widely publicized success of the prolific '70s coincided with an unprecedented rush of speculative money into clarets bearing names of at least some international reputation. There has always been speculation in Bordeaux wines, but it has largely been a professional affair, conducted within the trade in Bordeaux itself. Of course, there has been a fringe of private speculators too, and this fringe certainly broadened in the latter half of the sixties, as the ever-rising prices in the London wine auction rooms demonstrated. However, with the arrival of the highly recommended '70 vintage, the investment-in-wine movement reached proportions impossible to quantify because of the great number of trade outlets – but certainly sufficient to affect prices throughout the Gironde.

It was not that the 1970 prices started high, for a record-sized vintage naturally made the growers nervous, and Baron Philippe de Rothschild, doubtless with an eye to checking the first-growth price race, slashed the opening price of his Mouton-Rothschild to 36,000 frs. – less than half the first-*tranche* offer of the previous year. An average second-growth price, including keeping charges, was about 9,200 frs. However when it became apparent that there was a tremendous demand for the '70 clarets from investors as well as normal trade buyers, prices shot up for the second *tranches*. Investment, inflation and a shortage of stock resulted in a sellers' market for the growers, and encouraged them to offer their '71s and '72s at much enhanced prices. The trend can be shown by the opening prices of Palmer over four vintages, '69, '70, '71 and '72: 10,000 frs., 12,000 frs., 31,000 frs., and 55,000 frs. per *tonneau* respectively. The pattern can also be seen in the prices, rising as each *tranche* was offered, of two of the most popular second-growth St-Juliens. Léoville-Las-Cases first offered its '70 at 8,700 frs., followed by 13,000 frs., 14,000 frs., 16,000 frs. and 18,000 frs. Ducru-Beaucaillou for the same vintage rose more modestly: from 8,000 frs. to 11,500 frs. Then when the '71 was offered, Léoville-Las-Cases began at 20,000 frs. and went on up to 35,000 and 45,000 frs. Ducru-Beaucaillou started much higher at 28,000 frs. and eventually rose to 40,000 frs., and other popular classed growths, including Beychevelle, Brane-Cantenac and Lynch-Bages all sold their *deuxième tranche* at 40,000 frs. a *tonneau*. A *tonneau*, it is worth recalling, should produce a yield of 100 dozen bottles, but for many years the leading châteaux only gave 96 dozen, though one result of the ensuing slump was that the full yield was passed on to the buyer. At the exchange rate then ruling 400 frs. per case was equivalent to about £30 or $72, on top of which was the brokerage, profit of the Bordeaux firm that bought it, freight, insurance, import duty if shipped abroad and retail mark-up; to which in Britain from April 1973 onwards VAT had to be added, at first 10 per cent, later 8 per cent. This would mean a probable opening price to the consumer of totally immature wines of £5 a bottle, although earlier buyers might have paid less.

Not that the prices quoted above were the highest for properties on the *deuxième-cru* level. Growths like Pape-Clément, Figeac and Vieux-Château-Certan, which a few years earlier had been offering their first *tranches* at between about 7,000 and 9,000 frs., including keeping charges which represented about 15 per cent of the price, asked (and secured) no less than 42,000, 40,000 and 48,000 frs. respectively for their opening offers. It would be difficult to equate these prices let alone those of the first growths with value for wine. Those whom the gods wish to destroy . . .

A little more sympathy may be felt for the *crus bourgeois*, with the more renowned selling their '71s for 12,000 to 15,000 frs. (and even more in a few cases) in place of the 3,000 frs. or so that they had been accustomed to receive and which undervalued the quality of many of their wines. They were making a little hay while the sun shone on their vineyards.

The same was true of the growers of generic wines, from simple Bordeaux Rouge up to Médoc and St-Émilion. Certainly this important part of the market went mad too. Bordeaux Rouge which less than ten years previously had been selling for a mere 900 frs. a *tonneau* had risen to at least 4,000 frs. by the beginning of 1973, while Médoc '72 – at best an indifferent wine – was being offered at 8,500 frs. and St-Émilion at up to 10,000 frs. Three years later, in spite of inflation running at about 10 per cent a year within France, the price of Bordeaux Rouge was fixed at 2,000–2,500 frs., a price considered profitable to the growers.* In the meantime the excessively high prices of these generic wines, particularly of Bordeaux Rouge, had a seriously adverse effect on the market for such wines within the country.

The last to benefit in this boom were the sweet white wines. Yquem was the only Sauternes whose prices at all marched with the increases of the top growths. World taste has for the time being turned against sweet white table wines, and Bordeaux has suffered, though – as explained in the chapter on sweet white Bordeaux – neither growers nor merchants are blameless for the decline. On the other hand the medium-quality white Graves and other sound white Bordeaux have found ready markets abroad, particularly in Germany, though overall at the expense of the lesser reds. Yet if Germany were not the biggest buyer of Bordeaux Blanc the white wine growers would be in great difficulties; for not all can be taken over by the government for distillation. However, the exceptionally poor vintage record in the Sauternes in the sixties led to an acute shortage of stock, so a marginal increase in demand about the end of 1971 lifted prices threefold within twelve months. A distinguished growth such as Climens, which had been securing only 5,000 frs. a *tonneau* for its young wine, found its '71 – an excellent year for Sauternes – fetching 15,000 frs.; and as they had never scaled the price heights the *cru-classé* reds reached, so they did not have to fall back. The better first-growth Sauternes were selling their '75s and '76s at between 15,000 and 18,000 frs.

This period of rising prices coincided with a sharp increase in château-bottling. Indeed this tendency was encouraged by the higher prices, since the price advantage to the consumer of bulk shipment in cask diminished as the cost of the wine itself

*Comparative average prices for the 1978 generics were: Bordeaux Rouge 4,300 frs., Médoc 7,000 frs., St-Émilion 8,500 frs., Bordeaux Blanc 2,300 frs., Graves Blanc 6,400 frs. and Sauternes 8,200 frs.

rose. Compulsory château-bottling also became a matter of prestige, as well as of additional profit to the proprietors. For it implied not only the resources to make this possible, but also an ease of sale at the higher price demanded for wine offered by the case rather than by the cask. This trend towards château-bottling extended beyond the classed growths – it became compulsory for the Médoc *crus classés* from the 1972 vintage – and is likely to grow, while more and more of the lesser wines will be bottled in Bordeaux or in the region of production. By no means all those proprietors who have opted for château-bottling have taken the necessary steps to equip themselves for this, and it is yet to be seen whether the bottling in the *chais*, carried out perhaps intermittently, is superior to the professional bottling carried out by the receiving wine merchants.

The boom conditions described above were halted in the spring of 1973, and by the end of that year prices, particularly of the classed growths, began to retreat. Before the end of 1974 the retreat had become a rout, affecting the over-priced clarets of recent vintages and especially those subject to speculation within and without the trade.

The reasons for this were complex. First, speculation had encouraged growers to ask and secure prices unrelated either to the cost of production or to the ability or willingness of the consumer to pay. Then when the shadows of world economic recession were accompanied by historically high rates of interest, buying stopped and selling began. Within a few months a sellers' market turned to a buyers'. In Britain and the U.S.A. large firms who had over-bought recent vintages at excessive prices started to unload; and outside speculators, embarrassed by the high interest charges and tight credit, began to sell, often through the London auctioneers. The public outside Bordeaux became clearly aware of the change in the market first, when the London auction prices for first growths, which had been mounting for at least two years, declined, and second, when huge quantities of wine began to be unloaded in these London sale-rooms, beginning with a two-day sale in July 1974 of Bass-Charrington Vintners, on behalf of its Bordeaux subsidiary Alexis Lichine & Co. This attracted buyers from America and the Continent as well as those within Britain, and the knock-down total of £961,000, of which the majority was Bordeaux, included thousands of dozens of classed growths, including 1,200 dozen of Mouton-Rothschild '70 and 500 dozen of Latour '70, as well as lesser quantities of the other firsts of this and other vintages from '61 to '71. Mouton-Rothschild '70 and Latour '70, which in 1973 had risen to record prices of £160 and £125 a dozen respectively, now went down to £54 and £50 for those who could afford 100- and 50-case lots. Other trade disposals followed and in June 1975 Lafite and Mouton-Rothschild joined in an unprecedented auction at Christie's of 6,000 dozen of their wines, which realized £430,000. In normal times such a by-pass of the Bordeaux trade would have caused a furore, but it was quite obvious that the *négociants* were in no position to absorb such quantities. Indeed several of them joined the auction queue, including Delor, Sichel, Calvet and Cordier, who wound up the series with a sale in September 1976 from their own properties alone. By then the recession in Bordeaux had spent itself and trade was on the mend; but after this period of boom and bust, lasting about five years, it might fairly be said that the Bordeaux trade would never be the same again.

The turn-about was accentuated by the immediately un-attractive '72 vintage and the record '73 crop, followed by a scarcely smaller '74 *récolte*. By the end of 1974 stocks of *A C* Bordeaux wines had risen to 5 million hl compared with 3 million only two years previously. With Bordeaux's overseas customers holding an excess of stocks there was virtually no market in the fine clarets, almost entirely dependent on foreign demand. The situation was not helped by the wine scandal revealed in the late summer of 1973. As already described in this book Bordeaux has always been a centre of *coupage* (blending), some of it justified, a good deal not. The 1973 scandal, which principally affected the respected firm of Cruse, was chiefly the product of the hectic price rises of even modest Bordeaux Rouge. Contracts entered into when prices were much lower could not be honoured without loss. M. Pierre Bert, a small *négociant* whose family had been growers and merchants, somewhat ingeniously altered *Appellation Contrôlée* documents covering white Bordeaux to authenticate *AC* Bordeaux Rouge wine from outside the Gironde. The ease with which he did this must have caused some red faces in the *Institut National des Appellations d'Origine* as well as in the *Répression des Fraudes*, and after this case some tightening up of surveillance took place. In December 1974 M. Bert went to prison for a year and was heavily fined, but that did not prevent a book appearing in 1975 under his name, entitled *In vino veritas*, an amusing, cynical account of the Bordeaux wine world. MM. Lionel and Yvan Cruse received similar sentences, though these were suspended. It was said that other leading Bordeaux merchants had been recipients of this fraudulent wine, but were not proceeded against. One result of the case was that for a time at least Cruse wines were sold under the *sous-nom* label of Schröder & Constams. Although it appeared that the firm had recovered part of its former position, the rather sad end of the affair came in March 1979 when the firm was bought by the Société des Vins de France, a huge concern best known for its Margnat branded wines.

The affair could not have come at a worse time for Bordeaux, just toppling over into the worst crisis since the world slump of 1929–33. The world always enjoys a wine scandal, partly because it seems to prove that wine expertise is a lot of nonsense and many of those who drink wine are snobs. The scandals that have been revealed from time to time, not least in Italy, have reinforced this view. The Bordeaux scandal received world-wide coverage in the press from the moment that the story broke in August 1973 to the trial in December 1974, and it was blown up out of all recognition in relation to its importance in the context of Bordeaux wines. Nevertheless, coming on top of the extravagantly high prices asked and obtained for recent vintages, it appeared to show that everyone in the wine business in the Gironde, from growers to merchants and perhaps their customers too, were *tricheurs* if not *fraudeurs*. This view was particularly widespread in the United States, most of whose wine drinkers had not served a very long apprenticeship yet had often paid very high prices for their claret. The market, loaded with stocks, collapsed. So it did to some extent in Britain, but as the figures show there was less panic, and the drop in imports was as much the result of the country's economic problems as of scepticism about the authenticity of Bordeaux wines.

For at one point the U.S. imports rose much more sharply than the British, and between 1970 and 1972 they exceeded them. In the early post-war years British imports from Bordeaux had been limited owing to official restriction, and between 1947 and 1959 had only averaged 36,000 hl. Then from 1968 to 1972 they rose to an average of 75,000 hl, but by the latter year shipments to the United States rose to a peak of 130,000 hl. However, when the decline started in 1973 and was sharpened in 1974, American demand fell as low as 70,000 hl, while U.K. imports were still high at 141,000 hl. Nevertheless, U.S. demand soon recovered, though at a lower price level than previously and in 1978 surpassed any previous total, importing nearly 168,000 hl to the value of 244 million frs. The U.K., after dropping further in 1974–5, improved thereafter with a total in 1978 of 176,000 hl, valued at 178 million frs. The difference in the pattern of imports of the two countries is that practically all the American purchases are in bottle, while about 50 per cent of British imports from Bordeaux are still in bulk, although as elsewhere the proportion of wine exported in bottle is rising steadily and has reached about 60 per cent. In 1977 total Bordeaux exports were a record 1·4 million hl and in value surpassed 1,000 million frs. for the first time. In 1978 the total dropped to 1·23 million hl (these figures are concerned only with physical movements of wine abroad, not sales made), but the value rose to 1·36 billion frs., reflecting the sharp rise in prices.

In this hectic period of boom and bust, the total of stocks in relation to current demand was an important factor. One reason why prices rose in the early seventies was a feared shortage of stocks, a major determinant depending on nature itself. It is impossible to predict even a few weeks in advance the quantity let alone the quality of the approaching vintage. It was the shortage of stocks that was an important element in forcing up prices in the boom period; not just the internationally known and bought wines, but the basic Bordeaux *appellations*. For it must never be forgotten that there are *two* red Bordeaux trades: the international one, though including some basic wines and comprehending the top level of the French domestic market, including hotels and restaurants; and the bread-and-butter business, confined almost entirely to the basic *appellations* of Bordeaux Rouge and the Côtes, and dependent largely on demand in Paris and Northern France, where it competes with Côtes du Rhone and Bourgogne Rouge. In the 1974–5 slump it was the firms largely in the export business and without an adequately based home market that suffered most.

The risk in the future lies at the lower end of the business, for there is a shortage of supply in relation to demand for the 250 or so estates of greater or less renown and international reputation. It is among the growers of the basic *appellations* and of wines sold only as *vins de consommation courante*, of which the Gironde produces large quantities, that the problems lie. For they are often only marginally profitable in a region subject to the vagaries of vintage. Since 1948 the Bordeaux *vignoble* has been contracting sharply. In 1948 it was rather larger than in 1939, totalling 134,000 ha. Helped by government grants to marginal producers who agreed to pull up their vines, it was down to 112,000 ha by 1960, and to 97,000 by 1978, of which the *AC* area, increasing steadily, was 78,000 ha – over three quarters. Owing, however, to improved methods of cultivation and increases in permitted yields there is no shortage of Bordeaux wine: production between 1962 and 1969 averaged 3 million *AC*, and the record 1973 produced nearly 3·8 million hl plus almost 1·9 million non-*AC*. The number of growers declaring a crop in the department of the Gironde has dropped from 58,500 in 1945 to just over 25,000 in the late seventies.

In recent times the peak of stocks of red Bordeaux was reached at the end of 1976, when, counting the very large 1976 crop, they amounted to 5·5 million hl, compared with 3·01 million hl at the end of 1972; it was the lower classification most in surplus with regards to 1972. By the end of 1978 *AC* red wine stocks were down to 4·6 million hl. The white wine stocks were much less of a problem, with amounts in 1976 only 10 per cent up in relation to 1972. Indeed, when trade revived there was a shortage of white Bordeaux: only 1·4 million hl at the end of 1978, compared with 1·85 million hl at the beginning of the 1970s. This partly reflects the reduction of the white wine *vignoble*.

In order to reduce in future the risks of abrupt rises or falls in price of the generic types of red Bordeaux, in 1976 the *Conseil Interprofessionnel du Vin de Bordeaux* (*C.I.V.B.*) took a useful step. For at these levels the thousands of small growers have all too often been in a position either of near-bankruptcy because the prices they could obtain for their wines did not permit a fair return, or, after a short period of relative prosperity, priced out of the highly competitive market because their prices were too high, as happened in the boom years of the early 1970s. The *C.I.V.B.*, under the then president

M. Jean-Paul Jauffret of Dourthe, devised a scheme known as
the Contract of Bordeaux by which growers of the basic nine
red and eight white *appellations* – among them Bordeaux
Rouge, St-Émilion, Entre-Deux-Mers, Médoc and Sauternes –
agreed to sell only between an upper and lower limit, called
the *fourchette*. If the market fell below a certain figure, the
unsold wine would form part of a buffer stock; if higher,
then the growers would not sell, as in order to do so the
documents would have to include the *C.I.V.B.*'s authorization, and this would not be given for sales above the top figure
of the 'fork'. Most important are the reds and initially the top
figure for Bordeaux Rouge was 2,500 frs. a *tonneau*, for
Médoc 4,000 frs. and for St-Émilion 4,760 frs. However, the
marked recovery in trade early in 1977 led to the top of the
bracket being increased by 20 per cent; and after the very short
1977 crop, a further upward adjustment was made, and the
control, intended originally only to apply to the *vin nouveau*,
was in this case continued briefly to take in also the 1976s.*
Owing to the buoyancy of the market no buffer stocks have
come into being as yet. Opinions have remained divided on
this scheme, as might be expected in such an individualistic
trade, with the merchants more sceptical than the growers.
Yet all admit that this control did reduce a too-vibrant up-
swing in prices when the market improved from the beginning

*For 1978-9 the *fourchettes* for the generic wines were as follows:
Bordeaux Rouge 3,800-4,300 frs., Bordeaux Supérieur and Côtes de
Bordeaux 4,300-4,800 frs., Entre-Deux-Mers 2,550-3,200 frs., Côtes
Blaye (white) 2,000-2,600 frs., Graves (white) 5,000-6,200 frs., Bordeaux
Supérieur St-Macaire (sweet white) 2,500 frs.-3,000 frs., Loupiac-Ste-
Croix-du-Mont 3,300-4,200 frs., Cérones 5,500-7,000 frs., Sauternes
7,000-8,500 frs. What was described as an 'indicative price' was given
for Médoc (6,500 frs.) and St-Émilion (7,500 frs.). A 10 per cent increase
or decrease is permitted on the *fourchette* prices. Although no doubt the
progress of inflation will cause these prices to be raised, the above figures
demonstrate the comparative standing of these basic *appellations* on the
Bordeaux market. (See also average 1978 prices on p. 181.)

The Bordeaux Wine Trade 189

of 1977. This in its turn influenced the higher *appellations*, for obviously enough if generic Médoc and St-Émilion prices start going through the roof, the 'château wines', for reasons of prestige as well as of profit, will increase their prices proportionately. While Bordeaux remains the kind of speculative market it is, control will never be wholly effective, but that does not mean that there should be none.

Whether the domestic market for Bordeaux remains good depends to a great extent on the economic and political state of the country. The international market reflects these factors too, but the world market for Bordeaux's wine should increase, for new markets could open. The latest example, not altogether happy, was Japan, where the rise in demand was swift and the subsequent decline scarcely less so. In 1970 Bordeaux exported only 3,549 hl of red and white wine there; less than half the amount shipped to Finland. By 1973 this had risen to 29,835 hl with Japan suddenly becoming Bordeaux's seventh largest customer. Yet by 1975–6 the total had fallen back to 9,904 hl, putting Japan in twelfth place from which it showed no appreciable recovery by the end of 1978. The demand had mostly been for expensive classed growths, including the *premiers crus*, and in 1972–3 Japan clearly exceeded both the U.K. and the U.S.A. in the average price paid per bottle of Bordeaux wine: 18·85 frs. compared with 15·12 frs. and 11·49 frs. respectively, a figure unlikely to be matched for years thereafter. However, retail and restaurant prices in Japan for such wines were spectacularly high, and demand proved to be more a matter of prestige than appreciation. Nevertheless the market could again become important.

There are other potential markets too. Before 1917 there was a steady Bordeaux trade with Russia; and up to 1939 good business was done with countries in Central and Eastern Europe now within the Socialist bloc. It would be surprising if the rising standard of life in these countries did not eventually lead to renewed demand for the red and white wines of the Gironde.

7. The Wine Merchants of Bordeaux

Although in these historical chapters some survey of the Bordeaux wine trade in modern times has been given, this book is not a history of the wine trade in the Gironde. I lack occasion, knowledge and space to write one, although it is a striking subject awaiting a delving author. However, while the châteaux and sometimes their proprietors receive a good deal of prominence and attention, the wines of Bordeaux owe so much to the merchants (*négociants*) and their enterprise, and they are so entwined in the history of Bordeaux's growth and production as well as the sale of wine, that to give them in this work no more than the passing attention they have received so far would be inadequate as well as ungenerous.

The earlier story of the wine trade has been sketched in the previous chapters dealing with the history of Bordeaux. Here we are concerned with the firms who have been associated with the modern Bordeaux trade, which began in the seventeenth century, but like the development of the châteaux really dates from the eighteenth century. The arrival of the Dutch merchants has been mentioned; one of these was the founder of the oldest existing firm in Bordeaux today: Jean-Simon Beyerman, who arrived from Rotterdam in 1620 and began trading in wine. Today the firm is in the Cours Xavier Arnozan, formerly known as the Pavé des Chartrons (but changed in 1928 and named after a well-known doctor). In 1974 control of the firm passed to the London house of Atkinson, Baldwin, already British agents of Ch. Cantemerle.

The significant fact about the Bordeaux merchants was that, as in other wine-exporting regions such as Oporto, they were mostly foreigners. As such in earlier times they were not permitted to reside within the city walls, and this partly accounted for the rise of the Chartrons area, so called from association with a Carthusian monastery; today the Chartrons still remains the traditional centre of the trade. Up to the end of the last century it was considered inconceivable that a merchant should have his cellars and offices anywhere else than by the Quai des Chartrons, for there they would be conveniently near the docks and the brokers. When in 1899 Eschenauer's moved out to what is now the Avenue Émile Counord they were regarded as very eccentric indeed. In fact of course they were wise, as the Chartrons area is congested and the possibilities of expansion are very limited. Nevertheless when the firm of Alexis Lichine, established in the early fifties, sought cellars and then offices in Bordeaux they set up on the Chartrons.

These foreign merchants naturally came from the countries and regions where the wines of Bordeaux had penetrated: England, Scotland, Ireland, Scandinavia, the Low Countries and Germany. They came to export Bordeaux wines first to their own countries and then elsewhere. Some carried on an import–export business in other goods as well. Many of these merchants were Protestants and maintained their faith through succeeding generations, although religious as well as national assimilation with their French Catholic neighbours also took place. It was largely on account of religious persecution by Cromwell and others that so many Irish came to Bordeaux, part of a flood of emigrants who left Ireland for France from the second half of the seventeenth century onwards, some of them to form an Irish brigade in the French army and fight against the English at the French victory of Fontenoy. Some of the names of the Irish who joined the wine trade in Bordeaux are still known today, such as Barton and Johnston (though these were Protestants), but others are long since forgotten, if occasionally still commemorated in a château name. They include Dillon, Exshaw (the cognac house), French,

Kirwan, Lawton, MacCarthy, Mitchell, O'Byrne and O'Quin; and later of course came the Lynches. The first was John Lynch, who served in the army of James II in Ireland and left for France after the latter's defeat by William III in 1691. He married a Bordelaise in 1709 and was naturalized in the following year. Initially the family was not in the wine business, but became very prosperous. John Lynch's grandsons, Thomas-Michel and Jean-Baptiste were very rich men, who owned an array of châteaux in the Médoc, including Dauzac, associated with Jean-Baptiste Lynch, Mackline in Macau (later called La Maqueline and owned by Nathaniel Johnston), Castelnau, Cussaux (a home of Thomas-Michel), Pontac-Lynch, Lynch-Bages and Lynch-Moussas. Jean-Baptiste, a dedicated royalist like his brother, had to emigrate to London for a period during the Revolution, but later became first a councillor of the Bordeaux Parlement and then the Mayor, as related later on.

The most prominent merchant house in the eighteenth century was probably Barton & Guestier, established in 1725 by Thomas Barton, an Irishman of Anglo-Irish stock. He was then about thirty years old. He must have been one of the earliest wine merchants to acquire property in the Médoc, when in 1747 he bought Le Boscq in St-Estèphe. By the time he died in 1780 he had amassed a considerable fortune. Barton was the largest buyer of the first growths. For example in the middle of the eighteenth century he is described in contemporary documents as the normal buyer of Lafite's crop. This was one of Bordeaux's periods of prosperity, although not on account of the wine trade with England, which was at a low ebb owing to the discriminatory duties, but through demand from the Low Countries, northern Germany and the developing French colonies.

In 1764 there was a great commotion on the Chartrons arising out of an edict of the local Parlement forbidding the blending of Bordeaux wines with those outside. This row arose from the seizure of several English merchants accused of this practice. Led by Thomas Barton, the most important Anglo-Saxon merchant, his fellow-countrymen drew up a protest, in spite of the fact that some Dutch and Irish merchants declared themselves perfectly satisfied with the new decree. However, it is fair to say that the leading Dutch houses along with the principal French exporters rallied to the English cause. Among the signatories were Cornelis Beyerman, Schröder & Schÿler, J. Lynch and other firms of foreign and French origin.

The protest pointed out that some years previously a body of twenty-four Irish merchants and bottlers had complained that Bordeaux wines were mixed with Spanish. However there were 'at least a thousand wine merchants in Ireland who all mixed the wines of Bordeaux with the wines of Spain'. More recently such concoctions had taken place at lower cost in Bordeaux, and this had increased the consumption in Ireland, where it was much to the local taste. It consisted of adding 10 per cent Benicarlo to a 'pot' of unfermented Bordeaux wine must. This created a new fermentation and apparently made the wine clear and bright. The Bordeaux brew was so successful that it put the Irish 'brewers' out of business. The merchants then brought forward the wonderfully specious argument which has by no means exhausted its value today, that if blending, on which foreign taste insisted, was prohibited it would go on just the same, but by merchants abroad who would be more shameless about the operation, and this would be a serious detriment to the Bordeaux trade. *On ne cuit bien que chez soi!*

Further, while the Dutch took a great deal of white wine from the Entre-Deux-Mers, they chose to improve and strengthen it with a quarter to a fifth of Barsac and Sauternes. Also the Spaniards liked to lighten the colour of their red wines from the *palus* by adding some white wine; while the Irish and the Scots preferred to toughen the red Graves and

Médocs with wines from Queyries and Montferrand. Anyhow, protested the merchants, in bad years in the region it was a good idea to improve their wines with those from outside.

After an interval the merchants more or less had their way, but these accusations contributed to the loss by the Bordelais of their famous 'privileges', removed briefly in 1776, restored again and then finally abolished under a more radical regime in 1790.

Jefferson, the American Minister in France, in his southern France tour-notes of 1787, stated that:

the principal English wine merchants at Bordeaux are Jernon, Barton, Johnston, Foster [Forster], Skinner, Copinger and McCartey [MacCarthy]. The chief French wine merchants are Feger, Nerac, Brunneau, Jauge and du Vérget. Desgrands, a wine broker, tells me they never mix the wine of first quality: but that they mix the inferior ones to improve them. The smallest wines make the best brandy.

The American envoy clearly had no great respect for the merchants, for elsewhere he had written to a friend, warning him to buy direct from the best vineyards, 'and can assure you that it is from them alone that genuine wine is to be got and not from any wine merchant whatever'.

A little later on there is evidence from the Latour archives that the merchants were no more popular with the growers. Most of the firms mentioned above were regular customers of this château, as well as Fennwick and Chalmers. About them and particularly about the brokers (*courtiers*) the Latour *régisseurs* were consistently scathing. Lamothe, manager for the first quarter of the nineteenth century, wrote, 'Yesterday I had the visit of M. Pierre François Guestier, surnamed Pierre the Cruel, but no matter, he is solid' (i.e. financially sound). He particularly distrusted the 'inexorable' broker Lawton and also Merman. 'The rapids of Cordouan are not more dangerous for ships than these two personages are for the proprietors.' He described them as 'our skinners'.

The rapids of Cordouan lay at the mouth of the Gironde, and were caused by some partially exposed rocks near the left bank of the estuary. To mark them a lighthouse was built on a rock in the reign of the French King Henri II (1519–59), and still exists today after many restorations. Over the centuries the rocks have sunk into the river bed, but on occasions when the water is exceptionally clear they may still be seen from the air. However big ships still pass to the north of the lighthouse.

The power of the merchants in relation to the growers then and indeed up to very recent times has not always been realized. In the eighteenth century the important estates might be owned by rich men, many of them members of the Bordeaux Parlement. Though they or more accurately their managers and workers could make the wine, they had no means of selling it except through the well-heeled merchants of the Chartrons, most of them English, though this term also included the Anglo-Irish, who perhaps predominated, notably Barton and Johnston. There were others too, now forgotten, including Jacob Albert, who also had a property in Talence, Kater, Bonfield and MacCarthy, prominent in the middle of the eighteenth century. They were powerful because they alone had commercial access to the U.K. market which absorbed almost all the first growths and the other superior clarets.

Moreover, although they competed with each other they were often able to present a fairly united front to the growers and divided the latest vintage on offer between themselves. For example, as shown from the Latour archives, when in February 1786 the château offered 95 *tonneaux* of its 1785 *grand vin*, they were bought by twelve merchants. Of these eight were 'English', including Barton, Bonfield, Johnston, Keyston, Eady & West, MacCarthy and Bossière & Morgan, and they bought more than 78 *tonneaux* at a price, no doubt agreed between them, of 1,100 livres *tournois* the *tonneau*. In February 1789 William Barton bought the whole crop of the *grand vin*, 91 *tonneaux*, at 1,400 livres per *tonneau*. It was the second wine that was chiefly left to the lesser merchants, many also, it would seem from their names, of foreign origin, such as Luetkins, Schellschuyp and Brauer & Schmidt. The last-named bought 24 *tonneaux* of Latour's second wine of the 1789 vintage. It was a mediocre vintage, but the last one of any size in the Revolutionary period that followed, for after the emigration of the Comte de Ségur-Cabanac his part of the property was confiscated by the state, as was the property of other émigrés.

Thomas Barton's son William was born in 1723, joined his father in the business in 1743 and died in 1791. Unlike most of the other foreign merchants the Bartons have always maintained links with their country of origin, and some of the family continued to return to Ireland to live and work. So it was William's fourth son Hugh, born in 1766, who carried on the firm with his French partner, Daniel Guestier. Hugh Barton married Anna Johnston, daughter of another merchant of foreign origin, Nathaniel Johnston. In the Revolution Hugh Barton was imprisoned in 1794 as an alien, but with the help of his wife he escaped and, it is said, burnt the local guillotine en route for Ireland. In his absence Daniel Guestier ran the business. Barton later returned but died in Ireland. In 1830 his son, Nathaniel, born in 1799, and Daniel Guestier's son, Pierre François, were admitted as partners. Nathaniel died in 1867, also in Ireland, being succeeded by his son Bertram Francis (b. 1830), who in his turn was followed by his son Bertram Hugh (b. 1858), the father of Hugh Ronald Barton, until 1969 the head of the firm, and uncle of Anthony Barton, whose father took no part in the business. Ronald Barton (b. 1902) is the owner of Langoa and that section of the Léo-ville estate bearing the Barton name. The last of the Guestier family was killed in a car crash, and Barton & Guestier is now owned by Seagrams, the large American concern. In 1969 Ronald Barton resigned as head of Barton & Guestier though for a time maintaining a connection with the firm which in 1973 moved to new premises in Blanquefort.

Barton & Guestier had their offices in the erstwhile Pavé des Chartrons until their move out of Bordeaux. Even today this remains the most splendid street of private houses in Bordeaux, although almost all the houses now accommodate offices, with flats on the higher floors of the lofty buildings. Curiously enough, much of one side of this street, shaped like a dog's hind leg and with trees down the middle, is occupied by fine and very solid warehouses constructed in the first third of the nineteenth century. They were built by Daniel Guestier (1755–1847) in 1830, and run through to the Rue Foy and the Rue Vauban, both of which lead to the Quinconces. Guestier bought the site from the municipality and paid the considerable sum of 140,000 frs. for it. Both Bartons and Guestiers used their substantial profits to buy châteaux.

Unfortunately records of these Bordeaux firms are very scanty, and little remains of Barton & Guestier's archives. They possess, however, an interesting account book, including records of the purchase in 1790 of the 1788 vintage vines. This shows clearly the way in which Bordeaux wines were blended. The firm bought 56 *tonneaux* of Lafite 1788. Some was sold to Dublin and some to London. Then they bought another 10¾ *tonneaux* of 'Lafite peur', along with 41¼ *tonneaux* of Latour, plus 10¾ *tonneaux* of 'Latour peur'. As the account books were kept in English, 'peur' of course means pure. Also bought were 13 *tonneaux* of a wine named Casterede, and 3 per cent of this was blended into the Brane-Mouton, Margaux, Larose, Léoville (spelt Lehauville), Listrac, etc. Also 'Ermitage' 1788 was used half and half with Casterede for blending. Elsewhere in the accounts is a note of the purchase of 2½ *tonneaux* of that erstwhile notorious Spanish blending wine, Benicarlo, mentioned in connection with the blending charges in 1764 and much denounced by English writers on wine in the nineteenth century. It gave colour and body.

An interesting later note also in this account book is an early reference to La Mission-Haut-Brion, with the record of the purchase in 1793 of 7 *tonneaux* of 'Lamission graves', and also 20 *tonneaux* of 'Leauville' 1791.

The 'hermitaging' of red Bordeaux was an accepted practice, the alleged purpose being to strengthen these delicate wines for the voyage abroad. It was implied that the pure wine usually went to the British Isles, and it was the Netherlanders, Belgians and Germans who liked their wines 'filled out' with a dollop of something stronger and fruitier. One may take leave to doubt whether only the best came to Britain, as may be judged below.

The letter-books of Nathaniel Johnston, quoted by H. Warner Allen in his *History of Wine* (1961), show what was done. Of the Lafite 1795 (a fine year), he wrote that 'made up with Hermitage [it] was the best liked of any of that year'. Only the finer wine had Hermitage added, for it was expensive; the cheaper had Benicarlo and Alicante blended in. For himself he ordered some 'neat Lafite' of the celebrated 1798 vintage, and when dealing with the well-known London wine merchants, Barnes, who had a great reputation for claret, he recommended that their wines 'should be neat or very lightly made up'. It must be remembered that there was no *égrappage* in those days, the stalks went into the fermenting vats with the grapes, and the wines were very hard and tannin-ridden. The softer, if fuller wines from the Rhône and Spain mollified them.

However Henderson in his *History of Ancient and Modern Wines* (1824) stated 'there is a particular manufacture called *travail de l' Anglaise* which consists of adding to each hogshead of Bordeaux wine three or four gallons of Alicant or Benecarlo, half a gallon of stum wine, and sometimes a small quantity of Hermitage.' This of course was long before the days of Algerian wine and blending 'scandals'. In the *Manuel du sommelier* (third edition, 1826) A. Jullien wrote: 'The wines of the first growths of Bordeaux as drunk in France do not resemble those sent to London; the latter, in which is put a certain quantity of Spanish and French Midi wine, undergo some preparations which give them a taste and qualities, without which they would not be found good in England.' Somewhat ironically to us today, Jullien dedicated his book to Chaptal.

Even later a writer on wine in the seventh (1842) edition of the *Encyclopaedia Britannica* complained 'it is plain that few of those who imagine they are drinking the first growths of Bordeaux can even be drinking the second'. The sceptical contributor also wrote, 'The most extensive operations of this nature [blending] are carried on at Bordeaux with the wines we now call Claret, but not one-thousandth part of which are of good quality, or unmixed in some way, and the one half of which, perhaps, are not French, but Spanish wine.' Although other writers bear witness to the fact that this was an era of wine sophistication, the envenomed tone of the encyclopaedist suggests that he was a confirmed drinker of port.

A particularly revealing example is given in the Goudal–Scott correspondence from Lafite, as recounted by Pijassou in his work on this château. In the difficult oidium years of the 1850s, the *régisseur* was anxious to dispose of old stocks of indifferent wines, still lying in cask in the *chais*. Such long keeping in wood was then normal, for there was no château-bottling for the trade and so the wine had first to be sold. In 1858 Goudal sold some 1848 still in cask to a Paris merchant, at the good price of 5,500 frs. a *tonneau*. In 1853 he disposed of quite large amounts of the 1836 and 1838, miserable vintages even originally, to the leading London firm of Cunningham. But the wine when bottled had some deposit and the Londoners suggested that it might be reinforced with *Cantenac vieux*. The *régisseur* replied that the only wine to strengthen these two weak wines was some 1849 St-Émilion, which at a price of about 200 frs. the *barrique* would reduce the price of these wines and reinforce them. The St-Émilions were almost as full-bodied as Hermitage. Cunningham accepted this advice and imported 4 *barriques* of St-Émilion 1849, but six months later complained that the wine was 'pure vinegar'. Goudal replied that the wine must have been badly handled in London, as it had been very good. He added that he had tasted perfectly good thirty-year-old St-Émilions still in cask.

Goudal was well aware of the charges of falsification against Lafite and other growths, and mentioned complaints from Brussels and Cologne. It was said of Lafite and others that none was sold at Bordeaux, and all went to England. Such rumours had been spread widely for twenty years by the Bordeaux firms, with a few exceptions, notably Cruse. Goudal also told Scott that in 1854 he had been told by M. Clossmann that in 1836 Clossmann had sent to Mr Crawford of the St James's Club 100 *barriques* of Latour 1831 under the name of Lafite! No doubt at Latour they would feel that the members of that distinguished club had had the better bargain!

To try to stop this, Goudal came forward with the revolutionary suggestion of the château itself bottling all its wine in good vintages and carrying the château's name on the cork, capsule and on the packing case. The poor vintages would continue to be sold in bulk, but without the château's name and only under the denomination of Pauillac. The wine bearing the château's guarantee would be sold direct. Scott, who seems to have been excessively conservative in matters affecting Lafite, refused to adopt this suggestion which had to wait a further seventy years before being adopted.

To return to the merchant families, the Johnstons, already mentioned, came originally from the Scottish Border, but William Johnston was sent to Northern Ireland by the English Government and the family became part of the Protestant Ascendency there. In 1716 William Johnston, grandson of the first Irish settler, sent to Bordeaux to learn French, did business in Holland and after returning to Ireland to marry an

Irish girl, settled in Bordeaux in 1729 and worked in the firm of Pierre Germe. After the death of his principal he set up on his own in 1734. The firm dealt not only in wine, but were general merchants and continued in this mixed trade for many years. A price list of the 1820s shows that they imported everything from cotton, sugar and coffee to incense, oil (castor, whale and cod), and exported apples, liquorice and walnuts, as well as brandy and wine. The last was divided into 'Red common cargo', 'Red East-India ditto', 'White cargo', 'Red in bottles comm.', 'Ditto in bottles better' and 'Good Médoc'.

The firm became William & Nathaniel Johnston in 1765, and in the same year their cellars and stock were partly transferred to Blaye and the rest to Guernsey. This move was dictated by fear of blending being prohibited in Bordeaux and of increased taxes. Later on they moved back to the Rue de Pessac in Bordeaux.

The Johnstons always had good connections with America, and when trade with England was severely hindered in the Napoleonic Wars, the Johnstons did their best to increase their American business. In 1807 a member of the family sailed for New York, armed with an introduction from General Lafayette to General McHenry, an Ulsterman who became secretary to George Washington and Secretary of War (1796–1800). By 1809 the Johnstons had over 1,000 customers for wine in the U.S.A. The firm prospered throughout the nineteenth century and, like other wine merchants, branched out into château-ownership, members of the family becoming proprietors of Ducru-Beaucaillou, Dauzac, and La Maqueline (a *palus* estate), but unlike some of the other foreign merchants the Johnstons took French citizenship. Today the firm of Nathaniel Johnston is still independent.

Another Johnston family, although at one time in the wine trade, is celebrated in the annals of Bordeaux for a different calling. Walter Johnston, born in Ireland of Scottish descent, came to Bordeaux in the years before the Revolution and founded a wine firm. His son Céline, also known as David, was born as that great social movement was beginning, in September 1789. David inherited his father's firm in 1819, married Marguerite (known as Peggy) Barton and became so prominent in the municipal affairs of Bordeaux that he became Lord Mayor in April 1838 and remained so for four years. A few years earlier, in 1834, he had acquired 'Les Moulins des Chartrons' at 77 Quai de Bacalan, an extension of the Quai des Chartrons, and there established a pottery and porcelain factory, which ran with varying fortunes. In 1845 Johnston's firm was in liquidation and was turned into a company, J. Vieillard, which continued operations until 1895. The prosperous wine families of Bordeaux and even out in the Médoc were good customers of the firm, and to this day large dinner services as well as other pieces of china are to be found in houses and châteaux. Issan, a home of the Cruses, is particularly well endowed with examples, but in the Bordeaux wine trade the Johnston-Vieillard firm is particularly celebrated for the charming series of plates bearing transfer pictures of the leading châteaux and vineyard scenes. Rare and much sought-after, they include engravings of all three Médoc *premiers crus* and Yquem in the Sauternes. Others depict Issan, Pichon-Longueville, Langoa, Gruau (*sic*) Larose and Gironville, a château in Macau which no longer exists as a wine producer. Others portray a view of Pauillac and the vintage in the Médoc. In all there were about fifteen such plates, but in 1970, at the instigation of Guy Schÿler, the firm of Haviland of Limoges reproduced some of the old châteaux plates and added newcomers, including Angludet and Loudenne. David Johnston himself died in 1854 and is commemorated in a street in Bordeaux near the Jardin Public; he is probably remembered more as a civic leader than for his less than financially successful crockery business.

Another very old firm is Schröder & Schÿler, which opened its doors on 1 January 1739 at exactly the same address as it occupies today: 97 Quai des Chartrons. The two original partners came from Germany, although the Schÿlers had been Dutch, and this is said to account for the unusual *umlaut* on the 'y' in their name. They soon built up a big trade with north Germany. Like Hugh Barton they were arrested at the Revolution and brought before the Military Tribunal. However they were acquitted on the grounds that they had 'never shared the ideas of those greedy speculators who, for too long, have grown fat upon the substance of the people'. This throws a light on conditions in the Bordeaux market as well as on the integrity of the Schröders and Schÿlers. The last Schröder was killed while serving in the French army at the Battle of the Marne in September 1914, but M. Marc Schÿler and his son M. Jean-Henri Schÿler still run the firm, while they own Kirwan in Cantenac. The firm's fine arched stone cellars on the Chartrons date back to the early eighteenth century, and are nearly 100 yards in length. While being general wine merchants, the firm has been associated with branded wines, of which the dry white Graves Rosechâtel is the best known. For many years they had the monopoly of the sale of the wines of Carbonnieux. M. Guy Schÿler, another well-known Bordeaux personality, is a cousin – who has his own firm, Alfred Schÿler, and is also associated with publicity for Lafite.

A neighbouring Chartrons firm (at No. 60), founded in 1740, is Tastet & Lawton, the famous *courtiers* or brokers, to whose incomparable records of vintages and prices this book owes no little. Abraham Lawton came from Cork, and the family took French nationality just before the Revolution. Guillaume Lawton retired in 1825, and M. Tastet was taken into partnership in 1830. The present head of the firm is Daniel Lawton, whose wife is the sister of Christian Cruse. Indeed all the wine families are so connected with each other by marriage that a Jewish family gathering has nothing in the way of kinship on a large dinner party of the Bordeaux wine trade. Daniel Lawton is also renowned in Bordeaux as holding the expectorative record. It is said to be 2 metres 31 centi-metres. His son, also Daniel Lawton, is in the firm too. Their records of the vintages since 1795, and the quantities produced and the opening prices attained by the leading wines since 1830 are unique. Jean Lawton, a cousin, is head of the firm of Lalande, mentioned below, and was proprietor of Cantenac-Brown until its sale in 1968.

Also founded in 1740, but across the rivers in Libourne, was the house of Beylot, whose offices by the river are on the same site as they were then. Among some pre-revolutionary docu-ments in their possession is a letter dated 1 September 1782 in which M. Beylot *père* informs his customers that he has taken his son into partnership, and asks them to accept, as being equally valid as his own, the appended signature of Beylot *fils* on wine transactions. In the past the firm dealt in Cahors and other Haut-Pays wines, but today they are largely concerned with the wines of St-Émilion, Pomerol and Fronsac, with family properties in the area, including Moulinet in St-Émilion and Junayme in Fronsac. The head of the firm today is M. Conynck.

A French house founded just before the Revolution and still in business is Dubos Frères. Jean-Baptiste Dubos began business in 1785. It was principally an export house, and in particular was concerned with selling wine to Canada. At one period it was the sole supplier to the Quebec Liquor Board, but also had connections in the U.S.A., and in northern Europe. Part of the firm now is the old house of Cunliffe, Dobson who began business at the beginning of the nineteenth century in the Cours Balguerie Stuttenberg. Later on Mr Dobson achieved a financial coup by buying a large amount of wine just before the phylloxera at the end of the 1870s and selling it thereafter. At the beginning of this century the firm was amalgamated with Dubos, but it still trades under the name of Cunliffe, Dobson in the British market.

Most of the early Bordeaux merchants had special associations with certain overseas markets, often the countries of their origin. Beyerman, for example, were for centuries associated with the Dutch wine trade, and the firm possesses the passport issued by the mayor of Leiden, 'in the name of Napoleon, Emperor of the French', to Jean Henri Beyerman, wine merchant of Bordeaux, in April 1811, allowing the latter to circulate freely in the district during the ensuing year. Jean Henri died in 1835 – after being part-owner of Haut-Brion – and the firm became Henri & Oscar Beyerman. Then in 1899, Robert Binaud, great-grandson of Jean Henri, took over and his son Henri Binaud ran the firm until 1977, as well as being joint-proprietor of Cantemerle, whose produce the Beyermans were long accustomed to sell in the Low Countries. The firm used to have its premises in the Chartrons, but is now in the adjacent Cours Xavier Arnozan, where Barton & Guestier had their offices. Henri Binaud was long prominent in Bordeaux wine trade affairs and in matters of national wine concern.

Another industry associated with the Bordeaux wine trade was started by foreigners: glass bottle manufacture. At the beginning of the eighteenth century the bottles were imported, but the first bottle glass-works in Bordeaux was founded in 1723 on the Chartrons by an Irishman, Pierre Mitchell. The second was started two years later in Bourg by a German named Fouberg. These two pioneers secured certain privileges which for a time gave them a monopoly, but in 1748 two more glass factories were opened in Libourne, another followed in Bordeaux in 1751, and several others when the original privileges lapsed. By 1789 there were three glass-works for bottle-making in Bordeaux and five others not far outside the city. Altogether they were making 3,200,000 bottles a year.

After the restoration of the Bourbons in 1815, a number of firms prominent today began business. The earliest chronologically was Mestrezat. Domeine Guillaume Mestrezat was a Swiss citizen from Geneva who became Swiss Consul in Bordeaux. The firm was actually founded in 1814, the year when Napoleon was exiled to Elba, but operations as general exporters and importers began the following year. The family was prominent in Bordeaux affairs in the nineteenth century. D. G. Mestrezat himself was an administrator of the Bordeaux–La Teste–Arcachon Railway, one of the earliest in France. Like other railways it was not as successful as expected, and Mestrezat and his firm were only rescued from bankruptcy by his banker parents in Geneva. Later, fortunately, the local line was bought out by the main line railway from Paris to Bordeaux. D. G. Mestrezat's son Paul was also Swiss Consul. He married Anna Jackson, whose family came from England. His nephew Willy became an oenologist and colleague of the celebrated Ulysse Gayon, director of the *Station Oenologique* in Bordeaux; later he joined the Pasteur Institut in Paris. Paul's son James was the last Mestrezat in the firm, for his son, also James, was killed in the Battle of the Somme in 1916. The elder James died in 1925, but his daughter had married Jacques Anglivel de la Beaumelle, whose family has directed the firm ever since, the present head being René de la Beaumelle. However in 1926 the firm and chairman of Preller, M. L. Preller, joined Mestrezat and since then the combined concern has borne the name of Mestrezat-Preller. Three other directors today are Jean-Pierre de la Beaumelle, Édouard Lawton of the well-known family and Georges Roullet. The firm has always had the same premises, but now bearing a different street-name, in the Cours de la Martinique. It has long conducted a world-wide export trade. The family has not gone in for château-owning, but at one period around the end of the last century and the beginning of this one, it used to purchase the whole crop of Haut-Bailly. Today it has the exclusive sale of Rieussec.

In 1816 Léon Hanappier arrived in Bordeaux from Orléans and began his career as a wine merchant. There have been four generations of the family in the firm since, and the present representative is M. Michel Hanappier, who is Swedish Consul in Bordeaux, as his father and grandfather were before him. His family was joined by the Peyrelongue family in the inter-war years, Pierre and Gérard Peyrelongue having been grandsons of Charles Hanappier of the second generation of the family. Both of them left sons now in the business. Hanappier, Peyrelongue, besides having a good wine export trade, particularly in Scandinavia and Belgium, have been unusual in having a distillery in the Rue du Jardin Public, where they produce liqueurs and, alas, whisky from imported Scottish malt. The Peyrelongue family are joint proprietors of Calon-Ségur with the Gasqueton family, the two ancestors of the present generation having bought it on an equal financial basis in 1895. Their premises are in the Cours du Médoc, near the Quai des Chartrons. In 1968 the firm made certain commercial and technical arrangements with Calvet, but retained its independence.

The most patriarchal firm and prolific wine family in Bordeaux is that of Cruse. The first of them was Herman Cruse, born in 1790 in Schleswig-Holstein, then part of Denmark. He came to Bordeaux and began trading in 1819. Cruse had a very large trade with north Germany, and the firm was Cruse and Hirschfeld before it became Cruse et Fils Frères in 1850. Two or three years before that the family fortunes were established by Herman Cruse's daring speculation on the 1847 vintage. The output was very large and the quality excellent although light. However, the whole trade was thrown into confusion by the rumblings and then the Revolution of February 1848, when Louis-Philippe fled to England. Moreover the series of revolutions in Germany, one of Bordeaux's best customers, made things worse. Consequently prices slumped, many merchants were unable to meet their obligations, and in some cases a moratorium on debts was declared.

In these adverse conditions Herman Cruse bought at very low prices enormous quantities of the abundant 1847s, particularly the *crus bourgeois*. Whereas the leading wines of this class in the excellent 1844 vintage had sold for up to 800 frs. a *tonneau*, Cruse paid as little as 300 frs. in January and February 1848. In April he bought 35 *tonneaux* of Cos d'Estournel for 350 frs. and thereafter 50 or 60 *tonneaux* apiece of Rausan, Léoville-Barton, Pichon-Longueville and Durfort at 525 frs. and 150 of Léoville-Las-Cases at the same knock-down price. In September 1848 he acquired 140 *tonneaux* – just about all the crop unsold – of Lafite at 1,025 frs. He was still buying these '47s in 1849, with 24 *tonneaux* of Margaux at 1,000 frs., 12½ *tonneaux* of Yquem at 700 frs. and 29¾ *tonneaux* of Suduiraut at 675 frs. To compare prices, the '44 first growths had been in the 3,000–4,000 frs. range, and the seconds about 2,500–2,800 frs. Later the '48 Lafite was back at 2,800 to 3,000 frs. Altogether Cruse bought 13,650 *tonneaux* from more than 130 growths. A proportion he sold off on the Bordeaux market to Barton & Guestier, Johnston and Clossmann, and these bottled their purchases. It is interesting to note from the full list that nearly all the red wines came from the Médoc, and nothing of importance from St-Émilion or Pomerol.

Like other successful merchants the Cruses moved into château-proprietorship. In 1852 Herman Cruse bought Laujac in Bégadan in the Médoc from one of the Cabarus family, and it is still in the Cruses' possession. In 1865 they acquired Pontet-Canet for 700,000 frs. and Giscours in 1875 for 1,000,000 frs. They also bought du Taillan on the border of the Médoc nearest to Bordeaux. When Adolphe Cruse, son of Herman and inheritor of Laujac, died in 1892 he left 30 million frs. The prosperity of the Cruse family is a symbol of the most affluent period for the Bordeaux wine merchants. This prosperity is reflected even today in the charming antique furniture, decoration and ornaments which adorn the châteaux and merchants' houses throughout the Gironde.

The Cruse firm's offices have always been on the Quai des Chartrons (No. 124). The Cruse family is prolific. The doyen of the partners for years was Christian Cruse, who for over fifty years visited Britain to sell Bordeaux wines. He died in 1975. With an unrivalled memory of the past events, personalities and vintages, he was of immense help over many details of this book. Throughout his life he took a keen interest in wine affairs, and for long was on the Council of the *I.N.A.O.* Many of his travelling activities were later taken over by his son Édouard. However the senior member of the Cruse family of that generation was Christian Cruse's brother Roger, who married a de Luze and was a partner in the Cruse firm for over sixty years. The other pillar of the Cruse firm for many years was Christian Cruse's brother, Emmanuel, proprietor of Issan and one of the keenest commercial brains in Bordeaux, as well as a most charming personality. He died in June 1968. If in the 1847 speculation the firm paid scant attention to the wines of St-Émilion and Pomerol, today the firm of Cruse has made something of a speciality of these attractive wines; until his retirement in 1976 Édouard Cruse had always taken a special interest in these. Apart from Britain, Cruse have always had special connections with Scandinavia, and more recently with the U.S.A., where they have a very important share of the trade in Bordeaux wine.

Two years after Herman Cruse arrived in Bordeaux, Louis Eschenauer left Strasbourg, and opened his doors on the Chartrons in 1821. He ran an expanding business, particularly with Germany, until his death in 1873. Eschenauer also had a good domestic trade inside France. Louis Eschenauer was succeeded by his son Frédéric, who took into the firm his third son Louis and his nephew-cum-son-in-law Louis Lung. After Frédéric's death in 1899 these two directed the concern, with Louis Eschenauer concentrating on the German, Scandinavian and Russian markets, and Louis Lung on Britain. It was in the year of Frédéric's death that the firm moved from the Chartrons to the present huge premises in the Avenue Émile Counord. It has no less than 20,000 square yards of cellar space, including a private cellar in which I once saw such pre-phylloxera wonders as magnums of Lafite '74. So far as seeking vineyard properties went, the Eschenauers turned not to the Médoc but to the Graves. Camponac in Pessac near Pape-Clément was their chief property, although now the name is used as a brand only. The three other vineyards associated with them are Smith-Haut-Lafitte, Olivier and La Garde.

Louis Lung died in 1913 and Louis Eschenauer became sole director, and remained so until his death in 1958 at the age of eighty-eight. 'Oncle Louis' was one of the great personalities of the Bordeaux wine trade. If, probably mistakenly, during the German occupation in the Second World War, he maintained connections with those with whom for many years he had been accustomed to do business, it is also fair to say that he was no little responsible for the Germans leaving Bordeaux intact, and particularly its famous Pont de Pierre, when they withdrew in 1944. After his death the firm was sold to John Holt & Co. of Liverpool. In 1969 Holt's themselves were acquired by Lonrho, a big group with trading interest in Africa. The actual running of Eschenauer's since has still remained in French hands, the head of the firm being Jean Roureau; the sales director is Yves Fourault.

Another firm founded in this period of new wine merchants was de Luze, who began business in 1820 at 88 and 89 Quai des Chartrons where they still have their offices and cellars. The de Luzes were of French origin and had emigrated to Germany, but the founder of the firm, Alfred de Luze, was brought up in Switzerland with his brother, Louis Philippe. Together in 1817 they set off for New York and established an import business there. Three years later Alfred, the younger brother, returned to Europe to help organize trade with the New World, and in order to set up in the convenient port of

Bordeaux. However, by 1824 he had decided to concentrate on wine, including Burgundy and Cognac as well as Bordeaux. Alfred became Consul-General for the Grand Duke of Hesse, and for that service was made a baron, a title still in the family. In 1862 the family bought Château de Paveil and added their name to its own. Since 1964 they have also administered the vineyard of Domaine de l'Ermitage Lamourous, belonging to the Sisters of Mercy, in Le Pian, near Ludon and Macau. In 1961 de Luze absorbed a firm which was one of the leaders in the last century, Clossmann. This very old firm had been founded by a German immigrant in 1785, and was a well-known buyer of classed growths. The de Luze firm has always had a special connection with Scandinavia, and particularly with Denmark, whose Royal Court they supply. In 1968 they acquired Cantenac-Brown.

New firms were, of course, always springing up in Bordeaux, but this short survey is principally concerned with those who have survived. After the four houses that opened their commercial doors in the early Restoration period, there is a gap, and the next important concern was Lalande, who began business in 1844, five doors along from the de Luzes, at 94 Quai des Chartrons. They are still there. Armand Lalande the founder was also prominent in Bordeaux affairs, becoming a Deputy for the Gironde. Yet another Lawton – Henry Lawton – was his grandson, who died in 1933, and the latter's son, Jean, is now head of the firm and owned Cantenac-Brown until 1968. At one time or other members of the Lalande family have owned Léoville-Poyferré, La Couronne and Senilhac. Eighty per cent of their trade today is export, particularly with Britain and northern Europe.

A well-known broker who flourished at this period, but whose firm no longer exists, was Merman, a partner in the firm of Merman & Baguenard, and already mentioned adversely by the *régisseur* of Latour. He owned the curiously named Le Crock in St-Estèphe, which one passes on the main road from Pauillac to the Bas-Médoc; also Marbuzet in the same commune and later owned by Ginestet. He was one of the jury judging wines at the 1862 International Exhibition in London, at which Cheval-Blanc was awarded a bronze medal. In Bordeaux he lived at 29 Pavé des Chartrons (now Cours Xavier Arnozan). The Merman family were one of the earliest Protestant Dutch families to settle in Bordeaux. They arrived there in the sixteenth century but for a long time their principal interest was in shipping.

As might be expected the period of prosperity in the 1860s encouraged the formation of new wine merchants' businesses, and three firms well known today were established: Delor, Calvet and Kressmann.

Delor was founded in 1865 by Alphonse Delor, and soon became one of the big 'names' in Bordeaux. They specialized in business with South America. Their extensive premises were in the Rue de Macau, but at the beginning of this century these were gutted in probably the most spectacular fire in a wine merchant's premises until Calvet's establishment in the Cours du Médoc was seriously damaged in 1966. The Delor family were at one time owners of Durfort-Vivens. They were one of the houses well known for carrying large stocks of bottled wines, including the classed growths. In 1955 they bought the whole crop of Lafite '55. In 1962 Harveys of Bristol acquired a majority share in the firm. They are now a subsidiary of Grants of St James's, the wine division of Allied Breweries.

Unlike many of the Bordeaux merchants, the Calvets were French, and Octave Calvet was born in Tain l'Hermitage on the Rhône. Indeed when he first came to Bordeaux in 1870, it was with the somewhat suspect-sounding purpose of selling Hermitage to the Bordeaux trade. However, even then many of the foreign markets, notably Belgium, Scandinavia and the Hanseatic cities of Germany, still liked their Bordeaux *hermitagé*. Calvet set up his premises in the Cours du Médoc, the broad avenue which runs down to the Chartrons and the river. Here very large cellars were constructed and remained the headquarters of this leading firm until the disastrous fire of 1966. These premises have since been rebuilt. Jean Calvet specialized in the British market, and he used to spend about half of each year travelling his wines in Britain. The original family home was Château Tauzia in the Graves, and today this is the name of their branded claret. Unlike many other Bordeaux merchants they had no ambitions to be classed-growth château proprietors. Like Delor they had extensive business in South America, and opened a branch in Buenos Aires in 1886. Calvets have never restricted their interests to the wines of Bordeaux; they have a substantial Burgundy trade in Beaune, and they also market Cognac.

The third firm of substance dating from this period, Kressmann, was of German origin. Édouard Kressmann first came to Bordeaux in 1858, but worked in other firms until 1871. He then began well with a speculation reminiscent of Herman Cruse's with the 1847; and Kressmann's was also linked with a period of social upheaval. He bought at bargain prices the initially disregarded vintage of 1871, including 163 *tonneaux* of Lafite and Carruades de Lafite. The first wine of Lafite cost only 1,800 frs., and Kressmann paid but 1,400 frs. for Mouton-Rothschild. These prices may be compared with 4,500 frs. and 3,000 frs. respectively for the 1870 wines of these two growths; and for the next good vintage of 1874 Kressmann paid 4,200 frs. for Mouton which had produced a record crop of 190 *tonneaux*. The purchase and successful sale in England, Holland and north Germany of these '71s set up the house of Kressmann. They are known for their La Tour-Martillac in the Graves, discussed in the chapter on that district.

It is surprising to find any firms setting up in the unpropitious eighties which have survived, but that is when Sichel's started. They opened their premises in 1883 on the Quai de Bacalan, a continuation of the Chartrons, and they are still there. They were a branch of the Mainz firm of Sichel. However when the First World War began, Herman Sichel in Bordeaux formed a completely separate French company. After that war Allan Sichel and his brother Herbert joined the firm, while the German firm set up its own Bordeaux house, which only reunited with its cousin firm in 1966. Allan Sichel became one of the best-known wine shippers in England where he lived until his death in 1965. He was a dedicated, outspoken *amateur* of Bordeaux wines, with a mischievous pleasure in being controversial. Many lovers of claret in Britain today remain in Allan Sichel's vinous debt. The firm also deals in Burgundy, and has considerable connections in the United States as well as in Britain. They are associated with Palmer and Angludet. In the latter lives Peter Sichel, son of Allan and head of the firm in Bordeaux. Following difficulties arising out of the slump in the mid 1970s, the firm has now divided, with Peter controlling Maison Sichel, and H. Sichel & Sons of London being responsible for Sichel, Fils, Frères.

Another firm, now part-owners of Palmer, began in the 1890s: Mähler-Besse. They are of Dutch origin.

The next important firm to open was that of Ginestet which began in the auspicious vintage year of 1899, setting up at 132 Quai des Chartrons. Fernand Ginestet faced a difficult period ahead, but did succeed in building up a large trade in the north and west of France, and later began to develop an export trade with the Low Countries and Britain. In 1916 he joined with another merchant, Latrille, and the firm was Latrille & Ginestet until they separated in 1929. Meanwhile Ginestet had begun to purchase vineyards. In 1919 he acquired Clos Fourtet and Cos d'Estournel, and in 1925 was a member of the syndicate which bought Château Margaux. After the last war he relinquished control of Clos Fourtet in order to become sole owner of Château Margaux. His son Pierre, a prominent figure in Bordeaux wine circles, became head of the firm, which has controlled the sale of seven lesser red and four white growths in the Graves, Sauternes, Premières Côtes and Bourg districts, as well as Domaine de Chevalier. In the 1960s the firm moved its premises to the Cours St-Louis. Bernard Ginestet, son of Pierre, was the third generation in the firm, which was particularly badly hit by the slump that began in 1973; as a result the Ginestets had to dispose of Ch. Margaux, a separate company, in 1976.

A smaller but distinguished house was that of Woltner. Around the turn of this century Frédéric Woltner, who had already served his wine apprenticeship in a Bordeaux firm, opened an office in Paris but also maintained cellars on the Chartrons. Not long before the last war these were moved round the corner to the Cours du Médoc. His two sons, Henri and Fernand, joined the firm in 1926, and until their deaths in 1974 and 1977 respectively these two were the sole partners. Although they had a general wine merchandising business, and were for long the agents in France of Pol Roger champagne, their best-known activities were connected with their three properties in the Graves: La Mission-Haut-Brion, La Tour-Haut-Brion and Laville-Haut-Brion, to be described in the Graves chapter. Lacking suitable successors, the firm closed down in 1977.

One of the largest Bordeaux firms today is Cordier. Désiré Cordier had founded his business at Toul in 1877, but opened a Bordeaux branch during the First World War. The firm was to some extent involved in supplying wine to the French Army during the war. Like Ginestet, Cordier began to buy châteaux when peace arrived, securing Gruaud-Larose, Talbot and later on five other growths. The firm nowadays has a substantial domestic trade, particularly with northern France. Since 1953 all wines from the Cordier châteaux have been sold through agents at home and abroad and are not offered on the Bordeaux market. Jean Cordier, the present head of the firm, owns one of the most attractive eighteenth-century houses in Bordeaux, Labottière, built by the architect Laclotte.

Two firms which have come to the fore since the last war but which had their origins earlier are La Bergerie in Pauillac and J-P. Moueix in Libourne.

La Bergerie actually dates from as long ago as 1904, as the commercial outlet of Mouton-d'Armailhacq, and it was included in the sale of that property to Baron Philippe de Rothschild in 1933. Originally it had traded and developed under the name of the Société Vinicole de Pauillac, until the present name of La Bergerie was adopted in 1954. The premises in the middle of Pauillac include a charming eighteenth-century house with a courtyard. The firm is basically concerned with the brand wines of Baron Philippe's concern, including the best-selling Mouton-Cadet, but it also carries on a general wine merchandising business, buying from other estates, including of course the two Moutons. It has a large American trade. The energetic managing director is Philippe Cottin, a source of much information on Bordeaux wines.

The expansion of the house of Moueix is one of the features of post-war Bordeaux. Jean-Pierre Moueix has built up his business since the 1930s largely by acquiring the production or marketing rights of important châteaux in the St-Émilion and Pomerol area, also buying control or part-ownership in local châteaux. In St-Émilion his firm owns Magdelaine and Fonroque, and in Pomerol La Fleur-Pétrus, La Grave-Trigant-de-Boisset and Lagrange. In addition he is co-proprietor of Pétrus itself. The company is responsible for 'farming' several properties, including Latour-à-Pomerol and La Clotte, and has exclusive or part selling rights of nine estates in the two districts, including Pavie, Clos Fourtet and La Fleur. Further, it sells a third of the crop of Ausone and a quarter of Cheval-Blanc, as well as important parts of a number of other leading growths in the neighbourhood. The firm also controls the old Libourne house of Danglade, which was founded in 1780. Both Moueix and Danglade have their offices on the quayside in Libourne. The head of Danglade now is Patrick Danglade. His grandfather was the first Bordeaux merchant I met, who welcomed me on my first visit to Bordeaux in 1939. Moueix also owns the firm of Duclot in Bordeaux.

The most recently established firm of size in Bordeaux is that of Alexis Lichine, the Russian-born American who did much to publicize French wines in America after the last war. Following the purchase of Lascombes and Prieuré by American syndicates with which he was associated, he began a substantial merchandising business in Burgundy and Bordeaux. More recently he concentrated all his stocks of French wines in Bordeaux, where on the Chartrons the firm has cellars that formerly belonged to Cruse. At one time his offices were in the old château of Lascombes in Margaux, but they too are now on the Chartrons. A feature of these cellars, like others in the locality, is their great length and narrow width. They run back from the Quai des Chartrons for 365 metres, with bins placed at right angles to a central *piste*. In order that the staff may move quickly from one end of the cellars to the other, bicycles are provided, and these dash to and fro along the *piste*, summoned often by a public address system originating in the office. Lichine claimed to have the biggest trade in château-bottled wines with the U.S.A. In 1965 his business was bought by the British brewery group of Bass-Charrington. This was yet another example of the influx of foreign capital and control into Bordeaux in recent years. Lichine is no longer concerned with the firm.

Formerly associated with Lichine's firm, but now operating on his own is William Bolter, probably the most recent addition to the Bordeaux merchants who trade with Britain and the United States, an agreeable revival of the tradition of English merchants in Bordeaux. He, like many other merchants, ran into difficulties in the mid-seventies, but continued his business.

There are other substantial wine merchants in Bordeaux whom I have not mentioned because they are little associated with the type of Bordeaux wines familiar in Britain or America. In general the wine merchants are not so dominant in Bordeaux as they used to be, owing to the advent of big foreign groups. The role of the Bordeaux wine merchants is that of middle-men, between the growers whose wine they select with the aid of brokers who receive 2 per cent commission on sales, and their trade customers. In addition to the broking firms in Bordeaux, there are individual brokers in every district whose business it is to know the quality of the wines throughout their area. They are the link between the local growers and the merchants.

I have only mentioned the brokers *en passant*, as they are little known to the general public, to whom the merchants' names may be familiar. But in addition to those referred to, well-known names include Damade, Chauvot, Moreau (briefly the owner of Ch. Margaux), de Rivoire, associated with the great Paris concern of Nicolas and a former president of the Syndicat des Courtiers en Vins de Bordeaux, and Daniel Lacoste, who was the principal white wine broker of his time.

In times of prosperity as recently, the role of the merchants with the leading growths in short supply is little more than that of brokers, but for the mass of wines they have considerable responsibilities in buying wines and holding them. Often they have arrangements with particular growers, whom they have to support through bad vintages as well as good. Most Bordeaux wine merchants nowadays, in addition to supplying the home and export trade with wines bearing château names, are concerned to develop the sale of their own brands, as a safeguard for the future. With the exception of Mouton-Cadet and perhaps one or two other brands, these so far have proved more successful at home than abroad.

The slump in the Bordeaux trade in the 1970s hit the merchants collectively as well as individually. They could no longer afford to finance the purchase of young wines on a large scale, or hold stocks for later – and in some cases much later – sale in bottle. As can be seen from the preceding pages, many of the Bordeaux houses are now foreign-owned. Indeed if they had not been financed by outside groups such as British brewery groups and conglomerates, they might not all have survived the slump that hit them so suddenly and severely in the seventies. One result of this slump was that many of the smaller growers increasingly sold direct to consumers within France, a tendency to be observed everywhere in the wine-growing districts. This *vente directe* even affected some of the *crus classés*. For they had increasing difficulty in selling their wines to the Bordeaux merchants. There was also a growing amount of what might be termed *achat direct* with the merchants being by-passed by big British and American concerns. Nevertheless, the wine region of the Gironde and the Bordeaux market are so large and complex that the experience and skill of the merchants are necessary for the selection and disposal of wine from thousands of estates. However, control of the firms by families, particularly those with long traditions, has obviously weakened in the post-Second World War epoch, and this trend is likely to continue. Behind the tall grey façades of the Chartrons things are not what they were for so long.

The boom of the early 1970s and the succeeding slump caused big changes in the structure of the Bordeaux market and the position of the merchants. In the earlier years the signing of exclusivity agreements between growers and merchants, who then obtained the sole world rights to market the wines of these estates, led to many well-known and some less well-known growths being removed from the Bordeaux market. They provided the proprietors with a guaranteed market, almost irrespective of the quality of their wines each vintage. The catastrophic results were shown with the '72s. Not only did the agreements tend to force up the price in good times, for the grower usually had the whip hand, but they also perhaps led to a certain carelessness in cultivation and vinification. There has always been a limited amount of this exclusivity business in Bordeaux, as described in these pages, though in earlier times the merchants holding the five- or ten-year contracts expected to off-load part of their purchases on to the Bordeaux market. However, the situation never went so far as in the late sixties and early seventies, when firms like Gilbeys and Lichine held a wide range of such exclusivity agreements. What followed is well known, and by the late seventies few still existed.

The slump certainly assisted the decline of what may be generalized as the Chartrons, even if not all the firms still had their offices and cellars there. In a way this is to be regretted, for although no doubt at times they were overbearing and arrogant – as history shows was the case in the eighteenth and nineteenth centuries – they represented a long historical tradition and they served Bordeaux and its customers well. In spite of the over-centralizing policies of all French governments for hundreds of years, Bordeaux has retained a cultural identity common to few other cities of France, and to this the Chartronnais contributed; and their houses and châteaux bear the marks and ornaments of their taste. This cannot be said of many other groups of prosperous merchants elsewhere. The Bordeaux scandal of 1973–4 hit worst the most patrician family of them all, the Cruses; and no doubt in this there was an element of jealousy. Nevertheless, as the records of the firms mentioned in this chapter show, the Chartrons and its occupiers established a firm place in the history of Bordeaux and of France.

8. The Médoc I
Pauillac and St-Estèphe

To the *amateur* of fine claret the Médoc is surely the Holy of Holies. I yield to no one in my admiration of an outstanding St-Émilion like Cheval-Blanc of a great year, or of the voluptuous qualities of a rich Pomerol like Pétrus or Vieux-Château-Certan; and the leading Graves may fairly consider themselves the peers of their historically junior rivals to the north. I cannot follow a distinguished Médoc château proprietor who said he found Graves not to his taste and St-Émilions and Pomerols 'common wines'; but as to the latter pair I see what he means. They lack the elegance and distinction of a great Médoc.

The late Maurice Healy who wrote as engagingly and enthusiastically about claret as any man, and who sharpened my early knowledge and appreciation of Bordeaux, yet proved an apostate at the last jump. In his *Stay Me With Flagons* (1940) he wrote: 'For let there be no doubt about it: Burgundy at its best overtops claret at *its* best.' He added that one would only drink four or five bottles of truly first-class Burgundy in one's life, and be lucky to find so many; he had only come upon three. They were Volnay Caillerets 1889, La Tâche 1904 and Richebourg 1923.

One cannot argue about wines that one has not drunk, but I would claim to have drunk with fitting appreciation more than three bottles of top-rank Burgundy. They would include ... but this is a book about Bordeaux. It comes down to the kind of taste and flavour one ultimately prefers. There is no need to denigrate a Burgundy – to me the second of red wines – to express a preference for red Bordeaux. There is more flavour, more variety and distinction about claret; it is a more interesting wine than Burgundy; a violin compared with a trumpet, a baritone as against a bass. But then some prefer basses.

Maurice Healy went on to admit that one may drink claret of the highest class several times in the year, and this is certainly true or was in his time, when relatively such were not expensive. Today it is different. This also makes it that much more difficult to pick out the peak bottles. What claret team can I select from my experience to match Healy's Burgundies? It is not so easy. For one thing Burgundy is usually drunk rather young, and it is rare to open one more than fifty years old – although I have drunk a splendid 1865 Musigny from the Comte de Vogüé's estate. Burgundy can seldom compete in antiquity with Bordeaux. Yet with an aged, perhaps a pre-phylloxera claret, it is difficult not to be influenced by its seniority, by the dusty, often hand-blown bottle, by the fine nose and fruity flavour of old wine still in possession of its faculties. Unconsciously one may make allowances. Yet age is not enough to win laurels. The oldest bottle of claret that I have ever drunk and ever expect to drink was in Bristol at the table of Ronald Avery in April 1967. It was Lafite 1803, re-corked in October 1957 at the château, and is described on page 237.

Much of course depends on memory, the circumstances as well as a touch of nostalgia. A wine may have made such an impression that no other can erase it; and I wonder if that happened to Maurice Healy with his three Burgundies. I cannot put in an opening pair, but I would include in my team, in ascending age order, Ch. Margaux 1953, Lafite 1949, Cheval-Blanc 1947, Lafite 1945, Léoville-Poyferré 1929, Léoville-Las-Cases 1929, Pichon-Longueville-Baron 1929, Latour 1929, Léoville-Las-Cases 1928, Cheval-Blanc 1921, Latour 1920, Cheval-Blanc 1920, Latour 1899, Haut-Brion 1899, Mouton-Rothschild 1878, Lafite 1875, Langoa 1870 and Grand-Puy-Ducasse 1868.

In the reserve team I might include Margaux 1961, Mouton-Rothschild 1949 and 1961, Pétrus 1949, Léoville-Barton 1948, Cheval-Blanc 1948, Pétrus 1947, Mouton-Rothschild 1945, Pontet-Canet 1929, Cheval-Blanc 1928, Haut-Brion 1920 and others of that year now past their best. Among the very old wines that have left a great impression are Branaire-Ducru 1899, Mouton-Rothschild 1895, 1880, 1870 and 1869, Lafite 1870 and 1869, and Latour 1865 and 1863.

No doubt there are firmer favourites for other people's selection, but one cannot drink everything. One thing, however, will be noted: most of the wines are Médocs. In a 'colts' team I would spread my net wider, including perhaps La Mission-Haut-Brion 1948 and Vieux-Château-Certan 1947, along with other lesser Pomerols and more than one Cheval-Blanc, but greatness surely implies a certain survival, and although I have put several post-war wines in my two leading lists, their inclusion may be premature. But the '61s have mostly yet to show their form.

But I do not doubt the primacy of the Médocs. Being rather harder and firmer wines than the St-Émilions and Pomerols, they take more time to come round, while the latter may often make more agreeable bottles when young. A Médoc of a fine vintage, as Ronald Barton, part-proprietor of the Léoville vineyard and sole owner of Langoa, has observed, should not be drunk until it is ten years old.

Physically the Médoc is triangular in shape, with the Atlantic and the Gironde enclosing it on the two long sides and Bordeaux on the short, southern line. The vineyards lie on the eastern side of the triangle, forming a narrow strip only three to six miles wide and about forty-five miles long. The general aspect of the country is flat, and the best vineyards lie on slopes that are never more than 150 feet above sea level and fall gently towards the estuary. Although now well drained there is some marshy land; with occasional little streams, known here as *jalles*, slipping down into the broad river. The best known of these is the Jalle de Blanquefort, for that forms near Bordeaux the 'frontier' between the Médoc and the Graves.

The soil, washed down by the rivers, is gravelly and sandy, and the visitor can only wonder that so many fine wines are produced from such poor ground. It has to be fertilized moderately to give of its best. The sub-soil varies, from chalk and clay to iron and sand; but even the top soil varies imperceptibly and this is what accounts for the astonishing variation in the wines made from adjoining properties. The Bas-Médoc is more sandy and has clay, which results in a greater output but a lower quality than in the Haut-Médoc. One reason at least for the difference in style between Latour and Lafite is that the former has a shallower top soil than the latter, so that the roots more effectively penetrate the chalk sub-soil, thus giving a rather fuller, harder wine. To produce a *tonneau* of wine in the Médoc the grapes from about four thousand vines are needed; so a big château vineyard includes over half a million vines to be cared for.

In the middle of the last century and at the period of the 1855 classification the Médoc *vignoble* extended to 20,000–25,000 ha (2·47 acres = 1 hectare). In his book on the Médoc published in 1855, d'Armailhacq gives the lower figure and a total average production of 40,000 *tonneaux*, two per hectare, equivalent of only 18¼ hl per hectare, compared with a minimum *rendement* allowed today of 40 hl per hectare. Of this amount, wrote d'Armailhacq, only 4,500 *tonneaux* were derived from the *vins classés* and an equal quantity from the *crus bourgeois*. The remainder was 'assimilated to the *vin ordinaire*'. He reckoned the cost of production, not counting first planting or replacements, was 685 frs. a hectare (about £27 10s. in the English currency of the day, but at least ten times that figure in today's value). The cost of replanting he gave as 6,000 frs. per hectare.

Today the *vignoble* is little more than a quarter of its 1855 size, owing to the successive crises that have hit Bordeaux from the 1870s onwards. In recent years, however, prosperity has led to replanting, while production is increasing; too much so, some say. Total annual output of the Médoc is now averaging about 350,000 hl, of which three-quarters comes from the Haut-Médoc. The six communes entitled to their own *appellation*, as listed below, produce about 175,000 hl a year. All these figures are substantially higher than in the sixties.

In 1824 Franck gave the normal Haut-Médoc and Bas-Médoc output as 286,000–346,000 hl, of which the Haut-Médoc accounted for between 243,000 and 293,000 hl. St-Estèphe was the most prolific producer, averaging 40,500–45,000 hl, followed by Pauillac with 31,500–36,000 hl. Neither of the other two qualitatively important communes, St-Julien and Margaux, produced as much as a third of these totals; and Macau production was double either of them, while Blanque-fort equalled each. Today the average output figures for St-Estèphe and Pauillac are roughly 50,000 hl and 38,000 hl respectively. Owing to the prosperity that started strongly in the 1960s, these figures, like those of the entire Médoc, are much on a par with those early in the last century, but they conceal a shrinkage in the *crus bourgeois*, the disappearance of the *palus* wines and a general rise in yield, as a result of more scientific methods of viticulture and wine-making.

Evidence of increased production in the *crus classés* is that in March 1965 the permitted quantity per hectare for the Médoc *appellations* was raised by the *Institut National des Appellations d'Origine (I.N.A.O.)*. The maximum *rendement de base* per hectare now allowed to be sold with the appropriate *appellation* is as follows:

Pauillac	40 hl	St-Julien	40 hl
Margaux	40	St-Estèphe	40
Listrac	40	Haut-Médoc	43
Moulis	40	Médoc	45

Already in October 1974 the *AC* regulations for permissible yields had been amended throughout France. For details of the changes for the Bordeaux *appellations* see Appendix A. In 1966 the total *AC* production throughout the whole Médoc was 223,000 hl, while in the record years of 1970 and 1973 it was 362,985 hl and 423,035 hl respectively.

There are twenty-two communes in the Haut-Médoc in which wine is produced and, as can be seen above, only six are entitled to an *appellation* of their own. The rest are only allowed to label their wine Haut-Médoc. In the Bas-Médoc* (*appellation* Médoc) there are sixteen wine-producing communes.

Although the Médoc resounds with 'big names', there are in fact remarkably few large estates. However these do produce between two-fifths and one-half of the total quantity of wine. The largest of these probably is Lafite with a vineyard area of 80 ha. I write 'probably' advisedly, and would like to warn readers that throughout this book such figures, and the totals of output, may be approximate rather than accurate. For they vary not only with time and vintage but from source to source. In many cases the figures have been given me by the proprietors, their *régisseurs* or *maîtres de chai*; otherwise from official returns or standard works of reference. They seldom all agree with each other. It may be that a vineyard has been extended since the official figure. For example it was M. André Portet, then *régisseur* of Lafite, who gave me the total of 80 ha, but the latest official figure is 78 ha. No doubt there has been some additional planting in the meantime. The same applies to the composition of the vineyards, in nearly all cases given me by the men on the spot. Sometimes I have been mildly surprised by the percentage precision with which a *maître de chai* or a *chef de culture* has replied to my question with some such formula as: Cabernet-Sauvignon 53 per cent,

*Although this name is no longer official (see page 359), I have used it throughout to distinguish it from the Haut-Médoc.

Cabernet-Franc 24 per cent, Merlot 21 per cent and Petit-Verdot 2 per cent. How do they measure up those few rows of Petit-Verdot? However, it does not matter, and such accuracy is possible from the vineyard records. The significance of such figures is to give the balance of the vineyard, which may give a clue to the style and quality of the wine we drink; few of us are going to lose much drinking time if the percentage of Petit-Verdot is in fact 1 per cent or even 3 per cent. It is there in the vineyard, and the juice of its grapes is in the bottle.

Sometimes the acreage and output given me at the château have seemed rather large in relation to other sources, and perhaps they owe a little to proprietorial pride; although growers in the Médoc and elsewhere in the Gironde are usually more reliable about their own property than about their neighbours'. In cases where I suspected a little rounding-off of the totals, I have done my best to take account of this. It is a fact, however, that since the sixties many, if not most, leading estates have increased their area under vines and output.

To return to the Médoc, in addition to the big estates, which do not much exceed fifty in number, there are about 450 small growers making their own wine and accounting for roughly one-sixth to one-eighth of the total, and fourteen co-operatives making the balance of total production. These co-operatives are nearly all in the northern part of the district and half of them in the Bas-Médoc. The most southerly is at Arcins in the Haut-Médoc; Bégadan in the Bas-Médoc is the largest.

In discussing the wines of the Médoc there are two possible ways of covering them; by geography and by classification. Either method on its own has obvious shortcomings, so I decided to combine them as far as possible; and I have followed this procedure in the other districts with classified or outstanding wines. In the case of the Médoc, where the order of the 1855 classification had meaning, I have described the classed growths in sequence commune by commune.

So far as the history of the older growths is concerned firm

THE 1855 CLASSIFICATION OF RED BORDEAUX*

Premiers Crus		Troisièmes Crus (cont.)	
Lafite	Pauillac	Ferrière	Margaux
Latour	Pauillac	Marquis d'Alesme-Becker	Margaux
Margaux	Margaux	Boyd-Cantenac	Margaux
Mouton-Rothschild	Pauillac		
Haut-Brion	Pessac (Graves)	Quatrièmes Crus	
		St-Pierre-Sevaistre	St-Julien
		St-Pierre-Bontemps	St-Julien
Deuxièmes Crus		Branaire-Ducru	St-Julien
Rausan-Ségla	Margaux	Talbot	St-Julien
Rauzan-Gassies	Margaux	Duhart-Milon	Pauillac
Léoville-Las-Cases	St-Julien	Pouget	Cantenac
Léoville-Poyferré	St-Julien	La Tour-Carnet	St-Laurent
Léoville-Barton	St-Julien	Lafon-Rochet	St-Estèphe
Durfort-Vivens	Margaux	Beychevelle	St-Julien
Lascombes	Margaux	Le Prieuré-Lichine	Cantenac
Gruaud-Larose	St-Julien	Marquis-de-Terme	Margaux
Brane-Cantenac	Cantenac		
Pichon-Longueville	Pauillac	Cinquièmes Crus	
Pichon-Longueville-Lalande	Pauillac	Pontet-Canet	Pauillac
Ducru-Beaucaillou	St-Julien	Batailley	Pauillac
Cos-d'Estournel	St-Estèphe	Haut Batailley	Pauillac
Montrose	St-Estèphe	Grand-Puy-Lacoste	Pauillac
		Grand-Puy-Ducasse	Pauillac
		Lynch-Bages	Pauillac
Troisièmes Crus		Lynch-Moussas	Pauillac
Kirwan	Cantenac	Dauzac	Labarde
Issan	Cantenac	Mouton-Baronne-Philippe	Pauillac
Lagrange	St-Julien	Le Tertre	Arsac
Langoa	St-Julien	Haut-Bages-Libéral	Pauillac
Giscours	Labarde	Pédesclaux	Pauillac
Malescot-St-Exupéry	Margaux	Belgrave	St-Laurent
Cantenac-Brown	Cantenac	Camensac	St-Laurent
Palmer	Cantenac	Cos-Labory	St-Estèphe
La Lagune	Ludon	Clerc-Milon	Pauillac
Desmirail	Margaux	Croizet-Bages	Pauillac
Calon-Ségur	St-Estèphe	Cantemerle	Macau

*plus 1973 amendment adding Mouton-Rothschild to the *premiers crus*, and taking into account other changes in name.

facts are by no means easy to secure. In many cases it is surprising how little is reliably known about the past, and often fact is difficult to disentangle from fiction, or perhaps tradition. Several important-looking French books published in the heyday of the Médoc in the 1860s and 1870s are inclined to 'write-up' the châteaux they describe, and when it comes to the earlier history they sometimes contradict one another as to events, proprietors and dates. This is often owing to a paucity of solid information. An exception is Latour. The English proprietors who secured the property in 1962 found voluminous records that were edited and published in 1974.

Then there are certain legends which probably arose through some skilful public relations work of the time. For example it is said that Marshal Richelieu, when Governor of Guyenne, was advised by his doctor to drink Lafite as being the most powerful and most agreeable tonic. Thereupon Louis XV (1715–74) complimented him on looking twenty-five years younger. The Marshal explained why, gave the king some bottles and the fortunes of Lafite and its proprietor M. de Ségur were made. It is also said to have been equally appreciated by Mesdames de Pompadour and Dubarry. All this may be taken with a pinch of salt, particularly as the later French kings were always having thrust on them 'favourite wines', invariably with tonic qualities. Such stories are often told about more than one growth.

PAUILLAC

Accordingly I begin with the Haut-Médoc, starting – a shade arbitrarily perhaps but arguably without difficulty – in Pauillac. To enter the Médoc on paper from the south by crossing the Jalle de Blanquefort would entail a dull, prosaic progress, while to land at St-Estèphe might be logical topographically but ill-balanced vinously. No doubt partisans of Ch. Margaux and St-Julien would have no difficulty in pressing their claims for 'first footing', but whatever the merits of the 1855 classification, discussed later, it does include more growths from Pauillac than any other commune: 18 in all, after various subdivisions of properties. They tend to cluster at the top and bottom end of the five classes, with three *premiers crus*, two *deuxièmes*, one *quatrième* and no fewer than twelve *cinquièmes*.

With exceptions to be noted, this range is justified, for the sumptuous leading growths near the estuary are worlds away from the small, farm-like properties lying inland amid the woods and rather scrubby land of the thinly populated 'outback' towards St-Laurent and the forest of the Landes. So far as the vineyards are concerned, the commune of Pauillac is really split into two: north and south, with the little estuary town of Pauillac in between. In the northerly section lies Lafite (which adjoins Cos-d'Estournel in St-Estèphe), Mouton-Rothschild and the attendant Mouton-Baronne-Philippe (formerly Mouton-d'Armailhacq and then until 1976 Mouton-Baron-Philippe, as explained below) and then Pontet-Canet. To the south-west of these stretch such growths as Grand-Puy-Lacoste and Lynch-Bages. There is a cluster of smaller growths around the town, among them Duhart-Milon, now owned by Lafite, Haut-Bages-Libéral, part of which has been incorporated into Pontet-Canet, and Grand-Puy-Ducasse, whose château, though not its vineyard, is on the riverfront.

Then there is something of a gap, as one proceeds south on the famous *Route-des-Grands-Crus* (*D.2*). Indeed Latour, on the river side of the road, is only marginally a Pauillac and at one time was registered as being in the hamlet of St-Lambert. The other two major growths, Pichon-Longueville-Baron and Pichon-Longueville-Comtesse-de-Lalande, whose châteaux stare across the road at each other (rather sultrily I always fancy), are similarly placed, and at one time the *appellation contrôlée* authorities insisted on part of the latter being labelled as St-Julien. This, however, was carrying bureaucracy a little too far, and has now been stopped, but it demonstrates the distinct physical position of these 'southern' Pauillacs.

The commune as a whole has a fairly heavy gravelly soil, with a stony sub-soil and then iron below. To some extent Pauillac is the wine capital of the Haut-Médoc, with the *Maison du Vin* there, and the headquarters of the *Commanderie du Bontemps*, the publicity organization promoting the wines of the Médoc and the adjacent Graves.

In discussing the Pauillac growths, I deal with them in the order of the 1855 classification, since the approximate class sequence is widely known and less confusing than if the estates were considered only on a geographical basis within the commune. This pattern I have adopted for the other communes and districts. For reference purposes the 1855 classification is printed on page 228.

First in Pauillac, therefore, comes Lafite, whose claim to first-growth status is long-lived and unchallenged. Even its immediate neighbour at Mouton-Rothschild would not aspire to more than parity of esteem although not perhaps averse to stealing an occasional priority of price in the open market. However, I have yet to meet a proprietor of a classed-growth Médoc who does not publicly or secretly believe that on the day – or in the evening – his wine is the peer of any other.

As mentioned earlier, in the Christie's sale in 1788 of the cellar of the retiring French Ambassador, Count d'Adhémar, his Lafite fetched the high price of 66s. a dozen, compared with 49s. for the Margaux. No vintage was listed in either case. In these early years Lafite's name was often spelled in varying ways, sometimes with two 'f's, and often with two 't's, variations not unknown in print even today. In the eighteenth and the first third of the nineteenth centuries it was occasionally called La-Fite or La-Fitte.

As with other Médoc estates, the date when the vineyard was established as an entity is not known; it was probably around the turn of the seventeenth–eighteenth centuries, when

many of the Médoc growths began to take shape but it may
have been earlier. Lafite then passed to the important vineyard
proprietor, the Marquis de Ségur, who also owned Latour
and Calon, now named after him. He was also a Vice-
President of the Parlement of Guyenne, already described.
On his death in 1755 the estate passed to his grandson Nicolas-
Marie Alexandre, Comte de Ségur. It was then that Latour
and other properties passed into the hands of other descendants
of the Marquis, while as Nicolas-Marie was a minor his
father Alexandre administered his affairs. The separation
actually took place in 1760, although until 1785 Latour and
Lafite shared the same *régisseur*, Domenger. When after about
ten years the young Count took over Lafite, he was, unfortunately, well on the way to ruining himself and by 1774
he was so deeply in debt that the official Garde des Sceaux
had to intervene; and in 1776 he took flight to Holland to
avoid his debtors, an event by no means rare among the
nobility attendant upon the Royal Court. Finally Lafite was
sold in 1784 for 1,012,000 livres. This sale, like another later,
seems to have been something of a blind, for a year later the
estate was resold to Nicolas Pierre de Pichard, who was a
distant cousin of the dispossessed Count. Pichard was immensely rich and the first Président of the Bordeaux Parlement. According to Jefferson, Pichard had sold 175 *tonneaux*
of Lafite in 1780 at prices averaging 1,500–2,000 livres a
tonneau. A millionaire in contemporary terms, he drew 30,000–
40,000 livres a year from Lafite after the production costs had
been met. He owned Lafite from 1784 until he was guillotined
in Paris ten years later for illegally aiding the emigration from
France of his daughter. Along with the owners of Ch. Margaux, he was perhaps the only important Bordeaux vineyard
proprietor to be guillotined. Owing to his daughter's flight,
Lafite like the properties of other émigrés was confiscated. It
had been greatly improved by the Ségurs, or in fact by
Domenger, and its fame may be gauged by the printed notice

of sale which may be seen in the hall of the château today. It was described as being the property of *La Fille de Pichard émigrée*. The sale was notified as being in the Fifth Year of the Revolutionary Calendar (1796–7) and the property was described as *Le domaine de Lafite, premier cru du Médoc, et produisant le premier vin de Bordeaux*. Whether or not the last remark was an example of auctioneer's enthusiasm, it is significant to note that it was described as a first growth. This is amply confirmed in the later chapter on the Classification of 1855. It was valued at the large and precise sum of 1,286,606 frs. 25c. The notice stated that the vineyard did not suffer from frost and was well maintained throughout. It was sold on 12 September 1797 for 2,000,000 frs. to Jean de Witt, former minister of the Batavian Republic and a businessman living in Paris. In 1800 he re-sold the property, probably because he was unable to pay the last instalment of the purchase price, to a Dutch syndicate.

At this moment enters the mysterious figure of Ignace-Joseph Vanlerberghe, a wealthy grain merchant who had done well out of supplying Napoleon's armies. For many years it was thought that, after the Dutch syndicate, the proprietor was Sir Samuel Scott, a London banker, but then it was suggested that the syndicate sold Lafite to Vanlerberghe in 1803. However, Pijassou has disproved that there was any such sale, and Goudal, the *régisseur*, continued to report to the owners in Amsterdam. What did happen was that in 1818 Mme Barbe-Rosalie Lemaire, ex-wife of Vanlerberghe and mother of Aimé Vanlerberghe, who is recorded as having visited Lafite to help with the 1819 vintage, paid 1 million frs. for the property. In 1821 she apparently re-sold Lafite to Sir Samuel Scott, partner in the banking firm of Sir Claude Scott, Baronet & Co., for 1 million frs. (The Scott bank was absorbed in 1894 by Parr's Bank, which in turn was amalgamated with the Westminster Bank.) When Sir Samuel died in 1849 he was succeeded at Lafite by his son, Mr Samuel Scott. It would appear that the 'sale' was made to ensure that the property was not split up, as it would be under French law, among the four children of the late Ignace-Joseph Vanlerberghe. Instead the English banker would act for the only son, Aimé. He, however, died in 1866 without issue, and it was then that the other members of his family decided to clear the matter up and pay the fines for not registering the name of the real owner back in 1821. So after nearly half a century the facts came to light. The first to reveal the main aspects of this story was Cyril Ray in his *Lafite: The Story of Château Lafite-Rothschild* (1968), but it was left to Pijassou to clarify the affair completely. An astonishing story!

Accordingly the property was put up for sale on 8 August 1868. It was keenly fought for by a Bordeaux syndicate, led by the merchant Gernon. These merchants wanted to avoid its falling into the hands of 'outsiders', but after a struggle it was acquired by a representative of Baron James de Rothschild for 4,140,000 frs., plus 300,000 frs. for the Carruades vineyard. With the cost of the auction and the reimbursement of the costs of cultivation that year, Lafite cost Baron James just on 4·8 million frs., the equivalent of about £3 million or $5·7 million in 1978. Baron James almost certainly bought Lafite purely as an investment, as did other bankers, including the Foulds (Beychevelle) and the Pereires (Palmer). As he died in November 1868 it is unlikely that he ever visited the château he had owned for just three months.

After the château had been sold, there was an auction in October 1868 of some of the old vintages from 1798, the date of the establishment of the famous *Vinothèque* mentioned on page 236. Seven bottles of this wine fetched only 12 frs. apiece (25 frs. to the £), and 60 bottles of the celebrated 1802 went for 11 frs. Of the 1803, there were 69 bottles offered, and they fetched 13 frs. each. The real interest lay in 21 bottles of the already mythical 1811, the *Vin de Comète*. M. Delhomme, proprietor of the Café Anglais in Paris, had come down specially for this sale and he started the bidding for the 1811 at 50 frs. But he had an opponent in M. Gremailly of the Hôtel des Princes in Bordeaux. When finally it was knocked down to the latter for the enormous price of 121 frs. a bottle, the victory for Bordeaux caused the locals to cheer. The price, equal to £5 at the time, would be at least the equivalent of £50 today.

Later vintages were also sold at this remarkable auction. The celebrated 1815 made 31 frs. for each of 35 bottles, and the 1823 – a vintage with a poor initial reputation but a fine one in later life – reached 60 frs. for each of 33 bottles, while 47 of the excellent 1834 made 70 frs. apiece. The fine 1847 was not offered, but 191 bottles of the robust 1848 went for 65 frs. each. The effect of the oidium scourge could be seen in the price of the 224 bottles of the 1854 – 18 frs. a bottle – while the first fine post-oidium year of 1858 made a high price for a ten-year-old wine: 195 bottles for 36 frs. each. The already renowned 1864 made 20 frs. apiece for 274 bottles, and a similar quantity of the château's second wine went for 10 frs. while six *barriques* of the 1865, still in cask, achieved between 2,850 and 3,200 frs. each.

Maybe there was an element of auction-room fever in some of these prices, for at about this period at Christie's in the doubtless more restrained atmosphere of St James's, the 1858 Lafite, château-bottled and 'bought of M. Goudal in 1864' (M. Émile Goudal was the manager of the château) fetched no more than 105s. a dozen, while the 1848 from the same source had gone for 126s. and the young 1864 had made only 68s. Nevertheless these were high prices for claret at the time.

In the French Rothschild family Lafite has remained ever since, the branch particularly associated with the bank in Paris being the chief shareholders, with generally a third or a sixth share in the château. Today there are five proprietors, with Baron Guy the major shareholder but Baron Élie taking the chief administrative burden until 1977 when Baron Éric, son of Guy, took over the main responsibility. Each of the proprietors is given annually *gratuit* two *barriques* of the new wine. The charming château, with its corner turret and terrace made familiar by one of the most elegant, unassuming Bordeaux labels, is furnished in the Second Empire style current when the house was acquired by the Rothschilds: a little heavy and bourgeois perhaps, but with the solid lavishness of a rich nineteenth-century family. In fact the furniture mostly came from Ch. Ferrières, the family mansion east of Paris where the terms of the Franco-Prussian Treaty were drafted at a desk now at Lafite. It was the Rothschilds who made possible the speedy payment of the 5 billion frs. indemnity, intended by the Prussians to be crushing, and the ink stain on the desk's surface is said to have been caused by Bismarck thumping it in fury at the quick payment by the Rothschilds. Around the walls of the reception rooms are comfortable-looking family portraits, many of the men bearing an unmistakable kinship; and up on the roof is a weathercock bearing the familiar five Rothschild arrows.

Below the stairs lies the celebrated *Vinothèque* of Lafite. Here rest the wines of one vineyard in a collection whose only rival is that of Schloss Johannisberg in the Rheingau. It was started by the manager, M. Goudal *père*, in 1798, the year after the public sale, and there are still eight bottles of the 1797 vintage, reputedly a poor thin year, lying in the rectangular trays that house the older wines. There are two bottles of the much finer 1798 vintage, and then follow varying numbers of the succeeding twenty years or so; of some vintages there are none, and of the famous 1811 'comet' year only one bottle remains. This was the wine served at the château on a famous occasion in 1926 and declared to be in perfect condition by the 300 guests to whom it was offered.

This alas was before my time, but I can claim to have drunk a Lafite senior in vintage and older in years. Towards the end of the 1950s the château for some reason decided to sell off a small quantity of unwanted wines. Most were of poor years, but there were one or two good vintages put in as *bonnes bouches*. Ronald Avery, the Bristol wine merchant, chanced to be in Bordeaux at the time, and he bought a mixed two dozen bottles, including the 1897 and three bottles of the 1803. This had been re-corked at the château in October 1957. I was privileged to share in the last of these three bottles, in April 1967, the others present being Ronald Avery and his son John, W. E. Newton a director of the firm, André Simon and George Rainbird. Although not surprisingly the colour was tawny, rather like that of a fine old Madeira, the aroma was very fine as it developed after being decanted immediately before being poured out. There was no doubt from the 'nose' and the flavour that this was claret. It had great distinction and for its age was surprisingly fruity; that it had maintained this fruitiness for just on 164 years was extraordinary. Only after half an hour in the decanter did the wine begin to show some sign of decline, but not much even then. The previous two bottles had both, I was told, been excellent too. It was the oldest bottle of claret that André Simon, then aged ninety, ever drank. The bottle itself, curved in shape rather like the bottle now used for Haut-Brion, was pitted. The 1803 vintage was average in quantity, and although good in quality, it had not been the equal of 1802, a rival of the exceptional 1798. After that there was not to be another really fine vintage until the fabled 1811.

It is worth digressing slightly here to mention that until well into the nineteenth century, vintages did not have the importance they have assumed since. There were the outstanding vintages which were known to wine drinkers, such as 1798, 1802, 1811, 1815 and 1819. When a first growth of one of these years turned up, the vintage would be mentioned. For example at Christie's in 1811, some Ch. Margot (*sic*) 1798 was sold and described as of 'celebrated vintage, bottled at London in 1802'. Four years earlier the same château's 1802 wine had been listed. Otherwise the wine would generally be sold as from Lafite or one of the other first growths, without a vintage date. Quite often it would be described purely as 'first growth claret'. There were exceptions as when the ordinary vintage of 1804 was mentioned at a sale of Lafite in 1814, but that was at the end of the Napoleonic Wars when claret was very hard to come by in England, and it fetched the good price of 80s. a dozen.

Vintages also came to the fore with the rise of the other classed-growth châteaux. No doubt in Bordeaux both growth and vintage had *réclame*, but so far as England was concerned it was not until well into the nineteenth century that any but first-growth clarets were sold by the name of the growth. Instead they relied on the names of the wine merchants who imported and bottled the wines. These were described as 'Barnes's Claret', Plasket's, Payne's, etc.

In May 1967 there was an outstanding sale of ancient wine at Christie's in London, and among these were some notable clarets from the cellars of the Earl of Rosebery. These included bottles and magnums of Lafite 1858, a single magnum of Lafite 1864, triple and double magnums of Lafite 1865, bottles of Lafite 1871, magnums and bottles of Lafite 1874 and two magnums of Lafite 1878. I was invited to taste a small selection of the wines before the sale, and one bottle of the famous Lafite 1858 was opened; it was drinkable but in decline, and nothing like so good as a bottle of Latour 1874. The top price was £155, given for a triple magnum of the Lafite 1865, but on a per-bottle basis the record item was the magnum of 1864, which fetched £82. The quantity of wines was as remarkable as the prices. There were 19 magnums of the 1858[*], as well as six bottles, 12 double magnums of the 1865 and no fewer than 40 magnums and 60 bottles of the 1874.

[*] It is interesting to note that in the sale at Christie's in 1867 already mentioned magnums of the 1858 'bottled on the estate' went for 150s. a dozen.

Nearly all were declared to be in good condition, i.e. with good corks and not ullaged. The only other clarets were a few bottles of Latour 1874 and Pichon-Longueville of unknown vintage. This also I tasted and it had a firmness that might have suggested an 1870. An indication of the increased interest, almost entirely American, in these celebrated old clarets is the sharp rise in prices when wines from the Rosebery and other cellars have been re-sold in the London auction rooms. By 1974 a magnum of Lafite 1874 that made a maximum of £38 in 1967 fetched £82; and a single bottle of Lafite 1870 that brought just over £18 a bottle in the Glamis Castle sale in June 1971 made £270 in December 1977, while in the following September a magnum of the same wine that had realized £83 at this auction went for £960.

The most remarkable range of Lafite vintages that I was privileged to taste was at the château itself at the beginning of October 1977, just before the late vintage that year, and consisted of a specially organized tasting of vintages from 1976 back to 1961 and three meals at which older vintages were drunk, back to 1869. The occasion was arranged by Baron Éric de Rothschild and the *régisseur*, M. Jean Crété, with a home team that also consisted of M. Yves Lecanu, the administrator, M. Guy Schÿler, the Bordeaux wine merchant who also organized publicity for Lafite, and M. Émile Peynaud, the celebrated Bordeaux University oenologist who was the technical adviser of Lafite, as of so many other estates in and outside of the Gironde. The guest tasters were Mme Odette Kahn, editor of the official *Revue du Vin de France*, Mr Frank Prial of the *New York Times*, Mr Abdallah Simon, well-known American importer of leading Bordeaux wines, M. Daniel Lawton, of the old-established brokerage firm of Tastet & Lawton, and myself. At the meals in the charming green and white dining-room, entirely candle-lit in the evenings, there were some changes among those present, the wife of M. Crété and my own being added to the company while M. Peynaud missed the second dinner at which the 1869 was served.

The older vintages tasted at this remarkable gathering are referred to in the later chapter on the vintages. Of the fourteen vintages laid out for tasting in the château's office – for the occasion transformed into a tasting-room, with white table-cloths, bread, water, spittoons, etc. – the '76 and '75 were cask samples; the first comparatively easy to taste in spite of its youth and big colour, the second, on the eve of being bottled, very 'oaky', hard and backward. Of the other vin-tages, the best were agreed to be '70, '66 and the magnificent though still backward '61. The '73, '67 and '62 were all light in their various ways, the '62 probably the best, while the '71 was lighter than expected. Most of the twelve wines opened at the meals – half of them magnums and two bottles apiece of the others – are mentioned in the vintages chapter. Among the others the '59 in magnum was perfect in its way, beautifully complete with a lovely aroma and a fruity, almost sweet flavour. I could not pretend to be very enthusiastic about the '34, for although it retained good colour and some elegance, it was the hard, tannic wine that nearly all the '34 Médocs have remained. The '18 was understandably brown in colour for a nearly sixty-year-old wine from such a moderate, though initially well-publicized vintage. The flavour was 'oaky', and if the wine was drying up yet it was still sur-prisingly drinkable.

One result of this extensive 'exercise', in which twenty-six vintages of Lafite were tasted and drunk in not much over twenty-four hours, was that the special character of this château's wines came through: claret with an elegant but fruity nose and a body that owed more to its balance than to 'size'. In light years, however, this sometimes led to lack of backbone. An unusual aperitif served before one of the meals was a 1959 'white Lafite'. It derived from a small patch of white grapes in the vineyard, now no longer grown. It tasted, as might be expected, rather like a dry white Graves, now slightly heavy, but with a flowery nose. In the early nineteenth century some white wine was made both at Latour and Lafite but this was gradually eliminated. This used to be made only for domestic drinking, as was the case at other châteaux. In 1977 some Mouton d'Armailhacq Blanc 1889 was sold at Christie's and some white Palmer 1920 also appeared in the sale-room.

When considering the naturally controversial matter of the relative placing of the first growths in the last century, it is material to note that in England, far and away the most important market, Lafite undoubtedly seems to have been the first. The evidence is to be found in the remarkable series of country-estate cellars 'unearthed' by Christie's in the 1960s and 1970s. In the Rosebery (1967), Meyrick (1970), Glamis Castle, Scotland (1971), Gladstone (1972) and Woodperry (1976), Lafites, usually of pre-phylloxera vintages, were always prominent and usually predominant. Latour came next, but a long way behind, while Ch. Margaux and Haut-Brion were very thinly represented and Mouton hardly at all. As the opening prices in Appendix C show, this supremacy was not by any means always represented in the prices that the other *premiers crus* were able to screw out of the Chartrons merchants and their brokers. Latour often sold for the same price as Lafite and occasionally more. Perhaps the merchants most influential in the English market, such as Barton & Guestier, favoured Lafite. Certainly the South-Wales cellar sold by Christie's in 1877, mentioned on page 144, included nine vintages of Lafite between 1847 and 1870 and only three apiece of Latour and Margaux. Where the shipper's name was given in the catalogue all were handled by Barton & Guestier or Cruse. Maybe Lafite was the snob name discreetly to be whispered by the butler as he poured from the claret jug. Whatever the reasons, Lafite undoubtedly appears to have enjoyed a definite priority in these islands in the second half of the last century; and the evidence remaining to us would at least confirm the fine quality of many of the wines.

Some of the Lafites of the 1870s in the Rosebery sale were château-bottled, but for many years, from the 1885 vintage in the phylloxera period until the 1906, it refused to accord château-bottling to the purchasers of its wine. In December 1976 and in the following year a large collection of château-bottled Lafite was sold at Christie's in London, including examples of vintages within these twenty-one years. However, these had come from members of the Rothschild family, and therefore had naturally been bottled at the château. Any château-bottled Lafite of the vintages 1885–1905 that may have found its way onto the open market will have come from this or other Rothschild family sources. It was only in 1925 that Lafite decided henceforth to bottle the whole of each *récolte*. Châteaux Margaux and Haut-Brion had started bottling the whole crop in 1923, Mouton-Rothschild followed in 1924, with its revolutionary 'modern art' label by Carlu, and Latour did the same in 1925.

The refusal of Lafite to allow château-bottling was perhaps occasioned by the fact that, although part of the 1884 crop had been bottled at the château, the buyers found the wine not up to standard and brought an action against the proprietors. Not until over twenty years later when the whole crop was bought by two Bordeaux merchants, Lebègue and Rosenheim, did Lafite again consent to château-bottling. (Château-bottling for part of the crop of the finer wines of Bordeaux only became general shortly before the First World War, about 1910 and 1911. At first it was regarded as an accolade of quality bestowed by the château only in good years, but this aspect has long since been abandoned.) Many years later Lafite also had trouble with a vintage. This was the 1928, which the Bordeaux merchants who had bought it declared not up to sample, and it had to be taken back after a court case. It was said to have been pasteurized.

Like the other leading growths Lafite has many other fine wines in its private cellar, for it was the practice of the château proprietors each good vintage to exchange a few cases with each other, and still is. In the Lafite *caveau*, for example, I noted Mouton-Rothschild 1869, Larose 1870, Smith-Haut-Lafitte 1878 and Léoville-Barton 1899 – a bin of about 15 dozen of this last wine. There were also some Carruades de Lafite 1907.

As already stated, the vineyard of Lafite is one of the largest of the classed growths, with an area of 80 ha (about 200 acres). However not all the production of this area is sold as Lafite. There is the plateau known as Carruades, which in fact runs across into Mouton-Rothschild, and at one time only the wine from this area was sold as Carruades de Lafite. Owing to the fact that for many years Lafite sold its second wine from the younger vines – generally those less than twelve years old – under this label, many people have thought that this was a less good part of the vineyard. In fact it is one of the best, and might well today be exclusively the property of Mouton-Rothschild. Until 1844 it was part of Mouton d'Armailhacq, and was then bought by Goudal, the *régisseur* of Lafite. Its 10 ha were at that time not under vines; it was then planted, but its wines were kept separate from those of the main vineyard. In the early 1850s Samuel Scott, the nominal owner of Lafite, expressed a desire to sell the Carruades. Goudal urged him not to do so, saying that it was a very fine part of the vineyard, and that it would be eagerly snapped up by the new owner of Mouton – Baron Ferdinand de Rothschild. This would be disastrous, said Goudal, and would give countenance to the already-heard claims of Mouton to be a first growth. Indeed Mouton made an attempt to buy it, but were just beaten by no less than M. Vanlerberghe, the undercover real owner of Lafite. So in fact this part of the Carruades remained part of Lafite, though some belongs to Mouton.

There was some excellent wine sold under the Carruades

label, one fairly recent one being 1953. Then in 1966 it was decided to discontinue the use of the name for the second wine, because it caused confusion among the less knowledgeable and in restaurants, where it was sometimes listed as Lafite itself. There used to be a third wine, Moulin-de-Carruades, all château-bottled and normally reserved for exclusive sale within France by the Paris firm of Nicolas. In 1974, however, it was decided to use this name generally for the château's second wine from the young vines, thus avoiding the word Lafite on the label.

While on the subject of second wines, most châteaux have one or more *sous-noms* and very confusing they can be, for often they are not widely known. Sometimes they are used because some of the wine in any given vintage comes from vines too young to have their produce sold under the château label, or the wine is otherwise not up to the standard of what at first-growth level is called the *grand vin*. Another reason for their use may be a possible limit to the sale of an estate's wine under its château name, whereas purchasers may be found for the wine under an alternative label. This applies particularly to the *crus bourgeois* and is said to be particularly prevalent in St-Estèphe. In 1974 the authorities in Bordeaux recommended that no château should be allowed more than two names under which to sell its wine. This emphasizes what should never be overlooked: that Bordeaux estate names are brand names and can be used indiscriminately so long as they do not violate the *AC* regulations or those of the *crus classés*.

However, about 250 *tonneaux* of wine are sold as Lafite, which is usually more than the other first growths. In 1973 a record total of 387 *tonneaux* was made, including the Carruades. Lafite is generally rather a delicate wine for a Pauillac, much less robust than its neighbour at Mouton or at Latour. This is partly to be ascribed to the soil, partly to the composition of the vineyard which is said to contain more Merlot than its neighbours, and partly to the method of vinification.

At the château I was told that the vineyard was 68 per cent Cabernet-Sauvignon, 13 per cent Cabernet-Franc and 18 per cent Merlot. What is not always realized with regard to these statistics is that the various grapes do not perform uniformly vintage after vintage. The Merlot may be caught by spring frosts, the Cabernet-Sauvignon develop particularly late and even not ripen adequately, so its proportion will be reduced when the *assemblage* for the *grand vin* is carried out. For example, where there was 20 per cent Merlot in the Lafite 1949, the 1961 only contained 11 per cent, precisely owing to spring frosts catching the early-budding variety. So while the 1970 contained 18 per cent of Merlot and the 1971 a mere 10 per cent, in 1975 and 1976 the percentages were 24 and 20 respectively. It might be an interesting if perhaps confusing exercise to try to detect differences in the wines according to the proportions of each grape. These figures were given me at the château. In successful years Lafite is the acme of fine claret, well-balanced, elegant and supple with a delicious aroma. Its 1945 is generally regarded as the top wine of the vintage, although this might be contested by those who like a more full-bodied wine. In less good vintages it lacks the stamina of Latour and may be rather thin and disappointing. In recent years its opening price has risen astronomically.* Whereas the highly esteemed 1953 was first offered to the British and American trade at the equivalent of £100 or less a hogshead, the 1964 went for £572 and the 1966 for £695. The 1967 was sold for the same price in francs as the 1966, but owing to sterling devaluation in November 1967 the price in Britain was nearly £800. In spite of franc devaluation in 1969, that year's short-crop Lafite opened at £1,325 a cask. The 1971 vintage was first offered at 110,000 frs. per *tonneau* and the opening price to the trade in the U.K. was £2,800 per cask. These extravagant prices were the result mostly of a world-wide and particularly an American demand for the

* *See* Appendix D.

first-growth clarets, but partly also to the well-known rivalry between Lafite and Mouton-Rothschild. But Nemesis was at hand.

No ancient *premier cru* vintages seem to match Lafite for prices in the saleroom today; possibly because of its special reputation, as well as of the surprising amount that has come to light. At Christie's in September 1977 a record price was paid for a single bottle of wine: £8,300 for Lafite 1806; and in 1978 at a Heublein sale in Texas, conducted by Christie's, a jeroboam of Lafite 1864 brought another record of $18,000.

If historic Lafites have fetched extraordinarily high prices at auction, this is true also of the vintages of the post-Second World War epoch. In November 1978 at Christie's a case of Lafite '45 passed the £150 a bottle mark, and was sold for £1,900, while the '47 rose to £700 a dozen and £840 per six magnums, the '49 to £620 and the '61 to £820. At such prices – and they were nearly matched and occasionally exceeded by the other first growths – the question must arise as to whether these wines are for drinking or for trading. For they are not rarities in the way that the historic bottles are.

Latour has a longer history than Lafite, more dramatic in the earlier times, less eventful until recently, less known later on. Or this was so until 1963, when a huge hoard of documents, most of them hitherto unknown and none properly worked on, was discovered in a bureau on the retirement of the eighty-four-year-old *régisseur*, M. Pierre Brugière. Covering a period of 600 years, they cast new light not only on the estate of Latour itself, but on its neighbours and on wine-making in the Médoc as a whole. The value of these was at once seen by Mr David Pollock, the chairman of the company, and his colleagues, and they enlisted the help of Professor Charles Higounet of the history faculty of Bordeaux University and editor of a valuable seven-volume history of Bordeaux, then in course of publication. Of a team of the professor's colleagues the main task of writing the history fell on Pijassou, officially a geographer, but best known for his historical works on the Médoc, for which he received a doctorate in 1978. The two-volume work, running to almost 700 pages, was commissioned both by the château and by the university; it was published in 1974 under the title of *La Seigneurie et le vignoble de Château Latour*, and is certainly the most important work on a Bordeaux wine château to be published. This is not to underestimate the value of Pijassou's accompanying work on Lafite, but the documentation, so plentiful for most of the period since Latour became a wine-producing estate, is lacking there. For while absentee land-lordism is generally to be deplored, it has its compensations for later generations if it results in correspondence that would otherwise not have taken place. There are over 1,000 letters written between 1775 and 1865, and after a gap another long series between 1883 and 1932. Unfortunately Brugière's correspondence, if there was any, has not survived, but the annual reports made by one or other of the family adminis-trators have, and Pijassou has been able to call on other sources, including the unique records of prices kept by Tastet & Lawton. As it is highly unlikely that these tomes will be translated into English, I am able, with due acknowledgement, to pass on in this book a small fraction of the information contained in them.

According to the *Histoire militaire de Bordeaux* (Ribadieu), in the early days of the English in Gascony the châtelains of Latour were pro-Plantagenet, a record that may be con-sidered satisfactory by the present British owners. The tower was one of a line of fortifications, erected as a kind of pre-Martello line, against the ocean-going pirates. It is said that this particular link in the chain lay to the south of the existing domed tower, whose appearance owes more to the evocative quality produced by the name of the wine than to any great distinction of its own. Apparently the Latour proprietors did not hesitate to take tribute from the Bordelais navigators as well as from the more suspect Breton mariners who ventured up the Gironde. At some point it evidently passed into French hands, as Jean de Neuville, described as a lieutenant of the English King in Gascony, took it from the French under siege in 1378. Curiously enough this siege was mentioned by Froissart in his *Chronicles*, the tower being designated as 'Saint Maubiert', its name in fact then being St-Maubert. Later this became Saint Mambert, then Saint Lambert, a name which still exists as a suburb of Pauillac. In 1444 it was retaken by Bertrand de Montfaucon, but a few years later recaptured by the pro-English Gaston de Lisle, Baron de la Brède. How it finally passed into French hands is not clear, but there is no truth in the story that the remnants of Talbot's army passed beneath its walls in 1453 after the Battle of Castillon. Possibly it was confiscated after the emigration of its owner, for other sources have suggested that it was owned by the Sire de Larsan on the English side, who when defeated sought refuge in England, and the *manoir* was sacked and burnt. The tower, incidentally, was not round but square, and it appears to have stood more or less on the site of the existing *chais*.

At this period the *seigneurie* was not in the hands of one family, but of many; after several generations of de Lisles, Gaston de la Touche became the principal owner in 1571, and he was followed by Arnaud de Mullet, whose family consolidated their hold on the whole property. At this time wine was certainly grown in the commune of St-Maubert, but it cannot be said that there was a separate *domaine* of Latour until near the end of the seventeenth century. An invoice made out by a Bordeaux merchant in 1714 for a cargo of wine to be shipped to Holland specifically mentions Latour, with a price of 450 livres a *tonneau*, compared with 550 livres for Pontac (Haut-Brion) and 410 for Lafite. So by then the vineyard must have been well-established.

The estate which had been bought in 1670 by M. de Chavanas, passed in 1677 to the Clauzel family and then by marriage to the Ségurs. As already mentioned in the chapter on the rise of the estates, Latour was valued at over half a million livres at the death of the Marquis Nicolas-Alexandre de Ségur in 1755, and it passed, along with Lafite, to his four daughters, one of whom married a cousin, Alexandre de Ségur-Calon, a member of the Bordeaux Parlement and later provost of Paris. In due course in 1760 he handed over Latour to his three sisters-in-law, and this established the independence of Latour from Lafite, and encouraged its development. Of the three Ségur sister co-proprietors, Marie-Antoinette-Victoire's family became the most important, as her two daughters married the Comte de la Pallu and the Marquis André de Beaumont, who acquired or inherited all but 27·6 per cent of the property, which fell to the Comte de Ségur-Cabanac, part-recipient of the share of his mother, and an aunt.

This division was to cause a good deal of trouble later on, for the Comte de Ségur-Cabanac fled abroad at the Revolution and his part of Latour was confiscated and sold in the same way as Lafite. Divided again, this part passed into several hands, including a prominent ship-owner, a doctor and a widow; and they paid a total of 219,724 livres for it. Unlike Lafite and Margaux, Latour was not directly affected by the Revolution. The *régisseur*, Domenger, who had run both Lafite and Latour from 1774 until 1785, when M. de Pichard acquired the former, continued on at Latour until his death in 1797. He was the first of the *régisseurs* whose letters survive. He was succeeded by Poitevin (1797–1807), who did much to improve the estate, and Lamothe (1807–35), who, as the volumes on the history of Latour show, combined technical skill and a ready pen and wit with considerable skill in lining his pockets at the expense of the absentee proprietors. The wines of his own property at Mousset in Pauillac near Lafite were *élevés* at Latour and perhaps blended with the first growth.

The whole estate was still cultivated as one, but in 1833

Barton & Guestier succeeded in purchasing nearly half the financially hived-off portion, and in 1840 Nathaniel Johnston bought the rest. This curious episode in the estate's history might well have led eventually to the loss of control by the descendants of Ségur. However, by then the family pro-prietors had seen the danger and when the other 13/144ths of the shares had been auctioned in 1839 they had re-acquired ten of the shares, but Barton & Guestier picked up the other three, so that the trade now had a not inconsiderable twenty-nine shares (20 per cent) of the equity. Since 1833 Barton & Guestier had taken their share of the profits in kind, repaying some to cover the costs of production; and Nathaniel Johnston was advancing money to cover these costs, so acting as a banker. In 1840 he announced his intention of giving up this role for Latour. So the noble owners – five of them by then – decided the following year to put the estate up to auction, with an estimated value of 1,200,000 frs. The final price that the family had to pay was 1,511,000 frs., which meant that the three merchants secured 311,286 frs. – not much of a capital gain on their investment – and the family regained all the estate after nearly half a century. Taking no more chances, in 1842 they formed a private company, with the associated peers taking shares varying between 35 and 25 out of the total still of 144. This did not lead to a breach with the merchants, who indeed held the whip-hand when it came to buying the wine, and from 1844 to 1853 Barton & Guestier held the exclusivity of the whole crop. At this time it was valued at $1\frac{1}{2}$ million frs., and in the prosperous 1860s the wine sold for much the same price as Lafite. The manager was M. Roux, a notary and mayor of Pauillac. The vineyard was then said to be in excellent condition. It is impossible here to follow the fortunes of Latour or of the three families who owned and administered it through the head of one of them. Some further historical information is to be found in other chapters.

One incident, however, is worth recounting, as it shows the

value of a *premier cru* at a not conspicuously favourable period. It was mentioned in the chapter on the estates that the family nearly sold the property in 1889. In November of that year an offer, on behalf of an unknown client, was sent by a prominent notary in Bordeaux to the administrator for the family share-holders, the Vicomte A. de Courtrivon. The price named was 3 million frs., based on an average revenue of 200,000 frs., derived from an estimated price of 3,000 frs. per *tonneau*, i.e. a purchase price of 15 years' turnover. The family response was well disposed, but favoured negotiation for a higher figure, and within a few days the Vicomte had signed an option to sell at 3,350,000 frs. This worked out at nearly 80,000 frs. per ha (£1,290 an acre), an exceptionally high price considering that the Rothschilds had paid 60,000 frs. for Lafite in 1868, and in the intervening years Bordeaux had experienced the phylloxera, oidium and economic depression. Pijassou, writing in the early seventies, states that this was the equivalent of 400,000 (new) frs. today; a very high price, although on the basis of a first growth being worth double a second, whose market value was at least 250,000 frs. per ha, it might have been higher still. In view of inflation since Pijassou was writing, these figures might well be nearly doubled for the end of the seventies. The contract was due to be signed on 22 December, but in the preceding week the notary wrote to say that his client was not prepared to go ahead, but the whole negotiation would remain 'the deepest secret'. And so it did until the Latour papers were examined.

In the later years it was the Beaumont family who took the lead in administration until in 1962 the property was sold to an English company representing the family interests of Viscount Cowdray. This company took 51 per cent of the shares, Harvey's of Bristol, the well-known wine merchants, acquired 25 per cent and the remaining 24 per cent of the shares stayed in French hands, with Comte Hubert de Beau-mont, the former chairman, and Comte Philippe de Beaumont

representing them on the board. The English buyers are said
to have paid over £900,000. This sale did not go through without some protest from those who thought that control of so
famous a first growth should not pass into foreign hands. However it was pointed out that Haut-Brion had been American-
owned for many years, and General de Gaulle to whom the
matter was said to have been referred is alleged to have remarked that the English company could scarcely remove the
soil. Judging from the fact that the estate's published profits
for 1970 were £254,000 before tax and for 1971 were
£542,000, the deal must be considered amply successful; and
in 1972 the profits were estimated at over £1 million.

Latour was the first *premier cru* château to be listed with
vintage date in a Christie's wine auction. This was the Latour
1785 of which 500 bottles were sold in a trade sale in 1792.
The top price was 44s. per dozen in bond. Later, in 1824, its
output was given by Franck as 70–90 *tonneaux*.

It is interesting that when the present owners of Latour took
over they found small parcels of the vineyard in the hands of
peasant proprietors. These totalled several hectares and were
gradually acquired from them. Only in 1790 did Latour come
into Pauillac; previously it had been in St-Lambert.

The vineyard of Latour, substantially smaller than Lafite
and also seldom subject to frost, comprises 60 ha of Cabernet-
Sauvignon (80 per cent), Cabernet-Franc (10 per cent) and
Merlot (10 per cent); and it produces an average approaching
200 *tonneaux* a year of the *grand vin*. Since it was taken over
by the present owners, there has been a great deal of replanting,
part in a separate vineyard, some way back from the main
one, near Batailley. In the exceptionally prolific year of 1970
the production was 216 *tonneaux* of *grand vin* and 81 *tonneaux*
of a second wine. Very sensibly it was decided to sell this 1970
second wine separately, but not to put it onto the market until
it was reasonably mature. Labelled Les Forts de Latour, it
consisted initially of wine made from vines less than twelve

years old, but as the average vineyard age has increased this may not be strictly adhered to, and this second wine will be derived from the *cuves* considered not good enough to be included in the *grand vin*. The first vintage of Les Forts de Latour was 1966, and it was not sold until 1972, along with the lighter 1967. The 1970 was not generally disposed of until 1978, after the 1971. The price is about the equivalent of that asked for the more popular second growths. In the record year of 1973 no less than 419 *tonneaux* were filled, but some was sold as plain Pauillac, and some even as *vin de consommation*.

Latour is a powerful wine of a style largely derived from the high proportion of Cabernet-Sauvignon – 80 per cent – in the vineyard. That this has always been its characteristic may be gauged from Franck's comment in 1824 that Latour had 'more body' than Lafite but needed to be kept a year more in cask. Also a chemist, M. Faure in his *Analyse chimique des grands vins de la Gironde*, quoted in Danflou (1866), stated that the wines of Latour had a stronger nose and a more pronounced flavour than those of Lafite and Margaux. Its character no doubt also arises from the soil, situation and vinification, for the proportion of Cabernet-Sauvignon at Mouton-Rothschild is no less, but the wines are quite distinct in type.

So powerful and strong, almost coarse, is Latour in youth that it is difficult to taste and even not very agreeable, particularly in fine years. In any tasting of fairly mature first growths, Latour is almost invariably the most backward. Good examples of this were 1945, 1949 and 1961. On the other hand Latour has wonderfully fruity qualities, and if it lacks the elegance of Lafite, the concentration of Mouton and the charm of Margaux, it has a splendid depth and richness of flavour. This can still be seen in the 1920 and 1929 wines, and the former surely remains as it has always been, the best wine of the vintage.

Moreover Latour usually makes exceptionally good wine in off or indifferent vintages. In about 1966 a special tasting of off-vintage Latours was arranged for me at the château. They started with '63 and continued with '56, '54, '51, '46, '44, '41, '40, '39 and '33. The last was not by any means an off-year, but it was put in as a *bonne bouche* at the end, and to show the lasting power of Latour in a light vintage. Otherwise these years were not only generally poor, but the older wines of most other growths would long since have died. However with Latour only the '56 was non-agreeable, but that was an exceptionally bad vintage. The '39 was definitely on the way down, but who could blame it a quarter of a century after such a deplorable harvest? The wartime examples were brown in colour but perfectly drinkable. I picked out the '40; but my choice of them all was, unexpectedly to me, the '46 which was surprisingly full and well-balanced. It is fair to say that M. Metté, then the *maître de chai*, gave his vote to the '51, an excellent wine for its year which I have drunk a number of times. On this occasion the '58 was not on show, but that was another excellent Latour in a lightweight year, and the '60 is the best wine of the year.

An even more exceptional if concentrated opportunity to taste Latour vintages was given by Christie's in June 1977 at an evening pre-sale tasting, prior to an auction of 81 vintages of this château's wine, including every vintage from 1916 to 1974; at the tasting cask samples of the '75 and '76 were also available, in addition to a selection of 37 vintages of those to be sold – an occasion unique in my not inconsiderable experience of tasting a range of one château's wines. Clearly more extended than the Lafite tasting three months later, there was little more than an hour in which to taste almost 40 vintages. So, as I always abide by the rules of starting at the youngest and finishing with the most senior, by the time I reached the 1865 it had been decanted well over an hour, with the bottle tipped up many times, so it tasted very thin, with little fruit and body remaining; but I was told by those more precipitate or agile on the palate that it had been splendid. Moreover, as will be seen in the chapter on vintages, it had been very fine at the château nine years earlier.

In such a marathon which had to be run more or less at a sprint, fleeting impressions could not be all that significant, but for the record the best vintages, in ascending order of age, seemed to me to be '70, '66, '61, '49, '29, '26 and '97. Some might expect the '28 to have been in my first 'team', for it is commonly said that the '28 is now superior to the '29. However, I compared closely the two bottles of each available, and the '29 was still a beautifully round claret of great character, whereas the '28, though fine, retained the slight severity that has nearly always marked that vintage. So I preferred the '29*. My second team included '71, '67, '64 (exceptionally well-balanced for this unequal vintage, and with a lovely aroma, this was one of the surprises of the tasting), '55, '46, '45 (although described in the catalogue as 'one of the greatest ever' this particular bottle was oxydized or out of condition, but the catalogue stated that it had been re-corked in 1967; see my note in the vintage chapter), '28 and '90. The '59 was disappointing, with some acidity. The '20, though two bottles were later sold at £170 apiece, was not in the tasting. The '99 was, but this too was rather dry on the nose and palate. It is scarcely fair to judge such very old clarets lately moved from their original resting place. Both the young cask samples showed very well, particularly the '75, but they were too young to be included even in a junior 'eleven'.

Prices at the subsequent sale – an exercise in prestige and publicity rather than an off-loading of surplus stock – were often phenomenally high. The first lot, an imperial of 1900, went to an American bidder for £2,800, a jeroboam of '06 made £700, and other notable prices for the 'modern' vintages were £540 for an imperial of '24, £280 for a magnum of '29, £920 per dozen for the '45, £740 for a dozen of the

---

* This conclusion was confirmed by those present at a dinner in my home in October 1978. Both bottles had long been in my cellar.

'47, £620 for a dozen of the '49, £560 for a jeroboam of the '52, £600 for a jeroboam of the '59 and £540 per six magnums of the '61. Of the nineteenth-century rarities, the top price for one of the three bottles of 1863 was £380, single bottles of the 1865 made up to £310 and the 1899 sold at the rate of £110 a bottle. Many of the successful bidders were American. Remarkable prices were also paid for such off-vintages as '31, '32 and '41 – often well over £30 a bottle. It was believed that some of the buyers were eager to commemorate their birth years! This extraordinary sale realized over £76,000.

The virtual reconstruction of the *cuvier* and *chais* at Latour in the sixties included the installation of nineteen stainless steel fermentation vats, the larger holding 200 hl and costing £1,500 apiece. The only other château to install stainless steel vats throughout, though of different design, is Haut-Brion, though experimentally Lafite put in three. These have caused controversy and head-shaking in Bordeaux, but at Latour they state that better control can be secured during the fermentation, cold water can be poured over them to reduce temperature and the fact that vats are of stainless steel is irrelevant; the wine is normally only in them for ten to fifteen days and thereafter is matured in wood. They were first used in the 1964 vintage, in which Latour came out particularly well; so time alone will show. Certainly the '66 is a big fruity wine, and so is the second wine of Les Forts de Latour, also vinified in the stainless steel vats. The '67 appears a bigger wine than many others of the vintage.

For consistency over the years, I am inclined to think that Latour leads the firsts (with which I must in this and other contexts now include Mouton-Rothschild). It is not always so distinguished a wine as the others at their best, but it has fruit and quality. In any one fine vintage, it may be beaten by its rivals: by Lafite in '45, Mouton in '49, and by several in '53. Yet overall its record is impressive, and faced by the need to select one bottle from all the leaders in a vintage unknown to me or of lesser repute I would certainly select the Latour. But of course I could be wrong.

The actual château of Latour is a small, post-Tuileries Second Empire building which has now been redecorated by its English owners. The interior is as charming and comfortable as a small English country house, and to its dark-papered dining-room are brought up notable bottles from the small private cellar below. From the windows is a fine view of the Gironde, the only first growth with such a prospect.

The small *caveau privé* of Latour is notable for the representation of its own wines, but for a general collection not so much as the other leading châteaux; the reason being that in the past Latour did not exchange so regularly as the others. The earliest Latour is the 1863, an off-vintage in a remarkable decade, and there were 30 bottles when I first saw them. A bottle shared in 1970 was remarkably fruity. There were also 18 bottles left of the famous 1865, and this was proclaimed remarkable in the year of its centenary. It was no less remarkable when I was privileged to drink it at the château three years later: an amazingly full-bodied, fruity wine. Further comments will be found in the chapter on Bordeaux vintages. There are many gaps, but of the great 1899 I noted 100 bottles, and many more of less ancient years, including several hundred of the 1929, of which no fewer than ten dozen were sent to London for André Simon's ninetieth birthday banquet in February 1967. A curiosity is a number of glass-stoppered bottles full of wine and of age unknown; to open them it would be necessary to remove the neck. I believe that elsewhere examples of glass-stoppered Lafites have been found.

At the Rosebery sale in 1967, already mentioned, the highest price reached for old wines in bottle, rather than in magnums or larger sizes, was for 13 bottles of Latour 1874. All were bought by Harvey's at 6,200s. a dozen, or £25 16s. 8d. a bottle. This was one of the wines which I sampled beforehand; it was in excellent condition, showing no sign of decline.

In the last century Latour was particularly popular in Britain and, according to the 1853 edition of Franck's *Traité sur les vins du Médoc*, in favourable years the English were the largest buyers. In those days it averaged between 70 and 90 *tonneaux* a year, compared with 100 to 150 for Lafite.

The chairman of the board of Latour until 1978 was David Pollock. By an odd coincidence, facing the title page of Michel's *Histoire du commerce et de la navigation à Bordeaux* (1867) is a long pull-out English map of the siege of Blaye in 1592. The places on the Médoc side of the estuary are marked and Pauillac is spelled Pollock. The chairman is now Clive Gibson.

The controversial question of Mouton-Rothschild and its standing in the classification is discussed elsewhere,★ but there is no doubt that Mouton, its image and its ambience, add a good deal of colour as well as quality to Bordeaux and the repute of fine claret. There are those who disapprove of what they would call the publicity-consciousness, the restlessness which insists on a new label, designed by a well-known artist, each year. When I first visited Mouton not long after the Second World War, the richly furnished *salle de réception* with its visitors' book covered with the large-scale signatures and gushing praise of American visitors, and the indirectly illuminated Mouton arms at the end of the great *chai*, struck an unusual note among its fellows. To visit Lafite afterwards was like entering a monastery. But now nearly all the leading châteaux and some minor growths have *salles de réception*; most of them designed with far less taste and skill than at Mouton.

This growth is presided over by one of the great 'committed' proprietors of Bordeaux. All the vineyard owners are proud of their wine, but some whom I have met have a special attachment, differing widely in expression. Among these I would place Henri Binaud of Cantemerle, Ronald Barton of

★ In June 1973 Mouton-Rothschild was made a first growth.

Léoville and Langoa-Barton (though more quietly as befits an Anglo-Saxon), Henri Woltner of La Mission-Haut-Brion, Raymond Dupin of Grand-Puy-Lacoste, Jean-Eugène Borie of Ducru-Beaucaillou and above all Baron Philippe de Rothschild. Although his father, Baron Henri, was the proprietor before him, the former was more interested in literature and the theatre. Philippe, brought up in Paris, scarcely visited Mouton before he was grown-up. His grandmother ran the estate, efficiently but perhaps without special flair, from the death in 1881 of her husband, Baron James, to 1920. For many years the labels bore the name of the actual director, Baron de Miollis. The Baroness's name was Laura Thérèse and she came from the Frankfurt branch of the family. When in 1920 the Baroness James was seventy-three she partly handed over to her son, but within two years he had passed the property on to the twenty-year-old Philippe, who ran it on his own from 1922 onwards. There is no doubt that he transformed the estate and its reputation.

As mentioned earlier, the name Mouton has none of the ovine significance to which the heraldic supporters of the arms give credence. A *motte de terre* is an eminence, and indeed in relation to the slightly lower ground towards the estuary, it is such. Originally part of the Lafite estate, the growth seems to have been established as an entity in the reign of Louis XV, when it belonged to the Brane (or Branne) family, later associated with Brane-Cantenac, and previously with a link to Haut-Brion. According to Armailhacq, neighbour of the Branes, writing in the 1850s, it was the first Brane, grandfather of the one in his day, who had acquired the seigneurial rights of the barony of Mouton, which no longer existed; this gave him the right to call his *domaine* Mouton, though he and his family lived in Le Pouyalet and it was the Armailhacqs who lived at Mouton. As will be seen when discussing Mouton-Baron-Philippe later in this chapter, Armailhacq was a little sensitive about being criticized for appending the name

Mouton to the wines of his estate. Baron Hector de Branne was one of the great improvers of the Médoc vineyards, like his neighbour A. d'Armailhacq, and together they are said to have been responsible for introducing the Cabernet-Sauvignon to the Médoc. If so they largely made claret what it has become. The wine of Branne-Mouton had a reputation in Bordeaux, but it was not widely known before the Revolution. The first mention I can find of it in a Christie catalogue was in 1834, alongside Lafite and Latour, and all without vintage date. It was noted again in 1842 and some eight dozen Branne-Mouton, bottled 1835, were in one of the mammoth sales of the cellar of Crockford's Club in 1852. It fetched the moderate price of 59s. a dozen. But even at this time named clarets were the exception, and they were still mostly sold under such merchants' names as Randolph Payne or Maxwell & Keys. In fact after Branne sold Mouton in 1830 to M. Thuret it appears to have been somewhat neglected, which is partly why Baron Nathaniel Rothschild, a member of the English branch of the family, was able to buy it in 1853 comparatively cheaply and for less money than M. Thuret had paid for it (*see* page 124). However, the Mouton production had been considerable, and was given in 1824 as averaging 120–140 *tonneaux*.

The other reason was probably the current oidium then ravaging the Médoc; and it was five years before the new owner could harvest a good vintage. The vineyard was greatly improved by the manager, M. Galos, and he planted it with Cabernet-Sauvignon. Previously it had not been an entirely united vineyard, having strips detached from the rest, a not uncommon situation in the Médoc. To this day two of the three parts of the Léoville vineyard are somewhat intertwined, and below the walls of Ronald Barton's château of Langoa lie parts of Poyferré's portion.

What there was not at Mouton was a château or house of any size; merely a farm. Baron Nathaniel was more interested in improving the property than in building a house, and it was his son Baron James, succeeding his father in 1870, who in the middle of the *chai* courtyard in 1880–83 built the small and charming Second Empire style house now known as Petit-Mouton. Here the family lived until the late fifties, when the first floor of the adjacent stable buildings was converted into a series of splendid apartments, including an open-beamed library and a long gallery overlooking the vineyard. In this gallery are assembled and skilfully placed an ingenious variety of eye-catching *objets d'art*, including an Italian Renaissance painter's wooden model of a horse.

Petit-Mouton, still used for guests and occasional meals, is also full of interesting *objets*, including a collection of English needlework pictures, assembled by Baron Philippe when he was in England during the last war. However, vinously the most interesting item is a fine French carpet presented by Napoleon III to Queen Victoria in 1860. The design shows a slim Napoleon holding one end of a scroll inscribed, 'THE TREATY OF COMMERCE – A further proof of our FRIEND- SHIP'. The other end is held by Queen Victoria, less kindly depicted as already somewhat generous in girth. In the side panels are 'N' and 'V' and across the bottom is written '*LA RÉCIPROCITÉ EST LA BASE VRAIE ET DURABLE DE LA PAIX.*' For some reason this curious carpet was ejected from the royal household and subsequently bought by Baron Philippe; it is highly appropriate that this memorial of a treaty which did so much to increase the Bordeaux trade with Britain should find a place in the Médoc.

Under the Rothschild regime, production was increased and by 1865 140 *tonneaux* were produced, and 170 in the following year. There were by then 55 ha under vines.

Mouton is unusual for the high proportion of Cabernet- Sauvignon in the vineyard, perhaps as high as 88 per cent, with 7 per cent Cabernet-Franc and the balance Merlot and Petit-Verdot. Its output is now about 200 *tonneaux*. The wine is distinguished for its fullness and concentration of flavour. It is a rich wine, and more than once I have mistaken it for one of the top Pomerols such as Pétrus. Sometimes almost burgundian in its power, it is probably the most individual of all the Médocs. As already mentioned, the classification problem is discussed in Chapter 17, but if a Bordeaux classification was to mean anything Mouton-Rothschild should in 1855 have been in the top class. A very different style of wine is produced at Mouton from its neighbours, but no serious wine drinker can doubt the exceptional quality or the record of fine vintages in the last hundred years or so. Mouton is said to have *un goût de capsule*, but I have seldom captured this, although on occasion its other alleged point of individuality, an aroma of cedar-wood, or lead pencils, has come home to me. The special quality of Mouton must lie in the soil and in the method of vinification. The *cuvier*, with its seventeen large fermenting vats all made of oak, is built on the traditional two-storey principle, with the vats being filled from above. This is also to be seen at the neighbouring Pontet-Canet. When the fermentation is over, the wine stays in the *cuves* for another fortnight before being transferred to brand new oak casks. One of the sights of Mouton and of the other leading châteaux is the carefully aligned ranks of new oak casks for the new wine. Only the top growths can afford these days to have entirely new casks every time, for they cost over £50 apiece. To spend about £40,000 a year on new casks as they do at Mouton even for a bad vintage is a formidable outlay. They must certainly make some difference to the style of the wine, for young oak does give a flavour quite distinct from the rather disagreeable taste of a wine which is 'casky'. Mouton like all the fairly large châteaux has several cellars: one for the first year's wine, and another for the second year's. Save in very poor years, the leading growths do not normally bottle until the winter or spring of the third year after the vintage. In this case the older wine generally stays in the second-year cellar.

The vineyard of Mouton-Rothschild is 75 ha in extent, and 70 are now in production. To the north it is separated only by a cart track from Lafite. Elsewhere it adjoins Mouton-Baronne-Philippe, and to the south-east it marches with Pontet-Canet.

Mouton, like Latour, often makes good wine in off-years, but this is less true of the other top growths. At tastings at Mouton in the sixties I sampled such vintages as '60, '58, '56, '54, '51, '50, '46 and '44. The best of these were the '58, '51 and '46. The '60 was very fair and so was the '54, and only the '56 – a terrible Bordeaux year – and the '50 were unattractive. The '44 had a fine nose but lacked fruit, while the '46, also so good at Latour, was remarkably round and fruity for very much of an off-year.

Mouton has always been more publicity- or sales-conscious than the other châteaux, although this is now considered less 'bad form' than it used to be. One aspect of this was close attention to the design of the labels. The first one which broke away from a traditional style was the brightly coloured design by Carlu employed from 1924 to 1926, and distinctly advanced for its time, with the famous Rothschild arrows prominent. In 1934 the idea was hit upon of inscribing on the label the number of bottles produced in each size, and numbering each. For example the label of the famous 1945 reads:

> Cette récolte a produit
> 24 jéroboams numérotés de A à Y.
> 1475 magnums numér. de M 1 à M 1475
> 74,422 bout. et $\frac{1}{2}$ bout. numér. de 1 à 74,422
> 2000 Réserve du Château marquées R.C.
> Cette bouteille porte le No. . . .
> > Philippe de Rothschild

The 1945 was a small vintage but in 1959, for example, the number of bottles and halves was given as 151,744 and the proportion between the two was probably much the same as before. There were 2,091 magnums and 116 *Grands Formats*, which is the formula now used to include double magnums, jeroboams and impériales. There have been several large vintages since. The label on the 1970 vintage, one of the biggest in Bordeaux, reads:

> Cette récolte a produit
> 315,000 Bordelaises et ½ Bses, de 1 à 315,000
> 7,000 Magnums de M 1 à M 7,000
> 615 Grands Formats de G. F. 1 à G. F. 615
> double-magnums, jéroboams, impériales
> 5,000 Réserve du Château marquées R.C.

The number reserved for the château varies, but it is never less than 2,000; in 1947 it was 4,000, and 3,000 in 1955. The only two years when the numbered label was omitted were 1953 and 1973. The former commemorated the centenary year of the Rothschild acquisition of Mouton. It carried a medallion of Baron Nathaniel, ovals containing the names of the two subsequent family owners and underneath, signed by Baron Philippe, a dedication of the vintage to three of his predecessors. Fortunately Mouton made an exceptionally good wine that year. The second occasion when the details of the bottles were not on the label was in 1973, when the label carried a reproduction of a gouache by Picasso in the Mouton museum, and an inscription 'en hommage à Picasso', who died in that year.

It was in 1945 that Mouton started its custom of inviting a different artist every year to design the label for the vintage, in the form of a strip at the top. The first was 1945 – *Année de la Victoire* (a year when even Lafite unbent sufficiently to emboss the year's date on the bottles, but whether this was to commemorate the victory over the Germans or the fine vintage is an open question). Since then many distinguished artists have been commissioned to provide this decoration, including Jean Cocteau (1947), Marie Laurencin (1948), Dignimont

(1949), Braque (1955), André Masson (1957), Salvador Dali (1958) and – a compliment to an English artist – Henry Moore (1964). Of more recent years, the 1970 label was designed by Chagall, the 1971 by Kandinsky and the 1974 by Motherwell. Following the visit to the château in 1977 of Queen Elizabeth, the Queen-Mother. the device of her Royal Arms formed the design for the vintage of that year – unfortunately not one of Bordeaux's more successful.

From here it is appropriate to pass to Mouton's other positive contribution to the relation between art and wine: the *Musée du Vin*. This remarkable collection, open since 1962 to all who care to apply in advance to the secretary of the château, is assembled in a former cellar, lying between the *cuvier* and the other *chais*. This is a book devoted to wine and not to the arts, but here surely is one of the most brilliantly conceived, collected, arranged and displayed small museums in the world. Every object, whether a fourteenth-century B.C. Mycenaean *krater*; a James II silver cup; a series of fifteenth-century Rhine Valley tapestries, on work in the vineyard, reunited here after being as far afield as the U.S.A. and Italy; a Picasso gouache; or an ingenious eighteenth-century Italian painting whose strips turn to display the Three Ages of Man; all have a vinous association. It is wonderfully uncluttered and every piece is of the highest quality in its genre. Even the warm terracotta-coloured floor in the main hall and the black tiles of a side room all contribute to produce a closely considered effect. The placing of the articles is superb and the lighting spectacular without being obvious. For example, engraved glasses are lit from below and this sharply shows off their design. The assembly and planning of this museum took the Baron and Baroness many years, and the design and layout were done by the Baroness Pauline, the American-born wife of Baron Philippe. Her artistic knowledge and sensibility are also very evident in the living apartments on the other side of the gravelled courtyard where white doves wheel and beat the air with their wings. Mouton, relaxed and almost informal, provides a strange contrast to the tightly buttoned-up *Deuxième Empire* period charm of the other Rothschild mansion just across the way at Lafite.

The *Musée du Vin* has steps leading down to another museum – the private and reserve cellars of wine. There is no wine in the Mouton cellar so old as that at Lafite and the oldest Mouton vintage in the private cellar is 1859, but there is a greater collection of old wines of its own and from other châteaux than any other, not excepting the fine collection at Château Margaux. There are 20,000–30,000 bottles in one cellar, 100,000 in another. The specially locked and segregated cellar of Mouton wines has a 'reference library' of twenty-four bottles, five magnums and two jeroboams of each vintage. In the older bins lie, like elephants half submerged in a sea of mud, ancient jeroboams and magnums encrusted with a dark kind of fungus which has almost to be chipped off when the bottle is taken out for its appointed day of opening. To the visitor the wealth of wine is inebriating without a bottle being opened. For example, I observed fifty-nine bottles, two magnums and two jeroboams of the famous 1870; but it would be difficult to call in vain for any vintage not lying there in considerable quantity. These bottles are re-corked and if necessary topped up from the same wine every twenty-five years; the last occasion was in 1957.

Mouton has always been a big exchanger and buyer of the wine of other châteaux. Indeed it is the custom there, as in other Médoc châteaux, to open for another proprietor invited to lunch or dine a fine bottle of his own wine; and at Mouton very often it may be something that he lacks in his own cellar. The second cellar consists of a 70-metre-long 'corridor', with all the first growths on one side, among them a fine selection of the vintages of the 1870s. The wines are not confined to the Médoc, and there are some enviable modern vintages of Cheval-Blanc, Pétrus and various other Graves, St-Émilions and Pomerols. There is also a section where the reserve stock of Mouton is kept. Once after a conducted tour by the taciturn though amiable chief *maître de chai*, M. Pierre Blondin (his voluble brother Raoul is the other), who dropped the remark that the best *vieux Moutons* are the 1870, 1878 and 1899, I emerged dizzy into the sunlight.

The next two stars in the Pauillac galaxy of classed growths are the pair of Pichons, which once were one. Jacques Pichon Baron de Longueville was the first Président of the Parlement of Bordeaux in the seventeenth century.

If there is less to be said about the past of these distinguished châteaux and indeed hereafter about nearly all the other classed growths, it is because neither they nor their wines have captured the attention and imagination as the leaders have. Nor have many of them preserved much historical material. Some of them were long in the hands of old families like the Pichons, Barons de Longueville, who held their châteaux for two hundred years, but as wine makers they lacked wide *réclame*.

This can be gauged from the already quoted Christie's wine catalogues. The first mention of a non-first-growth Médoc château that I could find was in 1829, with some Léoville 1820 shipped by Barton & Guestier, a firm already well known in the British market. Probably for that reason they put on the label the name of the vineyard, which Hugh Barton was partly to buy in 1821. Otherwise the nearest to a name was usually a wine sold as St-Julien. In 1832 there is mention of Cantenuc (*sic*), and in 1834 La Rose and Mouton are listed. Apart from these three growths, catalogued occasionally thereafter, I can find no other until Rauzan 1845 in 1848, Cos-Destournel (*sic*) 1848 in 1860, and Pichon 1841 in 1861, when Barton & Guestier's Langoa (1857), an English club favourite, also appeared. In 1862 Pontet-Canet 1841 from Cruse et Fils Frères was offered. Slowly then the other well-known names began to appear before a conservatively-minded public. For the nobility drank either one of the first growths, with Lafite predominating and Haut-Brion rarely seen, or they drank their wine merchants' claret, *tout court*.

The first Pichon-Baron, so designated in the sale lists I came across, was the 1851, which fetched 78s. a dozen in 1867. The Baron had a mother born Lalande, and when the estate was divided before the 1855 classification, in the proportion of two-fifths and three-fifths, the larger, 'feminine' part of the château took its name from a Comtesse de Lalande, *née* Pichon-Longueville. At one time the Baron enjoyed the wider repute, although the smaller of the two, and its 1929 was one of the best wines of the vintage. Today it is owned by M. Bouteiller, also proprietor of Grand-Puy-Ducasse and Lanessan. At least until recent years it seemed much less distinguished and often rather a hard wine. The vineyard is 60 per cent Cabernet of both varieties and 40 per cent Merlot. Its area is only 18 ha, compared with 63 for Lalande, which has always struck me as a lighter wine. This may be accounted for partly by the fact that strictly speaking two-fifths of the vineyard lie in St-Julien (and was at one time obliged to label part of its *récolte* as a St-Julien) and partly by the composition of the vineyard. The *cépage* is 45 per cent Cabernet-Sauvignon, 12 per cent Cabernet-Franc, 38 per cent Merlot and 5 per cent Petit-Verdot. The last-named ripens late and produces a powerful wine, rich in alcohol, but a harvesting risk in a late vintage. For its size Lalande often makes a good deal of wine, but the hazards of the Bordeaux producer may be gauged by the fact that whereas in a good year Pichon-Lalande will produce up to 250 *tonneaux*, in the fine but short vintage of 1961 its total output was only 30 *tonneaux*. Today the production of Pichon-Baron is about 90 *tonneaux* annually, and the quality is improving.

Pichon-Lalande is owned by the Miailhe family, who also own Siran and in 1966 bought Dauzac, adjacent to the latter. William-Alain Miailhe is principally concerned with these estates. In recent years a good deal of work has been done in the vineyard and *chais*, and in 1966 a new cellar was completed, with a terrace on top which looks down on the vineyard of Latour – if such condescension be permitted of a second growth to a first. For a long time the Comtesse has been superior to the Baron, which though fruity has tended to be tannic and tough. The more elegant 'lady' has produced some charming, well-balanced wines from about 1966 onwards, and initially I was impressed by the '75 and '76, particularly the latter; but that was drawn from the cask with years to pass before a more reliable assessment could be made. The '75, also still in cask, was a bigger wine, less hard perhaps than many other wines of this vintage at that stage.

After this galaxy of *premiers* and *deuxièmes* there is a big gap in the Pauillac hierarchy until we come to Duhart-Milon among the *quatrièmes*. Placed partly on the Carruades plateau adjoining Lafite, it is not altogether surprising that Lafite acquired the vineyard in 1962. At one time it belonged to M. Castéja, a lawyer who was elected Mayor of Bordeaux, and it passed to his widow before becoming, like so many of the main Médoc properties, a limited company or *société civile*. The vineyard had decreased over the years to no more than 20 ha when the Rothschilds bought the property, but they engaged in extensive planting and replanting, and the vineyard area was increased to 48 ha. The proportion of each area under vines was broadly brought into line with that of Lafite: 70 per cent Cabernet-Sauvignon, 12 per cent Cabernet-Franc, 15 per cent Merlot and 3 per cent Petit-Verdot. At one time this last variety had occupied half the Duhart-Milon vineyard, a peculiarity of the estate and producing a very hard wine. It is not a wine that has often come my way, though one of those that I had in my early days of wine-collecting was Duhart-Milon 1923 (a vintage not much seen in Britain), and aged about sixteen years, a very fine wine it seemed to me. Then I drank a 1947 when it was more than twenty years old, and for that somewhat variable vintage in the Médoc it remained round and fruity. Otherwise I have never come upon a really exciting bottle. But then it takes time – at least twelve years – for young vines to achieve maturity, and when I tasted the 1975 and 1976 in the autumn of 1977 these appeared wines of true character, particularly the former. The wine is now labelled Duhart-Milon-Rothschild, and the engraved label is similar in style to that of Lafite.

Pontet-Canet, which heads the *cinquièmes*, must be one of the best-known châteaux of Bordeaux, particularly in Britain where it has always enjoyed a special popularity. It is named after M. Pontet, who created the vineyard in the location called Canet (spelt Cannet on the stone front of the *cuvier*) and is one of the oldest Haut-Médoc vineyards. Jean-François Pontet was major-general of the Médoc and assistant to the intendant. His vineyard estate was certainly in being before Boucher's edict against planting in 1725, and by 1743 had nearly 20 ha; he added to them in various parcels as he was able, in competition with his neighbour at Lafite and Joseph de Brane at Mouton. It was sold by his heirs in 1865 to M. Herman Cruse, head of the Bordeaux firm of Cruse et Fils Frères. At that time this large vineyard (it had averaged 120–140 *tonneaux* according to Franck in 1824) was somewhat split up, with part at Canet, part at Milon and part in Bages. It has long been reunited; and when in the sixties the Cruses bought Haut-Bages, a 9-hectare portion of the vineyard adjoining Pontet-Canet was added to the latter, which now has a vineyard of 70 ha, and may produce more than any other classed growth. In 1964, for example, the output was 382 *tonneaux* compared with the next largest producer, Gruaud-Larose, which made 349 *tonneaux* from the same area. In the same year Lafite, the largest in area of all the *crus classés* with 80 ha, made 290 *tonneaux*, including Carruades. These figures are the quantities declared for *appellation*; total production may well have been higher. The vineyard composition is 79 per cent Cabernet-Sauvignon, 1 per cent Cabernet-Franc and 20 per cent Merlot.

Pontet-Canet is a very attractive, well-run property, and is rare in the Médoc for having very fine underground cellars. The *cuvier*, overlooking the vineyards, is in two storeys so that the grapes can be hauled up and loaded from above into the large vats. The house itself, with fine trees, lawn and flower-beds in front, is one of the most agreeable and *familial* of the Médoc châteaux, some of which are more remarkable for their architectural eccentricity than for their domestic appeal. Pontet-Canet, on a slight rise, has a wide view of the neigh-bouring vineyards, looking across to Mouton in one direction and Lynch-Bages, Grand-Puy-Lacoste and the 'outback' of Pauillac in another. It is a château that I visited many times, and under the guidance of Christian Cruse and his son Édouard acquired as much information about Bordeaux wines and drank as many of the best and most interesting bottles as anywhere in this hospitable region. Not least of the latter was the notable Pontet-Canet '29, an extraordinarily full-bodied, almost rich wine, that stood out even in that fine year. In May 1962 Christian Cruse gave a dinner in London to celebrate fifty years of visiting English wine merchants. For this occa-sion bottles of Pontet-Canet 1929 and magnums of Mouton-Rothschild 1929 were decanted in Bordeaux into clean bottles, topped up, re-corked and then flown over to London. It was no disrespect to the Mouton, a fine wine but beginning to show its age, that the general view of the assembled company was that the Pontet-Canet was the finer. In March 1975 Pontet-Canet was sold for 30 million frs. to Guy Tesseron, son-in-law of the late Emmanuel Cruse, and some associates. This was an unhappy outcome of the 'Bordeaux scandal' affecting the Cruse family.

Until recently Pontet-Canet shared one feature with only one other *cru classé* – Langoa. It refused ever to have any of its wine bottled at the château, although a proportion was bottled in Bordeaux under the label of Cruse et Fils Frères, as Barton & Guestier bottled Langoa. This policy was a subject of controversy and suspicion. It was suggested that the absence of château-bottling made the authenticity of these wines less assured. The fact that both were sold under non-vintage labels in the restaurant cars of the French Railways was also sometimes adduced as a slightly doubtful feature. However I would think this was a useful way of disposing of the embarrassingly large quantities of off-vintage years from so large a property as Pontet-Canet (in the poor year of 1965 it made 420 *tonneaux*). The argument used at Pontet-Canet was always that it was cheaper for them and their customers to sell the wine in cask. However, with château-bottling made compulsory for all classed-growth Médocs, Pontet-Canet fell into line in 1972.

Batailley, which lies inland, has an attractive nineteenth-century château with a *parc anglais* behind, but the estate is much older. The name is said to have originated from the fact that there was a battle here between the French and English. Later it was owned by an old Pauillac family named St-Martin, and in 1819 it was bought by Daniel Guestier of Barton & Guestier for 118,000 frs. When his heirs sold it in 1864 to M. Constant Halphen of Paris the sum realized was 500,000 frs. The present proprietress is the widow of Marcel Borie, of the firm of Borie-Manoux, and the estate is run by Émile Castéja. However, since the war, the estate has been divided in two; the other part, called Haut-Batailley, whose vineyard is dominated by a Virgin-crowned tower, is owned by the widow of Francis Borie. For a time this wine was made at Ducru-Beaucaillou, but from 1974 onwards it has been vinified in the modernized *cuvier* of La Couronne in Pauillac. Ducru and Haut-Batailley are run by Jean-Eugène Borie. Batailley comprises 26 ha and Haut-Batailley 18. Like other 'outback' classed growths, the large, sprawling *cuvier* and *chais*, long, low and supported by iron posts, have rather more of a farmyard air than the show-places nearer the Gironde. In my experience Batailley consistently makes sound, rather

unexciting wine, often rather on the hard side and inclined
to be unyielding in the way Pauillacs can be. Of Haut-
Batailley I have had limited experience, but they made an
excellent '61, '67 and '70. As M. Borie has greatly improved
the previously disappointing Ducru-Beaucaillou, I am not surprised, judging from tasting more recent vintages, to find
Haut-Batailley looking up. Some excellent wine was made in
the better vintages of the seventies. The vineyard is composed
of Cabernet-Sauvignon 68 per cent, Cabernet-Franc 12 per
cent and Merlot 20 per cent. Production averages 70–90
tonneaux.

Next are the two Grand-Puys: Ducasse and Lacoste. The
first is unusual in that the château is separated from its vineyard; the former is right on the waterfront at Pauillac, and the
actual dwelling is now Pauillac's municipal *Maison du Vin*,
which is worth visiting as it gives an idea of the situation of
the estates in the commune. Alongside are the small old-
fashioned cellars of Grand-Puy-Ducasse, with the vineyards
lying outside the town and split into three parts. It is one of
the smallest of the classed growths, with a vineyard of only
10 ha and an output of 30 *tonneaux*. Formerly owned by M.
Bouteiller of Pichon-Baron, it is now part of the Mestrezat-
Preller group, associated with others, including M. Roland
Dumas and the Société Promodes. The wine is not much seen
in Britain, and the one I remember best is the fruity but rather
hard 1948. But after drinking the 1868 with Christian Cruse
at Pontet-Canet I shall always have a soft spot for Grand-Puy-
Ducasse. The name came from an *avocat* in the pre-revolutionary Parlement of Bordeaux.

Grand-Puy-Lacoste, however, enjoys quite a wide esteem,
and I have a special regard for it since it was the first château-
bottled 1924 claret I ever acquired, as part of a modest consignment bought from a wine merchant in Nantes. Why
Nantes? Because the firm had been recommended to me as
having supplied Hilaire Belloc, who had a certain reputation

for good living, and was then still alive. The Grand-Puy-Lacoste was about fifteen years old and was probably the first fine claret that I had ever consciously drunk. I remember now the wonderful 'nose' of blackcurrants, a mark of well-matured claret; but nowadays it is blackcurrants that remind me of claret.

After that Grand-Puy-Lacoste passed out of my life for many years. I sampled one or two not very exciting post-war vintages at London tastings, but then in October 1965 when in Bordeaux I was invited to lunch at the château. There I met the sparkling, sprightly Raymond Dupin, a short man full of genial enthusiasm for his wine. The château like many others is not regularly lived in or kept up, but there are at least the essentials: a kitchen and a dining room, the latter embellished with oval carved cask ends more familiar in Germany than in France. When I lunched there, on the simply laid table were bottles of the year-old '64, drawn from the cask; but that was only *pour le soif*, and we went on to drink the delicious '53, the remarkably well-preserved '47 (a very uneven Médoc vintage considering its reputation) and a magnum of '43, which was surprisingly full and complete for a year generally by then considered well past its best. Between the dining room and the kitchen run lofty corridors, and to the English guests was allotted the slightly embarrassing role of summoning each succeeding course of the plentiful meal. This involved advancing to the double doors of the dining room, opening them and yelling *fortissimo* 'Antoinette!' This was soon followed by the smiling appearance of a buxom maid and her companions, bearing heavily laden trays. My own vocal performance was as nothing compared with that of a fellow guest, Sir Solly Zuckerman, the Chief Scientific Adviser to the British Government and later Lord Zuckerman. To adapt Ouida, none yelled louder than he.

The Lacoste part of Grand-Puy assumed its separate identity in the first half of the eighteenth century, when acquired by the Lacoste family, who owned it at least until the phylloxera. The full name has Saint-Guirons added, commemorating another former owner. Judging by old records, in those days it was larger than now, but today consists of 24 hectares, and in a good year produces about 110 *tonneaux* of wine. There is a big proportion of Cabernet-Sauvignon, and this château is today making excellent wine, notably the '75. In September 1978 Jean-Eugène Borie of Ducru-Beaucaillou took over, with M. Dupin's approval, the running of the estate and 50 per cent of the shares. He made the 1978 wine.

Not far away is the better-known growth of Lynch-Bages, formerly belonging to one of the 'characters' of Pauillac, M. Cazes. Bages is a hamlet. The château was named after its proprietor of Irish descent, Count Lynch, the Mayor of Bordeaux, who in 1814 displayed his Bourbon-like memory in excitedly welcoming the return of Louis XVIII. He also owned Lynch-Moussas and Dauzac in Labarde. On his death in 1835, it passed to his brother the Chevalier Thomas-Michel Lynch, who died in 1840. After an intervening owner, it was acquired in 1865, the heyday of the Médoc, by Maurice Cayrou, yet another Bordeaux merchant. After it had passed to his daughter it was acquired by Jean-Christian Cazes and made into a company. It is now run by M. Cazes junior.

Lynch-Bages is a large estate of just over 50 ha, and the *chai* buildings have much the same traditional, agricultural appearance as Batailley. Casks are piled three-high, and the typical long, low cellars are dimly lit. I have heard Lynch-Bages described as 'the poor man's Mouton-Rothschild'. However, there is no marked expenditure on electricity in the Lynch-Bages cellars, as may be found at Mouton. But there are some large new concrete fermenting vats, installed in 1965. There is a high proportion of Cabernet-Sauvignon – 75 per cent – with the balance made up of Cabernet-Franc, Merlot and Petit-Verdot. Production in a good year may be as high as 150 *tonneaux*. Lynch-Bages has indeed something of the 'concentrated' flavour of Mouton, but without its distinction; fair enough considering its status. I find it rather a heavy and often over-sweet wine, but at the same time it can be agreeable when not all of its rivals are; for example, in that hard vintage of 1957, Lynch-Bages made an attractive wine. The '53 also had the 'size' that some other wines rather lacked. Lynch-Bages is a wine I used to like more than I do now, but it is probably I who have changed rather than the wine, and I am quite prepared to be surprised by picking it out in a blind tasting. It is an easy-to-drink claret.

To reach Lynch-Moussas one really has to penetrate the backwoods of Pauillac, bumping along a very minor road that runs from near Batailley, with only the château signpost, common in these parts, to indicate the destination. It lies tucked away in the woods, to the south-west of Grand-Puy-Lacoste. As the name indicates the vineyard once belonged to the Lynchs, and in the middle of the last century to a M. Vasquez. It is now owned by Émile Castéja, of the family that used to hold Duhart-Milon and still possess Doisy-Védrines in Barsac. It is a small property of 5 ha producing only 15–20 *tonneaux*, the least of all the *crus classés*. Indeed one wonders why it was included, for it is sometimes suggested that the only reason why Ausone, the leading growth of St-Émilion, was not listed, was that its output of about 15 *tonneaux* was so small. Perhaps the magic of the name Lynch secured entry. Not that size is a necessary criterion of excellence, and maybe in 1855 the wine's quality elevated it above its *crus bourgeois* rivals. Yet for many years the wine has been little seen abroad, and I have never done more than meet it at trade tastings. In fact the vineyard was practically wiped out by the severe frosts of 1956 and nearly the whole vineyard had to be re-planted, a heart-breaking matter for a small proprietor. So only recently has the necessary balance been achieved, which is why I found the '64 very strong, when tasted in the *chai*. My arrival was greeted with some curiosity by the small band of *vignerons* who were assisting at the vintage, and with pleasure by the proprietor and his wife; this welcome because an English journalist a few years ago had written that Lynch-Moussas no longer existed! I can testify that it does and shall look forward to tasting vintages already said to be better in a restored *vignoble*. Recently it has been seen occasionally on English merchants' lists.

With Mouton-Baron-Philippe we are back among the bright lights. It runs alongside Mouton-Rothschild, with its incomplete classical-style château (built in the 1820s) – the money ran out less than half-way along the pediment – standing at right angles to the gravelled, flower-bordered drive up to Mouton-Rothschild and facing across to Pontet-Canet. Until the eighteenth century the two Moutons were one property, and part at least was leased from the Lafite estate. In 1730 an Armailhacq, who was probably a member of the Bordeaux Parlement, bought a portion of Mouton, while the other part passed into the hands of the Baron Hector de Brane. M. d'Armailhacq, like other proprietors of his time, sought to increase and consolidate his *vignoble* by extracting it from neighbouring peasants, to whom he first lent money and then evicted when they could not repay it. (One need not be surprised that the French Revolution occurred, only that it did not happen earlier.) Armailhacq was in competition for parcels of land with his neighbour, the Chevalier François de Pontet who was establishing Pontet-Canet and had consolidated it by the second half of the eighteenth century. After the Revolution a later Armailhacq bought some of the plateau of Carruades, part of which belonged to the commune of Pauillac, and this tried to recover it. Only in 1840 did Armailhacq win his fight in the law courts. Reference to the contest between Lafite and Mouton for the Armailhacq portion has already been made in the section on Lafite. The reason why it was then sold was that the family ran into financial difficulties in a time of very bad trade, caused partly by the protectionist policies of Louis-Philippe. These suited the industrialists of the north, but hindered trade with England, the natural market for the fine wines of the Médoc. Mme Odette d'Armailhacq borrowed 400,000 frs. from a group in Bordeaux, who three years later decided to foreclose and sell the property. However, Mme d'Armailhacq, now separated from her husband, bought it for 390,000 frs., but in the following year had to sell the 10·2 ha of Carruades. M. Thuret, who then owned Brane-Mouton, refused to buy, and instead M. Goudal of Lafite acquired it and began to plant. By the 1860s the property was in the hands of the Comte de Ferrand, who married an Armailhacq, and it was his grandson who sold the estate to Baron Philippe in 1933. He also sold a company that he had formed in 1921, at the beginning of another bad trade period, to sell his own and other wines. It was called the Société Vinicole de Pauillac. This company formed the basis of La Bergerie, the trading company of Baron Philippe, known best for its marketing of Mouton-Cadet.

Whatever the sharp practices of the early Armailhacqs at Mouton, the family's good name was restored by A. d'Armailhacq, who in 1855 published a classic work on the Médoc: *De la culture des vignes, la vinification et les vins dans le Médoc*. It was reprinted several times, and Armailhacq, formerly a magistrate, was awarded *une médaille d'honneur* for his book by the Agricultural Society of the Gironde. He wrote it to improve the standards of viticulture and wine-making, but comments at the beginning that 'most proprietors and *vignerons* of the Médoc think there is no need to study and that books are valueless to them'. This could equally have applied to many proprietors up to about 1950. The only solution to the difficult trading conditions, wrote the author, was to change ancient practices and to produce if possible a cheaper wine to reduce the price without making a loss. That is why a less expensive, more productive method of cultivation was vitally necessary. Armailhacq then set out the proper methods of cultivation, including the choice of the best grape varieties.

One other comment of this author is worth quoting, as still having some relevance. He refers to the *amour exagéré* of the growers for their own wines. 'Each believes he makes it better than his neighbours, often even better than those whose reputation is much superior. This confidence in himself, an almost excessive *amour-propre*, destroys all progress, since each is convinced of having reached perfection.' His remarks on the attitude of the trade in the first half of the last century are apposite too:

The brokers and merchants do not encourage improvement. They concern themselves solely with maintaining the Classification and never pay for a wine according to its real quality, but according to its reputation. So the best the owner can do will be to sell the first of his class, but not above those who, rightly or wrongly, are considered his equals.

One interesting point about the two Moutons is why the Armailhacqs called their property by this name. A. d'Armailhacq pointed out that when his forebears acquired the estate, they actually lived in the leading house in the hamlet of Mouton, while the Branes, proprietors of the greater part of the vineyard, lived in Le Pouyalet, the village on the main road between Pauillac and St-Estèphe, where the Mouton cellars are to this day. The Armailhacqs were therefore quite entitled to the name Mouton, and it was not for any reasons of false ambition, of which they were sometimes accused. This also explains why there was no house at what became Mouton-Rothschild until Petit-Mouton was built in 1880.

To return to our own day at Mouton d'Armailhacq, the estate was large when acquired by Baron Philippe in 1933: from 60 to 75 ha of vines, but it was gradually cut down drastically, with the aim of improving quality. In 1964 the productive area was only 32 ha. Now, however, it is back to 50 ha, composed of 70 per cent Cabernet-Sauvignon and 30 per cent Merlot. Production averages 200 *tonneaux*. In 1966 the *cuvier* and *chais* were entirely rebuilt, and cement vats installed. After the fermentation is finished the wine is transferred to big vats in order to secure early malo-lactic fermentation, as this helps to round out the flavour. As at Mouton-Rothschild the grapes are hauled up to an upper floor and then go straight into a stainless steel *égrappoir*.

In 1956 the name was changed to Mouton-Baron-Philippe, and then again in 1977 to Mouton-Baronne-Philippe in memory of Pauline de Rothschild who died in 1976. Although a fifth growth, this associate estate of Mouton-Rothschild is run very much on first-growth lines except for the cement vats. Also entirely new casks are no longer used for the new wine; they are too expensive for the price the wine can command. A proportion of this wine is said to go into the Mouton-Cadet.

As a side-light on the curious way the French wine laws work, it would be quite possible for this lesser part of the Mouton vineyard to have been incorporated in the major one, and the whole production sold as Mouton-Rothschild. Lafite could have done the same with Duhart-Milon. In each case of course, the overall quality would show a deterioration, but less scrupulous proprietors might be tempted to make even a short-term gain on wines normally sold for a fraction of the first-growth prices. Contrariwise, if a *bourgeois* growth proprietor were to buy part of a classed-growth vineyard and incorporate it into his own, the former would lose its classed status.

Before leaving Mouton it is well to mention Mouton-Cadet, claimed to be the best-selling claret in the world. Some people believe that it is a second wine of Mouton-Rothschild, a sort of Carruades. In fact it is a branded wine which may be drawn from anywhere in Bordeaux, but is claimed to be essentially Médoc. The *appellation* is Bordeaux. It really originated with

the very poor 1927 vintage. It was decided that the wine of
Mouton was not good enough to sell under the château label.
Not wanting to dispose of it at a low price as plain Bordeaux,
Baron Philippe thought of the name 'Carruades de Mouton',
since the estate included a large part of the plateau so-named.
An attractive label bearing a red bunch of grapes was designed,
and the wine sold with the 1927 vintage; two magnums
turned up in a Christie's auction in the mid-seventies. But, as
Baron Philippe frankly admitted, it was not a success. The
problem did not arise again until the even poorer 1930 vintage.
Baron Philippe was the *cadet*, the youngest of the three
children of his father, Baron Henri, and it was decided to try
the experiment attempted with the 1927 again, but under a
new name. The 1931 and 1932 vintages were no better than
the 1930, so the new branded wine was launched, a blend of
the three vintages. Initially this was to have been called 'Cadet
de Mouton', but at the last moment it was switched to
'Mouton-Cadet', and was an immediate success, demonstrating as Baron Philippe told me when recounting its origin,
'the power of words'. At first other *crus classés* were included,
though the Mouton-Cadet 1938 was largely from Mouton-
Rothschild.

However, an earlier example than any generally known
appeared at Christie's in April 1976 in the form of a magnum
of 1929, described on the label as 'Grand Vin de Médoc,
Sélection Rothschild', and a lead capsule embossed 'Mouton-
Cadet Médoc'. This must have been a second wine of Mouton-
Rothschild in that famous vintage, and presumably sparked off
the idea of a branded wine to follow a few years later. In 1976
it was bought by a trade buyer for £52. Since then the blend
has always included, I was told, some Mouton-Rothschild in
it – perhaps wine made from the younger vines – and particularly a proportion of Mouton-Baron-Philippe. Sales
started in France, Belgium and Sweden in the thirties, but the
wine spread to the United Kingdom after the last war, and

Britain is now the largest buyer, although it is expected that the United States will soon overtake us. The wine is always sold with a vintage label and so far as Britain is concerned it has had two years in bottle before being marketed. I have found Mouton-Cadet an agreeable, consistent but not very distinguished wine, which is much as one would expect. Owing to the fact that it has to bear a trade mark-up, like other such branded wines, it is rather expensive. The chief sale is in hotels and restaurants.

The small estate of Haut-Bages-Libéral, which owes its title to the name rather than the politics of a mid-nineteenth-century proprietor, was partly divided in location. Part lay alongside Latour, and another part was on the side of Pauillac adjoining Pontet-Canet. So when the Cruses bought the property in the mid 1960s they incorporated the latter, lesser portion into Pontet-Canet, as they were quite entitled to do. The other part which produces about 40 *tonneaux* from its 20 hectares is still sold under the Haut-Bages-Libéral label, but like other Cruse-owned properties was not château-bottled before this became obligatory for all *crus classés*, starting in 1972. For some time the wine was made and kept at Pontet-Canet, but more recently a modern *chai* was constructed on the old site. For a long time it had seemed rather an undistinguished wine, but it appeared to improve in the seventies, and the '75 achieved a certain reputation when still young.

Two of the remaining three Pauillac *crus classés* are small and not very widely known, and both have their *cuviers* and cellars separated from their vineyards. Pédesclaux's wine is grown in an area adjoining Mouton and near to Lafite, by the main road to St-Estèphe. Its extent is 16 ha, of which 70 per cent are Cabernet-Sauvignon, and almost 30 per cent Merlot, with the balance made up with a little Cabernet-Franc. Output may go as high as 70 *tonneaux*. The *chai* is enmeshed in Pauillac itself, lying between the church and the river. The young wine as I tasted it in the modest cellars seemed supple for a Pauillac.

Most Pédesclaux is sold abroad, with the U.S.A. taking 30 per cent of the crop, and Switzerland and Belgium as the next best customers. The name was from a member of Mermans, the brokers. In 1950 it was bought by M. Bernard Jugla, together with some lesser *crus bourgeois*, Grand-Duroc-Milon, Belle-Rose and Haut-Padarnac.

Clerc-Milon-Mondon has its cellars in the hamlet of Mousset, which adjoins the village of Pouyalet, on the outskirts of which is Mouton-Rothschild. Until 1970 the owners were Mlle Marie Vialard, sister of a well-known notary of Pauillac much concerned with the wine trade, and Mme L. Hedon, but in that year it was bought by Baron Philippe de Rothschild for about 1 million frs. All the wine is produced in a *cuvier* little larger than a good-sized drawing room. The output averages about 50 *tonneaux* but may be expected to rise under the Rothschild ownership, for its vineyard increased from a mere 10½ ha in the sixties to 32 ha by the middle of the seventies. (In 1855 it was 50 ha, but later 18 of these were divided among several owners.) Part is on the fine territory between Mouton and Lafite, and as Mlle Vialard once reminded me, the local Médocain saying is that 'the wine is good if one can see the river from the vineyard'. When Baron Philippe bought the property the average age of the vineyard was considerable, and the '70 had a remarkable depth of flavour when young, with a high proportion of Cabernet-Sauvignon. With a newly designed label, depicting an early seventeenth-century, silver gilt, German drinking cup in the Musée, it is now simply called Clerc-Milon.

Croizet-Bages, last on the official list of classed Pauillacs, is better known. It is one of the relatively 'inland' Pauillacs, and it lies to the left of the road from St-Lambert to Pauillac, on the rising slopes around the hamlet of Bages, in which its *chai* lies. It is also near Lynch-Bages. The vineyard is 25 ha in area, and the composition is unusual for Pauillac: 50 per cent Cabernet-Franc, 30 per cent Merlot and only 20 per cent

Cabernet-Sauvignon, although I was told that the proportion of this last is increasing. In a good year 100 *tonneaux* are produced in the small cellars, whose white columns are an echo of the grandeur of Château Margaux's lofty *chai*. Croizet-Bages, named after two brothers Croizet who owned it in the eighteenth century, has no château to speak of. After other owners it passed to M. Julien Calvé in 1853 and remained with the same family until 1930. The present proprietor is M. Paul Quié. The wine is distinctly robust, even coarse when young, but it has plenty of flavour and occasionally I have drunk mature bottles that surprised me by their roundness. Generally it is a typically big, 'gutsy' Pauillac wine, with more body than beauty.

The *bourgeois* wines of this big commune are more numerous than in the neighbouring St-Julien, and some of them find a ready market. A neighbour of Croizet-Bages is Haut-Bages-Avérous, which unlike Haut-Bages-Libéral is not a classified growth. From its 6 ha are made 25–30 *tonneaux* in distinctly old-fashioned premises but none the worse for that. Other well-known Pauillac *bourgeois* growths are La Couronne, which belongs to J.-E. Borie of Ducru-Beaucaillou, Fonbadet, Monpelou, La Tour-Milon, Pibran and La Tour-Pibran. There are a number of variations on the themes of Bages and Milon. Of these *crus bourgeois* La Couronne is almost certainly the best. In its old cellar by the Médoc railway line, its proprietor now also makes his Haut-Batailley, and ten new vitrified steel vats were installed in 1974. The vineyard area is only 4 ha, composed of 60 per cent Cabernet-Sauvignon, 10 per cent Cabernet-Franc and 30 per cent Merlot, with production averaging 25–30 *tonneaux*. If there were a new re-classification of the Médoc La Couronne would be a candidate for advancement.

One of the best-known lesser Pauillac names is La Rose Pauillac, the wine of the Pauillac Co-operative. This organization, the first of its kind in the Médoc, was founded in the difficult times of 1932. It 'farms' 520 ha belonging to classed growths and 300 of other properties. It has 180 producing members, who own from three ha to only one-half; output varies from 6,000 to 8,000 hl (666–888 *tonneaux*). At one time its wine was sold as Château Pauillac. The wine can be very agreeable and I remember with pleasure the soft 1959 La Rose. Wicked tongues in the district maintain that the Co-operative is a useful source of wine for proprietors whose own stocks have run low. But then the stock of wicked tongues is perhaps high in the Médoc. For many years the Co-operative had handled the wine of Ch. Colombier Monpelou, but in 1973 it was bought by M. Bernard Jugla of Pédesclaux.

ST-ESTÈPHE

I must here confess at once that the St-Estèphes have never been great favourites of mine. It may be that I have been unlucky; certainly I can never remember being offered a really great St-Estèphe, and I have always found them rather strong, sometimes coarse wines, green and stalky when young and full of tannin. I have been told that in St-Estèphe wine is made more in the traditional way than elsewhere in the Haut-Médoc, and certainly most of the properties I have visited have been impressively conservative. Under the *appellation* laws, since 1965 they have been permitted to make 40 rather than 36 hl per hectare. Principally, however, it must be a matter of soil and situation. Cos d'Estournel adjoins Lafite, but the wine is as different as Lafite is from Mouton. The soil is heavier and more fertile, the gravel being mixed with clay over lime. The wines are robust, full-bodied and repay keeping.

St-Estèphe boasts two second growths, Cos d'Estournel and Montrose. The first of these has certainly the most curious buildings of all the eccentric structures in the Médoc. Originally the property was just called Cos (pronounced like the lettuce, not like the common abbreviation for 'company'), and it belonged to the Estournel family who sold it in 1811, only to re-buy it in 1821 and then greatly to enlarge the vineyard from 16 to 57 ha. M. d'Estournel built a splendid series of *chais* in the Chinese style and today these have the agreeable appearance of a folly. When a passing traveller asked of a worker, 'What is this palace?' the latter replied, '*C'est le parc à bœufs de M. d'Estournel.*'

In giving proper precedence to the vineyard and winemaking this oxen-parking proprietor omitted to build a château at all, and he spent so much money on the former that a year before his death in 1853 he had to sell the property to a Mr Martyn of London. Mr Martyn lived in Paris, and his purchase of Cos d'Estournel was aided by the banker Fould whose family later owned Beychevelle. The price stated was 1,150,000 frs. but this possibly included Pomys and two other minor estates that this rich Londoner (was he a banker?) acquired simultaneously. He also bought Cos-Labory next door. With the purchase in 1853 of Mouton by Baron Nathaniel de Rothschild, a member of the English branch of this family, and the ownership at least in name of Lafite by the Scotts, there was a period in the 1850s and 1860s when three famous adjoining estates could be said to be in English hands. Mr Martyn, like his neighbour at Lafite, left the affairs of Cos d'Estournel in the hands of a manager. This was the very experienced M. J. Chiapella, owner of La Mission-Haut-Brion. Martyn's money and Chiapella's skill further improved the standing of Cos, so that in 1866 the Agricultural Society of the Gironde awarded the English proprietor its *prix d'ensemble* for the high standard of the vineyard, of the buildings and the general conduct of the estate. Specially picked out for commendation was a 'free medical service' for the workers. Like many other vineyard owners Martyn remains a somewhat shadowy figure, except that he was apparently generous as well as rich.

A year after Lafite passed to the Rothschilds in 1868, Martyn sold the property, which passed through several hands, including the Charmolue family who owned Montrose. In 1919 it was acquired by M. Fernand Ginestet, the Bordeaux merchant and later owner of Château Margaux, and so passed to his son Pierre. In 1971 the ownership was transferred to M. Ginestet's sister, Mme Prats and her family. Her son M. Bruno Prats now runs it. Although Cos d'Estournel is usually given the château prefix, in the past at least it was often written without this; possibly because there was no château. Its productive area is about 47 ha, and the output is considerable: 180–200 *tonneaux*. The vineyard is composed of 60 per cent Cabernet-Sauvignon and 40 per cent Merlot.

Early in the sixties the 1945 wines, château-bottled, of the three leading St-Estèphes – Cos d'Estournel, Montrose and Calon-Ségur – were opened at a lunch at Christopher's, the then Jermyn Street, London, wine merchants. Of the three Cos was certainly the finest, and a very good wine, less 'spiky' than I had expected. Montrose was adjudged second. Cos often produces good wine in indifferent years; its '58 was excellent and among the best wines of that light vintage. It also made a good '55, not an off-year, but sometimes rather a disappointing one. For a time Cos took to selling a non-vintage blend, the first being made up of the '63 and '64 vintages, but later they gave this up. This matter is discussed when Château Margaux is reached.

To enter the low-ceilinged *chai* of Montrose is to give traditionalists a sense of confidence. One may be convinced chemically, statistically and intellectually by concrete or steel vats, but there is something about the massive old oak fermenting vats that appeals. At Montrose they have a few concrete vats, but most are of wood, extending almost up to the low ceiling. The *cuvier* is lit by attractive brass lamps. The vineyard extends to about 50 ha and the output may be as high as 130–140 *tonneaux*. St-Estèphe is, in general, real Cabernet country, and this may partly account for the heavy tannin content of most wines. At Montrose 70 per cent of the vineyard is Cabernet-Sauvignon, 10 per cent Cabernet-Franc, 15 per cent Merlot and 5 per cent Petit-Verdot. The commune's *crus bourgeois* often have a heavy Cabernet percentage.

Montrose, in spite of its rather traditional appearance, is not a very old vineyard. The vineyard was carved out of the woodlands belonging to Calon, and the first vines were planted in 1815 by Théodore Dumoulin, whose father had acquired the land from Alexandre de Ségur in 1778. The charming little château was built by M. Dumoulin. In 1825 this still very small vineyard of about 5 ha was accepted as a second growth, which was curious as Calon-Ségur was only a third, and this rank was confirmed in the 1855 classification. In 1861 M. Dumoulin's heirs sold the estate to a M. Mathieu Dollfus, a financier, for 1,050,000 frs., and he designed the fine cellars that remain much the same today. On his death in 1887, the vineyard was bought by M. Jean-Jules Hostein, at that time owner of Cos d'Estournel and Pomys. Nine years later M. Hostein sold Montrose to his son-in-law M. Louis Victor Charmolue in whose family it has remained ever since. It is now run by Jean Louis Charmolue. The estate buildings are very pleasantly set on a slight rise overlooking the Gironde, towards which the vines slope. There is a fine avenue of plane trees leading to the *chais*. Montrose is a powerful wine and all the wine is bottled at the château. The strength that can make it rather aggressive in successful vintages stands it in good stead in off-years, such as '58 and '60, when Montrose was rated particularly high. The apparently Scottish name is said to earn it a special popularity in Scotland, but the name is said to arise from the pinkish colour of part of the estate when the heather is in bloom.

Calon-Ségur, lying slightly inland, is a very old estate, which belonged to a M. Gascq in the seventeenth century and then passed by marriage to the celebrated Président de Ségur, who also owned Lafite and Latour. The heart on the château label is said to commemorate the remark of Ségur: 'I make my wine at Lafite and Latour but my heart is in Calon.' He gave his name to the large vineyard, which is now a third growth. The first part of the name is taken from the little river-boats that once ferried timber across the estuary. It belongs to the Gasqueton and Peyrelongue families, after having passed through the well-known Médoc family of Lestapis. Calon has an impressive château with a vineyard of about 60 ha and production up to 220 *tonneaux*. The vineyard is, untypically in St-Estèphe, 50 per cent Cabernet-Sauvignon and Cabernet-Franc and 50 per cent Merlot. A hundred years ago a writer described its wines as the most *corsé* (full-bodied) and alcoholic of the Médoc. Today they are more rounded than most St-Estèphes, but perhaps a little at the expense of character. Sometimes they have struck me as being rather on the sweet side and a shade dull, possibly owing to the high proportion of Merlot. But they are consistent wines, and if I have never been particularly elevated by a bottle of Calon-Ségur, I seldom remember ever having been let down. The estate has a wide reputation and is certainly among the better-known classed growths.

Lafon-Rochet lies on St-Estèphe's vine-crowded plateau. Although a fourth growth, it seems not to have had a very distinguished history, and for many years at least it was one of the more obscure *crus classés*. In the post-war years it was owned until 1960 by a proprietor from the north of France, but in that year it was bought by Guy Tesseron, the well-known Cognac merchant who specializes in selling brandy to the trade rather than to the public. His wife is a member of the Cruse family. In 1965 they decided to rebuild the somewhat nondescript *chartreuse* (one-storey) château, replacing it by one on the traditional low-lying pattern of the district. It must be the only new classed-growth château to have been built for many years, indeed perhaps in this century. The *chai* is unpretentious. The vineyard area is 33 ha (75 per cent

Cabernet-Sauvignon, 10 per cent Cabernet-Franc, 10 per cent Merlot and 5 per cent Petit-Verdot) and production goes up to 150 *tonneaux*. The wine is more supple than many St-Estèphes, but has the typical big colour, flavour and backbone of its district.

Cos-Labory, which has a nineteenth-century turreted château of modest size, lies over the road from Cos d'Estournel, looking across to the vineyard of Lafite beyond the low-lying marshy ground separating St-Estèphe from Pauillac. It belonged to the same Mr Martyn who owned Cos d'Estournel, passed to a M. Louis Peychaud, was more recently in the hands of the Ginestets, and in 1958 was bought by its present owner, M. François Audoy. Compared with its imposing neighbour, Cos-Labory like many of the other lesser fifth growths has a pleasantly farm-like air, and the proprietor himself runs the estate. The 15-hectare vineyard is made up of 40 per cent Cabernet-Sauvignon, 20 per cent Cabernet-Franc and 40 per cent Merlot, mingled with a trace of Petit-Verdot. The output is 40 to 50 *tonneaux*. Half of this is sold to Great Britain and the U.S.A., and the balance divided between France and Germany. The wine is kept three months in the fermenting vats and bottled after two years.

St-Estèphe is great *cru bourgeois* country. It abounds in large properties producing between 50 and 200 *tonneaux*, and based for the large part on rambling, old-fashioned traditional wine buildings. Ch. de Pez is a good example, with a vineyard comprising 70 per cent Cabernet-Sauvignon, 15 per cent Cabernet-Franc and 15 per cent Merlot. The small amount of Petit-Verdot, which gives strength to the wine, is a very irregular producer and was pulled up after the 1970 vintage. It is owned by Mme Bernard, a cheerful widow proud of the 400 hogsheads of wine she makes in a good year. The estate today is largely run by her nephew M. Dousson. In 1965 the Merlot rotted so badly that the wine was made only from Cabernet-Sauvignon, and as a result was surprisingly fruity for such a poor year. The old *chai* is long and lofty, with *barriques* lying in three tiers. The wine is typical St-Estèphe; but de Pez has been making much more supple wines, and for my taste they are now one of the more agreeable wines of the commune.

Meyney, which like Montrose lies near the river, is rather more modern in appearance, with concrete vats and virginia creeper-covered buildings lying round a neat square court-yard. From its well-cared-for 52 ha as much as 250 *tonneaux* can be produced, as in 1966. A peculiarity is that the wine is aged in very large oak casks, each of which holds the equiva-lent of 20 *barriques*, or 4,500 litres. The purpose is to save ullage by evaporation, which is much less in big casks. However this does slightly retard the development of the wine, so after the first year the wine is transferred to the normal casks. A few of these are also filled during the first year, in order to make comparisons. Meyney belongs to Jean Cordier, proprietor of Gruaud-Larose and Talbot.

There are many other St-Estèphe properties with more than a local reputation. This is partly perhaps because their wines are inexpensive by Médocain standards, and so have found customers abroad, including Britain. On nearly every repu-table wine merchant's list will be found some bourgeois growths from this broad commune, which normally produces more than any of the other five *appellation*-named Médocs. These will include the handsome Marbuzet, belonging now to the Prats family of Cos d'Estournel, Phélan-Ségur (once the property of the Martell family of Cognac), La Tour-de-Marbuzet, Le Boscq, Beauséjour, Capbern, Canteloup, Ormes-de-Pez, owned by M. Cazes of Lynch-Bages, Tron-quoy Lalande, owned by M. Jean Castéja, Pomys, Plantier-Rose and Beausite, owned by the Borie-Manoux family and run by M. Émile Castéja of Batailley. There are a number of others. In recent years some St-Estèphe estates in order to sell their large crops more easily have labelled part with subsidiary names which most of them own; very confusing for consumers. More than a hundred of the small proprietors sell their wine to the St-Estèphe co-operative, which markets its wine under the name of Marquis de St-Estèphe. The commune's total output averages nearly 50,000 hl. In the large village, which in one direction looks out over the adjoining Bas-Médoc there is a Wine Museum.

Visitors to Pauillac and the adjacent part of St-Estèphe since mid-1970 will have been astonished and dismayed to find in operation a large Shell oil refinery extending along the estuary banks to the north of the town of Pauillac. While opinions differ as to whether the vines and the wine will suffer from the exhalation of the prominent chimneys, there is a general agreement that the siting of this large complex, which cost many millions of francs, adjacent to probably the most valuable and prestigious agricultural land in France, was an extraordinary act of folly. That its construction over a period went little challenged until near-completion appears to reflect on the vineyard owners of the district. Following somewhat delayed agitation, it has since maintained what for a refinery might be called a 'low profile'.

9. The Médoc II
St-Julien, St-Laurent and Margaux

ST-JULIEN

Retracing our steps through Pauillac, we are in the splendid commune of St-Julien-Beychevelle, which unhappily advertises its produce by a huge, hideous bottle placed prominently on a corner of the main road. Otherwise it is an inconspicuous enough village, with a church whose nineteenth-century Gothic spire contrasts with the classical tower of Pauillac. The commune is straggling. For some reason St-Julien is a name that has caught on and is a Médoc *appellation* known to those who know no other; not even that it is a Médoc. This was usually just as well, for, until we entered the EEC and had to apply the *AC* regulations, very few of the bottles labelled 'St-Julien' in British off-licence windows can have contained a high proportion of wine from this commune. For one thing there are too few small proprietors who would find it profitable to sell their wine under the commune label only, and for another, it is far too expensive a wine to be sold as a sort of superior Bordeaux *vin supérieur*, roughly what it was in the old pre-*AC* days. The basic wine was sold as Bordeaux and one up the scale was Médoc or St-Émilion. The next step, with perhaps an infusion of the real thing, was St-Julien, or for the more knowledgeable, St-Estèphe or Margaux. You paid your money and got your worth. Nowadays the maximum basic quantity of *AC* St-Julien is 40 hl per hectare, but often more under the new annual quotas.

St-Julien contains no fewer than eleven classed growths, ranging from seconds to fourths; more than any other commune bar Pauillac, and with more second growths than any other. St-Juliens at their best are perhaps the quintessence of claret. Grown on a fine gravelly soil with iron in the sub-soil, shallower than in Pauillac, they have less body and 'power' than most of the latter, but more than the Margaux and Cantenacs. They combine fruit with delicacy and have a splendid aroma when fully developed. According to Franck, the St-Julien wines with more colour and vinosity than the Pauillacs took a year longer to achieve maturity, and he stated that they required five to six years in cask. This seems excessive even by the standards of a hundred years or so ago. Today certainly the St-Juliens do not stay more than two and a half years in cask and often less than two years. One wonders if they used to be quite different in style.

Unfortunately until recently at least all too many of the classed growths of this great commune were not making consistently the quality of wine that their classification and reputation implied. This no doubt was partly owing to a long period of unprofitability for the Médoc properties until about the mid-1950s. This may be surprising to those who know only the proud reputation of these classed growths; yet several château proprietors have told me how small until recently was their return. From the 1955 vintage onwards they secured much better prices, and now enjoy something of a boom, comparable with but probably not as great as in the 1860s. The leading châteaux are said to earn at least 8 per cent on their capital, and there has been until recently at least no lack of buyers for any classed-growth Médoc château of good repute that may be in the market.

These earlier poor profits may explain why some St-Julien growths over many years did not make such good wines. Another factor is the personality, interest and experience of the proprietor, and equally of his *régisseur* or *maître de chai*. The latter post may be almost hereditary in some estates, and the reputation of a château may well vary according to the skill and expertise of these key men. A *maître de chai* without a suitably equipped son to follow him means a problem in store for the proprietor. In St-Julien there is also the question of site to be considered. As in Pauillac there is a wide difference between the vineyards near the estuary and those in the backwoods towards St-Laurent and the Landes.

In the eighteenth century the Léoville estate must have been the largest in the Médoc, comprising as it did the three separately owned vineyards of Las-Cases, Poyferré and Barton that exist today. It was originally known as Mont-Moytié – another example of the Médocain propensity to make mountains out of little more than molehills in this flat country. M. Moytié, a merchant of Bordeaux, had created the estate in 1638. Then a century later it was re-named after another Président of the Parlement of Bordeaux, M. Léoville, who died in 1769. He was a member of the Abbadie-Léoville family. In the Revolution the Marquis de Las-Cases-Beauvoice, who owned a quarter of the great vineyard, emigrated and as a result the whole property was sequestered. The rest of the family who had not emigrated demanded the restoration of the remaining three-quarters, and this was granted. The émigré's portion was eventually sold to Mr Hugh Barton, of the firm of Barton & Guestier, partly in 1821 and partly in 1826. Another quarter came into the hands of the Baron Poyferré, who sold it in 1866 to Armand Lalande, a Bordeaux wine merchant and the proprietor of Cantenac-Brown. This portion, sold in 1920 for 1,300,000 frs., is now owned by Cuvelier. The rest of the estate remained in the Abbadie family's possession, represented by the Marquis de Las-Cases, who inherited it from his father in 1815. For many years now this has been a limited company. At one time the Poyferré château was equally divided between the owners of the Poyferré and Las-Cases vineyards.

Las-Cases is much the largest of the three portions, with a vineyard of 65 ha, compared with about 54 for Poyferré and 35 for Barton. Its composition is 70 per cent Cabernet-

Sauvignon, 12 per cent Cabernet-Franc, 15 per cent Merlot, and 3 per cent Petit-Verdot. The average *A C* output of Las-Cases is about 300 *tonneaux* (227 in 1967), considerably more than the other two. The Las-Cases vineyard is not parcelled but Poyferré and Barton are much intermingled. Also Ronald Barton told me that among the lines of his part of Léoville run some vines officially designated as Langoa. The low-built Léoville château, rather less neglected-looking recently, belongs to Poyferré. Las-Cases has no château, but the Bartons have Langoa, which they bought with the vineyard in 1821. The charming mid-eighteenth-century château is built on one storey only, with cellars below. This style of building, common in these parts, is known as a *chartreuse*. Until the latter part of the last century all three wines were customarily sold just as Léoville.

Poyferré, once so fine and elegant, is one of the St-Julien growths that for many years I found disappointing. After making superb wines in the 1920s (for elegance combined with fruit, it produced perhaps the best '29 of all) and some acceptable wines in the disappointing 1930s (particularly '34 and '37), it thereafter produced wines that all too often seemed green, stringy and pinched. From time to time it was said that the wine was improving, and in view of the time it takes to raise the standard of a vineyard, this seems now to be true, for the *vignoble* was replanted to a large extent in 1962. The 1970 certainly has had a certain reputation, though I do not recall tasting it, but the '75 in cask at the château certainly showed well, and was less tannic than some of its neighbours. One must hope these and other vintages turn out well, for Léoville-Poyferré is one of the great names of Bordeaux. The vineyard composition is quite different from Las-Cases: 50 per cent Merlot, 30 per cent Cabernet-Sauvignon and 20 per cent Cabernet-Franc. Production has risen and now averages as much as 250 *tonneaux*, compared with 180 in the late sixties; not, one trusts, too much. The second wine is Ch. Moulin-Riche.

Las-Cases too had a long bad patch. Again, they made wonderful wines during the 1920s, with the '28 leading the Médocain field, and the '29 in the front rank. But then came a similar decline to Poyferré's, possibly owing to the fact that the wines were made under the same management. With the recollection of those few fine bottles of the twenties in mind, in the post-war decade at trade and other tastings I used to look for better things in Las-Cases, but was always disappointed. The '48, '49 and even the almost universally good '53 were thin, ungenerous wines. The '55 was unexciting, but so were many others, and then the tide seemed to turn with the '59. Not a great wine by any means, but a true if rather damped-down St-Julien, with elegance on nose and palate. By the late seventies it was already somewhat attenuated, but good in style. With the '61, a very fine, fruity wine, it had really returned to form, and Las-Cases is now judged to be one of the best estates in the Médoc. The '62 had a good reputation too, though not a favourite of mine, but the '64 was one of the successes of that variable vintage. Since then its reputation has been maintained with the '70, '75 and '76. From 1968 to 1975 the *régisseur* was M. Jean Crété, who then took over at Lafite. It was in 1968 that cement *cuves* were installed in the *cuverie*. Here too production has been increased with no less than 350 *tonneaux* in 1970, though no doubt some of this was sold under a lesser label, of which they appear to have two: Clos du Marquis and Ch. du Grand Parc. These are made from the younger vines. To judge from advertisements that appeared in *Country Life* from time to time in the mid-seventies, Las-Cases seemed to invite *vente directe*, surprising in view of the château's standing in the trade; but I did not find the prices so inviting!

On the other hand Léoville-Barton has come much to the fore since the Second World War. Until 1929 they refused to bottle at the château, and that particular vintage suffered from not too good corks. In England I have found it rather disappointing on the few occasions I have drunk it, but at the château it has sometimes been delicious. This may have been owing to the defective corking of some bottles sold, or to the fact that the wine at Langoa had never been moved. Ronald Barton assured me that his stock was no different from that sold, yet although in Bordeaux châteaux the wine from the different vats is equalized, some may be more equalized than others, and one would not expect the château to retain the worst casks. In this case I think it was not an outstanding '29.

In the 1930s sometimes above average, in the post-war era Barton was certainly the most consistently good of the Léovilles. The 1945 is very fine, and the 1949 too, but perhaps its greatest unusual success was its 1948. This year was a particular favourite of mine, although coming between two such famous vintages as '47 and '49, the intermediate year was largely overlooked. Barton '48 was firm, like all '48s, but wonderfully fruity even when about ten years old, and it became the epitome of a full-flavoured yet truly claret-like wine of its age. Later, however, in the seventies it seemed to turn a little acid, like so many '48s. Ronald Barton is a conservative wine-maker, and in off-years his wines can be a little thin, but in fine years like '53 and '59 they have been among the best. The latter was at one time second only to Lafite, but when nearing its twentieth anniversary became a little variable, some bottles showing abnormally sweet; though they were certainly not chaptalized. The '61 that should have been so good turned out disappointingly, and there followed a period in which the previous distinction seemed a little missing, though it must be said that in the generally disappointing vintage of '67 the Léoville-Barton showed well, and much better than the Langoa. High hopes were held for the '75, certainly a very fruity wine when young. The wine is made and kept at Langoa in the clean but traditional *chais* abutting upon the château's charming garden. New cellars were built in the seventies when compulsory château-bottling became the

THE MÉDOC

Royan
Pointe de Grave
Soulac
GIRONDE
St-Vivien
D2
D1
Bégadan
Lesparre
St-Christoly-de-Médoc
St-Germain d'Estenil
St-Yzans
St-Seurin-de-Cadourne
Vertheuil
St-Estèphe
Cissac
St-Sauveur
Pauillac
St-Laurent
St-Julien
BLAYAIS
Fort de Médoc
Cussac
Blaye
Listrac
Arcins
Lamarque
Moulis
Castelnau
Soussans
BOURGEAIS
Avensan
Margaux
Cantenac
Arsac
Labarde
Bourg
Macau
Le Pian-Médoc
Ludon
Parempuyre
Le Taillan
Blanquefort
ENTRE-DEUX-MERS

0 2 4 6 8 10
Km

BORDEAUX

MÉDOC (BAS-MÉDOC)

HAUT-MÉDOC

rule. At one time neither wine was seen on the Bordeaux market, as both were funnelled through Barton & Guestier, a subsidiary of Seagrams, the American distillery group, but this ended after the 1975 vintage. The composition of the Léoville part of the vineyard is 70 per cent Cabernet-Sauvignon, 7 per cent Cabernet-Franc, 18 per cent Merlot and 5 per cent Petit-Verdot. The proportion of Cabernet-Sauvignon has been increased. The 23-hectare Langoa section is 55 per cent Cabernet-Sauvignon, 7 per cent Cabernet-Franc, 20 per cent Merlot, 10 per cent Malbec (rather unusual these days) and 8 per cent Petit-Verdot.

Gruaud-Larose is a handsome stone château lying rather back from the riverside. At one time it was known as Fond-Bedeau, but M. Gruaud acquired the estate in 1757 and re-named it. It was 116 ha in extent and second only to the then united Léoville property. In 1787 the growth was bought by M. Larose, who married M. Gruaud's daughter and added his name to his father-in-law's. After his death and those of his heirs, it was sold in 1812 to a group of three men, including Baron Sarget. After several later deaths the vineyard was divided into two: Faure and Sarget, although until 1867 the wine was made together, producing an average total of 110–120 *tonneaux*. In England the wine was generally sold and known as Larose. The Sarget part was bought in 1918 by M. Désiré Cordier. The two vineyards were reunited by purchase in 1934 and since then have been sold as Gruaud-Larose *tout court*. The proprietor today is Jean Cordier, grandson of Désiré, who owns both this, as well as Talbot and other vineyards in the Gironde, and one in Sancerre on the Loire. I drank quite a number of the vintages of the 1920s when the two parts were still separate, and my view then was that the Faure was rather the better. I remember the excellent '20 and '29. The Sarget tended to be a little lighter. On the other hand I drank a '24 Sarget at the château in 1966 that had plenty of colour and depth of flavour, and showed little of the decline obvious in most '24s; yet a magnum drunk in London the previous year was much more obviously on the way down; as usual, wines not moved keep best.

Gruaud-Larose is a big fruity wine and is no doubt made that way, as is Talbot. Neither is my conception of a typical, fine St-Julien (such as Beychevelle, Ducru-Beaucaillou and the Léovilles): elegant and fruity, though Léoville-Barton is a bigger wine than its neighbours. On the other hand, what both the Cordier wines lack in elegance they make up in fruit; they are often more agreeable in lesser or variable years, such as '64, when Gruaud-Larose was one of the best, '67 and '73. The '62 Gruaud-Larose also lasted exceptionally well, and the very rich '61 is regarded as one of the great successes of the vintage. If it is compared with the equally esteemed Léoville-Las-Cases '61, the difference in styles will be clear. This difference may partly be the result of the situation of the two Cordier châteaux, well back from the riverside.

Although the two Cordier wines are similar in style – and allied to them in this way to some extent are their other properties, Meyney in St-Estèphe and Clos des Jacobins in St-Émilion – they do not taste alike. Before the big Christie sale of these wines in September 1976, there was a large tasting, going back to '45, and in most cases the Gruaud-Larose was the better. This was true a few days later at Talbot in a tasting of both wines from every passable vintage from '75 back to '61. A possible exception was the '67.

Gruaud-Larose now extends to 77 ha, with 82 per cent Cabernet-Sauvignon, 8 per cent Cabernet-Franc and 10 per cent Merlot, and sometimes produces more wine than any other classed growth save Pontet-Canet, averaging 300 *tonneaux* but often producing more. A special bottle introduced about 1960 for the Cordier red wines originally included an oval seal on the neck, somewhat incongruously reproducing a photograph of the late Mr Georges Cordier wearing a 'derby' hat. With the 1970 vintage this was replaced by his initials cut in the mould. In June 1965 Gruaud-Larose suffered a very bad fire, and no fewer than 547 *barriques* of the 1964 vintage were lost. Fortunately the crop was exceptionally large and over 800 casks survived. As a result some of the cellars have been rebuilt. The *cuvier* is very long, with large wooden vats on one side and glass-lined vats opposite, as at Talbot, although the properties are operated completely separately so far as work in the vineyard and making the wine are concerned. At Gruaud-Larose the wine is transferred from the fermentation vats immediately after the fermentation into the wooden vats opposite, where it is left for one or two months before being racked into the normal-size *barriques*. At Talbot, however, the wine is kept in big casks for eight months. The difference between wine in big and little casks, Jean Cordier told me, was the difference between wines in magnums and bottles. All the Cordier properties are immaculately kept.

Gruaud-Larose has an exceptionally fine private cellar, with vintages extending back to 1815, and as mentioned later I was privileged to drink the splendid 1875 in October 1977. At the Christie sale referred to, single bottles of 19 nineteenth-century vintages were sold, extending back to 1825, which realized £300 the bottle. Other exceptional prices were 1833 (£105), 1834 (£200), 1848 (£190), 1851 (£210 – a magnum), 1852 (£64), 1862 (£155 – a magnum), 1865 (£120), 1871 (£54), 1876 (£64) and 1878 (£80). The respective ratings of some of these vintages will be found in Chapter 18, and as will be seen not all were high.

Not far from the river, Ducru-Beaucaillou's outwardly somewhat grandiose near-classical style building is familiar from its label – in itself certainly distinctive if not exactly attractive from a typographical or design point of view. But then how many château labels are? Inside, the house is charming, and is one of the relatively few Médoc *crus classés* permanently lived in by its proprietor, M. Jean-Eugène Borie and his wife. One reason for the considerable size of the château, facing the Gironde across an agreeable, sloping garden, is that the *cuvier* and the cellars lie beneath the house. In the eighteenth century it was just called Beaucaillou, and was owned by a M. Bergeron, but by 1795 it was in the hands of M. Bertrand Ducru, who died in 1829. He left it to his two children, J.-B. Gustave Ducru and Marie-Louise, who married M. Antoine Ravez. In 1860 the daughter, now Mme Ducru-Ravez, became sole proprietor of what was by then known as Ducru-Beaucaillou. However, she soon disposed of it in 1866 for 1 million francs to Mme Nathaniel Johnston, *née* Dassier (see also under Ch. de Parempuyre). Nathaniel Johnston, of the leading *négociant* house on the Chartrons, did much to restore both vineyard and mansion, but fortunately neither the Johnstons nor the Cruses sought to immortalize their family names by changing those of the wines of the estates they owned.

Some time before the First World War the Johnstons, who owned Ducru-Beaucaillou, began making a sparkling wine. They had owned since 1892 a large estate in the *palus* of Macau, Cru La Maqueline, once the property of the Lynch family, and from the date of their purchase had made sparkling wine by the champagne method, taking the red must off the skins, as in Champagne. It comprised wines from other estates, including probably some from St-Julien. The sparkling wine was matured in cellars across the river in Bourg, and later in another cellar in the limestone of St-Émilion. Others imitated the Johnstons, but without their success. At some time or other the marketing company was situated at Ducru-Beaucaillou, though later in Bordeaux in the Place de la Bourse. At one period this somewhat unusual Médoc sparkler must have been sold under the Ducru label, for the International Exhibition Co-operative Wine Society of London certainly sold it as such from 1903 to the 1930s, although when writing this book I was assured that it contained none of the wine from the distinguished *deuxième cru* vineyard. Since the Wine Society has always enjoyed a reputation for probity, I assume that this curious labelling was permitted. To have tasted it would have been interesting, but not to have done so remains one of the lesser vinous regrets of my life.

In 1928 the Johnstons sold Ducru-Beaucaillou to M. Desbarats de Burke, of the once important merchant house of Gernon, then Gernon, Desbarats. Then in 1942 it was acquired by M. Francis Borie, whose son Jean-Eugène now runs it.

Ducru is another St-Julien property that made distinctly disappointing wine for many years, and I suspect that in the latter years of the Johnston ownership, matters were not too good financially and the estate was allowed to run down; not the only one in those difficult times. Even the 1929 was poor in that great year. However, since the early fifties the wines have steadily improved. I once drank the excellent '53 at the château and have often drunk the '59 and '61. The vineyard make-up is now 65 per cent Cabernet-Sauvignon, 10 per cent Cabernet-Franc, 25 per cent Merlot and a trace of Petit-Verdot. In 1970 the vineyard was increased by the purchase of 18 ha of the Lagrange estate, but the wine is sold separately as Ch. Lalande-Borie. Ducru now totals 43 ha, with an average production of 150 *tonneaux*. M. Borie, who also owns Haut-Batailley and La Couronne in Pauillac, is generally regarded as one of the most serious wine-makers in the Médoc, and Ducru-Beaucaillou certainly ranks among the leading second growths. For M. Borie's second wine, Ch. Lalande-Borie, The *cépage* is 70 per cent Cabernet-Sauvignon, 10 per cent Cabernet-Franc and 20 per cent Merlot. Average production is about 60 *tonneaux*.

Lying far back in the commune and near the boundary with St-Laurent lie the massive buildings of Lagrange. From 1791 to 1842 it was owned by the Cabarrus family, a famous name in revolutionary Bordeaux, as a Mlle Cabarrus married a famous revolutionary, Tallien, and is said to have saved many people from the guillotine. Then Lagrange was bought by Comte Duchâtel, minister of King Louis-Philippe. At that time it was the largest of all the Médoc properties, 300 ha in extent, with 120 under vines, and it had the biggest output of all the *crus classés*: 250 *tonneaux*. Nowadays it is much reduced, with a *vignoble* of 40 ha or less, and a production in a good year of 100 *tonneaux*; yet in the prolific 1964 it made only 80. As mentioned above, part of the property was sold to Ducru-Beaucaillou in 1970. The vineyard is almost half Cabernet-Sauvignon, with a little Cabernet-Franc, and half Merlot. The lines of solid buildings look as if they might have been the stables of a demolished palace. Opposite the Lagrange *cuvier* is another inscribed outside with the names of growths no longer in cultivation or in the same ownership: Ch. St-Julien, and Ch. Latour-Rauzan, now in other hands. The cellar at Lagrange is dark, low and old-fashioned like so many of these establishments. The proprietor now is M. Cendoya. I must confess that I have never drunk a Lagrange of real distinction although a 1926 opened in 1968 was fruitier than I anticipated. Indeed I have drunk very few bottles at all of Lagrange. Nearly all the wine has been château-bottled, one reason in the past why seldom seen in Britain.

However the next third growth, Langoa, is a particular favourite in Britain as well as in Ireland, and this no doubt can be ascribed partly to the nationality of the proprietor, Ronald Barton, who has contrived to support his Irish origin, English education and French domicile. In 1940, when the Germans arrived at Langoa and began to pillage the cellar, as belonging to an enemy alien in England, it was Ronald Barton's 'neutral' Irish nationality that saved most of the precious contents of the private *cave*. By that time the 'neutral' was in the British Army.

Langoa is made in the same *cuvier* and kept in the same cellars as Léoville-Barton, but there is no confusion, and Ronald

Barton maintained, as the only proprietor of a second and a third growth, that he could demonstrate the superiority of the former over the latter. Each year he made both as well as he could, but the Léoville always won; it is a slightly softer, more rounded wine with greater 'flesh'. Yet the Langoa can be very good, and in particular the '53 which Barton said was the best Langoa he had ever made. Nevertheless to the outsider, the difference in quality between wines made on very similar ground is one of the fascinations of claret. Until the 1971 vintage, like Pontet-Canet, the wines of Langoa were never château-bottled. This was partly at least, as with the Léoville, because Ronald Barton found it an additional 'chore', for which his property was not regularly geared. However all Léoville-Barton is now château-bottled in a newly built *chai*. The production of Langoa is now around 50–60 *tonneaux*.

The one-storey *chartreuse* style château of Langoa is one of the most charming in the whole Médoc. It was built and owned by a judge, M. Pontet, in 1758. He had exchanged his old holding in St-Laurent for the much more promising site in St-Julien. It was bought by the Barton family in 1821, and thus provided them with a home and a *chai* for the portion of the Léoville vineyard they soon acquired. In the pre-phylloxera period Langoa was said to fetch more money than any other third growth, and among its well-known successes was the 1846. The château in its central part is only one room deep, and in plan not unlike that of the rather grander Beychevelle. It is curious in having the main floor, the *piano nobile*, leading off a first-floor terrace, so that the private cellars and kitchens are on the ground floor level. Behind it is a *jardin anglais* and a *potager* which have more than a whiff of England. Both Langoa and Léoville-Barton are the personal property of the Barton family.

The two St-Pierres, Bontemps and Sevaistre, are now one, although a section of Bontemps is said to be included in the *bourgeois* growth of Gloria. St-Pierre owes its name to a baron of that name who bought it in 1767. In 1832 the property was divided among his descendants, part being kept by Colonel Bontemps-Dubarry, the rest going to his daughter, who became Mme de Luetkens. That part was sold in 1892 to M. Léon Sevaistre. It now belongs to a firm of Antwerp wine merchants, Van den Bussche Fils, and is run by M. Paul Castelein. For this reason the wine is frequently to be found in Belgium. The vineyard is fairly small, about 13 ha, but it generally makes sound enough wine to make an interesting fourth growth. For a period it was unusual in not blending its wine from the Cabernet and Merlot grapes, and they were sold separately. At a time when the '49s were generally rather hard and edgy, the St-Pierre-Sevaistre was an agreeable soft wine; clearly the Merlot wine. This separation stopped about 1955. The '53 was light and attractive too.

It is curious, in a way, that St-Pierre heads St-Julien's *quatrièmes*, as it is certainly the least known of them today. Not far from the disfiguring publicity bottle of St-Julien is the entrance to Branaire-Ducru, once known as Duluc, after the name of the owner in the late eighteenth and early nineteenth centuries. Between 1856 and 1868 it passed into the hands of M. Gustave Ducru of Ducru-Beaucaillou, and then in 1879 it became the property of his nephews, Ravez and Carbonnier, the sons of Mme Ducru-Ravez, former owner of Beaucaillou. Between 1874 and 1881 the owners added the name Ducru, and on the labels was printed 'Château Branaire (Du Luc-Ducru)'. Recently the Ducru was dropped, and it is now plain Ch. Branaire. From about 1880 to 1952 the property was owned by M. Mital and his successors; they sold it in 1952 to M. Tapie, whose son Jean-Marie now conducts it. The charming low house, two storeys high, was built in 1770 and like Langoa is only one room deep. The attractive staircase in the hall mounts between columns and behind the house is a pleasantly rural garden and a fine orangery recently well-restored.

Branaire is a growth that used to make fine wine and then fell on bad times. I remember their 1899 of which I once had a few bottles from Avery's of Bristol; they were superb in the 1940s. I cannot remember an exciting bottle of any vintage since, but that may have been my misfortune. Certainly in the post-war period this château, with a considerable vineyard of 45 ha that can produce 130–140 *tonneaux*, made rather thin wine. But the proprietors have been enterprising. The composition of the vineyard is 70 per cent Cabernet-Sauvignon and Cabernet-Franc, 25 per cent Merlot and 5 per cent Petit-Verdot. M. Tapie has introduced new methods of vinification, which owe something to Algerian systems. Nor should this put anyone off, for some very enlightened viticulture and wine-making has been practised in Algeria. Moreover at Branaire they went in for producing a non-vintage wine, like Château Margaux and Cos d'Estournel. I sampled the first blend in the autumn of 1966. It was made from the light, elegant '64 which I had tasted on its own, and the definitely rather slight '63. Certainly the result was much more agreeable than the unblended '63. It is easy to shake a purist head at such things, but what is a classed-growth proprietor to do with his off-vintages like 1963 and 1965? However, this practice has now been given up.

Talbot, not a little assisted by its name, is a popular wine in Britain. Named after the English commander who fell at the Battle of Castillon in 1453, any direct connection with him is legendary. Nor is the label correct in describing him as 'Gouvernour de Guienne 1400–1453'. He wasn't and there was no such post. It used to be called Talbot d'Aux, because at one time it was owned by a marquess of that name. In 1919 it passed into the hands of Georges Cordier, who had an English wife and was the son of Désiré Cordier, who bought Gruaud-Larose. It now belongs to his son, Jean, who also owns Gruaud-Larose and other châteaux, as well as a large merchant business in Bordeaux. Talbot has always been a very big property, running behind the Léoville and Langoa vineyards, and to the north of Gruaud-Larose. A hundred years ago it was producing 120–130 *tonneaux*, and today in a plentiful year it can make 300 *tonneaux* from its 85 ha, one of the half-dozen largest classed growths. The house has something of a comfortable English nineteenth-century appearance but the extensive *chais* are very much up-to-date. As already mentioned in connection with Gruaud-Larose both have glass-lined fermentation vats, and large wooden casks for maturing the young wine. The vineyard is made up of 80 per cent Cabernet-Sauvignon, 5 per cent Cabernet-Franc, 10 per cent Merlot and 5 per cent Petit-Verdot. There is none of the last-named at Gruaud-Larose. Although all the Cordier properties in the Bordeaux area are under one *régisseur*, M. Georges Pauli, each château is responsible for making its own wine, under his general supervision. The backbone that Talbot lacks in comparison with its stable-mate can make it very drinkable in rather hard tough years, like 1952 and 1957; and an excellent, well-lasting wine was produced in 1948.

To me one test of a château's reputation is the Unknown Wine List. Upon inspecting the list of a restaurant, hotel or club, it can happen that one knows none of the wines. It is therefore necessary to pick by vintage and/or château. Assuming that the really expensive first growths and the like are out, then I would certainly short-list Talbot, as well as Gruaud-Larose, and if I would not hope for a surprise, as I might with some others, I would expect and almost certainly drink a well-rounded and sometimes slightly rich wine by Médoc standards.

From a separate piece of vineyard of 2 ha Talbot also produces about 10 *tonneaux* of a white wine called Caillou-Blanc, which is of course rather like a Graves in style. The *cépage* is 50 per cent Sauvignon and 50 Sémillon. At one time it was quite common for the Médoc proprietors to make a little white wine, mostly for their own drinking in summer, as they did a *vin rosé* known as a *vin de goutte*; both are referred to elsewhere. Talbot is probably the last to do so, certainly to commercialize it, and of course, the *A C* is only Bordeaux Blanc, for there is no white Médoc *appellation* – fortunately, one may think, in view of a certain publicity delight and public fondness for drinking wines of the 'wrong' colour. The dry white wines of Bordeaux are not all that easy to dispose of, without the additional complication of a Médoc-Blanc.

The long line of St-Julien classed growths ends with one of the best known: Beychevelle. This fine eighteenth-century château, basically built on one storey only, like Langoa and perhaps by the same architect, lies beside the main *D.2* road which passes so many Médoc châteaux. From its terrace looking across the vineyards and meadows, there is an excellent view of the estuary, and this explains the theory that the name comes from *baisse voile*, because the autocratic Admiral d'Épernon demanded that all passing ships should dip their sails. At any rate this story gave the château an opportunity to put a ship on its label and so achieve a suitably nautical touch in a district which is inclined to be introspective from a label point of view. To pass Beychevelle by road is to enjoy one of the not too common architectural pleasures in the Haut-Médoc; and horticultural too, as the parterres are splendid. So is the garden on the other side of this well-kept and beautifully furnished house, which contains one fine room after another.

Beychevelle has usually enjoyed well-off owners. It was the property of the Abbadie family in the first half of the eighteenth century, but they neglected it. The château itself was built in 1757 by the new owner the Marquis de Brassier, but the property was lost in the Revolution because his son, the Baron de Brassier, killed an opponent in a duel; he was exiled and the property was sequestered. However the family contrived to win it back, only to sell it to M. Conte, a rich *armateur* or shipowner of Bordeaux. In turn he sold in 1825 to his nephew, P. F. Guestier, connected with the wine firm of

Barton & Guestier who during a bad time for Bordeaux wines held it until trade improved as a result of the Anglo-French Commercial Treaty in 1860. In 1874 he sold out to M. Armand Heine for 1,600,000 frs., who left it to his daughter, mother of the late owner, M. Achille Fould, Minister of Agriculture in one of the pre-war French governments and whose son was Deputy for the Gironde. The area under vines is 70 ha, the property is productive, and in 1964 made over 200 *tonneaux*. Beychevelle is one of the classed growths particularly well-liked in Britain and is common on wine lists here. In the post-war period it appears to have suffered some decline, with wines less fruity than one would expect. It is said that Beychevelle was an 'early picker', with a consequent lack of stamina. Possibly the vinification methods were varied, and certainly the casks containing the young wines were turned over with their bungs on the side rather than on top earlier than in other châteaux where the top position is normal for the first year. This would appear to indicate that the wines were brought on earlier. However that might be, Beychevelle certainly returned to form with the 1964 and the 1966. The 1970 and 1975 also promised particularly well. Like its neighbour, Ducru-Beaucaillou, it produces an elegant wine in the classic St-Julien style. Its opening price now is on a par with the leading second growths, and if there were a re-classification, there is no doubt that it would be elevated to this rank. The vineyard composition is 70 per cent Cabernet-Sauvignon and 30 per cent Merlot, into which, regardless of percentages that cannot be exact, must be squeezed a tiny amount of Cabernet-Franc. Beychevelle is fairly uncommon in the Médoc for having a fine underground cellar.

St-Julien is almost certainly the claret name most taken in vain in Bordeaux and abroad, and the outsider might imagine large stretches of vineyards in the commune, which are most happy to sell their wine under the sole *appellation* of St-Julien. Nothing could be further from the reality. The classed growths occupy nearly all the available vineyard area, and the twelfth edition of Cocks et Féret's *Bordeaux et ses vins* (1969) mentions a mere 20 *crus bourgeois* and *crus artisans*, which together only account for about 600 *tonneaux*. In addition there is a note of fifteen small proprietors who make between 2 and 5 *tonneaux* apiece. Any growers who thought it worth while to sell their wine under the commune name only would certainly demand a price that would put it well above the price of 'commercial' St-Julien; so the wine would have to be sold under a château label. The vineyard area is about two-thirds of Pauillac's. As with other Haut-Médoc communes, both area and production increased from the sixties onwards, although they had stabilized by the mid-seventies. Average output rose to nearly 30,000 hl, though it was over 35,000 in 1973 and 1974 (almost 36,000 in that year), but only 23,600 in the short 1975. In 1976, which produced a red Bordeaux crop second only to 1973, St-Julien registered only 30,000 hl. Margaux and its associated communes always produce rather more than St-Julien.

The best-known *bourgeois* growth in St-Julien now is certainly Gloria, owned by Henri Martin, for a long time also the manager of Latour, and a prominent figure in Bordeaux wine affairs, including being formerly the president of the *Conseil Interprofessionnel du Vin de Bordeaux*. It includes part of the old vineyard of St-Pierre-Bontemps, and now has 46 ha in production, with a *cépage* of 60 per cent Cabernet-Sauvignon, 30 per cent Merlot, 5 per cent Malbec and 5 per cent Petit-Verdot. Wine labelled Haut-Beychevelle-Gloria is a special *cuvée* made exclusively for Gilbeys, an arrangement come to in the seventies, but is unlikely to vary in style. The wine is full, perhaps a little sweet for some tastes, but this contributes to making it an easy-to-drink glass of claret. This extra roundness often makes Gloria appear more attractive when young than its more aristocratic neighbours. The 1953 was notable for being drinkable very early. Production is about 150 *tonneaux*. Its 1971 opening price was 18,000 frs. a *tonneau*, about three times the opening figure of the 1970, and the following year the 1972 – no more of a success than others – was offered at 32,000 frs. Not too much should be made of the crazy state of the Bordeaux market in these boom years, but the exceptionally advanced prices of Gloria were attributed less to the excellence of the wine or to the financial expectations of the proprietor, than to the prospect of a re-classification of the Haut-Médoc wines. If this took place (which at that time it did not), position would depend to a large degree, as in 1855, on the price obtained *sur la place de Bordeaux*, the Bordeaux market. Gloria was not alone in appearing to adjust its prices for what may be termed class rather than cash reasons. When early in 1979 M. Martin offered his 1978 at more than 50 per cent higher than the 15,000 frs. a *tonneau* of the 1977, some accused the imperturbable *cru bourgeois* of hubris – and promptly increased their own projected opening prices. Such always has been Bordeaux!

Another *bourgeois* St-Julien is du Glana, an imposing if perhaps rather out-of-place mansion near Langoa, but backed by a large new *chai*; the production of a wine obscure for some time is now rising. In the village there is a Ch. Médoc – a name one would think less than genuine on a bottle were it not for the fact that it truly exists – which belongs to Eugène Borie, and is partly used for bottling wines of his châteaux. There is also an equally suspicious-sounding but actual Ch. Grand St-Julien.

ST-LAURENT

Inland from St-Julien lies the commune of St-Laurent, centred on the village of that name on the straight *D.1* road, the *crus classés* by-pass which runs direct to Lesparre, the Bas-Médoc and the Pointe de Grave, where a car-ferry crosses the mouth of the Gironde. St-Laurent has an attractive spired church and also three classed-growth châteaux: a fourth and two fifths.

St-Laurent has no *appellation* of its own, but the wines bear the Haut-Médoc *AC* and the maximum *rendement de base* with this qualification is 43 hl per hectare, 3 hl higher than for the six Médoc communes entitled to their own *appellations*. The soil is gravelly towards the St-Julien side, where the best wines are produced; on the west it shades off into the sand of the Landes.

La Tour-Carnet really has a tower, a rectangular medieval one that puts Latour's affair to shame; there is a moat too. The vineyard, a very old one, once belonged to Jean de Caranet or Carnet. In the eighteenth century it passed to a Swedish family, de Luetkens, and remained in their hands for about a century. Then after several changes it became a private company, but in 1962 was acquired by M. Lipschit, who embarked on a replanting of the vineyard and a renewal of the cellars. When I first visited it, in the *cuvier* were five brand new oak vats and two others. The whole estate, including the house and gardens, had a thorough renovation, and this is indeed to the good, for it is a growth that has to some extent fallen out of public notice. In 1962 it had produced only 5 *tonneaux* instead of the 70 credited to it by Cocks et Féret. But by 1966 the total had been increased to over 30 *tonneaux*. The vineyard make-up is unusual: 80 per cent Cabernet of both varieties, 15 per cent Merlot and 5 per cent Petit-Verdot. Although La Tour-Carnet has not often come my way, I always have had a soft spot for it, because it was one of the wines that introduced me to the 1920s. Early in the last war the distinguished old Bath grocery firm of Cater, Stofell & Fortt – original producers of the Bath Oliver, one of the best biscuits to go with cheese and claret – had some of its own bottling of La Tour-Carnet as well as Pontet-Canet. Priced at 6s. 6d. a bottle and very good too, it was a real bargain at a time when wines doubtfully labelled Liebfraumilch were already fetching £1 or more.

Belgrave is rather better known or more widely distributed.

Until the present proprietor, M. A. Gugés, took over in 1955 the property was run together with La Tour-Carnet. It is a real backwoods property, tucked away in St-Laurent on the poor soil that yields rather slender crops. It adjoins the St-Julien boundary, behind Lagrange, and I was told that at one time Belgrave was counted as a St-Julien and part of it was a fourth growth. The untraditional *chai*, built in concrete in 1934, has vats of the same material and after the fermentation the wine is left in these vats for three months. The more traditional-looking cellars were, on my visit in 1966, full of the odour of ripe apples as well as of wine, for the estate also grows apples for the market. The *vignoble* is 33 ha and at present produces 120 *tonneaux*. The vineyard is 40 per cent Cabernet of both types, 40 per cent Merlot with the balance Petit-Verdot and Malbec. In the cellars was a large bottle stock of 1961, 1962 and some 1959, which probably demonstrates the problems of selling that faced these smaller properties. I have often found Belgrave a sound claret in the good Médoc tradition, fruity but not very refined. I remember a good 1953.

When compiling the first edition of this book I tried to make it my business to visit every *cru classé* in the Médoc and to taste the wine; but I was defeated at Camensac. The rectangular old farmhouse, which claims the château name, lies on a plateau not far from La Tour-Carnet, and faces a square courtyard. Life there appeared to be at a low ebb, and when I did find someone to ask if I might visit the *chai* and taste the wine I was told that the *maître* was away and no one else had the key. I retreated. In 1977, however, I had better luck and there was a good deal of activity in the days just before a late vintage. The owners used to be the firm of Cuvelier, proprietors of Léoville-Poyferré, but in 1964 the property was bought by three people, headed by a Spaniard, M. Émile Forner; it was then in a very run-down state. In 1968 I was told that the area under vines was only 13 ha and the current production no more than 35 *tonneaux*. It is now 58 ha and the average production is 250–260 *tonneaux*, from 60 per cent Cabernet-Sauvignon, 20 per cent Cabernet-Franc and 20 per cent Merlot. Camensac is unique among the *crus classés* for having an automatic picking-machine, used as well at the extensive Larose-Trintaudon, also owned by M. Forner. This time M. Forner offered to allow me to taste the '76, '75 and '70. The first seemed good-coloured, fruity and easy to taste, as the '76s were only a year after they were made, while the '75 was just as typically hard and backward after two years. The '70 had a big nose and colour, and should turn out a bold, fruity wine. It was encouraging to see that this fifth growth was being restored to a state of good and careful production from the depressed condition that long affected many of the lesser names on the list. As yet Camensac is little known in Britain, but with such a large production it should make its way here.

Motorists travelling from Pauillac to the main D.1 road at St-Laurent for many years passed massive, deserted buildings, on one of which could be detected the name Larose-Trintaudon. This was once a well-known vineyard, planted on land which had formerly belonged to M. Larose of Gruaud-Larose, and later to one of his heirs. It was reckoned unofficially as a fourth growth and produced about 25 *tonneaux*. A victim many years ago of the slump in Bordeaux wines, it was deserted. Then in 1964 it was acquired by M. Forner, who had also bought Camensac, and replanting began the following year; very ambitiously, for by the mid-seventies the *vignoble* had grown to 158 ha, consisting of 60 per cent Cabernet-Sauvignon, 20 per cent Cabernet-Franc and 20 per cent Merlot – the same proportions as at Camensac. Average production was already 700–800 *tonneaux* and it was aimed to increase it to 900 – the biggest output in the Gironde, it was said. No doubt the vineyard encompasses part at least of what used to be its neighbour, Perganson, which was much larger and once made 50 to 80 *tonneaux*, but was another victim of the post-phylloxera slump. The long-deserted pair of estates were a grim reminder of the problems that even growers in the favoured Haut-Médoc have from time to time had to face. Can such a large production of a *cru bourgeois* of St-Laurent be absorbed on the Bordeaux market? In essence there is a shortage of fine Médoc in relation to world demand, and much must depend on the quality of the wine itself.

MARGAUX

With Margaux, however, we are again in the main stream. Such, indeed, is its *réclame* that a number of the neighbouring vineyards in Cantenac, Soussans, Arsac and Labarde are now allowed to sell their wine under the *appellation* Margaux, which carries a 40-hectolitre-to-the-hectare *A C* maximum. Those who look at a map of the Haut-Médoc are often surprised by the gap in the famous vineyards between St-Julien and Margaux. After one leaves Beychevelle on the outskirts of St-Julien no great 'name' greets one until Lascombes heaves in sight, whose line of flagstaffs and flags used to represent, no doubt, Alexis Lichine's customers in many countries. The reason for the gap lies in the poor quality of the land: heath and marsh much of it. The Bordelais vineyards are often on marginal land, and in the thirsty gap between the two world-famous villages great wines are impossible, although reputable crops are produced in Cussac, Arcins and Soussans. Up until 1914 the gap was much smaller and less thirsty for there were many *bourgeois* growths on the now vine-deserted stretches.

Although Margaux possesses a nominal eleven classed growths, the commune is dominated by its celebrated *premier cru*, Château Margaux. To wine drinkers of many generations it has symbolized fine claret, and the name of commune and château alike have been familiar to those who could not readily give, let alone pronounce, the name of the commune of

Lafite and Latour. Judging by the prices of the first growths in Christie's wine auctions, Margaux seemed particularly sought-after during the first half of the nineteenth century. It had the advantage of being sold as Château Margaux, to distinguish it from a wine of the commune, while the other wines seldom had this prefix until well on into that century.

Margaux has undergone so many changes and had so many owners that to recount them would be valueless. It used to be called La Motte or Lamothe, and was said to have been the property of Edward II. It is also alleged that English soldiers ravaged the vineyard at the end of the fourteenth century, so presumably by then it was in French hands. The owner commonly thought to have enlarged the vineyard and planted it with top quality vines in 1750 was M. de Fumel, also owner of Haut-Brion. There is a story that the next owner, the Comte d'Hargicourt, the godson of Mme Dubarry, the mistress of Louis XV, attracted the attention of that sovereign by wearing buttons of unusual lustre. The king said that to wear such stones he must be the richest man in his kingdom, whereupon the owner of Château Margaux replied, 'I am wearing the diamonds of my soil.' These were the plain stones of the Médoc, cut and polished. Whether true or not (the anecdote is also told of Latour) this public relations story stood the estate in good stead. In the cellar of Count d'Adhémar, Louis XVI's retiring Ambassador to the English Court, in 1788 there was some Ch. Margeau (*sic*).

The Comte d'Hargicourt acquired Margaux by marrying in 1768 the daughter of the Marquis Joseph de Fumel and during the Revolution both were guillotined, so that Château Margaux like Lafite was sequestered by the state. In 1804 the *régisseur* of Latour estimated that Margaux was worth 1,200,000 livres, the same price for which Lafite had been sold five years earlier, but it was bought by the Marquis de la Colonilla in the same year for 652,000 frs. and the old building was pulled down without his even seeing it. From that year dates the splendid classical First Empire building whose colonnaded portico is so familiar from the label. The architect was J. Combes, a pupil of Louis. In 1836 the château was acquired for 1,300,000 frs. by M. d'Aguado, Marquis de Las Marismas, who also bought the little port of Margaux on the estuary. The Aguados were the first of a number of bankers who acquired Médoc châteaux in this period; others were to include the Rothschilds, Pereires and Foulds. In 1879 it was transferred to the Comte Pillet-Will for 5 million frs., and his name across the label may be remembered by those who have had bottles of Margaux prior to 1920, when a company acquired it. The owner after Pillet-Will was his godson, the Duc de la Tremoille. In 1925 M. Fernand Ginestet, the Bordeaux wine merchant, and a syndicate began to buy shares in the company owning the château, and slowly the Ginestet control was increased, so that in 1949 his son Pierre Ginestet was able to complete the purchase on his own; to effect this he sold Clos Fourtet in St-Émilion. He furnished Margaux with great taste in the First Empire period of the building. This décor makes an interesting comparison with that of the Second Empire furnishings of that other first growth, Lafite. It seems likely that Margaux was less profitable and more of a financial problem in the post-war period than the other first growths. Even in 1949, it has been said, M. Ginestet sought some financial association with Baron Élie de Rothschild of Lafite, but the latter desired control of the company, which M. Ginestet was, understandably enough after all his family's efforts to secure sole ownership, unwilling to accept.

Moreover, Margaux has for many years always secured a much lower price for its wine than the other first growths, although its production costs were probably not markedly less. It was generally thought in the 1970s that the vineyard and cellars were in less good condition than might be expected of a first growth. Then in 1975 it was announced that the estate was for sale. This was not owing to loss on the part of Ch. Margaux, but to difficulties run into by the Ginestet firm in Bordeaux as a result of the severe slump that followed the speculation period of 1971 to 1973. As a result, prices of wines had risen sharply, and Ginestet et Cie were bound by exclusive contracts with more than sixty growers which they were obliged to honour. Moreover the exports of Ch. Margaux, like the other classed growths, suffered a severe setback after the over-high prices of the preceding years. Ch. Margaux was in effect pledged as security, but then M. Ginestet was required to dispose of it. At first it was said that it would be bought by the Cognac house of Rémy Martin, but the large U.S. group, National Distillers, came in with a much larger bid of 82 million frs. (equivalent then to £9¼ million). However, the French Government would not permit another first growth to pass into foreign hands. Then in December 1976 it was announced that the estate had been purchased by the grocery and finance group, Félix Potin, headed by M. Mentzelopoulos, a Greek domiciled in France. The price was said to be about 52 million frs., but with a quarter of a million bottles in the cellar, including three unsold vintages, the total payment was 72 million frs. (about £8 million). At the time of the sale it was confirmed that the firm of Ginestet would continue to market the wines. Nevertheless, great sympathy was felt in Bordeaux for Pierre Ginestet, a leading statesman and diplomat of the Bordeaux wine world and one of the most charming men in a milieu where they are not lacking. On the other hand, it was undeniable that vineyard, *chais* and château had suffered from financial stringency for a number of years, and the new owners not only had the requisite resources but also great enthusiasm in the cause of a great estate. Both M. Mentzelopoulos and his wife, who take an active interest in the château's affairs, have pledged themselves to carry out the necessary changes in the vineyard and estate buildings to restore Margaux to its rightful position. Mme Mentzelopoulos told me in 1977 that she thought it would take ten years for Margaux to regain its peak; for one cannot renew a vineyard overnight.

The cellars of Margaux are among the finest in the Médoc, particularly the lofty building, supported by a line of white pillars, where the young wine is kept for its first year. Adjoining this is the splendid private cellar, in the form of a long gallery built of stone from the Charente at the same time as the château. The stone bins, three rows high on either side, can each hold 50 dozen, the contents of two *barriques*. There are 60,000 bottles there, including the wines of other leading châteaux. This long gallery-cellar makes a fine sight, but Pierre Ginestet said it is no longer big enough and another is planned. One of the reasons for this is that Château Margaux is large and conveniently near Bordeaux to make it an attractive place for celebrations and the visits of distinguished persons. These may make calls not only on the private cellars but on the young wines still in cask. When the late Chancellor Adenauer visited Bordeaux he was taken officially to Margaux with his suite and French hosts. In the course of the day it is said that two *barriques* of samples of the young wine were consumed by the visitors! During the month of August alone, when tourists descend in coach-loads, no fewer than eight *barriques* might be emptied in this way. Expensive publicity, or – now stopped!

Fortunately Margaux is a big estate, although only a relatively small part is planted with vines: about 80 ha, with an average production of 200 *tonneaux*. The composition of the vineyard is 50 per cent Cabernet-Sauvignon, 10 per cent Cabernet-Franc, 35 per cent Merlot and a small balance of 5 per cent of Petit-Verdot, which is providential in a wet year, as it provides the acidity and backbone that will be lacking, especially in the Merlot. The soil is gravelly, except in one part where it is soft-water chalk, rare in the Médoc. This is where the white wine, sold as Pavillon-Blanc de Château Margaux, comes from: 40 *tonneaux* of it on average. The *cépage* is 50 per cent Sauvignon and 50 per cent Sémillon. It is a pleasant, dry wine but does not aspire to be in the same class as Haut-Brion-Blanc. Pavillon-Blanc, of course, relies on the cachet of Margaux. The soil of the commune is very thin, a coarse gravel with lime sub-soil. The average yield is small, and production may be phased out. A second red wine used to be sold as Pavillon Rouge, and this may be re-introduced.

The wine of Château Margaux is noted for its fine bouquet and the delicacy of its flavour. At a blind tasting of young first growths it may often be picked out by its 'nose'. On the whole it is a wine particularly successful in fine years, but sometimes correspondingly disappointing in off-vintages; although the excellent 1950 is an exception to this. Yet, for example, the 1953 is still fine, and the 1961 had an outstanding reputation. The 1966, a well-balanced wine, also shows very well, yet the 1964 proved disappointing. Over the past half-century the château has had its ups and downs, and for a period was making wine well under its class. Along with Haut-Brion it was the first of the first growths in 1923 to establish compulsory château-bottling. But in 1930 this rule was abandoned and for twenty years Château Margaux could be bought in wood, the only one of the *premiers crus* to whom this applied. (1949 was the last year it was shipped in wood, but later at least one cask appears to have got away. For Château Margaux 1952, bottled by Skinner and Rook of Nottingham, was sold at Christie's in February 1968.) No doubt this gave the wine some competitive advantage in the difficult thirties, but good vintages were rare then, and in the intermediate post-war period the wine was not very inspiring; but the 1950 was first-class. The last really good old Margaux that I have tasted was the 1924, a perfectly balanced wine and probably the best Château Margaux of the decade. Part of the 1929 was excellent too, but some was thin and poor, owing, I believe, to problems during the fermentation.

Château Margaux is a difficult wine to taste young, and this applies to other wines in the neighbourhood. For they tend to taste astringent and thin, lacking the 'flesh' of the Pauillacs and the fruit of the St-Juliens. Until recently it has often been the least dear of the *premiers crus*, although these days that is but a relative term. When Château Margaux is successful, this is, one may feel, the essence of claret – fine, delicate but fruity – and its rivals up there in Pauillac can seem a little heavy-footed. A splendid example of this was the '61. But when it falls short, even in a reasonably successful year like 1955, it is not a very attractive, though refined, glass of fine claret.

To solve the problem of off-vintages, in 1966 Pierre Ginestet decided to produce a non-vintage wine on his properties, including Margaux and Cos d'Estournel. This was a blend of young vintages, good and indifferent, and the first batch, of about 10 *tonneaux* so far as Margaux was concerned, was to be a blend of 1963 and 1964. When I first tasted the blend it had not been in bottle many months, but it was certainly better than the 1963 on its own. This move was the subject of controversy, and at first thought it seems somewhat below the dignity of a *premier cru*, and even of lesser classed growths, to market their wine like this. As recently as 1936 Lafite sold most of its crop of that year as Pauillac *tout court* and even today proprietors sell off part of their crop not considered good enough to be sold under the château name, although it does not cost any less to produce a bad wine than a good one. In 1975 Latour sold wine from young vines as Pauillac. There was no wine produced at Château Margaux in 1965 sold under the château label, and if sold as plain Margaux or even as Bordeaux Rouge, it secures a fraction of the price of the wine sold as a château wine. In 1963 there was not a Médoc proprietor who did not lose money, and 1965 was even worse. The experiment was not a success, and subsequently this N.V. Ch. Margaux was first suspended and then dropped.

Rausan, along with Léoville and Larose, were probably the first named growths outside the *premiers crus* to establish a reputation abroad. Originally this Margaux vineyard was united and belonged to the Mesures de Rausan family, merchants, one of whose descendants, M. de Rausan, was a member of the Bordeaux Parlement in the eighteenth century. The story goes that, dissatisfied with the price offered for his wine in Bordeaux, he chartered a ship which he loaded with casks from two good vintages and sailed for London. Using his ship in the Thames as an office, his initiative brought him both publicity and orders. But he still did not consider the price high enough, so he announced that, unless he secured what he considered a fair price, he would throw the casks into the river, barrel by barrel. After four casks had thus been jettisoned the onlookers could stand it no longer and surrendered to the vendor.

Later on the vineyard was divided, with two-thirds remaining to the Baronne de Ségla, born a Rausan. In 1866 this portion passed to M. Eugène Durand-Dassier, the father-in-law of M. Frédéric Cruse, for 505,000 frs. The Cruse family owned it until 1956 and turned this charming, low-built house into a kind of private museum, with rooms furnished in the style of various French epochs. In one room, I remember, there was a replica of the curious bath in which the unfortunate Marat was murdered. Other rooms were more comfortably adorned and the house was of considerable interest. The Cruses sold it for 36 million old frs., and after an intermediate owner, M. de Meslon, a descendant of the Rausan family, it passed at an advanced price, after much replanting, in 1959 into the hands of John Holt & Co., the Liverpool firm of West African merchants, who thus began their involvement in the wine trade. Later they were acquired by the financial conglomerate, Lonrho. The reception rooms are now furnished with eighteenth-century English furniture.

The vineyard of Rausan-Ségla now lies compactly in front and at the side of the low château buildings, but – an illustration of the parcelization of Bordeaux vineyards – until 1933 it was divided into no fewer than 240 strips. In particular it was deeply mixed up with its neighbour, Rauzan-Gassies, but in 1933 an exchange was made with them and other neighbours, and it is now contained in only 16 'parcels'.

As a wine Rausan-Ségla had a particularly distinguished record in the 1920s, and the '29 was outstanding for its balance of fruit and delicacy. Meanwhile the vineyard and its output had been allowed to decline. Whereas in 1899 and 1900 it had produced 62 and 122 *tonneaux* respectively, this was down to about 20 *tonneaux* in the 1930s, and the vineyard area had dropped sharply to only 34 ha. Replanting took place in 1934, but even in the post-war period the crop was small: 30 *tonneaux* in 1945, a very short vintage, and only 44 in 1953. By the time the Cruses disposed of the property, the active area was again reduced to scarcely 20 ha, and in 1959 only 35 *tonneaux* were made. However, much replanting with a large proportion of Cabernet-Sauvignon took place under de Meslon and this continued under Holt's, so that it had risen to 95 *tonneaux* by 1962, although the general shortage of the '61s is demonstrated by the production of only 35 *tonneaux*. Now the vineyard area is 42 ha and the average crop about 100 *tonneaux*. The *cépage* is 51 per cent Cabernet-Sauvignon, 11 per cent Cabernet-Franc, 37 per cent Merlot and 1 per cent Petit-Verdot. Since 1961 when the château celebrated its tercentenary of being known as Rausan with a special label for this vintage, the wine has been bottled in a newly designed, embossed bottle. Rausan-Ségla was the last Bordeaux estate of importance to tread the grapes; it ceased after 1956, with the transference of ownership. A curiosity by which I remember Rausan-Ségla is its *vin rosé*, known as a *vin de goutte*. In common with other properties, they occasionally made a few hogsheads of this wine for domestic consumption; the wine is taken off the skins after passing through the *pressoir fouloir* and fermented in hogsheads, so there is little contact with the skins. After twenty years the '47 was still delicious. Ronald Barton has also made a *vin rosé* periodically at Langoa, and Alexis Lichine commercialized this in recent years at Lascombes. The most interesting *vin de goutte* I have tasted was the remarkable Léoville-Poyferré 1898, referred to in the vintages chapter.

Rauzan-Gassies – whose variation in the spelling of the first part of its name, called after a seventeenth-century owner, is often mis-rendered in wine lists – was sold in 1866 to M. Charles Rhoné-Pereire. It is much smaller than its neighbour, consisting of 22 ha, but relatively produces quite a large quantity: about 110 *tonneaux*. Perhaps too much. Rauzan-Gassies has one of the most attractive labels, but almost consistently I have found the wine thin and disappointing. A few years ago I shared in a splendid magnum of 1920, but otherwise I have been unlucky, and years ago even the 1929 was lacking in fruit. It is unfortunate that one of the pair that top the *deuxièmes* after Mouton, which has long since shrugged off this ascription, should not be better. It is fair to add that the '61 was the best wine from this growth for many years.

Although Durfort-Vivens stands high in the 1855 classification, this has not been a prominent wine in the last generation. It has hardly ever come my way, although once I had some 1934 from the Wine Society which was softer and more agreeable than most of the Médocs of that hard year. Originally named after a proprietor, M. Durfort, the next owner, M. Vivens, added his own name when he acquired it in 1824. In 1866 his great nephew sold out to MM. G. Richier and E. de la Mare for the considerable sum of 500,000 frs. At that time it was 30 ha in extent and produced 50–55 *tonneaux*. Towards the end of the century Durfort-Vivens was the property of the family and firm of Delor, who disposed of it during the difficult times in the 1930s. After that it was owned by Pierre Ginestet until 1963 when he sold the vineyard, the *cuvier* and the name, but not the château, to Lucien Lurton, the owner of Brane-Cantenac, another second growth. Pierre

Ginestet told me that he sold it because he did not want to own adjoining first and second growths. The château, with its name on the wall, is on the outskirts of the village of Margaux, and is now occupied by Pierre Ginestet's son Bernard. For some time the area of the Durfort vineyard was much reduced, but is now said to be on the increase, perhaps with the transference of part of the large Brane-Cantenac vineyard. The output is about 40 *tonneaux*. The *cépage* is 60 per cent Cabernet-Sauvignon, 20 per cent Cabernet-Franc and 20 per cent Merlot.

It must be understood that these château names are in effect brand names, and can be used at will inside a commune, but without violating the gap between classified and non-classified vineyard areas, already mentioned. A classed-growth proprietor cannot buy a *bourgeois* vineyard and add the production to his own, but he can acquire another classed growth and use the name and/or the vineyard. This is what Palmer did with Desmirail.

Margaux's fourth *deuxième*, Lascombes, was yet another highly-placed classed growth that somehow had not shone for many years, until in 1952 it was bought by a large American syndicate headed by Alexis Lichine, an American of Russian origin who certainly created a name for himself and an increased market for French wines in the United States. The price is said to have been very low; only a five-figure sum in dollars, but much money had to be spent on the property. Lascombes was named after the Chevalier de Lascombes, and then it passed into the hands of the Johnston family, and later to that of M. Petit who owned it a century ago. At one point it was well known for its 1847 and 1848, but the production was small, and during the present century it has had many masters, which no doubt accounted for often disappointing wines. The original château was a charming small eighteenth-century building, still standing, but in the last century a rather ugly if more imposing building was erected, and this has housed both annual exhibitions of pictures associated with wine and a shifting flock of young wine students. In 1971 Lascombes was sold to Bass Charrington Vintners (later renamed Hedges & Butler after the Regent St, London, merchants owned by the brewery group) for $1·9 million. They were responsible for erecting an imposing new *chai*, somewhat resembling that of Mouton-Rothschild.

Lascombes has a common Médoc vineyard make-up, though with less Cabernet-Sauvignon than many classed growths: 48 per cent Cabernet-Sauvignon, 11 per cent Cabernet-Franc, 33 per cent Merlot, 7 per cent Petit-Verdot and 1 per cent Malbec. From about 80 ha in the 1950s it was increased to 92, which in area alone must make it the largest in the Médoc; its average production rose from 180 *tonneaux* in the late sixties to 300 ten years later – another example of the growth of the classed-growth *vignoble* in the Médoc. Although great things were promised under its new American owners – some of whom, it was said, had inscribed on their visiting-cards *Propriétaire dans le Médoc*, or words to that effect – and although it is understood that it takes ten to fifteen years radically to raise the standard of a vineyard, it does not seem to me that Lascombes has regained the status that in 1855 placed it in the middle of the *deuxièmes crus* and just above the classic, long-established Gruaud-Larose. The wine has been round and fruity, but lacking in the elegance and style that one looks for in Margaux wines. Perhaps it is still to show its best. Until recently, at least, most of the wine went to America.

It is convenient to take Malescot St-Exupéry and Marquis d'Alesme-Becker together, for both have been under the same ownership for many years. Malescot – which at one time enjoyed, I am told, a certain popularity in Canada when pronounced as Male Scot – was named after Simon Malescot, *procureur* in the Bordeaux Parlement, who bought the property in 1697. In 1827 it passed to the Comte de St-Exupéry who added his name, and the estate changed hands again in 1853, being acquired by M. Fourcade. At that time the vineyard was very large, amounting to 77 ha, producing well over 100 *tonneaux*, but this diminished over the years, and now production is much smaller, yielding 50–60 *tonneaux* from 22 ha. Becker, said to be one of the three oldest Médoc vineyards, on the other hand was always one of the smallest classed growths, and a century ago was making only about 7 *tonneaux*. Now the figure is 40–50 from 12 ha. For a period this pair of estates was English-owned because in 1919, after being in German control, they were acquired by the London wholesale wine firm of W. H. Chaplin, best known for their connections with the Australian wine trade. Soon after the last war they sold out to Seager Evans, the distillers, who in their turn in 1955 sold the two Margaux growths to Paul Zuger, who had been running the estate on their account. The handsome house, associated with the St-Exupéry family, stands in the middle of Margaux. The former Becker château is elsewhere in the village. Paul Zuger has done a good deal of replanting and worked very hard to improve his property. The *cuvier* adjoining the château is on two floors as at Pontet-Canet, and contains five wooden vats and four of the concrete type. Both wines are made in the same *chai*, and the vineyard composition of each is similar: 40 per cent Cabernet-Sauvignon, 20 per cent Cabernet-Franc, 30 per cent Merlot and 10 per cent of Petit-Verdot. Until recently neither wine had been much seen in England, but the '48 Malescot has been an outstanding example of that vintage and since the sixties it has usually been making excellent wine. Malescot has the style and elegance associated with Margaux; Becker is rather more *corsé*. The estate also has a second wine, Domaine-du-Balardin, which has the *appellation* Bordeaux Supérieur.

By one of the many irrationalities of the Médoc, Boyd-Cantenac is indeed a third-growth Margaux, and was entitled to this *appellation* in 1855. A hundred years later its now associated growth, Pouget, a *quatrième* in Cantenac, also became entitled to sell as a Margaux. Of the two, Pouget is the older property and used to belong to the monks of Le Prieuré. Mr Boyd must surely have been of Irish or Scottish origin but this is not clear, although the present owner believes that this gentleman lived in the time of Napoleon III. Boyd-Cantenac used to belong to the Ginestet family and was bought from them in the mid 1930s. Both are owned by Pierre Guillemet and his energetic wife, who won my heart when I called to taste their wines, by insisting that I preserved my health from the ravages of young wines by eating bread and cheese at the same time. Together the two properties form 25 ha and produce 100 *tonneaux*. After the vintage the best *cuves* are set aside to be called Boyd-Cantenac, the less good are sold as Pouget. (Another example of the brand element in these wine names.) The vineyard is 70 per cent Cabernet-Sauvignon, 10 per cent Cabernet-Franc, 15 per cent Merlot and 5 per cent Petit-Verdot. The reason why these wines are not very widely known is that the Boyd part is normally sold to one or two wine merchants only, while the Pouget goes exclusively to private clients. I thought the Boyd-Cantenac in particular a soft, supple wine in good years, and improving steadily in the seventies.

Margaux seems somewhat the home of lost châteaux. Desmirail has disappeared as a vineyard, Durfort is divorced from its vineyard, Ferrière has been somewhat marginally active recently, and Dubignon-Talbot, a classed growth in 1855, no longer exists.

Of these Ferrière is the senior in the classification lists. It was named after Gabriel Ferrière in the mid eighteenth century, and was in the hands of that family until 1914. The production was always tiny, and in 1867 was given as only 6 *tonneaux*. The modest château lies in the middle of the village, and part of the small vineyard is actually walled; the remainder is near Lascombes. In 1962 a fifteen-year lease to Lascombes was arranged, and the wine is still made and kept there. There has been replanting of the 6½-ha vineyard and production, now 10–12 *tonneaux*, might rise to 15. It will be interesting to see how the wine develops.

The Château of Desmirail, a third growth like Ferrière, is also situated in the middle of Margaux. Originally the vineyard was part of the large Rauzan estate and was split off when a M. Desmirail married a Mlle Rauzan de Ribail in the eighteenth century. Production of this vineyard was never large, about 25 to 30 *tonneaux*, but it had an excellent reputation. I remember a '28 that was much less hard than many of its peers. In 1938 M. Edmond Ritz, a mining engineer from Alsace, bought Desmirail from its then owner, M. Michel; the latter had already sold two or three ha of the vineyard adjoining Palmer to M. Miailhe, part owner of the latter estate, and had also sold part of the cellars. Finally in 1957 the property was sold to Palmer, and the vineyard incorporated in that estate. It is now a brand name seldom used.

Marquis de Terme, the one fourth growth of Margaux, has its *cuvier* on the outskirts of Margaux near the Rauzan-Gassies vineyard, but the other *chais* are a mile away. The wine is not very well known in Britain, although production can be as high as 200 *tonneaux* from a rather small vineyard of 24 ha. Perhaps the output is excessive, for a hundred years ago when it was owned by M. Oscar Sollberg the production was given as 50–60 *tonneaux*. The present owner is M. Pierre Sénéclauze. Certainly the wine is made unusually in the tile-lined vats in the *cuvier*, for the *maître de chai* told me that, after the fermentation, the wine is kept in these vats for a year and then in casks for a further two years. All the wine is château-bottled. The make-up of the vineyard is unusual too, for it is split up equally between the four main grapes, Cabernet-Sauvignon, Cabernet-Franc, Merlot and Petit-Verdot. There must be a higher proportion of Petit-Verdot at Marquis de Terme than in any other classed growth in the Médoc. The young wine as I tasted it from the vats seemed full and fruity, but I cannot recollect ever drinking a mature bottle. Most of the average output of 150 *tonneaux* is sold direct to private customers and the remainder exported, so it is not seen on the Bordeaux market.

A former classed growth that has now completely disappeared is Dubignon-Talbot. It ceased production in the phylloxera period, was revived, but in the early 1960s Cordier bought the brand name, presumably to avoid a rival Talbot to his own, while the tiny vineyard was divided between Ginestet and Zuger.

Margaux *tout court* is a name not infrequently to be found on wine labels, but there can be scarcely enough of such wines from proprietors, content to sell them only under the commune label, to inspire confidence in most of such bottles; so the contents are unlikely to have originated solely in the district. Of course, some may come from the outlying communes which, as already explained, are entitled in part to call their wines Margaux. These are the whole of Soussans and Cantenac and part of Arsac and Labarde. This authorization was given first in 1955. However the balance of proprietorship can be seen from the fact that thirty large proprietors account for 85 per cent of the wine sold under the *appellation* Margaux, while seventy small owners take up the remaining 15 per cent. Counting the 'satellite' communes, the area under vines is nearly as large as Pauillac and St-Estèphe: about 820 ha, but on the thin soil average output is much less, around 35,000 hl – as elsewhere, a good deal more than it was in the sixties.

CANTENAC

Adjoining Margaux is the leading commune now allowed to
sell its wines as Margaux: Cantenac. As a result the name has
almost disappeared so far as wine lists are concerned, except
for the growths that have the commune name incorporated in
their own. The wines of Cantenac tend to be a trifle fuller, less
delicate than those of Margaux, although Palmer, whose
vineyard adjoins Château Margaux, is somewhat similar in
style, with perhaps a little more body, which I find agreeable.
The vineyards of these adjoining communes are considerably
intermingled.

According to the classification, Brane-Cantenac, a second
growth, is the leader of the Cantenacs. It was named after the
former proprietor of Mouton, who moved south after his
sale to M. Thuret in 1830 and then concentrated his talents on
this vineyard, which was once called Gorse-Gui. It then passed
through various hands rather quickly, including those of M.
Roy, owner of Issan. Today it is the property of Lucien Lurton
and is situated rather back from the river and near the woods.
Behind the small château, one storey high except for a central
upper room, lies a very green lake. The aspect of the wine
buildings is traditional but the vineyard is large, with some
80 ha producing well over 200 *tonneaux* a year. The vineyard is comprised of 75 per cent Cabernet-Sauvignon, with
the balance made up of Cabernet-Franc, Merlot and a very
small quantity of Petit-Verdot. Brane-Cantenac used to be a
big, sometimes rather coarse wine, with a good deal of fruit
but not overmuch delicacy; or that was my experience. But
I remember one or two splendid wines in the 1920s, not-

ably the 1924 and 1928. The latter, in a vintage that remained hard longer than any vintage should, became one of the better-balanced wines. Again in 1948 it turned out exceptionally well. Since then it was disappointing for at least a decade. Perhaps the vineyard was being replanted, for the wines improved considerably in the sixties, and have become a deal more elegant and Margaux-like in style, which is as it should be. The '64 was one of the better examples, possibly because it was one of the earliest to pick in the Médoc, along with its companion estate of Durfort-Vivens, and finished as the pene-trating rain descended. The '66 turned out well too, and the estate's *deuxième-cru* rank is deserved. Production is large, and it is to be hoped that the quality of a wine without a great deal of body will be maintained. Like its Brown neighbour, it is notable for its resplendent black and gold label. It has a second wine, Ch. Notton.

Ch. Kirwan (is the name Irish in origin?) is something of a curiosity. At one time it must have made distinguished wine and in the 1855 classification Kirwan was placed at the head of the third growths; a position of note. About this time the estate was owned by M. Godard who became Mayor of Bordeaux, and when he died about 1882, he left it to the city of Bordeaux. No doubt this was intended as an act of civic piety, but as in similar cases one may suspect that the gift was an embarrassment, for although municipally-owned vine-yards are not unknown in Germany and Switzerland, they are not part of the Bordeaux scene. So in 1885 the well-known firm of Schröder & Schÿler made a contract to buy the whole crop every year, and for a long period the wine was sold as a *monopole* without vintage date, although a small part of the crop was disposed of with a vintage year on the label. Then I remember the wine being marked in a pre-Second World War list of Avery's of Bristol as 'ten years old'. In 1904 the city of Bordeaux divested itself of the property and sold it to two other well-known wine merchants Daniel and Georges

Guestier. Alfred Schÿler married Daniel Guestier's daughter and when his father-in-law died in 1924, Schröder & Schÿler acquired the property whose crop they had been marketing for about forty years. It used to have a considerable sale in Germany, where much of the firm's business lay. The eighteenth-century château and its gardens, somewhat tucked away behind the Médoc railway line, are particularly attractive. The vineyard is 25 ha in extent and now makes 80–100 *tonneaux* of wine. In the 1956 frosts 100,000 vines out of 250,000 were lost. After a bad period the wine is now improving again. Considerable replanting began in 1972 and before the end of the seventies production is expected to be doubled. Nowadays the wine is sold with a vintage label.

With the exception of Ch. de Lamarque in that commune, Issan could almost be described as the only original old château of the Médoc, complete with towers and moat. The oldest part dates from about 1600. It lies between the *D.2* Médoc road and the river; down on the flat land which is almost a drained marsh, with dykes. Much of the vineyard, however, is on a slightly higher ground, not far from Château Margaux and opposite Le Prieuré. Its early days are associated with those of the last of the English in Bordeaux. For after the capture by Dunois in 1451 of Blaye across the river, the English had to evacuate the country and fought a skirmish at Issan on their way out. The legend is that they succeeded in extricating some of the local wine as well as themselves and carried it off to England where the wine of Issan became known. More recently there was apparently a special demand for Issan in Britain in the last century. In 1848 it belonged to M. Deluc, whose family sold it to M. Gustave Roy, also owner then of Brane-Cantenac. The wine had a high reputation in the nineteenth century – and its label motto had been *Regum Mensis Arisque Deorum*. It was said to be a favourite of the Austrian Emperor Franz Josef; particularly the 1899. But from the middle of the 1920s it declined, under the proprietorship of M. Grange who also owned Giscours. The estate certainly passed through not very good times in the first third of this century, but was purchased just after the war by the late Emmanuel Cruse, part-owner of Rausan-Ségla. Restoration was not taken in hand until after the sale of the latter in 1956. A great deal of money was spent not only on the charming château, with its fine rooms and furniture, but also on the cellars and vineyards. One of the *chais* has timber rafters, recalling an old dining hall, and is registered as an historic monument.

The vineyard area, after extension, is 26 ha; its composition is 75 per cent Cabernet-Sauvignon, 5 per cent Cabernet-Franc and 20 per cent Merlot. Production is about 80 *tonneaux*. Like other Cruse properties, Issan was shipped in bulk or bottled in Bordeaux until in 1972 it fell into line with the other *crus classés* and was entirely château-bottled from that vintage onwards. Perhaps, owing to its Cruse ownership, and like the other wines not sold on the Bordeaux market – generally a mistake in my view whatever the commercial acumen of the firm responsible for its marketing – Issan was not always as well-known as it deserved. From the sixties onward I have usually found its wines well-balanced and elegant, in the Margaux style. The '61 and '66 were fine, and even the '67 well above average. At one time there used also to be a wine from the neighbouring *palus*, sold as Moulin d'Issan; as much as 200 *tonneaux* were produced in the days when large quantities of wine were made in the riverside strip that runs up to Cussac. The late Christian Cruse once told me that Moulin d'Issan was said to be particularly liked by the Protestants of Paris, as the proprietor was of that faith. Such marketing by faith is not, I believe, entirely dead today, for I am assured that wines with religious names, such as Angélus in St-Émilion, have a particular attraction for some Catholics. If so Pape-Clément, Magdelaine and L'Évangile should have certain commercial advantages, although the high prices of these particular wines might reserve them for Church adherents of the higher socio-economic group. Future purchasers of estates in the Gironde, where proprietors have long been accustomed to change the names of their properties on arrival, might well consider this marketing point; and nowadays this would not have to be confined to what might be summarized as the two-party system, especially with such people as the Japanese in the market. Moulin d'Issan, however, has long been gone, and the Parisian Protestants have had to become oecumenical in their claret drinking.

Cantenac-Brown was formerly called Brown-Cantenac, but no doubt the confusion and pronunciation problems arising from the adjacent Brane were too much, and the name was reversed. Mr Brown was a Bordeaux merchant, and a century ago his vineyard was very large, running to 70 ha under vines, compared with about 20–25 today. It was bought in 1860 by the owner of Léoville-Poyferré, M. Armand Lalande, from a banker, M. Gromard, who had let the property run down. M. Lalande set to work to erect a large and curious-looking brick and stone château, which in the 1860s was described as 'one of the architectural beauties of the Médoc'. Whether nowadays this looks more out of place than some of the other Médoc châteaux is a matter of opinion, but I would not have been surprised to come upon it equally incongruously placed in some Highland glen or forming the back-drop for *Lucia di Lammermoor*. This house belonged to M de Wilde, whose father owned du Tertre in Arsac, and was for a long time divorced from the vineyard; another that had been in the doldrums for a long time, although one sees it now and again on British wine lists. Yet it made one of the outstanding '29s that I remember. The proprietor was Jean Lawton, head of the firm of Lalande, but in 1968 it passed to Comte Bertrand du Vivier, on behalf of the Bordeaux firm of de Luze, of which he is chairman and managing director. The price was said to be in the neighbourhood of 1,800,000 new francs. At present the vineyard composition is 40 per cent Cabernet-Sauvignon, 20 per cent Cabernet-Franc, 30 per cent Merlot and 10 per cent Petit-Verdot, but it is proposed to increase the proportion of Cabernet-Sauvignon at the expense of the Merlot. Cantenac-Brown has been due for a revival, and with another proprietor and a vineyard with a good proportion of old vines, it will be interesting to see how the wines show in future.

Palmer, on the other hand, is commonly accepted as one of the most successful châteaux of its class and the wines among the most distinguished in the Médoc. Before the Cantenacs were permitted in 1955 to call themselves Margaux, Palmer was known as Palmer-Margaux and this seemed fair enough, for the vineyards adjoin those of Château Margaux, and its wines are similar in style. By some they are also considered to have an affinity with Lafite, perhaps because both are soft wines and have a fair proportion of Merlot in their vineyards, although Lafite claims to have much less than Palmer.

Even by Médoc standards the vineyard is not very old, having been constituted by General Palmer, who is said to have taken a liking for the Médoc and its wines when the English army occupied the region in 1814, near the end of the Napoleonic Wars. He bought what was then called Château de Gascq from the family of that name and energetically expanded the property, including a somewhat remote part called Boston. Unfortunately the general's resources or commercial acumen did not match his enthusiasm, and in the 1840s he went bankrupt without even building a château. However he had been successful enough with his wine to establish it as a *troisième cru*, and this was confirmed in the 1855 classification. Two years previously it had been bought by one of the great Second Empire banking families, the Pereires, who gave their name to the Place Pereire in Paris. At one period they were rivals of the Rothschilds. The Palmer property, badly ravaged by the oidium and entirely replanted, was bought for 425,000 frs. and in 1856 the present château was erected, built in what may be called the 'château style', with some affinity with Pichon-Longueville-Baron. The château today bears the initials of Émile Isaac and Isaac Rodrique Pereire, whose descendants in 1938 sold out to a consortium of three. The biggest shareholder is the Bordeaux firm of Mähler-Besse, and the balance is held by Sichel & Co. of Bordeaux and M. Alain Miailhe, proprietor of Pichon-Lalande and other growths. Until his death in 1965 the late Allan Sichel largely represented the English interest of Palmer. I have already referred to him. He was one of the most enlightened, enthusiastic, downright and fluent exponents of Bordeaux. His geese were never mistaken for swans, and if he thought that his beloved Palmer had produced a disappointing vintage he never hesitated to say so, and to dissuade, if possible, his customers from buying the wine. To illustrate the difficulties that faced even well-known châteaux until a few years ago, he once told me that Palmer made no money from the time it had been acquired just before the last war until after the 1953 vintage. Baron Philippe de Rothschild has more than once said the same about Mouton, except that his first profitable year was 1955. From the beginning of the sixties, however, Palmer was recognized as making exceptionally good wine, and this was later reflected in prices higher than even the leading second growths. For example, the opening figure for the 1971 was 31,000 frs. a *tonneau*, compared with 12,000 for the 1970. The better second '71s averaged about 26,000 frs. for opening prices. In 1972 Palmer came out at 55,000 frs. but this and other prices for that vintage are best forgotten.

Starting with the moderate '60, Palmer has seldom disappointed in the context of the varying vintages. The '61 rose to secure the highest price outside the first growths, and in 1979 secured a record figure of £580 a dozen – a beautifully full, round wine with a splendid nose. Then the '62 was one of the best clarets of the vintage and lasted remarkably well. The '64, however, was a disappointment, disproving the widely-held view that the early pickers did well; Palmer started on 21 September and finished on 8 October, the first day of the continuing rains. The '66 was exceptionally fruity, and there are those who believe it superior to the '61; the '67 was fruitier than many others in that rather thin year. High hopes of the '70 are also expressed.

A curiosity that came to light at an auction at Christie's in April 1976 was several dozen bottles of Palmer Blanc 1920. Other vintages have also been seen. No white wine has been made at Palmer for many years and, like the white Lafite 1959 already mentioned, it was probably produced just for the proprietors' drinking. When it was first made is not known today. Also unknown is the origin of the fine gold and midnight-blue château label, but at Christie's I saw an 1883 vintage with a label of the same design and colours. It is one of the most striking in a large gallery of classed-growth labels scarcely notable for the quality of their design or typography. Apart from the ever-changing Mouton-Rothschild, among the more distinctive and agreeable of those classified in 1855 are Lafite, Haut-Brion (now returned to the design it abandoned in the 1920s), Rauzan-Gassies, Beychevelle and perhaps Margaux.

On the top of the steep roof of the château, which the French call *Pal-Mehr*, flies the Union Jack along with the French Tricolour and the Dutch flag, representing the other two proprietors, and they look across the vineyards to the Union Jack flying from Rausan-Ségla. Allan Sichel's son, Peter, now lives at Angludet in the same commune.

The vineyard of Palmer is about 38 ha, having been increased slightly by the accession of Desmirail, which was bought in 1957 and absorbed. The reason for this incorporation is that wine can be sold more advantageously under the Palmer label than under that of Desmirail, and this is quite legal. However in the poor year of 1963 the whole Palmer crop with *appellation* was sold under the Desmirail 'imprint'. Otherwise Palmer, hemmed in as it is by surrounding vineyards, has not expanded like some other châteaux; and this may partly account for its fine quality. The composition of the vineyard is 45 per cent Cabernet-Sauvignon, 10 per cent Cabernet-Franc, 35 per cent Merlot and 10 per cent Petit-Verdot; in the last replanting the proportion of Cabernet-Sauvignon was increased appreciably. The normal output is just over 100 *tonneaux*. Yet in that fine but short vintage of 1961 they only made 30 *tonneaux* of a splendid wine. In off-years it is sometimes a little thin, like its neighbour, Château Margaux. There is little doubt that Palmer is under-classed. Some of its successful vintages are mentioned in the chapter on vintages. A hundred years ago the first Pereire was ambitious to make it a second growth, and so it should be.

Also foreign-owned is Prieuré-Lichine, whose charming little square-built eighteenth-century château, looking more English than French, is approached through an archway on the main road. It was indeed once a priory, and the house almost touches the parish church of Cantenac. Always a small property, a hundred years ago it belonged to a M. Rosset, and the output was 15–20 *tonneaux*, but now from 55 ha it produces about 200 *tonneaux*. The vineyard is 50 per cent Cabernet-Sauvignon, 5 per cent Cabernet-Franc, 40 per cent Merlot and 5 per cent Petit-Verdot. It was bought in 1952 for about 150 million old francs (equal to 1·5 million new francs) by Alexis Lichine and, although nominally owned by a company, it is essentially his property. The vineyard was replanted and is certainly now producing more distinguished wines, though rather on the full side for my Cantenac taste. The small château, in which I have stayed, is attractively furnished and decorated. In the converted kitchen, with its fine scrubbed farmhouse table and galaxy of copper cooking utensils, the serious business of the day takes place when the American proprietor is in residence. Surprisingly for a *cru classé*, it now displays a *vente directe* sign by the road.

One of the lesser Cantenac châteaux not very widely known is Pouget. This, in fact, is run in harness with Boyd-Cantenac, as already mentioned on page 329.

That ends the classed growths of Cantenac, but certainly Angludet, which belongs to the Sichel family, deserves promotion. It claims to have had classed-growth status up to the Revolution, when it acquired the temporarily topical name of La République, but was split up when the 1855 classification was being considered. This low, friendly-looking château lies out in the country from the village; both vineyard and wine-making have improved since the war. The '53 Angludet is still a delicious wine. The vineyard contains 30 ha made up of 52 per cent Cabernet-Sauvignon, 10 per cent Cabernet-Franc, 30 per cent Merlot and 8 per cent Petit-Verdot, and production is around 110 *tonneaux*. There are few other Cantenacs of wide repute. There is Martinens belonging to Mme Dubos, and producing sound wine; another is Pontac-Lynch. The lesser growths are sold as Margaux.

ARSAC

It is convenient to mention here the wines of those neighbouring communes who harbour *crus classés* and are entitled in whole or in part since 1955 to sell their wines as Margaux. Arsac boasts one classed growth in its territorially large commune, which lies inland and broadly south of Cantenac. This is du Tertre, a fifth growth. It is a vineyard which had considerable *réclame* in the nineteenth century, and when it was bought in 1870 by M. Koenigswater he paid 530,000 frs. A later owner was Achille de Wilde, whose family had owned Cantenac-Brown. For many years the property certainly fell into some decline, but it is now owned by the Gasqueton family, co-proprietors of Calon-Ségur, who bought it in 1962 and considerable replanting of the vineyard, remote on a plateau, took place. Tastings of later vintages indicate a marked improvement in quality. Production is about 100 *tonneaux*. Otherwise the Arsac wines are not very well known.

LABARDE

Labarde adjoins Arsac and Cantenac, on the river side of the former, and has two classed growths, Giscours and Dauzac. With the first of these the story is once again of a fine earlier reputation, then the decline which, mainly owing to hard times, affected many of the leading Haut-Médoc properties, and more recently of active revival. Giscours claims records going back to 1330 when it was a fortified keep. In 1552 it was sold to a Sieur Delhomme for 1,000 livres, and apparently was one of the wines served, in 1656, to Louis XIV to encourage the monarch's interest in the wines of Bordeaux. At the Revolution its owner, M. de Saint Simon, joined the émigrés, so his estate was confiscated and was sold to a Mr Michael Jacob, who oddly enough had two American merchants as associates, John Gray and Jonathan Davis – surely the first American proprietorial sortie into the Médoc. But this partnership did not last long, and in 1825 the property was sold to M. Marc Promis, a Bordeaux merchant whose family name is incorporated in the Sauternes growth of Rabaud-Promis. It was he who really developed the estate and built a new château, but in 1847 he in turn sold it to a rich Paris banker, Comte M. J. P. Pescatore, for 500,000 gold francs. The Count replaced the Promis house, destroyed by fire, with the existing ample château, which has something of the air of a seaside or spa hotel. When the banker died in 1855 his nephew, Guillaume, took over, and twenty years later disposed of it to M. Édouard Cruse, great-uncle of the late

Christian Cruse, for 1,000,000 frs. Cruse restored both château and vineyard, and the family owned the property until 1913 when it was sold to M. Émile Grange. Grange was already the owner of several other properties in the Médoc, including at one time Issan and an associated vineyard in the *palus* of Cantenac, Moulin d'Issan, which formed a company that he administered. Unfortunately the property deteriorated. It was bought and re-sold by a number of people not really interested in producing fine wine, and the 60 ha planted by the Pescatores and Cruses fell to a mere 7 ha. Then in 1952 the estate was bought by M. Nicolas Tari, a wine grower from Algeria, and at once he set to work to increase the vineyard and improve its status. The château was renovated and the fine *chais*, too small for the increased production planned, were extended and modernized. At the same time a reception centre was formed out of the old farm buildings, and this is used for parties and banquets, including the celebrations of the *Bontemps du Médoc et des Graves*.

The Giscours *vignoble* now runs to 75 ha, planted with 65 per cent Cabernet-Sauvignon, 15 per cent Merlot and the balance divided between Cabernet-Franc, Petit-Verdot and Malbec. The proportion of Cabernet-Sauvignon has been greatly increased at the expense of Cabernet-Franc and Merlot. Average production is about 200 *tonneaux*. As with other proprietors with Algerian experience M. Nicolas Tari imported some modern methods of vinification, and these have been continued by his son, Pierre, one of the more active of the relatively few *cru-classé* proprietors to live on the spot. Giscours is now a full, fruity style of wine, with plenty of colour and body. If it lacks the elegance of Margaux, to the *appellation* of which it is entitled, then that applies equally to others similarly placed. When mature it is a round, easy-to-drink claret. Since the 1972 vintage Gilbeys have been the world distributors.

Dauzac has also had its ups and downs. The estate lies on the

Gironde side of the commune, and the vineyards touch those of Giscours. At the Revolution it was owned by the celebrated Count Lynch, Mayor of Bordeaux at the Restoration. When he died in 1835 it went to his brother, Chevalier Lynch, but he died in 1841, and with one intervening owner the property passed in 1863 to Nathaniel Johnston of the Bordeaux family. It was at Dauzac that Bordeaux Mixture, which successfully combated the mildew in the 1880s, is said to have been devised. But it is also alleged that it had originally been used by Johnston to colour unpleasantly blue the grapes near the road which might be eaten by the local children. At one time a great deal of wine was made at Dauzac, and the 1900 crop was no less than 1,000 *tonneaux*, although most of this was sold as La Maqueline. At one time the prolific Dauzac had its own railway line; but in the inter-war period this fifth growth fell on hard times and production declined. In 1966, however, the Miailhe family, already proprietors of Siran next door and of Pichon-Lalande, bought Dauzac and set about its complete remodelling. By the later seventies the vineyard had been extended to 30 ha, with an *encépagement* of 58 per cent Cabernet-Sauvignon, 9 per cent Cabernet-Franc, 15 per cent Merlot and an unusually high 18 per cent of Petit-Verdot. Average production had then reached 130–150 *tonneaux*. M. Alain Miailhe, responsible for the administration, at one point attempted to rename the property Dauzac-Lynch, and for some time this name appeared on the roadside walls. However, as already mentioned, château names are brand names, and the other properties bearing the name Lynch objected, and this fifth-growth Labarde remained Dauzac *tout court*.

Sparkling Ducru-Beaucaillou has already been mentioned. Nathaniel Johnston also used the wines of Dauzac for making sparkling wine, which was actually produced on the other side of the estuary in Bourg.

Adjoining Dauzac is Siran, into which the Miailhe family

invested a good deal of money in the sixties, and transformed the vineyard. When Dauzac was acquired, some four or five hectares were transferred to Siran, including the top part of the Labarde plateau called Bellegarde, which had been acquired by Count Lynch in the early part of the nineteenth century. This *cru bourgeois* property would have a claim to a higher status should there be a re-classification. The area under vines is 18 ha, and the *cépage* is 40 per cent Cabernet-Sauvignon, $16\frac{1}{2}$ per cent Cabernet-Franc, $25\frac{1}{2}$ per cent Merlot and, like Dauzac, 18 per cent Petit-Verdot. Production averages 80–90 *tonneaux*. A separate part of the vineyard, 10 ha, produces 10–15 *tonneaux* of wine labelled Ch. St-Jacques, *appellation* Bordeaux Supérieur. From a rather sandy soil Siran itself makes a well-balanced, Margaux-style wine of elegance in good years.

Not the least remarkable feature of Siran is behind the old two-storey house: the garden filled with cyclamens. Many of the Médoc châteaux have the charming little white and pink varieties in their gardens, but nothing approaches the display in the early autumn at Siran, where they grow as thickly in the long grass as bluebells in an English wood in spring. Siran is a Margaux first growth for cyclamen.

In this part of the Médoc now entitled to the *appellation* Margaux there are some of the best-known and respected *crus bourgeois*. In Margaux itself there is a series of three growths with a variation of the name Labégorce. They are de Labégorce, L'Abbé-Gorsse-de-Gorsse and Labégorce-Zédé, and to rival such complexity one probably has to go to Germany. This cannot assist their distribution. The third of these extends into Soussans and is said to be the best, but some favour the first, which has an agreeable Louis XVI château. It produces 70 *tonneaux* of wine, exclusively sold by Dourthe of Moulis. In Margaux also is the curiously named La Gurgue, whose name is pronounced as if the last two letters were omitted and not like the noise the last of the bath-water makes as it disappears down the plug-hole. The only time I drank it I found it rather a hard wine.

The area includes two of the somewhat curious six or seven *crus exceptionnels*. Curious because although some but not all of them are rather more widely known than most of the *bourgeois*, they have not benefited much from this unofficial promotion. Also the list is a shifting one. The two candidates in the Margaux fold include Angludet, already mentioned, and Bel-Air-Marquis d'Aligre, a splendid name, whose length is little calculated to secure its success in foreign markets, although the wine enjoyed popularity in the Low Countries. Though the production is now small, it heads the list of Soussans wines.

Much better known, however, is La Tour-de-Mons. This property, which often makes excellent wines, lies out in the country towards the estuary and is named after a Belgian family who bought it in 1623 (M. Pierre de Mons also owned Angludet). It is now run by Bertrand Clauzel, grandson of Pierre Dubos, the owner for many years of Cantemerle, whose wine-making M. Clauzel also controls. The large *chai* at La Tour-de-Mons is traditional in appearance, and production averages 100 *tonneaux* from 25 ha. The *cépage* is 40 per cent Cabernet-Sauvignon, 10 per cent Cabernet-Franc, 45 per cent Merlot and 5 per cent Petit-Verdot. It is one of the properties that would be in line for promotion if a re-classification of the Médoc were ever to take place, and its '53 was one of the most distinguished Médocs in an outstanding year.

Another Soussans growth of repute is Paveil-de-Luze. The first word is a derivation of *pavillon*, as there is an old seventeenth-century tower attached to the low-lying vineyard buildings. In the eighteenth century it belonged to a M. Bretonneau who married a daughter of the Chevalier de Rauzan, but in 1862 it was bought by a member of the Bordeaux firm of de Luze. Today its chief owner is Baron Francis de Luze. Production, in a vineyard which is 35 per cent Cabernet-Franc, 30 per cent Cabernet-Sauvignon, 30 per cent Merlot and 5 per cent Petit-Verdot, is not large, around 50–60 *tonneaux*, but the wines are particularly well known in Denmark. A bottle of '24 was still sound and fruity if showing its age in 1968. A little white wine is made, bearing of course the *appellation* Bordeaux Blanc. Its composition is 50 per cent Sémillon and 50 per cent Sauvignon.

There are not many other well-known *bourgeois* properties in the area permitted to sell their wines as Margaux. In Labarde, Rosemont used to be fairly well known in Britain, but its production is now very small. Arsac, already mentioned above, is vinously a small commune, but adjoining it is the more important one of Macau, whose best-known growth is Cantemerle.

MACAU AND LUDON

Those who point to the inadequacy today of the 1855 classification often mention the fact that Cantemerle is the very last of the fifth growths, whereas most people would certainly put it much higher. From 1579 until nearly the end of the last century the property was owned by the Villeneuve family, and a hundred years ago the proprietress was the Baroness d'Abbadie de Villeneuve de Durfort, which must have been quite a formidable name to announce when she went visiting her neighbours. I suspect that the low rating in 1855 was owing to the fact that at that period its sale was almost exclusively confined to Holland, and compared with other growths the wine was therefore hardly known in the Bordeaux market. The original manuscript copy of the classification shows that Cantemerle was added at the end in a different hand. The special popularity of the wine in the Low Countries continued until a generation ago, but nowadays its best export market is probably Britain, where it is esteemed. Certainly the quality has risen ever since 1892 when Pierre Dubos's parents acquired the château for 770,000 frs. Curiously enough Cantemerle was bought by Calvet for 600,000 frs. – the only moment when the Calvets were classed-growth château proprietors – but a fortnight later it was bought by Dubos. Dubos junior ran the property for over sixty years and was famous for the detailed weather records that he maintained over the years. He was one of the most expert and charming of the last generation of Médoc proprietors. When I visited the château after the 1966 vintage Henri Binaud was able to show me that the weather conditions that year had closely resembled those of 1920 – no bad omen for the '66s, which have yet finally to prove themselves. The château, in parts very old, is approached by a long avenue. The *chai* buildings are exceptionally extensive and solid with a fine stone façade.

Henri Binaud, who married a daughter of Pierre Dubos, was until his retirement in 1977 not only head of Beyerman, the ancient Bordeaux firm of Dutch origin, but in effect the proprietor of Cantemerle, as well as being a prominent figure in the Bordeaux wine world. He has always been among the most extrovertly enthusiastic of Bordeaux château proprietors. When at a private dinner early in the sixties in London Latour '53 and Cantemerle '53 were both served blind, and the Cantemerle was judged the finer wine, the latter's director was not only gratified but clearly felt that the judgement could only be correct. Later when the old custom among Médoc proprietors of exchanging cases of their wine led to Lafite swopping an equal number of cases of its wine for those of Cantemerle, Binaud obviously believed that the first of the firsts had obtained the better bargain at the expense of the last of the fifths. But that is not untypical of the views of a Médocain château owner, and I have heard Baron Philippe de Rothschild say that his choice after Mouton would be Cantemerle.

Cantemerle has one advantage over some of its classed neighbours to the north. The *appellation* is Haut-Médoc and therefore entitled to the extra 3 hl per hectare more than the vineyards in the Margaux 'consortium' of communes limited to a basic 40 hl. This of course also applies to the other growths in Macau and the adjoining Ludon. So while Binaud at classed-growth Cantemerle may make up to 43 hl from each of his 20 ha, on *cru bourgeois* La Tour-de-Mons, with which his family is associated, permitted *A C* production under the Margaux label is 40 hl. It must be emphasized here that, from vineyard to vineyard and vintage to vintage, the maximum is by no means always reached (at Cantemerle the average is only 27 hl), and even when it is the proprietor may not declare all his wine with the *appellation*. He may prefer to de-class a proportion to maintain a high quality for his wine. On the other hand in plentiful years, and 1967 and 1970 were examples, some châteaux have been making quantities far in excess of the permitted maximum, and this cannot be for the good of their reputation or the quality of their wines. The maximum as increased in recent years is agreed by most growers and merchants to be generous enough. Yet it is not uncommon for part at least of the excess production to be allowed the top *appellation*.

In Macau we are near the end of the fine wine area of the Médoc, and on the road to Bordeaux only one classed growth is nearer the city: La Lagune. It is surprising, therefore, that Cantemerle in semi-isolation is so distinguished. The composition of the vineyard is 45 per cent Cabernet-Sauvignon, 15 per cent Cabernet-Franc, 35 per cent Merlot and 5 per cent Petit-Verdot, and the average production about 85 *tonneaux*. The wine is fairly full-bodied and rather 'bigger' than the Margaux wines. As it has been regularly listed since the Second World War by the Wine Society in London, I have drunk a considerable amount of Cantemerle, which often contrives to make good wine in off-years, such as '58 and '60. The '53 was one of the most successful Médocs. I have also drunk older vintages of Cantemerle, back to the excellent '16, '20 and '21 and the still fine '06. More recently I have been somewhat disappointed in the vintages from the mid-sixties onwards, but the '75 has a good reputation.

Château Cantemerle must not be confused with Cru Cantemerle across the Dordogne in the commune of St-Gervais. (There is also another Château Beychevelle nearby on the same river.) Not many other growths in Macau are well known, but a lesser wine there but sold as Bordeaux Supérieur is Beau-Rivage. In view of the old association of Cantemerle with Holland it is interesting to note that in the first edition of Franck's work in 1824 he makes the comment about Macau wines that their roughness depreciates them in Holland, where they only like soft wines. This remark was omitted in later editions.

The last of the important Médoc wine communes now is Ludon, with its third growth La Lagune. The vineyard was originally planted about 1724, to the extent of 50 ha. The production has varied very much. A century ago it was 70–80 *tonneaux*, but until recently it had dwindled, coming down to as little as 15 *tonneaux*. Indeed the whole vineyard was very run-down, but in 1957 it was purchased by a company which replanted nearly all the vineyard in 1958 and 1959; ever since production has been increasing, so that it is now about 250 *tonneaux*. The *chai* has also been reconstructed on the most modern lines, with series of steel pipes running from the vats along above the rows of casks. If this all looks a little factorial to those accustomed to more traditional cellars, conditions are certainly changing in Bordeaux, and it is the results that as elsewhere will count at La Lagune – which now likes to be known as Grand La Lagune. Another break with tradition is a female *régisseur*, Mme Boirie. The property, beautifully kept and administered by M. Ducelier, is owned by the heirs of M. Chayoux, who was also a champagne merchant. La Lagune used to be regarded as a particularly long-lived wine and indeed took time to come round. It was popular in Britain and made an excellent '26, which I have drunk a number of times. After the replanting, for some years the wines usually seemed to me excessively sweet, as if it had been necessary to add sugar to mask the greenness of the young vines. Indeed more than once I have mistaken the '61 for a burgundy, and a rather suave, velvety one at that. However they improved in the latter part of the sixties and it will be very interesting to see the vintages of the seventies when the vineyard is mature. Already the wines are much improved.

The only other Ludon wine known to me is the *bourgeois* growth of Nexon-Lemoyne. Its production is small, about 10 *tonneaux*, and the wines that I have tasted have been rather hard. Another estate, once well known, is Agassac.

THE LESSER COMMUNES OF THE HAUT-MÉDOC

As Bordeaux is approached the soil becomes more like that of the Graves. At one time a good deal of *bourgeois* wine came from the communes of Blanquefort, Parempuyre, Le Taillan and Le Pian-Médoc, but most suffered with the decline of these wines; and the city has been advancing into the vineyards. At Blanquefort is the local School of Agriculture, in Château Dillon, where some wine is made on an experimental basis. Before the last war it used to be sold in England and occasionally still is. At Le Taillan is the very fine Château du Taillan, which belongs to the Cruse family. In addition to the red wine, there is white wine produced, which can only be called Bordeaux Blanc Supérieur, as it is a mile or so from the edge of the Graves. So Cruse sell it as La Dame-Blanche. At Parempuyre is another substantial mansion, built during the palmy days of the Bordeaux wine trade in the last century and known as Château de Parempuyre. Durand-Dassier, a connection of the Cruses, had it built, and until about 1970 it belonged to the same family. Centuries earlier this was the territory of the Pichon family. At Blanquefort also is the not unknown Maurian, but broadly speaking this is not now the wine area it once was.

This leaves to be mentioned a number of communes in the Haut-Médoc, lying between the best-known districts and the Landes, and possessing no classed growths. The most important are Moulis and Listrac, and these alone have a wider reputation. Both communes at one time had much more extensive vineyards than today. Just before the First World War Listrac alone had 1,345 ha under vines. Today, even after some recent recovery, the area is only about 420 ha. The average production of Moulis is 10–12,000 hl of *AC* wine, and of Listrac about 20,000 hl. They were among the eleven communes stretching from Le Taillan to Cissac called by Franck in 1824 'Le Derrière du Haut-Médoc'.

Moulis, indeed, boasts in Chasse-Spleen one of the *grands crus exceptionnels*, with an output of about 120 *tonneaux*. As with other Moulis wines I have tended to find the vintages of this growth that have come my way to be rather hard and astringent. However at the *Ban de Vendange* dinner in the great pillared *chai* of Château Margaux in September 1967, the '61 Chasse-Spleen was served, and was an admirably fruity wine with more roundness than normal. In recent years there have been renovations at Chasse-Spleen, including a new, semi-underground cellar. It also boasts ambulant peacocks. The Moulis wines are entitled to their own *appellation* and a number of them incorporate the name Poujeaux in their frequently long titles. There are Poujeaux-Castaing, Gressier-Grand-Poujeaux, Poujeaux-Marly, Poujeaux-Theil and Dutruch-Grand-Poujeaux. Poujeaux is a gravelly sub-area of Moulis, and generally regarded as the finest. The best of these that I have had some experience of is the Dutruch, which can be rounder and less austere than many Moulis wines, which have an inner core of firmness, also associated with the Listracs. Among other Moulis growths of repute – and the estates are quite considerable – are Pomeys, Mauvezin, Duplessis, La Closerie, Renouil-Franquet and the somewhat confusingly named Moulin-à-Vent.

In about 1950 La Closerie gave me an object lesson in how quite minor growths can on occasion produce outstanding wine. Some cases of the 1920, 1929 and 1934 vintages then became available in London and I tasted them all several times and acquired a few bottles of the '20. This was a splendidly round and complete wine, and at a time when the '20s of far greater repute had passed their best. The '29 was also good, and the '34 very fair for that hard, tannin-struck year. These were all château-bottled stock released by the proprietor. In youth the '49, bottled in England, was good, but latterly it turned somewhat acid. Maucaillou is owned by the firm and family of Dourthe, who from Moulis run a wine business which specializes in the exclusive sale of the wine of a number of Médoc and other châteaux. Maucaillou itself produces 120 *tonneaux* and is a very sound wine.

Moulis wines are for the long haul, unless one overlooks their firmness and drinks them young as fruity, youthful claret; and much the same applies to the Listracs, except that no very interesting bottles have come my way. The soil is gravel with some clay and sand. It was from this and surrounding areas that came the red Bordeaux *crus bourgeois* which were purchased in great quantities by pre-Nazi Germany. They were bought in the spring following the vintage and carried off at once to be matured in the Hanseatic cities. When Hitler seized power the trade dropped, and has never been resumed on anything like its old scale; nowadays the Bordeaux which the Germans overwhelmingly buy is white.

The Listrac wines which are perfectly respectable if rather hard come from such growths as Fourcas-Dupré, Fourcas-Hosten, Clarke and Pierre Bibian. The first of these probably makes the best wine today. However, Fourcas-Hosten was bought by a basically American group in November 1971 for 2·8 million frs., and considerable developments then took place, with 20 ha being added to the vineyard within a few years, making a total of 44 ha, yielding an average production, from Cabernet-Sauvignon, Cabernet-Franc and Merlot, of 180 *tx*. Clarke now belongs to Baron Edmond de Rothschild.

It is claimed that the hardness and the lack of 'generosity' in many of the wines of Moulis and Listrac have been caused by their being kept far too long in cask. This may be attributed either to the short-sightedness of the owners in awaiting orders in bulk for bottling or to their lack of financial resources to bottle at the proper time all that remained unsold. Certainly in the not too distant past the wines of these communes were not easy to sell, but with better prices they should have the chance to improve and to be more saleable.

There is also a co-operative, founded in 1935, which sells its wines under the title of Château Grand Listrac. Moulis and Listrac *A C* output is limited to 40 hl per ha as being two of the six named Haut-Médoc communes, though this is now variable. See Appendix A.

To the south of Moulis is the small commune of Avensan, which contains another of the *crus exceptionnels*, Villegeorge, whose vineyard, but not the château, belongs to M. L. Lurton. Its production is under 20 *tonneaux*. I have only tasted it when very young and it has seemed to me a sound but not exciting wine. Much larger is the only other widely-known Avensan growth, Citran-Clauzel, which makes over 60 *tonneaux* and is owned by Jean Miailhe. A century ago its production was between 250 and 325 *tonneaux*, an indication of the scale of *cru bourgeois* production in that period. There are a scattering of other growers in Avensan.

Further north and nearer to the estuary, on the *D.2* Médoc road, is Arcins on the edge of the 'thirsty gap' in the vineyards of quality. Between St-Julien and Soussans-Margaux near the river, and St-Laurent and Listrac further inland is a considerable area of scrubby, plantation-filled country, looking about as infertile as a rather neglected piece of English common land. It demonstrates the essential role that the soil and situation play in viticulture. A stranger visiting the Haut-Médoc for the first time might reasonably expect an almost uninterrupted stretch of vines from Blanquefort to St-Estèphe and beyond; and if aware of the high value of good vineyard land in the Médoc he might think it extraordinary that the frequent, extensive gaps in the vineyards have not been put under vines. In fact there used to be reasonably well-known wine made in Lamarque, now best remembered for its ferry to Blaye, and Cocks et Féret still lists some growths now. Properties such as Lamarque, Cap de Haut-Lamarque and Malescasse made wine in considerable demand in Germany up to 1914. Indeed this last growth has now been bought and expanded by a group of Americans. It will be interesting to watch its future, for considerable outlay has been made in the vineyard and *chai*. Christian Cruse once told me that the area of the *crus bourgeois* here and elsewhere in the Médoc occupied little more than 10 per cent of what it did early in this century. Over 400 *crus bourgeois* recognized in the Médoc less than forty years ago are now reduced to about 100. The others have gone out of production or sell their grapes to the co-operatives. Much the same decline applies to Cussac, although that still retains two fairly familiar châteaux, Beaumont and Lanessan, mentioned below. Yet in relation to the market demand as it has existed for many years the land here is as marginal as in the once so productive *palus*, adjoining the Gironde. Even if wine were grown on a large scale in this gap it would often not secure a higher *appellation* than Bordeaux Supérieur, and the price would be correspondingly low.

Arcins (the 's' is pronounced as is common with a final 's' in these parts) is a very small area, and the best known of its few *bourgeois* growths is probably La Tour-du-Roc, but there is also a Ch. d'Arcins and a co-operative which uses the name

Chevalier d'Ars. The village had also the distinction of having a small estate in English hands. For Nicolas Barrow cultivated Courant for about ten years from 1964 onwards. Using traditional methods he produced about 20 *tonneaux*. Later he became, for a time, manager of Malescasse, which was bought by an American group; the Courant vineyard was amalgamated in the Lamarque vineyard of that château.

Moving up the Médoc, Lamarque, as already indicated, need not detain us further, but Cussac on the main road is more of a wine village, with one or two houses notable for the mid-nineteenth-century exuberance of their architecture. Lanessan is a large estate with a reputation which is rising. It provides another example of the fact that not only the greatest names make fine wines. For several years I had a few bottles of Lanessan '29, which had been lying in a central London cellar since before the Second World War. With one or two exceptions, owing probably to the cork rather than the wine, they remained deliciously fruity, strong-flavoured and complete. One could not then say the same about a number of the leading '29s.

Lanessan lies in a large 'park', and is approached by a long avenue from the *D.2* road. The substantial *chai* buildings indicate that it was once a very large estate. Nowadays the vineyard runs to 30 ha, two-thirds Cabernet-Sauvignon and one-third Merlot, and produces 125 *tonneaux*. It has a certain fame in the district for having a small carriage museum installed in one of the old *chais*. There is a mail coach and nine carriages, including an odd-looking four-wheeled *Américaine* with canvas hood and an open *Break de Chasse*. There is a fine display of horse equipment and a stable in whose opulent marble feeding troughs 'Darling', 'Tommy' and 'Whisky', according to their inscribed names, once regaled themselves. Lanessan is owned by M. Bouteiller, proprietor also of Pichon-Longueville-Baron and Grand-Puy-Ducasse.

One Cussac estate mentioned above that used to be famous

in the popular *bourgeois* claret trade was Beaumont, but its production is now much reduced. Better known is Lamothe-de-Bergeron.

From there northwards we are again in the belt of famous châteaux but from the north-west of Pauillac there is a small string of lesser Haut-Médoc communes running round to the estuary and mostly adjoining the Bas-Médoc. These are St-Sauveur, Cissac, Vertheuil and St-Seurin-de-Cadourne. They are the last communes entitled to the *appellation* Haut-Médoc before the descent to the Bas-Médoc. In the first of these is the very extensive Liversan, producing well over a hundred *tonneaux*, and at one time well known in Britain. Nowadays Peyrabon, which makes a well-balanced wine, has a wider reputation. St-Sauveur also has a co-operative, which calls its wines Ch. St-Sauveur. Cissac has a château of that name as well as a co-operative, and there is a Lamothe here too, as well as La Tour-du-Mirail. Ch. Cissac, owned by M. Louis Vialard, has been making particularly good fruity wine for many years and is a *cru bourgeois* to watch. The 26 ha in production are composed of 65 per cent Cabernet-Sauvignon, 10 per cent Cabernet-Franc, 20 per cent Merlot and 5 per cent Petit-Verdot; a fairly typical make-up in this part of the Médoc. Total production averages 125–150 *tonneaux*, but only the best wine will be sold under the château label, and the rest as Domaine de Martiny. Ch. Lamothe, whose proprietor is M. Gabriel Fabre, is larger and expanding; soon it will extend to 50 ha. The Vertheuil wines are not much known under their own names, but I have come across Le Bourdieu. There are co-operatives both here (the brand name is La Châtelerie) and at the neighbouring St-Seurin, which is a little more prominent in wine annals. There are Coufran, owned by Jean Miailhe, who also owns Citran in Avensan, Verdignan, Bel-Orme, Sénilhac and Sociando. Most of these are considerable producers on large rolling vineyards, many of them adjoining St-Estèphe.

The wines from these communes have something of the quality of St-Estèphe but with less distinction. They can make excellent, inexpensive bottles. Coufran stands out in my mind as the last château of the Haut-Médoc. Physically the epithet 'Haut' in this flat country is strictly relative, but in fact on passing Coufran, still on the *D.2* which has given us so much vicarious wine pleasure since we joined it before Blanquefort, one does descend a hill to the Bas-Médoc. The contrast is emphasized by a little international rivalry. For in the vineyard of Coufran there is a small tower from which waves the *tricolor*, and this looks down physically, as well no doubt as philosophically, on the first estate in the Bas-Médoc, which happens to be Loudenne, in English hands ever since it was bought by the Gilbeys in 1875. This too has towers in its vineyard, constructed in Victorian Flamboyant. On one of these facing Coufran, and on the château terrace overlooking the Gironde, flies a defiant Union Jack.

THE BAS-MÉDOC

Nowadays the word 'Bas' is officially discarded, for to foreign ears and eyes it suggests inferiority. For the same reason the *départements* of Loire Inférieure and Charente Inférieure were constrained to change their names to Atlantique and Maritime respectively. The Bas-Médoc's geographical name is now Médoc-Maritime but is seldom used. It so happens that a Bas-Médoc wine is likely to be inferior to an Haut-Médoc one, though this is not the case in the Armagnac country, where the Bas-Armagnac is the best. However there is not necessarily much to choose between the lesser *Hauts* and the better *Bas*. With all respect to Coufran, whose wine I have drunk with pleasure, a good Loudenne is likely to be at least as good. Nevertheless the term *Haut* is worth something in terms of cash, even if the plain Médoc *appellation* allows two more hectolitres to the hectare.

A hundred years ago they were not so class-conscious on the lower levels of *appellation*, and when, as mentioned earlier, Alfred Gilbey and his colleagues bought Loudenne in 1875 they were probably looking for a source of good, sound, inexpensive wines as well as a base for their Bordeaux operations. So I do not suppose that they cared much that their estate lay in the Bas-Médoc commune of St-Yzans just across the way from Coufran in St-Seurin in the Haut-Médoc.

Indeed it is clear from the splendid series of diaries of the visits of the proprietors, their associates and their friends still preserved at Loudenne, that the Gilbeys were delighted with their acquisition.

The Gilbeys could scarcely have bought at a more unfortunate time, for not only did a general depression develop – a factor now forgotten when the classic vintages of the period are recalled – but within four years came the phylloxera scourge, dealt with earlier. In the diary for 1878 there is reference to the large vintages of '74 and '75, with the statement that production was far ahead of consumption and that many of the Haut-Médoc proprietors had three vintages in hand, owing to 'the general depression of commerce through Europe'. In the following year is the first reference to the phylloxera in the Médoc, although it was already well established in the Charente and the Midi.

Nevertheless the Gilbeys consolidated their position at Loudenne and built the extensive brick and stone *chais* still in use today, and a good example of what has now been upgraded to 'industrial architecture'. Down by the waterside they constructed a small 'port', once used for shipping their wines, but long since disused. Since the sixties the charming château has been restored and redecorated, and externally is pink-washed. Over the years the fine *chais* have been remodelled internally, and constitute an up-to-date base for the company's French operation. The château has welcomed many visitors from Britain, including myself, and at one meal I drank a Loudenne

'24, which although showing its age after more than forty years was still fruity and surprisingly good for a lesser growth. At the same meal, David Peppercorn, then my host and a most serious-minded *amateur* of claret as well as being a professional wine merchant, opened a bottle of Château Margaux of that 'over-productive' year of 1875 when the Gilbeys became owners of Loudenne. The wine was almost *rosé* in colour and very light, but not entirely gone.

Loudenne now makes white as well as red wine in considerable quantities and the quality is good. It is now all bottled on the spot. The vineyard for the red wine extends to 32·5 ha and for the white 6·50. The red part of the vineyard is 49 per cent Cabernet-Sauvignon, 39 per cent Merlot, 9 per cent Cabernet-Franc, 1·5 per cent Malbec and 1·5 per cent Petit-Verdot. The *cépage* for the white is 65 per cent Sauvignon and 35 per cent Sémillon, thus resulting in a crisper, fresher wine than is often the case with Bordeaux Blanc, which is the *appellation* here. Moreover, the white wines are fermented in stainless steel tanks in the immaculately clean *cuverie*. The red wine is fermented in enamel-lined fermentation tanks. The vineyard, after a good deal of replanting in the sixties, is now mature, and some excellent full-bodied well-balanced red wine has been produced since the 1970 vintage in particular – though it must be said that the 1961 was remarkable for its status in the Bordeaux hierarchy. All the wine sold under the Loudenne label comes from the estate, but a branded *A C* Médoc, blended from local wines and bottled at Loudenne, is sold under the name of La Cour Pavillon. I have found it excellent on the one or two occasions I have encountered it. The average production of Loudenne is 120 *tonneaux* of red and 10 *tonneaux* of white wine.

I do not propose to give a château-by-château account of the Bas-Médoc for two reasons that appear relevant. First, with a few exceptions the wines are not widely known in the Anglo-Saxon world, and secondly, my experience is limited.

The low-lying level country, intersected by drainage channels and with English-looking church spires standing up against the sky-line, has something of the appeal of Lincolnshire. Although well cultivated, and in recent years fruit farmers have been developing the region, this part of the Médoc has a rather lost, back-of-beyond air. History seems to have passed it by, and Bordeaux, some forty to fifty miles down the straight *D.1* which by-passes most of the Médoc vineyards, seems in a different country.

The chief town of the Bas-Médoc is Lesparre which, with its suburb of St-Trélody, appears quite large and animated after the silence of the surrounding countryside. It has a pleasant eighteenth-century town hall. Lesparre was of course in English hands in the Middle Ages and the fine old churches of the area, mostly much older than those of the more recently developed Haut-Médoc, show that it had a prosperous past. The Romanesque apse of the church at Bégadan is particularly fine.

The region's wine growing has never quite recovered from the effects of the phylloxera and the following slump in the lesser wines of the Médoc. Abandoned and ruined buildings here and there testify to this. The proportion of Cabernet-Sauvignon grapes tends to be smaller, and that of the Merlot and Malbec larger. The permitted basic output per ha is 45 hl compared with 43 in the Haut-Médoc. Most of the wine properties lie towards the base of the area, thinning out near the sea, but there are even a few vineyards in the commune of Soulac, which abuts on to the Atlantic. Many of the growers make white as well as red wine in properties which often produce altogether no more than 10 *tonneaux*. In the near-record vintage of 1976 the output of red Bordeaux entitled to the *appellation* Médoc was 110,006 hl, compared with 100,171 for the Haut-Médoc. The first figure omits the white wines, as they are entitled only to a Bordeaux *appellation*, and the second does not include those wines from the six communes allowed a higher *appellation*. In the same year St-Estèphe produced 49,855 hl and Pauillac 38,450 hl so the relatively limited production of the large Bas-Médoc can be seen; it is less than 25 per cent of total Médoc output.

The chief wine communes are Bégadan, Blaignan, St-Germain d'Esteuil and St-Christoly-de-Médoc. Bégadan contains Laujac, a large property bought in 1852 by M. Herman Cruse and still in the family. It now makes 100 *tonneaux*, but used to produce much more: 1,000 in 1901. Cru Patache d'Aux and La Tour-de-By are both well-kept and the latter wine is excellent in its class. In St-Germain the Livran estate was familiar in England as it was owned by an English firm, Denman; du Castéra is also known. I have drunk well-made wine from Ch. St-Christoly and another reputable growth is Potensac, under the same ownership as Léoville-Las-Cases. Perhaps it owed something of its wider reputation to the 'growers' market' period in the early 1970s when those who wished to buy the Léoville had also to undertake to acquire a stated quantity of Potensac. In this case perhaps, the buyers were not badly done by, but such conditional sales were undesirable, unworthy of leading *crus classés* and scarcely in the interests of the lesser growths. Fortunately these practices ceased when the boom was followed by the slump, but are not an unknown tradition in the Gironde. Nevertheless Potensac is an example of a number of Médoc châteaux that have improved their wines and their status in recent years.

Another is Cardonne in Blaignan. For many years this was, unusually, owned by a bank, the Crédit Foncier, and from 1953 to 1973 by M. Ludovic Cattan, but it was bought in March 1973 by the Rothschilds and added to the Lafite estate, although like its other property, Duhart-Milon, it is operated entirely separately. The price paid was 8·5 million frs. It has a vineyard area of no less than 97 ha, but only 77 ha are in production – substantial enough at a basic 45 hl to the hectare – and in 1976 it was already making 330 *tonneaux*. Cabernet-

Sauvignon and Cabernet-Franc account for 60 per cent of the vines, and the rest is Merlot with a little Petit-Verdot. Within a few years of the Rothschild purchase the wine seemed very good of its class. Another large estate is La Tour St-Bonnet in St-Christoly, and it makes some of the best wine in the lower Médoc. The main communes all have co-operatives. For example, that at Bégadan sells under the name of Ch. Béga-danais. The recent sharp rise in *cru classé* prices has created a new interest in the Bas-Médoc wines, whose prices also have sud-denly increased heavily.

To complete this record of the Médoc it is worth mentioning the wines of those Girondin isles which are near the shore of the Médoc. They are not now entitled to the *appellation* Médoc as they used to be, but are Bordeaux or Bordeaux Supérieur. Those on the other side are Bourgs or Blayes. At one time a good deal of wine was grown on these islands, but now the most important is the Île de Patiras, and one growth that is seen on British wine lists is Valrose, a pleasant light wine. Both red and white wines are made.

To end this tour of the Médoc in mid-stream seems in-congruous, although it will be the first view of those who cross on the ferry from Blaye to Lamarque. Little shows among or above the trees except the occasional church spires, the riverside bastion of the Fort de Médoc and the inland white water tower of St-Julien, less offensive to the eye than its black bottle. Few travelling the length of the Gironde estuary from the Pointe de Grave to the Bec d'Ambès and the Garonne would guess that behind the fringe of mud, projecting fishermen's huts and green trees lay perhaps the greatest red wine vineyard district in the world; certainly the most varied. Such glimpses as one has – the terrace of Lou-denne, the half-deserted waterfront of Pauillac (though now somewhat revitalized by a marina), the modest-looking château of Latour, the wider splendour of Beychevelle – hardly reveal much of the energetic, competitive yet friendly world of wine beyond. A world of such fine distinctions of commune, soil and individual growth, that one is hard put to it indeed to describe them. The variations are much greater than in the other districts that make up the Bordeaux *vignoble*. This variety is the chief attraction of the Médoc for dedicated claret drinkers, and even in cases where my comments have been less than enthusiastic, I am always more than willing to review the situation by way of practical application.

11. The Graves

The Graves district was the wine cradle of Bordeaux. In the Middle Ages wine was grown in the suburbs and gradually spread nearly all round the city. It is not a coincidence that Haut-Brion was the first known of the *premiers crus* and perhaps the first Bordeaux château wine to be mentioned in English literature. On 10 April 1663 Samuel Pepys recorded that he 'drank a sort of French wine called Ho Bryen that hath a good and most particular taste that I never met with'. The vineyard of Haut-Brion possibly existed from the beginning of the sixteenth century when it was owned by Jean de Ségur. Once well outside the city in Pessac, it has now been more or less engulfed, as has La Mission-Haut-Brion across the road in Talence.

Thomas Jefferson, American Minister in France from 1785 to 1789, whose comments on the Bordeaux red wines are given in the chapter on the classification of the Médoc, said of the white wines:

Those made in the canton of Grave are most esteemed at Bordeaux. The best groups are 1. Pontac, which formerly belonged to M. de Pontac, but now to M. de Lamerl. He makes 40 *tonneaux* which sells at 400 l. new. 2. St Brise belonging to M. de Pontac, 30 *tonneaux* at 350 l. 3. De Carbonius, belonging to the Benedictine monks who make 50 *tonneaux*, and never selling till 3 or 4 years old, get 800 l. the *tonneau*.

Throughout the last three centuries many Graves vineyards have fallen to the house and factory builders, some of them in recent years. Much of Mérignac was swallowed up by the airport of Bordeaux and the military airfield although at least one good growth remains: Pique Caillou. In theory, however, the Graves begins where the Médoc ends at the Jalle de Blanquefort.

To most people Graves indicates a fairly dry white wine, and indeed there is a preponderance of white, although this may change. In the sixties there was an average production of about 60,000 hl of white to 20,000 hl of red, but by the late seventies the *A C* Graves and Graves Supérieures average had dropped to about 50,000 while the red was averaging over 40,000 and in the prolific vintage of 1966, the red (and *rosé*) was close on 58,000 hl, compared with a much-above-average of nearly 62,000 for the white. Although there is no great problem in selling this relatively small quantity of *A C* Graves – the *A C* Bordeaux Blanc total is upwards of 700,000 hl – the changeover from white to red reflects a general trend throughout the Gironde.

Indeed at first the region was basically a red wine area, and today in those communes nearest to Bordeaux the red wines predominate. Certainly they are more important than the whites, although there is a small band of fine white wine vineyards; and as will be seen a number of the growths contain both red and white.

As the name indicates the Graves soil is gravelly and sandy. It produces red wines quite distinct from the Médocs, although some declare that the wines of the communes nearest to the Graves, such as those from Ludon and Macau, resemble the Graves. The difference is not at all easy to detect, although the Graves red wines have a certain *goût de terroir*, a slightly earthy taste, often more easy to recognize when one knows that the wine is a Graves than beforehand. They are usually rather drier, more austere than the Médocs although in style the Graves are nearer to the Médocs than to the St-Émilions and Pomerols. But I know at least one Médoc proprietor who declares his lack of liking for Graves; for many of the Médoc-ains, of course, the St-Émilions and Pomerols are beyond the serious wine pale as well as across the two rivers. I am inclined to believe that, nowadays at least, many of the red Graves do not last so well as the Médocs.

For the red wines the best soil is a mixture of pure gravel which on its own produces rather light wines, with a somewhat heavier mixture of heavy gravel and clay. Upstream the gravel becomes heavier and the soil contains more clay. There the white wines are sweeter. Indeed in the three communes of Cérons, Podensac and Illats those white wines made in the Sauternes way, the grapes picked as they become ripe and achieving the *pourriture noble*, are entitled to the *appellation* Cérons; those made in the usual way, with one picking through the vineyard, have a Graves *AC*. The Graves area goes even beyond Sauternes and ends in the Bazadais at St-Pierre-de-Mons and St-Pardon. Consequently there are really two styles of white Graves: the dry and the fairly sweet. Only about thirty communes produce wine on any scale, including the three around Cérons just referred to. As mentioned earlier the two chief grapes are the Sémillon and the Sauvignon. In the less distinguished wine communes the former predominates, and up to 5 per cent of Muscadelle may be found. The basic permitted quantity per ha is 40 hl compared with 43 hl in most of the Haut-Médoc and 40 in the named Haut-Médoc communes. The minimum strength for red Graves, however, is the same: 10 degrees.

I should say here and now that for white Graves my enthusiasm is limited. I can enjoy the few at the top, and on occasion – not too frequent an occasion – I can pleasantly employ the modest near-anonymous well-cooled Graves Supérieures to wash down an equally modest meal in summer. Yet to me too much white Graves seems to smell of sulphur, used to keep the wine stable and pale; and that applies to many of the sweeter Bordeaux too. Though perhaps more the fault of the wine-makers than of the wines, this takes much of the fresh, flowery, even honeyish aroma out of them and deadens the flavour too. It is fair to add that the Sauvignon grape produces a slightly smoky aroma and flavour that may be taken for sulphur. Often too the Graves are rather sweet and that does not provide the suitable prelude to a dry red wine that a white Burgundy affords. Much dry white Graves strikes me as rather dull, and although I am assured that this is at least owing to the way it is made nowadays, I have my doubts.

CLASSED GROWTHS OF THE GRAVES

Red Wines (classified in 1953 and confirmed in 1959)

Château Bouscaut	Cadaujac
Château Haut-Bailly	Léognan
Château Carbonnieux	Léognan
Domaine de Chevalier	Léognan
Château Fieuzal	Léognan
Château Olivier	Léognan
Château Malartic-Lagravière	Léognan
Château La Tour-Martillac	Martillac
Château Smith-Haut-Lafitte	Martillac
Château Haut-Brion	Pessac
Château La Mission-Haut-Brion	Pessac (Talence)
Château Pape-Clément	Pessac
Château Latour-Haut-Brion	Talence

White Wines (classified in 1959)★

Château Bouscaut	Cadaujac
Château Carbonnieux	Léognan
Domaine de Chevalier	Léognan
Château Olivier	Léognan
Château Malartic-Lagravière	Léognan
Château La Tour-Martillac	Martillac
Château Laville-Haut-Brion	Talence
Château Couhins	Villenave d'Ornon

★ Apparently at the request of the proprietor Haut-Brion Blanc was not included.

Yet they are often very moderately priced; except for the top flight, some of which in my view are often over-priced. So if any of my succeeding comments on various white Graves appear a little hard or tepid, I hope some allowance will be made for my lack of enthusiasm and my sulphur-conscious nose. Others enjoy them with abandon. They are improving.

PESSAC

The senior commune of the Graves is Pessac. Not only is Ch. Pape-Clément probably the oldest single vineyard of Bordeaux (although it did not at first bear that name, or so far as I know any prior title in the Middle Ages), but Pessac includes the only red Graves admitted to the 1855 classification: Haut-Brion. It also heads the official classification of 13 red Graves made in 1953.

Haut-Brion has had many owners, perhaps 25 since the beginning of the sixteenth century, when it was in the hands of Jean de Ségur. In 1525 it passed to Philippe de Chabot who was a mayor of Bordeaux as well as being an admiral. A few years later it was transferred to the daughter of a mayor of Libourne, de Bellon, and she married a Pontac, a family which intermittently owned or was connected with the estate for the ensuing 200 years. The present château was built in 1550.

According to another story, Jean de Pontac, a property owner, was the real creator of Haut-Brion as a vineyard, by buying it in 1533 from Jean Duhelde, a Bordeaux merchant of Basque origin, for 2,650 livres. The currency used in Bordeaux was the *livre tournois*, until supplanted at the Revolution by the roughly equivalent franc. According to Malvezin's *Histoire du commerce de Bordeaux* (1892), the value of the livre fell by nineteen-twentieths between the reigns of Louis XV (1715–74) and Louis XVI (1774–93). Either way the Pontacs became large landowners, including proprietors of vineyards, throughout the Bordeaux region, among them several in the

Graves communes and in St-Estèphe. Even today Ch. Myrat in Barsac is owned by the Comte de Pontac. Pontac was indeed the familiar name for Graves in seventeenth-century England. In the eighteenth century Haut-Brion was certainly sometimes known in England as Pontac, although Pontac was also a white wine.

In 1748 Haut-Brion passed into the hands of Catherine de Fumel, *née* Pontac, and the Fumel family owned the property until the Revolution. The first Fumel, Comte Louis, managed to acquire a fine assortment of first-growth titles, for not only was he Seigneur of Haut-Brion, but also of Margaux and Baron de Pauillac. He it was who in 1749 divided the estate into two parts: the château and one portion of the vineyard, and another smaller part known as the *Chai-Neuf*. In 1770 the latter part passed to the Marquis de Latresne and was detached from the rest of the property until 1840.

The Revolution produced a complicated situation for the rest of the château, as part was confiscated by the state owing to the emigration of Joseph Fumel, but his brother J. P. Fumel and his sister, Mme Branne, owned the other two-thirds and did not leave France. The brother acquired the confiscated portion for 237,666 frs. and 50 centimes (no less!) and bought out his sister. In 1800 he sold the whole to Talleyrand, who thus added the role of vineyard proprietor to that of his many other profitable callings from bishop onwards. He paid 255,000 frs., but in 1804 it was bought from Talleyrand, then Foreign Minister, by a banker, M. Michel, for 300,000 frs. He in his turn sold it twenty years later to M. Beyerman, the well-known Bordeaux merchant, and M. Comynet, a stock-broker of Paris, for 525,000 frs. The former ran the estate and paid his partner a rent of 25,000 frs. This arrangement appears not to have worked very satisfactorily, for there was a lawsuit and the property was once more put up for sale. The notice of the sale on 12 March 1836 can be seen in the château. It was valued then at 250,000 frs., but in fact at the auction it fell to

M. Eugène Larrieu for 296,000 frs. In the sale notice the area of that part is given as 91 ha, of which 40 to 50 were under vines, a similar total to that existing today for the whole, for it is now about 42 ha.

In 1840 M. Larrieu succeeded in reuniting the portion of the vineyard which had been split off in 1770 and paid 60,000 frs. for it; and the property has remained one vineyard ever since.

The estate remained in the Larrieu family until a few years after the First World War. Prior to that war Cocks et Féret recorded Haut-Brion as producing 100 *tonneaux* of first wine and 20 of second. This second wine used to be sold under the label of Château Bahans-Haut-Brion with a vintage, and this name is still used today, as a non-vintage wine. Output is from 20 to 30 *tonneaux* and the wine is mostly sold in French restaurants, although it may be found in the U.S.A. and Britain.

In the earlier part of the eighteenth century, Haut-Brion was still probably the leading red wine of Bordeaux, but thereafter it certainly declined, perhaps as a result of the division of the property. Although clearly it had a high reputation just before the Revolution, as exemplified by Thomas Jefferson's high praise of it, quoted in the chapter on the classification of the Médoc, little more than thirty years later Franck in the first edition (1824) of his book was writing about it: 'for several years it has lost its reputation because too much manure is used. It cannot be put in bottle until six or seven years after the harvest, although other first growths are drinkable at the end of five years.' Haut-Brion's lack of *réclame* may be shown by the fact that up to the end of the nineteenth century its name appeared far less in the Christie's auction catalogues than the other *premiers crus*. However, it improved after the reunification in 1840, and the wine had an excellent reputation in the latter part of the nineteenth century, though perhaps not in Britain where Lafite and Latour predominated. In the great vintage of 1899 Haut-

Brion's opening price of 2,600 frs. a *tonneau* was 400 frs. higher than Margaux, 600 frs. above Lafite and Latour, and 800 frs. above Mouton. It is generally agreed that the quality of Haut-Brion fell off later. From 1907 to 1916 the sale of the first wine was the monopoly of the Bordeaux firm of Richard et Muller, a by no means uncommon practice at that time when prices were steady for good quality wines. Under a later proprietor, the house of Rosenheim bought all the 1929 crop.

After the First World War Haut-Brion passed through several hands, not with the best of results for the wine. The Larrieu family died out and the last M. Larrieu divided the estate between two god-children, M. Milleret and Mme Taconet. The latter sold her portion to M. Milleret, who, to effect the purchase, had to borrow from a bank, the Compagnie Algérienne. Unfortunately the new owner did not run the property efficiently and soon, with the value of Bordeaux vineyards in decline during a difficult period, his debts to the bank exceeded the total value of the estate, and the creditor company foreclosed on the unfortunate M. Milleret. The bank, unlike the Rothschilds fifty years or so earlier, was uninterested in owning a vineyard, and sold the property to the Société des Glacières de Paris, who were looking for just such an estate. However in 1923, one of its directors, M. André Gibert, who had made a fortune in Algeria as well as in France, decided to retire from the company, and received as his share of the assets not only a considerable sum in cash but also the whole estate of Haut-Brion. Unfortunately within a year or two M. Gibert was permitted to sell off as building plots a large part of the château's splendid gardens and park. The new owner formed a company of the property, but that did nothing to improve the quality of the wine, much criticized at this period in Bordeaux. Then in 1935 it was bought by Mr Clarence Dillon, the American banker, with Mr Seymour Weller as the president of the company. It is said that not only was Haut-Brion then in the market but also

Cheval-Blanc and Ausone. Mr Dillon could have acquired Cheval-Blanc for 2·5 million frs., but on the day he visited St-Émilion the country was swathed in fog. So he decided not to buy Cheval-Blanc, but instead acquired Haut-Brion for 2·35 million frs. It is an open question which would have turned out the better buy, but in those days Cheval-Blanc's international reputation was less than now. In 1958 the property became the Domaine Clarence Dillon, S.A. The direction was essentially in the hands of Mr Douglas Dillon, son of Clarence, but in the mid-1970s the former's daughter Joan, now the Duchesse de Mouchy, took an active interest in the château's affairs.

Production remained fairly constant over the last century at around 100 *tonneaux* of red wine although in 1970 the crop made 150 *tonneaux*, and the average now is 130 *tonneaux*. The 42½-hectare vineyard is composed of 55 per cent Cabernet-Sauvignon, 22 per cent Cabernet-Franc and 23 per cent Merlot, a higher proportion of Cabernet and a lower one of Merlot than a few years earlier.

In its own way Haut-Brion is quite a 'big' wine. Cyrus Redding writing in the Beyerman era described it as follows: 'The flavour resembles burning sealing wax: the bouquet savours of the violet and raspberry.' These parallels are nearly always lost on me, but I pass this one on, in the hope that it will strike a chord with others.

The fine turreted château is widely familiar from its appearance on the label, surely one of the most attractive in Bordeaux. For about fifty years (from the early 1920s onwards) the finely engraved representation of the château was abandoned for progressively poorer versions. However, the original stone on which was engraved the fine picture was still in existence, and from the 1974 vintage the label has been essentially the same as the first style. The agreeable, rambling house lies in a grassy *parc anglais* with little of the horticultural precision that marks some of the greater châteaux. Inside it is charmingly decorated, with the drawing room furnished in the French style and the dining room in English Regency lacquer. The private cellar is small, rather like that of Latour, but leads out of the *chai* and not under the house. It is finely arched and has specimens of Haut-Brion back to the 1890s but, perhaps because the proprietor has seldom been in residence, there appears to have been little exchange with other owners' wines.

Vinously the château has had its ups and downs in this century and it must be said that, outside the United States where its American ownership has given it a special cachet, the wine has not enjoyed the reputation of some of the other first growths or of Mouton-Rothschild when it was still a second. Earlier on it was splendid, and I had a few bottles of 1899 and 1900 that were all that old claret might be expected to be, especially the '99. In the mid-sixties I drank the '08 at Mouton and that was surprisingly full and firm, with that slightly burnt taste which Redding referred to. The '20 was very fine indeed, but like most other '20s has now passed over. At the château I have drunk the '26, which had the typical dry finish of the wines of that vintage, but was very distinguished. But after that there was an off-period – with a very poor '28 and a not very good '29 – until the 1945 retrieved the situation. Of all the '45 first growths Haut-Brion was the first to come round and be drinkable, and remains a first-class wine.

Since then Haut-Brion appears to have varied. In off-vintages it has sometimes struck me as over-sweetened, notably the '50 and '60. The '49 I have not much liked, but the '52 and '53 are certainly good, and the '55 one of the more interesting first growths of a not outstanding vintage. It has also come out well in succeeding vintages. The '59 was certainly one of the best first growths of a vintage that did not always hold up as well as had originally been expected. The Graves often develop rather more quickly than the Médocs,

GRAVES

and this certainly applies to Haut-Brion as compared with the other firsts, save Ch. Margaux. So in '61 and again in '66 it was already very attractive when the Pauillacs were still rather closed-up and backward. The '62 was a light, elegant wine, and the '64 was among the more successful and when ten years old came first in a tasting including not only the Médoc *premiers crus* but also Cheval-Blanc and Pétrus. Its '67 had style and made an unusually successful wine in the generally disastrous year of '68. Haut-Brion is an elegant wine, with that 'earthy' taste of the finer red Graves. Under its *régisseur*, Jean Delmas – one of the most experienced wine-makers in Bordeaux – it has been making very well-balanced wines. Compared with its 'big brothers' in the Médoc it is perhaps a little undervalued; in the 1973 re-classification of the *premiers crus* it was set down as *assimilé* rather than as one of the 'regular' firsts (as in the 1855 categorization), which might appear to give it a mere 'associate' status. If so, this is the fault of the classification and not of Haut-Brion.

One must mention here that in 1960 Haut-Brion startled Bordeaux by installing stainless steel vats, which Latour were later to adopt, but of a rather different pattern. The purpose was to secure better control of the wine during the fermentation period. When fermented the wine is left in the vats for one month, during which time part at least of the malo-lactic fermentation takes place.

Opinion in Bordeaux is both conservative and critical, and when the steel vats were installed, eyebrows were raised (an exercise much practised and enjoyed in the region). By this time the shock had passed of the enamel-covered vats of La Mission-Haut-Brion across the road, the first of which were put in during 1926 and the rest in 1951. After nearly twenty years at Haut-Brion and not much less at Latour it would be hard to argue that the quality of these wines had deteriorated or that they are less likely to enjoy a long life. The great period of risk in wine-making is obviously enough the fermentation one, and such scientific control as can be best effected in these vats is surely desirable. At Haut-Brion one central panel administers the whole range of vats in the *cuvier*.

Another small change at Haut-Brion was the design of a new bottle, with a longer neck and a more rounded body, very much in the style of earlier claret bottles. This was first used for the 1958 vintage.

Haut-Brion is also known for producing one of the leading white Graves, Haut-Brion Blanc, although oddly enough in the 1959 Graves classification it was not included, according to the wishes of the owner. Production, restricted to $2\frac{1}{2}$ ha, is small – from 8 to 15 *tonneaux* – and the wine is much sought after, particularly in the United States. I first came upon it in the 1949 vintage, when part at least was shipped in cask and bottled in England. That and succeeding vintages were fine, honey-nosed wines with a good deal of flavour and distinction. Later on, however, when it was all bottled at the château it often seemed to me over-sulphured, though a bottle of the '59 was a beautifully full wine, rich on the nose but dry on the palate, when it was at least fifteen years old. Nevertheless, when over the years the young wines in cask have been sampled this sulphuring has not been noticeable, and from the early seventies onwards the wine appears to have been much fresher. It is, however, a decidedly expensive wine, with very restricted production.

It is perhaps worth mentioning here that, contrary to a fairly widespread belief, these fine dry white Graves deserve a fair amount of bottle-age in order for them to round out. The late Henri Woltner, who made nearby Laville-Haut-Brion, always maintained that a fine vintage white Graves should not be drunk until it was at least ten years old, and he demonstrated this successfully to me a number of times at his own table. I have drunk Laville-Haut-Brion bottles of twenty and even thirty years old that were wines of unexpected character and distinction.

The second wine of the district and in recent years something of a rival to Haut-Brion is La Mission-Haut-Brion, which lies just across the main road to Arcachon. Although the reference books place it in Pessac, in fact La Mission is in Talence, for 13 of its 16½ ha are in that commune and only 3½ in Pessac. The agreeable château, with at one end the seventeenth-century chapel that contributes to the estate's name, is also in Talence, but in view of its accepted status, it is convenient to include the wine here among the Pessacs.

The Mission was one conducted by the order of St-Vincent-de-Paul, and the interior of the charming little chapel is full of objects of interest. So indeed is the château, including a collection of holy-water stoups and a splendid assembly of superb Delft dishes brought by the Dutch merchants who came to collect Bordeaux wine. The *cuvier* and the cellars are impeccably kept.

La Mission-Haut-Brion was owned in the last century by M. Chiapella and then by M. Coustau who sold it in his old age in 1920 to Frédéric Woltner, father of Henri and Fernand Woltner. Until his death in 1974 the active partner was Henri Woltner, certainly to be classed as one of the most infectiously 'committed' Bordeaux château owners. In my time I have had my share of meals at which on sitting down an array of glasses has faced one like sentinels, but I can remember no comparable number at a private lunch as on a notable occasion at La Mission; in front of the four places at table, there were ten apiece for M. and Mme Woltner, his manager and myself. First we had four white Graves, two of them different vintages of his own Laville-Haut-Brion but not including the neighbour's across the road – then five red wines, and a Barsac to end up with. That did not include, of course, the bottle of Pol Roger (the Woltners used to have the French agency) beforehand or the glass of cognac afterwards. Fortunately we were not expected to finish all the bottles, although it was not easy to refuse replenishments of such wines as La Mission '47 and Cheval-Blanc '47, and La Mission '29 and '20 (these last two at my request, and very fine too).

However in Bordeaux one can certainly drink safely much more than in London, and any soporific tendency was checked by Henri Woltner's enthusiastic discourse. For he was indeed a man with a mission; not a religious one, but for his *fermentation froide* system of vinification.

During the period of fermentation the main aim of a château's *maître de chai* or *régisseur* is to secure a continuous vinification without extremes of temperature. If this falls too much the fermentation may stop and be difficult to re-start, leaving dangerous unfermented sugar in the must. If the temperature rises too high – the danger point is variable but 35 degrees C. (95 degrees F.) is very near it – the wine may turn to vinegar.

In M. Woltner's vitrified steel *cuves* at La Mission the temperature may be more easily controlled than in wooden vats, and this obviates the exhausting manual work and watching that may be necessary if the temperature is running too high. Thus at La Mission the temperature never goes above 30 degrees C. (85 F.), and is more likely to run at 27 C. or 28 C. (80·6–82·4 F.). Had it not been for the Second World War, all the vats would have been replaced long before 1951 when the changeover was completed. The stainless steel vats at Haut-Brion and Latour are designed for the same purpose, although one may suspect that Henri Woltner believed his own to be more satisfactory, as well as being a good deal less expensive. It can be seen that the term *froide* is a relative one, and does not imply any degree of refrigeration. After the vinification in the vats is finished, the wine is transferred to oak casks, and normally bottled about two and a half years after the vintage. Until recently this operation took place not at the château, but in a specially authorized annexe of the firm's cellars in Bordeaux. Now the wine is all bottled at the château.

M. Woltner's system is not to the taste of some other proprietors, and of course it involves considerable capital outlay, but there can be no doubt that La Mission produces splendid, 'meaty' wine. At one period in the sixties some comparative blind tastings of Haut-Brion and La Mission-Haut-Brion took place, and at one the balance of opinion appeared to favour the latter. Apart from the fact that Haut-Brion was not always making exceptionally good wine in the early post-war epoch (though its '45 was outstanding), but thereafter produced very distinguished clarets, in my view such a comparison is misconceived though of course interesting. For La Mission-Haut-Brion is no less different in style from its neighbour than Mouton-Rothschild is from the adjoining Lafite. La Mission is powerful, with a decided *goût de terroir*, while Haut-Brion is more elegant and lighter. La Mission probably takes more time to come round, but thereafter stays rich and concentrated. Among the vintages of the latter that I have enjoyed are the remarkably big '49, '53, and, for the year, exceptionally good '58. The '61 has a big reputation, but I have found the '62 and '64 variable. La Mission usually commands an opening price higher than any other non-first growth, and is usually fixed at about two thirds of the price of its neighbour.

The composition of the vineyard is 65 per cent Cabernet-Sauvignon, 10 per cent Cabernet-Franc and 25 per cent Merlot. The average output is 80–90 *tonneaux*, but only 40 *tonneaux* were made of the very powerful, full '75, whose opening price per *tonneau* was 35,000 frs.

The Woltner family (Fernand Woltner died in March 1977) own two other vineyards: La Tour-Haut-Brion, a red wine growth of Talence, and Laville-Haut-Brion, which is devoted entirely to white wines. The composition of the former is identical to that of La Mission; the latter is 60 per cent Sémillon and 40 per cent Sauvignon. La Tour is a small vineyard with an area of only 4 ha, and an output of 10–12 *tonneaux*. Although it has not the distinction of La Mission, the wine is fruity and well balanced, and made in the same *chai* as La Mission. La Tour-Haut-Brion formerly belonged to M. Coustau but he did not sell it to Frédéric Woltner along with La Mission. He died not long afterwards and his widow arranged for the vineyard to be run and the wine made *en fermage* (i.e. on a rental basis) by La Mission. This was done so successfully and profitably for Madame Coustau that when she died some years later she left the property to Mme Woltner, who had befriended her. A valuable bequest indeed! Although La Tour-Haut-Brion is not the second wine of La Mission, a small part of its production may be included in the *assemblage* of the latter, and vice versa. Laville-Haut-Brion, also in Talence, was in fact carved out of the La Tour vineyard, in a part where the quality of wine from black grapes was not entirely satisfactory. So a small white wine vineyard was planted – at first 50–50 Sémillon and Sauvignon – and the first vintage took place in 1928. Average production is about 20 *tonneaux*. Laville-Haut-Brion is certainly in the first flight of dry white Bordeaux. Indeed along with Domaine de Chevalier I would put it top on current showing.

The next most important Graves of Pessac is Pape-Clément, whose archiepiscopal origin has already been mentioned. It belonged to the Church until the Revolution, when it was sold to a wine merchant in 1791. In the 1824 edition of Franck the proprietor is given as Jarrige and the output as 30–40 *tonneaux*. This château has a long tradition of excellent wine-making, and not least in the 1920s; the '20, '24 and '29 were splendid wines. Then the property fell into some eclipse, and indeed it was rumoured that the estate had been sold to builders. Certainly production dwindled and was at a very low ebb after the last war. The property belongs to the family of M. Léo Montaigne, who bought it in 1939 and replanted the vineyard which now runs to 27 ha; there is a handsome park adjoining it. But not until 1953 did the wine recover its old form. Both then and in 1955 the wine was excellent, though the latter, like many '55s, was not a great keeper. There was a very fine wine in 1961, when only about 20 *tonneaux* were produced instead of a normal 120–150; but the '75 output of a wine at first generally regarded as one of the best red Graves was only 85 *tonneaux*. Among other vintages in which particularly good wine was made here were '62 and '64, the former one of the best in the Gironde. Pape-Clément is generally a bigger, fuller-flavoured wine than other red Graves such as Haut-Bailly and Domaine de Chevalier. The vineyard is said to be 58 per cent Cabernet-Sauvignon and 42 per cent Merlot. In 1974 a new *chai*, 75 m long, was built with a capacity, rather like that of Mouton-Rothschild, of 1,000 *barriques*. This *chai* is also hired out for weddings and receptions, and when I was there in September 1977 a band on the higher level at one end was tuning up for a double-wedding party. I only hoped that the wine in the casks beyond would not become as warmed up as seemed likely with the guests, who were able to help themselves from Pape-Clément *vin de l'année* as well as rather more senior papal wine in magnums. Compared with the growths discussed above the wine is made very traditionally at Pape-Clément.

One Pessac vineyard that has been swallowed up by the bulldozers is Laburthe-Brivazac, which sixty years ago ranked high among the wines of the commune. M. Brivazac was a councillor in the eighteenth-century Parlement. A few years ago it was sold, but Ronald Barton bought for his firm a stock of several thousand bottles of the fine 1929. I acquired a few bottles, and although the wine was a little dry at the end, it was still very fine and enjoyable. There is something a little melancholy in drinking wine from a vineyard no longer in existence.

With the remaining small collection of Pessac growths I can claim no acquaintance. The best known is Camponac, which was bought by Frédéric Eschenauer in 1875, but is now used as a brand name of the firm. Several other growths managed to weave the magic words Haut-Brion into their name, but they had no wide reputation and in the late twenties legal action was taken against one or two of these; one was forbidden to use the name Haut-Brion, but Larrivet-Haut-Brion, some way away in Léognan, was permitted to do so, on the grounds of long usage, but it was forbidden to print the name Haut-Brion in larger type than the Larrivet, as it had done previously. Les Carmes-Haut-Brion is a small vineyard, almost engulfed by Bordeaux like its neighbours in Pessac. Its name comes from the Carmelite monks who owned the property from 1584 to the Revolution. Thereafter it was nationalized and passed through several hands, until it was bought more than a century ago by the ancestors of the present owner, Mme Chantecaille. The vineyard area is about 12 ha and the production (of purely red wine) is around 15 *tonneaux*. Although not among the classified Graves it has a good reputation, but is not widely found outside France. There is also listed La Passion-Haut-Brion, with an output of only four *tonneaux*, but this exciting-sounding claret has yet to come my way.

LÉOGNAN

Talence need not delay us apart from the growths already mentioned, and the next important Graves commune for red wines is Léognan, which includes six of the thirteen classified growths.

First in general standing is Haut-Bailly. Its reputation was established in the last century by a proprietor, Bellot des Minières, a famous grower known as *le roi des vignerons*. According to the firm of Mestrezat, which used to buy the whole crop around the turn of the last century, one at least of the 'secrets' of Haut-Bailly's success was that he 'cleaned' out his *cuves* before the vintage with a few litres apiece of Grande Fine Champagne cognac. This drop of spirit at the bottom of each vat was conveniently 'forgotten' when the grapes were shovelled in, and the result in the wine was nothing but beneficial. Fortunately or not this no longer takes place. Like Pape-Clément in Pessac, Haut-Bailly had a great reputation and then temporarily rather lost it. In the inter-war years some splendid wine was made, notably a fine '28 and a supple, fruity '37, no mean feat in that hard year. After the Second World War it had two disastrous years in 1959 and 1960, owing to frost. In the former, production was 10 *tonneaux* only, instead of a normal 50, and in 1960 was down to 1·5 *tonneaux* – six hogsheads. Fortunately the château made a very sound '64 in that uneven year. Its '66 and '70 were judged fine, but the '71 less distinguished. The '75 promised well. Haut-Bailly was bought in 1955 by M. Daniel Sanders, a Belgian, and the production averages 75 *tonneaux* from a 20-hectare vineyard bounded by woods. The *cépage* is 60 per cent Cabernet-Sauvignon, 10 per cent Cabernet-Franc and 30 per cent Merlot. The Graves vineyards tend to lie among woods off the main roads and are difficult to find. More than once I, and even Bordeaux merchants with me, have lost the way in the small cross-country roads. Haut-Bailly is one of these remote-seeming châteaux, although not in fact very far from Bordeaux.

Equally high if not higher in repute is Domaine de Chevalier, whose white wine carries a renown equal to the red, and is certainly among the top three or four white Graves. Like Haut-Bailly, the Domaine de Chevalier is tucked away in the countryside, and its modest appearance can be gauged from the photograph on the old labels. The property is only 15 ha in extent, 2 of them devoted to the white wine, which is 70 per cent Sauvignon and 30 per cent Sémillon. The red is 68 per cent Cabernet-Sauvignon, 2 per cent Cabernet-Franc and 30 per cent Merlot. Production is 40–45

tonneaux of red and 8 of white. The latter is bottled after eigh
teen months. For some years in the seventies Ginestet had
the exclusive selling rights.

At one time Domaine de Chevalier was very much of a
connoisseur's claret, for production was small and the growth
was not widely known; being a domaine in a country of so-
called châteaux did not altogether improve the sales prospects.
Although dating back well into the last century, I am inclined
to think that the Chevalier's more than local reputation dates
from this century only. The estate was founded by M. Ricard
in the last century, and today his grandsons of the same name
cultivate the property. In between came a relative of the first
M. Ricard, M. Gabriel Beaumartin, who ruled over the
domaine from 1900 until his death in 1942. André Simon in
Vintagewise (1945) includes the 1899 among the fine wines of
that vintage which he had enjoyed, but I never came on it
anything like so early; not even the 1907 which he reckons to
have been the best wine of that very light vintage, nor the
1909, which was generally another uncertain year.

Yet Domaine de Chevalier really introduced me to the red
Graves. During the last war I bought from Justerini & Brooks
some excellent bottles of the '24, domaine-bottled I suppose
one must say. They had a great deal of elegance, but plenty of
fruit and were fine true claret right up to my last bottle in
1952. The '23 was a notable wine of Chevalier, but this I did
not drink until a few years ago, when it was going downhill.
Nevertheless I did drink the '28 in its prime and, along with
Léoville-Las-Cases and Cheval-Blanc, it was certainly the best
'28 that has ever come my way. Indeed the Chevalier '28 was
a wine with a considerable reputation in Bordeaux, for it
lacked the hardness of most '28s. The '29 I only drank once,
but remember it as good, and so was the '34. I have even
heard tell that a very fair wine was made in that deplorable
year '31, and again in '35, but I have never sampled them.
Another success in a generally disappointing vintage was the

Chevalier '37, which I bought not very long after the last war, and finished with regret early in the 1960s. It was wonderfully supple in that hard year, and even better than Haut-Bailly.

Gabriel Beaumartin must have been a particularly fine wine-maker, for he triumphed when others failed. One reason for his success was that he was also a timber merchant with a large labour force. At the vintage he waited until he believed the moment of full maturity had arrived. Then at once he brought in his workers and cleared the relatively small vineyard in two or three days instead of the more normal ten to fourteen days. He was also very selective with his grapes, eliminating any that were unripe. Whatever art he added to nature, the result was a success. Unfortunately in 1945 much of the vineyard was wiped out by frost and had to be replanted. The wine was certainly disappointing in the next few years, but showed signs of revival in 1953. I confess to having tasted it seldom since, but the '58 – a year in which Beaumartin might have pulled something out of the bag – was thin and disappointing. The '62 is agreeably fruity, while the '70 is well thought of.

The white wines have kept a more consistent path and were good in the inter-war years. I had bottles and half-bottles of the '37, which were excellent after nearly twenty years. Later came a beautiful 1947, followed by fine wines in the fifties. The '64 Chevalier was certainly among the best of the white Graves. I hope that the more recent red Chevaliers will exhibit the old form of this vineyard, for they rank among the most expensive of the non-first-growth clarets. Certainly recent vintages have been distinguished.

The four other classed Léognans are Malartic-Lagravière, Carbonnieux, Fieuzal and Olivier. All four also make white wine. I have drunk the red Malartic several times, but, apart from an ageing but fine '26, recently have found it rather a hard and not altogether well-balanced wine; yet I may have been unlucky, for Alexis Lichine places it high. I have found the white '64 excellent. The vineyard area is only 10 ha.

Carbonnieux, once the most famous dry white Graves and as a red wine on a line with the top Léognans, has until recently generally disappointed me. The property once belonged to the Abbey of Ste-Croix in Bordeaux but in 1956 it was bought by M. Mark Perrin, formerly of Algeria. Here I may repeat the famous story that in order to fool the innocent, wine-forbidden Turks, the not so innocent, not so scrupulous Benedictine monk-exporters labelled their wine as *Eaux Minérales de Carbonnieux*. Later, in the last century, Carbonnieux rather unusually took to growing a wide variety of grapes taken from all over Europe, although the main vines in the vineyard were the normal Bordelais types, Cabernet-Sauvignon, Verdot, Malbec and Merlot.

The vineyard today is 50 ha in extent, the majority being planted with white grapes: 65 per cent Sauvignon and 35 per cent Sémillon, the more productive of the two. The *cépage* of the red part of the vineyard is 60 per cent Cabernet-Sauvignon and 30 per cent Merlot, with the balance made up of Cabernet-Franc and Malbec. For many years the red and white wine rarely lived up to their well-known name, and the wines were seldom seen in Britain. Moreover, although M. Perrin obviously set to work to improve matters this is a lengthy job for any wine estate, and until the seventies the wines did not show particularly well, the dry whites being rather heavy. However, in 1973 began the installation of nine stainless steel vats in the *chai* for the white wine; this is now bottled about nine months after the vintage with the result that it is much fresher and crisper, and able to take its place among the very small band of fine dry white Graves. The red wine too shows much more of the true Graves style. It should be mentioned that the turreted château of Carbonnieux is one of the more attractive in the region. It includes a very agreeable, arcaded, creeper-covered courtyard.

I cannot recollect ever tasting Fieuzal, another small vine-yard with 14 ha, except in the modern *chai*. The wine is seldom seen in Britain and probably little exported, for it is not easy to sell red Graves, simply because they are not well publicized. Fieuzal mostly produces red wine, but there is a little white also. In 1973 it was bought by M. Négrevergne.

Olivier is certainly much better known, but mostly for its white wine, which has been sold as a monopoly by the owners, the firm of Eschenauer. Some red wine is made there but much less than white. Olivier is not in the top class of white Graves, but is a sound wine, sometimes seeming rather sulphury to me, but well above the average. The moated château, owned by M. P. de Bethman, is very picturesque, but the vineyard property is rented to Eschenauer. It extends to 25 ha. Since Eschenauer was bought by the Liverpool merchant firm of John Holt, a good deal of money has been spent on all their estates, including those in the Graves. Incidentally, Holt is now a subsidiary of the large merchant/finance group of Lonrho, with considerable interests in Africa.

There are a number of other quite well-known Léognan estates, including Larrivet-Haut-Brion, whose red wine I have enjoyed in the past, but not seen recently; and La Louvière, best known for its white wine.

MARTILLAC

The next best-known red Graves commune is Martillac, which adjoins Léognan, and includes two classed growths: Smith-Haut-Lafitte and La Tour-Martillac. The former is another Eschenauer property, and one always well known in Britain, initially perhaps because the first of its three names had a familiar ring to the not so knowledgeable and the last suggested quality to the rather more sophisticated. I remember a very fair '29. Like other Graves it seemed to decline or merely not sell over here for a long period, but with the arrival of new owners, there have been fresh developments, including a special bottle, which in Bordeaux is sometimes the outward and visible sign of change within; others content themselves with a new label. The area is 30 ha, and an average of 90 *tonneaux* of red wine is made. In 1968 white wine production started. The château is separately owned, and the wine although made on the spot is then transferred and kept in Eschenauer's cellars in Bordeaux. The fruity '61 has turned out well, and the '66 when I sampled it in cask was a supple wine with plenty of colour. I would place the estate among the good, second-rank red Graves, which might well improve in the next few years.

La Tour-Martillac is an exceptionally interesting small property, for it includes what must be among the oldest vines producing grapes for wine in Bordeaux today. If the estate were not run by one of Bordeaux's leading wine enthusiasts, Jean Kressmann, knowledgeable about the history and background of Bordeaux, one can imagine that these ancient white wine vines would have been dug up; for they were planted in 1884, in the middle of the phylloxera, and were grafted on to immune American stocks. Throughout his vineyard, which also produces red wine, the average age of the vines is 30–40 years, which must be nearly twice the normal average. How little old vines yield may be seen from his production. From 4 ha of white wine grapes, including the 1884 plantation, he secures only 20 hogsheads of wine, whereas the 8 ha under black grapes yield 112–120. But the old vines give the quality, and Kressmann is justifiably proud of them, although the oldest section must soon be replanted. Jean Kressmann is also proud of the careful way he makes his white wine, and says it is unnecessary to use sulphur – the bane of so much white Bordeaux. Indeed I have heard it suggested that since the prohibition in the United Kingdom of the use of sorbic acid in white wine, the application of sulphur has increased. The wine is kept in Bordeaux before bottling in the cellars of the firm of Kressmann. The tower which stands before the charming small château was apparently built by an ancestor of Montesquieu.

There is yet another Eschenauer property in Martillac, La Garde, which seems particularly tucked away in the woods. A rural-looking establishment with a fine two-storeyed stone *chai*, this is predominantly a red wine vineyard, producing about 50 *tonneaux*, of which only a few are white, but the proportion of white is increasing, owing to the demand for good quality white Graves and the corresponding difficulty of selling the lesser-known red wines. The red wine that I tasted seemed particularly full-bodied for a Graves, and in 1968 in Bordeaux I was surprised to find the '47 still so fruity, with a slightly strong flavour.

VILLENAVE D'ORNON

Before we reach the white wine area proper there are a number of small communes in the neighbourhood of Bordeaux which make red wines of fairly wide reputation. In Villenave d'Ornon there is Baret, which makes both red and white wine, and Couhins, which is owned by the Hanappier and Gasqueton families, associated with Calon-Ségur. Here they make a well-known *rosé*, which is among the best in Bordeaux. White Baret I have often drunk in England, and it can be very agreeable of its kind. At Villenave also there is Pontac-Montplaisir; its name sufficient to make one order a bottle; a very fair wine. The property formerly belonged to the Pontac family. The estate used to be planted with Riesling vines.

CADAUJAC

Cadaujac has the important and very well-cared-for estate of Bouscaut, to be seen from the main road from Bordeaux to the Sauternes country. Until 1968 it was owned by Victor and Robert Place, but was then sold for 5.5 million new francs to an American syndicate, Domaine Wohlstetter-Sloan. This vineyard has been largely replanted in the last thirty years; it extends to 40 ha, producing 180 *tonneaux*, of which two thirds are red and one third white. The composition of the red part of the vineyard is 30 per cent Cabernet-Sauvignon, 20 per cent Cabernet-Franc, 40 per cent Merlot and 10 per cent Malbec. The white wine is made from 60 per cent Sémillon and 40 per cent Sauvignon. When making the white wine the uncommon practice is followed of putting the white grapes into a cement vat for one night prior to pressing. This apparently results in the impurities falling to the bottom of the vat. Thereafter the fermentation of the juice pressed from the skins takes place as usual in the hogsheads. The owners are go-ahead people, and all the property, including the charming château, rebuilt after more than one fire, is in first-class order. Both young red and white wines that I tasted seemed good, the red supple and fairly forward, the white fresh, but neither outstanding. So far they seem to lack style.

Although there is plenty of red wine made in the communes to the south of Cadaujac, more and more the white wines take over. As already indicated at Bouscaut, the two grapes used are Sauvignon which produces an elegant, perfumed wine and the Sémillon which results in wine lighter and less distinguished in aroma and flavour. White Graves is usually bottled after about 16–18 months. White wine is normally more difficult to make than red as it suffers much more from the risk of oxidation and darkening of colour, or *madérisation*. To counteract this sulphur is used, all too often to excess. So a great deal of white Graves suffers from too much sulphur and too little freshness. Contrary to common opinion white Graves is a fairly strong wine, for to be entitled to the *appellation* of Graves Supérieures it must have a minimum of 12 degrees, although the plain Graves *appellation* calls for only 11 degrees. In good years white Graves may be 12–13 degrees, while the red will be a minimum of 10–11.

One of the show-places of the northern part of the Graves is the Château La Brède, where Montesquieu (1689–1755) was born and lived. He took a prominent part in the affairs of Bordeaux, but was also a substantial vineyard owner, both in the Graves, where he owned Rochemorin in Martillac, and in the Entre-Deux-Mers at Raymond in the village of Baron. Both estates still exist. On one occasion Montesquieu said, 'What makes me love being at La Brède is that there it seems to me that my money is beneath my feet.' Nevertheless he was aware of the comparatively low value of his wines, the nearest of which was in competition with the more famous estate of Carbonnieux, whose average price was no more than 215 livres per *tonneau*; although as mentioned at the beginning of this chapter, thirty years later Jefferson gave its price as 800 livres. Although the charming, turreted and moated château is more of a show-place (and open to the public) than a wine-château, a very agreeable white Graves is made there in relatively small quantities and is now all château-bottled. The owner is the Comtesse de Chabannes.

As one travels south in the Graves region, the wine tends to become less distinguished and rather sweeter. There is Graves de Portets which is cheaper and less good than most Graves to the north. The red Graves de Portets, while lacking the special 'bricky', earthy quality of the leading red Graves, are generally superior to the white. They and some of their neighbours are wines that appear once on the cheaper end of a wine merchant's list, and then disappear, probably not because they are disappointing but because the broker or the Bordeaux merchant does not happen to have them in his portfolio. Three red Portets that I have drunk with pleasure are Cabannieux, La Tour-Bicheau and Bernard-Raymond. In spite of the often resplendent names on the châteaux's gates and in the books of reference, the area becomes largely one of anonymous Graves and Graves Supérieures. Only the local brokers really know the lie of the wine land, whose wine is good and whose is less good. On British wine merchants' lists will usually be found one or two white Graves with unfamiliar château names, and they probably come from this southern part of the district, which in fact extends round and beyond the sweet wine area, down to the town of Langon. There the *appellation* is not Sauternes as might be imagined, but Graves. The whole Graves district is about 60 km long with an average breadth of 10 km.

It should be pointed out here that a wine labelled Graves de Vayres is not a Graves, but in effect an Entre-Deux-Mers, for it lies more or less near the *RN.89* which runs from Bordeaux to Libourne. It is referred to in the chapter on the Entre-Deux-Mers.

12. St-Émilion

Many wine drinkers first 'discover' claret through the St-Émilions. For the fruitiness and earlier maturity of these wines makes them more immediately attractive than the rather drier and, when young, austere Médocs. Hence the St-Émilions and their neighbours in Pomerol are referred to as the 'Burgundies of Bordeaux', although that simile is unlikely to appeal to either party. The wines are soft and full because the soil is distinctly richer than in the Médoc or the Graves; this is obvious to any visitor. Also the high proportion of Merlot and the presence of Malbec grapes, both of which produce softer wines than the Cabernet-Sauvignon, are factors in the style of the St-Émilions. The Cabernet-Franc variety is known as the Bouchet in these parts; the Malbec as the Pressac. On the whole St-Émilions mature and decline sooner than the Médocs, though there are exceptions from the Côtes area.

The Merlot and Malbec are prolific bearers, but the basic St-Émilion *appellation* permits 42 hl per hectare, compared with 43 in the Haut-Médoc and 40 for the six named communes of that district.* As against that the wines must be 11 degrees in strength compared with the Haut-Médoc's and Médoc's minimum of 10 degrees. This is not a factor of concern to the general run of St-Émilion proprietors. The Merlot and Malbec have the further advantage of being early ripeners, so the vintage in St-Émilion normally begins a few days earlier than in the Médoc. However they also have their disadvantages: they are subject to frost, mildew and *pourriture grise*. In unfavourable weather just before or during the vintage, rot can spread through the vineyard with alarming speed, and

*But see Appendix A on 1974 *rendement* regulations.

this is another reason for early vintaging in St-Émilion. The susceptibility to frost was demonstrated in the terrible disaster of February 1956, when the St-Émilion and Pomerol districts were far worse affected than the Médoc. This was partly owing to situation as well as frost, but the result was that a great number of vines were killed outright, and even ten years later the unexpected collapse of apparently healthy vines was attributed to their weakening in the 1956 frosts. The effect of rot was shown at the 1968 vintage, when St-Émilion and Pomerol were devastated after a wet late summer.

St-Émilion is viticulturally a large district by Bordeaux standards. The output of wines entitled to its *appellation* averages 250,000 hl a year from about 700 growths, compared with about 350,000 from the whole of the Médoc. In addition there are five fringe communes attached to St-Émilion which together produce about another 130,000 hl. So there is plenty of St-Émilion available, much of it inexpensive.

Until the coming of motor transport, the local wines were all shipped from the quay at Libourne. Several important firms including the old house of Beylot, along with Danglade and Moueix, have their cellars there yet; and there are still barrels of wine on the quayside. In the pre-1914 days, the Gilbey family and their friends on their way to Loudenne in the Bas-Médoc used to take the steamer from Libourne. If the place is now quieter than it once was, it is a pleasant but by no means sleepy town, known chiefly to foreign visitors as lying at the end of an essential bridge – blown up by the retreating Germans in 1944 in spite of a promise to the contrary – on the way to St-Émilion, Fronsac and the north.

St-Émilion, which likes to describe itself as 'the pearl of the Gironde', lies four miles inland from Libourne. It is as charming a small wine town as is to be found in France, occupying a splendid position on top of a hill with wide views over the Dordogne valley. There is a famous monolithic church excavated from the limestone, which locally provides admirable cellars for a number of the châteaux, topped by a spire that rises above the town's small main square. There is also the alleged cell of the hermit, Aemilianus, who gave his name to the town, but there is no evidence that he had any wine associations. Nor are the local wine connections of the fourth-century Latin poet Ausonius, First Consul of Rome, clear. It is maintained that he owned a villa, and Château Ausone is said to have been built on the foundations. He was born in Bordeaux but his vineyard was probably in the Premières Côtes.

Parts of the town walls still remain, along with a rather grand collegiate church which has a finely proportioned cloister and the remains of a monastery. It also has two well-known restaurants in the main square, and is notable for its macaroons, though these cannot be recommended as a suitable accompaniment to the local wines.

The heart of St-Émilion is divided geologically and physically in two: the Côtes and the Graves. The first part, as the name implies, is on the slopes, which are in fact the sides of the river valley. The soil comprises silica, clay and chalk. The leading growth of these is Ausone, and its vineyard, lying below the château terrace, is sited on a considerable slope. This Côte is not the unbroken line of hillside one associates with the Côte d'Or, but is irregular. Nevertheless most of the vineyards are on a hillside, and other well-known growths include La Gaffelière, Bel-Air, Canon, Magdelaine, Pavie and Clos Fourtet. The second and smaller area, lying on the fairly flat plateau which also includes Pomerol, has a more gravelly, sandy soil. Hence the name which misleads some into thinking that the wines are from the Graves. Cheval-Blanc is the pre-eminent château, and other well-known growths include Figeac and a clutch of neighbours who have added the name Figeac to their own; also another group with variations on the name Corbin; and others such as La Dominique and Ripeau. The plateau is partly a saucer,

ST-ÉMILION

l'Isle

N 674

N 89

CÔTES DE FRONSAC

LALANDE DE
POMEROL

NÉAC

POMEROL

Lussac-St-Émilion

COMMUNES WITH ST-ÉMILION *AC*

LIBOURNE

Dordogne

GRAVES-ST-
ÉMILION

St Georges-
St-Émilion

Montagne-St-Émilion

Puisseguin-St-Émilion

SABLES-ST-
ÉMILION

Parsac-St-Émilion

St-Émilion

St-Christophe-des-Bardes

GRAVES DE VAYRES

N 670 A

St-Hippolyte

St-Étienne-des-Lisse

St-Laurent-des-Combes

ST ÉMILION

ENTRE-DEUX-MERS

St-Pey-d'Armens

Vignonet

N 136

N 136

Castillon

Battle of Castillon

Castillon

1453

N 136

N 670

Pujols

BORDEAUX

0 1 2 3
Km

with higher ground on more than one side, and this was a frost pocket in 1956, with Cheval-Blanc, Figeac and Ripeau among the most severely devastated, while the Côte vineyards escaped much more lightly.

Until 1955 St-Émilion had a classification of its own making. It sprouted first growths like generals in a military dictatorship, and to soften the descent to the ranks an ingenious system of *deuxièmes-premiers* was devised. All the rest were seconds and there were no *cru paysan* troops at all. This was said to give offence to the highly class-conscious men of '55 enrolled in the Médoc classification and to cause immense confusion abroad, not least in the United States where, it was alleged, a first growth was a first growth all the world over. One may doubt whether most of the Médoc proprietors were so put out or the overseas buyers so confused as was said, but the case sounded convincing. So in 1954 the *Institut National des Appellations d'Origine* moved in and set up an official classification formalized in the following year. This was to be a purely temporary affair for ten years, because it was thought that the 1855 Médoc classification would be amended or superseded by then. However this was not to be, and like other provisional arrangements the St-Émilion classification remains in force, with a slight modification in 1969.

The *I.N.A.O.* was careful to eliminate some of the gold-lace trimmings of the previous self-classification, and set the leading growths into two categories: *Premier Grand Cru* and *Grand Cru*. There are eleven of the first, with Ausone and Cheval accorded a certain priority, and seventy of the second category. This official if provisional classification did not reduce the alleged irritation or confusion, as the now officially ennobled eighty-one growths of St-Émilion had some basis for their status, but even if and when the Médoc classification is altered or superseded, it may well be that the other districts will maintain a local grading. This classification is given in the table below.

Premiers Grands Crus Classés

A. Château Ausone
   Château Cheval-Blanc

B. Château Beauséjour
   Château Bel-Air
   Château Canon
   Clos Fourtet
   Château Figeac
   Château La Gaffelière
   Château Magdelaine
   Château Pavie
   Château Trottevieille

Grands Crus Classés

   Château L'Angelus
   Château L'Arrosée
   Château Baleau
   Château Balestard-la-Tonnelle
   Château Bellevue
   Château Berget
   Château Cadet-Bon
   Château Cadet-Piola
   Château Canon-La-Gaffelière
   Château Cap-de-Mourlin
   Château Chapelle Madeleine
   Château Chauvin
   Château Corbin
   Château Corbin-Michotte
   Château Coutet
   Château Croque-Michotte
   Château Curé Bon
   Château Dassault
   Château Fonplégade
   Château Fonroque
   Château Franc Mayne
   Château Grand-Barrail-Lam-arzelle
   Château Grand-Corbin-Figeac
   Château Grand-Corbin Des-pagne
   Château Grand-Corbin Pec-resse
   Château Grand-Mayne
   Château Grand-Pontet
   Château Grandes Murailles

Grands Crus Classés

Château Guadet-St-Julien
Château Haut-Corbin
Château Haut-Sarpe
Château Jean Faure
Clos des Jacobins
Château La Carte
Château La Clotte
Château La Cluzière
Château La Couspaude
Château La Dominique
Clos La Madeleine
Château Larcis-Ducasse
Château Lamarzelle
Château Laniote
Château Larmande
Château Laroze
Château Lasserre
Château La Tour-du-Pin-Figeac
Château La Tour-Figeac
Château Le Châtelet
Château Le Couvent
Château Le Prieuré
Château Matras
Château Mauvezin
Château Moulin-du-Cadet
Clos de l'Oratoire
Château Pavie-Decesse
Château Pavie-Macquin
Château Pavillon-Cadet
Château Petit-Faurie-de-Souchard
Château Petit-Faurie-de-Soutard
Château Ripeau
Château Sansonnet
Château St-Georges-Côte-Pavie
Clos St-Martin
Château Soutard
Château Terre-Daugay
Château Trimoulet
Château Trois-Moulins
Château Troplong-Mondot
Château Villemaurine
Château Yon-Figeac

The army of St-Émilions also has a kind of temporary 'local-acting-unpaid' rank of *Grand Cru*. This is confusing in a district in which *Grands Crus Classés* proliferate, as it takes a knowledgeable person to recognize the extra significance of the word *Classé*. This *Grand Cru* status is subject entirely to tasting and applies to one particular vintage only of the wine thus awarded; but it may be put on the label for that vintage. No wonder that adjacent Pomerol refuses to have anything to do with a classification!

At one time the top growth of St-Émilion was Ausone, and it is said that if in 1855 the production had not been so small – about 15 *tonneaux* for many years, and given as only 8 *tonneaux* in the 1893 edition of Cocks et Féret – the château would have been included in the classification, as Haut-Brion was. I rather doubt this, because in the middle of the last century the St-Émilion wine district was not highly regarded in Bordeaux. Although, along with the Graves, St-Émilion was the senior *vignoble* of the Gironde, it was, and indeed largely remains today, a district of small proprietors, without the development and the prestigious château-building that went on in the Médoc in the eighteenth and even more in the nineteenth centuries. This is shown by the scarcity of reference in old books on Bordeaux wines to St-Émilion châteaux.

In the first edition (1850) of Cocks et Féret's *Vins de Bordeaux* thirty-seven first growths and twenty-one seconds were listed. In the third (1853) edition of Franck's then standard work, which describes all the districts of Bordeaux in spite of the short title limiting it to the Médoc, no single St-Émilion château is mentioned in the text as being outstanding, as was the author's custom in most other areas. There is however a classification, the basis of which is not declared. It divides the St-Émilions into wines of the *première marque* and *seconde marque* with 42 in the first category and 17 in the second. The first includes Ausone (with an output of 12–15 *tonneaux*), Beauséjour, Bel-Air, Canon, etc., but Cheval-Blanc (25–30 *tonneaux*) and Figeac (40–45 *tonneaux*) are only in the second category, although the latter is marked as *très-bon cru*. None of the Graves-St-Émilion wines is in the first class, although some of the Côtes, including Gaffelière are in the second. Well-known Graves-St-Émilion growths today like La Dominique and Ripeau do not appear at all, and it would appear that the vineyards in this part of St-Émilion had then little reputation.

Moreover Charles Lorbac in his section on the *Crus Classés* of Bordeaux in *Les Richesses gastronomiques de la France* (1867) makes scant reference to the St-Émilion wines in comparison with the space given to the Médocs. He states that the wines were then well known, but the demand was so great and the quantity so small that much of it sold as such was nothing of the sort. Wines labelled St-Émilion *tout court* were more often than not fraudulent. True, Lorbac goes on to repeat the story that when Louis XIV visited Libourne in 1650 he is said to have compared the wine of St-Émilion with the nectar of the gods; however one may fairly attribute the remark to the publicity-conscious Libournais who had sent a special deputation to ask the king to visit the town. Moreover as *Le Roi Soleil* was at that time but twelve years old, his appreciation of wine must have been rudimentary and his opinion worth little. Anyhow thirty-five years later his savage as well as stupid Revocation of the Edict of Nantes which had given toleration to the Protestants in 1598 showed his mature view of at least the Huguenot citizens of Libourne.

Evidently St-Émilion had a share in the Second Empire prosperity, for by the second edition of Cocks et Féret (1868) the number of first growths had increased to 44, many of them with divided ownership (Magdelaine had four different proprietors), and 26 second growths. Surprisingly, in this edition Bel-Air is placed firmly at the head of the list, followed by Troplong-Mondot, Canon, Ausone and Beauséjour in that order. Bel-Air, it is stated, had 'always been placed at the head

of the first growths of St-Émilion', and included among its
earlier owners Ausonius, Robert Knoll, the English Governor
of Guyenne, whose name became frenchified into Canolle,
and the Baron de Marignan, who acquired the château as the
dowry of a Mlle Léontine de Canolle, and was in possession
in 1868. There is no comment on Ausone, but then experienced
readers of this bible of Bordeaux are aware that the footnote
puffs are not altogether objective and were doubtless paid
for. Ausone adjoins Bel-Air, and the alleged Ausonian origin
may have been shared. In any case Bel-Air's production in
1868 was given as 20–28 *tonneaux*, compared with only 10–12
for its neighbour.

By 1868 what are now known as the Graves St-Émilion
were given a separate identity, but only to the extent that they
are listed separately, and described as having a special character,
lying among the wines of St-Émilion and Pomerol. Figeac is
placed top, followed by Cheval-Blanc, and their production
appears to have increased since 1853, as they are given as 50–70
tonneaux apiece.

However the comparative obscurity of the St-Émilion
wines was partly at least caused by the traditional jealousy of
the then dominant Bordeaux trade. Thus it was the Médocains
who stole the show at the 1855 International Exhibition. Mind-
ful of this the St-Émilionnais decided not to be left out in the
cold at the next International Exhibition in Paris, to take place
in 1867. Accounts differ as to whether the Bordelais refused
to include St-Émilions in their display, or whether the St-
Émilionnais decided anyhow to act on their own, but the
result was a collective stand of St-Émilion wines. According to
Cocks et Féret's listing, thirty-seven of the principal growers
combined to show their wines, and collectively they won a
gold medal. This certainly helped to put St-Émilion on more
extensive maps.

What is interesting about this collective exhibit is that the
names of the exhibiting châteaux are known, and they include

Ausone, Beauséjour, Bel-Air, Canon, Clos Fourtet, Ferrand, Les Grandes Murailles, Laroque, La Magdelaine, Troplong-Mondot, Pavie, Les Trois-Moulins and Trottevieille. The vintages they showed are also known. Ausone, then owned by M. Cantenat, displayed its '47, '48 and '62, Canon the '58, '61 and '62, Clos Fourtet '58, '59 and '64, Trottevieille '59, '61 and '64. A château now little known called Sarpe, in the associated commune of St-Christophe-des-Bardes, showed a '34. It will be noted that the range of vintages on display was considerable. The 1859 vintage in the Médoc was not at all good, and the 1861 like its successor a hundred years later was very small, owing to a notorious frost in May.

The other significant point is the absentees. Cheval-Blanc, Figeac and Ripeau, for example, did not collaborate. Cheval-Blanc at least cannot have been averse to exhibitions, as one of the two medals shown on the château's label to this day is a bronze one won at the 1862 International Exhibition in London (successor to the more famous 1851 one). La Dominique also won an award in 1862. Figeac was of course a well-known estate locally, and indeed at one time had extended all over the present Cheval-Blanc vineyard. La Gaffelière was probably there under the name of Puygenestou, for that was the property of the Comte de Malet-Roquefort, whose family now own La Gaffelière and Puy-Blanquet in the lesser St-Émilion village of St-Étienne-de-Lisse. It rather looks as if the joint exhibit at Paris in 1867 was largely a Côtes St-Émilion affair.

At this Exhibition the Médoc châteaux were not overshadowed by the St-Émilions, for the leading growths were represented and showered with gold medals. Among those thus rewarded were Lafite, with its 1848 vintage, Latour also showing 1848, Margaux with 1825 and 1848, Léoville with 1848, and Haut-Brion, Mouton and Larose, with no vintages particularized.

It seems likely that a good deal of the St-Émilion wines at

this period were not well cared for. Lorbac stated that the best wines were made in St-Émilion itself and the adjoining St-Christophe-des-Bardes, St-Hippolyte and St-Laurent-des-Combes, and that between them only 690 *tonneaux* of first quality and 2,100 of second quality were produced. According to Cocks et Féret in 1868, the prices *en primeur* of St-Émilions ranged from 600–1,200 frs. for first growths down to 300–600 frs. for third growths. However, in the fine year of 1865 the first growths opened at 1,500–1,700 frs. and two years later had risen to 2,000 frs. As will be seen by comparison with opening prices of the classed Médocs in Appendix C (on page 658), the St-Émilion leaders fetched less than third growths like Langoa, and were more on the level of the fifths.

Although, no doubt, the status of St-Émilion wines improved after their success at Paris in 1867 – sixty of them went on to win the collective *Grand Prix* at the 1889 Exhibition – their progress was slow. True the 1893 edition of Cocks et Féret lists the prices over recent years as from 1,200–2,400 frs. for the first growths, 800–1,600 frs. for the seconds and 500–1,000 frs. for the thirds, thus showing a relative advance towards the classed Médoc prices for the vintages of the eighties and of 1890 as shown in the Appendix on page 659. But the range is so wide that it looks very much as if the top prices referred only to a few wines, such as Ausone, Bel-Air, Cheval-Blanc and Figeac. For probably a few of the better growths alone had much of an international reputation until after the First World War.

Even then the more esteemed Médocs were so inexpensive in the depression years that the lesser St-Émilions had not much chance of widening their repute. Since the Second World War they have, along with the Pomerols, come into their own; for that extra body and fruitiness combined with their relatively early maturation have proved attractive to many who find young Médocs rather hard and astringent.

Today Cheval-Blanc is certainly the most esteemed St-

Émilion – and one cannot imagine the proprietor now being satisfied with a bronze medal at an international exhibition – but there is no doubt that fifty and more years ago Ausone was the leader. In the early 1950s the late proprietor, M. Dubois-Challon, had been told of some derogatory remarks about the lasting quality of St-Émilion wines. So he organized a small luncheon party at which various old vintages of Ausone were opened, running back to 1869 and even to 1834. Present at this lunch was Ronald Avery of Bristol, who made careful notes on the wines, and later told me that the 1834 was still 'just there'. As recently as 1967 I myself drank a bottle of the not-very-highly regarded vintage of 1880, and the wine was perfectly sound and agreeable, in spite of having been moved several times in its life.

On the other hand, many would agree that for a long time Ausone has not made wine up to first-growth standard. Years ago I remember an excellent '20 and a good '24, but since the last war I have never met an outstanding Ausone. It is true that in recent years a new *cuvier* has been built, with new vats and equipment, including a horizontal cooling apparatus for use during the fermentation. The proportion of Cabernet-Sauvignon has been increased in a vineyard extended from 7 to 8 ha, and will diminish the total exclusivity of 55 per cent Merlot and 45 per cent Bouchet (Cabernet-Franc). Over the years the very small production has been increased and in 1964 the output was as large as 45 *tonneaux*, though only 35 in 1966. It was extremely small in 1975 when perhaps we may look for better results, as the wine was very promising while still in cask. The situation of the vineyard should be ideal, and behind the terrace above it, the fine cellars, excavated from the limestone, are suitably humid, so that the barrels have mould on them. One hopes shortly to find Ausone again at the top.

In these cellars is also kept the wine of the neighbouring Bel-Air, which was acquired by the Dubois-Challon family in 1916. The château itself, a very old building with turrets wedged into the rock, lies along the terrace from Ausone, and the two growths are worked together. The soil here is more chalky and Bel-Air is usually a lighter wine than Ausone but often very agreeable. Output is about 40 *tonneaux* from 13 ha. Its earlier *réclame* has already been mentioned.

On the plateau just above Ausone lies Canon, with a pretty courtyarded château, adjoining an old church and owned by the lively Mme A. Fournier, one of the senior but not least energetic wine-growers of the region. The vineyard area, enclosed somewhat uncommonly in these parts by a wall, is 18½ ha. The *cépage* is 60 per cent Merlot, 30 per cent Bouchet and 10 per cent Cabernet-Sauvignon, with an insufficient quantity of Malbec to be allotted a percentage. By St-Émilion standards, production is on the high side: about 80 *tonneaux*. The fermentation is carried out in unusually small wooden vats, as Mme Fournier believes this leads to more regular fermentation. One of the leading St-Émilions, it is a big, firm, fruity wine. There was an excellent '37 and a fine '59. However unquestionably the finest Canon I have drunk was the '21 which showed that Cheval-Blanc did not have it all its own way in that famous vintage. This was served in September 1965, appropriately enough at lunch in St-Émilion, but in fact had been decanted in Bordeaux at 8.45 a.m. and brought by Édouard Cruse in his car. When drunk at 2 p.m. the wine was remarkably full and sweet-flavoured in spite of a very brown colour, with a firm, almost hard background that no doubt had preserved it. Otherwise Canon is a wine that I have, to my regret, drunk too seldom. New *chais* were built in 1974.

Immediately below Ausone is La Gaffelière, which a few years ago removed the supplementary 'Naudes' from its title. The château was built on the site of an old leper colony and the name comes from the medieval word for a leprosarium. For many years the proprietor was the late Comte de Malet-Roquefort, who combined running a vineyard with owning a pack of hounds; he told me his family was connected with the English Malet family. La Gaffelière is a medium-sized St-Émilion property, producing about 100 *tonneaux* from 23 ha. It has now become rather expensive, like several other classed St-Émilions. The *cépage* is 60 per cent Merlot, 20 per cent Cabernet-Sauvignon and 20 per cent Bouchet.

I remember in particular two vintages of La Gaffelière, '34 and '29, and put them in that order, for it was the excellence of the former over a period of more than fifteen years that led me to taste the latter. The '34 La Gaffelière was in the first case of wine that I bought from Avery's of Bristol in the month that the Second World War broke out. It cost 3s. 4d. a bottle, and the initial bottle was opened in November 1939 – my note reads, 'a fine bouquet and an almost creamy wine'. The following year, having joined the International Exhibition Co-operative Wine Society, I bought a further quantity for no more than 2s. 7d. apiece and continued to buy from both sources, until the last half-dozen from Avery's in 1951 cost 11s. 6d.; in all, counting half-bottles, over 5 dozen. I do not remember a bad bottle, and that in a year so disappointing in the Médoc considering its fame. This '34 was always a splendidly rounded wine.

Accordingly when I visted the château some years after the last war and prior to lunch in St-Émilion the proprietor in his private cellar asked me what wine of his I would like to try, I thought it would be interesting to see what the vineyard could produce in a really notable year. So I asked for a bottle from the bin of the '29s. I then noticed that the bottling dates were on all the bin labels and this was given as August 1934, almost five years after the vintage. Thinking that the wine would be thin I feared the worst until we tasted it an hour or so later; the wine was still wonderfully fruity and showing absolutely no sign of decline. The Count explained that it had been a very big wine and that is why it had been left so long in cask.

In the post-Second World War epoch I bought or otherwise enjoyed most of the well-known vintages: '52, '53 and '55.

And '50 was agreeable too for a moderate year. From the sixties onwards, however, I have met with several disappointing vintages, not least in the seventies. There are not all that number of leading St-Émilions, particularly in the Côtes, so it is to be hoped that my disappointments were misplaced or temporary. La Gaffelière should not be compared with Canon-La-Gaffelière – an acceptable but often dull wine, now German-owned – which has seldom appealed to me.

The other St-Émilion of renown from the Côtes area is Clos Fourtet, situated on the outskirts of the town, opposite the collegiate church. It has the most remarkable limestone cellars of the neighbourhood, extending under the town. This property belonged for many years to the Ginestet family, but Pierre Ginestet sold it after the last war in order to complete the purchase of Château Margaux. It made a famous 1899 and in the 1920s Clos Fourtet made some remarkable wines: '21, '23, '24, '28 and '29. The most remarkable was perhaps the full, rich '24. Yet since the last war the vineyard's reputation has declined and I have not come upon a distinguished bottle since, though the '70 is well spoken of and I found the '75 in cask to have a good deal of style and finesse. As already suggested, St-Émilion could do with a few more wines of impeccable quality. The Clos Fourtet vineyard is 18 ha, with Bouchet predominating. Adjoining Clos Fourtet is Grandes Murailles, named after the ruins of a monastery in its vineyard.

A neighbour of Ausone that has been making particularly good wine in recent years is Magdelaine which belonged to the Chatonnet family for nearly 300 years, but since 1952 has belonged to Jean-Pierre Moueix, who owns several other châteaux, as well as the firm on the quayside at Libourne. Magdelaine and Fonroque of St-Émilion and Trotanoy, Latour-Pomerol and Lafleur-Pétrus in Pomerol are all bottled in the Moueix *chai* on the Quai du Priourat in Libourne, but under the château-bottled label. M. Moueix bought Magdelaine in 1952, and as with all his other properties he has considerably improved production, under the general supervision of his oenologist Jean-Claude Berrouet. The Magdelaine vineyard is 10½ ha, with 75 per cent Merlot and 25 per cent Bouchet, resulting in about 45–50 *tonneaux* a year. There is said to be a good market for it in America, as well as in the Low Countries, perhaps on account of its religious name as already suggested for another St-Émilion, Angélus. The wine is very fruity and round, with more than a touch of Pomerol, although it is a neighbour on the Côtes of Ausone and Bel-Air. The '75 in cask seemed a particularly deep-flavoured wine. The other classed growths in this part of St-Émilion are Pavie, Trottevieille and Beauséjour, which is divided into two. Pavie, owned by M. Valette, is certainly the largest of the top-level St-Émilion vineyards, and extends over a large steep hillside to the south of the town. The cellars are in the very large galleries of an old quarry. Pavie has long been well known in Britain. Production is 120 *tonneaux* and the 42-ha vineyard is made up of 50 per cent Merlot, 30 per cent Bouchet and 20 per cent Cabernet-Sauvignon. Trottevieille also makes very sound wine.

There are so many *grand cru* St-Émilions of the Côtes area that it is difficult to single out those with a particular reputation, or which I know myself. Grand-Pontet, acquired some years ago by the firm of Barton & Guestier, now seems good, and so does La Clotte, oddly named to English ears. The proprietor, the ebullient M. Chailleau, was pleased to show me the cave in the limestone cliff overhanging his vineyard which was excavated by 'you English'. The reference was not to some recent archaeological 'dig' but to the English soldiery in the days of the English rule of Gascony. La Clotte is a pleasant, supple wine, with an average production of 20 *tonneaux* from 5 ha. Troplong-Mondot (partly named after S. E. M. Troplong, President of the French Senate in the 1860s, who owned this once more prominent property), Villemaurine and Tertre-Daugay are all to be found on English

wine lists from time to time. So are that religious trio Grâce-
Dieu, L'Angélus and Le Couvent; and the more secular
sounding Clos des Jacobins, although in fact named after a
religious order. It is owned by the Cordier estate. Just off the
main square is the Couvent des Jacobins, whose deep cellars
include monastic remains. The average production of its
suburban vineyard is 35–40 *tonneaux*. I have enjoyed agreeable wines from all of these and other growths lying deeper
in St-Émilion's long list. There is a Cheval-Noir, no connection with any other stable in the district, but owned by the
Bordeaux firm of Mähler-Besse, and a La Fleur-Pourret
formerly belonging to Ginestet and now owned by his sister,
Mme Prats.

The difference in style of the Graves St-Émilions lies in
situation and soil. The growths lie on a plateau which also
includes Pomerol. This is prosperous, profitable land and the
prospect is entirely vinous, with the lines of vines occupying
every piece of ground not lying fallow prior to replanting.
The soil is much more gravelly and sandy than on the
Côtes.

The outstanding wine is certainly Cheval-Blanc, which
does not mean that it is always the best wine. Over the past
couple of generations it has advanced in reputation probably
more than any other single property in Bordeaux; the much
smaller Pétrus, whose wider reputation is even more recent,
is its only rival in this respect.

Cheval-Blanc's reputation, as M. Fourcaud-Laussac, one of
the two brother proprietors, confirmed to me, really began
with the famous 1921. Not that this was the first outstanding
Cheval-Blanc vintage. The '20 was a splendid wine too, and
when in the mid-1950s I opened together bottles of the '20
and '21, the majority opinion preferred the '20 as a more
complete wine; but I was in a minority at my own table in
preferring the '21 for its extraordinary sweetness and depth
of taste. The merits of various vintages are discussed in the

chapter on Bordeaux vintages, but '21 Cheval-Blanc was as famous as '21 Yquem. That the château was making excellent wine earlier on was confirmed by the 1904 and 1911, mentioned in the vintages chapter.

The secret of the special appeal of Cheval-Blanc lies partly in that it is almost a Pomerol. Only the width of a cart-track separates it from La Conseillante in Pomerol, and on the minor road to Montagne-St-Émilion, the vineyard of Cheval-Blanc is on one side and L'Évangile in Pomerol on the other. The rich, full flavour of Pomerols is embedded in Cheval-Blanc, but the rather greater distinction of the best St-Émilions gives Cheval-Blanc a unique quality.

This individuality, showing a fruity, welcoming aroma and a big rich, almost sweet flavour, makes Cheval-Blanc of a good year, and sometimes an indifferent one also, a very easy claret to drink. A fine Médoc often retains for some years a marked austerity and even astringency, calling for a certain experience to appreciate fully, but the softer St-Émilions in general and above all Cheval-Blanc come out to meet one. Rich but not so experienced wine drinkers, buying by name, often go for wines like Cheval-Blanc '21, '34 and '47, and this inevitably increases demand, in the same way as an international *prima donna* attracts to Covent Garden Opera the not-so-musical as well as the regulars. As an admirer of Cheval-Blanc but not at present prices, I am constrained to misquote a celebrated remark and say, let them drink Burgundy! Cheval-Blanc is at its best a wonderful claret, but it is no more the consistent summit of all clarets than Lafite, Haut-Brion or Pétrus are. Not, it is fair to say, that it is more expensive than these are.

The Médocains would certainly enter a protest at any undue elevation of a non-Médoc wine, and more than one château proprietor would deprecate the integration of St-Émilions in a new classification. Yet it was at Langoa that Ronald Barton opened for me a beautifully rounded bottle of Cheval-Blanc 26. When at Mouton-Rothschild and given a choice of wines,

I asked for the '29 to precede a Mouton 1900, the *maître de chai* paid the wine (and me) the compliment of saying it was one of the best wines in the cellar. Although I would not pick a Cheval-Blanc as the finest claret I have ever drunk, I think I have had greater enjoyment of more vintages of this château than any other; the frequency is partly owing to the fact that it used to be inexpensive by first-growth standards; but this is no longer the case.

The vineyard of 33 ha is, with the neighbouring Figeac and Pavie, one of the three largest in the district. The vineyard consists of 37 per cent Merlot, 43 per cent Bouchet and 20 per cent Pressac (Malbec). In the sixties a little Cabernet-Sauvignon was introduced, possibly owing to its important part in the neighbouring Figeac, but it was not considered a success. When I was there one September loads of soil from the *palus* by the river were being spread on the vineyard as a form of fertilizer or humus. Production averages 120–130 *tonneaux*, but it is variable: 145 *tonneaux* in 1964, not much more than half that quantity in 1966, a record 200 in 1970, but only 70 in 1975 and 120 in 1976.

I was a witness of the devastation that affected this part of St-Émilion and Pomerol in February 1956, for I visited the area the following June; where there should have been an expanse of green leafage the black stumps of the vines stood bare; it looked like a battlefield. No wonder, for there had been 24 degrees C. of frost. Fortunately fewer of the vines were dead than at first thought, and they sprang up again, although at Cheval-Blanc as elsewhere some died throughout the following decade. The immediate result at Cheval-Blanc was that their crop for 1956 was precisely three *barriques*. The following year it was about 120 *barriques*, or 30 *tonneaux*, and reached 100 *tonneaux* only in 1959. It was not until 1961 that Cheval-Blanc recovered something like its pre-frost quality, but with an output of only 40 *tonneaux*. The '61 is certainly a fine wine and will be better, but no other vintage has yet come up to the outstanding post-war run that finished with the '52. But that applies also to other St-Émilions and Pomerols.

For many years visitors to the *chai* at Cheval-Blanc will have noticed how small it was for the size of the vineyard and in comparison with other châteaux producing similar quantities of high-quality wine. The *cuvier*, adjoining the pleasant but modest house, was even smaller, and it was a wonder that the wine could be accommodated for the fourteen-day fermentation in the crowded cluster of vats. One result of this was that the wine was bottled not at the château, but in Libourne in an officially-designated annexe, as with La Mission-Haut-Brion in Bordeaux. However, in 1974 a splendid new *chai* was built, from the flat roof of which can be viewed the wide St-Émilion/ Pomerol plateau. Here the wine is bottled. Incidentally, Cheval-Blanc was the last growth on *premier cru* level to sell part of its output in cask. This ceased in 1969. Modest too is the private cellar of this famous growth ranking with the *premiers crus* of the Médoc. It contains no very old bottles, and I saw only a few of the famous '21, but there were some bottles of the '29 and '34. The fact is that by Médoc standards Cheval-Blanc and the adjoining Pomerols do not enjoy long life. They tend to go brown early (though not the Cheval-Blanc '21) and after twenty years or so may look and taste much older. This applies even more to the Pomerols, whose '45s now show distinctly brown while still tasting well. In my experience the '20 Cheval-Blanc began to 'descend' in the fifties, and the same happened to the '28, one of the outstanding wines of this variable vintage. So the Fourcaud-Laussac family are probably right not to make too much of a museum of their private cellar, but to drink their wines while still at their best. However, M. Fourcaud-Laussac did tell me that the '93 and the '99 had been wonderful wines, lasting well, but he had possessed neither for many years. Acquired in 1853, the estate is now run by M. Jacques Hebrard.

Adjoining the Cheval-Blanc vineyard is that of Figeac,

which in the eighteenth century owned all the estate of its chief rival (which as already indicated it led by a short head a hundred years ago), as well as those other Graves-St-Émilions which have captured the name Figeac with prefixes and suffixes. It is a very old property which in the hands of its present proprietor, M. Thiérry Manoncourt, has made considerable progress since the last war, although severely stricken by the 1956 frosts. The vineyard, very stony and sandy in appearance, is unusual in these parts for its large proportion of Cabernet-Sauvignon, which accounts for about one-third of the *cépage*, and no doubt gives Figeac its special quality. The detailed figures are 35 per cent Cabernet-Sauvignon, 35 per cent Bouchet, 29 per cent Merlot and 1 per cent Pressac. The vineyard area has been expanded from 27 ha in the sixties to 37 ha, but the normal production remains between 125 and 150 *tonneaux*. In 1975 the crop yielded 100 *tonneaux*, in the much more prolific 1976 it was 130. When young the wine often strikes me as having an unusual 'smoky' nose and taste which is perhaps a *goût de terroir*. Yet it seems to disappear with maturity. M. Manoncourt is an 'engaged', albeit modest, vineyard owner, and he and his charming family live in a somewhat English-looking late-eighteenth-century château with flanking buildings overlooking a courtyard led up to by a fine avenue of trees. The château has been burnt down twice. Although Figeac had a considerable reputation in the last century, greater even than Ausone so far as international reputation was concerned, later it suffered some eclipse. Apart from the excellent '28 and '29 I have not come upon the inter-war vintages, but since the fifties it has usually been on my buying list. M. Manoncourt told me that the best post-war vintage for him was '53, but there have been many other interesting vintages, including '55, '61 and, for the vintage, the exceptionally good '64, while '66 and '70 were fine. At the château in October 1977 M. Manoncourt produced two bottles of his '52: one made from Cabernet only, the other from Merlot alone. The former had more aroma, suggesting cedar wood, and had much more character than the Merlot, which was also lacking in nose yet was quite complete – an interesting, unexpected result for a 25-year-old St-Émilion, traditionally Merlot country.

St-Émilions along with Pomerols have achieved a special popularity in the post-war epoch, particularly in Belgium and Holland, and so have tended to be expensive. In the boom of the early seventies Figeac rose to unprecedentedly high prices, from 16,000 frs. for the '70 to 40,000 for the '71, and 42,000 for the '72. However, as throughout the Gironde, prices tumbled in the slump and the '75, a far better wine than the '72, was offered at 18,000 frs. Nevertheless, Figeac is a fine wine, and in some years, such as '55, '62 and '64, it has at least rivalled Cheval-Blanc. Like his neighbour, M. Manoncourt sensibly ploughed back his profits in the boom period; in 1973 a fine new *chai* and *cuvier* with stainless steel vats were built.

In the neighbourhood are a number of smaller properties which have been able to adopt the name Figeac. The proliferation was also caused by division of the properties. For example La Tour-Figeac, split off from Figeac itself in 1879, was subdivided into three, of which the original château retained 16 ha. The other two parts were both called La Tour-du-Pin-Figeac, each with vineyard areas of about 8 ha. One part is owned by M. G. Bélivier, the other by M. Jean Marie Moueix, a cousin of M. Jean-Pierre Moueix, and like him also a wine merchant. The two La Tour-du-Pin-Figeacs make big, fruity wines which can be very agreeable, without having the distinction of Figeac itself. Between them they produce about 100 *tonneaux* compared with 100 from La Tour-Figeac. Yon-Figeac also makes at least 100 *tonneaux*. On the other hand Petit-Figeac, until lately owned by Pierre Ginestet and now owned by the Prats family, produces an average of 3–6 *tonneaux*. All but the last are in the *Grand Cru* class as is Grand

Barrail-Lamarzelle-Figeac, which turns out over 100 *tonneaux*
but which is seldom referred to by its full name. There are also
Franc-Petit-Figeac and La Grave-Figeac, but I have not met
either. La Tour-Figeac is now German-owned.

All these growths are near the Pomerol 'frontier' road.
Another which also adjoins Cheval-Blanc is La Dominique,
whose '55 has much of the character of its neighbour. Although
not as widely known as it might be it is a growth with a good
reputation, and its wines of the vintages of the first half of the
seventies showed well at a tasting in Bordeaux in 1977. The
vineyard is of 17 ha, producing 50 *tonneaux* from a *cépage* that
is 50 per cent Bouchet and 50 per cent Merlot. Until 1970 the
proprietor was the cheerful M. de Bailliencourt, also the
owner of Gazin in Pomerol; but in that year he sold it to
M. C. Foyat. The modest house at La Dominique still showed
the scars of the last war when I visited it nearly a quarter of a
century after the Germans had left it, the only house in the
district which had been fought over. Next along this Montagne road is Ripeau, a fair-sized property but the few bottles
I have drunk of it have not impressed me particularly. The
road here leaves Pomerol entirely, and on the left side is now
Croque-Michotte, a typically full St-Émilion whose '47 I
remember with particular pleasure.

I should here state that for me to pretend to have an inti-
mate knowledge of even all the better known 70 St-Émilion
Grands Crus and their unclassified peers in Pomerol would be
misleading. Few outside the local *courtiers* have, let alone even
the Bordeaux merchants. For the latter tend to follow certain
growths and perhaps have contractual relations with them.
It is virtually impossible to know all the St-Émilions and
Pomerols all of the time, and the best one can do is to follow
some of them some of the time.

There is, for example, a cluster of Corbins in this part of
St-Émilion: Grand Corbin, Corbin Despagne, even a Corbin-
Michotte, etc. The land is claimed to have belonged to the

Black Prince. I have come upon several of these Corbins from time to time, and they have never seemed more than middling wines, but I may have missed some winners. One such excellent wine that came my way not long after the last war was Chauvin '29, which was listed by Nicolas, the famous Paris chain wine-stores. Since then I have once or twice chanced on Chauvin at some tasting of young wines, and have always paid it special attention in recollection of its '29, but I have never found one that stood out in any way. The property adjoins Ripeau.

The list of Graves-St-Émilions is much shorter than that of the Côtes, and the 'other ranks' of the old *Deuxièmes Crus* are even fewer.

The third section of St-Émilion which is part of the commune proper and not associated with one of the seven adjoining villages entitled to that *appellation* pure and simple, is the small area of Sables-St-Émilion. This is near the Dordogne on the flat riverside plain, and it begins just outside Libourne on the road to Castillon and Bergerac. There are very few vineyard properties and more than one of these is threatened by the expanding factory zone of Libourne. The best known is certainly Martinet, which has a charming late-eighteenth-century château, resembling an English country house. It is owned by the family associated with the old Libourne wine merchant firm of H. Beylot, and the wine is light and agreeable.

Near here is the very agreeable Ch. Videlot, not a wine château but the eighteenth-century home of Jean-Pierre Moueix, set in a park extending down to the Dordogne, and looking very English in this ensemble. It is notable for its fine collection of modern paintings, including more than a dozen Dufys, two Picassos, a Derain, etc. There is also a splendid array of modern French illustrated *éditions de luxe*. As a change from vineyard visiting an invitation to Videlot makes a welcome diversion and the cellar is not exactly lacking.

The seven associated St-Émilion villages which lie on the

east and south of St-Émilion, extending down to the right bank of the Dordogne, once came under the jurisdiction of St-Émilion. Collectively they make a good deal of wine, but little of it has a wide reputation. The districts, with the names of one or two better known properties in brackets are St-Christophe-des-Bardes (Haut-Sarpe), St-Laurent-des-Combes (Larcis-Ducasse), St-Hippolyte (de Ferrand, Lassègue), St-Étienne-de-Lisse (Puy-Blanquet owned by the Comte de Malet-Roquefort of La Gaffelière), St-Pey-d'Armens, St-Sulpice-de-Faleyrens (Monbousquet, Castelot) and Vignonet. The first two of these villages used to include a number of properties of *soi-disant* first growths. Among these Larcis-Ducasse, very near Pavie, has made some very attractive wine in the seventies. The proprietor is Mme Gratiot-Alphandery, and her 10-hectare vineyard produces 40–50 *tonneaux* from a *cépage* one-third each of Merlot, Bouchet and Cabernet-Sauvignon.

In addition, to the north-east of the St-Émilion plateau and on higher, more undulating ground are five communes entitled to add St-Émilion to their names. These are St-Georges, Montagne (Plaisance), Lussac (Lyonnat), Puisseguin and Parsac. To ease the multiplicity of *appellations* these might well follow the Burgundian custom and call themselves St-Émilion-Villages. Nearly all have co-operative societies, and there are some very large estates as well. Outside the central area of St-Émilion the vine is less ubiquitous and the country becomes more interesting, more rural. The 'montagne' to the north-east of the plateau is not a very considerable one, but it affords a pleasant view of the heart of St-Émilion, with the fine monolithic church spire on the horizon, and Pomerol's church spire prominent on the plateau, as it is everywhere in the neighbourhood. Montagne itself has a church with a fine Romanesque apse, and for those who like a little sight-seeing as a change from wine tasting, on the outskirts of the district there is Château Monbadon, an historic monument standing rather gloomily on a hill with a fine slope below it. Broadly speaking as the road rises out of the plateau the reputation of the vineyards descends, but the wine though less distinguished may still be agreeable. Some of the smaller, lesser-known St-Émilion properties can often produce most agreeable claret. An example that comes to mind is the '61 Domaine de la Chapelle, a modest St-Étienne-de-Lisse bottled by Berry Bros. in England. In 1977 it was more enjoyable than many of its social superiors.

The co-operatives are important in the large St-Émilion district, and the leading one, the *Union des producteurs de St-Émilion,* is on the Côtes not far from the town itself. Founded in 1932, it has 400 members cultivating 1,200 ha with an average output of about 50,000 hl. The name under which most of the wine is sold is Côtes Rocheuses, and another is Royal Saint Émilion, but it is unusual in including among its members twenty owning vineyards with château names entitled to be labelled *Grand Cru,* subject to tasting. Though all *Grand Cru* St-Émilions must be bottled at the château, this is allowed to take place in the co-operative cellars. Of course the wines are all kept separate. The leading one of these is Berliquet, commanding a rather higher price than all the others, which are sold at the same level. Among the others are Haute-Nauve, Lamartre, Destieux, Grangey, Paran-Justice and de Lisse.

One should mention St-Émilion's *Jurade.* As elsewhere this was the assembly of town councillors, but it is now a publicity and propaganda organization to spread the fame of the wines of St-Émilion. It meets several times a year, and enrols candidates who pledge themselves to quaff St-Émilions. It has, however, rather more of an unbroken link with the past than its rivals in the Médoc and Sauternes.

Before leaving the region of St-Émilion a visit is worth while to the site of the Battle of Castillon which effectively put an end to English power in Gascony. This is outside the wine area of St-Émilion, and lies beyond the small town of Castillon. On the hillside above the town, which is on the Dordogne, stand reminders of medieval warfare in the shape of fifteenth-century towers. The busy main road to Bergerac and a railway line run across the battlefield, which is surrounded by a semi-circle of wooded hillsides, partly covered also by vines. The flat valley is described on a notice board as a *Zone Industrielle* and there is one token factory and a few bungalows to disturb a landscape that only the road builders and railway makers have altered since the Middle Ages. On the river side of the road the land falls away in tree-lined meadows to the fast-flowing stream.

The battlefield on which old Talbot led his army against the French is marked by a monument, sited perilously near the road on which the *camions* thunder past. The monument was erected only eighty years ago by a 'union of patriots' with an evident surge of chauvinist emotion. It reads:

> Dans Cette Plaine
> Le 17 Juillet 1453
> Fut Remportée la Victoire
> qui délivra
> du joug de l'Angleterre
> Les Provinces Méridionales
> de la France
> et termina
> La Guerre de Cent Ans

As described earlier on, the Bordelais were by no means overjoyed at being liberated by their semi-compatriots, and for a period after Castillon preferred the English yoke to the French embrace. But at least we English should have a special regard for the wines of St-Émilion.

13. Pomerol

The finer wines of Pomerol are the most immediately attractive red wines of Bordeaux; even more than those of the neighbouring St-Émilion. They are soft, lacking much of the tannin that marks the Médocs and the Graves when immature and they may be drunk fairly young, a consideration these days when the accent is on quick turnover. Consequently it is no surprise that the Pomerols have won many adherents in the last twenty-five years; and with demand prices have risen sharply too.

Sometimes one finds Pomerols described as being half-way between St-Émilions and Médocs, with the softness and roundness of the former and the intensity and some of the distinction of the latter. I cannot see this. The really typical Pomerols to me have the intensity of aroma and flavour all right, but to resemble St-Émilions only more so. If the aroma of Médocs often recalls blackcurrants, the Pomerols for me evoke brown sugar.

A fine Pomerol has a wonderful concentration of perfume – and I use the word advisedly here – and flavour which marks it out from other clarets. The wine has a rich, but not an enriched, taste that is seductive. If I cannot follow the late P. Morton Shand – that pioneer writer on wine to whom all serious wine drinkers have been grateful for over fifty years – in detecting in Pomerols 'a rich truffle scent, which leaves just a whiff of hidden moss and violets in its wake', this must be because these similes seldom reflect what I seem to smell and taste in wine. In a blind tasting of clarets, Pomerols should be the easiest to pick out although I confess that I have confused them with Pauillacs and vice versa.

Such comments refer to the more successful wines. There are Pomerols which lack this concentration of aroma and flavour, and are merely full-bodied and St-Émilion-like in style. These I find dull and prefer a sound St-Émilion. If all Pomerols are open to some criticism, it is that they tend to lack 'centre'. Whereas a fine Médoc has an inner core which keeps the flavour 'true' to the end, a Pomerol is 'all over one' immediately, and its flavour may slightly 'depart' or soften out at the finish. However this is high-level criticism, and I am particularly fond of fine Pomerols. Owing to their richness they are sometimes rather difficult to accommodate on an occasion when red wines from the other Bordeaux districts are being served. A Pomerol will often 'blanket' a Médoc, as I remember when I served to a Médoc proprietor a splendid La Croix-de-Gay '47, followed by the then outstanding Léo-ville-Poyferré '29. The finely balanced though fruity '29 had to struggle to surmount the rich concentration of the '47. It succeeded but afterwards my guest remarked, 'Never serve a Pomerol before a Médoc.' This is perhaps an exaggeration, and that distinguished *amateur* of Pomerols, Édouard Cruse, to whom I recounted this remark, strongly disagreed. 'The great thing', he rejoined, 'is to give a vintage of the Médoc corresponding in reputation to that of the Pomerol, and always a considerably older Médoc. The finesse of the Médoc will usually show up better even after a powerful Pomerol.'

Yet serving a Médoc after a rich Pomerol can come close to drinking claret after burgundy; but although there is much less variety in the Pomerols than the Médocs, it is always interesting to show a range of vintages from the same growth.

By Bordeaux standards Pomerol is a 'new' district, for up to much less than a century ago the wines were sold as St-Émilions, in the same way as other outlying villages of that area. If then the wines of St-Émilion were not highly considered, those of Pomerol attracted even less individual attention. Being powerful and fruity they were often used for

424 *The Wines of Bordeaux*

blending with lighter wines. In 1853 Franck dismisses Pomerol in a five-line paragraph, and mentions one growth only: Château de Curtan (*sic*). He says they last well, are inexpensive, and that the wine on the low-lying part is inferior to that on the high ground; true enough today. Moreover the production total he gives of 600–700 *tonneaux* is less than a quarter of to-day's average of 3,000 *tonneaux* made by 135 growers. Even in the 1868 Cocks et Féret the list of seventeen principal proprietors is headed *crus bourgeois et 1ers artisans*. First is Vieux-Ch.-Certan, followed by Trotanoy and Pétrus. Although Pétrus won a gold medal at the 1878 Paris Exhibition, in the 1893 edition of Cocks et Féret Pomerol was included as part of the St-Émilionnais. In this edition 31 first-growth Pomerols were listed and 25 seconds.

Nevertheless Pétrus's gold medal must have helped it to sell its average output of only 16 *tonneaux*. For it apparently sold the 1879 – generally a moderate year only – for 2,800 frs. per *tonneau* and the 1891 for 1,600 frs., equal to the price of the Médoc second growths.

Much later, in George Saintsbury's *Notes on a Cellar Book* (1920), the St-Émilions are dismissed because he did not care for them; the Pomerols are not even mentioned. Even Alexis Lichine in his valuable *Wines of France*, first published in 1952 but revised later, gives hardly any space to Pomerol, although some amends are made in his *Encyclopaedia of Wines and Spirits* (1967). The commune of Pomerol only secured separate delimitation in 1923.

One reason for this earlier neglect is the small size of the properties on the roughly 700-hectare plateau which includes all but the outlying sub-districts of Lalande-de-Pomerol and Néac. For the most part individual production is small, less than 50 *tonneaux*, and the châteaux are little more than farmhouses or villas. Nénin, with an output of 100 *tonneaux*, is the largest of the better known growths, and Pétrus, the most celebrated, until its enlargement in 1970 averaged only 30,

POMEROL

Dordogne

l'Isle

LIBOURNE

N 10 bis

Barbanne

LALANDE-DE-POMEROL

Lalande-de-Pomerol

POMEROL

Pomerol

Néac

NÉAC

N 89

0   1   2   3
Km.

including the *vin de presse*, which is usually not included at the *assemblage*. Accordingly these small estates have with one or two exceptions not the quantity or the resources to make much individual mark among wine drinkers. This has not, however, inhibited their proprietors from disposing of their relatively modest crops at good prices. The *appellation contrôlée* output is limited to 40 hl per hectare.

The small *récolte* of Pomerol must always be remembered, and is a factor in the prices. Even a plain *A C* Pomerol will usually command a much higher price than an *A C* St-Émilion, which is usually marginally dearer than an *A C* Médoc *tout court*. In the record crop of 1973 Pomerol only produced 41,720 hl (compared with just on 39,000 for Lalande-de-Pomerol). This was smaller than the Médoc communes of Pauillac and St-Estèphe, and not much larger than Margaux and St-Julien. In that year the St-Émilion harvest produced 306,087 hl, plus over 180,000 hl from the associated villages. In the prolific year of 1976 Pomerol production totalled 33,445 hl as against 21,110 in 1975; and in 1977 the crop was but a third of normal. In 1978 it was 27,216 hl.

I have already observed that St-Émilions of the plateau do not normally last as long as Médocs, and this certainly applies to Pomerols, which after fifteen years or so generally acquire the tawny colour of age. With one or two exceptions, among them Pétrus, the '45 Pomerols are now fully stretched, whereas this is not true of most of the Médocs; and such Pomerols of the twenties as I have drunk have seemed older than their Médocain coevals. However this is little cause for complaint, and I do not quite agree with the *maître de chai* of Pétrus, who told me that his wines were at their best at ten years old; but then the French like to drink vigorous, *corsé* wines.

The soil in Pomerol is similar to that of Graves-St-Émilion on the same plateau, but in one part there is some iron in the ground. Yet there are small but sharp changes in the composition of vineyards close to one another. The clay in the gravel accounts for the rather special character of Pétrus, including its fuller, heavier style compared with the neighbouring Vieux-Château-Certan. On the edge of the plateau the soil is sandier, and the wines are lighter.

The make-up of the vineyards is similar to that of St-Émilion, with perhaps an even greater emphasis on the Merlot, which gives soft wines. A number of the growths have even a majority of Merlot, although a general indication is one-third apiece of Merlot, Bouchet and Malbec.

Of the famous major Bordeaux red wine areas Pomerol is the only one now unclassified, and, as in pre-officially classified St-Émilion, first growths abound as well as second-firsts in front of a small rank of seconds. However an unofficial classification has some support and if and when the *I.N.A.O.* decides to produce an authoritative one, this is unlikely to differ very much from the present list except that it might be longer. This places Pétrus on a similarly slightly elevated level, like Ausone and Cheval-Blanc in St-Émilion. Nine or ten other growths follow, including Vieux-Château-Certan, Certan, La Conseillante, Petit-Village, L'Évangile, Trotanoy, Gazin, La Fleur-Pétrus and one or two others according to personal choice. One reason why an official Pomerol classification may be unlikely is that there are so many growths of similar quality in this compact area. Their local 'guild' calls itself the *Hospitaliers de Pomerol*.

Nearly everyone would agree that Pétrus is the best Pomerol, and none can deny that it is the most famous. Combined with the quality and appeal of the wine itself, this is very largely owing to the efforts of the late Mme Loubat, a woman of great personality who never made the mistake of underestimating the value of her product. She affirmed that her wine was equal to the first growths of the Médoc, and accordingly should sell for the same price. Personality and perseverance, aided by a limited supply of an excellent wine, won through, and today Pétrus sells at about the same price as the top first growths. From the eighteenth century to the First World War, Pétrus was owned by the Arnaud family, who then turned it into a company. About 1925 M. Loubat bought part of this estate, but after his death Mme Loubat gradually acquired the rest, finally achieving this about 1945. After Mme Loubat's death in November 1961 the estate was owned by her niece, Mme Lily Lacoste, and M. Jean-Pierre Moueix. Its rise in reputation is much more recent than Cheval-Blanc's, and although the 1893 was listed at a fair but not first-growth price on the International Exhibition Co-operative Wine Society lists in the later 1890s, it was hardly seen in Britain, and the wine was not offered generally before the last war by two firms in England who had first featured it in the post-war years: Avery's and Harvey's of Bristol. True it had a special French reputation and in an unofficial classification in the 1920s Pétrus was listed as *premier des grands crus*, followed by Vieux-Château-Certan and Certan as *grands premiers crus*. The 1906 was listed in the 1933 edition of the famous special illustrated lists of Nicolas of Paris, who only included notable wines therein. I have twice drunk Pétrus '20, but the bottles had come from Switzerland. One bottle was good, the other *passé*. No Pétrus is mentioned in André Simon's *Vintagewise* (1945), which describes the wines he and later the Saintsbury Club had drunk over many years.

The rise in the popularity of Pétrus and of Cheval-Blanc in the early post-war years may be demonstrated by their opening prices per *tonneau* in comparison with those of the established *premiers crus*. As such prices vary, the exactness of the figures may be questioned but the trend is clear. Moreover it should be noted that first-growth prices include keeping charges while the wine is in cask, but this did not apply to Cheval-Blanc and Pétrus, and this added 15–20 per cent to their prices.

1945 *Vintage*		1949 *Vintage*	
All *premiers crus*	200,000–240,000 frs.	All *premiers crus*	c. 250,000 frs.
Cheval-Blanc	100,000 frs.	Cheval-Blanc	175,000 frs.
Pétrus	80,000 frs.	Pétrus	225,000 frs.

1947 *Vintage*		1953 *Vintage*	
All *premiers crus*	c. 200,000 frs.	All *premiers crus*	c. 300,000 frs.
Cheval-Blanc	130,000 frs.	Cheval-Blanc	200,000 frs.
Pétrus	100,000 frs.	Pétrus	275,000 frs.

Cheval-Blanc '53 was not considered as successful as in some vintages, and this may account for the comparatively low price. Today Pétrus sells for the same price as the most expensive *premiers crus*, as can be seen from the opening prices in Appendix D. (Unfortunately the opening prices prior to the 1961 vintage have not been preserved by the estate.) At the London auctions Pétrus consistently fetches higher prices than the other *premiers crus*. In 1978 at Christie's the '47 reached £820 for six bottles, three of the '49 went for £250 and even the '70 rose to £340 a case. The following year the very fine '61, exceptionally small in quantity and seldom seen in the saleroom, brought £500 for only three bottles. Americans have been the most voracious buyers of Pétrus, – and, it is to be hoped, drinkers rather than speculators – partly no doubt for its quality and partly perhaps because of its relatively small production. Such excessively high prices are to be regretted, for not only do they put such wines and all the other first growths out of the even occasional reach of other than very affluent *amateurs*, but they discourage the opening of bottles fetching such extravagant figures. It is difficult to believe that in 1956 I paid £7 10s. for a dozen of Pétrus '52, bottled by Harvey's of Bristol, but I did and it remained excellent for twenty years.

Pétrus is indeed a modest estate, with no very grand château, and one comes on the building quite suddenly amid the network of small roads that cross the plateau. Until the acquisition in 1969 of 5 ha from Gazin, the *vignoble* was only 6½ ha –

much about the size of Ausone – and consisted of 70 per cent
Merlot and 30 per cent Bouchet. However, the wine from the
Gazin vineyard was added very sparingly to the Pétrus *grand
vin* for a long time: the crop from about half a hectare was
used first in 1970. (The average age of the Pétrus vines is over
forty years; some are over eighty years old.) Since then the
proportion of Merlot has been increased even more and by
1977 had reached 95 per cent, with only 5 per cent Bouchet;
quite different from the neighbouring Vieux-Ch.-Certan, as
will be seen below. As already stated its output was about 30
tonneaux, but it suffered as severely as Cheval-Blanc in the
1956 frosts. No wine was produced at all that year. In succeeding years the output was as follows:

Year	Tonneaux	Year	Tonneaux	Year	Tonneaux
1957	8	1964	37	1971	30
1958	24	1965	none	1972	32
1959	18	1966	27	1973	47
1960	31	1967	28	1974	40
1961	17½	1968	7	1975	32
1962	30	1969	21	1976	38
1963	none	1970	45	1977	12
				1978	38

The exceptionally small crop in 1961 was the result of spring
frosts, while the unusually large one in 1970 partly reflected
the contribution from Gazin.

These figures were based on the number of *barriques* filled,
but evaporation and the resultant topping up will reduce the
final quantity of this and other Bordeaux by 10 per cent or
more, which strikes hard on a small growth. The best post-
war vintage of Pétrus was probably '47, although the fine '61
has yet to show its full paces. There are those who find Pétrus
almost too full and rich, too heavy and concentrated and prefer
a rather lighter Pomerol such as Vieux-Château-Certan, where
the flavour is more subtle. I understand the criticism, but do

find Pétrus a splendid wine in a good year. I have drunk the '47 against Cheval-Blanc '47, and found that the latter had more character though not so much concentration. On this occasion I was in a minority in preferring the St-Émilion. The '49 has been very fine too. Until the 1956 frosts Pétrus was sold in cask as well as in bottle, and wines like the '50 (an excellent wine in this variable, lesser year), '52 and '53 could be bought in Britain for 15s. or so a bottle, English-bottled. Now the whole crop is château-bottled, usually about two to two and a half years after the vintage. The name is of course taken from St Peter, who figures on the excessively old-fashioned label; a proprietor of M. Moueix's taste should not have any difficulty in matching Baron Philippe de Rothschild at Mouton. M. Moueix markets the whole production and also a quarter of Cheval-Blanc. The great majority goes to the U.S.A.

Vieux-Château-Certan which lies very near Pétrus is generally accorded now the unofficial first rank given it many years ago. Until 1858 it belonged to the May family and was then bought by M. Charles de Bousquet. In 1893 the average output was only 15 *tonneaux*. The vineyard area is nearly twice that of Pétrus and about equal in production. The 13 ha average 70 *tonneaux*, made up of 50 per cent Merlot, 25 per cent Bouchet, 20 per cent Cabernet-Sauvignon and 5 per cent Pressac – an interesting variation from its close neighbour, as well as from Cheval-Blanc and Figeac, though its make-up is nearer that of the last-named. It is a remarkably full, velvety wine and like its neighbour the château's reputation in Britain has greatly increased in the last twenty years; although this wine has always been sought after in Belgium, possibly because the owners, the brothers Thienpont, are Belgian wine merchants. In recent years the whole crop has been château-bottled. I myself have only drunk post-war vintages with the exception of a bottle of '28, powerful, deep-coloured but with a curious burnt taste, which I drank in Bordeaux in 1967. However the '47 was an exceptionally fine wine, and the '55 was one of the most successful wines in a vintage often disappointing to me considering its early *réclame*. In that year Vieux-Château-Certan may well have surpassed Pétrus. The '61 sampled at source in 1970 was splendidly rich, and this impression was amply confirmed later. The '64 was among the most agreeable wines of that variable vintage, and in my view superior to the Pétrus, which at any rate in the mid-seventies was rather disappointing. The '70 promised well, and so did the '75 while still in cask, but there have been some rather disappointing vintages here too for its class and in comparison with earlier performance. Like Figeac its prices rose to extraordinary heights in the early-seventies boom. From an opening price of 18,000 frs. for the '70 the '71 opened at 48,000 frs. This may be compared with 33,000 frs. for the '75, 26,000 frs. for the more plentiful '76 and 38,000 frs. for the '78. As at Figeac M. Thienpont wisely spent part of his boom proceeds in having a new *cuvier* and *chai* built in 1973.

I have two recollections of visits there. During the vintage I was surprised to see a baboon tethered just out of reach of the vines, which the animal was making strenuous, noisy efforts to reach; and a number of ponies similarly staked. M. Thienpont explained that the pickers were gypsies who came every year, bringing with them their livestock. He then led me to taste the previous year's wine. At first he seemed uncertain into which cask to insert his *pipette*. This was partly because the *égalisage* had not taken place, so his Merlot was in one cask and Bouchet in another; but also because he wanted me to taste from a good cask. For never, said he, taste from a cask near the cellar door, as the wind gets at it; always taste from a cask in the middle of the cellar. An inside tip.

Just across the road is Ch. Certan, once part of the same estate as its neighbour, and more recently known as Certan-de-May. (There is also a Certan-Giraud and Certan-Marzelle, both less renowned.) This growth is only about a quarter the size of Vieux-Château-Certan in output, but at times it has made some admirable wine, of which the '47 was an outstanding example and the '49 no less so. Since then it seems to have lost a little ground, although the '50 and '53 were both very agreeable; yet I have not come upon a particularly fine post-frost vintage.

There are a number of other claimants to leading rank in Pomerol. Possibly because they are small and perhaps owe their position to one man – or woman – their reputations seem to vary. For example L'Évangile was a Pomerol with a considerable reputation in the 1920s, and its vineyard signs immediately opposite Cheval-Blanc bear the inscription 'L'Évangile Haut-Pomerol', although it would be difficult to say how the situation was any higher than its neighbours. I remember a '24, from Avery's, which though a little tenuous aged twenty years and more was still a wine of distinction. I may have been unlucky but I did not come upon another vintage for many years. Then I drank the '59 several times, and very good it was, although not in the top flight. The proprietor is M. Louis Ducasse and his vineyard covers 14 ha, with two-thirds Merlot and one-third Bouchet. The production averages 60 *tonneaux*. This wine like its peers in Pomerol secured very high prices in the seventies boom, and a new cellar was added in 1973. The '75 in cask seemed a splendidly deep, concentrated wine, of which only 30 *tonneaux* were made in the short vintage.

Another in the same class is its neighbour La Conseillante, which also adjoins Cheval-Blanc. Before the last war this château was one of the best known of all Pomerols, and still today has a good reputation; but once again I have not found it outstanding in recent years, although the '49 was very fine, and the '53 agreeable. Yet it has been surpassed by others which would have been little known a generation earlier. Its 12 ha produce 40–45 *tonneaux* from a *cépage* of about 70 per cent Merlot and 30 per cent Bouchet. The wine has always been expensive, and like most Pomerols became excessively so in the boom, rising from 16,000 frs. for the '70 to 40,000 for the '71. One reason for the unusual if short-lived success of the Pomerols and some St-Émilions was extensive American buying. Both La Conseillante and L'Évangile are popular in Belgium.

Yet another estate is La Pointe, one of the larger Pomerol growths and prominent to the left of the road from Libourne. As Pomerols went a hundred years ago it was fairly well known and its 1865 was sold at 1,500 frs. the *tonneau*, on a level with fifth-growth Médocs. One of the most enjoyable '34s from any Bordeaux district was La Pointe, and, bottled by Avery, it was still good when over thirty years old; a wine of great concentration of flavour. Even in that *annus mirabilis* for Pomerols, 1947, La Pointe stood out. Since then I have drunk acceptable but generally rather unexciting wines from this property (one of the largest estates in Pomerol), which produces about 100 *tonneaux* from 20 ha. The grapes employed are 60 per cent Merlot and 40 per cent Bouchet. Among more recent vintages that I have enjoyed are '64 and '71.

Many other châteaux are making excellent wine, and often they are growths that used to be little known. One is La Croix-de-Gay, situated in the main street of the village of Pomerol, and directed from a modest enough villa. My attention was drawn to it by a superb '47 bottled by Harvey's, and one of the finest Pomerols of that year; although now beginning to show age it still is a delicious wine, and my only regret is that I have never had the chance to drink the château-bottled wine to discover if it were even better. I then acquired the '45, also bottled by Harvey's, a beautifully mature claret with a brown tint that makes one at first think it must be a wine of the 1920s. The '43 was very good too, and, coming forward, so was the delicious '49, in this case bottled by the Wine Society. The '52, with that toughness but fullness of flavour that marked the best Pomerols of that year, was also a good wine. I believe the château was less successful for a few years, but in 1973 it was bought by M. J. Janoueix of La Croix (Pomerol). La Croix-de-Gay has always been liked in Belgium.

Another up-and-coming Pomerol has been Clos René, a further Harveian find for me, with the '53 at 9s. a bottle: a soft, but deliciously rounded wine. The '52 was bigger and firmer, and the '61, bottled by Christopher's of London had all the flavour one could expect from a Pomerol. I have particularized the English bottlings here, because until the seventies one is unlikely to find many château-bottlings of these smaller, less famous Pomerols. Making the wine is their concern, and they would rather sell it in cask. So one quite often comes upon Bordeaux bottlings, not least by Cruse who made a speciality of interesting Pomerols. With reference to Clos René '61 a comparison between a Bordeaux bottling and one by Christopher's gave the palm unquestionably to the latter. Maybe the wine in France had been left too long in cask, a not infrequent occurrence when lesser growths are concerned. Clos René, situated in the village of Pomerol, with a garden round the house, is a typically unselfconscious Pomerol vineyard. The wine, in which there is a large proportion of Merlot and some Malbec, is powerful and well flavoured. Production is now around 60 *tonneaux* and Clos René is no longer the inexpensive wine that it used to be.

Nearby is a third property in the same excellent class, L'Enclos, which produces 40–50 *tonneaux* from a *vignoble* which is 70 per cent Merlot, 20 per cent Bouchet and 10 per cent Cabernet-Sauvignon and Malbec. This may be regarded as a common Pomerol vineyard make-up. The cellar in which one tastes the wine is below the house itself. The oldest L'Enclos I have drunk was a '29, opened in the company of Cruse's London agents, Rutherford, Osborne & Perkin, in the mid-sixties. Certainly it was showing its age, and the colour was very brown, but the wine was delicious. Much younger, the '45 was another exceptional vintage of this area, while the '53 remained a rival of the Clos René.

There are other Pomerols with no very wide reputation which I have met perhaps only in one or two vintages, and they have then passed me by. One of these has the unwieldy name of La Grave-Trigant-de-Boisset (the three latter words were a former owner's name), whose '55 was another Harvey find in the days when that great claret lover Harry Waugh was their claret scout and buyer. With more acidity than many '55s, it was that much more successful and agreeable, but I have not met it since. The property now belongs to M. Jean-Pierre Moueix's son, M. Christian Moueix, and as with all Moueix properties much trouble has been taken to replant and improve it; the '76 in cask was attractively fruity. The 7-hectare vineyard is 80 per cent Merlot and 20 per cent Bouchet. This produces about 35 *tonneaux*. Another '55 in the same class was Lacabanne, just near the Pomerol church with its prominent spire. This is quite a fair-sized property making 40 *tonneaux*; the '35 was excellent but I have not seen it again. Pomerol is indeed an area worth exploring, but one can easily lose the way there amid the jig-saw pattern of small vineyards.

Although Pomerol is a smaller area than St-Émilion, with less than 700 ha under vines, there appears to be a larger number of fairly well-known vineyards. Of these Gazin is one and Nénin another. These are among the largest Pomerol vineyards and their wine probably the most exported. Each produces between 80 and 100 *tonneaux*. Gazin was particularly badly stricken in the 1956 frosts. In spite of its wide reputation I have usually found Gazin a rather clumsy, sometimes coarse wine, although the '45 has been exceptionally fine. As noted above, Gazin has sold 5 ha (out of 28) of its best part to Pétrus. Nénin, which is opposite La Pointe, has always seemed to me rather dull, although the proprietor, M. Despujol, is an engaging enthusiast for his wine. In the sixties he built new cellars and is constantly concerned for the improvement of his vineyard. While being a sound wine, Nénin lacks the appealing concentration of flavour so attractive in the best Pomerols.

There is also a Lafleur-du-Gazin which makes very amiable wine; a small growth, producing 25–30 *tonneaux* from 6 ha of 60 per cent Merlot and 40 per cent Bouchet. The proprietor is M. Borderie, but in 1976 M. Moueix rented part of it. It takes its name partly from Lafleur, which is near Pétrus and is owned by the Mlles Robin. Although this small property, producing only 12–15 *tonneaux*, has always enjoyed a good name, apart from a fine '61 – which the Lafleur-du-Gazin also had – I have never found it outstanding; the same applies to the 14-hectare Le Gay.

The swapping of names is no less prevalent in Pomerol than in St-Émilion, and there are a number of combinations adopting names calculated to bring prestige to less well-known growths. It would be impossible to do this today, as charges of 'passing-off' would soon be made, but these names have the acceptance of tradition. Indeed it is not rare to find that a growth can use several names, and might do so for a second wine. A well-known double name is Lafleur-Pétrus, now owned by Jean-Pierre Moueix. For some reason it has a flag on its label, giving it a shipping-line appearance. It is only 9 ha, two-thirds Merlot and one-third Bouchet, producing 30–40 *tonneaux*. I may have been unlucky but I have never found it a very exciting wine, though it was among the better '64 Pomerols that I acquired, and the '75 in cask promised a good deal of style. It has always been fairly well-known in Britain. In general I much prefer Trotanoy, also owned by M. Moueix or his firm. This property is on the western slope of the Pomerol plateau, and the small but charming château used to belong to a M. Giraud, when the area under vines was much larger than today: a mere 8 ha now; the average age of the vines – 80 per cent Merlot, 15 per cent Bouchet and 5 per cent Pressac – in the late seventies was thirty-five years. The crop is never larger than 35 *tonneaux*. Its curious name is apparently derived from the mixture of gravel and deep clay that in a dry summer can become so hard and compact that it is *trop ennuyeux* – too hard to work. Prior to a sale at Christie's in January 1978 I was invited to a tasting in London by its London agents, Corney & Barrow, with a range of ten vintages from '74 back to '61. The other tasters were Michael Broadbent of Christie's and Harry Waugh. We all agreed that the '61 was outstanding, with plenty more to give, and the next best was the '66, big and backward, as was the '70. For early drinking the '62, '67 and '71 were excellent examples of their year in the district. In the two previous autumns I had been able to taste in the Moueix offices in Libourne the '75 and then the '76 in cask. The former was a very fine, very concentrated wine, the latter much lighter, but with a good deal of style; and this may well turn out the verdict for 1976 Pomerols, which were certainly less good than the '75s.

Another fine property is Petit-Village, which belonged to M. Pierre Ginestet before it was passed over to his sister Mme Prats and her son, the owner of Cos d'Estournel. The vineyard, which was wiped out in the 1956 frosts, produces about 45 *tonneaux*, and the wine is always highly priced, which is perhaps why over the years it has not been much seen in Britain. It made a particularly distinguished '47, and then I hardly saw it until the very deep, typical '75 was shown in London. For these parts, it has an unusually large Cabernet-Sauvignon proportion of 55 per cent, with 35 per cent Merlot and 10 per cent Bouchet. The reason why in general one does not find a great deal of Cabernet-Sauvignon in Pomerol and St-Émilion is that it does not ripen well there. In the Médoc, of course, it also ripens after the Merlot and Cabernet-Franc.

A Pomerol growth that has confused not a few drinkers is Latour-à-Pomerol. It has not always been made clear on wine lists that this is a Pomerol, and on occasion it has at least been ordered if not drunk as the more famous Pauillac *premier cru*. It was owned by the famous Mme Loubat of Pétrus, and is now in the hands of her niece Mme Lacoste; on the few occasions that I have drunk it, the wine has seemed fruity and full but lacking a little in character compared with some of the others. The 9-hectare vineyard is made up of 70 per cent Merlot and 30 per cent Bouchet, and the output is about 30 *tonneaux*. The vineyard is run by the ubiquitous J.-P. Moueix, who also owns (through his firm) Lagrange, a small 8-hectare estate right in the centre of the commune, producing 30 *tonneaux* from a vineyard of which 75 per cent is Merlot and 25 per cent Bouchet. I have never found it outstanding, though the '75 in cask was fruity enough. Sometimes it is mistaken for its namesake in the Médoc. Another Pomerol not in the first class but one of the very largest producers (40 ha) is de Sales. Until the mid-seventies I had never been much impressed when occasionally I encountered it, but then I tasted the '73 and the '75. The former was not a great Pomerol year, nor indeed great anywhere in the Gironde, but the de Sales was unexpectedly fruity even though the natural sugar was assisted. Then I was much taken with the '75 in cask. It had a big colour, a rich nose and plenty of body. However, it shows the uneven path that clarets often traverse. For more than a year later I tasted it in England, shortly after it had been château-bottled and shipped: certainly the colour was there, but the nose was very tough and the wine was as hard as nails, lacking all the generosity of the earlier occasion. The '75s are hard and backward, but that does not mean that they will not develop well.

Indeed there are so many Pomerol wines that have edged into my drinking and then not been encountered again that it is impossible to generalize about them. Among those which I remember are: Plince, a well-known name but not one that has impressed me; Rouget which has produced one or two very agreeable wines; Domaine de l'Église, a medium-to-good quality wine; Clinet, a wine with a traditional name but not remarkable in my experience; Bourgneuf, a medium wine that can show well in good years, but is not exceptional; La Commanderie, run-of-the-mill; Moulinet, respectable but not exciting. I offer these comments for what they are worth, and would not claim too much for them. There may be other surprisingly good wines among the ranks of *soi-disants premiers crus*, *deuxièmes premiers crus* and *deuxièmes crus* which march across the Pomerol plateau. In the 1949 edition of Cocks et Féret was listed L'Enclos-du-Presbytère. Its production was given as a mere 3 *tonneaux* and its owner 'le curé de Pomerol'. Alas, with other such small properties, it is not in the 1969 edition, but it is to be hoped that his vineyard is still a substantial assistance with his pastoral problems. How many of his parishioners emerge from the Pomerol presbytery with the comfortable delusion that 'presbyter is but priest writ large'?

One straight main road (*RN.10-bis*, Bordeaux–Paris) runs through Pomerol from Libourne in a north-easterly direction and crosses the small stream named the Barbanne, which flows from the east to join the Isle just before the latter enters the Dordogne on the west side of Libourne. Nearly all the better growths of Pomerol are on the east side of the road, with one or two exceptions such as Clos René and L'Enclos. The vineyards shade off into the commune of Libourne. Beyond the Barbanne lie the two associated sub-districts of Pomerol: Néac on the right and Lalande-de-Pomerol on the left. On the eastern side of Néac is Montagne-St-Émilion, but if one enters this small area by the road from Montagne one notices a difference at once. The anonymity of the vineyards gives way to name-plates, and by a hamlet a notice board announces *Néac – Ses Grands Vins*. The country is more broken up and the miniature valley of the Barbanne *en passant* looks agreeably rural and remote, affording some relief from the monotony of vineyards. The village of Néac is by the stream, and then one ascends a slight hill on to the Pomerol plateau, with Pétrus and other well-known names at hand.

The Néac wines are not very well known, although entitled to their own *appellation* until 1954 when they were merged with Lalande. Total output of the two is about 30,000 hl. I suspect many of them dodge under the net and are sold as Pomerols. There are Tournefeuille (one of the best), Belles-Graves, Moncets, Siaurac and Moulin-à-Vent, all producing 40 *tonneaux* or more a year, but I claim little experience of them. Siaurac, formerly owned by a deputy of the Gironde, is now the property of the Baronne Guichard and yields 100 *tonneaux* from 30 ha. The wine is sound.

Some of the Lalande wines are better known, and among my early purchases before the last war was a delicious Bel-Air '29 – not to be confused with the growth in St-Émilion. This growth, which in the 1868 Cocks et Féret headed the small Lalande list, still has a good reputation and is near the main road dividing Lalande from Pomerol proper. The district was once the property of the Templars, and the village of Lalande has a twelfth-century church, with a *clocher* over the round-arched west door. There is a sharp change in the aspect of the country and the vineyards as soon as one crosses the main road from the highly cultivated, disciplined-looking commune of Pomerol. Although Lalande-de-Pomerol also proclaims *Ses Grands Vins*, this is mixed farming country, as in Néac, and the vines are less dominant and concentrated, less well cared-for in appearance. No doubt this reflects not only the smaller reputation of the wines but the prices they can command. In style the wines of these two lesser communes are rather coarser and with less finesse than the Pomerols. Not far away to the west, beyond *RN.10-bis*, from Libourne to Coutras, lies Fronsac whose 'mountain' overlooking the Dordogne is clearly visible from Lalande; and perhaps the wines slightly resemble each other. In addition to Bel-Air the better-known châteaux selling under the Lalande *appellation* include La Commanderie, La Croix-de-Chenevelle and Perron. Considering how near Libourne is, this little strip of country is very quiet. A railway line runs through it, and to return to the town one had to summon the keeper of an apparently not too greatly used level-crossing to raise the gates for the car.

The wines of the commune of Libourne are not of great significance and are entitled only to the *appellations* Bordeaux or Bordeaux Supérieur. They are either wines of the *palus* by the river or *sables*.

The reader will have gathered that I have a particular affection for the wines of Pomerol, without in any way wavering in my ultimate allegiance to those of the Médoc and the red Graves. It is common for serious wine drinkers in France to maintain contact with small growers in the various wine areas, and these latter furnish them with regular supplies of their wine. If I lived in France I do not doubt that one of my *petits fournisseurs* would be in Pomerol; and to keep him up to the mark regular visits would be necessary.

14. Fronsac, Bourg and Blaye

Large quantities of wine are made in the lesser districts on the right bank of the Dordogne and Gironde. They amount so far as the local *appellations* are concerned to about 15 per cent of the total Bordeaux *AC* output which averages 3 million hl. Then there are the Bordeaux and Bordeaux Supérieur *appellations* which are not confined to this area, and which altogether account for well over a half of Bordeaux's output. The best of these lesser right-bank wines are red; the Fronsadais have the highest reputation and fetch the best price, while the white Blayais are probably the least good.

As is normal the best wines come from the Côtes. In Fronsac the two *appellations* of Canon-Fronsac (formerly Côtes de Canon-Fronsac) and Côtes de Fronsac (there is no Fronsac *AC* now) carry equal weight, but the Canon wines are usually judged the better. Côtes de Bourg, Bourgeais and Bourg are also parallel *ACs*, but Premières Côtes de Blaye is slightly superior in red wine and rather more so in white. Côtes de Blaye is a white *AC* only.

The Fronsac wines are big and fruity, but by no means coarse, and in style like the lesser St-Émilions; the Canon wines in particular can be very agreeable, though without the finer points of the better St-Émilions. The country is picturesque and the Tertre de Fronsac rises to a high point overlooking the Dordogne and across to the Entre-Deux-Mers. But the vines do not climb as high as the top of this hill. The district begins a mile or so to the west of Libourne, across the little river Isle, which here joins the Dordogne, its last tributary of any size. Down by the river are level *palus* vineyards, which produce only Bordeaux or Bordeaux Supérieur wines, but higher up the growths are entitled to one or other of the two Fronsac *appellations*.

The whole area of Fronsac consists of between 15 and 20 villages spreading inland from the river across a plateau. On the west it approaches the two long bridges that carry the Bordeaux–Paris railway and *RN.10*, the Paris road. One of these bridges was built by Gustave Eiffel. The best known of the villages apart from Fronsac itself on the eastern fringe are St-Michel-de-Fronsac, La Rivière and St-Germain-la-Rivière. The last-named of these is entitled only to Bordeaux and Bordeaux Supérieur *appellations*, but one or two of the other villages, such as St-Aignan and Saillans, which are indeed on the Côtes, are allowed the Côtes de Fronsac *appellation*. Part of St-Michel is entitled to the Canon-Fronsac *appellation*. The large output of 50 hl per hectare is permitted under the basic Bordeaux *appellation*, but this is cut to 40 for the Supérieur, which is 2 hl less than allowed the two Fronsac titles. For these and the Bordeaux Supérieur *appellation* a minimum strength of 10·5 degrees is prescribed, but Bordeaux may be as low as 10 degrees, which is light for a red wine. White wine is only made in the minor Fronsadais areas, and this is only allowed the two Bordeaux *appellations*, with output of 50 hl and 10·5 degrees and 40 hl and 11·5 degrees respectively. Canon-Fronsac produces about 13,000 hl, and Côtes de Fronsac 30,000.

The best-known château is probably Canon in the Côtes Canon-Fronsac area. It must not be confused with the well-known St-Émilion growth, nor indeed with several other adjacent châteaux in Fronsac which have adopted the name. There is even another Canon in St-Michel-de-Fronsac, with a pleasant view over the river. Such a prospect is shared by several of the other attractively placed Côtes châteaux, including Junayme whose conspicuously prosperous nineteenth-century house is enclosed in very fine magnolia trees. The soil is rich hereabouts and the wine correspondingly powerful. Another well-known growth is Bodet, which has given rise to several little Bodets, not forgetting Vrai-Canon-Bodet-La-Tour. Also in Fronsac itself are Gaby, Domaine de Toumalin, La Dauphine, not unknown in Britain, and La Croix. Down by the river is the extremely prolific Château La France, whose name no doubt helps it to dispose of an enormous crop of about 500 *tonneaux*.

Names of Fronsac growths are not of great importance to wine drinkers outside France, but most British wine merchants will have a Fronsac or two early on their claret lists. The first Fronsacs I remember bore the imposing name of Larchevêque, and before the last war I bought the 1934 vintage from Berry Bros. at the even then very moderate price of 3s. a bottle. It was a well-balanced, not too strong wine and the late Charles Walter Berry told me that the celebrated and fashionable doctor, Lord Dawson of Penn, physician to George V, was so impressed with a trial dozen, that he ordered first another 20 dozen, and then called in at the famous St James's Street premises to secure yet another 20 dozen. He liked a reliable bottle of claret a day. It had been sold to Berry's by M. René Danglade, and when I visited the latter in the summer of 1939, with an introduction from Charles Walter Berry, I was asked if I would like to be shown the source of this wine. It turned out to be a very modest seat for an archbishop.

I must mention M. Danglade's own property, Ch. Rouet, situated high up in St-Germain-la-Rivière. From the terrace of the eighteenth-century château is probably the finest view anywhere in the region, looking across the Entre-Deux-Mers. In a fit of pique the German detachment which occupied the château in 1940 departed from their general policy of being *toujours correct* towards the Bordelais, and burnt the place down. After the war it took M. Roger Danglade, a wine merchant like his father, many years to restore this charming house. Rouet is a large estate and produces over 100 *tonneaux* of red wine.

To sum up, Fronsac wines can be excellent and they are

often under-appreciated, partly perhaps because of careless vinification in the past; also, because like their neighbours in Bourg and Blaye they are often drunk too young. The best Fronsadais are certainly worth keeping for up to ten years.

North of Fronsac lie the two small communes of Coutras and Guîtres, both in the Isle valley, with the former lying upstream beyond Lussac and the lesser St-Émilion villages. In the Middle Ages Guîtres was quite a well-known vineyard area, largely owing to its river communications, and to being near the Roman road from Bordeaux to Périgueux. It is amusing to note that the Guîtres wines suffered from the same disabilities *vis-à-vis* St-Émilion as did the Haut-Pays production in Bordeaux: they could not be transported by water or road to St-Émilion, including Libourne, until St Martin's Day (11 November).

These wines are not of great importance today; production limitations are those of their Bordeaux and Bordeaux Supérieur *appellations*, and white wine is made in the twenty-four villages which comprise the two communes. This area is one of those to have suffered a decline in vineyard area over the last twenty years. After the 1956 frosts many growers accepted compensation to pull up their vines.

Also worth mentioning here is a half-circle of lesser wine villages, entitled to the two basic Bordeaux *appellations*, which begins in Libourne, runs round the outside of the Pomerol and St-Émilion communes and south of Coutras, and joins the Dordogne at Castillon. There are twenty-two of these communes, all small villages with the exception of Libourne at one end and Castillon at the other. Probably the best known of them, on historic rather than viticultural grounds, is Monbadon, whose château I have already mentioned. Here is produced 120 *tonneaux* of red wine, much more commonly grown in this area than white. No doubt in earlier times the wines from all these outlying parts were sold as St-Émilions.

In and around Castillon there are now two small *appellations* authorized by the *I.N.A.O.* In Castillon itself and eight other nearby communes, the red wines may be labelled Côtes de Castillon after the *appellation* Bordeaux. To the north of Castillon the red and white wines of Francs, Monbadon and three other communes may be labelled Bordeaux Supérieur Côtes de Francs; and the white wines of Monbadon commune are entitled to the same labelling. One village, Les-Salles-de-Castillon, is divided between these two *sub-appellations*, which, although superior to the two basic *ACs*, are not significant enough to have their *récoltes* output listed separately; they are included in the Bordeaux and Bordeaux Supérieur totals. The soil in this undulating country is largely lime or clay, with alluvial deposits from the Dordogne. The chief red grape is the Merlot, the most popular white the Sémillon.

Rather more significant is the Cubzaguais, which runs to the west of Guîtres and across the north of Fronsac, and the chief town is St-André-de-Cubzac, well known to motorists on the Paris–Bordeaux road. Its wines carry the two basic Bordeaux *appellations*, and large quantities of white wine are made as well as red. The red wines are inclined to be rather 'plummy', but of course they can have that touch of quality which Bordeaux gives. There are nine communes, and the soil is chiefly lime and clay.

In the area there are two well-known properties. The first, Château du Bouilh, is an historic monument better known for its vast though incomplete range of buildings than for the wine. Designed by the famous Bordeaux architect, Victor Louis, for the family of La Tour du Pin, if completed this would surely have been his masterpiece, and on a scale almost comparable with that of Versailles. Only one side of an enormous 'quad' was completed, and a building now known as *Le Grand Pavillon*, but even that was not finished. What is charming is a *Hémicycle* of two-storey buildings, with a chapel preceded by columns and pediment in the centre of the half-circle. Other 'works' of this huge architectural concep-

FRONSAC WITH COUTRAS AND GUÎTRES (1)

0 2 4 6 8 10
Km

CÔTES DE FRONSAC

CÔTES CANON-FRONSAC

Guîtres

Coutras

L'Isle

N 10 bis

St-Germaine-la-Rivière

N 89

La Rivière

Saillans

St Aignan

St-Michel-de-Fronsac

Fronsac

POMEROL

NÉAC

LIBOURNE

LALANDE-DE-POMEROL

St-Émilion

ST-ÉMILION

Dordogne

Castillon

BORDEAUX

tion may be seen. The whole was planned to welcome Louis XVI on a progress that he intended to make in the region. Before this could take place, the Revolution arrived and the building operations were stopped. It is well worth a visit.

The wine is kept in the limestone caves which abound in this area. No less than 300 *tonneaux* of red wine, and 75 of white and *rosé* are made here, and the cellars and ex-quarries are full of casks. Much of the wine here, as throughout the right-bank wine districts, is disposed of direct to private customers throughout France. A proportion is sold in small casks for home-bottling.

The other property is Terrefort in Cubzac-les-Ponts, which is owned and well publicized locally by Marcel Quancard, a substantial firm of wine merchants at La Grave-d'Ambarès. Terrefort produces 100 *tonneaux* of red wine and 50 of white, and the wine is well made. The estate used to belong to the Monbadon family. Two well-known names occur in the Cubzaguais. At St-André there is a Ch. Beychevelle and in St-Gervais a Cru Cantemerle. (In Blaye there is a Ch. Cantemerle too.) These produce substantial quantities of wine, but have, of course, no connection with the Médoc properties, although I have seen them offered in Britain; if wine drinkers see these names at surprisingly low prices they had better look at the *appellation* on the label. The wines are by no means bad. I have sampled all of them, but they are not on the *cru classé* level. The vineyard area in the Cubzaguais has declined in recent years.

Bourg wines have a wider reputation than those of Cubzac, and the best reds can be very attractive. They are usually more vigorous and with more character than the neighbouring Blayais; the red are certainly better than the white. Franck, writing more than a hundred years ago, says that the Bourg wines were preferred to the Médocs, by which he meant the general run of wines in the latter district, and not the *crus classés*. This was because the Bourgeais wines were fruity and

BOURG AND BLAYE
WITH CUBZAGUAIS (2)

0 2 4 6 8 10
Km.

CHARENTE MARITIME

N 137

N 10

CÔTES DE BLAYE

GIRONDE

Île de Patiras

Îles de la Gironde

HAUT-MÉDOC

Blaye

N 137

CÔTES DE BOURG

Bourg

Bec d'Ambès

Dordogne

Garonne

Ambès

CUBZADAIS

St-André-de-Cubzac

Cubzac-les-Ponts

BORDEAUX

had plenty of body; and Franck goes on to say that the Bordeaux trade would only use Bourg wines to mix with the *petits vins* of the Médoc. As evidence of the 'bigness' of the Bourgeais, Franck states that unless they had undergone 'the fatigue of the sea' (i.e. suffered a sea voyage), they had to be kept for eight to ten years before drinking; and they did not begin to decline before they were 25 to 30 years old. Both Bourg and Blaye were, of course, wine-growing areas long before the Médoc was developed. This does not mean, however, that when the great estates came into being on the left bank, their wines were thought less of than those across the Gironde.

This is very agreeable, rolling country, providing a contrast with the flat Médoc on the other side of the Gironde. From the terrace of Bourg, near the confluence of the two rivers at Bec d'Ambès and on a level with Margaux, there is a fine prospect of the Dordogne, the Gironde and the Médoc. Inland the country is not so bold and the hills and valleys not so steep as in the Entre-Deux-Mers, but they are very attractive, with farms and *chais* attractively set on the hillsides. The 'frontier' between Bourg and Blaye is only a small rivulet, the Brouillan, on its way to the estuary; physically all the countryside near the Gironde is similar, but the Blaye wines are lighter and generally less good. It will be noted that while Bourg wines are allowed 50 hl of red and white wine, the Blaye vary from 50 to 42. In both the *encépagement* is common in this part of the country, with equal proportions of Merlot, Malbec and Cabernet-Franc. The white is Sémillon, Sauvignon and some Colombard. The soil varies from alluvial deposits near the waterside, to clay and lime on the hills. The land generally is rich by Bordeaux vineyard standards and viticulture is not the only form of agriculture practised in these parts. Bourg used to have a reputation for its potatoes, and today the landscape has a varied appearance, with crops of cereals, vegetables and fruit. Until about a hundred years ago both Blaye and Bourg were not unimportant ports, particularly the former, which shipped up to 15,000 *tonneaux* a year, partly to Rouen and the north of France and partly upstream to Bordeaux. But as Bordeaux's influence grew and road communications improved, the two ports of the estuary lost their carrying trade, and Blaye's nautical life today is centred round the ferry across to Lamarque in the Médoc. Blaye was a much fought-over town in the Anglo-French Wars, and even later; the massive fortifications of Vauban still overhang the river front.

The *appellations* of these two districts are somewhat complicated. In Bourg there are three *appellations* of equal standing: Bourg, Côtes de Bourg and Bourgeais. An excess quantity of red wine above the permitted maximum may be de-classed and called Bordeaux, but not the white. About 125,000 hl of red wine and 10,000 of white are produced. In Blaye also there are three *appellations*: Premières Côtes de Blaye, Cotes de Blaye and Blaye or Blayais. For all intents and purposes the first of these is restricted to red wine, and produces about 90,000 hl. On the other hand, Côtes de Blaye is exclusively white, with an average output of only 10,000 hl. Blaye and Blayais are almost exclusively white, and make an average of 45,000 hl. White Côtes de Blaye may be sold as de-classed Bordeaux, but not Blaye/Blayais. Following government offers in 1953 of premiums to growers who pulled up their over-productive hybrid vines, these two areas' production has fallen, especially in white wine.

Many of the Bourg estates have an old tradition of sound wine. Like the Fronsadais most Bourg wines are drunk too young, although in good years they still have a reputation of lasting twenty-five years or more. Both Bourg and Blaye have a hierarchy of estates without official backing, but this is an indication of relative quality. It runs: *premier cru bourgeois, cru bourgeois, premier cru artisan, cru artisan, en palus*. There is also a *premier cru de Bourg*. In the first rank in Bourg there is du Bousquet, belonging to the de Barry family for well over a century. It produces 150 *tonneaux*. An even larger production comes from another well-known growth, de Barbe, which makes 220 *tonneaux*, mostly red. The composition of that part of the vineyard is 50 per cent Cabernet-Franc, 40 per cent Merlot and 10 per cent Malbec, which can be seen to differ considerably from the norm. This is a typical 'country growth', with a big old-fashioned *chai* on one side of a court-yard reached through an archway. Inside the *chai* are rows of cement tanks. I have found the red wine fruity and 'substantial' and better than the slightly sweet though acceptable white. Among the other better-known estates are Croûte-Charlus, Tayac, Eyquem (does the name confuse anyone?), La Croix-Millorit, Blissa, Rousset, Thau (a romantic-looking fortified castle on a hill), Mendoce and La Tour-Séguy and Mille-Secousses, whose 'shaking' wine was served on the old Great Western Railway to the delight of Maurice Healy. The list is arbitrary and nearly every Bordeaux merchant would produce a different one. Indeed this is unknown country to most of them, and when I have visited Bourg, Blaye and Fronsac growths in their company, they have usually brought with them a broker to act as pilot to estates which lie, outwardly unnamed, up narrow roads and down winding lanes.

The co-operatives play a considerable part in these areas. There are at least five in Bourg and four in Blaye. The one I visited at Tauriac in Blaye is typical. Situated opposite the derelict Château du Pia, another work attributed to Victor Louis, its large concrete bulk has the factory air common to wine co-ops. This one turns out about 16,000 hl of white wine and 12,000 of red, and the variations in quality largely rest on alcoholic strength. There are 180 members, and I found nothing to complain about in the wine, much of which is sold to the Bordeaux merchants for blending.

So far as Blaye is concerned, my own experience of vine-yard visiting is even more limited. There is a Barbé, distinguished from the Bourg growth by the elimination of a 'de' and the addition of an acute accent on the final 'e'. I remember a surprisingly good '58 when the wine was about seven years old. I have visited the pleasantly situated and attractively built Lescadre, where M. Paul Carreau makes 150 *tonneaux* of a wine big and fruity for a Blaye. Other well-considered growths include the curiously-named Sociando, Virou, Petits-Arnauds and Monconseil. Off the main track there is Menaudat, associated with the Cruse family and whose wine one may see on an English list. The better-known estates of Bourg and Blaye find regular customers in Belgium and Holland. In the more outlying communes of Blaye white wine increasingly predominates. North and east they almost reach the departmental border, and beyond that is the Charente-Maritime, where the grapes one sees will be made into brandy, though not of the finer quality which comes from much further north.

My comments on these right-bank wines have been scattered like the properties themselves. This is charming country in which to wander, and the village restaurants will not fail to provide a satisfying midday meal and a local wine list wherever one happens to find oneself between midday and 2 p.m. With the left-bank red wines now so dear, there is a case for taking a leaf out of the book of the growing thousands of French wine drinkers who enjoy the wines they order regularly from Fronsac, Cubcaz, Bourg and Blaye. In our case it is not wise to order direct but to rely on our wine merchants, who already usually list one or two and may turn more to them. Not distinguished wines, they are however the essential red Bordeaux which for centuries have helped to build the reputation of claret. Just because they are cheap they should not be quaffed young, but kept until they are fully mature. However, they must not be expected to match their rivals across the estuary, although with the prices of the *crus classés* and even the *crus bourgeois* now so high, increasingly we may find on merchants' lists more and more wines with hitherto little-known names but coming from these areas.

Now that every district has its own dressing-up publicity organization, it is not surprising that Blaye, Bourg and the Premières Côtes de Bordeaux are united in the *Connétablie de Guyenne*, which assembles in the fine château at Cadillac in the Premières Côtes. Even the Bordeaux and Bordeaux Supérieurs have their *Compagnons de Bordeaux*.

15. Sweet White Wines

The Sauternes district lies about 25 miles south-east of Bordeaux, and is generally reached by the *RN.113*, which leads on to Toulouse and to the Central Pyrenees. Just short of it lies Cérons and opposite, on the right bank of the Garonne, are the two small districts of Loupiac and Ste-Croix-du-Mont. To reach them from the left bank, the river must be crossed either from near Cérons to Cadillac, or beyond the Sauternes area at Langon. This left-bank area is a very old one and there is the mention of a vineyard in Preignac in the eighth century A.D. The soil is poor, composed of chalk and stony gravel with a sub-soil containing clay. In Barsac the soil is less gravelly, contains more clay and has a chalky sub-soil. The clay is more prominent on the low hillsides of the district. The Cérons district is more gravelly and flinty, with sub-soil of clay and stones. Across the river on the hillsides the vineyards of Loupiac and Ste-Croix-du-Mont are a mixture of stones, clay and chalk, but rather more gravelly on the top of the slopes.

These lesser districts are allowed to produce with *appellation* more wine than the five Sauternes communes: 40 hl per hectare compared with 25. While the latter must have a minimum alcoholic strength of 13 degrees, and so must the two right-bank districts, Cérons need only be 12·5 degrees. Throughout, only the sweet wines are entitled to these *appellations*; the dry varieties are Bordeaux Supérieur.

The main grapes throughout are the Sémillon, which accounts for from two-thirds to four-fifths of production, and the Sauvignon, which represents the remainder, except for a certain amount of Muscadelle, as detailed below in referring to the individual vineyards. There is even a little Ugni-Blanc.

The fine sweet white wines of Bordeaux are currently the most under-appreciated and under-valued table wines in the world. This is not because people do not like them, for I have never known anyone refuse a glass of a fine Sauternes or Barsac at the end of a meal; and the engagingly luscious liquor often elicits more appreciative comment than the red wines that have preceded it. The drop in demand is part of the decline in popularity of all dessert wines, unless we include therein the so-called 'cream' sherries. Also nowadays a bottle of sweet white Bordeaux does not seem so integral a part of a meal as a bottle of dry white wine from Bordeaux or elsewhere earlier on. However, genuine Sauternes cannot be among the very cheap white wines, for the method of production is expensive, and at the lower end of the market no doubt many people have fallen for Spanish 'Sauternes', a wine which bears no resemblance to the original except that it is sweet. Finally many of the Sauternes producers have not done their wine much good in the last forty years by the way they have made it.

Taking this last point first, unfortunately it became the custom on the Bordeaux market in the inter-war years to buy these sweet white wines by alcoholic strength; the higher the strength the better the price. This still obtains. The minimum strength of a Sauternes entitled to the *appellation* is 13 degrees, but by the use of additional sugar the wine may be forced up to 15, 16 or even 17 degrees. The result is a heavy, unbalanced wine, and the public taste is rightly not in favour of such wines. Further, a good deal of the Sauternes so-labelled was for years nothing of the kind.

This 'blending', as it is perhaps fairer to call it rather than falsification, has been the result of an alleged refusal of the consumer and the wine merchant to pay for the real thing. So most of the basic 'Sauternes' one sees in off-licences or on wine merchants' lists is a blended wine, with probably a good proportion of sweet Premières Côtes de Bordeaux 'cut in'. Since we had to accept the *A C* regulations on entering the EEC this situation should have improved.

However, in the last few years it is possible that the Sauternais did see the error of their ways and the desirability of eliminating the errors of others. In 1967 a scheme was adopted according to which there should be a minimum price per *tonneau* for *A C* Sauternes (it was fixed initially at 2,500 frs.) in return for which the growers promised to make better wine, to be subject to the tasting approval of independent committees. Further, *en principe*, all Sauternes should be bottled at source. This, however, was seen to be impracticable in the immediate future, so a number of approved Bordeaux merchants were allowed to buy and even to re-sell in cask.

These measures were greeted with some disfavour and scepticism by the Bordeaux merchants. They claimed that there was no improvement in standards of wine making in the next year or so, and that the tasting committees were too apt to pass inferior wines. On the other hand the growers alleged that few merchants were paying the legal minimum. In fact it did not work effectively.

Meanwhile Sauternes suffered a series of very poor vintages, particularly from 1963 to 1965, and produced no really first-class crops in the sixties, although '61 and '62 were good, and '67 and '69 at least acceptable. So the plight of the Sauternes growers was a sad one, and in a number of cases even classed-growth properties were turning over to produce red wine, most of which bore only the *appellation* Bordeaux Supérieur. Not only was this saleable, but had an output double that permissible or obtainable for the sweet white wine: for, whereas the basic Sauternes *appellation* limits production to 25 hl (often not achieved), Bordeaux Supérieur allows 40 hl, although the price is low.

However a turn for the better occurred in 1972, when prices for red Bordeaux of all classes were advancing rapidly; those in the Sauternes district more than doubled. Whereas a growth as distinguished as Climens had only been able to obtain 5,000 frs. a *tonneau* for its young wine, the price now rose to 15,000 frs. This was partly assisted by much more successful vintages, particularly by 1970 and 1971. It is to be hoped that higher prices will be matched by better quality; otherwise the Sauternes growers will have thrown away their prospects of long-term recovery, menaced by the slump from 1973 to 1975.

The decline in the standard of Sauternes did not, of course, affect all the leading classed growths, but most suffered from the side-effects.

Five communes alone are entitled to the *appellation* Sauternes: Sauternes, Barsac, Bommes, Preignac and Fargues. In addition Barsac may call itself Sauternes-Barsac, but usually leaves out the first name. Descriptions such as Haut Sauternes or Haut Barsac have no official standing.

The particular quality for which Sauternes is esteemed, its aromatic richness, is caused by the *pourriture noble*, or noble rot, which attacks the ripe grapes if weather conditions are suitable from September onwards; but only if the weather is right. Rather warm, slightly humid atmosphere is necessary. If the weather is wet, particularly if this is followed by finer, humid weather, *pourriture grise* sets in, a form of decay caused by excessive damp against which farmers all over the world have to contend. The skins are easily broken, which is not the case with *pourriture noble*, which is the same as the German *edelfäule*, responsible for the luscious *beerenauslesen* and *trockenbeerenauslesen* wines. When attacked by *botrytis cinerea* the grapes at first have a slightly rosy hue, then they begin to shrivel up; and indeed look decidedly rotten. However, when one tastes a grape, there is no disagreeable flavour of rot, but instead the juice is sweet beneath the unpunctured withered skin. Under good conditions the *pourriture noble* may set in during the second half of September.

SAUTERNES AND BARSAC

BORDEAUX

LOUPIAC

Cérons

Loupiac

STE-CROIX-
DU-MONT

Barsac

BARSAC

Preignac

Ste-Croix-du-Mont

Le Ciron

N 113

Garonne

GRAVES

Langon

SAUTERNES

Bommes

Fargues

Sauternes

G R A V E S

0   1000   2000
m

The vintage tends to take place later than elsewhere in the Gironde, in order to ensure the greatest amount of *surmaturité* in the grapes. The picking normally begins about the end of September and may go on as long as six or seven weeks; but if frost occurs, which is rare, the remainder of the crop is picked at once. There is no *Eiswein* in Sauternes! The great estates alone can afford to maintain this slow tempo of picking the grapes only when they are nearly all shrivelled up; a St Martin's Summer is looked for but does not always arrive. At Yquem the vintage may take the better part of three months, with the vintagers going through the vineyards nine or ten times; elsewhere five or six times is usually the maximum. The small growers may wait until as much of the crop as possible is ripe and affected by *pourriture noble* and then pick quickly.

When was the importance of this noble rottenness first discovered in Sauternes? Almost certainly it was known much earlier in Germany. It is said to have originated at Schloss Johannisberg owing to the delayed arrival of a messenger from the Prince-Bishop of Fulda giving permission to start the vintage. In the intervening fortnight the grapes were attacked by rot, and when picked were kept separate from the others to prevent contamination. In fact, however, the wine from these grapes turned out superbly luscious. The date given for this anecdote is 1716, but certainly Tokay was made from grapes affected by *botrytis cinerea* long before that, and probably as early as the beginning of the seventeenth century, for there was a famous cellar of Tokays dating back to this period in Warsaw until it was destroyed by the Nazis.

The late proprietor of Yquem, the Marquis Bertrand de Lur Saluces, whom I asked about the origin of the deliberate use of rotten grapes in the production of Sauternes, was of the opinion that it began about 1860. He thought also that a German oenologist with experience of the *botrytis cinerea* in the German vineyards helped to develop its acceptance and use in Sauternes. However M. Jean Bureau, a former *maître de chai*, told me that the earliest wine of Yquem he ever drank was the 1845, and he believed that it had been made essentially in the same way as today. The earliest that has come my way has been the 1869. This was but a sample in a medicine bottle and decanted from an ordinary bottle a day or so earlier; the wine was certainly remarkably luscious and deep-coloured.

Yet it is said that there was not much *botrytis* in the district in 1855 when the Sauternes alone were given the distinction of classification alongside the Médocs. There was then as now a certain amount of red wine produced in the district. Nevertheless there is no doubt that the finest wines there were wonderfully luscious, and in the middle of the last century the Russian Tsar's brother Constantine, one of those traditionally sweet-toothed Russian Grand Dukes, paid 20,000 frs. (*c.* £800 then but the equivalent now of £8,000) for a cask of the 1847 Yquem. In 1861 and 1864, when the first-growth Sauternes sold for the same prices as first-growth Médocs, Yquem made up to 6,000 frs. a cask, higher than for Lafite. In successful years 24,000 frs. a *tonneau* was not infrequently paid for Yquem.

It was in the exceptionally fine year of 1868 that the house of Cruse bought the whole *récolte* from the properties owned by the Marquis de Lur Saluces in Sauternes and Barsac: Yquem, Filhot and Coutet. There was no château-bottling for these wines then, but the whole quantity was bottled by Cruse in their Bordeaux cellars, bearing a label 'Monopole des Crus du Marquis de Lur Saluces'. Most of this was then shipped to the firm's customers in Moscow and St Petersburg. An indication of the wealth – as well as the taste – of some Russians then was that an important Moscow customer demanded that his Yquem should be bottled in cut-glass decanters, with the inscription Château Yquem 1869 engraved in gold on the glass. Although these decanters were corked, they also bore glass stoppers, tied to the neck of the decanter with a silk ribbon.

When comparing the finest Sauternes with the German *trockenbeerenauslesen*, one must bear in mind that whereas the latter seldom attain more than 7–8 degrees of alcohol after a long and frequently assisted fermentation – and the same is true of Tokay Essence – the Sauternes may go up to 17 degrees of alcohol quite naturally; often they are 14 or 15 degrees. The German wines, particularly the Moselles, may have more acidity. In comparing them with their French rivals, it should be remembered that while very small quantities of these wines are made in exceptional years (perhaps 100–250 bottles), the fine Sauternes are produced in quantity. A celebrated comparison between the two wines in 1867 is mentioned later in connection with Rayne-Vigneau.

THE CLASSIFICATION OF THE SAUTERNES IN 1855

Grand Premier Cru		*Deuxièmes Crus*	
Yquem	Sauternes	de Myrat	Barsac
Premiers Crus		Doisy-Daëne	Barsac
La Tour-Blanche	Bommes	Doisy-Védrines	Barsac
Lafaurie-Peyraguey	Bommes	d'Arche	Sauternes
Clos Haut-Peyraguey	Bommes	Filhot	Sauternes
Rayne-Vigneau	Bommes	Broustet	Barsac
Suduiraut	Preignac	Nairac	Barsac
Coutet	Barsac	Caillou	Barsac
Climens	Barsac	Suau	Barsac
Guiraud	Sauternes	de Malle	Preignac
Rieussec	Fargues	Romer	Fargues
Rabaud-Promis	Bommes	Lamothe	Sauternes
Sigalas-Rabaud	Bommes		

The high repute of the Sauternes in the last century is demonstrated by their inclusion in the 1855 classification, when Yquem was placed as the sole *Grand Premier Cru*, eleven châteaux were classed as *Premiers Crus* and twelve as *Deuxièmes*

Crus. The list, as amended by subsequent sub-divisions of properties, is above. A hundred years ago Yquem fetched about 20 per cent more than the better first growths, while the seconds sold for 20–25 per cent less than these.

Yquem was certainly well known in the previous century, for Thomas Jefferson who, as mentioned earlier, visited Bordeaux in May 1787, wrote in French in December of that year to 'M. d'Yquem' asking to buy some of his wine for drinking in France and even after his return to America. 'I know that yours is one of the best growths of Sauterne [*sic*], and it is from your hand that I would prefer to receive it directly, because I shall be sure of receiving it natural, good and sound.' He went on to ask if he could let him have 250 bottles of the 1784, via the American consul, John Bondfield, in Bordeaux.

The Comte de Lur Saluces replied from Yquem on 7 January 1788 that he would draw and bottle the wine desired and hoped he would like it. (The Lur Saluces family had bought this property only in 1785.) Evidently Jefferson did, for in November 1788 he wrote to Bondfield that 'the Sauterne sent me by the Marquis de Saluces turns out very fine'. The following year Jefferson bought five more cases (250 bottles) of Yquem, and these cost 340 livres, including packing and freight.

To judge from Christie's catalogues Sauternes château names were not well known in England. The first mention of Barsac, *tout court*, was in a sale in 1787, and occasionally thereafter, but 'Vin de Sauterne' (with the final 's' omitted as by Jefferson and for American wine today) seemed to appear only in 1808; at 60s. a dozen it was fairly highly priced, but 4s. cheaper than a Barsac. In 1788 there was a 'Prigniac' for sale and the following year a 'Vin de Langon', but entries were infrequent compared with 'Vin de Graves'. However this was in the years of revolution and the wars with France, and the import of all French wines was severely discouraged. Moreover the British devotion to port must have limited the demand for sweet French wines. Certainly they did not appear very frequently at auctions, and the first mention of Yquem itself that I was able to find in the Christie catalogues was in 1862 in the sale list of a large cellar from Herefordshire. No vintage was given, although clarets in the same sale bore dates. Four years later some Yquem '58, described as *vin de goutte*, sold for the respectable price of 96s. a dozen. Then the following year Yquem appeared several times, the '47 (120s.), '51 (92s.) and the '58 again (80s.), with the Marquis de Lur Saluces mentioned as proprietor. Up to that date I could find no other Sauternes château named in the auction catalogues.

It is no disparagement to the other leading Sauternes to say that Yquem is the quintessence of these great luscious wines. Its charming setting on a small hill, the courtyard of turreted buildings dating back to the twelfth century and the Renaissance, and the easy appeal of its wine have made Yquem a focal point for visitors to the region. So much so that casual visitors are now discouraged, and appointments must be made; and no wonder, for one must be surprised that the *maître de chai* and his staff find any time for their work.

The château buildings themselves have the pleasantly old, informal air of a *manoir*, and the late Marquis, who died aged eighty in December 1968, used to spend most of his time in an attractive house in Bordeaux near the Jardin Public, with a fine music room built by the famous Louis, architect of the Théâtre. But in the base of one of the turrets at Yquem there is a small but fine private cellar, with bottles of Yquem going back to 1892 and of Coutet to 1888 and 1890. The bottles, which include samples of the '21, most famous Sauternes of this century, are re-corked every thirty years. It was odd, it occurred to me as I looked over the bins of old Sauternes, to come upon a purely white wine cellar in France. The present member of the Lur Saluces family in charge of Yquem is Comte Alexandre.

Yquem is as traditional in its equipment as Mouton. Everything that comes into contact with the grapes is of wood, and the pressed juice ferments in new oak casks. During the period of fermentation in these white wine *chais* the whisper of the bubbling wine in the bung-less casks reminds one of a muted apiary. Thereafter the wine remains in wood until bottled three to three-and-a-half years after the vintage. Since 1922 the whole crop has been bottled at the château. When the wine is a year old the *égalisage* or *assemblage* takes place, with the wine from each cask brought together for blending. For the casks will vary, since some will contain wine that may have started its life as long as two-and-a-half months earlier than the wine from the last picking. Each *barrique*, therefore, bears the date of vintaging. Standards are high at Yquem, and they can afford to be, for sometimes as much as 60 per cent of the crop may be de-classified and not sold as Yquem; this in addition to the fact that although the permitted *A C* output is 25 hl per hectare, at Yquem only about 9 hl are produced from each of the 100 ha under production. The vineyard is made up of 80 per cent Sémillon and 20 per cent Sauvignon. Yet over the years the average total production is around 70 *tonneaux* or 80,000 bottles. A century ago its average was higher: 100–130 *tonneaux*.

For, as everywhere in this part of the world, the dreaded risks are frost and hail. In 1950 there was only a half crop owing to frost, and because of hail there was no Yquem in 1951 or 1952. Recently a very bad run of vintages has adversely affected all the Sauternes, and there was no very acceptable year between 1962 and 1966. Yquem, unwisely, did offer some '63 but it was very dark-coloured by the time of its bottling, and grew even darker thereafter; certainly not up to the level of quality that Yquem often produced even in off-years like 1954 and 1958. There was no 1964 Yquem and only a little 1965, for 60 per cent of the crop was sold off as Sauternes. The 1966 and 1967 bear the château label, and 1968 also, owing to late picking in a fine autumn of that generally poor year. The 1967 is generally regarded as one of the best Yquems for many years. The 1970 was good and the 1971 also, but there was no 1972 or 1974 bottled under the château label, and it might have been as well if there had been no 1973 either, owing to the poor weather at the vintage; but it is hard even for Yquem not to market its wine as such for three consecutive years.

Unlike its peers in the Médoc who bottle the whole of their *récolte*, Yquem is not offered *en primeur*. The wine is not sold until bottled, and then is marketed in three successive portions or *tranches*, in the Bordeaux term. The late Marquis explained to me that it had been his policy over many years to sell each year no more than his average production, or about 80,000 bottles; the surplus in the good, prolific years, made up for the deficit in others. Yquem is the one Sauternes whose price has more or less kept level with those of the red *premiers crus*, or did until the exceptionally high opening prices that began in 1969. Whereas it used to cost only a quarter to a third more than the best of its neighbours, now it is more than double; for their price remained low.

In 1959 Yquem rather startled the wine world by producing a dry wine, which it called Ygrec. A number of other Sauternes growers have been selling a dry wine, notably Filhot and Doisy-Daëne, but that was mostly owing to the difficulties of selling a sweet wine. The Ygrec has the full, honeyish nose one associates with Sauternes but the flavour is fairly – and to me disappointingly – dry on the palate. The wine is made from 50 per cent Sauvignon and 50 per cent Sémillon, and is not marketed every year. The initial vintages offered were '59,

'60, '62, '64, '65 and '66. About 20 *tonneaux* are usually made, but the quantity varies from 15 *tonneaux* of the '59 to 26 of the '62. To my mind it is not a great success.

The hazards and heavy costs of producing Yquem go a long way to account for its high price. So does its unequalled reputation. It is irrelevant whether some of the other fine Sauternes and Barsac châteaux have often produced as successful wine, for world opinion has rated Yquem a consistent first. There have been three particularly outstanding vintages: 1869, 1893 and 1921. These were all exceptionally hot years, and wonderfully sweet white wines were made not only in Bordeaux but also in Germany. If one may count the spoonful of the '69 from a medicine bottle, I have been lucky enough to drink them all. The '93 and the '21 I have actually owned to the extent of two or three bottles apiece, and both came to me in an unusual way.

When Sir Arthur Evans of Knossos fame died early in the last war, part of his cellar was included in the sale of his house on Boars Hill, near Oxford. By this time Britain was cut off from Continental wine supplies, and prices were rising fast. A friend of mine attended the sale, and while anonymous St-Julien and doubtful Liebfraumilch fetched about 30s. a bottle, six or seven times their pre-war value, some old bottles of Burgundy and Sauternes were largely disregarded and went very cheaply. My friend bought five or six bottles of Yquem '93 for 15s. apiece, and some Clos de Vougeot '98 for the same price. He passed me a proportion of each, and I also shared more than one of his bottles. When I drank the '93s they were either side of fifty years old, the colour was dark, but the flavour wonderfully complete and luscious.

My few bottles of the '21 – certainly the most celebrated Yquem of this century and on a par with the Cheval-Blanc of the same year – came to me soon after the end of the last war from a doctor friend in Swindon. Swindon, then a railway town in southern England reminiscent of the industrial north, is not the place where one would expect to find a small cache of Yquem '21, but it had belonged to the departed husband of a patient, who asked my friend to take eight or nine bottles of this precious wine, along with a few other old Sauternes, including Coutet '21 and '24, in settlement of his account. In due course several of these found their way into my cellar, and I drank the last bottle of this Yquem '21 in 1955. It was still pale and in excellent condition, whereas, according to Harry Waugh who shared in this splendid bottle, a number of examples he had had in Bordeaux in previous years had been *madérisé* (madeira-coloured and having lost its freshness) and past their best. One up for Swindon and its cold climate!

I have drunk Yquem '21 several times since, and the last occasion was in October 1966 at lunch in the London office of Sichel & Co. Although this 45-year-old Sauternes was a little dark in colour, it was far from being *madérisé*; still a wonderfully rich, velvety, deep-flavoured wine.

These three years are not the only vintages in which Yquem had a special *réclame*. Among others in my own recollection were '24, '28, '29, '37, '45, '47, '49 and '55. I remember the 1929 being served at the dinner given in London in May 1962 by Christian Cruse to commemorate his fifty years of 'calling on' his English wine trade customers. When the Yquem was poured out, my apprehensions were aroused, as the colour of this 32-year-old wine was distinctly dark. The nose was old too, but the flavour was magnificently full and without any sign of decay.

The '28 was equally fine, although I have had variable experience of it. The reason is that white wines are much more susceptible to the conditions of keeping than red wines. The last time I drank it was in Bordeaux in October 1974, when it was very deep-coloured, certainly maderized, but with a splendidly luscious aroma. The '37 was very fine too, but in this year I consider that Climens beat it; indeed that wine had a special reputation. The '45 is certainly the most highly

considered vintage of the post-Second World War epoch: a
single bottle fetched £105 at Christie's in November 1978.
The '49 had all the richness that one looks for in Yquem, but
was showing rather dark after twenty-five years or so.

Thanks no doubt to the ready sales facilities offered by the
London auction rooms, the price of old and even not-so-old
Yquems has risen to extraordinary heights, stimulated by European
as well as by American bidders. At Christie's in June
1978 a record London auction price for a Sauternes was recorded:
£700 for a single bottle of Yquem 1858. In the same year
the following record prices were paid in this saleroom for
single bottles: 1869 (£440), 1871 (£250), 1893 (£165), 1900
(£400), 1921 (£165), 1928 (£150) and 1929 (£160). Even the
'49 made £82 a bottle in May 1977. The other leading
Sauternes have risen to some extent too, though usually
nothing like as much. In 1976 a single bottle of Coutet 1868
went for £125; in the same year one of Lafaurie-Peyraguey
1900 was knocked down for £68, and some high prices have
been recorded in the sales that Christie's have conducted in
the United States.

I suppose it is just possible to defend such prices in terms of
interest, especially in inflationary times when the value of
money in relation to commodities is in understandable debate,
but scarcely in terms of quality. I was privileged to drink the
Yquem '24 twice in 1977: the first time from a magnum
bought for £230 at auction and generously opened at a dinner
in London, the second time at a dinner in Mouton-Rothschild.
Both were very deep-coloured, but the latter was the fresher,
perhaps because it had never been moved. I have always been
interested to taste old wines, whether or not they have gone
'over the top', but to pay such prices for them seems out of
proportion.

The criticism has been made of Yquem that it is too heavy
and too liquorous; even allowing for the number of poor
vintages in the sixties onwards, I am not sure that Yquem

has been up to form. Perhaps the very conservative methods of fermentation and maturation in cask have led to a certain loss of freshness and to consequent early maderization, reflected in deep colour. Even the '61 and '66 showed colour at an early age. Nevertheless the '67 is an outstanding wine, very rich though also showing some colour after ten years. The development of the '70, '71 and '75 will be watched with interest. Meanwhile it must be said that to taste a bottle of Yquem is always an experience.

Although Sauternes is the omnibus name for all the wines grown in the five privileged communes, there are only five growths within the village area of Sauternes itself. This village lies right at the back of the commune, and considering the fame of the name it is probably little visited, compared with Barsac on the main road. Not that it is a village of any character, being unexpectedly dull and nondescript.

The only *premier cru* in the commune is Guiraud, formerly known as Bayle. It lies on a plateau rather higher than Yquem and to the south. This large estate belongs to M. Paul Rival. The courtyard and *chai* are substantial, with big wine cellars. The vineyard is of 65 ha, made up of 50 per cent Sémillon, 35 per cent Sauvignon, 14 per cent Muscadelle and 1 per cent Ugni-Blanc. The average production is 400 *barriques* of sweet wine; but there are also about 12–15 *barriques* of dry wine, which is sold as Pavillon Sec de Château Guiraud. In addition an increasing amount of red wine is being made, under the label of Pavillon Rouge. This started in 1961 and about 40 *barriques* are now produced annually. The composition of this section of the vineyard is 50 per cent Cabernet-Sauvignon, 25 per cent Cabernet-Franc and the balance of Merlot and Malbec. When I visited the *chai* in 1968 I was surprised to find the 1961 and 1962 sweet white wine still in cement tanks, in order to keep them fresh; but the former was already rather heavy. This is symptomatic of the difficult times through which the Sauternais have been passing. It is sad that a first-growth château like Guiraud should have such difficulty in selling its wine. I have had good examples in the past.

It must be borne in mind that the sequence of châteaux within the 1855 classification was significant; those at the top of each class were considered better than those lower down. The three other classed Sauternes were all among the *Deuxièmes Crus* and not particularly high up. D'Arche and Filhot were fourth and fifth respectively and Lamothe was bottom.

Ch. d'Arche, named after a wealthy eighteenth-century proprietor, is on a hill near to the village of Sauternes. The buildings are single-storeyed on three sides of two courts which look across to Lamothe on a hill opposite. The proprietor is A. Bastit Saint Martin, and he owns part of Lamothe too. The vineyard of d'Arche is 50 ha in extent, producing 200 *barriques*. The vineyard composition is 20 per cent Sauvignon and 80 per cent Sémillon. The better *cuves* are sold as Ch. d'Arche, the less good as Ch. d'Arche-Lafaurie. It is bottled after two years. The wine is usually well balanced.

Filhot, set in an English-type park, is much grander. Indeed the château, with two projecting wings, is the most imposing in the Sauternes region, and the ensemble has rather an English look. It was the home of the Lur Saluces family, and indeed belonged to them until 1936 when it was sold to the Comtesse de Lacarelle, herself a Lur Saluces. Out of a total property of 320 ha only 45 are under vines. The soil here is quite different from Yquem, and is a mixture of sand, gravel and clay. Filhot makes a dry wine as well as a sweet one, and total production is about 100 *tonneaux*, although these days it is kept not in wood but in glass-lined vats for three years before bottling. The dry wine is sold as Grand Vin Sec de Château Filhot, and about 10 *tonneaux* only are made. Sémillon is, of course, the predominant grape, and here the grapes are said to ripen later than at Yquem, and it is normal to go through the vineyards five times. No wine of the '63, '64 and '65 vintages was sold as Filhot. Not only is the proprietor of Filhot a woman, but the *gérant* or manager also: Mme Cazeaux Cazalet. These days Filhot seems less to be seen on wine lists than it deserves.

Lamothe, prominent on a crest facing d'Arche, also near the village of Sauternes, is exactly divided in two. M. Bastit St Martin owns 15 ha and produces about 100 *barriques*, and M. Jean Despujols makes the same amount of wine from an equivalent area of land. Neither is widely known outside France.

There are several other fairly well-known *bourgeois* growths in the Sauternes commune, including Raymond-Lafon, Arche-Vimeney, and Lamothe-Bergey which claims classed-growth status. There is also Lafon, whose wine is exclusively marketed by Dourthe of Moulis.

Adjacent to Sauternes is Bommes, which includes no fewer than seven classed growths, among them La Tour-Blanche, in 1855 placed immediately after Yquem. It is something of a curiosity for it was owned by a M. Osiris, an umbrella manufacturer in Bordeaux and a friend of Pasteur. In 1910 he gave the whole property to the state on the condition that it was used as an oenological and viticultural school. Today there are fifty students who do a two-year course. The vineyard, with a stony soil, is exploited separately, and is of 25 ha, of which nearly 90 per cent is Sémillon, 10 per cent Sauvignon with a little Muscadelle, but the proportion of Sauvignon is increasing and will be 25 per cent. Production averages 200 *barriques*, and since 1967 a little dry wine has been made. There is a second wine sold under the name of Cru St-Marc. At one time the marketing was done by the firm of Cordier, but nowadays the estate does its own selling; a good deal is disposed of direct to the private consumers, a practice not uncommon in this part of the world where trade is difficult. La Tour-Blanche is not as well known as one would expect in view of its distinguished placing in the 1855 classification. The installations are modern and, unlike at Yquem, the fermentation takes place in concrete vats, on the grounds that the fermentation is more rapid, being completed in about ten days, more economical and that there is less oxidization. Here is quite a different school of thought from the traditional Yquem. They also have a different attitude towards fining, for at La Tour-Blanche it is done two or three times before bottling, while at Yquem the first fining only takes place in the second year. A curiosity was a half-bottle of La Tour-Blanche '46 opened in London in 1974. It had been bought for no great price as an odd lot in a sub-urban wine merchant's shop. Astonishingly pale for its age and vintage, it was not very luscious and a little dry at the end, but very well balanced. It must have been very well made.

Lafaurie-Peyraguey, the next Bommes on the list, is a much smaller estate, with a fine château surrounded by an old crenellated wall. Part of it dates from the thirteenth century, and the property, owned by Cordier, is as well kept as his other estates. The vineyard is only 18 ha, with a composition of 60 per cent Sémillon, 30 per cent Sauvignon and 10 per cent Muscadelle. Average production is 120 *barriques*. The wine is bottled after three years and is an excellent example of the slightly lighter type of Sauternes. I remember a remarkably fine '24. In October 1976 at Talbot I had the unusual experience, at least for a non-Bordelais, of drinking the same Sauternes both at the beginning of a meal with *foie gras* and at the end with a sweet. The wine was Lafaurie-Peyraguey '37. Very brown in colour, it had a lovely nose and in fact was not maderized on the palate, and it tasted delicious at both ends of the meal, particularly at the beginning. The property which adjoins Yquem, was owned in the eighteenth century by the Président Pichard, proprietor of Lafite. In his account of Bordeaux Jefferson mentions that in 1780 Coutet produced no less than 150 *tonneaux*, which Pichard sold for 280 livres per *tonneau* and 600 livres when mature, which probably meant no more than two or three years old. The relatively low price that even so distinguished a Barsac as Coutet then obtained is shown by the fact that Pichard sold his Lafite for between

1,500 and 2,000 livres a *tonneau*. Like the latter this property was confiscated as a *bien national* after the death of its owner in the Revolution, and sold to M. Lafaurie who greatly improved its standing.

Adjoining this estate is the small one of Clos Haut-Peyraguey, originally part of its neighbour and non-existent as a separate entity in 1855. The vineyard is 8 ha, and in addition there are 4 ha of a *cru bourgeois*, Haut-Bommes. Both are owned by the company of Pauly Frères. The composition of each vineyard is 80 per cent Sémillon, 17 per cent Sauvignon and 3 per cent Muscadelle and bottling takes place after two to three years. Average production is 60 and 30 *barriques* respectively. From my limited experience of the wine I would not say that Haut-Peyraguey is in the same class as Lafaurie-Peyraguey, but as one of the smaller Sauternes estates its problems are certainly greater.

Rayne-Vigneau is one of the biggest properties of the district. The large turreted nineteenth-century château is similar to several of those in the Médoc, such as Pichon-Baron, and there are substantial out-buildings including two very big cellars well over 100 yards long. Standing on a slope the château commands a fine view over the Sauternes vineyards and across the river to the hills of the Premières Côtes. For many years the estate was owned by the Pontac family, well known for its association with Haut-Brion, and a hundred years ago was generally considered second to Yquem. In 1961 it was bought by M. G. Taoux, a Bordeaux wine merchant, and sold again in 1975, without the château, to a group of five Bordeaux wine merchants; the price was said to be 1½ million francs.

A common dispute among *amateurs* of sweet white wine concerns the relative superiority of the Sauternes and the richer products of the Rhine and Moselle. At the 1867 Paris International Exhibition a notable success was scored by the 1861 Vigneau-Pontac, as it was then, when a mixed jury of

French and German tasters in equal numbers awarded the palm to the French wine. The triumph of the Vigneau was underlined by the fact that its samples came from the whole, equalized crop, while the German wines, as customary, were from two selected casks of extra-luscious wines out of several hundred casks produced in the vineyards.

The vineyard of Rayne-Vigneau extends to 45 ha, producing 350 *barriques* from a grape composition of 65 per cent Sémillon, 30 per cent Sauvignon and 5 per cent Muscadelle. The vineyard is notably stony, and at the château I was assured that this contributed to the fine quality of the wine which I have certainly found one of the more delicious Sauternes. Ninety per cent of the wine is château-bottled and this takes place after three years. It is one of the fuller Sauternes.

Rabaud, the last of the classified Bommes – as Peixotto, its only *deuxième* in the 1855 classification, was later absorbed into this estate – is named after Mlle Marie Peyronne de Rabaud who married into one of the Parlement families, the de Cazeaus. The family sold it in 1819, and then it was re-sold in 1864 to M. Henri de Sigalas, who in 1903 parted with more than half the estate to M. Adrien Promis. Reunited in the 1930s, they were divided again in 1952. This explains why there are now two Ch. Rabaud wines: Sigalas-Rabaud and Rabaud-Promis. The former is only of 15 ha, made up of 60 per cent Sémillon and 40 per cent Sauvignon, and the average production is 160 *barriques*. The wine is fermented in concrete fermenting vats, and then kept in concrete tanks for a year before being transferred to wooden casks for another year or so. Bottling takes place between two and three years after the vintage, according to the state of the wine. The proprietor is the Marquis de Lambert des Granges. This is a lighter and generally regarded as a better wine than its neighbour, which is owned by M. Lanneluc. This latter is 30 ha in extent, of which over 80 per cent is Sémillon and the rest Sauvignon save for a little Muscadelle. Average production is 400 *barriques*.

The wine is not only fermented in cement vats but also kept in vats until bottled after two years. It does not lie at all in wood, and it is claimed that the wine keeps younger and fresher this way. The variation in practice between the two Rabauds demonstrates the individuality of Bordeaux. Rabaud-Promis has large arched cellars below the house, claimed as a work of Victor Louis. The tops of the *cuves* have covers in the cellar floor. For the 1962 vintage Rabaud-Promis had numbered bottles, but this is not a common practice. The best market lies in Germany.

There are few *crus bourgeois* in Bommes, the smallest of the Sauternes communes, but M. Lanneluc owns the small foreign-sounding Ch. Cameron, which should commend itself north of the Border.

Fargues is the most southerly of the Sauternes communes, but these are so intermingled that it is not easy to say at any given moment in which commune one is standing. All are sparsely populated, and it is hard to find one's way about, for few of the châteaux bother to put up a name-plate. Not even the natives are very familiar with the whereabouts of the various growths. A villager of Sauternes, when asked the way to Rieussec, replied, '*C'est à Fargues*', with the air of one describing a far-away commune of which he knew little. They adjoin!

Rieussec is indeed in Fargues and is the only *premier cru*. The wine is distinctly lighter and less liquorous than some of the other Sauternes, notably Yquem on which it abuts. It is an estate of 50 ha, producing 320–350 *barriques*. The vineyard composition is 80 per cent Sémillon, 15 per cent Sauvignon and 5 per cent Muscadelle. The soil is decidedly gravelly. Wine considered not good enough to be sold under the château label is marketed as Clos Labère, non-vintage. It is a well-kept property with underground cellars, rare in this part of the world. In 1971 it was bought for about 1,100,000 frs. by the Aquitaine group of multiple grocery stores.

The other Fargues *cru classé* is Romer, little known these days, and tucked away among woods, and much nearer the main Bordeaux–Langon road (*RN.113*) than Rieussec. It is only 7 ha, and is a real peasant property, with the small *chai* abutting on a little farmyard. The soil here is also very gravelly. The composition of the vineyard is 60 per cent Sémillon, 20 per cent Sauvignon and 20 per cent Muscadelle – a very high proportion of this last grape. The wine is heavy and not very distinguished. It is sold exclusively to Calvet.

A Fargues *cru bourgeois* of note is Ch. de Fargues. It is owned by the Lur Saluces family, and is run by the *régisseur* of Yquem. The wine is all bottled at the château and the label, which bears the name of Lur Saluces, is very similar to that of Yquem. An excellent example was the 1967.

Preignac, nearer the Garonne, is a much larger commune but also with only two classed growths, of which the sole first growth is the Ch. de Suduiraut. The fine old turreted seventeenth-century château lies at the end of a long drive and avenue of trees, with no prior indication of the identity of the large house. For, unlike in the Médoc, as already mentioned, few of the owners identify their properties by signposts, and in view of the need of publicity for Sauternes this is surprising. Although the local wine growers' association has devised a *Circuit du Sauternais* which is alleged to pass deviously by all the leading growths, my experience of château-visiting in the district takes me back to that hazardous-halt-provoking, diversion-creating nursery game, Peter Rabbit's Race Game. Amid the obscure, winding, unpopulated roads one always seems to overshoot the mark, to be two roads away, if not in the wrong commune and heading straight for the Landes or the Garonne!

To return to, or rather arrive at, Suduiraut, whose hard-to-pronounce name cannot be a sales asset in, say, Texas or Manchester, the house itself is a classified building of historical interest and has been owned since 1940 by M. Léopold Fonquernie, a wealthy industrialist from the north of France, who has devoted a great deal of attention and money to improving the property, which for many years previously had been sadly neglected and made little wine. From the courtyard with buildings on both sides, one passes into the château, which externally is rather severe, but agreeably furnished within. Beyond a finely panelled hall lie formal gardens said to have been laid out by Le Nôtre. The cellar buildings are thick-walled and traditional, but there are concrete vats. For although the wine is made in the traditional way, with the vineyard traversed six or seven times, the young wine is transferred after about eight months from wood into concrete vats, in order to keep it fresh and to avoid oxidization; a practice already noted elsewhere. Of course development is also delayed or prevented, but the results seem good when the wine is bottled three years after the vintage. The *maître de chai* told me that Suduiraut has a micro-climate warmer than its neighbours. As a result the vintage usually begins earlier. The wine is rich and luscious even by Sauternes standards, and fairly high in alcohol. Sémillon now forms 95 per cent of the 85-ha vine-yard, Sauvignon the small balance and there is no longer any Muscadelle. Production ranges from 300 to over 400 *barriques*, and all the wine deemed worthy of the château label is bottled on the spot. In the past the reputation of Suduiraut suffered from lack of care, but since about 1955 onwards the wine has been reckoned among the best in the region. The '67 and '70 showed very well. In a Christie's sale in November 1978 of twenty-one vintages from the private cellar – from 1820 to 1972 – one half-bottle of 1820 made £500, and single bottles of the 1900 and 1945 reached £76 and £54 respectively.

The other classed Preignac, de Malle, is also a classified historic building and certainly the finest in the district. Dating from early in the seventeenth century it has a courtyard in front, and round pepper-pot towers on each flank. At the back is a very formal Italian garden. The interior is open for public visits and well worth seeing. There is a splendid panelled hall with a marble floor, and the Italian influence can be seen. Most attractive is a seventeenth-century round chapel in one of the towers. The Duke of Wellington stayed here during his campaign against Napoleon. For many years de Malle belonged to the Lur Saluces family and the last owner of that name was Comte Pierre, but by marriage it has descended to the young, energetic Comte Pierre de Bournazel, an electronics engineer who devotes all his spare time – and his spare cash too, one would hazard – to restoring both château and *chai*, and to improving the quality of this *deuxième cru*, which lies very near the border of Barsac and also of the Graves. Nearly all the vineyard had to be replanted after the savage winter of 1956, and is now 36 ha in extent. Half of this is planted in white grapes and half in red. Until the last century the château always made red as well as white wine, the former being entitled to the *appellation* Graves, as part of the vineyard is in Graves. This red part is made up of 80 per cent Cabernet-Sauvignon and 20 per cent Merlot, while the white is 65 per cent Sémillon, 30 per cent Sauvignon and 5 per cent Muscadelle.

The red wine is made by the method of carbonic maceration, as described at the Cave-de-Bel-Air at St-Maixant (p. 493). It is bottled within the year and sold under the label of Ch. de Cardaillan. The wine is for early drinking, and up to 400 *barriques* are made. Of the rest, 200 *barriques* of sweet wine are produced, and bottled after about eighteen months, while 150 *barriques* are made of a dry white wine, fermented out. Both sweet and dry white wines are fermented in cask for a week and then as the fermentation slows up the wines are transferred into concrete tanks. The dry white is sold under the name of Chevalier de Malle, having been bottled after eighteen months. The *appellation* for this is Bordeaux Supérieur. It will be seen that the young Count is enterprising in these difficult times for the Sauternes. The sweet wine is on the light side, the dry is fresh and clean-flavoured.

In Preignac there are quite a large number of *crus bourgeois* and the best known is Bastor-Lamontagne, which produces about 250 *barriques*. There is also the Domaine du Mayne, and Domaine de Lamothe, Ch. des Remparts, so-named to distinguish it from the other Lamothe in Sauternes. It is very near the little stream, the Ciron, which divides the Sauternes communes from Barsac.

This last is much the largest of the fine sweet wine communes, producing about 30 per cent of the total crop, averaging 13,000 hl. The total production in the five Sauternes communes is about 40,000 hl. Barsac is probably the best known. 'A nice bottle of Barsac' has provided many drinkers of tender years with their introduction to wine. The Barsacs are generally considered a little heavier and a trifle less distinguished than the best growths of the other villages. No doubt the lesser properties of which there are several dozen are more plebeian, but this certainly does not apply to the leading châteaux among whom Coutet and Climens stand out.

In the 1855 classification, which included eight Barsac growths, but which subsequent division has increased to ten, Coutet leads Climens, although over the years many people would place the latter first. Climens is rather a fuller wine than Coutet, but both can be excellent. In its best years Climens can be a challenger of Yquem. A celebrated Climens was the '29, often reckoned the best Sauternes of the vintage. Early in the 1950s I had bottles and halves of the '37 of both Yquem and Climens, and I thought that the latter had the edge on its rival, being rounder and fuller. The last time I drank Climens '37 was in 1965. The wine had the tint of a well-coloured cognac, but the flavour was complete and clean, whereas Suduiraut of the same vintage opened in the same year was well past its best. Climens '47 was another outstanding wine;

but then so in its own style was Coutet '50, delicate and fruity. Another vintage in which I believe Climens was superior to Yquem was '61, as it was less coloured by the mid-seventies. So indeed was the seductive '59 at about the same time. The Coutet '61 was very good too.

To visit, the two châteaux afford a marked contrast: Coutet spick and span, with a well-kept garden beside the small turreted château, and a very neat *chai*; Climens, with an un-ambitious low house facing a somewhat uncared-for-looking forecourt, and an old-fashioned *chai*. Until 1977 Coutet was owned by M. Rolland-Guy, and in the years following the Second World War he clearly spent a good deal of money on it. As mentioned earlier, a former proprietor was a member of the ubiquitous Lur Saluces family and the father of the Marquis Bertrand, who died in 1968. Coutet came to M. Rolland-Guy via his wife's father. The proprietor now is M. Marcel Bally, an industrialist from eastern France, who bought the property for 4,350,000 frs.

Climens for over a century was in the hands of the Gou-nouilhou family, but in 1971 it was bought, reputedly for 2½ million frs., by M. Lucien Lurton, proprietor of Brane-Can-tenac. If Climens is less smart than Coutet I have continued to find the wine good. Unlike Yquem, both produced some '64 under their château labels, but Coutet had to de-class three-quarters of its production.

The area of Coutet is 33 ha, made up of 80 per cent Sémil-lon, 15 per cent Sauvignon and 5 per cent Muscadelle. Average production is 330 *barriques*. Climens which has a more chalky soil also extends to 33 ha of vines, but with a greater proportion of Sémillon: 95 per cent, with only 5 per cent of Sauvignon. It all depends on which grape suits best the particular soil. Climens usually bottles after three years, Coutet after two-and-a-half, but much depends on the vintage. Both wines are sold in cask as well as château-bottled. Some people, noting the great difference in price between Yquem and wines like these, like to ask whether the former is 'worth all that much more'. The question might be better put as 'are the first-growth Sauternes worth all that much less?' The answer is certainly no.

The next on the list of the classed growths and the top *deuxième* is a château whose wines are certainly little known in Britain nowadays: de Myrat. The mid-eighteenth-century, single-storey château, with an upper floor only in the middle – a *chartreuse* like Beychevelle and Langoa in the Médoc – is a charming building set in a pleasant park. It used to belong to the Martineau family but the owner is now the Comte de Pontac, of the family which once owned Haut-Brion. He has devoted a great deal of attention to restoring the house and furnishing it suitably. The vineyard is 22 ha, and curiously enough contains no Sauvignon. The reason for this, I was told, was that the soil is very chalky and this does not suit the Sauvignon grape. So the *cépage* is 95 per cent Sémillon and 5 per cent Muscadelle. The production is 200 *barriques*. None is currently château-bottled, and I found this wine rather on the heavy side. The Count told me that sometimes the strength went as high as 19½ degrees. This is perhaps a doubtful recommendation. In 1976 it was announced that he was giving up the unequal economic struggle and would produce no more wine. This was a sad comment on Sauternes's problems.

Not far away are the two Doisys: Védrines and Daëne. (Doisy-Dubroca, once a small vineyard of 4 ha, producing 40–50 *barriques*, is now part of Climens.)

Doisy-Védrines is the larger of the pair, with a vineyard of 20 ha, of which almost 80 per cent is Sémillon, 20 per cent Sauvignon and the balance a small quantity of Muscadelle. The average output is 200 *barriques*. It lies between Coutet and Climens, and is run by Mme Castéja on behalf of her husband, a brother of the proprietor of Lynch-Moussas and a Bordeaux wine merchant. As an example of the difficulties of selling even classed Barsacs these days, at Doisy-Védrines in the sixties they planted red wine grapes which could only be made into wine with the *appellation* Bordeaux Supérieur. I have drunk several very attractive sweet Doisy-Védrines, a rather full wine.

On the other hand Doisy-Daëne (pronounced Denne) has become known for its dry wine. Under the enlightened proprietorship of M. Pierre Doubourdieu, who described his modest house to me as a 'cabine' and not a château, this dry wine has been developed and 120 *barriques* are made from a vineyard which is 60 per cent Sauvignon, 20 per cent Sémillon and – very unusual – 20 per cent Riesling. This dry white wine is bottled after six months and with a fresh nose and clean flavour, it is reckoned to be drunk young. The whole estate is 13 ha, with about 80 per cent Sémillon and 20 per cent Sauvignon for the sweet wine, of which 120 *barriques* are made in good years. This is bottled after two years. Daëne is the more widely known of the two Doisy growths.

The remaining four classed Barsacs are not now well known widely whatever they were in the past. They follow each other in the 1855 list. Broustet is the first, consisting of 16 ha, with 60 per cent Sémillon, 30 per cent Sauvignon and 10 per cent Muscadelle. Production averages 165 *barriques* in the small, low-ceilinged *chai*. The proprietress is Mme Veuve Pierre Fourneu.

Nairac, named after an eighteenth-century Bordeaux merchant, ship-owner and deputy of Guyenne, is a fine two-storeyed château facing the main road on the outskirts of the village of Barsac. In 1971 it was acquired for between 800,000 and 1,000,000 frs. by Mr Tom Heater, the American son-in-law of M. Tari of Giscours. The 14-ha vineyard is immediately behind, made up of 90 per cent Sémillon, 6 per cent Sauvignon and 4 per cent Muscadelle. Production is about 120 *barriques* and some red wine is made.

Caillou, a lofty building lying further into the countryside is a larger property owned by the active M. Bravo. The area under white grapes is 22 hectares, planted in the proportion of

65 per cent Sémillon, 25 per cent Muscadelle and 10 per cent Sauvignon. Just over 400 *barriques* are normally made, including 30 *barriques* of dry wine called Domaine Sarraule. Some 3 ha are planted in Cabernet-Sauvignon and Merlot to produce 25 *barriques* of red wine, sold as Clos du Clocher. There is even a little *rosé* produced, known as Rosé St-Vincent. To illustrate the difference in wine-making methods within a small area, M. Bravo begins his white wine fermentation in cask for two to three weeks, and then transfers the wine to cement vats for a month. After that it returns to casks early in the year following the vintage, and at the beginning is racked as often as once a fortnight, and later on every two months. In the third year before it is bottled it is racked twice more. I found the wine on the light side, as is to be expected. Most of it is sold privately. M. Bravo also owns or runs one or two other *bourgeois* Barsacs.

The last classed Barsac is Suau, situated between the main road from Barsac to the south and the railway from Bordeaux. The château is small, but rather like a small English country house, except that it has a round turret at one corner. It is owned by M. Biarnez, and production is only about 60 *barriques*. A little red wine is made here.

There are a considerable number of *crus bourgeois* in Barsac and some of them are well known. There are several Roumieux. The Goyaud family own 13 ha, and the Bernardet family 8, while a third section is owned by the Lacoste family. In all, the three make about 240 *barriques* from 55 per cent Sémillon, 30 per cent Sauvignon and 15 per cent Muscadelle. I have seen this wine on one or two lists.

Piada was once in the hands of the Lur Saluces family, and at one point adjoins Coutet. I was told at the *chai* that the property dated back to the times of the English King Edward I. The present proprietor is M. J. Lalande, and he makes dry as well as sweet wine from his 13 ha. Of this 150 *barriques* are sweet and 50 dry, sold allusively perhaps as Clos du Roy. I found it sweeter than the dry Doisy-Daëne. This dry wine comes from two-thirds Sauvignon and one-third Riesling. Before bottling the wine is heated sufficiently so as to be slightly pasteurized; another variation in local production. Other fairly well-known Barsacs are Dudon, Liot and Menauta. The last of these has an enclosed walled courtyard in the style of Yquem.

A quick way to sample Barsacs is to visit the Office Viticole in the middle of the village, opposite the fine sixteenth-century Gothic church. It is possible to taste and buy wines, as well as obtain information about the local châteaux and their situation. The nearness of the Garonne is demonstrated by two high flood marks in the church: one mark is dated 7 April 1770 and the other 6 March 1930.

Adjoining Sauternes are four other small sweet white wine areas: Cérons, St-Pierre-du-Mons, Ste-Croix-du-Mont and Loupiac. At one time both Cérons and St-Pierre-du-Mons used to be part of Sauternes, and no doubt some of their wines contrive to be sold as Sauternes still. Cérons, situated on the left bank of the Garonne, downstream from Sauternes, is the largest and its *vignoble* is part of the Barsac plateau. The *appellation* is Cérons for wines with an alcoholic strength of 12·5 degrees (half a degree less than for Sauternes), and this extends to the communes of Podensac and Illats. In style the Cérons wines are between those of Graves and Barsac, but nearer the latter in their sweetness which owes something to the *pourriture noble*. However in order to meet the current taste for dryer wines a certain amount of dry Cérons is produced, although in my view it is the richer wines that represent the true Cérons. These are not widely known abroad, but in fact can be delicious, and are very modestly priced. Although the name-boards of châteaux greet passing motorists on the main road, and there is even a Château de Cérons, owned by Jean Perromat, yet château names are not all that important. The *cépage* is much the same as for Sauternes, but there tends to be a higher proportion of Muscadelle. For those who enjoy sweet wines but find the Sauternes either too luscious or too expensive, Cérons is an excellent alternative; discriminating wine merchants usually list one or two. St-Pierre-du-Mons produces wines similar in style. The Cérons output averages 11,000 hl.

Ste-Croix-du-Mont and Loupiac adjoin each other on the right bank of the river, opposite Sauternes and Barsac. Their wines are similar enough to treat them as one. Loupiac was delimited as recently as 1926. Each has its own *appellation*, with a minimum strength of 13 degrees like Sauternes, but with a much larger permitted crop of 40 hl to the hectare, the same as Cérons. Physically these two small districts are part of the Entre-Deux-Mers, and vinously adjoin the Premières Côtes de Bordeaux. From the terrace by the nineteenth-century Romanesque-style church whose tower is a landmark from the Sauternes country opposite, there is a splendid view. Below is the river and the 'port' of Barsac, and beyond spread out the network of vineyards, with their châteaux, *chais* and clumps of woodland. Right behind, the horizon, dark with the trees of the Landes, forms a great arc. Ste-Croix-du-Mont and Loupiac together produce about 20,000 hl, considerably less than Sauternes. However, both communes are subject to frost and in 1963 the former produced hardly any wine with its *appellation* and Loupiac only 25 per cent of normal. The wines are perhaps rather heavier, less distinguished and 'simpler' than those on the opposite bank, but they can be very agreeable for all that. Their chief markets used to be in Holland, Prussia and pre-revolutionary Russia, but all these fell away after the First World War, and their growers have been in difficulties since the world slump in the thirties.

The best known Ste-Croix growth is probably de Tastes, formerly owned by Pierre Ginestet and now controlled by his sister Mme Prats. The *vignoble* area under production is only 6 ha. Another is Lamarque owned by the Rolland family, who were associated with the old Parlement de Guyenne. As at many other properties here, red wine is also made. Loubens is also a well-known Ste-Croix.

Many of the sweet white wines of this area have suffered from the general lowering of demand and standards in the last thirty years or so, and all are ripe for a revival. Their two publicity organizations are the *Commanderie du Bontemps de Sauternes et Barsac* and the *Commanderie du Bontemps de Ste-Croix-du-Mont*.

The local main town on this side of the river is Cadillac, just to the north of Loupiac. It is an attractive old walled town, dominated by the Renaissance château of the Ducs d'Épernon, which is now state-owned. To the south of Ste-Croix is Verdelais, best known not for its wine but for the burial place of Toulouse-Lautrec. His grave lies up a flight of steps across the street from the village church, and is situated somewhat incongruously among the artificial flowers that are the normal cemetery furniture of French burial grounds.

16. The Entre-Deux-Mers, Côtes de Bordeaux

The Entre-Deux-Mers, whose name dates back to the Middle Ages deriving from the Latin *Inter Dua Maria*, is an extensive, expanding tongue of land between the rivers Garonne and Dordogne. The distance as the crow flies from the confluence opposite Bourg to the southern limits of the Gironde department is roughly the same as the length of the Médoc, about fifty miles, but the land broadens out as the two river valleys diverge. The country and the soil change, from the flat land round the confluence at Bec d'Ambès, rising to the district of Carbon-Blanc through which the Bordeaux–Libourne main road runs, and thereafter presenting a generally hilly appearance of great charm. The Entre-Deux-Mers and the Premières Côtes, physically one and only vinously separate, certainly form the most agreeable and varied country in the Bordeaux region. The 'frontier' towns which once prevented – and at other times connived at – the entry of wines from the 'Haut Pays' are Castillon and Ste-Foy on the Dordogne and St-Macaire and La Réole on the Garonne.

Vinously this triangular region is sub-divided and split up. Entre-Deux-Mers itself has three main areas: in the north-west and west the districts of Carbon-Blanc and Créon; in the north the communes near the Dordogne around Libourne (left bank only), Branne and Pujols; in the centre and south the districts of Targon, Sauveterre, Monségur and La Réole. The southern part of this is the Haut-Benauge region.

There are also enclaves with *appellations* of their own. In the north, across the Dordogne from Libourne, is the small area of the Graves de Vayres, whose white wines can carry that *appellation*, with a maximum output of 43 hl per hectare. The gravelly soil earned them their name, but the wine is less good than Graves. The main market is Germany, where it is often sold as plain Graves and popular because cheap. Output is about 15,000 hl. A little red wine is also produced bearing the same *appellation* (averaging 6,500 hl). On the other end of that part of the Dordogne valley in the Gironde department is the rather larger Ste-Foy, with its *appellation* of Ste-Foy-Bordeaux. Then on the other side of the region and bordering on the Garonne is the thirty-mile-long strip of the Premières Côtes de Bordeaux, which runs downstream to the north of Bordeaux and upstream to the slopes opposite Langon. The old archiepiscopal vineyards in Cenon and Lormont were in what is now the Premières Côtes. Set into this long strip are Loupiac and Ste-Croix-du-Mont, and beyond them the Côtes de Bordeaux-St-Macaire, which hinge on the riverside town of that name.

The best red wine in the area comes from the northern part of the Premières Côtes, for the southern section of that long strip, about thirty miles long but only three to four miles wide, is largely but not exclusively devoted to white wines. To secure the *appellation* the red wine must be at least 10·5 degrees and the white 12. Both may produce up to a basic 40 hl per hectare. The best red wine communes in the Premières Côtes are Camblanes, Quinsac and Cambes; and the best whites come from Monprimblanc and Gabarnac. Average production for the district is 45,000 hl of red and 40,000 of white. For the Côtes de Bordeaux-St-Macaire only the white wines are entitled to that *appellation*, and they are allowed to produce 42 hl per hectare at a minimum strength of 11·5 degrees. Average output is 6,000 hl. They are fairly sweet wines. The reds are ordinary with only the basic Bordeaux *appellations*. Yet in Ste-Foy on the borders of the Dordogne department the large output per hectare of 45 hl is permitted, and the strength of red and white wines is 10·5 and 12 degrees respectively. The white wines are the better, but somewhat heavy and more like those of the Dordogne. Production averages 4,500 hl, including a little red. From the Haut-Benauge area on the Garonne side comes rather ordinary white wine. A new *appellation contrôlée* for Premières Côtes whites was formulated in August 1973: Cadillac. Centred on the Garonne-side town of that name, it includes twenty-two communes of which the best-known are probably Cadillac itself, then Langoiran, Rions and Tabanac. The *cépage* is confined to Sauvignon, Sémillon and Muscadelle, the minimum alcoholic strength must be 12 degrees, and the basic maximum yield is 40 hl per hectare. However, in accordance with the regulations passed in October 1974 this may be increased on the basis of tasting by a further 20 per cent, i.e. a maximum of 48 hl per hectare. Average production is less than 4,000 hl. No doubt the purpose behind the new *appellation* was to raise the standard of production and thus the level of sale in this district.

To complete this statistical picture, the extensive vineyards of the Entre-Deux-Mers are only entitled to that *appellation* for their white wines; the red must be sold as Bordeaux or Bordeaux Supérieur. The somewhat low status of the Entre-Deux-Mers white wines is shown by the fact that up to a basic 50 hl with an 11·5 degree minimum may be produced, while a white Bordeaux Supérieur of the region has to be 11·5 degrees with a 40 hl maximum and fetches a correspondingly higher price. The red Bordeaux can be as low as 10 degrees, and the red Bordeaux Supérieur 10·5 degrees. (But see new *rendement* regulations on p. 651.)

It should be mentioned here that these proletarian wines of Bordeaux and Bordeaux Supérieur *A C* have their own guild – the *Compagnons de Bordeaux*.

It will be seen that these are very much the basic wines of Bordeaux, particularly the whites. It is a reasonably safe assumption that a wine labelled Bordeaux Blanc comes from these parts, and possibly a Bordeaux Rouge also, but either might originate in Bourg or Blaye, where rather low-grade white wine is also grown. Much of the wine made in the geographical Entre-Deux-Mers region is used for blending. As the visitor can see, this is a region of mixed agriculture, with lines of grapes running beside other crops. The attractive countryside is dotted with fine old *manoirs* and farmhouses. A large proportion of the wine is made in the fifteen co-operatives in the Entre-Deux-Mers. One I visited at Romagne, founded in 1936, each year makes 35,000 hl of wine for its 180 members. The largest co-operative in this area makes as much as 120,000 hl; these co-operatives have done much for the survival as well as the improvement of local viticulture. The trend here and in the Premières Côtes is towards red wine, which hitherto has accounted for only about 10 per cent of the output in the region. Soon it might be 20 per cent. The Entre-Deux-Mers white wines are dry, but the Premières Côtes are largely sweet. Most of the former wines are sold without vintage as they do not vary much. An average price of Entre-Deux-Mers in 1979 was 2,550 frs. a *tonneau*, compared with 3,000 frs. for the Premières Côtes. Both look a long way off prices now current in the classed-growth districts. Much of the decline in the Gironde *vignoble* area in the past twenty years has taken place in the Entre-Deux-Mers.

One feature of this part of the world is the high-culture system of vine-growing. This originated in its present form in Austria, where it was developed by Lenz-Moser in vineyards on the Danube near the Wachau. There and in Germany whither it has spread, the system is called after Lenz-Moser. The lines of vines are much more widely spaced than normal and are allowed to grow to a height of four or five feet. The result is that the same quantity is produced from half the number of vines, a useful economy in itself. Also this permits tractors and ploughs to work among the rows. Nearly all planting in the Entre-Deux-Mers district is now being done by the high-culture system, and this may well spread to the other areas of mass-production. However it does call for fairly rich soil, and would not be suitable for the Médoc, or so I was told. Another limiting factor is that the sugar content is slightly reduced, as the moisture on the long grape stalks does not rise so easily. It is said that this high-culture system is in fact a reversion to ancient practice, for in Roman times when the vineyards were hand-worked the vines grew high; only when ploughing with oxen came in were the straight, narrowly spaced rows of low vines introduced.

Over the past generation there has been a decline in the standards of the less fine white Bordeaux. In pre-war days chaptalization was chiefly used to raise the alcoholic strength of a wine that was too light. Each 1·8 kg of sugar per hectolitre will raise the strength by 1 degree, and it is permitted under certain conditions to add a maximum of 3 kg per hectolitre. There is a tax on sugar used for this purpose. After the war the taste for sweet wines spread beyond the borders of France, and as in the Sauternes district across the river such wines were sold by alcoholic strength, the temptation to pile in the sugar was seldom resisted. So white Bordeaux lost its character, became flabbily sweet and disagreeably heavy instead of being fresh. In recent years, however, determined efforts have been made by the *C.I.V.B.* and others to improve the quality, and with some success; the dry wines are generally much crisper.

The move to change this in the Sauternes district has already been mentioned, but this is also needed across the river. One interesting development is a *Cave de Vinification* opened in 1966 at St-Maixant. Run by the Bordeaux firm of Sichel & Co., the object is to buy grapes from neighbouring proprietors and make fresh, dry white wines with plenty of acidity as well as light, fast maturing reds. The white wines, sold under the name of Domaine-de-Belair, are certainly fresh and reasonably priced. The red wines are subjected to a process of carbonic maceration, which is used in the Côtes du Rhône. The whole grapes are put in the vats for four or five days, and

ENTRE-DEUX-MERS AND
CÔTES DE BORDEAUX

BOURGEAIS

Dordogne

Garonne

Carbon-Blanc
Lormont
Vayres
LIBOURNE
ST-ÉMILION
Castillon
Cenon

ENTRE-

STE-FOY-
BORDEAUX
Pujols

Camblanes
Quinsac
Cambes
PREMIÈRES CÔTES DE BORDEAUX
Créon
DEUX-
Romagne
MERS
Targon
Sauveterre
Monségur
Cadillac
Loupiac
Monprimblanc
Gabarnac
La Réole
Langon
Canal
Garonne

0 2 4 6 8 10
Km

BORDEAUX

CÔTES DE
BORDEAUX-ST-MACAIRE

LOUPIAC

STE-CROIX-DU-MONT

PREMIÈRES
CÔTES DE BORDEAUX

STE-FOY-BORDEAUX

ENTRE-DEUX-MERS

CO_2 is added to keep them healthy. The weight of the volume of grapes breaks the skins and the juice flows out. Then the grapes are taken out and pressed before being put back into the vats for another eight days. The result is a fresh, non-tanniny wine that can be bottled in four or five months. The young wine seemed to me to lack some of the Bordeaux character, but after a year or so it should make a fair *vin de table*.

The St-Maixant *cave*, built on the side of a hill to allow for a natural fall of grapes and juice into the fermenting vats, is in a superb situation, and at vintage-time the ripe country looks more like Italy than the Gironde. Adjoining is Ch. Malagar, home of the late François Mauriac, novelist of the region, and from the ridge one can look across the vast Garonne valley with the forest of the Landes a dark line on the horizon. It is an unfortunate fact that few of the best wines are made in the most picturesque surroundings, but there would be much to be said for having a house in the Entre-Deux-Mers and accepting the ordinary wines of the neighbourhood, in the knowledge that the finer bottles of Bordeaux lay at hand for special occasions.

At the extremity of the Bordeaux region in these parts lies the district of Bazas, across the river from St-Macaire and La Réole, and to the east of Langon. Once quite important quantitatively, the Bazadais has long been one of the declining areas of the Gironde. In six or seven communes both red and white wines are one-third Malbec and two-thirds from one of the other 'noble' grapes, Cabernet, Merlot or Petit-Verdot. The white wines are partly made from the Sauvignon and Sémillon grapes, but also from an ordinary variety known as Enrageat. The most interesting feature of Bazas is its cathedral, exceptionally long by French standards, with a nine-bay nave that is rather English-like in relation to the height. There is a fine portal too. During the Wars of Religion the cathedral was badly burnt by the Calvinists.

17. The Classification of the Médoc

Beginning his chapter with the same heading in French as above, Wilhelm Franck, writing before the famous 1855 classification, starts off with: 'Now we arrive at the most delicate section of our work.' This remains true today, for while there are many who say that the classification is irrelevant, meaningless or outdated, it is a factor still to be taken into consideration in any survey of Bordeaux. That the grading remains a subject of controversy is the best demonstration that it still counts for something; and the value of some kind of classification is shown by the fact that in recent years the leading Graves and the St-Émilions have been classified. I have heard no voices to suggest this should not have been done, although there are those who maintain that they should have been included in a comprehensive new classification embracing all the fine red wine areas.

For about the white wines there is little controversy. The urge for promotion and change is not apparent among the Sauternais who received recognition in 1855, and if the omission of Haut-Brion Blanc in the Graves Classification of 1959 caused a stir, this exclusion was at the owner's request. So this chapter is almost exclusively concerned with the red wines. However, in spite of the title, it is impossible to discuss the Médocs in isolation from the wines of the other leading red wine districts of Bordeaux.

The origins of the Médoc classification are not clear, but it existed at least a century before 1855 and probably earlier, and the essential point was that class was based on price. It was not the reputation of estate or owner, the size or style of the château which counted, but the hard commercial facts as they existed on the Bordeaux market. I suspect that this classification began largely as a matter of convenience for the trade. By grouping the vineyards in classes – there were originally only four – it was easier to establish a price-structure for the roughly fifty to sixty best growths of the Médoc. Both the long standing of the classification and its basis are confirmed in letters written in 1823 by Lamothe, the *régisseur* of Latour, to the proprietors and quoted by Pijassou in his chapter in *Bordeaux au XVIIIe siècle* (1968). 'It is the trade itself which fixed the prices and formed the different classes of the wines of the Médoc a very long time ago.' He also referred to the fact that the relation of prices between the first and second growths had been established by the trade 'more than a hundred years ago'. Pijassou regards this as a slight exaggeration and dates its beginnings as between 1725 and 1735.

Also included was Haut-Brion, probably the senior of the first growths, for the Graves had been the original centre of Bordeaux wine growing; but other red Graves such as La Mission-Haut-Brion and Pape-Clément seem either to have been in a period of recession or were few enough not to have caused difficulty in pricing. There is a record of Haut-Brion being sold to the English in 1684 at 400–450 livres a *tonneau*, while other red wines (? of the Graves) only fetched 84 livres.

That some sort of classification existed by the mid-eighteenth century is shown by the fact that there was a fixed scale of prices for all the growths in each class, with an equal step between each. No doubt the quality of wine produced by individual vineyards caused periodic variations from the norm, but in the eighteenth and early nineteenth centuries there seems to have been much more uniformity of price in each class than exists today. Nor does there appear to have been any substantial movement from class to class. If not the good God, then the Bordeaux brokers made them high or lowly and ordered their estate. The classification probably grew up gradually, and without any preconceived idea that there should be so many different classes within it. The earliest reference I have found is a report dated 1730 and quoted by André Simon in *Bottlescrew Days* (1926). In this report are mentioned three principal classes of red wine. 'The first comprises the growths of Pontac, Lafitte and Château de Margo, which produce as a rule only about three hundred tuns a year; this is, however, the wine most highly esteemed of the province and it usually sells for 1,200 to 1,500 livres per tun. It is the English who buy the greater part of this wine.' After that came 'a very large number' of second-class growths, selling for 300–500 livres, and exported to England, Ireland, Scotland, Holland and Hamburg. Then there were the third class which went to northern France for 100–200 livres. Finally were mentioned the 'unclassified' wines of the '*Palu*', the 'fine' costing 150–180 livres per tun, and the 'big' going for 90–100 livres. The first were bought in Holland, England, America and northern France; and the latter in America and Brittany.

Further, according to the Archives of the Gironde department, referred to by Pijassou, in the years 1735–40 the four *premiers crus* achieved the highest prices on the Bordeaux market; rarely below 800–900 livres a *tonneau*, more commonly they sold for 1,200–1,800 livres, and even reached a peak of 2,000 livres. This is attributed to the fact that they were owned by the rich Parlement families, able to spend money on improving their profitable estates.

The first organized though not official classification arose from two reports addressed to the intendant by members of the Chamber of Commerce about 1750. It was called: *Tableau des paroisses d'où viennent les vins de Bordeaux et leurs différents prix*. Price, as will be seen, was an in-built feature; it is worth examining how this was worked out. The red Graves were included, and the leading growth of Pontac (Haut-Brion) was rated at 1,500–2,000 frs. per *tonneau*. It was, however, based much more on communes than on particular growths, although that too was considered. For example the leading wines of Pauillac and Margaux fetched 1,500–1,800 frs. Yet the wine of M. de Ségur (Lafite), although fetching at least as much as 1,500–1,800 livres, could sell for 2,000. The wines of St-Julien, St-Mambert, Cantenac and St-Seurin de Cadourne made 800–1,200 livres, the same price as the wines of Pessac other than Haut-Brion. It is interesting to see the 'border' commune of Haut-Médoc, St-Seurin, included among the leaders, for even a hundred years later its wines were not highly regarded. St-Mambert, later called St-Lambert, is the small commune lying between St-Julien and Pauillac. Latour and Pichon-Lalande were at one time not Pauillacs but St-Lamberts; we may be thankful for the take-over, with one less commune-name to grapple with.

The second-growth communes were Soussans and Labarde, whose wines were worth 600 livres a *tonneau*; Ludon (Agassac, 400–500 livres); Arsac, Arcins, Listrac and Moulis (400 livres). At the lowest level in the Médoc were St-Laurent, St-Estèphe, Le Pian, Macau and Ludon (300–400 livres); and the Gradignan and Cadaujac growths even less, at 200–300 livres. These low prices for the Graves demonstrate their comparative obscurity in the eighteenth century.

Malvezin reprints a list from the intendants' archives, giving a classification as in 1767. It is very similar to the slightly earlier one. The price is by commune, and there are three classes apiece for the red Graves and the Médoc, and two each for the *vins de palus*, which include the Fronsadais and the white wines. In addition to the sweet wine communes, Blanquefort is included among the first white wine growths, but these only fetched 300 livres. A note records that 36 communes in what was then the *Sénéchaussée* of Bordeaux made wine only for distillation into *eau-de-vie*. Also the St-Émilion wines were normally sold only on the home market.

That there was an accepted classification by the last quarter of the eighteenth century is shown by the notes that Thomas Jefferson, United States Commissioner and Minister in France, made after a tour of southern France in 1787. He visited Bordeaux in May of that year, and with his usual industry and attention to detail wrote the following report on the classed growths.

There are 4 vineyards of first quality, viz. 1. Château Margau, belonging to the Marquis d'Agicourt, who makes about 150 *tonneaux* of 1,000 bottles each. He has engaged to Jernon a merchant. 2. La Tour de Segur, en Saint Lambert, belonging to Monsieur Miromésnil, who makes 125 *tonneaux*. 3. Hautbrion, belonging 2/3 to M. le Comte de Femelle [Fumel], who has engaged to Barton a merchant, the other 1/3 to the Comte de Toulouse. The whole is 75 *tonneaux*. 4. Chateau de la Fite, belonging to the President Pichard at Bordeaux who makes 175 *tonneaux*. The wines of the three first are not in perfection till 4 years old. Those [of] de la Fite, being somewhat lighter, are good at 3 years, that is the crop of 1786 is good in the spring of 1789. These growths of the year 1783 sell now at 2000 l. the *tonneaux*, those of 1784 on account of the superior quality of that vintage, sell at 2400 l., those of 1785 at 1800 l., those of 1786 at 1800 l., tho they sold at first for only 1500 l.

He goes on to mention the '2nd quality wines:

as Rozan, Dabbadie or Lionville, la Rose, Quirouen, Durfort; in all 800 *tonneaux* which sell at 1000 l. new.

The 3d. class are Calons, Mouton, Gassie, Anboete, Pontette, de Terme, Candale; in all 2000 *tonneaux* at 8 or 900 l.

After these they are reckoned common wines and sell from 500 l. down to 120 l. the tun. All red wines decline after a certain age, losing colour, flavour and body. Those of Bordeaux begin to decline at about 7 years old.

While in Bordeaux Jefferson sent a relative in America six dozen 'of what is the very best Bordeaux wine. It is of the vineyard Obrion, one of the four established as the very best, and it is of the vintage of 1784, the only very fine one since the year 1779'.

Jernon (Gernon), the merchant who took and sold the wine of Ch. Margaux, was one of the English traders of the time.

From Jefferson's description of the state of readiness of the first growths it would appear that for the most part they must have been drunk very soon after bottling.

Jefferson's own purchases throw an interesting light on the predominance of the first growths even before the Revolution. He bought Ch. Margaux 1784 and wrote:

It is the best vintage that has happened in nine years, and is one of the four vineyards which are admitted to possess exclusively the first reputation. I may safely assure you therefore that, according to the taste of this country and of England, there cannot be a bottle of better Bordeaux produced in France. It cost me at Bordeaux three livres a bottle, ready bottled and packed. This is very dear.

In February 1788 he wrote to Président Pichard asking to buy 250 bottles of La Fite 1784, asking him to put it in bottle and '*emballer chez vous*', as this would be a guarantee that the wine was natural and the racking, etc. had been well done. He also requested that while in France and after his return to America he might apply to him for his wines.

The letter was sent on to Pichard at Libourne, as the Parlement was then situated there, but in April the Président replied that he had no '*vin de Laffite*' 1784 left, and though he would like to serve Jefferson in future he only had the 1786 which was not yet drinkable.

The American Consul in Bordeaux, J. Bondfield, in enclosing this negative reply, mentioned that the 'vins d'Hautbrion, belonging to Monsr. le Comte de Fumel' were esteemed as next in quality and a few hogsheads of the 1784 were still available. Thereupon Jefferson settled for 125 bottles of this wine. However, it turned out that the Comte only retained 4 hogsheads of the 1784, and refused an offer of 600 livres for 1 hogshead, so Jefferson was to have two cases (more than a dozen and probably 50 bottles apiece) of the first hogshead bottled.

Bondfield added, 'It is urging and too much to pay three

livres in Bordeaux for a Bottle of Bordeaux Wine, but so great has been the demand for that Vintage that the holders obtain that exorbitant price.' Three livres were about the equivalent in English money then of 2s. 6d.

Shortly before the Revolution, according to André Simon, the prices per *tonneau* of the Médocs were as follows:

1st growths – 1,600–2,400 livres	3rd growths – 900–1,400 livres
2nd growths – 1,300–2,100 livres	4th growths – 600–850 livres
Other Médocs – 400–500 livres	

The range of prices in each class reflected variations in the quality of the vintages.

André Simon gives the English prices per hogshead (*barrique*) of the classed growths at the end of the eighteenth century as being:

1st growths – £24	3rd growths – £18
2nd growths – £20	4th growths – £12

Then Wilhelm Franck, in the first edition of his *Traité sur les vins du Médoc* (1824), in an appendix to a table of Bordeaux prices from 1782 to 1823, lists by communes the prices of the red wines of the 'good years of 1745, etc.' Some communes have four classes, others fewer. Margaux and Cantenac, bracketed together, are given first and Château Margaux is the single *premier cru* (1,500–1,800 livres a *tonneau*). Then follow eight seconds, including familiar names such as 'Rosan ainé' and Durfort (1,000–1,300 livres), twelve thirds (600–1,000 livres) and nine fourths (400–600 livres). Growths are listed in seven other communes, including Labarde, Macau, St-Julien, St-Lambert, Pauillac, St-Estèphe and St-Seurin-de-Cadourne, in that order. They all have a *premier cru* but at very different prices. For example, the one in Macau is Villeneuve (Cantemerle), but its price is only 300 livres. Giscours, the top wine of Labarde, is in the 1,500–1,800 livres price-bracket, while Brane-Mouton, the only named second growth is, surprisingly, only priced at 400–600 livres, while Pichon-Longueville in St-Lambert is 400–500 livres.

Interesting too is a list of six red Graves communes, which include Pessac, Mérignac, Caudéran, Taillan and Blanquefort (these last two now the southern 'frontier' communes of the Médoc), Léognan and Gradignan. Haut-Brion is the only first growth of Pessac, in the 1,500–1,800 livres price range, followed by La Mission and Savignac as seconds, with the surprisingly high price of 1,200–1,300 livres. There are two thirds, one belonging to Mme Sabourin (800–1,200 livres) and Giac (500–800 livres). Three fourths follow, and even Mérignac, now largely lost to wine under the developers' excavators and the aircraft runways, has three classes, headed by Bouran (500–800 livres). Of the others only Caudéran has any growths mentioned and Léognan, esteemed today, sold for 300–400 livres only.

A further note by Franck shows that the price of Château Margaux in 1822 was the same as in 1722, 2,500 livres (frs.). Its output averaged 100–120 *tonneaux*. The stability of Bordeaux wine prices over very long periods is difficult to understand in these inflationary times. In 1824 Lafite commonly secured the top price, followed by Latour and Margaux in that order.

The prices given above are, of course, growers' prices, i.e. what they received for their wines when sold to the merchants in Bordeaux. The latter, responsible for the expenses of stockholding and sale, have traditionally secured a good margin on their purchases. From the point of view of merchants' prices to their trade customers at home and abroad, as well as from that of the classification, a price list of Beyerman of this period is doubly interesting. The date is probably 1828, for the red wines of 1825 and 1826 are offered, and the whites of 1827. As the prices show, 1825 was a far better vintage than 1826, and the wines were, of course, a year older at the time of offer. The main listings are as follows:

Vins Rouges	1825	1826
	frs.	frs.
1 *Crus*, Ch. Margaux, Latour, Lafite, Ch. Haut-Brion	6,000	2,000–2,100
2 *Crus*, Rauzan, Léoville, Larose, Branne-Mouton	5,500–5,700	1,600–1,800
3 *Crus*, Kirwan, Pichon-de-Longueville, Ch. d'Issan, etc.	4,800–5,200	1,200–1,300
4 & 5 *Crus ou Bourgeois supérieurs* de Margaux, St-Julien, Pauillac, St-Estèphe	4,200–4,400	700–1,100
Bons Bourgeois de Médoc	3,500–3,800	500–600
Bourgeois Ordinaires de Médoc	1,900–2,800	360–400
Graves, Pessac, Talence, etc.	1,800–3,000	400–850
Graves, Pessac, Talence, *Ordinaires*	700–800	—
St-Émilion & Canon *1er qualité*	800–900	380–400
St-Émilion & Canon *2e & 3e qualité*	650–750	300–330
Bonnes Côtes & Bonnes Palus	400–450	—

Vins Blancs		
Haut-Preignac, Ht. Barsac, Bommes, Sauternes	900–1,200–2,600	500–800
Bas Preignac, Bas Barsac	600–700	400–425
Cérons, Ste-Croix, Dumont, Loupiac, et St-Pey, Langon, Fargues, Virelade, Landiras, etc.	450–700	280–425

The spelling of the names is as on the list. It is interesting in particular to note the relatively small difference in prices between the 1825 classed growths, and their relation to the other wines. Also the relatively low prices of the best Graves and the very modest position of the St-Émilions are shown. At this period Beyerman was part-proprietor of Haut-Brion.

It will be observed that the prices of the 1825s, although a distinguished vintage, were high in relation to the likely cost of the wines at source. Franck in 1824 was listing the average growers' prices for the three Médoc *premiers crus* as 2,300–

2,400 frs. a *tonneau*, and 2,000–2,100 frs. for the same four *deuxièmes* as offered by Beyerman. For the eight *troisièmes*, which included Gorse, Pichon-de-Longueville, Cos, Calon, Lascombes and Bergeron (St-Julien), the growers' prices were 1,500–1,800 frs., while for the 18 *quatrièmes*, headed by Kirwan and ended by Boyd, they were 1,200–1,400. There were no *cinquièmes* in Franck's list of 33 classed growths. Neither in his list nor in the merchant's did the first growths then greatly exceed the seconds in price.

Franck makes clear that at this period the first growths went to England. Of Latour he wrote that the English were the biggest buyers, and of Lafite 'nearly all is drunk in England'. 'The English also normally buy all the other *premiers crus* of this commune' (Pauillac).

The fifth class gradually evolved from the fourth, which at one time was divided into the first fourths and the second fourths. Franck in the first edition of his book (1824) in listing the prices of the classed and other growths from 1782 to 1823 gives the same prices for what were to be fourth and fifth growths, but in later editions shows them separately and at different average prices. A. L. Henderson in his *The History of Ancient and Modern Wines* (1824) lists five classes in tables of prices for the 1815, 1818 and 1822 vintages. Three firsts sold for 3,100 frs. and six seconds at 2,300 frs. Then follow six in the next rank, including Malescot, Castelnau, Brane-Cantenac, Gorse, Pichon-de-Longueville and Cabarrus (Lagrange) at 1,800 frs.; a fourth rank, including Giscours, Pouget and Laujac at 1,400–1,500 frs.; and a fifth and final one, with Pontet-Canet and St-Guiron (Grand-Puy-Lacoste) at 1,200 frs. A long way below these comes St-Émilion at 500–600 frs. and Sauternes and Barsac at 650–800 frs. Some of the Médoc prices look very high.

It would be wearisome to follow all the price variations over the years up to 1855, and a selection taken from the more successful vintages will be found in Appendix C. The essential factor in each vintage was the basic price of the first growths; the others then fell into line. In general the norm in the 1820s and 1830s in a good year was 2,400–3,000 frs. a *tonneau* for the first growths, and then a descending scale of 300 frs. less per class; so the fifth growths sold at half the price of the first. However, there was so much variation in this that it was only a rough guide, and as the century advanced, the first growths tended to draw ahead of the others, as has happened much more dramatically in the past dozen years. Henderson mentions that the four first growths fetched 20–25 per cent more than any other wines of the region, and also says that Brane-Mouton sold for one-third less than Lafite. These differences, however, varied from vintage to vintage, and according to whether or not a vineyard made particularly good wine in a certain year. Although Lafite usually headed the list, in the excellent vintage of 1831 Latour's price was 2,600 frs. a *tonneau*, compared with 2,400 frs. for Lafite, 2,100 frs. for Mouton and 2,500 frs. for Rausan-Ségla. It was rare, nevertheless, for a second growth to challenge a first growth in price.

Perhaps before 1855 the classes were less rigid, because unofficial. For example, Cyrus Redding in 1833 says:

The wines are classed by the brokers, who decide to which class the wine of each grower shall belong. The latter use all their efforts to place their wines in a higher class, and thus emulation is kindled, and they are justified in their efforts by the profits. The price of their wines, too, is less governed by particular merit, than by the number they occupy in the scale of classification. It often costs them sacrifices to reach that object. They will keep their wine many years to give it a superior title, instead of selling it the first year according to custom. By this means an individual will get his wine changed from the fourth to the third class, which he had perhaps occupied before for many successive years.

However, it is not clear that any proprietors were successful in their efforts but if the 1855 classification had been similarly flexible, who can doubt that Bordeaux would have been occupied with a non-stop game of snakes-and-ladders ever since?

That the pre-1855 classifications were not closed corporations, as their successors turned out, is shown by the admission of Montrose and Palmer in the 1820s, when these vineyards were new and their wine young. Montrose, partly carved out of Calon's estate, was generally accepted as a second growth in 1825, and Palmer, based on Gascq, a third about the same time. However, allowing for changes of name and some variations in grading, the pre-1855 lists, as printed by Franck in his 1853 edition, are surprisingly similar to those set forth for the Paris Exhibition of 1855. Franck was careful to print his list of seconds to fifths in alphabetical order, to avoid controversy that was evidently as brisk then as later, but the only omissions from his list of second growths were Montrose and Ducru, both then placed as thirds. The third-growth list, with this pair added and Palmer subtracted, is little different from 1855, allowing for some changes of name, and one or two other relegations, including Calon and La Lagune, to the fourth class. Here and in the fifth growths the pattern is a little more confused, but the well-known estates such as Beychevelle, Talbot, St-Pierre and Duhart-Milon are there; and among the bottom rank the variations between the pre- and post-1855 listings are surprisingly small, although Château Popp may not immediately be recognized as Camensac. There are one or two outsiders in the list, notably La Mission 'près Haut-Brion', with the surprisingly small output of 30–40 *tonneaux*, compared with 80–90 today. Also Liversan and Monpelou are now no longer classed growths. It is interesting to see Cantemerle listed in 1853; it was not sold generally on the Bordeaux market but exported to Holland *en totalité*.

Too often the 1855 classification has by inference been presented either as the beginning of things, rather like the Creation; or, to use another biblical simile, like the Tablets of the Law, handed down by the brokers of Bordeaux to the Médocain proprietors assembled on the Quai des Chartrons – with Haut-Brion's owner smuggled in on the old-boy network. As will have been seen already, the 1855 was no more produced suddenly out of thin air than Man was created in Seven Days. It was little more than a codification of previous practice and classification. Devised on the occasion of the Universal Exposition of Paris in 1855, and carried out by the Syndicate of Brokers, it was then endorsed by the Bordeaux Chamber of Commerce, which was careful to point out that 'this classification has been sanctioned by experience extending back more than a century'. It included twenty-two Sauternes and Barsacs in addition to the sixty-odd Médocs and the solitary Haut-Brion from the Graves. Ostensibly the classification was of the Gironde, but in fact with this one exception the red wines were confined to the Médoc, the whites to Sauternes and Barsac and so the claret list is here throughout conveniently called a Médoc one.

What was fresh, however, was a new or at least newly formalized order of the growths in the classification. Whereas Franck in the appendix to his first edition had thought alphabetical order by commune was the better part of valour – so he put Ch. Margaux of Margaux at the head of the firsts, Haut-Brion as an outsider being tacked on at the end of this class – the brokers boldly placed the growths, red and white, in order if not of merit then certainly of price. So Lafite is at the top of the firsts and Mouton-Rothschild, however unwillingly later, leads the seconds.

This order of precedence continues throughout the list, demonstrating that they considered Rausan-Ségla superior to its neighbour Rauzan-Gassies, the Baron to the Comtesse of Pichon-Longueville and Grand-Puy-Lacoste to Grand-Puy-Ducasse. They may or may not have been right at the time, but that is how they saw it. The only errors on their showing at the time may have been the classification of Palmer as a third and the placing of Cantemerle at the bottom of the whole list; for the former was in the hands of receivers, and the latter was normally sold on the Bordeaux market only the year before the classification, so therefore there was no list of prices to use as a guide. But even this is only speculation. In Appendix C will be found representative classed-growth prices in some of the more important vintages.

It is a highly debatable point whether the 1855 classification has been of assistance to Bordeaux or to the consumer; but it has certainly helped the châteaux at the head of the list. The immediate result was a widening of the price differential between the first growths and the rest. D'Armailhacq in the third edition of his treatise *De la culture des vignes* (1867) comments that between 1855 and 1865 the first-growth prices rose from 2,800 to 5,600 frs. but the seconds only from 1,500 to 2,100 frs. and the fifths from 900 to 1,300 frs. It appears that the new 'official' classification may have done no more than hasten and emphasize a trend already in existence.

It is probably true that the first growths have helped indirectly to raise above those of the non-classed properties the prices of the seconds and of all the classed growths, but whether this has been beneficial is again arguable. The *crus bourgeois* have probably secured less than their worth, and some at least of the *crus classés* have from time to time been 'carried' by their classmates. They still are. Moreover the rigidity of the 1855 classification over more than a century has removed even the theoretical incentive to betterment mentioned by Redding prior to 1855. So far as I am aware none of the Médoc classed growths below *premier cru* level advertise their rank in the classification on their labels except Issan, a third growth, unlike the army of *premiers crus* in St-Émilion and Pomerol; and Lafite, 'first of the firsts', apparently scorns to do so. Indeed, so far as the consumers are concerned, there is little evidence of class-consciousness, except for the first growths.

However this has not prevented periodic skirmishes in the

Médoc class war, particularly from the Rothschilds of Mouton. In the description of Lafite, reference was made to the desire of Baron Ferdinand, the new owner of Mouton, to become a *premier cru*, and to the fact that he felt he would be helped to do this if he were able to acquire the portion of the Carruades that Lafite was purporting to sell. (Mouton has always owned two-thirds of the Carruades.) In fact it would seem as if the ambition for Mouton to become a first growth only developed when the Rothschilds secured it in 1853. Only three years later M. Goudal at Lafite wrote to Sir Samuel Scott that 'after being informed that Larose, a second growth, had sold at 4,000 frs., I suspect that the Baron de Rothschild would have much higher claims for his Moutons'. Goudal had told the broker Merman that before he fixed the price of Lafite he wanted to know Mouton's, for he knew that Merman had bought it. (In fact the brokers only acted for their merchant clients.) Merman affected not to know, so Goudal asked 6,000 frs. for Lafite, but said he would take the highest offer. This was made by Tastet at 5,700 frs. and Goudal settled for that. In fact Mouton had sold for 5,000 frs., as Goudal delightedly reported to his master: 'You will have heard with pleasure, I hope, the revenge we have taken on the Baron de Rothschild.' He went on to say that it was the opinion of all the old brokers of Bordeaux that too much had been paid for Mouton, and it was one of the youngest who had bought it. M. N. Johnston was associated with the Baron,

and to give pleasure to this banker (certainly with interest), he is helping him in his plan to place his growth at the rank of the firsts; this will be difficult unless M. Johnston wishes to continue to squander money. Rely on me, Monsieur, to maintain the reputation of our flag. You see that has not taken long to arrive.

Then in 1867 Charles Lorbac, in his description of Mouton in *Les Richesses gastronomiques de la France*, says the question of making Mouton a first growth had been raised, for it always sold for more than the other seconds. Docteur Aussel in *La Gironde à vol d'oiseau; ses grands vins et ses châteaux* (1865) wrote of Mouton: 'this growth tends to achieve the first rank'.

Then Alfred Danflou in *Les Grands Crus Bordelais* (1867) writes somewhat rhetorically that he is convinced the classification is not definitive and the syndicate of brokers will be called to render justice to those growths which have risen to a rank they lacked at the time of classification. At one time, he continues, were not wines of Bourg the leaders, and eighty years previously some growths, scarcely known today, had a European reputation. He instances La Bégorce, Gorse, Prévôt de Lecroize in Margaux, Dubosc in St-Julien, Liversan in St-Sauveur and Angludet in Cantenac.

It may well be that Danflou had been listening to the complaints of Mouton, for he rather goes out of his way to depreciate the established *premiers crus*. According to him, Margaux was the only first with a reputation in the seventeenth century, Lafite was little known until the end of the reign of Louis XIV (d. 1715), while Latour and Haut-Brion's position dated in reality only from the end of the eighteenth century. This last point is certainly not true, as we have seen. He concludes by suggesting that Lafite and Latour might pay a public tribute to Mouton, state that the public considers it their equal and then admit it to parity. For good measure Danflou suggests that some unnamed other growths might also become firsts. (Seconds he particularly praises are Rausan, Léoville and Larose.)

According to Danflou, Mr Scott, described as one of the most important members of the Bordelais trade and presumably Scott the Consul, as well as M. Merman, the well-known broker, who were both members of the jury at the 1862 London Exhibition (when Cheval-Blanc secured its still label-publicized bronze medal), stated that Mouton above all equalled them (the first growths) in many years.

In the famous vintage of 1858 Mouton, Lafite and Haut-

Brion all sold for the same price – 4,000 frs. – but Margaux, which had a special reputation *en primeur* fetched 5,000 frs. and Latour 4,800. Among the seconds Léoville-Poyferré made 3,500 frs.

In 1865 Mouton sold for 4,000 frs., compared with 2,750 for Palmer and 2,400 for Léoville-Barton. But Lafite, bought by a syndicate of six Bordeaux merchants, fetched 5,600 frs. However, it is not easy to compare prices at this period, because it was not uncommon for a merchant to make a contract for five or ten years to buy the crop each year, irrespective of quality. Obviously such a speculation on the part of a Bordeaux merchant or group of merchants meant a lower price for the best years, so from 1863 to 1872 Margaux was sold for 4,200 frs. to an English syndicate of three merchants: J. Alnutt, Trowers & Lawson, and Boord, Son & Beckwith. The terms of this contract, which had been negotiated by a Mr Clarke, were not disclosed, but in Bordeaux no deals remain secret for very long, and not only did the price emerge, but also the fact that in a crop averaging 130 *tonneaux* the first wine was sold for £42 per *barrique* and the second wine for £21.

At the height of the pre-phylloxera golden era, the 1868 edition of Cocks et Féret included a table (see page 513) showing the relative prices of the various classes of the excellent 1865 vintage, both *en primeur* and two years later. Mouton, as will be noted, is singled out from the second growths. Also the lower classes appreciated proportionately more in price than the first growths.

These prices do not always coincide with those given for Mouton and Palmer above, taken from Tastet & Lawton's records, which of course reflect their own dealings. Other prices given in this chapter and elsewhere are subject to normal market variations, but show the general trend. Cocks et Féret commented in 1868 that the first growths fetched about 25 per cent more than the seconds, the fifths always sold more or less at half the price of the seconds, while the thirds and fourths were roughly half-way between the seconds and the fifths. These rough approximations made business much easier.

	En primeur	Le 16 Novembre 1867
1ers Crus	5,600 frs.	7,000–8,000 frs.
2e Cru Mouton	3,500	5,500–6,000
2es Crus autres	2,500–2,600	5,000–5,500
3es Crus	1,900	3,600–4,000
4es Crus	1,500–1,600	3,000–3,400
5es Crus	1,200–1,400	2,500–2,800
Bourgeois supérieurs	1,000–1,200	1,800–2,000

Broadly speaking up to the phylloxera period Lafite generally secured the top price, which was sometimes equalled by the other first growths but not by Mouton. But the latter was, nevertheless, much more expensive than any of the other seconds, and usually by more than 1,000 frs. a *tonneau*. In 1874, for example, Mouton was sold immediately after the vintage for 4,200 frs. and its nearest rival among the seconds was Gruaud-Larose-Sarget at 3,000. Yet Lafite went for 5,500 frs. and Latour for 5,000.

After the phylloxera Lafite appears to have gone through a bad period, with one or other of the other first growths securing higher prices. For example, in 1890 Latour made 4,100 and Margaux 4,000 frs., compared with 3,000 for Lafite, and in the great year of 1899 Haut-Brion achieved the top price of 2,600 frs., followed by Margaux at 2,200, and Latour and Lafite at 2,000. But Mouton was in a disappointing patch too, so far as opening prices were concerned. According to the Tastet & Lawton records, the 1890 Mouton was not sold until 1894 and then for a knock-down price of 2,000 frs. while the 1899 only went for 1,800. Later, however, the reckoning might have been different, as Mouton-Rothschild 1899 turned out one of the finest '99s.

During the first twenty years of the present century prices

of the first growths in comparison with others are difficult to compare, because it was a period of extensive contract-making. In the golden vintage epoch from 1858 to 1878 the contracting proprietors probably did less well than the merchants, but in the poor succesion of vintages after 1900, the boot was on the other foot. For trade was not very good. Mouton was the monopoly of Calvet between 1907 and 1912, but the 1913 was so poor that Calvet refused it, and the contract ended. Lafite from 1907 to 1916 was the monopoly of Rosenheim and Lebègue, and then of Rosenheim alone. Both the other Médoc first growths made contracts for the same decade, Margaux with Schröder & Schÿler and Eschenauer, and Latour with Mestrezat and others.

The contract price for Mouton paid by Calvet was identical with the first growths: 1,650 frs. a *tonneau*. Whatever was the assessment earlier, in this century and particularly since 1920 or thereabouts, Mouton-Rothschild as a wine has, I believe it is fair to say, generally received the same regard as the wines classed as *premiers crus* in 1855, and often better, as the twenties were not the best period for all the latter.

In 1917, a dismal war year, most of the leaders renewed their contracts for five years, for an increased price of 2,650 frs. Eschenauer and Calvet headed the Lafite group, Calvet the Margaux, while Ginestet had the monopoly of Latour for 1917 and 1918 only. As a result several of these first growths, committed to 2,650 frs., did not receive very satisfactory prices for the fine 1920s while third-growth Palmer secured 4,500 frs. After that the monopoly/contract system declined, although Rosenheim had a monopoly of Haut-Brion in 1929. While it lasted this contract system distorted the price structure, for the *premiers crus* which had tended to set the pace were largely out of the running. At the retail stage the first growths, with which Mouton must now be classed in common parlance, were not much more expensive than the runners-up.

In the 1920s the franc ran into difficulties and prices in terms of money rose sharply. The 1926s were the most expensive red Bordeaux ever sold up to that date, for the crop was small and the franc revalued. All the leaders reached upwards of 40,000 frs., while Palmer went for 23,000. As a result this vintage was little bought in Britain and therefore seldom seen later. The '28s made up to 20,000 frs. for the leaders.

Sample prices of the famous '29s opened as follows:

First Growths	20,000 frs.	Cantemerle	9,000 frs.
Gruaud-Larose-Faure	12,000	Léoville-Barton	8,000
Léoville-Poyferré	11,000	Léoville-Las-Cases	11,000
Brane-Cantenac	10,000	Gruaud-Larose-Sarget	7,500
Beychevelle	10,000	Langoa	7,500
Pontet-Canet	9,000		

I quote a number of these opening prices as they demonstrate that position in the classification was now far less important than the estimated quality of the wine, although Léoville-Poyferré, as indicated in the chapter on vintages, was exceptionally fine and superior to most of the *premiers crus* as well as to Gruaud-Larose-Faure. This was the year of the New York Stock Exchange crash which in October 1929 heralded the world slump as the young wines were still in the fermenting vats. Within eighteen months the first-growth '29s could be re-bought for 10,000 frs., exactly half their opening prices. Not until after the Second World War were classed-growth prices to recover.

If time brought a readjustment of certain châteaux's standing, the surprising thing was that the classification by and large had retained so much of its validity after three-quarters of a century; and this is still true today. The subsequent downgrading of some growths may well be owing more to bad husbandry than to anything else; and the reverse applies. Yet in the mysterious way that certain vineyards are esteemed all over the world, it is situation and soil which count first.

Although I have devoted some attention to the question of

Mouton because it was the most obvious anomaly, and the one most felt by a proprietor, this is not the only one; and after the last war voices began to be heard suggesting a reorganization of the 1855 classification or an entirely new one. Some merely proposed changes in the Médoc growths, with or without accessions from the leading *crus bourgeois*.

This category of *bourgeois* growth appears to be of indeterminate origin. Franck in 1853 lists seven *bons bourgeois*, following the fifth class, and fetching between 700 and 1,000 frs., according to quality. These were, as described by him:

Growth	Commune
Bel-Air	Soussans
Paveil	Soussans
Le Boscq	St-Estèphe
Cru-de-Morin	St-Corbian, St-Estèphe
Lanessan	Cussac
Pédesclaux	Pauillac
Tronquoy-Lalande	St-Estèphe

Of these the first is now Bel-Air-Marquis-d'Aligre, the second is the well-known Paveil de Luze. There is a Morin in St-Estèphe, but it is not outstanding nowadays. Franck admits that his list of *bons bourgeois* is not comprehensive, and also mentions La Tour-de-Mons of Soussans, and Pommiers and Morange of Ludon. The former of this Ludon pair appears not to exist now, but in 1853 it had a solid reputation in Holland, like the neighbouring Cantemerle. The second edition of Cocks et Féret's *Bordeaux et ses vins* (1868) makes no such distinction among the better *crus bourgeois*.

Later on a category of *cru exceptionnel* was developed, but although no doubt similar in standing to the *bons bourgeois* was no more constant. In the 1929 Cocks et Féret it was limited to three – Bel-Air-Marquis-d'Aligre, Chasse-Spleen and Villegeorge. In 1932 what might be called an unofficial market classification of these *exceptionnels* was made by

Bordeaux brokers at the request of owners of *crus bourgeois*, but was repudiated. The title itself was not well received, as one might consider an 'exceptional' growth superior to a mere 'first'. The selection too was controversial, but here it is:

Growth	Commune
Angludet	Cantenac
Villegeorge	Avensan
Bel-Air-Marquis-d'Aligre	Soussans
Chasse-Spleen	Moulis
Moulin-Riche	St-Julien
La Couronne	Pauillac

In the authoritative Larmat maps of Bordeaux issued in 1944, Villegeorge, then in partial eclipse, was not in the list.

Several other minor 'orders' came into being many years ago: *cru bourgeois supérieur du Haut-Médoc*; *cru bourgeois du Haut-Médoc*; and *cru bourgeois du Médoc*. This last applied to the Bas-Médoc. At the same time there were *crus paysans* and *crus artisans*. More recently, however, the peasantry was wiped out, though the artisans were spared. However even the *crus artisans* disappeared in the 1969 edition of Cocks et Féret; all are Principaux Propriétaires now. To complete this *bourgeois* revolution, it only remained to ennoble some of the *haute bourgeoisie* or, in Bordeaux terms, the *bourgeoisie supérieure*.

During the last world war a significant official price grading, carried out in 1943, at the Vichy Government's order, by the National Syndicate of the wine trade, gave some idea of how the classed growths then stood in relation to each other and to the rest of the Bordeaux estates. The purpose of this was to establish maximum prices at which these wines could be sold per *tonneau* of 900 litres. From a list running to 26 pages I take a few examples of interest.

		frs.
Médoc	Lafite (and other first growths)	100,000
,,	Mouton-Rothschild	100,000

		frs.
Graves	Haut-Brion	100,000
St-Émilion	Ausone	100,000
,,	Cheval-Blanc	100,000
Graves	La Mission-Haut-Brion	88,000
Médoc	Other second growths	80,000
Pomerol	Pétrus	80,000
Graves	Haut-Bailly and Domaine de Chevalier	80,000
Médoc	Third growths (Giscours, La Lagune and Palmer)	75,000
,,	Fourth growths (Beychevelle and Branaire-Ducru)	75,000
St-Émilion	Canon, La Gaffelière and Clos Fourtet, etc.	75,000
Pomerol	Vieux-Ch.-Certan, Certan, La Conseillante, etc.	75,000
Médoc	Other third growths	70,000
,,	Fourth growth (Talbot)	70,000
,,	Fifth growths (Cantemerle, Mouton-d'Armailhacq and Pontet-Canet)	75,000
St-Émilion	Figeac, Belair, Trottevieille, etc.	70,000
Pomerol	Gazin, Lafleur	70,000
Graves	Fieuzal	70,000
Médoc	Other fourth growths	65,000
,,	Fifth growths (Batailley and Lynch-Bages)	65,000
,,	Other fifth growths	60,000
St-Émilion	La Dominique, Pavie, Bellevue, etc.	65,000
Pomerol	La Fleur-Pétrus, Le-Gay, Domaine de l'Église, etc.	65,000
Graves	Bouscaut, Olivier, Carbonnieux, Smith-Haut-Lafitte	60,000
St-Émilion	Cadet-Bon, Ripeau, Le Couvent, etc.	60,000
Pomerol	Beauregard, Croix-de-Gay, Nenin, etc.	60,000

The *bourgeois* Médocs of renown fetched between 40,000 and 50,000 frs., although Chasse-Spleen was listed at 58,000 and Angludet at 52,000. The St-Émilion and Pomerol *crus bourgeois* fetched similar prices to the Médocs. The lowest listed prices for red Bordeaux were 28,000 to 30,000 frs.

It may be noted that among the Sauternes Yquem was clearly top of all Bordeaux at 130,000 frs., while the first growths were fixed at 90,000, and the seconds from 77,000 frs. down to 70,000 frs. The price average in this region was high, around 65,000 frs. Even some of the Ste-Croix-du-Monts were as high as 65,000, while the Cérons and Loupiacs averaged 55,000 frs. Perhaps they were in demand to satisfy a wartime shortage of sugar; and the Germans like sweet white wines.

In passing it is of interest to mention that the prices fixed for Romanée-Conti and Montrachet were 32,500 and 28,000 frs. respectively per cask of 228 litres, while Chambertin and Musigny headed the other red Burgundies at 25,000 frs., and Bâtard-Montrachet and Corton-Charlemagne were only 16,000 frs. To compare these prices with Bordeaux they should be multiplied roughly four times.

Such was the state of play under wartime conditions thirty years ago, and this shows a somewhat different appraisal of various growths than they would receive today.

After the war some reformers began thinking not only of re-classifying the classed growths but of embracing all the important red wines of Bordeaux. During the 1940s controversy simmered rather than raged, but the growing importance of the American market was an argument used by the re-classifiers. Across the Atlantic the existing system meant nothing, and was in fact highly misleading; and there was the nagging problem of the St-Émilions, not to mention wines labelled *premier cru* from elsewhere in France. Yet no evidence was produced that Americans, armed with classification cards as well as vintage charts, dismissed such wines as Grand-Puy-Lacoste with the curt comment, 'only a fifth growth with a rating of five'.

Meanwhile, the red Graves were classified in 1953 and the leading St-Émilions were officially classified by 1955, the latter being a provisional classification originally designed only to last ten years, pending the hoped-for re-classification of the

Médoc. Among the major districts only Pomerol now remains unclassified.

At one point in the 1950s the classed-growth owners of the Médoc conferred together and there was a majority for a new classification. In 1959 a committee was set up in Bordeaux to examine the matter. Proposals were made by a commission to omit no fewer than nineteen of the lesser classed growths from a new classification. True, three or four of these no longer existed or had been amalgamated, but they made a clean sweep of St-Laurent's trio, as well as Lagrange, Dauzac, St-Pierre and other fourths and fifths. They also proposed to add a dozen *bourgeois* growths, including several of the *crus exceptionnels* and Gloria, Lanessan, Siran, Labégorce, etc., but left out others with fair claims to inclusion. Not surprisingly such proposals, although never made public officially, were badly received.

A suggestion was then made for an entirely new classification, based on a new 'competition' and an examination by an expert 'jury'. Who were to be the jurors? the critics asked suspiciously. In 1965 it looked as if this new classification scheme would go through, with the blessing of the French Government. However several distinguished classed growths let it be known they would boycott any such competition. It was also discovered nothing could stop growths classified in 1855 from continuing legally to announce the fact, even if compelled to add the information that it was of that classification.

Meanwhile Mr Alexis Lichine, associated with two classed growths and a member of the original examining committee, had in 1959 produced his own proposed classification. This took in the Graves, St-Émilion and Pomerol and added four of the *crus exceptionnels* and a dozen *crus bourgeois supérieurs*. The whole comprised nearly 150 growths, thanks to large contingents from St-Émilion and Pomerol. Numerical classification was avoided by the use of other terms in the five categories retained and within each class the wines were listed alphabetically. The top rank, occupied by the original four, plus Mouton-Rothschild, Cheval-Blanc, Ausone and Pétrus, was called *crus hors classe*. Then came *crus exceptionnels*, *grands crus*, *crus supérieurs* and *bons crus*. Who indeed could object to drinking just a *bon cru*?

Mr Lichine also pointed out that some of the existing classed growths no longer produced wines, others occupied somewhat different situations, while a third section no longer made good wine; some, however, were making much better wine. On this score he demoted Lagrange from third to fifth (*bon cru*) class and elevated Cantemerle to second (*cru exceptionnel*).

There was also a plan to classify thirteen *crus exceptionnels* and divide the other *bourgeois* into *Crus Grands Bourgeois* and *Crus Bourgeois*.

Basically these proposals seem sensible, both in drawing in wines from other districts and in avoiding a numerical sequence. Mouton-Rothschild has since secured elevation to the top rank, and Cheval-Blanc and Pétrus have secured it by popular vote and the price of their wines. I would be doubtful about placing Ausone there on present showing, though there is evidence of improvement in the quality, while the price is on a par with the first growths. I would have several other reservations and additions to suggest, but so would others, for the standing of vineyards can rise and fall in a decade or so. However, I believe that if there is a re-classification Alexis Lichine's proposals, which he slightly revised in 1966, would form the basis for reform.

Whatever the eventual outcome, this new initiative came to nothing; the somewhat maladroit way of elevating Mouton-Rothschild (an upgrading which few in Bordeaux would have opposed in itself) aroused too much opposition, and may indeed have further postponed national consideration of a new, comprehensive classification.

Then early in 1970 Bordeaux was surprised by an official

announcement of a *concours* or competition for the establishment in 1970 of *une hiérarchie de mérite au niveau des grands premiers crus hors classe de Bordeaux*. Lest there be any doubt as to who might enter, it was stated that it was open only to Bordeaux châteaux of unquestionable fame and whose products had obtained an average price over the past five years notably above the prices of the leading *deuxièmes crus classés*. This clearly pointed to Mouton-Rothschild, along, it was suggested informally, with Cheval-Blanc, Ausone and Pétrus. Many who supported Mouton's claim to parity with the established first growths felt that this was not the right way to go about it; and opposition grew in Bordeaux when it transpired that the leading organizations had not been consulted, although the leaders of two of them had been 'sounded'. Even the head of the C.I.V.B., M. Henri Martin – *régisseur* also of Latour – had not been informed. There was some doubt as to whether the brokers who would form the jury, as in 1855, would serve. Then at the end of April, the Chamber of Commerce appealed to the Minister of Agriculture, M. Jacques Duhamel, to suspend this new competition, and to consider a fresh approach to the question of a classification to cover all the *grands vins de Bordeaux*.

Nothing further happened. Then in June 1972, a later Minister of Agriculture, M. Michel Cointat, signed a decree for a new *concours* to select *par ordre de mérite des crus du Médoc*. This competition would be open to all growths entitled to the *appellation* Médoc, but would take place in several stages: first, the *crus classés*, a class at a time, and after that the *crus bourgeois*, which would be classified into *crus bourgeois exceptionnels*, *crus grands bourgeois* and *crus bourgeois*. All this might take years. However once again it became clear that, while there was little objection to Mouton-Rothschild being elevated to first-growth status, there was no enthusiasm for this to be done as part of an amendment to the 1855 classification, regarded as sealed and settled for all time by most of those included therein.

However it transpired that Mouton-Rothschild would achieve its century-old desire for promotion, and in June 1973 it was announced that as from that year Mouton would be a first growth. This was widely welcomed in itself, but it was hoped that this would be only the first step in the proposed new classification of the Médoc. Yet why should it be limited to that district when the opportunity has occurred to consider the claims and establish a classified list of the leading 150 to 200 red wine estates of the Gironde? Moreover, two years after the ministerial initiative, there was no firm news of the planned further re-classification of the other classed growths of the Médoc. Inertia, opposition by the established order and the onset of trade depression in Bordeaux all contributed to give the impression that a new competition would be an irrelevant irritant at a time when more serious problems were much more pressing.

It will be seen from the references above to the *crus bourgeois* that the situation regarding them has always been complicated, not to say fluid. The 1932 classification referred to a few pages earlier derived from the foundation in 1920 of the *Syndicat des Crus Bourgeois et Bourgeois Supérieurs du Médoc*. The classification, conducted 'under the double authority of the Chamber of Commerce of Bordeaux and of the Chamber of Agriculture of the Gironde', not only selected 6 *exceptionnels* but also 100 *Crus Bourgeois Supérieurs* from 19 communes in the Haut-Médoc only, ranging from Parempuyre and Ludon in the south to St-Estèphe in the north. The biggest concentration was, as to be expected, in St-Estèphe (17), followed by Moulis (14), Listrac (9) and Macau (8).

Below these came no fewer than 250 *Crus Bourgeois*, drawn from 26 Haut-Médoc communes, and 87 *Crus Bourgeois* from 10 communes of the then Bas-Médoc. Unfortunately first the world slump and then the Nazis intervened and when in 1943 two brokers made an inventory of the *crus bourgeois* only 250 still existed in the Haut-Médoc and 40 in the Médoc. The crisis had destroyed over 150 growths in one of the world's most famous wine-producing districts. By then the 1920 *Syndicat* had lapsed.

Undoubtedly it was the talk of a new classification which spurred a small body of growers to start a new syndicate in 1962. Founded as the *Syndicat des Crus Bourgeois Supérieurs et Crus Bourgeois du Haut-Médoc*, a few months later it was extended to the whole Médoc. In 1966 this *Syndicat* issued its 'classification', devised from within the membership of 110 estates, comprising 1,600 ha and producing an average of 40,000 hl. There were 62 *Grands Bourgeois*, of which 18 were ranked as *exceptionnel*. Thirty-eight properties were listed as *Crus Bourgeois* from 17 communes – only five of them in the Médoc. Of the *exceptionnels* of 1932 only Villegeorge was in the new list, for the others were not adherents of the syndicate.

However, this group made progress and, two months after M. Cointat issued the decree setting up a new *concours* (still-born, it seems, apart from the elevation of Mouton-Roths-child), his successor as Minister of Agriculture, M. Jacques Chirac, issued a modification, permitting a *concours* for the three classes of *Crus Exceptionnels*, *Crus Grands Bourgeois* and *Crus Bourgeois*. Thus the *Syndicat* in effect secured the official recognition hitherto lacking. A revision of what is called the *palmarès*, the prize-list, was set in train among the membership now of 122 proprietors, owning 2,500 ha, and producing an average of 70,000 hl – one sixth of the total Médoc output. Six other members were not considered owing to replanting.

In the new list, issued in January 1978, there were considerable changes, particularly among the *Crus Bourgeois*, with 44 new names out of a total of 68, and 17 out of 59 in the *Grand Bourgeois palmarès*. Four estates – Houissant, Lanessan, Le Boscq and Villegeorge – were no longer rated as *exceptionnels* and presumably had resigned from the *Syndicat*; and there were a few changes in rating. Obviously an organization that ranks its members through judges appointed from within is open to criticism. Yet it would appear that the ranking was fairly done. The two-men teams that visited the 140 members or potential members seeking to be classified (18 were refused), filled up questionnaires which included such questions as how long the proprietor had been in possession, the average age of the vineyard, the grape varieties employed, the proportion of wine château-bottled, the level of trade, the general appearance of the buildings, together with the facilities offered to visitors, and whether there was a *salle de réception*. Moreover there were fundamental criteria. The minimum vineyard area must be 7 or 8 ha, and the wine must be made by the owner – so no wine vinified in a co-operative could be eligible. Then the wine had to look and taste well to the visiting judges. A *Grand Bourgeois* must have a separate maturing cellar with oak casks, and the wine must be superior to the *bourgeois* level. The *exceptionnels* were restricted to properties lying in the area from which the 1855 *crus classés* were drawn – from Ludon to St-Estèphe. Finally the proportion of wines château-bottled by the *Grands Bourgeois* was important.

In the 1978 list the 18 *exceptionnels* were Agassac (Ludon), once a well-known growth but obscure for many years; Citran (Avensan); Chasse-Spleen, Dutruch-Grand-Poujeaux and Poujeaux (Moulis); Fourcas Dupré and Hosten (Listrac); Cissac (Cissac); Caronne-St-Gemme (St-Laurent); Glana (St-Julien); Andron Blanquet, Beausite, Capbern, Le Crock, Haut-Marbuzet, Marbuzet, Meyney and Phélan-Ségur (St-Estèphe).

The notable absentees include Angludet, La Couronne, Lanessan, Siran and La Tour-de-Mons – all, it will be noted, owned by proprietors of classed growths: Palmer, Ducru-Beaucaillou, Haut-Batailley, Pichon-Baron and Lalande, and Cantemerle. Another omission is Gloria (St-Julien). This independence arises in part from the wish, in the event of the proposed (but unlikely) re-classification of the Médoc, to be free of any grouping. Also, no doubt, they feel strong and well-known enough not to need the support of any organization. This may be true, nevertheless it seems to me a mistaken view. For if, as seems likely, the *crus classés* become more in demand and increasingly expensive, the *crus bourgeois* should find wider markets, not least if more equitable prices enable them to improve the quality of their vineyards and their wine, as many of the *crus classés* did from the sixties onwards. A united front of the *crus bourgeois* of the Médoc, to which they are now confined, would surely assist this. If all the important *crus bourgeois* became members of the syndicate, it might be possible for the *I.N.A.O.* to take over the rating, which, as in the St-Émilion *grands crus*, could vary with performance.

Meanwhile, it must be emphasized that one should not drink on class lines. The 1855 classification was criticized at the time on the grounds that it represented the views of the brokers buying these wines *en primeur*. That Lafite sold for twice the amount realized by Pichon-Longueville-Baron or Palmer did not mean in the end that a bottle of the former was necessarily better than or even as good as the latter pair. All that can be said is that all things being equal the top classed growths are more likely to make a finer wine than the lesser-classed vineyards; but things are often far from equal, as the comments on various châteaux and vintages in this book show.

Moreover in so far as the concentration on the first growths, nowadays principally sold to the U.S.A. (as they once were to Britain), has distorted the price structure of the leading clarets, the existing classification is to be deplored. Early in 1979 an American estimate, informal but probably fairly accurate, calculated that 40 per cent of the initial purchases of the first growths went to the U.S.A., and about 16 per cent of the other classed growths. Pétrus, officially unclassified, attracts a higher price than any of the classified *premiers*. Cheval-Blanc, 'temporarily' classified in 1955, is usually placed at least as high as Margaux and Haut-Brion. Yet excellent wines of lower official status have often not secured their due return. On the other hand third-growth Palmer secures at least as good a price as any second growth and often more, while fourth-growth Beychevelle certainly ranks with the leading seconds.

Much of the distortion must be attributed to the rivalry among the first growths. This, as already shown, long precedes the arrival of the Rothschilds in the Médoc, but from the 1920s onwards was certainly accentuated by Baron Philippe's intense conviction that Mouton-Rothschild was as good as any first growth and for his money better than most. The only way that this could be achieved was by asking a price as high as any other first growth and if possible higher than all. Thanks to the devotion of Baron Philippe and his staff to the quality of the wine and to its high reputation – not exactly diminished by the glamour of the name Rothschild, which Lafite also insists on – throughout the fine-wine world, especially in the United States, he was able to do this successfully. Perhaps a side-door entry to the corridors of power helped too. Not that he was satisfied entirely by elevation to the top rank, for several years later he issued a reminder that the 1973 classification listing was alphabetical and contained no element of ranking as was the case in 1855. It was fortunate perhaps that Mouton-Rothschild fitted in so conveniently after Ch. Margaux, and that Haut-Brion was included as *assimilé* – a little depreciatory, it might be thought. It is difficult to imagine what would have happened if Baron Philippe's more recently acquired property, Clerc-Milon, had been the candidate for promotion to *premier cru* instead of Mouton-Rothschild!

18. The Bordeaux Vintages

This chapter is largely a personal assessment of clarets of various vintages that have come my way, along with general information I have been able to acquire; but even of the more recent years I cannot claim even to have sampled all the representative wines, and for these in particular any comments must be of very provisional judgement. It must always be borne in mind that not even the professionals know exactly how a claret of a reasonably successful vintage is going to turn out. It is easy to discard the poor years, for the wines are unbalanced from the start, but to predict the ultimate qualities of vintages like, say, 1970 or 1975 is largely a forecast of probability; which does not of course mean that it is not interesting and amusing to do so. As a decade has passed since comments on individual vintages and wines were first made here, revision has been necessary, particularly for those of the post-Second World War period; but some remarks have been allowed to stand, even if now not strictly applicable owing to the passage of the years. There seems little point, I believe, in performing the obsequies on such splendid vintages as 1920 or 1929, because few bottles now are what they used to be, and expectations aroused by their former fame may be disappointed. Let the record stand.

Then, although minor revisions to this chapter have been possible from time to time in the new impressions printed and in the first paperback edition, the appearance of a properly revised, reset edition has provided the opportunity to include comments on some of the wines that have come my way in recent years. I regret the comparative paucity of comments on the white wines, especially the Sauternes, but they appear on our tables with far less regularity than the reds.

Lacking the longevity and experience of André Simon, revealed, for example, in his *Vintagewise* (1945) in which, *inter alia*, he surveyed the claret vintages from the 1840s onwards, I cannot properly discuss every vintage. Indeed I have never drunk a bottle of claret of the 1840 decade, although it is fair to add that in 1945 André Simon admitted to having drunk only one: Lafite 1846. So it would be for me an academic, somewhat arid account, and probably of little interest to readers today. Now and again a wine already mentioned in the various districts may be discussed again here, but in the context of its vintage peers.

Accordingly I take together all the pre-phylloxera vintages, then deal as a whole with the years to the close of the last century, and follow with those up to the end of the First World War and its immediate aftermath. Then a more regular, annual comment is possible up to the last vintage which is at this time assessable in bottle: 1973. In addition some tentative notes are given on more recent years.

In 1977 and 1978 I took part in extended tastings of runs of vintages from a number of châteaux: Lafite and Trotanoy in 1977, Mouton-Rothschild, La Mission-Haut-Brion, Ducru-Beaucaillou and Magdelaine in 1978. They were arranged for varying purposes. The tasting at Lafite, already referred to in discussing the château, might be described as an exploration of its splendid cellar, while that at Mouton was in connection with writing the text of the book on that château's labels from 1945 to 1977; the tasting at La Mission-Haut-Brion in September 1978 was the result of a decision by the owners to dispose of the surplus in the very well-stocked private cellar of the château. Prior therefore to its sale at Christie's, for a total, including some larger quantities of younger vintages, of £86,000, Michael Broadbent, head of its wine department, and I tasted in less than twenty-four hours no fewer than forty vintages of La Mission-Haut-Brion, La Tour-Haut-Brion and Laville-Haut-Brion. The tastings in London of post-Second World War vintages of Trotanoy and Magdelaine also preceded auctions of these wines at Christie's. The sampling at Ducru-Beaucaillou – 1977–1966 and earlier vintages opened at meals, back to 1953 – was kindly arranged by M. Jean-Eugène Borie at my instance, in order that I might write an article on the excellent wines of this St-Julien estate. Tasting a line of wines with no more food than cheese, biscuits and bread, is always a fascinating exercise, but is not to be compared with drinking them 'in depth'. On all the occasions mentioned here, at least a fair proportion of the wines were consumed with food: usually the better and the more mature years. Some, therefore, of the comments below have their origin in these tastings, sometimes described as 'vertical', but carrying the risk of leaving the *dégustateur* with a strong inclination towards the 'horizontal'!

THE PRE-PHYLLOXERA EPOCH

There was a succession of fine vintages in the 1770s, and 1784 was a celebrated year sought after by Thomas Jefferson. Another famous vintage was 1795. However what may be described as the first 'modern' fine vintage was the wonderful 1798. This can be called modern because it occurred not long after the development of the modern type of bottle which made it possible to lay down wine for maturing. Significantly perhaps, the *Vinothèque* at Lafite was established only a year before the remarkable 1798s, which had a very long life. At a Christie's wine sale in London in 1811 Château Margot (*sic*) 1798 'celebrated vintage, bottled in London in 1802' fetched the very high price of £9 2s. 6d. a dozen, and in the same sale 'Barnes's 1802 claret' (Barnes was a famous London merchant of the time and he had imported the Margaux 1798) bottled as late as 1806 fetched £8 2s. 6d. a case. This was of course at the height of the Napoleonic War scarcity, and after the 1798

the next famous vintage of the era was 1802. Other outstanding vintages in the first quarter of the nineteenth century were
1811, the famous 'Comet' year, 1815 a vintage long remembered, 1819 and 1825. Both 1822 and 1825 were exceptional
white wine vintages. The 1825 wine was made after a very
fine summer, prices were very high but as the wines took a
long time to come round, considerable losses were incurred by
merchants holding them. Fine were 1801, 1803, 1807, 1814,
1818 and 1822. I have already described the bottle of Lafite
1803 drunk at Bristol in 1967. The 1811 *Vin de Comète* Lafite
was served at a celebrated lunch to several hundred guests at
the château in 1926 and was proclaimed in excellent condition.

In the next quarter of that century the leading vintages were
1828, 1831, 1834, 1841, 1844, 1847 and 1848. The 1828s were
very famous in their day, and were described by Tastet &
Lawton as '*merveilleuse d'élégance, de grâce, de bouquet, goût
délicieux*'. The first growths were particularly esteemed but
the most celebrated of them all was the Mouton. There is a
story, well known in Bordeaux, about a dinner party given
probably about 1860 by the British Consul in Bordeaux, Mr
T. G. D. Scott, who so far as I know had no connection with
the Scotts of Lafite, and lived at what is now 29 Cours Xavier
Arnozan. The story is told in Paul de Cassagnac's *French
Wines* (1930) translated by Guy Knowles. One of the guests
was M. Duffau-Dubergier, Mayor of Bordeaux and a very
rich man. The crowning wine was the Mouton '28. It was
greeted with great enthusiasm and the mayor at once asked,
'Have you much of it left?' 'Alas, only a dozen bottles.' The
mayor replied, 'Well, my dear fellow, I'm going to make you
a proposition. Twelve bottles, twelve thousand francs' (almost
£500 and the equivalent today of at least £5,000).

'You are asking an impossibility of me, my friend,'
answered Scott, 'but to show you how much I desire to fall in
with your wishes, I'll agree to share it with you, and we'll say
six bottles, six thousand francs.'

'My dear Scott,' remarked M. Duffau-Dubergier, 'if I buy wine at a thousand francs a bottle, it is on condition that I am the only man that can give it to his friends to drink.'

Scott thought it over a moment. 'Right; we'll say no more about it.' Then, turning to his butler, he said: 'Bernard, decant us two more bottles of the 1828 Mouton.' Another version of the story gives the wine as Lafite.

The winter of 1830–31 was exceptionally severe with ice-floes on the Garonne, with temperatures of minus 10 degrees Centigrade, followed by heavy hail in August. The crop was small, but fine.* The white wines were particularly successful, as they were in 1834, when after spring frosts and summer hail storms the crop was again much reduced. That summer had been exceptionally hot and the vintage started on 9 September, the earliest year of the century until 1865, when picking began three days earlier. In 1834 there was bad weather later in September, and those who waited until October were rewarded for their patience. However conditions must have been not unlike the very hot year of 1921, and some of the wines were 'pricked', i.e. turned to vinegar in the vats; others had at first a taste of decay, but outgrew it to become a very distinguished vintage.

The next rank of vintages of the second quarter of the century included 1840 (for white wines) and 1846 (also for white wines). The 1840s were a period of exceptionally fine vintages. The 1841 was both excellent and plentiful, but initially a little hard and bitter, and there was no rush to buy it. As recorded by Pijassou in his work on Lafite, Émile Goudal, the *régisseur* (also a *négociant* who lived on the Quai des Chartrons), believed that the early prices were too low and decided to keep the wine, although a year after the vintage Latour, short of money after the case in which it bought out the merchant

*From 1831 onwards prices of representative wines in fine or for other reasons interesting vintages may be found in Appendix C on page 656.

shareholders, sold at 1,800 frs. a *tonneau*, and Margaux went for 2,500 frs. Lafite, on the other hand, only offered its 1841 in April 1844 – very late indeed for those days – when the reputation of the vintage had already risen sharply. M. Goudal demanded 5,500 frs. per *tonneau*; in addition this was conditional on buying an equal amount of the small, very ordinary crop of 1842 at 2,500 frs. This latter was so indifferent that Latour took from 1846 to the beginning of 1851 to dispose of its crop at from 1,200–1,700 frs. a *tonneau*. Such conditional sales have been a recurrent feature of the Bordeaux scene, and were demanded in the late 1960s and in the boom years of the early seventies. They were no more popular then than a hundred or so years earlier.

As may be expected Lafite's 'exorbitant price' aroused the fury of the Bordeaux merchants. Nathaniel Johnston actually sent a circular to his clients denouncing Lafite's action and saying that as the 1842 was worth no more than 1,500 frs., the real price of the 1841 was 6,500 frs. He did not want to buy any but some of his competitors did, and it meant a price to his customers of £80 the *barrique*, £320 a *tonneau*, or 8,000 frs., which was probably at least the equivalent of the opening price of Lafite 1975: 54,000 frs. Johnston went on to point out that the first growths were by no means always the best, and even in 1841 some of the seconds were more successful than 'certain firsts', though they were now, in 1844, selling for 3,500 frs. He suggested that the Chartrons merchants should band together and ask their British traders to buy their clarets by class rather than by the exact name of the property; the merchants would supply the best, with the implied suggestion that the wines would be 'treated', or subjected to blending and the *travail à l'anglaise*. Moreover with these high prices it seemed all too likely that the English customers would buy direct! In time of course this fury subsided, but it throws an interesting light not only on the contest between the proprietors and the Chartrons merchants, widely regarded as arrogant and grasping, but also on the vital importance of the English market.

In spite of this 'exorbitant' price for the 1841, it is of note that from about 1833 to 1852 (the eve of the oidium) the average price of Lafite remained constant, at about 2,000 frs. a *tonneau*. However, from 1844 they were able to achieve a superior price to that of their rivals, Latour and Margaux. For in that year both entered into ten-year contracts to sell at 1,800 and 2,500 frs. respectively. Certainly the miserable 1845 was sold for no more than 700 frs., but when the 1855 classification was decided, principally upon the price of each growth on the Bordeaux market, the advantage of Lafite in the preceding decade may have made its mark; in the same way Margaux was ahead of Latour, as indeed was shown in the 1855 listing. According to André Simon, 1846 was the first vintage of Lafite bottled at the château. Certainly château-bottled Lafite 1846 appears in Christie's wine sale catalogues later in the century, but the late Christian Cruse suggested to me that at least on a large scale it was 1847, when his great-grandfather bought the whole crop and asked the château to bottle most of the wine, as he had no room in his Bordeaux cellars. In this period Lafite merely branded its château-bottled wine with 'C.L.' accompanied by the date. There was no label, and the wine merchants who purchased the wine were accustomed to use their own labels. The 1847s were at first largely disregarded and very cheap, but later had a great success, particularly in northern Europe and the United States. The 1848s were even finer for reds, but not for the whites. The '47s and '48s form one of the famous 'pairs' of claret vintages.

It is interesting at this point to be able to give some indication of the strengths of Bordeaux wines in this pre-oidium, pre-phylloxera period, for this is a question sometimes asked. It so happened that in 1845 a pharmacist, M. J. Fauré, published in Bordeaux a study of the chemical and comparative analysis of the wines of the Gironde, and he tested the alcoholic strength of leading and lesser red and white wines of recent vintage. The surprising result was that, whereas the white wines were of the strength that one would expect today, the reds tended to be distinctly low in alcohol. This was of course long before the days of authorized chaptalization, but whether the benefits of M. Chaptal's assistance in raising the strength by the addition of sugar was known and surreptitiously practised, or whether 'assistance' was still sought by way of wines from the Rhône or Spain, is not apparent. Certainly the low degree of the classed growths that M. Fauré analysed does not suggest any such recourse. To quote some examples, of the 1840s Lafite was 8·7°, Latour 9·33°, Haut-Brion 9·33°, Brane-Mouton 9°, Léoville 9·15°, Gruaud-Larose 9·85°, Giscours 9·10°, La Lagune 9·30° and Tronquoy-Lalande (a *cru bourgeois* of St-Estèphe) was the highest at 9·90°. It should be mentioned that 1840 was a prolific year of moderate quality, and perhaps the abundance resulted in a lowering of the strength.

The following year, however, was an excellent one of normal quantity, but unfortunately M. Fauré did not repeat his examination exactly; however, he also covered some 1842, a poor vintage of small quantity, and some figures for these can be given. The strength of Haut-Brion for both years was 9° and La Mission-Haut-Brion 10·12° and 10° respectively, while Pessac *tout court* was 10° and 9°. Also from the Graves, Léognan was 9·50° and 9·15°, but white Carbon-nieux 1841 was 13·15°. In these two vintages Pauillac showed 9·70° and 9·25°, Margaux 9·65° and 9·75°, Macau 9° and 8·9° and Ludon 9° and 8·7°. St-Estèphe for 1841 only was 9·75°, but Phélan (Ségur) 1842 was 9·25°. On the right bank of the rivers St-Émilion was 9·18° and 9·21°, Bourg 10·30° and 10·15° and Blaye 10·25° and 10·50° – interestingly enough, the highest degrees recorded anywhere over the three vintages tested.

Among the white wines, Sauternes 1841 showed 15°, and Barsac *premier cru* 1841, 14·75°, but the *deuxième* only 12·65° and the *troisième* 11·25°. Bommes .1841 recorded 12·15° and Ste-Croix-du-Mont 1841 was 12·15°. White Martillac 1841 was tested at 11·15°, but two 1841 Entre-Deux-Mers, Sauveterre and St-Macaire, showed only 8·76° and 8·15° respectively. Reference to Appendix A will show the minimum required strengths today for the various *appellations* represented above, but in the Médoc they like to secure 12°, and if necessary will often chaptalize to secure this, but the sweet white wines must be 12·50-13°.

If the 1840s were prolific in fine vintages, the 1850s were the reverse, owing to the oidium from 1853 to 1857 (but first noticed in 1852). Gruaud-Larose, which produced 160 *tonneaux* in 1848, made 20 in 1854 and 35 in 1855. As already mentioned with reference to the oidium in Chapter 1, crops were decimated and prices rocketed, never to return to levels previously held for many years. 1855, the year of the Classification, was no more than passable; Latour and Mouton could secure no more than 2,800 frs. for their wine, Lafite 500 less. However, significantly perhaps, Mouton, just designated as a *deuxième*, held out and achieved the same price as Latour and Margaux, and therefore was 'one up' on its next-door neighbour. Desperate perhaps for a good vintage to sell, the merchants Cruse and Barton & Guestier bought Lafite 1856 – a short crop owing to the oidium – for 5,700 frs. a *tonneau* before Christmas of that year, and the two other Médoc firsts followed suit. Mouton-Rothschild, as mentioned in the chapter on the Classification, secured 5,000 frs., the seconds 4,000; after all that the 1856s were held of little account. As Tastet & Lawton's note stated: 'very mediocre, at first judged good and bought very dear'. By March 1858 Goudal, who had pulled off the remarkable deal with the Lafite 1856, was writing to Samuel Scott in London that 'the trade has lost too much on the 1856s to begin again' (to buy the 1857s)! After some delay the firsts were able to sell their 1857s for 4,000 frs., Mouton for 3,000 and the other seconds for 2,400. The crop was again small though increasing compared with the worst years of the oidium, but the quality was mediocre. Only in 1858 was quantity again allied to quality. Lafite, which had produced only 40 *tonneaux* of *grand vin* in 1856 and 80 *tonneaux* in 1858, now made 162¼ *tonneaux* of the 1858, plus 19 *tonneaux* of Carruades (still made separately) and 23¼ *tonneaux* of a second wine. The commercial consequences of this have already been related in the chapter on the Bordeaux wine trade.

In 1858 really began what is sometimes called the 'Golden Age' of claret, with a succession of vintages not only remarkable in themselves but in many cases with exceptional staying power. They provide most of the backing for the argument, impossible yet of resolution, that post-phylloxera clarets have never lasted so well. This period ended in 1878.

I have at least tasted one 1858 – the Lafite. This was from a remarkable collection of wines from the cellars of Dalmeny and Mentmore of the Earl of Rosebery, sold at Christie's in May 1967. These included no fewer than 19 magnums and 7 bottles of the 1858. Before the sale the auctioneers opened one bottle for two or three of us. It had a real aroma of fine claret, but on the palate there was some decay. Perhaps the magnums, which fetched up to £41 apiece, were fuller, but if not this is scarcely surprising as 1858 was the vintage with which George Saintsbury started his cellar in the late seventies, and he described them as then being 'a trifle old'. Yet André Simon in *Vintagewise* describes an 1858 as being perfect in Bordeaux in 1935.

It should be said right away there is little doubt that wines which have either never been moved from the château cellars or have lain a long age in Bordeaux are more likely to last well than those which have suffered a journey; especially difficult is movement when they are old. Therefore it would not be correct to assume that certain old wines that taste very well in the Bordeaux region will necessarily be good abroad; and one seldom knows how the latter wines have been kept meanwhile. More on this matter on p. 580.

With the 1860s we enter the great pre-phylloxera period proper. Early in the decade some good wine was made. In 1861 there was a very short crop owing to an exceptional May frost, and good wine was dear as the average was moderate only in quality. Christian Cruse told me that in 1966 he and his son Édouard drank with great pleasure a bottle of Lafite 1862. In 1970 and again in 1975 I drank at Latour their 1863, a reputedly poor year; it was remarkable for full colour, nose and flavour. Unlike the 1865, noted below, it did not fade in the glass, and if served blind I might have taken it for a wine of the early 1920s. Perhaps it lacked just a little of the concentrated flavour of the greatest pre-phylloxera clarets. The classic vintage, however, was 1864, plentiful as well as of the highest quality, and the leading growth was certainly Lafite. A magnum of this was sold in the Rosebery sale for no less than £82. In 1976 another fetched £125.

By the kindness of Anthony Berry of Berry Bros. & Rudd I was able to taste this famous wine in February 1968. Having read that I had never drunk Lafite '64 and did not expect ever to do so, he invited me to lunch with him and his partners, and with Harry Waugh as the other guest. Preceded by two bottles of the Gruaud-Larose-Sarget '74 – good wine but in decline – we then had two bottles of the famous Lafite '64, served in separate glasses. Both were distinctly better than the two '74s. One was showing its age a little but the other was perfectly round, gentle and soft and with a 'sweet' nose. All its faculties were present, though only just. The other bottle too was also remarkably 'sweet'. Both wines had been decanted over an hour before we tasted them, and they showed no decline in the glass for at least half an hour; by that time we had dispatched them.

Other '64s were also successful, and Yquem sold at 4,500 frs. a *tonneau*.

The 1865s were prolific and the quality good but they took some time to come round. Very large amounts of wine were made in this year, but the opening prices of the leading growths were even higher than for the '64s. Indeed, taking into account the changed value of money and allowing for the 1868s which did not keep their price, they were overall probably the highest for a normal vintage for about a hundred years, when the 1961 first-growth prices broke all bounds. Both Lafite, which produced 195 *tonneaux*, and Latour, where 103 *tonneaux* were made, sold for 5,600 frs. or £224 a *tonneau*. Allowing at least a tenfold decrease in the value of money since then, this was the equivalent of just on £2,200 a *tonneau*. In 1930 André Simon found the Lafite still excellent in London. Much more recently I had the privilege of drinking the Latour at the château. In October 1968 David Pollock, then chairman of the company which now controls Latour, opened a bottle of this wine when my wife and I were dining there. Decanted just before drinking, it had a remarkably deep colour for a centenarian wine, with a powerful nose and a flavour so full and deep that there was almost a suggestion of port in its richness; perhaps it had been *hermitagé*, although I doubt it. The wine began to fade about half an hour after first opening, but it was so big a wine that one would have thought it fifty years younger. Today 1859 is the oldest vintage in the private cellar at Mouton. The 1865 Mouton-Rothschild is also in the private cellar but the *maître de chai* told me that it was not so good as the 1870. The following two years were not of much account, but 1868 was better, and the first growths went ahead again in price, since the prosperity of the times gave the big 'names' an exceptional popularity, which was to be emulated in the 1960s. Some of the 1868 first growths fetched as much as 6,200 and 6,000 frs. However the wines were hard and unattractive, and the merchants who paid these prices made heavy losses, and one wonders whether history may not repeat itself over some of the exceptional prices paid at source for the 1971s and 1972s. However in 1965 I drank one superb example of the 1868s – and a fifth, not a first growth. This was Grand-Puy-Ducasse – the last bottle in the cellar at Pontet-Canet and opened for me by Christian Cruse. Although of course a little brown, yet full-coloured for its age, it had that incomparable 'sealing wax' nose of really fine old claret; full of fruit and flavour with no sign of decay. Returning to the glass after an interval I found the wine remarkably sweet; class differences count for little at such an age if the wine is still in good heart, as this one was. It is interesting to read Tastet & Lawton's note that this vintage produced big wines, 'hard without charm', similar to André Simon's view of them. Since then I have been fortunate to drink several other 1868s, the best of them Latour, once more generously opened at the château; this time in October 1971. It had the big colour, fine nose and firm character one associates still with this growth. One could readily believe André Simon's comment, but by now the wine had softened, though perhaps it lacked balance; this applied also to the Mouton-Rothschild, drunk within a week of the Latour. Baron Philippe thought it was 'too strong', perhaps a reflection of the same hardness associated with the year. The Mouton had plenty of colour and flavour too, but there was a little acidity noticeable.

However 1869 was another winner, well-balanced and again copious; the most plentiful of the decade, so prices fell. I have been fortunate enough to drink two fine examples of this vintage. The first was in October 1970 when a bottle of the Mouton-Rothschild was opened at the château. In perfect condition, it had that wonderfully waxy, concentrated flavour of a great old claret – a perfectly complete wine. Then at the tasting at Lafite in October 1977, described in the section on the château, the peak of the final dinner was the 1869, served from two bottles. (Out of the five nineteenth-century vintages shown, this was the only one of which four bottles had to be opened in order to find two in fine condition; and although both were excellent, one was agreed to be more complete than the other.) The wine had an extraordinary depth of colour for its age. The nose was slow to develop in the glass, though the wines had been decanted well in advance, but then the very fruity, concentrated flavour emerged. A rich wine, old but still complete and fuller than the 1893 that preceded it. Baron Éric produced this *bonne bouche* as it had been made a year after Baron James, whose bust looked down on the dining table, had purchased the property; it was really the first vintage made completely under the Rothschild auspices, for the vintage in 1868 began only a month after the sale. Moreover although Lafite has some of that year in its cellar, it was not a very good year, whereas in the Tastet & Lawton records the 1869 was noted as 'remarkable and complete'. One could say the same of it more than a century later. This was one of the famous years of Yquem, ranking alongside 1893 and 1921. As mentioned earlier, in the late fifties I was allowed a sample of this great wine from a medicine bottle sent from Scotland to London by the owner of a bottle, who had decanted and posted off this sample. Although very dark it was still sound and luxuriously rich.

On the other hand I have been lucky enough to drink a number of 1870s. This was another fairly prolific vintage, which began early after a hot summer, the wine fetching similar prices to the '69s, although Mouton-Rothschild at 3,000 frs. a *tonneau* was higher and the equal of Latour. However the '70s' chief repute for many years was that they were not ready for drinking; a classic slow-developing fine claret. Saintsbury talks about 'those unsatisfactory '70s', and regrets that for the money laid out on classed growths he did not buy three times the quantity of sound *bourgeois* wine. Incidentally he mentions that the seven dozen classed growths, including all four *premiers*, cost him 'at the high prices then ruling for claret' about £30. Presumably he bought these soon after he began his cellar when the wines were about ten years old; over 85s. a dozen was certainly not a very cheap price, particularly as the late Ian Campbell mentions in his *Wayward Tendrils of the Vine* (1947) that his firm bought a good part of the crop of Latour '71, bottled it in London, sold it to the trade at 26s. a dozen, and felt almost guilty of profiteering when later they raised the price to 36s.

Saintsbury described the '70s as 'dumb' at forty years of age, and friends in Bordeaux told me that they did not really unfold until about 1920. Thus later hard vintages, such as 1928, have often been queried as 'another 1870?'; but I doubt this.

The other side of this picture, so frustrating for our grandfathers, is that the wines lasted magnificently; and as they were rightly not considered ready to drink many were preserved. About 1960 my friend John Hadfield found himself the residuary legatee of nine or ten bottles of Léoville '70, which for many years had been lying in a Suffolk cellar near his home. I shared several of these bottles, and although those ullaged were not as good as the fuller bottles, none was undrinkable and the best were remarkable. One bottle was generously given me, and I drank it at home in June 1962 in the company of Ronald Avery, Harry Waugh and the late Douglas McClean. Surprisingly deep in colour, with a wonderfully full nose and flavour it had tremendous 'size', fruit and sweetness. This was a very distinguished wine on any count and it showed no sign of weakness, in spite of having been moved from one side of England to another in extreme old age. Even the next day the dregs in the bottle smelled sweet, and I count it among the finest bottles of claret I have drunk.

There were other remarkable '70s in my experience. The leading wine was said to be Lafite, and I drank that at Harvey's, thanks to Harry Waugh who returned the compliment of my Léoville. Some Lafite and Langoa '70, all bottled by Harvey's, had come up for auction at Restell's and the firm had bought them in the 1950s for what would now be the amazingly low price of £5 a bottle. I drank both wines and they had the same characteristics of deep colour and fruit noticed in the Léoville. The Lafite was somewhat ullaged and not so fine as the Langoa, which I drank in December 1965, while the Lafite was opened in August 1966. The quality of the Langoa may be gauged by the fact that when first tasted it was taken for a 1920. On the other hand a magnum of Lafite '70 from Glamis Castle – one of over forty sold at Christie's in June 1971 – was in splendid condition at a dinner at Christie's before the auction; a big, strong wine still with some tannin. They fetched up to £190 apiece.

Another celebrated '70 was the Mouton, and this I was able to taste on the spot – always a special pleasure and experience. I was able to drink this and other famous Moutons mentioned here owing to the kindness of Baron Philippe de Rothschild, who in the course of several of my visits – for the sake of the cellar, fortunately mostly brief – more or less gave me the freedom of his incomparable cellar. I had the temerity to ask for the '70, and other wines on further occasions. The Mouton '70 had the same splendid nose and depth of flavour of the other '70s, but was perhaps rather more backward. The Latour '70 I sampled at a pre-auction tasting at Christie's early in 1969. English-bottled, it still had a good deal of vigour. It was later sold for just on £13 a bottle.

I am keeping accounts of famous bottles to a minimum, for vicarious drinking is a limited pleasure to others, but such nineteenth-century wines are worth recording.

I have never drunk '71 or '72, although the first of these produced some notable, elegant wines, described by Tastet & Lawton as light but very elegant. André Simon described them as 'nearer the perfection of claret than any other, not excepting the wonderful '64s and '75s'. He particularly commended the Haut-Brion, Mouton and Lafite. Perhaps, unlike the '75s, they were too light to last. 1873 was a vintage that I came to particularly late in life: the Mouton-Rothschild at the château in October 1974, the Lafite three years later, as part of the tasting described earlier. The Mouton had good colour though with some brown tinge; it not only had a fine, concentrated nose but the 'lead pencils' aroma associated with Mouton, though often found elsewhere. It was beautifully rounded and complete, without a trace of decay. The Lafite also showed some brownness, but it had a lovely flowery nose that perhaps might be associated with this château's wines. It had a fruity flavour, but oddly enough still retained some tannin and this no doubt had kept the wine extraordinarily complete. As my notes (made at the table on each occasion) indicate, these two wines were as different then as they show in all subsequent vintages. The crop was very small in 1873 owing to terrible frost at the end of April, and Tastet & Lawton's verdict was 'ordinary'. Certainly these two bottles were not.

The '74s I have drunk several times, and some were past their best. It was a huge, expensive vintage, only surpassed in quantity by the record '75. The finest '74 that I have drunk was certainly Pontet-Canet (of which a tremendous crop of 275 *tonneaux* had been made), opened by Christian Cruse in Bordeaux in September 1967. In colour it was very brown, with almost a hint of orange, but the aroma and flavour were remarkable although not so big as the '70s. The nose had that concentrated, 'sealing wax' aroma of these great old clarets, and there was no lack of fruit. I was lucky enough to drink it again a year later at Christian Cruse's table. This bottle had more colour and was still quite a big fruity wine but was overshadowed by the Lafite '75 mentioned below. Not long afterwards, at a lunch given by Michael Broadbent, head of Christie's wine auction department, two magnums of Lafite 1874 formerly from the cellars of Viscount Boyne at Brancepeth Castle, Durham, were served. Both were slightly ullaged, one had been decanted the previous evening, the other immediately before lunch. Both had good noses but showed some decay on the taste, and the one decanted eighteen hours beforehand was the better. I suspect ullage was the trouble, as Latour '74 from the Rosebery cellar sampled in May 1967 had been a big rich wine for its age, with a real fine-claret nose. Another opportunity to taste the Lafite '74 was afforded in October 1976, following the 'unearthing' of another very distinguished English cellar of old wines – at Woodperry House, Oxfordshire, the home of Sir John Thomson, a former chairman of Barclay's Bank. In a cellar scarcely touched for many years, some of the older clarets had lain there for nearly a century. I was present at the pre-sale tasting at Christie's and tasted the Lafite immediately it was opened. It had a good colour for its age, very clear and an elegant nose, with a long taste, fruity and even rich, with the concentrated taste that I have always associated with fine pre-phylloxera claret. Yet a month later, also at a dinner at Christie's, another bottle lacked fruit and showed some decay, though with a very big colour and fair nose. That must be the luck of the game when dealing with 100-year-old claret, and even when it is half that age.

I have referred to the declining Gruaud-Larose '74 in connection with the Lafite '64, and in Bordeaux in October 1968 I drank a superb example of Lafite '75, the last wine in a remarkable assembly of nineteenth-century clarets which Christian Cruse opened for my wife and me. All find a place in these notes, but I imagined that a further bottle of the splendid Pontet-Canet '74 mentioned above completed the range. But then from the mantelpiece Cruse took an English claret jug, saying 'the gem of my cellar'. It was Lafite '75. The colour was light, almost like a deep Madeira, but the concentrated 'sealing wax' nose was that of really great old claret. The flavour was truly delicate and fine but with no hint of decay, and it had a distinctly fruity, sweet taste even two hours after decanting. For its delicate yet true flavour all the way, it was certainly one of the finest clarets I have drunk. As a souvenir Christian Cruse gave me the bottle, a hand-made one with a seal on the neck, inscribed *Château Lafite – Grand Vin*. The following day I showed this to M. André Portet, the *régisseur* of Lafite, and he told me that the bottle would have been supplied not by the château but by the merchant who then sent it to Lafite to be filled.

The 1875s from that record vintage were the reverse of the '70s. They were drinkable and delicate so early that in the eighties and nineties all the experts said they must be drunk up while they were so good. It was 'the wine of the evening' at a banquet given in 1895 by the Bordeaux Chamber of Commerce to representatives of the Corporation of the City of London. However, these wines in fact survived well into the inter-war period. Another example I have drunk was Ch. Margaux at Loudenne in October 1966. Alas both colour and nose had gone, although the wine was sweeter than one might have expected. Mouton was said to be one of the finest wines of the vintage. I twice drank Léoville-Las-Cases '75 with the Cruses in Bordeaux, early in the seventies. The first was very extraordinary, with a 'cough-drop' nose and an odd sweetness that was not at all agreeable. It must have been 'assisted' in some way. The second bottle had fine colour and nose, and it was surprisingly full and fruity, but somehow did not seem to have much character. Much finer was a Gruaud-Larose that M. and Mme Cordier very generously opened in their splendid Bordeaux château, Labottière, in October 1977. Decanted two hours beforehand, it had everything that one might expect. The aroma was fruity and sweet, and this was confirmed on the palate, with great concentration. It had come from the fine cellar at Gruaud-Larose, where it had lain undisturbed for a great many years.

The next year was not held in any esteem, though Christian

Cruse and his son Édouard opened for me a bottle of Dauzac '76 at Pontet-Canet in October 1966. Édouard Cruse had never tasted a '76 before. It was pale, almost *rosé*, the nose was very fine and the fruit was attenuated but just there. A moderate wine which had not survived at all badly for ninety years.

The 1877s were irregular, as André Simon, whose birth year it was, assured me, but there was good report of a number of bottles presented to him on his ninetieth birthday. The only one I have tasted was Pichon-Longueville in Bordeaux. One bottle in 1966 was delicious, a second in 1967 was decayed; but there must always be uncertainty with old bottles. Prospective buyers should be warned that only reasonably full bottles are likely to be sound.

The 'Golden Age' ended with the 1878s. The vintage was a fairly big one, but the wines were less expensive than the '74s or '75s. I have once or twice had thin, disappointing bottles in England, although at a lunch given by Rigby & Evens at Bristol in April 1967 one out of two magnums of Lafite was still fine claret, although near the end of its journey; the other had that 'mushroom' smell and taste of decay. At Mouton in October 1965 I had a superb bottle of its own wine. This had been decanted four or five hours before being drunk; nevertheless it was a splendidly complete, fruity wine, even better than the Mouton '70 which I drank a year later. Apart from periodic re-corking, the '78 had not stirred from its original bin since 1881. The Lafite, opened by Édouard Cruse in October 1972, was certainly an old wine, tired rather than decayed, but it had a remarkable colour and some distinction.

So ended the pre-phylloxera era. The American-derived louse had been active in Bordeaux for ten years, but it was not a widespread menace until after 1878. Whether or not the wines made from the ungrafted French vines were better or not must always remain a moot point, and most of us would settle cheerfully for wines of the quality of 1899 and 1900. It does seem more than likely, however, that these old wines did last longer than those made in the first sixty years of the post-phylloxera era. With one or two possible exceptions, it is almost certain they lasted better than will the clarets of the post-Second World War period.

THE PHYLLOXERA AND AFTER

Many people believe that the onset of the phylloxera, already discussed in Chapter 1, led to an immediate deterioration in the quality of the wines. This is not so. What did suffer was the quantity, because the vines that were attacked wilted and died. It was the mildew which began in 1882 that affected quality and resulted in miserably thin wines often with a taste of decay. Frequently too in the decade from 1879 the weather conditions were unfavourable, yet some good wines were made in the earlier years. André Simon has praised the Latour '79, and I have good reason to know that the Mouton '80, which also won his and Ian Campbell's commendation, was a very fine wine indeed. I drank this at the château in October 1966; the colour was deep, and the wine was extraordinarily full-flavoured and big. It could have been forty years younger. One could not wish for a better wine. In the same year I had Ausone '80 at Avery's of Bristol. The colour was *rosé*, and neither the nose nor the palate suggested claret; yet it was not decayed. However Ronald Avery had already given me a bottle and this I opened, without much hope, in March 1967. It was surprisingly good. The colour, though pale, was much truer than the previous bottle, the nose was fruity, and the body had a fullness that actually did suggest a St-Émilion. Indeed the wine evoked a distinct suggestion of the aroma and flavour of very old vintage port. It had been château-bottled, and perhaps was *hermitagé*. I suspect that the other bottle had been ullaged, whereas this was up to the base of the neck. With an old wine the cork is the decisive factor, and that is why the leading châteaux re-cork their reserves of old wines roughly every twenty-five years. I have more than once tasted Latour 1881, from the cellars of Sir George Meyrick in Hampshire and Anglesey, and sold at Christie's in 1970. Although hard and rather severe, with an excess of acidity, all the bottles were sound and the best were remarkably fruity for a little-considered vintage in the middle of the phylloxera.

The phylloxera–mildew years need not detain us. I have been told at Mouton that the '81 is still good. I once drank a surprisingly good Rausan-Ségla '85 when it was more than sixty years old, but '85 was not a good vintage, the quantity was the smallest of the decade, and only about a fifth of the output of '75. There was also a small crop in '87, but the wines were better though they do not appear to have lasted well. The '88s were light but good, and the Ch. Margaux had a big reputation. The only '88 that I have drunk on the spot is the Lafite, on the October 1977 occasion. Served in magnum, it was a curious wine: the colour was big, but there was little nose. The wine lacked fruit and charm, and though quite free of decay and in perfect condition, it was still 'green' after nearly ninety years. Quantitatively this was the biggest vintage of the decade. The '89s were launched with hopeful noises by a trade desperately looking for good vintages to offer. Not that the wines of the eighties were poured down the sink. They were sold and drunk. For example the Wine Society list of 1899 had Branon 1881 and 1884, both at 32s. a dozen, Léo-ville-Las-Cases 1883 at 43s. and Palmer-Margaux 1886 at 34s. (Branon-Licterie was listed as a leading Léognan in the 1868 Cocks et Féret but is not in recent issues.)

In recent years my experience of old – and indeed also of not so old – clarets has been extended by a series of dinners given in London by Joseph Berkmann, the Austrian-born restaurateur. At each, about a dozen vintages of a leading growth's wine have been 'discussed' by rather more than that number of guests; and two bottles of each vintage have been served so that it was possible to correct impressions that may be derived from a single bottle of an old wine or doubtful vintage. Accordingly in 1971 I was able to compare at the same table Ch. Margaux 1887 and 1888. The '87 was remarkably well-preserved but had an odd 'mildew' flavour that was not very agreeable. The '88 was much better, with a good colour and a surprising amount of fruit; a big, complete wine for its age and vintage, and well-balanced. The following year La Mission-Haut-Brion, opened at the château, was very dark brown in colour and still contained some fruit on nose and palate, but decay crept up on both; yet a good wine for an indifferent year.

Recovery began properly in 1890 – a very expensive year although not considered a great vintage, for the wines were hard; yet I have drunk at least one fine bottle, a magnum of Pape-Clément, opened in 1948. It was full-bodied, deep-coloured and with the nose of a fine old claret. Although vigorous, the wine had a slight after-taste which prevented it from being in the top class, but the flavour was good. Much older-tasting but with a fine 'sealing-wax' nose was the Gruaud-Larose from Sir Arthur Evans's cellar on Boars Hill, Oxford, which was drunk in 1961; in flavour the wine was well on the way down.

The next two years, 1891 and 1892, had no reputation, but 1893 was different. After an exceptionally hot summer, the vintage began on 15 August, the earliest in 170 years of Bordeaux records. Ch. Margaux started picking on 17 August, and Lafite finished before the end of that month – for the first time ever in the history of Lafite. Owing to the immediate fame of this vintage the opening prices doubled within less than three years of the wine being made. The vintage was, like 1921, particularly successful for white wines, and Yquem '93 was one of the great wines of that château.

The red wines lasted well, and David Peppercorn, late of the International Distillers & Vintners group and a serious-minded judge of claret, has written that in 1957 the Lafite '93 was still excellent, with a sweetness that reminded him of the '29s. Twenty years later I was to some extent able to confirm this at the château. Served at the final dinner in October 1977, it preceded the 1869, and save for the 1900, opened at the previous dinner, it excelled the other two nineteenth-century wines shown. It had a big colour for its age, a very fine old-claret nose and a 'sweet', fruity flavour, as noted by Peppercorn. Slight decay developed in the glass, but it remained an excellent wine. Unfortunately, as already recorded in the chapter on the Bordeaux trade, there was a profound slump, and although the '93s were years later regarded as exceptionally fine for the period, the prices obtained by the growers were very low. In the Médoc Latour and Margaux achieved the best figure at 1,800 frs., Lafite only made 1,600 frs. and Mouton-Rothschild 1,300. The best prices went to the Graves, with 2,500 frs. for Haut-Brion and 1,500 frs. for La Mission-Haut-Brion. One reason given for the low prices was the absence from the market of England – still the most important customer. The Yquem, also from Sir Arthur Evans's cellar, was remarkably fine in 1947 in spite of its dark golden colour.

Thanks again to Joseph Berkmann, I sampled the Ch. Margaux '93 at the dinner mentioned above. It had an extraordinarily deep colour for its age, and tasted surprisingly young and fruitily sweet. It was beautifully well-preserved, and many present at the dinner voted it the wine of the evening. More recently still, Dr Bernard Watney opened a bottle of the Latour '93. This had a big colour and a fine nose, but although one would have thought it younger, there was some decay in this particular bottle.

The 1894s were poor (a bottle of Branaire-Ducru, château-bottled, opened by Ronald Avery in July 1972, had a coarse, rather thin, dried-up but not decayed flavour). Then another very hot summer in 1895 produced a lot of wines that were 'pricked', i.e. turned to vinegar, a fate the '93s had escaped. The late Christian Cruse recounted to me an interesting story of that scorching late September vintage. Professor Ulysse Gayon (1845–1929), Director of the Bordeaux Station Agronomique et Oenologique from 1880 to 1920, pupil and friend of Pasteur, happened to be staying at Lafite. Observing that the temperature of the must in the vats was rising fast and likely to go over the top, to stop the fermentation and turn the wine to vinegar, he advised Baron de Rothschild to order a large quantity of ice to be sent immediately from Bordeaux, more than thirty miles away. The same advice was given to Mouton-Rothschild next door, blocks of ice were thrown into the vats and both wines were saved. The news spread to neighbouring châteaux and some of them, including Pontet-Canet, adopted this emergency measure; but elsewhere many wines went wrong. Cruse added that Mouton-Rothschild 1895 was one of the best clarets he had ever drunk. By good fortune I was enabled to drink this wine at Mouton in October 1968. I remembered Christian Cruse's story when going through the private cellar, and asked Raoul Blondin, one of the two *maître de chai* brothers, whether there was any '95 in the cellars, and if so what was it like. He replied that he did not think there was any and did not know the wine. However as the hovering candle light flickered over the bins I saw a label bearing the vintage in question behind a bin of other wines. There were indeed some bottles and two days later one was drunk with Philippe Cottin of La Bergerie, the firm that markets Mouton, and my wife. Cottin had not drunk the '95 Mouton either. In fact, it was a remarkable wine. The colour was deep, the nose was positively rich, and the flavour extraordinarily full and sweet. The wine was a complete claret, with no hint of decay. No doubt the residual sweetness was owing to the very hot year, as was the case with the '47 clarets. The following day I sought out Raoul

Blondin, who had tasted the wine when decanting it. Beaming, he said: '*Monsieur, c'était un grand vin.*' It was.

During the same visit to Bordeaux I drank another '95: the follow-up of Christian Cruse's story. For he opened a bottle of the Montrose, apologizing for his lack of Mouton. This was brown in tint, but there was no hint of decay in the nose or taste. It had a slightly strong taste, and probably in youth it was a rather coarse, powerful wine as indeed Montrose can be. Now it was a fine big wine, but lacked the roundness of a great claret; it had probably not had the advantage of the ice treatment. Such a measure would be illegal nowadays, since the melted ice dilutes the must, so today it is lowered into the vats in bags; but I have heard of more recent cases of the ice being thrown in whole, notably in 1921 and 1947.

André Simon praised the Mouton '95 as well as the Lafite, and I have heard that the Carruades de Lafite lasted well for at least sixty years. There were other successes, and David Peppercorn has mentioned the Pétrus as still being very fine in 1963. However in October 1971, Henri Woltner opened a bottle of his La Mission-Haut-Brion '95 which was perfectly sound. The colour was brownish, and the wine had a slightly perfumed nose and a very special scented flavour. It was very different in flavour from other very old wines, and perhaps the excessively hot summer had produced wines with an exceptional amount of glycerine. It was still very fine seven years later in September 1978, with that fine 'waxy' nose of fine old claret and almost a 'liquorice' flavouring.

The 1896s were light though agreeable (and Peppercorn has recorded an exceptional bottle of Lafite '96, drunk in 1954), but the following year was without reputation. The summer weather before the vintage was atrocious, the crop was small with many unripe grapes. The Gilbeys in the Loudenne diary refer to the 'complete failure of the 1897 vintage'. However, as recently as 1967 I drank a remarkable bottle of the Lafite, château-bottled from the property's own stock. This was the prelude to the 1803, already referred to. The colour was deep and the flavour was strong, full and firm, as if it had once been a very hard wine. It had plenty of distinction and character now. Oddly enough the Sauternes were doing well at the time. Yquem '97 sold for 4,000 frs. the *tonneau*.

In 1898 the crop was small owing to disease and lack of rain after a dry summer. In fact some good wines were made, but they were overshadowed by the extraordinary pair of years that immediately followed. In September 1967 I drank at the château the Mouton '98, which had an excellent colour for its age and a fruity nose, but the wine was showing its age; nevertheless a fine wine after just on seventy years of what was considered almost an off-vintage. A year later I drank with Christian Cruse a curiosity of the same vintage: Léoville-Poyferré 1898 Vin de Goutte. As already mentioned in the Médoc chapter on Margaux, a *vin de goutte* in Bordeaux is a *vin rosé*, normally made for summer drinking for the proprietor's own use. This was the case with the Léoville-Poyferré '98. The 70-year-old *vin de goutte* was the colour of a medium sherry rather than pink. It was still perfectly balanced, a light but still fruity and agreeable wine. The strength, I was told, was only 10·5 degrees, but it had survived. Indeed Cruse half-apologized to me for not serving the '78, but that was now finished.

The two final years of the nineteenth century did their best to make up for the unsatisfactory vintages of the previous twenty years. Both were prolific, 1899 making nearly 400,000 *tonneaux* (3,600,000 hl), and 1900 well over 600,000 *tonneaux* (5,400,000 hl), a figure not exceeded until the unhappy 1922s. The Bordeaux trade realized the exceptional quality of the '99s almost before they were made and the classed growths were snapped up as soon as they left the vats. Nevertheless as the opening prices in Appendix C show, the proprietors did not secure much satisfaction from the prices. They were probably even less happy with those they secured for the next vintage, which after a very fine summer was very prolific. The 1900 prices were often little more than half those of the 1899s, and not only for the new wine. The Gilbeys noted at Loudenne that Mouton-Rothschild '98, which had sold for £22 a hogshead in 1899, dropped to £7 in 1900. Suddenly there was too much good wine available – but for the last time for a score of years.

As early as 1903 the Loudenne diary records that the relative superiority of the 1899s or the 1900s was greatly discussed, comparisons being made with the '64s and '65s or the '74s and '75s. At that time it was thought that the '99s had more flavour and colour, while the 1900s had 'a remarkable softness and delicacy'. Such a comparison between two outstanding successive vintages was not to be possible again until 1928 and 1929. The prices of the 1900s were lower by one-third (they can be compared in Appendix C), and the Gilbeys bought large quantities. In 1904 their records showed stocks at Loudenne of 5,793 bottles of Latour and 5,830 bottles of Lafite: about 20 hogsheads-worth apiece. In 1912 after a tasting of their wines the Gilbeys stated that 'Latour was by far the best of the 1900s'.

Between them these two years provided, in the drought of good vintages in the first two decades of the present century, the stand-by for *amateurs* of claret until well after the First World War. They were the wines to crown a wine dinner, as the finer '45s might today. They gave the lie to the pessimists who said that really fine claret on the pre-phylloxera pattern was a thing of the past. Further they provided a splendid arguing point as to which vintage was the superior. The '99s were perhaps more delicate wines than the '00s (the abbreviation is irresistible). André Simon twenty or so years ago stated that the 1900s had stood the test of time better, and this is Ronald Barton's view, yet I have drunk some 1899s in first-class condition. I have not had the fortune to be able to compare them on the same occasion, and for some unknown reason, I have drunk more of the earlier year; with the 1900s so exceptionally prolific, one would have expected to have found a larger number of them surviving.

It must be borne in mind, however, that, as mentioned earlier, a great deal of the wines of these post-phylloxera vintages were made from ungrafted vines, in whole or in part. Replanting with grafted vines at Latour only began seriously in 1901–2 and continued at an annual rate of $1\frac{1}{2}$ to $2\frac{1}{2}$ ha until 1913.

The first '99 I drank was the Branaire-Ducru, bought in 1941 from Avery's for 14s. a bottle, château-bottled, and opened in June 1942. Unused then to wine of such quality I and my guests were quite overcome; by its character, not by its alcohol. It was vigorous but smooth with an aroma that could truthfully be called a bouquet. It was certainly the finest wine I had drunk to date. In all I had five bottles of this wine – the last cost me as much as 21s.! Although they varied, all were good, and the last, opened in October 1959 when exactly sixty years old, was superb, with the colour, nose, sugar and fruit that had impressed me over seventeen years earlier.

In 1942 I was invited to visit the then manager of the wine department of the Army & Navy Stores, A. M. Heath, a well-known claret-lover. Previous correspondence had shown him that I too was very interested in claret, and on his table was a splendid bottle of Mouton-Rothschild '99. We consumed it between us to the accompaniment only of wartime biscuits. He then sold me half a dozen bottles of another bottling. These were somewhat ullaged, and not as fine. It is fair to add that he said they were uneven and charged me only 9s. a bottle. Thirty years later the Mouton '99 was splendidly full and rich-flavoured at the château.

I will not recite a list of the '99s I have drunk, but one particular occasion stands out in my memory. It was a dinner given in May 1950 by Ian Campbell and his wife at the Hind's Head Hotel, Bray, the scene of many chronicled wine dinners, where he, then in his eightieth year, was living. The other guests were his publisher, Jack McDougall and his wife, John Betjeman, Maurice Platnauer, then Vice-Principal and later Principal of Brasenose College, Oxford, Harry Waugh and myself. After some excellent La Mission-Haut-Brion 1934 and delicious Ch. Margaux 1929 we had the very last magnum of Latour 1899 in what had been the late Barry Neame's cellar. It was superbly full and rich; what one might hope for in an 1899 and a Latour. The next time I drank it was at a dinner given in London in January 1967 to Harry Waugh by his former associates and friends at Harvey's. Two bottles of the '99 had been brought over three months earlier by Harry Waugh from the château, of which he was a director. They showed just a trace of tiredness, probably owing to the journey, but the wine had great colour, concentration of nose and a slightly 'roasted' taste. Two other '99s that deserve mention happened to come my way late in 1977. The first was a Carruades de Lafite, bottled by Eschenauer in Bordeaux and from the private cellar of Louis Eschenauer. It was opened by Michael Broadbent of Christie's, where he had acquired it. I never remember previously drinking a really old Carruades. This was pale but not brown and had what Michael Broadbent described as an 'ivy leaves' nose. There was evident decay, though the wine was drinkable; it was interesting primarily perhaps for its source. Then in December 1977 John Avery opened a bottle of Gruaud-Larose 1899, which he had bought not long previously at Christie's. This was a risk, but in fact the wine was excellent, with distinguished old-claret aroma and a concentrated 'waxy' taste that I associate with even older vintages. It was slightly dry in flavour but not drying up, and remained true in the glass.

In 1899 all the 'names' were good, and I had a couple of magnificent bottles of Haut-Brion. Also delicious was Haut-

Brion 1900, though not as good as the '99, but the other top
wines of 1900 had eluded me until 1967 at Mouton, where my
request to taste the 1900 was willingly acceded to. It was put
to a hard test, for my suggestion for the previous wine had
been Cheval-Blanc 1929, a tremendously sweet rich wine.
Yet the Mouton 1900 had more body, prospect of life and
distinction than the much younger St-Émilion. It had everything a really fine old claret in perfect condition should have.
Château Margaux was another celebrated 1900, and said to
be the finest Margaux of all, but I had never come across it
until Joseph Berkmann's dinner in 1971 already mentioned.
It had a good colour and was not brown; a soft old wine,
well-balanced and very fine for its age, with no hint of decay.
In the same year a bottle of Léoville-Las-Cases (served at the
same Christie's dinner of Glamis wines as the Lafite '70) was
even better, with a good colour, a perfumed nose and long,
elegant flavour that combined to make a soft but still perfectly
complete claret that would have been taken to be much
younger.

The rather few other 1900s that I have drunk, among them
Pape-Clément and Talbot, were all fairly delicate wines; and
that the Mouton, drunk much later, certainly was not: a big
fruity wine for its age. The 1900 Lafite was a celebrated wine,
but I never had the chance to drink it until it was served in a
magnum as the last wine of the first dinner at the October 1977
dégustation. It followed the 1929 in bottles, and in my view
out-distanced that well-known year, though not all agreed
with me – among those who did not was my wife! I was greatly
impressed by the deep colour of the 1900 for its age, the lovely
'sweet' nose and wonderfully full, fruity flavour, even if a
little decay eventually showed in the glass. It had not quite
the concentration of some of the older pre-phylloxera wines –
though, as mentioned earlier, it was still produced from the
vignes françaises.

It might be thought that these wines, which in a way

began as well as ended an era, would have been in great demand. Not, however, to judge from the lists of the I.E.C. Wine Society in the period before the First World War. True, this society, small then with only two or three thousand members, tended to concentrate on the less expensive wines. However in December 1902 was listed the Lafite '99, English-bottled as all this château's produce was at this period, and with a comment, unusual in those days, that it was 'one of the finest wines of this exceptionally fine vintage, suitable for laying down'. The price was 42s. a dozen, and it remained on the list at that price until 1910 when it was cautiously raised by 3s. a case, and a further 5s. in 1911. I have no idea of the quantity originally bought, but it is unlikely to have been large, yet the wine remained on the list for ten years and was only sold out in December 1912. It was of course not the cheapest '99 on a list no more heavily crowded by them than by the 1900s. In 1906 Pontet-Canet '99 came on at 25s. per dozen, Gruaud-Larose '99 at 28s. and Giscours '99 at the same price. In 1913 Gruaud-Larose '99, château-bottled, appeared at 58s. and Malescot 1900 at 43s. However, as George Saintsbury indicated in his *Notes on a Cellar Book*, this was a bad time for claret drinking; champagne had largely taken over. A few years earlier, in 1897, the Gilbeys had written, 'consumption in England has fallen off considerably for expensive after-dinner claret'.

1901–1919

This was not only a bad time for claret drinkers; it was a bad period for the growers and merchants too. It also provides a warning to those who believe that nature has to some extent been tamed by chemistry and nowadays a good average of fair vintages is assured. True, the worst may not be quite as bad as they were, but 1963, 1968 and 1977, to mention three recent disastrous Bordeaux vintages, show us what nature can still effect. In the first nineteen years of the present century only one year can just be squeezed into the 'very fine' category: 1906.

Of the first three years, 1901 was not bad though variable; yet no one was much interested in such wines after their predecessors. The 1902s and 1903s were poor and after the failure of the latter vintage the Gilbeys were noting, 'no marketable wine has been made in the Médoc since 1900'. The 1904 offered more hopes but the wines appear to have lacked backbone and did not last. This was one good reason why I have drunk very few, but the survival of two or three that I chanced to drink in the mid-1970s shows that good wines can be made in a moderate year – and 1904 was not a bad year, signalled by Tastet & Lawton as 'good without being of exceptional quality, disappointing in ageing'. It also shows that wines from good stables may last better than might be expected. In 1975 La Tour-Haut-Brion, drunk at La Mission-Haut-Brion, though very brown in colour was remarkable for its big nose and concentrated flavour. Two years later in London I shared a bottle of Cheval-Blanc with Michael Broadbent of Christie's. Extremely pale, pink rather than brown, it had an unexpectedly fine and fruity flavour which held up perfectly in decanter and glass.

Until then I had been rather luckier with the 1905s, a light but elegant vintage, and I have known vintages drinkable up to the early 1970s, including Léoville-Las-Cases and Figeac. However, on the whole they did not make old bones.

The 1906s were much sturdier. After a hot summer and a good vintage a rather small crop of exceptionally full-bodied wines was produced. Opinions have varied on the final outcome, and the only bottle I have ever cellared was a magnum of Lafite, château-bottled, which came from that treasure-house of old wines, Avery's of Bristol, just after the last war, and was opened in 1949. It had not then the powerful quality associated with '06s, but was light, soft and delicate, good all the way but at the end of the journey. On the other hand Haut-Brion, which I have drunk, was outstanding and perhaps the best '06 in my experience.

However, once again in Bordeaux in the autumn of 1968, bottles were generously opened for me in the interests of my incomplete vinous education. At Cantemerle Henri Binaud wound up a lunch of his wines with the '06 Cantemerle. The colour was light, but the nose was fine, followed by a concentrated fruity flavour, though the wine was beginning to show its age. I would have taken it for a '20 had I not known the vintage. Secondly, at Latour a bottle of '06 preceded the '65 mentioned earlier. Although a fine complete wine, it was rather lighter than expected for a Latour, and was to some extent overshadowed by a wine forty-one years senior; no mean compliment to the latter. A 1906 with a considerable reputation was La Lagune, but I have not drunk it.

The only 1907 I have ever had – two bottles of Ch. Margaux – also came from Avery's. The vintage was exceptionally large, but apparently considerably affected by oidium, and the wine was light. The two bottles of Margaux, château-bottled, were drunk in 1943 and 1947 respectively. The first was very fine, with a remarkably fresh aroma, and a light but complete flavour; the second showed signs of fading, but it was ullaged. The bottle in good condition must have been well above the average in a vintage that did not generally last.

Of the 1908s, André Simon has stated that the only one he enjoyed was the Lafite; it was a hard, unattractive vintage. I have twice drunk the Haut-Brion with interest; the first a magnum in London in May 1965, which was past its best and had some decay; the second a far better bottle drunk at Mouton in October 1966. Very light in colour and with a fine old-claret nose, it was surprisingly big with a rather strong burnt taste. Having, as is the custom at Mouton, been decanted several hours before dinner, it did decline in the glass, but was a distinguished wine while it lasted. The only other

'08s of note that I remember drinking were the Malescot and the Latour, the latter when it was about sixty-five years old. The former was mostly remarkable for its very brown, old colour, and the Latour was brownish too, but was much better balanced, with a good deal of sugar and fruit for such an off-vintage but rather pinched at the end. The Malescot was less agreeable but retained a strong taste.

The 1909s aroused some expectations, but on the whole these were not realized. I once drank an Ausone '09 that was good, and in 1971 a bottle was opened at Mouton. In the way that Mouton and Latour seem to have, it had retained a fine old nose even sixty years after an indifferent vintage. The wine was a little hard still and lacked fruit, but it was certainly well-preserved for the vintage and made interesting drinking. The 1910s have passed me by, and so did the 1911s until the mid-seventies. A bottle of Mouton-Rothschild at the château was surprisingly fruity, but finer still was Cheval-Blanc, first drunk at Loudenne in 1976. Though slightly brown it was remarkable for its 'sealing-wax' nose and rich, concentrated flavour: a real Cheval-Blanc in a very hot year, rather like 1921 and 1947 when this estate's most celebrated wines were made. I was later able to buy a few bottles at Christie's. Some were ullaged to 'mid-shoulder', as the catalogues have it, and these were no good, but the reasonably full bottles had re-tained their fruit, though they were not as fine as the bottle at Loudenne, and declined in the glass. It is risky, incidentally, to buy or to expect much of bottles of old claret ullaged as much as this, although there are exceptions. It means that air has been let in, and decay is very likely to result. The year 1910 was notoriously one of the worst and smallest vintages of the century throughout France. ('It is necessary to go back a hundred years in the history of the Médoc to find a vintage as poor as this year,' wrote the Gilbeys while staying at Loudenne during the vintage period.) The year 1911, much better after an exceptionally hot summer, was not a particularly successful Bordeaux vintage although a classic year in Burgundy. The intervention of the First World War resulted in many being bottled too late. The 1912s were affected by mildew, and the only two that have ever come my way were not very agreeable. The Cos d'Estournel in 1957 had quite gone and was in fact undrinkable. Eleven years later the Duhart-Milon was very brown and had a distinctly old nose, with a suggestion of decay. Yet it had some quality of fine claret and was at least palatable. At this age, of course, there may be great variations between bottles, and one might expect better or even worse luck, particularly with an off-vintage. Generally the 1912s suffered from a great excess of acidity. Much the same applied to 1913. As it happened to be my birth year Tom Whelehan very kindly opened a bottle of Lafite '13 for me in Dublin in May 1966; it was very thin and rather acid, although drinkable. Another better '13 was Ausone, reasonably fruity for an off-year fifty-three years old. Among the many off-vintages shown at Christie's in June 1977 in the pre-sale tasting of over forty vintages of Latour was the 1913, which showed some decay and was not agreeable; that did not stop it being knocked down for £42 a bottle, a high figure reflected in that sale for other notorious vintages. The buyers, it was suggested, were buying the vintages of their birth, but even that would not have moved me to bid for the 1913. The 1914s had a rather higher reputation, but did not last. Many of them were bottled too late. Yet an Haut-Brion '14 that I drank at Mouton in October 1966 was by no means disagreeable and had a distinction of flavour not lost under an end-taste of slight decline. It could fairly be called an interesting wine. This was a successful year for Sauternes, and Yquem made a fine wine, which I have enjoyed more than once in recent years.

Although 1915 was an outstanding Burgundy year, it was poor in Bordeaux, and the best year of the First World War was certainly 1916. The wines were big and hard and in their youth were said to lack charm as hard claret can. I have once or twice drunk them in England and they were not good, but two excellent examples encountered at source were the Cantemerle and Mouton-Rothschild. The former I drank first at the château in 1964 and again in Bordeaux in the flat of the proprietor, Henri Binaud. It was a surprisingly full, *corsé* wine, vigorous but without the distinction and completeness of the Cantemerle '20 which preceded it on the second occasion. A third bottle of the Cantemerle, drunk at the château in 1975, was the best of the three, as it had the aroma of classic claret in fine condition, and was complete in flavour. The previous year I had the good fortune to encounter the Latour *chez lui*. It had all the size, colour, nose and fruit that one would expect of a fine wine of this château and was likely to last, one would guess, for many years more. The Mouton '16 was from a magnum and in September '67 was in very good shape. Although there was some brownness in colour, for a wine of fifty years old its colour was deep. In flavour the wine was fairly delicate but had a fruity nose. It needed drinking and it was drunk. Not the least remarkable wine of the few of this year that have come my way was the Lanessan, opened at Loudenne by Martin Bamford. It had an amazingly deep colour for its age, and a full flavour too that gave the impression of a much younger wine; big and powerful, if probably a coarse wine in its youth; but the '29 turned out an unusually long keeper too.

André Simon blamed the war for the lack of success of the '17s, which were light and might have been better. One alone remains in my memory: Latour, which like the '93 was produced at a dinner by Dr Bernard Watney. It had been recorked at the château in 1960, as is the custom with all their old wines. It had a fine big nose, and tasted rich and surprisingly fruity at the onset, but aged quite quickly in the glass. What was strange was that this wine, made in the disastrous depths of the First World War, should have survived so long.

The 1918s were of course exuberantly hailed at the end of the war, and were quite widely bought. The great Paris wine firm of Nicolas must have plunged heavily on them, since for many years they appeared in their famous special lists issued annually before Christmas and a number were sold for high prices at the auction which the firm organized in November 1972 to celebrate its 150th anniversary; the proceeds went towards the preservation of Venice. However in general the vintage was not very successful, although in 1970 I was surprised at the quality of the Ducru-Beaucaillou drunk at the château. With a very fine old claret nose, good colour and plenty of flavour it was remarkably sound for its age and vintage. It is surprising that the 1919s were not better, for again this was a fine year in Burgundy, although there the wines were tough and hard. Nevertheless I was surprised in September 1967 to drink Latour '19 at the château and find it so good. But then Latour is a celebrated surpriser. It was full-coloured for its age, with that 'bigness' of flavour that is the mark of Latour. There was a slight descent in taste at the end, but I would certainly have taken it for *un grand millésime*. I cannot recollect many finer bottles of this sad claret period between 1901 and 1919, but we were now on the eve of one of Bordeaux's great periods.

TWENTY-FIVE VINTAGES, 1920–1944

1920 (22 SEPTEMBER)*

I have always regarded 1920 as the finest claret year which I have had the luck to drink in relative plenty. They were about twenty years old when I first drank them and probably the vintage as a whole was at its peak in the next twenty years,

*Date on which the vintage began. These dates are reproduced from the records of Tastet & Lawton, with the kind permission of these celebrated brokers.

up to about 1960. One has to admit that a good many of the wines have now been in decline some time. However this is one of the factors to be taken into account with all wine. If longevity is the first consideration then judgements must be revised on many vintages, although for a leading year it is fair to demand a minimum period of, say, fifteen to twenty years. The '20s certainly passed the age test, but it was a great vintage also on quality. Many, perhaps most, people would put '29 ahead, for the later vintage was quite remarkably fruity and 'sweet'. But one çannot have everything, and if the '20s were a little drier they were also more refined and delicate, in my view more 'clarety'; whereas the '29s lacked this delicacy. It is a matter of choice. Ian Campbell, for example, found most '20s 'disappointingly dry'. Others found them not up to expectations too. Maurice Healy in his volume on *Claret* (1934) in the Constable Wine Library described 1920 as 'that year, which has proved so disappointing to us all (except to Warner Allen, who always assured me that the 1920s would not last, and who may read here the record of his triumph over me).' He then called it 'that treacherous vintage', but had a good word for Latour. In 1936, as recorded in the *Wine & Food Quarterly*, at a dinner attended by André Simon, Maurice Healy, J. Murray Easton and James Laver, the last-named commented, 'there is no other 1920 to compare with it [Latour], but we were lucky to drink it when we did, for it will probably never be better. Its sugar is all but gone and, like all the '20s, it does not appear to have any future.'

However in *Stay Me With Flagons* (1940) Maurice Healy revised his opinion of the '20s, stating, 'The 1920s seem all to have come back.' I attended a lunch with André Simon in Bristol in April 1967, and before the nineteenth-century Lafites we had some 'younger' wines, which included the Latour '20. It was at the top of its form, with a deep colour, wonderfully full nose and great distinction of flavour; and it was still delicious several years later. Which goes to show. I have no doubt thirty years previously the '20s must have been passing through a bad phase, which certainly they had largely overcome by the 1940s.

It would be wearisome for the reader if I went through all the '20s I have had and enjoyed, but two in particular stand out: the Latour, already referred to above, and the Cheval-Blanc. The latter I will leave to discuss along with the '21, but the Latour '20 today is still one of the finest bottles of claret one could wish for, although I have had disappointing bottles, probably because they were not kept well over the years. But a bottle in good condition is still full, rich and yet not too 'bold', as some might think its rival, the Latour '29. The other leading growths I have tasted were distinguished too, the Lafite fine and delicate, the Haut-Brion fuller, and the Mouton also. The way in which old wines vary from bottle to bottle – the state of the cork is usually the determining factor – and the danger of pontificating, was brought home to me by the Ch. Margaux, which I have only drunk two or three times. Some years ago now a bottle seemed very old and tired, and in the first edition of this book I commented that it was probably too old. Yet, in 1971 at the Ch. Margaux dinner, already mentioned, two bottles of this wine were wonderfully complete and well-balanced. The nose was all that one would expect of an old Ch. Margaux, and the flavour was distinguished; a much better wine than the '29 drunk earlier on the same occasion. The Mouton, once outstanding, is definitely in decline to judge from drinking it more than once at the château.

In their day the Palmer, Pape-Clément and Ausone were very fine wines. I do not think I have tasted a really first-class Ausone since. Nor a Rauzan-Gassies, whose '20 in magnum was still excellent in 1964. There was the minor La Closerie from Moulis which was fine for a lesser growth as late as the 1950s. Much later still, Cantemerle was in light but perfect condition in Bordeaux in 1966, and in the same year I drank with no little pleasure the La Mission-Haut-Brion '20 at the château; an old wine but still fruity. However, when I again drank it at the château – my own choice – in September 1977, it was showing its age: brown in colour, though with remarkably sweet taste, yet dry on the taste. Lanessan, whose '29 is mentioned below, made an excellent '20, still full-coloured and only pardonably showing its age in 1968 when I drank it at Loudenne. All in all 1920 was a fine year for *amateurs* of fine but delicate claret.

1921 (15 SEPTEMBER)

Every other wine made after this exceptionally hot summer was overshadowed by the Cheval-Blanc, one of the most extraordinary clarets I have ever drunk. Rather like the '47 from the same growth, it became a legend early in its life, and was expensive at a time when most fine clarets were very cheap. I remember it on Avery's list in 1938 for 300s. a dozen, at a time when Lafite '20 could be bought for 120s. The reason for its success lay in its quite extraordinary sweetness and sugar. This excess of sugar at the vintage which began on 15 September had been the ruin of a number of '21s, notably the Lafite which turned vinegary in the fermenting vats in the course of a single night. So far as I know there never was any '21 Lafite; it was sold as Pauillac or to Calvet as *vin rouge* for 1,600 frs. a *tonneau*. The sun was so hot that the grapes were scorched, and I remember some Margaux '21, which seemed to me to have a slightly burnt taste; and the Gruaud-Larose in April 1967 had a curiously strong flavour, though also fruity. On the whole the Médocs were not very successful, although those that survived to old age were agreeable enough. For example Palmer '21, opened by Christian Cruse in Bordeaux in September 1966, was very brown but still fruity, sweet and of fine claret flavour. Quite remarkable, however, was a double-magnum of Mouton-Rothschild opened at the château in September 1977. The size was justified by the large dinner-party, chiefly of Americans, and it followed a similar-sized bottle of the wonderfully rich, concentrated, typically Mouton '47. That the '21 could stand up to it, with full colour for age, lovely nose and round fruity. body was a tribute to its quality; indeed it had more character than the richer '47. A few days later I had the chance to drink the Haut-Brion at the château in half-bottles. It too had plenty of colour, a very sweet nose and rich flavour. I suspect that both wines benefited greatly from never having been moved.

Another successful survivor was Cantemerle '21, which I drank twice when it had just about reached its half-century. The first was in the Bordeaux home of the proprietor, Henri Binaud, in October 1970; the wine showed big colour for its age, and was very fruity – a fine old bottle that only began to decline when it had been decanted two hours. The second bottle was a present from M. Binaud, and I opened it almost a year later to celebrate a friend's fiftieth birthday. Again the colour was excellent, and the wine had excellent flavour, if finishing a little dry.

About the same time I had the first chance to drink two red Graves of this vintage: Haut-Brion and Domaine de Chevalier. The former had a good nose, but the wine was clearly 'over the hill' and a taste of decay grew in the glass; the Chevalier had more colour, perhaps just a sounder bottle, but it also had a surprisingly scented nose and taste.

Certainly it was the St-Émilions that scored and not only the Cheval-Blanc. In St-Émilion itself in 1964 I drank Canon '21, with a fine nose that really came out of the glass. The flavour had a certain hardness that no doubt had preserved the wine, but it was a splendidly generous-flavoured wine, which had been decanted by Édouard Cruse in Bordeaux five hours before we drank it at the well-known La Plaisance restaurant in St-Émilion. Another remarkable '21 from a St-Émilion growth was La Magdelaine, which M. Jean-Pierre Moueix opened at his home, Ch. Videlot, in October 1971. The deep colour was truly remarkable, and both nose and flavour were those of a rich wine still youthful. One would have taken it for a wine of the second half of the forties. No doubt the rich flavour owed something to that extraordinarily hot summer. It was M. Moueix's last bottle. There was also the fine Clos Fourtet '21, which I drank in Bristol in 1964, on the last occasion I encountered the Cheval-Blanc, with Ronald Avery, André Simon and two or three others. The Clos Fourtet was by no means an inferior wine, yet there was lacking the peculiar richness of the Cheval-Blanc, by then distinctly pale, pinkish rather than brown, but still with a remarkable concentration of nose and flavour that reminded one strangely enough of a great luscious German white wine.

The most interesting occasion on which I drank the '21 Cheval-Blanc was at my home in Wiltshire in July 1954; interesting because the company, which included Norman Alexander, Douglas McClean and Harry Waugh, was able to compare it with the '20. Contrary to my almost invariable practice, I served the '20 first, because I thought otherwise the older wine would be overwhelmed by the astonishing sweetness of the '21. The '20 had more colour, for the '21 already had the rosy hue much more pronounced ten years later. The nose of the '20 was distinctly better, and on the palate it was more complete and velvety. On the other hand the '21 though markedly sweet was not cloying and revealed gradations of flavour that made its rival seem almost lacking in distinction and interest. The '21 'finished' with a special quality – almost a flourish. However this was by no means a unanimous view and the table was, as it were, split down the middle, with Alexander and McClean supporting the '20, Waugh and I backing the '21. Probably the '20 was the more complete wine – and outstanding in its year – but the '21 was the more interesting; its fruitiness and flavour were enhanced not cloaked by the sweetness, and at the same time I wondered whether the sugar would stay as the body ebbed; I think it did, as shown by the bottle opened ten years later. I may add I drank the '20 a number of times subsequently, and it did begin to go downhill; the last bottle, tasted in August 1965 against the Pétrus (which showed finely but tired and less good than the Cheval-Blanc), was good all the way but not the wonderfully rich wine it had been earlier.

Throughout Europe 1921 was a very great year for white wines, and not least in the Sauternes. Elsewhere I have commented on the Yquem, which among white Bordeaux enjoyed a similar reputation to Cheval-Blanc in the reds. Too much of this great easy-to-drink wine was, I fear, drunk on luxurious picnics or at race meetings, where a fine bottle of Sauternes took second place to more topical affairs. The other Sauternes were excellent too, and I remember a very fine Coutet. For sheer lusciousness the vintage has probably never been equalled since, certainly not excelled.

1922 (19 SEPTEMBER)

More wine was produced in the Gironde this year than ever before or since – 7,192,657 hl or just on 800,000 *tonneaux*. Owing to the operation since 1937 of *appellation contrôlée* restricting output, it is unlikely that this figure will ever be attained again. Unfortunately quantity was not matched by quality, although the wines, if light and rather lacking in acidity, were not bad. There had been three prolific years, no one much wanted the '22s, and I had never come upon one until the vintage was fifty years old. Then at an Haut-Brion dinner, given by Joseph Berkmann in November 1972, the '22 was served. I was by no means the only one present who had never drunk a '22, and all were pleasurably surprised. For the fruit was still there, and, though light, the wine was well-balanced, with the flavour finishing perfectly; if it didn't hold very well in the glass, it was perhaps the most interesting wine of an evening in which thirteen vintages were shown: from 1962 back to 1906. At the Christie Latour tasting already mentioned the '22 had little to recommend it in colour, nose or fruit, but there was no reason to expect more of it after fifty-five years. However, one other wine that did rather more than rise to the occasion was L'Évangile, drunk in London in March 1976. One does not expect Pomerols to last, particularly from such a vintage, but this had big colour for its age and a fruity nose, with some roundness on the palate. If it did not last in the glass and soon showed some decay, it remained drinkable though short – nevertheless an experience.

1923 (1 OCTOBER)

This also was a prolific year; indeed more wine was produced in Bordeaux in the twenties than in any other comparable period. It was a much better vintage than '22, but the wines were light and on the whole did not last. One of the celebrities was Domaine de Chevalier, but when I drank it in 1957 at home the wine was pale and in decline, although still fruity to the end. On the whole the vintage was past its best when I began to drink it shortly before the last war, and in any case this was not a widely-bought vintage in Britain; the merchants went more for the '24s. However, I did have a really splendid Duhart-Milon '23, which had come to me direct from France, and which drank beautifully from 1940 to 1950. In later years I came upon others: Ch. Margaux at Angludet in 1965, La Lagune and Ausone in Bristol. The first two were very light, but the Ausone was still surprisingly fruity and agreeable; a fine wine. A most charming light but true wine was the Palmer '23 which drank beautifully well into the 1960s and may do so still; and it was at Palmer in October 1972 that the Branaire-Ducru '23 showed as a still elegant, light but complete old claret. An outstanding St-Émilion was

Clos Fourtet, which when forty-five years old was still very fruity. At the same age Cantemerle, though brown, had a delicious aroma and a sweetness on the palate that suggested a '29.

1924 (19 SEPTEMBER)

This was really the vintage when, as it were, I came in, and so I have always had a special feeling for it. Not that it was my birth year, but it was the vintage of the first really mature clarets I drank when they were nearly fifteen years old. The wine was Grand-Puy-Lacoste, purchased from a wine merchant in Nantes, who was one at least of the suppliers of that omnivorous drinker, Hilaire Belloc. It was part of a small consignment, and of the Grand-Puy-Lacoste there were but three bottles which cost me all of 4s. apiece. I opened the first bottle in July 1939 and the last, fearing the worst from bombs, on my birthday in March 1940. Here for the first time I smelled that wonderful bouquet of fine mature claret, an aroma which I then associated with that of blackcurrants. They were delicious bottles and I have never forgotten them.

There were of course many more notable '24s, although some of them were hard and did not develop evenly. The crop was again large (5,605,405 hl), until then only surpassed since 1900 by 1922. Latour, Lafite, Mouton-Rothschild, Pichon-Longueville and Gruaud-Larose-Sarget were among wines I enjoyed from time to time, although I never owned more than three or four of each. They did vary and sometimes they seemed to be going through a 'dumb' patch. Latour, disappointing in 1942, was superb in 1955, but later declined. Some, like Ausone, were rather coarse. Ch. Margaux made the last really fine wine for its class for a long period, and a bottle drunk in 1967 was still surprisingly full and fruity. So too was Palmer in the same year, a wine that twenty-five years earlier had seemed fine but on the delicate side. Giscours made a notable '24 and, though old in flavour when drunk in 1968, it had more fruit than expected and was very enjoyable. All three Léovilles made excellent wines in 1924, and I do not think I have tasted a better Médoc of the vintage than the Poyferré, then in an exceptionally fine era. I drank that in 1949. Much more recently I had the Las-Cases which had faded badly. However in 1967 when staying at Langoa I persuaded Ronald Barton, no great admirer of the '24s, to open a bottle of his Léoville. The colour was deep, the nose and flavour almost powerful; an exceptionally fine wine, which I would have taken for a '29, except it had more finesse.

So far as I was concerned, the St-Émilions and Graves were particularly successful in '24. The Cheval-Blanc was a splendid wine and so was Clos Fourtet, rich and full. Pape-Clément, much more delicate, was fine, but perhaps the Graves I remember best was the Domaine de Chevalier, of which between 1942 and 1946 Justerini & Brooks let me have more than a dozen bottles, beginning at 9s. each and rising over the wartime years to what then seemed the high price of 20s., but was of course very cheap for the quality of the wine. I drank them between 1942 and 1952 and I never had other than really fine bottles: true, delicate, refined claret. Towards the end the wine seemed so light that the next bottle must prove to have lost its body, but this was not so. Haut-Brion made a notable '24, but when I drank it in 1972 the colour was very brown and the fruit gone.

Although I heard from time to time of other people's good bottles, I concluded that nearly all had gone down by the seventies, including at least four of the first growths. The last good bottle that came my way was La Mission-Haut-Brion at the château in October 1976. It had less nose but more colour than the '26 which preceded it, but was a very fine, complete old wine with plenty of fruit and none of the decay that marked many of the '24s a good deal earlier. Some people, including Ian Campbell, never liked them, but on the whole

I was fortunate. It was a fine year for Sauternes, and Yquem served at Mouton-Rothschild in September 1976 was still comparatively fresh and unmaderized, but other bottles of the same wine tasted at much the same time were very heavy. Sauternes appear robust because they are so sweet, but they seem more susceptible to how they are kept than some red wines.

1925 (3 OCTOBER)

A very prolific, undistinguished year in which the wines lacked maturity and tasted green. However even as late as May 1969 a bottle of Petit-Village, clearly an old wine, had a fine nose and a surprising amount of fruit and body for a Pomerol of this age and vintage.

1926 (4 OCTOBER)

Until the early seventies at least this was always spoken of as the 'most expensive claret vintage ever'. The high prices were caused not by the rapacity of growers and merchants after an exceptionally small vintage for the period (under 3 million hl), but through a revaluation of the franc. The vintage began late in the first week of October, the wines were hard and on the dry side. As trade was not too good and English merchants at least were well supplied with the earlier vintages of this bountiful decade, very little expensive '26 was bought here. So not many have come my way until recent years. No doubt they are fine claret, but they tend to lack softness and charm. The most immediately attractive I remember was Cheval-Blanc, still in good form as far as I know, with plenty of sugar. So too was Gruaud-Larose-Sarget when I shared in a magnum in 1965. In the same year Mouton-Rothschild '26 at the château was a shade dry but distinguished and fruity all the way, while Haut-Brion – making indifferent wine generally in this period – tasted well when consumed at the château in September 1967: brownish in colour, a little dry but distinguished claret all the same. Latour is, as might be expected, bigger and fruitier to this day, albeit with the typical austerity of the vintage. A special favourite of mine has been La Lagune, light though true, but which has varied from bottle to bottle owing to poor small corks. Another better-than-average '26 has been Cantemerle. Lafite was distinguished but dry. Probably the best '26 I have drunk in recent years was Cos d'Estournel, a surprisingly big and fruity wine, with a splendid nose and more 'generosity' of flavour than most of its fellows. Another successful survivor in the later 1960s was Lagrange, that back-country St-Julien which has seldom appealed to me. The '26 when forty-plus had more fruit than I would have expected. Ch. Margaux had a certain reputation for this vintage, and a bottle drunk in London in 1970 was a distinguished, if light claret, and certainly not dry. One of the best wines must be the La Mission-Haut-Brion. Opened at the château in 1976, though brownish in tinge, it had a lovely rich nose and beautifully complete flavour.

1927 (27 SEPTEMBER)

Certainly the worst vintage of the twenties, and so far as I know it has left no trace.

1928 (25 SEPTEMBER)

The most controversial vintage of the decade and perhaps of the century so far. In those days 'vintages of the century' were not so prolific as now, but when the 1928s turned up they were hailed as the next best thing. Many wine merchants who had not bought '26 and so had nothing since '24 were only too ready to accept the '28s, which had been made in conditions of great heat, and were plentiful. We have André

Simon's word for it that when bottled in 1931 they were 'as good as one can hope any young clarets to be'. They were bought widely. In fact they mostly turned out very hard wines, and although encouraging voices muttered 'another '70', there was not now the same inclination to wait for fifty years. When the fruity, easy-to-drink '29s came along the battle was joined between supporters of the two vintages, and it is not yet over; although there is no doubt that in popular estimation the '29s won. The protagonists of the '28s aver with some truth that they have outlived their juniors, but it is not agreed that they are all that attractive; for they tend to lack charm. In 1964 I was visiting Latour and asked the *maître de chai*, M. Metté, which vintage of the two he preferred for Latour. He replied 1928, but when later at luncheon we were able to compare the two, the unanimous view round the table was for 1929. However Latour '29 is an exceptional wine, and in some other cases, a château's '28 is now better than the '29, which is in decline. Mouton-Rothschild '28 and '29 are examples of this.

Two of the first growths made very disappointing wine in '28: Lafite and Haut-Brion. Owing to the extremely hot conditions at the vintage, the Lafite had to be pasteurized, and the same is said to have been done with Haut-Brion. The Bordeaux wine merchants who had bought Lafite *en primeur* were so disappointed with the wine that they brought a legal action against the château and returned the wine which had to be sold off later. I have drunk Lafite '28, and it had a curiously dead flavour, with none of the distinction associated with this great growth. Yet such is the way things go that in 1966 I heard of this wine being sold in California for $75 a bottle. Haut-Brion is distinctly odd too. Margaux has always been rather hard and disappointing when I have drunk it, and certainly Latour was the best of the first growths. Mouton '28, drunk at the château in 1966, was a fine big wine, still a little severe.

However, I believe the best Médoc of the year to have been Léoville-Las-Cases, a superb wine, with plenty of body and fruit that reminded one of a '29 and yet also with the breed and delicacy of fine claret. It is one of the few '28s that outdistanced a '29 at the same table; yet on the one occasion I compared it with its own '29, the younger wine won by being even fruitier. The '28 was still fine in the early seventies.

Léoville-Poyferré was not far behind it but without quite so much body, and both the Léoville-Barton and the Langoa were fine too. When the vintage was about forty-five years behind us I twice drank Palmer; on each occasion it was beautifully complete, with fine old-claret nose and rich concentrated body, and had all the charm that many '28s lacked. Other good Médocs of which I had experience were Brane-Cantenac and Gruaud-Larose-Sarget. Then in September 1977 I had the chance at La Mission-Haut-Brion of comparing the '28 and '29. In advance, the former was expected to be better, and initially it seemed fruitier and firmer, but then the '29, a very powerful wine typical of the growth, gained both in aroma and flavour. It had a strong *goût de terroir* so often to be found in La Mission. The '28 was good but drier and showed slight acidity.

However the two '28s which stand out in my mind alongside the Las-Cases are Cheval-Blanc and Domaine de Chevalier. For years the former was a wonderful wine, with enough sugar to overcome the traditional '28 hardness. Then rather suddenly early in the 1960s it seemed to go brown in colour and lose its fruit. I cannot remember another really fine wine declining so quickly. Figeac made a fruity, firm wine, surprisingly deep-coloured after forty years. The Domaine de Chevalier was of course much more delicate, and I drank the wine years ago, when it was still wonderfully complete. However I did have a fellow Léognan, Haut-Bailly '28, much more recently, and although still a little firm it had an abundance of fruit, and was in the top rank of '28s I had drunk. The oddest '28 that has come my way was Vieux-Château-Certan drunk at Henri Binaud's table in Bordeaux in September 1967. The nose was very rich, the colour brown, but the taste was so strong it almost seemed as if a dollop of port had been added. There was a hint of burnt taste too, no doubt owing to the torrid vintage time.

Although some '28s may have still to yield of their best, others seemed to have given up the unequal struggle with their tannin and have dried up. The Sauternes were very good, and Yquem was exceptional, better even than the '29.

1929 (26 SEPTEMBER)

One may argue the comparative merits of this vintage, but there is no doubt that so far it has proved the most satisfying vintage of the century. Most châteaux made a good and plentiful '29. Deep-coloured, fruity and undeniably sweet, they were drinkable from so early an age that many believed they could not last. Ian Campbell, whom I once asked what was the first thing he looked for in a claret replied 'sugar'; elsewhere he testified to a doubt about the '29s lasting, on account of their sweetness. True most are now in decline, but they stood up for a good thirty years.

To give a list even of the '29s I have drunk would be dull indeed, so I will mention only a few. Latour, there is little doubt today, is the finest of them, still so big and fruity a wine that one feels it must go on for some years still. However, one of the strange things about this almost universally successful year is that two and perhaps three of the first growths were by no means up to their class. Neither Lafite nor Haut-Brion were very attractive wines for many years, and Margaux varied considerably, because, I have been told, one part of the wine was good and another part was not. On the other hand Mouton-Rothschild, the *premier cru* challenger, was for many years considered the finest '29, and excellent it was too; but this fellow-Pauillac has failed to stay the course so well as Latour. For some reason the Mouton-Rothschild became a special American favourite in auctions, particularly in large-format sized bottles. Every now and again a jeroboam metaphorically hurtled through the saleroom fetching an enormous price: £2,850 at Sotheby's in 1971, $9,600 at Christie's sale for Sakowitz of Houston, Texas, a year later – both world records at their time. As late as June 1977 another of these monsters was sold at Christie's for £2,800. By a coincidence, just before this sale a generous American purchaser of one of the rather less costly jeroboams, Kerry Payne, invited a large company to share this and some other old wines in large bottles with him at a dinner in London. Unfortunately, although immensely interesting to drink, the wine was clearly on the way down; which made the invitation to share this great rarity none the less generous. At this period, it was maintained at the château that the really large sizes were still drinking very well.

As we are now discussing a famous vintage that will no doubt continue to excite interest and high prices for many years to come, it is worth saying a word here about the prospects of longevity for such wines. Obviously they must always have been kept in good conditions: cool, dark and not subject to vibration. In addition their survival prospects are much enhanced if they have suffered the minimum of movement since they were first made. That is why they stand the best chance in the original château cellar – provided that is a good one, which is not always the case. Obviously extensive movement of a bottle of old wine puts a special strain on the cork, which itself may be the original one. This could lead to ullage, and if this extends below the neck, the chances of the wine being in good condition are clearly reduced; and that applies to wines of any age, for the liquid can escape only through the cork, leaving room for the air and oxidation. The importance of minimum movement was shown in the old cellars that Christie's auctioned in the sixties and seventies: Rosebery (1967), Glamis Castle (1971), Gladstone (1972) and Woodperry (1976), when fine pre-phylloxera and nineteenth-century clarets were 'unearthed' after lying undisturbed for a great many years, many of them since the original binning.

The advantage to be derived from those fortunate enough to have the chance of drinking a senior claret at the château has already been mentioned in connection with the tasting at Lafite in October 1977; and this particularly applied to the '29 which, as noted above, had not been very satisfactory when encountered every now and again. Although I thought the two bottles drunk at dinner full but slightly 'cooked' on nose and palate, rich but at least on the turn and probably going down, this was not the only view. Some thought the wine 'superb', others 'slightly oxidized'; and this shows that when tasting wine judgements can vary even among experienced tasters. In any event, '29 is a good example of put-not-your-(entire)-trust-in *premiers crus*.

My favourite candidate for the top rank among the '29s is Léoville-Poyferré. It was a racehorse, whereas many of the '29s were chargers. Until May 1969 it had been some years since I had drunk a wine that had refinement and distinction as well as fruit, and a typical fine Médoc bouquet. Then Jack Rutherford opened a bottle in the company of Édouard Cruse and Christopher Tatham. It still maintained its elegance and fruit, and was not in decline. Cruse even preferred it to the succeeding Latour '20; but here he was in a minority. Las-Cases '29 has on more than one occasion seemed just about on a par with its neighbour. The Barton was more variable, as this was the first occasion when château-bottling was granted; the corks were not always up to standard. A bottle drunk at Langoa in 1966 was still very fruity, but showed some sign of decline; another in England in 1968 lacked finish. This was the last vintage for about thirty years in which the

Poyferré and Las-Cases parts of the Léoville vineyard were really good, although the Poyferré '34 was above average for that disappointing year. Two other fine '29 St-Juliens I have enjoyed were Gruaud-Larose-Faure and Talbot.

Two Pauillacs that achieved splendid wines in this year were Pichon-Longueville-Baron and Pontet-Canet. The first, in the past at least, seemed to me to have more distinction of flavour than the overwhelming Latour. In 1964 it was still at the top of its form but a later bottle showed signs of decline. The Lalande, while good, never had the vinosity and fruit of its neighbour. I have already referred to the Pontet-Canet served at a dinner in London in 1962. I have drunk bottles more recently at the château and these remained just as fine. Being so 'sweet' this has more than once been taken by me for a Pomerol; an exceptional wine. As an example of the trade prices ruling when these wines were first offered, the Pontet-Canet '29 was £36 a *barrique*; the '28 had been £28.

Among the '29s of Margaux and its neighbours, the Rausan-Ségla was one of the great successes, with the delicacy to be expected as well as the fruit; it was still remarkably complete though tasting a little old in 1971; it was still so sweet and must be accounted one of the best-keeping wines of the vintage. There were the same qualities in Ch. Margaux '29 – obviously from the good *cuves* – which I drank in 1964 in the office of Corney & Barrow, the City wine merchants. It had lain in the City since 1932, unharmed by the blitz. In its day Cantenac-Brown '29 was an admirable wine, distinguished as well as fruity; alas the last fine wine from this château that has come my way. Giscours, another growth later producing indifferent wine for many years, also achieved a very fine '29, which I drank in Bordeaux in 1966. The brown colour suggested a much older wine, but it was still fruity.

I have never leaned much towards the St-Estèphes but there were certainly some good '29s. The Cos d'Estournel was very fine in the fifties, and the Montrose, a big wine with a powerful flavour even as late as 1967, was rounder than I usually find this growth.

It should not be imagined that, some first growths apart, all the classed Médocs made excellent wine. I can recall thin, disappointing Rauzan-Gassies and d'Issan, while the Mouton-d'Armailhacq was so sweet as to suggest sugaring. On the other hand there were some very fine wines from such *bourgeois* growths as Lanessan (Cissac) – still a big fruity wine today – and La Closerie (Moulis). La Tour-de-Mons made a '29 still very fruity when nearly forty years old; and Martinens (Cantenac) was still very fruity, even rich, in 1971.

I did not drink many of the '29 red Graves in their prime, but Haut-Bailly was excellent when at its best in the late 1940s and still good though curiously 'coarse' in 1972. Was it pasteurized? As already described, La Mission-Haut-Brion made a fine '29. It had a distinguished nose. Domaine de Chevalier followed its outstanding '28 with a fruity '29. A lesser Graves of fine quality was the Laburthe-Brivazac, a vineyard no longer in existence, as already mentioned.

As might be expected, the St-Émilions scored in 1929, and Cheval-Blanc I rate among the leaders of the vintage. It lasted better than the '28, for the last time I tasted the wine was in 1967 at Mouton-Rothschild. It had a marvellously fruity nose. The colour was light but not brown. There was just a touch of age on the palate, and the fine wine was beaten by the Mouton-Rothschild 1900 that followed. I have drunk the Ausone several times but it has never seemed to me as outstanding as one might have hoped for. The Clos Fourtet, however, maintained its splendid tradition during the 1920s, a big 'warm' wine. An exceptionally fruity '29 St-Émilion, already referred to, was La Gaffelière-Naudes.

The Pomerols were not so popular in Britain before the war as they have since become, so they were not widely shipped. Accordingly my experience of '29 Pomerols has been limited; and as they do not last so well as Médocs those

I have tasted have been on the old side. An excellent example in recent years I do remember, however, is L'Enclos. Early in the last war, I acquired from the Wine Society some Bel-Air-Lalande '29, C.B., and this was fruity, round and bountiful up to the time when I drank the last bottle in 1951.

On the whole the '29s are, alas, now on the way down, but fine bottles, well kept, from successful growths, are still among the most enjoyable clarets to be drunk. Nothing as good appeared for another sixteen years, until 1945.

This was also a very fine year for the Sauternes, and Yquem hit one of its high spots. This is now very dark in colour, but still tastes better than it looks.

1930 (1 OCTOBER)

1931 (25 SEPTEMBER)

1932 (15 OCTOBER)

This was the worst trio of successive years in the Gironde since the phylloxera–mildew era of the 1880s; they are years not worth discussing separately. The 1930s produced light, thin wines little seen outside the region, though I have heard that the Cheval-Blanc was quite palatable. The 1931s were slightly better, and there were two successes, Cheval-Blanc and Domaine de Chevalier. As it rained heavily during the vintage and the wines generally were light and acid, it is fair to assume that these two wines were 'assisted'. One may suspect that a little sugar was added to save the wine, and why not? Thanks to Rigby & Evens of Liverpool, I had a bottle of the Cheval-Blanc in December 1968 and though brown and in decline it was still surprisingly fruity. This was English-bottled, but thanks to Édouard Cruse, in October 1970 we had a bottle brought from the château to Bordeaux. It had a fine nose at first, but the colour was very brown, and before long the taste of decay was dominant; the English bottling, drunk two years earlier, was superior. However the La Mission-Haut-Brion, by coincidence drunk at the château only a day after the Cheval-Blanc, though brown in colour, was surprisingly strong – even coarse-flavoured – but quite drinkable. Oddly enough Yquem '31 was much better than expected, and although light is still pale and fresh. In 1932 the beginning of the vintage was the latest on record this century, beginning on 14 or 15 October. Only once before in modern times had a vintage begun later; in 1816, which Tastet & Lawton described as *détestable*, while to the 1932 they awarded the comment *qualité exécrable*. At the 1977 Christie tasting of Latours the '32 was brown and decayed.

No doubt in the conditions of the world slump even the first vintages would have been difficult to dispose of, but these were hard years indeed for Bordeaux, and they stimulated the development of the co-operatives which spread throughout the Gironde and saved many of the small growers.

1933 (22 SEPTEMBER)

After three bad years, and accompanied by a slight lifting of the economic cloud over the world by the time that these wines were offered, there were optimistic expectations of the '33s. I drank a good many of them during the war years, but on the whole they were very light and rather short of fruit; some were acid. The wines lacked 'guts', and among the Médocs the Pauillacs came out best. Even in the seventies Latour and Mouton-Rothschild were light but fairly complete wines. Berry Bros. of London, who made several very large purchases of the '33s, including Beychevelle, shared the whole crop of Mouton-Rothschild with the firm of Cruse. The wine was of course château-bottled and kept at the château. Unfortunately, to distinguish their share, Berry's had their cases marked with their name and city. Most of this wine was still there in the Second World War when the Germans occupied

Mouton. The 'enemy wine' was at once confiscated, and some fine wine went down unworthy, occupying throats.

In the mid-1940s the Ch. Margaux was still a pleasing soft wine, and as late as 1966 a bottle of Lascombes '33, drunk at Alexis Lichine's Le Prieuré was surprisingly distinguished for its age. However over the years the most enjoyable '33 I drank was the Cheval-Blanc, a comparatively delicate foil to the more robust and round '34.

1934 (14 SEPTEMBER)

This is generally reckoned to have been the best vintage of the thirties, and after a series of small harvests since 1929, a very large crop was gathered: 6·8 million hl, only beaten in the last hundred years by 1922. Naturally it was a much publicized vintage, with varying views as to the respective merits of '33 and '34. Unfortunately the wines contained an excess of tannin, particularly the Médocs and the Graves, and they have never outgrown this; the hardness was too much for the underlying fruit and most of the wines dried up. The best of the first growths was Latour, but even that remained dry and tannic more than forty years later. I am inclined to think that the most agreeable Médocs came from St-Julien, for Léoville-Poyferré and Barton, as well as Langoa, were less uncompromising wines than others. Perhaps the best thing about the '34 Médocs was their low price. The Wine Society of London bought Beychevelle '34 for £12 5s. a hogshead; thirty years later the '64 cost them £150.

On the other hand the St-Émilions and Pomerols were remarkably good in '34, as they had less tannin and more fruit. Cheval-Blanc '34 was the best Bordeaux of the vintage, and from birth fetched a correspondingly high price. It was a very velvety, round wine in the best tradition of this château. Another excellent '34 which I bought before and during the last war was La Gaffelière-Naudes, a rich full-flavoured wine. It cost between 2s. 6d. and 3s. 4d. a bottle. I drank my last bottle, a Wine Society bottling, in 1958 and the wine was still full of colour, fruit and flavour. Clos Fourtet also produced a typically full wine this year.

The Pomerols were no less successful, but I have drunk fewer of them, and none better than La Pointe, bottled by Avery's: a rich full wine even in the seventies. I am told the Pétrus was good, but I have never drunk it. Among the Graves the same is true of Domaine de Chevalier, but I can vouch for La Mission-Haut-Brion at least up to 1972. It had a little of the '34 hardness, but well-above-average fruit for the year, along with a fine colour and nose. The Sauternes were good in this year.

1935 (30 SEPTEMBER)
1936 (1–4 OCTOBER)

Although '35 was a notable port year and a fine one for cognac, in Bordeaux this was an indifferent, rather late vintage and the grapes lacked maturity; much the same applied to the '36s, which were even worse. Neither year was generally shipped to Britain, although I once had some Pauillac '36 from Avery's, which was said to be declassified Lafite. It was very light, had a curious aromatic, almost resinous nose and was quite agreeable. I cannot recollect drinking another '36 until the beginning of 1969, when two of very different rank presented themselves. The first was Latour, which was still surprisingly – if one continues to be surprised by off-vintage Latours – deep-coloured and fruity. I would have taken it for a much younger wine, but when it had been open half an hour its age began to show and the fruit to depart; however a fair innings. The other was Coufran, on the edge of the Haut-Médoc. In 1968 Michael Broadbent of Christie's gave me as a curiosity a bottle of Coufran '36 château-bottled. Although indubitably brown and in decline this lesser wine from the outskirts of the Haut-Médoc was still palatable after about a third of a century. Another curiosity was the Cheval-Blanc, drunk on the same occasion as the '31 mentioned already: though very brown, it had more fruit – natural or injected – than its earlier year. However four years later after drinking the Latour, I shared a bottle of the Mouton-Rothschild, in January 1973. It was very similar in style to the Latour, brown in colour, but well-balanced for such a vintage; but it too faded in the glass, though it had been decanted a good hour by then. Like the two other first growths I have drunk, it showed what a fine estate can produce in such a poor vintage; wines drinkable, and even enjoyable, more than thirty years later – but not always!

1937 (20 SEPTEMBER)

This was the first vintage since the application in the autumn of 1936 of the new law of *appellation contrôlée*. Together with further decrees issued during the ensuing war, this restricted the permitted area, the types of grape allowed and the output per hectare in districts covered by the *AC* writ. The result was a big drop in output of wines of the higher *appellations*. The 1937 vintage was average only, and the Médocs were hard like the '34s, but even more so. This was the last vintage shipped before the Germans overran France in 1940. Indeed a good deal of wine belonging to British wine merchants was left in Bordeaux, and some of it miraculously survived to replenish their tiny stocks after the war. So the '37s were welcome enough to wine drinkers in the later 1940s and early 1950s, until the fine run of post-war vintages became drinkable. I have drunk all the first growths and none were very agreeable, on account of the excess of tannin. Over the years I have come across one or two more acceptable wines, notably Léoville-Poyferré in a magnum, which in 1965 was soft if a little old in taste; Léoville-Las-Cases, very fruity still in 1968, and Pichon-Longueville-Lalande which, though pale in colour, was so finely rounded that I took it for a light '29. This was opened at the château in October 1966. The following year at Langoa the Cos d'Estournel surprised me. Although rather hard and strong-flavoured, there was more distinction than one would have expected. And as recently as October 1972 at La Mission-Haut-Brion, Henri Woltner opened a bottle of his '37 and Mouton-Rothschild '37 for comparison, and both were more agreeable than I would have expected. The Graves was the browner, and rather drier than the Médoc, which had a powerful flavour, and was distinctly fruity for such a hard year. Both seemed on the point of decline. I see no future for the '37 Médocs, and believe they will dry up like the '34s; many have done so.

The Graves, St-Émilions and Pomerols were, as in '34, much better. I would put Domaine de Chevalier '37, which I drank a number of times up to the early 1960s, as one of the outstanding wines of '37, only excelled by Cheval-Blanc, which once more turned out a most agreeably fruity wine. Another excellent Graves was Haut-Bailly, while Canon and Gaffelière-Naudes showed very well among the St-Émilions, whose extra fruit masked the tannin. The Sauternes were excellent, notably Climens and Yquem, in that order, while white Domaine de Chevalier was a very fine white Graves.

1938 (28 SEPTEMBER)

1939 (2 OCTOBER)

Unattractive though the '37s generally were, this was the last relatively successful vintage of a disappointing decade. The '38s were light wines and under normal conditions might have been acceptable, for they were quite well balanced though without much body. Two that came my way in

London in the early 1970s were still not at all bad: Calon Ségur and Pichon Lalande. And both had come from the firm of O. W. Loeb, that source of lost claret vintages. Both started well on nose and palate, but the Pichon had the more body, and the Calon was light. Each showed some excess of acidity which developed in the glass. A little later I drank the Léoville-Las-Cases and not long after the Latour. The former, brown in colour and obviously an old wine, was nevertheless still fruity, well-balanced and showed no decay; the latter had still retained very big colour and big nose. It was slightly dry and acid on the palate, but remarkable for the year. A bottle opened at the château in October 1978, though brownish in colour, had a full aroma and extraordinary fruit for the vintage. The '38s were nearly all consumed during the war years, and this also happened to the much larger vintage of 1939, harvested at the beginning of the deceptive 'phoney war' period. In the late sixties I tasted Latour '39 at the château, but even at that home of off-vintages, the wine was brown, old-tasting and rather tired. Yet in the mid-seventies the La Mission-Haut-Brion at the château, though distinctly brown, losing fruit and somewhat dry, was still quite drinkable with no decay – good for such a vintage so long afterwards.

1940 (26 SEPTEMBER)

1941 (3 OCTOBER)

1942 (19 SEPTEMBER)

These years are not worth discussing separately. Crops were small and quality was good only in 1942. No doubt largely owing to the Second World War the '40s were little shipped to Britain, and the few I have drunk were advanced in years for a vintage written off by Tastet & Lawton as 'mediocre'. Not surprisingly the Latour, tasted on a number of occasions, one as late as 1976, came out the best – and in Oxford, not at the château. It still had the typical Latour big colour, a fine nose and was surprisingly fruity. One would certainly have guessed it as younger. Earlier in the seventies both Rausan-Ségla and Rauzan-Gassies retained their faculties, the former notable for its good colour and balance, the latter for a very fine aroma and flavour, though it faded a little in the glass, understandably enough. At about the same time I drank the Palmer: fairly fruity, but light and with slight decay. The Latour '42 was a bigger wine and surprisingly full-flavoured ten years ago. In the mid-fifties I drank the La Mission-Haut-Brion '42 and then that too was a distinguished wine. There may well be good bottles of these other wartime vintages still lying in Bordeaux, but very few were exported.

1943 (19 SEPTEMBER)

This was certainly the best vintage of the war years, and the one most commonly shipped to Britain after the war and available until the early fifties. The wines varied considerably, owing no doubt to the difficulties of wartime production, with labour short and the anti-disease chemicals even more deficient in supply. There was also a shortage of bottles, so one finds French-bottled wines often in light green bottles used for both red and white wines. Although I drank a fair number of them between 1947 and 1953 they have left little impression. Most of the wines were on the light side, including the first growths. Latour was a fair wine, Lafite less so, but the Médoc which I remember best was the Pichon-Longueville-Baron, a fine fruity wine for its year. In Bordeaux in 1967 I drank Beychevelle '43 and was surprised by its fruity quality; a little dry at the end, but what would one expect of a twenty-four-year-old wine originally light?

Other '43s have come my way in recent years, mostly in Bordeaux. At a lunch at Grand-Puy-Lacoste in October 1965, Lord Zuckerman (then Sir Solly), a fellow-guest, asked

Raymond Dupin, the proprietor, whether after his '53 and '47 wines we might conclude with the '43. A magnum was brought straight from the cellar and I expected disappointment. But in fact although the wine was obviously an old one, the colour was good and the wine was fruity, not dry. The following year a bottle of Rausan-Ségla in London had still a lovely nose and was surprisingly fruity, if a little 'short' at the end; eleven years later a bottle opened in Cambridge was no less good. But the most surprising pair of '43 Médocs I drank together in September 1967 with their proprietor, Henri Binaud, were La Tour-de-Mons and Cantemerle. The colour of the first was paler than the second and implied age, but on the palate was more complete than the rather bigger Cantemerle. Considering the style of this vintage they were remarkably good for those who like their claret to be delicate but fruity.

The St-Émilions were fuller, and for some years the Clos Fourtet '43 was very attractive, but fell away when eight or nine years old. Cheval-Blanc was made of sterner stuff. In 1965 I was given a bottle by a Swiss friend; it had lain in Switzerland for many years, probably since the initial shipment. I drank it in August 1966. The colour was surprisingly deep, the flavour unexpectedly full and complete; a fine wine by any standards.

I have drunk one or two Pomerols of this vintage, but the one I remember best was La Croix-de-Gay, the first of a series of delicious wines from this small growth. It lasted very well, and was fruity to the end, even when the colour, like most old Pomerols, had browned. Surprisingly, in a way, the Sauternes were good, and a Climens which I drank at Loudenne in October 1966 had everything one would expect of such a growth.

1944 (27 SEPTEMBER)

A plentiful but light year. The wines lacked body but some were attractive of their type; I remember Haut-Brion as almost *rosé* in colour at ten years old, and Lafite of the same age, soft and delicate if a little attenuated. An unexpected success was Rausan-Ségla. Latour, predictably, was a bigger wine and a bottle consumed in the company of André Simon and his son in 1966 had still a sufficiency of colour, a full nose and a light but true taste. Later in the same year I drank Mouton-Rothschild at the château. It had the delicious nose of fine claret, but the wine fell away. Yet another bottle at the château in 1975 had the rich nose and concentrated flavour of true Mouton, but it was drying up. This of course was made when Mouton was particularly discriminated against so far as disease-combating chemicals were concerned through being of Jewish ownership and Vichy-controlled.

Another surprisingly good '44 was Pontet-Canet. A bottle opened in London in 1967 was extraordinarily full and with so deep a flavour I took it for a Pomerol. No doubt it had been 'assisted'.

THE POST-WAR RECORD: 1945–1978

1945 (13 SEPTEMBER)

This vintage has had more *réclame* than any other in the post-war period, as therein it must narrowly be counted; the only, much younger rival in prestige has been 1961. Both vintages were similar in being exceptionally short. The '45s suffered from a disastrous spring frost on 2 May, and the crop was the second smallest of the century to date (only 1915 was smaller), and totalled 1·48 million hl. Moreover conditions in the vineyards were understandably far from perfect. Ronald Barton has told me that when he first returned to Langoa in the summer of 1945, the normally trim vineyards were covered with weeds. Although an excellent vintage, which began early, around 10 September, not all châteaux were able to produce successful wines. For example, Margaux often seemed to lack fruit and to have been disappointing in its class, while a considerable proportion of Cheval-Blanc was 'pricked', or vinegary. Moreover, the one fault of the wines was that they had an excess of tannin, and there have not been lacking long-memoried pessimists who have murmured, 'another '28'. This is unfair, but no doubt those who bought '45s when first offered between 1948 and 1950 have had to wait a long time before finding their wines ready. I am among these. Layers-down of vintage port may resign themselves to waiting a score of years before opening a bottle, but this is a long period for claret drinkers. Fortunately many more earlier-maturing vintages have intervened. At one time the '47s were more immediately attractive and had their champions as against the '45s, but the Médocs of '47 certainly did not hold up as expected. It is sometimes said that the '45s were the last clarets 'made in the old way', i.e. with a prolonged fermentation on the skins, resulting in slow development and fruity but tanniny wines; for the tannin comes from the skins and the pips.

With the possible exception of Margaux all the first growths and Mouton made very fine wine. There are those who place Lafite first, and it is indeed a wine of great breed and finesse, but Mouton-Rothschild is an extraordinarily full-bodied wine, quite different in style from its neighbour, but nonetheless remarkable. At times it has seemed far from ready, although there have been other periods when it seemed to be breaking through. Latour is still a great big fruity, but backward wine, with a powerful flavour and a 'strong' nose, while Haut-Brion has long been the most advanced of them, with the typical earthy taste of Graves. La Mission-Haut-Brion, similar in style and a little more rounded, was also excellent but distinctly hard; even in 1978 it was excessively tannic.

As a pendant to the above comments, shortly after this vintage had completed its first quarter-century, a small party was organized to taste at dinner the four *premiers crus* and Mouton-Rothschild, not then promoted. They were opened a good hour in advance and at first tasted in the following order: Haut-Brion, Margaux, Lafite, Latour and Mouton-Rothschild – an order incidentally, which generally seems satisfactory when tasting these wines, though sometimes one might reverse the order of the first two and of the last two. The Haut-Brion took a little coaxing in spite of a good pre-prandial airing, but it developed well in the glass, slightly brown in colour compared with the others, but with the typical 'bricky' taste of fine red Graves. When returned to, it tasted firm and fruity – always a test. The Margaux had fine colour, and an elegant Médoc nose, but it was hard and lacked fruit and finish. The Lafite had even more colour, and a lovely fruity aroma and the classic flavour of a great Médoc. Latour had its typical deep colour; a big fruity wine, still a shade green and with more tannin than any of the others. Mouton-Rothschild had more colour and a richer nose than the rest, with the special 'cedar-wood' aroma for which Mouton is famed. In flavour it was exceptionally rich, almost sweet and nearly burgundian in style. It did not taste like a typical Médoc; but then Mouton seldom does.

The final vote unhesitatingly placed Lafite first and Margaux fifth. Latour was broadly conceded to be the runner-up, partly on the score that it would outlive them all, but one person put Mouton-Rothschild second; and, after all, Baron Philippe predicted that Mouton-Rothschild would be *à point* in the year 2000. Haut-Brion was unanimously agreed to be a distinguished third, although it was broadly felt that, if this implied placing Mouton fourth, it misinterpreted the general feeling about a splendid wine, difficult to compare with the others.

Since this anniversary tasting, I have had opportunities to drink all these wines again, and they have shown similar form, allowing for the variation in bottles that must be expected. However, I did have one deliciously fragrant, well-balanced bottle of Margaux in 1975, opened for me by Harry Waugh; but this was followed a year later by a fruity but slightly acid one, drunk in Bordeaux. The Mouton-Rothschild showed consistently rich, deep and concentrated in flavour. In the summer of 1978 both a bottle and a half were opened at the château. The former was still backward, the latter much more developed; both had plenty to give. Many might put Mouton at the head of the list, although those who look for elegance as well as fruit might opt for Haut-Brion. The Lafite has remained for me a variable wine, always with the lovely aroma of a first-class Médoc of a leading vintage, but often rather hard and even dry to the taste. An opportunity to sample it under the best possible conditions was afforded me at the tasting at the château in 1977, described in the account of Lafite. Baron Éric de Rothschild kindly agreed to add a magnum to the wine list at the dinner at which it was preceded by the '53 and followed by the '18. The colour was very deep for the age, with slight dryness on both nose and palate at the end, though it was fruity enough. Was there enough to sustain it in face of the tannin, or was it tending to dry up? Opinions varied, some holding that it still had some way to go and needed keeping for quite a long time. Another view was that it would always retain this style but would keep, while a third opinion suggested that it might be past its very fine best.

Latour, a splendidly big fruity wine at its best, has varied for perhaps different reasons. In September 1976 at lunch at Harvey's of Bristol I was asked to taste blind two bottles of the '45: one with the original cork, the other re-corked in 1967, as faithfully recorded on the cork. Identification proved no problem: the originally corked one had more fruit, more life while the other tasted older, less rounded. Not that this indicates that old wines should not be re-corked periodically. As mentioned earlier, at Mouton they are re-corked every twenty-five years, and I would be the last to suggest that some of the wonderful old bottles might have been better than they were. It must be better to re-cork than allow an ullage to develop, but it can be a risky operation. At Latour they re-corked all the remaining stock of the '61 in 1969 owing to some variation in levels.

However, the '45 Latour at its best is a splendid wine that should be able to compete with the Mouton in the early years of the next century. This is less likely with some other '45 Médocs that I have drunk in the middle and later seventies. One should never judge adversely on the basis of a single bottle, and this is not a vintage likely to be encountered all that often these days, but some classed growths seem to be a little dry and showing some acidity at the end, which often indicates decline. Among the good examples have been the fruity, beautifully balanced Léoville-Barton, a big Cos d'Estournel and a full, if brown-tinged Palmer. Cantemerle showed well in the mid-seventies and that well-made St-Estèphe, de Pez, was a remarkably big and bold wine in 1977.

Particularly attractive, because they matured fairly rapidly, have been the Pomerols. Pétrus '45, drunk in 1966, lacked the graciousness and completeness of the '47, but if still a little hard, it had the typical 'concentrated' flavour. Gazin is another wine of the same character and such wines as L'Enclos and La Croix-de-Gay are highly agreeable, though they have recently begun to show their age.

I have had a number of disappointments with wines bottled in England, and can only think they were shipped and/or bottled too late, for they lack fruit, but an English-bottled Rausan-Ségla tasted remarkably full, almost rich, in 1972; and both colour and nose suggested a much younger wine. The best of the Médocs may well last into the next century. On the other hand if the pessimists are proved correct, some of the wines with an excess of tannin might dry up and lose their fruit, as indeed a number of the '28s have done. The more elegant wines, of which Lafite is the best example known to me, might not have enough 'behind them' to last so long as the bigger types. But 'size' is not everything, and balance is at least equally important. So '45 remains a controversial vintage.

This was a great year for Sauternes, albeit a small crop. I doubt whether Yquem '45 has yet been surpassed in the post-war era. Judging by the Laville-Haut-Brion – the only '45 white Graves of distinction I can recollect – these must have been exceptionally full-flavoured. Even in 1978 this had lovely honey nose and almost rich taste, but ending dry.

1946 (30 SEPTEMBER)

A distinct off-year, but one in which I have come upon two surprisingly good wines: Latour and Mouton-Rothschild. At a tasting in 1964 at the château of off-vintage Latours this unexpectedly turned up as my favourite in a selection stretching back from 1963 to 1939. Since then I acquired a small stock and drank it a number of times with enjoyment. The wine has plenty of fruit, flavour and expectation of life, but without quite the finish of a great year. The Mouton '46 was one of my 'discoveries' at the château in 1968. As Mouton-Rothschild, like Latour, often succeeds in off-years, and remembering the Latour, I inquired about the Mouton '46. Not surprisingly it is not one of the most frequently sought-after vintages in that famous cellar, and opinions on the wine were as vague as on the '95, referred to earlier, and in fact drunk on the same occasion as the '46, which immediately preceded it at table. Deep in colour, and with plenty of flavour, the wine had a little of the dryness at the end noticed in the Latour, but was well balanced for the year. Perhaps it was even better than the Latour. Certainly, I was heretical enough to have preferred the '46 as a glass of mature claret to the much more famous '45, of which a bottle from the adjoining bin had been decanted and drunk only the previous night. That does not imply, however, that the '46 has such prospects. On more than one occasion I have drunk Latour '46 alongside Mouton '46, and the latter has shown rather more fruit and flavour.

1947 (19 SEPTEMBER)

After a very hot summer wines of great charm were made, although the excessive heat was the undoing of some. There was so much natural sugar present during the fermentation that not all was converted into alcohol; as a result there was volatile acidity in the wine. So quite a number of them, particularly the Médocs, soon showed a little sourness in the tail. These included Lafite, Latour, Lascombes, Léoville-Barton and many other classed growths. Two exceptions were part at least of Ch. Margaux and Mouton-Rothschild; both very fine wines. The former, drunk at a Saintsbury Club dinner in October 1977, was surprisingly deep in colour, had a lovely full nose and a round, fruity flavour – top-class claret. A month earlier I had shared in a double-magnum of quite a different style of wine: Mouton-Rothschild, at the château. An enormously rich, 'sweet' wine for the year, with very concentrated nose and flavour, it was typical Mouton, and a normal-sized bottle drunk in the same setting two years earlier was no less good. La Mission-Haut-Brion was good and Grand-Puy-Lacoste and Angludet above average. For their first ten years or so the '47 Médocs were very attractive, with a sweetness reminiscent of the '29s, but they lacked that year's balance, and acidity began to obtrude.

However, it was the classic post-war vintage for Pomerol

and a fine one for St-Émilion where, of course, Cheval-Blanc was and remains the star wine. In Dublin in May 1966 Tom Whelehan, whose generosity is not bounded by the capacity of his guests, produced among other wines Cheval-Blanc '47 and Pétrus '47. Both were remarkable: Pétrus rather sweeter and more overwhelming, Cheval-Blanc slightly more restrained and yet distinguished. I was in a minority in preferring the latter for its greater depth of flavour, but both wines are among the most attractive post-war clarets of the richer, fuller type one could wish to drink. For the Cheval-Blanc '47 was as much *hors concours* as the '21, and for much the same reason: a very hot summer. It turned out an enormous port-type wine, untypical of claret. I have had the good fortune to own a number of bottles, English- as well as château-bottled, and it has been a wonderful wine. For some years one has been told that the wine was 'not what it was'. Indeed I heard this opinion when writing the first edition of this book in 1968. That, as with all fine claret, particularly of a certain age, there have been variations from bottle to bottle is more than likely. However, until fairly recently, on the rare occasions when I have drunk it, I have always found it tremendously rich and fruity, and I had a wonderful bottle in 1974, but now I am not so sure. In September 1977 I was permitted to select one for dinner from the private cellar of La Mission-Haut-Brion, and it was a little brown, and though still very sweet, slightly lacking in the concentration of taste for which this wine was remarkable. Then in the first half of 1978 I had opportunities to drink it three times: twice from magnums and once from a bottle of my own. On each occasion it was a very fine claret, but it was generally agreed that the wine had lost something of its richness and 'port-type' character. Whether or not this is true for the wine as a whole, the fame of Cheval-Blanc '47 is such that those with deep purses are unlikely yet to be deterred from paying £100 or more a bottle at auction.

No other St-Émilion I have had approaches it, but a number of the Pomerols have been more or less in the Pétrus class, including Vieux-Château-Certan, Certan, Petit-Village, Nénin and the fruity La Croix-de-Gay, bottled by Harvey's – my first introduction to '47 Pomerols and drunk with pleasure over the years.

White Graves do not figure much in these notes, not because they are unworthy of comment, but because they seldom remain in the memory. Moreover their standards of quality vary less from vintage to vintage than with the red wines, or with the Sauternes. However 1947 was a remarkably fine year for white Graves, and the most distinguished one I often came across was Domaine de Chevalier, a flowery honeyish wine with a dry finish; dry, that is, by white Bordeaux standards. No doubt Haut-Brion Blanc was good too, but I do not remember drinking it.

The Sauternes, produced after this hot summer, were also very fine, almost up to the '45s. The two I have found most attractive have been Climens and Yquem.

1948 (27–30 SEPTEMBER)

A neglected year between two celebrated successes. I remember tasting the '47s and '48s in cask in the summer of 1949; the former were charming already, the latter very astringent. The only one of the '48s I liked then was the Brane-Cantenac, and indeed this has turned out one of the best Médocs of the year. The wines have always been on the firm side, and some have an excess of acidity which has become increasingly apparent with the years. Both Lafite and Palmer which used to be fine examples turned acid. The finest Médoc of the year was, however, Léoville-Barton, a fruity, big wine that to my knowledge was excellent since 1957, when I was introduced to it by that great claret lover, Sir Guy Fison of Saccone & Speed. Unfortunately it too became somewhat acid and the other two '48 Léovilles are thin and disappointing. None of the first growths or Mouton equalled the Barton, though both Latour and Mouton were well above average. One of the most attractive wines was Malescot, and both Talbot and Cantemerle were agreeable. Among the Graves La Mission-Haut-Brion is still outstanding with a very distinguished flavour. The future of any '48 depends on its acidity–sugar balance, and unfortunately I have the impression that the acidity has grown with most wines.

On the other side of the river Cheval-Blanc has remained one of the most consistently good '48s, and at one time I preferred it to the '49, but not in the latter seventies. Since 1948s were hardly shipped to this country, except by Avery's of Bristol, they were originally hard to come by and were scarcely to be found twenty years later. Some bottles of the Cheval-Blanc started to show acidity at the end, but the château-bottled remained longer. Otherwise I have sampled few St-Émilions and Pomerols, though I once enjoyed La Dominique. In an earlier edition I referred to the Pétrus as disappointing, but when I drank it at Ch. Videlot, the home of M. Jean-Pierre Moueix, in October 1976 it was magnificently rich on the nose and palate, with plenty of colour too. It must be a very rare wine, for it appears not to have been sold in the London auction rooms between 1966, when Christie's re-started regular wine sales, and this edition.

1949 (27 SEPTEMBER)

This year was greatly acclaimed initially, but has not always fulfilled its promise, for many of the wines have an edge and hardness that have persisted. Others, such as Latour and Léoville-Barton, surely have yet to show their full qualities; both are fine, with plenty of body. Even after nearly a third of a century, it may be that another few years must pass before the status of this vintage is finally established. However, there is little doubt on present showing that the outstanding Médoc is Mouton-Rothschild. This is a wine of such enormous concentration of nose and flavour that it almost suggests a Burgundy, or at least a Pomerol. In this wine particularly have I detected the 'cedar-wood' or 'lead pencil' nose associated with Mouton. Like the '45 it is typical Mouton. This enormously rich, concentrated wine is miles away in style from its near-neighbour Lafite, of which I wrote in earlier editions that it was 'delicate, distinguished but perhaps over-light Lafite '49. The Mouton embraces one, while the Lafite slips away from one's grasp.' This judgement on Lafite, however, needs revising in the light of some bottles of my own opened over the years, and in particular of a magnificent magnum drunk at the château in the 1977 tastings there. My tasting note ran: 'Wonderfully flowery, developed aroma that came out of the glass. Beautifully elegant, well-balanced wine, typical Lafite at its best, and real Médoc in style.' This view was endorsed by the whole party, and it would be difficult to find a finer wine of its type and age. It was preferred to the '45, though this was not drunk at the same meal, for that wine though perhaps bigger was less well-balanced. Whether such an elegant if fruity wine has long expectation of life, it is impossible to forecast. Certainly the 'light' but well-balanced '75s lasted for many years; but perhaps that is another story.

Of the other Médoc first growths Ch. Margaux has been delicious too in a more delicate way, while the Latour has so far been fruity enough but rather lacking in shape. One might say, still not ready.

Other '49 Médocs I have liked have been the very fruity Lynch-Bages, Léoville-Barton and Cantemerle, but recently some '49 Médocs have seemed variable and may be in decline. But how good the '49 Pomerols have been: Pétrus, La Conseillante, Certan, La Croix-de-Gay – these and others have been of the same pattern as the '45s and '47s, although perhaps not quite so good as the latter. Yet the Pétrus '49 seems to have taken over the concentrated richness of the '47; a splendid wine. Although less *renommé* than the celebrated '47, in the latter seventies there seemed some reason to believe it superior, for it had rather more backbone, while having that beguiling, concentrated richness of aroma and flavour in a fine Pétrus. In October 1977 a magnum at Videlot – declared to be the last in the cellar – was perfect of its kind, but it had nothing more to give, so was probably right to be opened then. The Cheval-Blanc, described in earlier editions as a bit on the dull side, seemed to have developed more character in the seventies, though even a magnum early in 1978 had a brown edge to the colour, but was a deliciously well-rounded St-Émilion that slipped down. Gaffelière-Naudes was good when young but did not keep a great time. I recollect Ausone as being better than I expected for this long-disappointing growth, but I do not remember ever tasting Figeac or Canon, both of which may have been very good. This was not a successful period for many of the leading Graves. The Haut-Brion and La Mission-Haut-Brion were typical examples of the difference between the two adjacent vineyards: the former dry, elegant and slightly austere, the latter powerful, with the strong *goût de terroir* one associates with La Mission, and still more with its associated La Tour-Haut-Brion. The former was remarkably deep-coloured in 1978, with typical Graves flavour. Very well-balanced and one of the best wines of the vintage.

Another good white Graves and Sauternes year, with a wonderful Yquem, and splendid Coutet, Climens and Rieussec among others.

1950 (23 SEPTEMBER)

By the standards of the period vast quantities of wine were made in Bordeaux this year. The output of 3·17 million hl with *appellation contrôlée* was almost half as much again as in

1949, and the total was not matched until 1962. With three acclaimed vintages in the previous five years behind them, there was not much initial enthusiasm for the '50s, watered by a wet summer. However, they were very cheap and so were widely bought. For example in 1954 I bought Latour for 16s. 6d. a bottle; so many proved excellent bargains. A large number of them turned out better than expected and a few are still good drinking today. The pattern of success was uneven and depended no doubt on the skill of the wine makers, plus perhaps a judicious proportion of added sugar, although not legalized until the following year. The Pomerols and St-Émilions, which sometimes do better than the Médocs in a poor year, were the most consistent wines, with Pétrus, Certan, Cheval-Blanc, Figeac and Ausone as wines still good up to twenty years of age. They tended to be a little short in flavour compared with, say, 1949, but fruity and enjoyable all the same. Latour and Margaux were the best among the Médoc leaders, and when the latter in magnums was served as the final claret at the *Ban de Vendange* dinner in the magnificent white-pillared *chai* of Château Margaux in September 1967, it was as charming a light but true claret as one could have wished for; and so it continued to be several years later. Latour, of course, was made of sterner stuff and kept even better. In the first edition of this work I wrote that both Mouton and Lafite were disappointing. This view was based on rather occasional sampling, for I had neither wine in my own cellar. However, in 1977 I opened a bottle of Lafite, one among a mixed case given me as a memento of Maurice Platnauer, former Principal of Brasenose College, Oxford, and a wine *amateur* generous with his fine bottles. This Lafite had good colour, fine nose and a surprising amount of fruit for such an age and vintage. If it did not compare in quality with the '49 that followed, it introduced the latter admirably. As to Mouton, perhaps it was a privileged bottle, never having left the château cellar, but in July 1978 I was surprised by its good colour, fine nose and well-balanced, if light for Mouton, flavour.

An enjoyable Pauillac in the earlier days was Pichon-Longueville-Baron; Cos d'Estournel in St-Estèphe drank surprisingly well as late as 1975, while among the St-Juliens I remember Gruaud-Larose and Léoville-Barton with pleasure. Palmer was always light, but hung on successfully for the better part of twenty years. Haut-Brion I never liked, for it seemed too rich to be true, but La Mission-Haut-Brion scored another success, and I was surprised by its quality when more than twenty years old, with good colour, real Graves nose and fruit. I guessed it much younger, though it lacked a little roundness. La Tour-Haut-Brion, its junior partner, was good too.

Although I had drunk and enjoyed Haut-Brion Blanc '49, I think it was the '50 that first attracted me to this often distinguished wine. In those days it was possible to ship the wine in cask, so that it was not over-expensive for the quality. I acquired a few bottles for not much more than 16s. 6d. a bottle, imported and bottled by Harvey's. Along with Domaine de Chevalier of the same year, this was an unusually good recommendation for white Graves; with a honeyish nose which at first led one to expect a rather sweeter wine than showed on the palate. Sauternes came up exceptionally well in this year, and some Sauternes enthusiasts place 1950 as among the greatest post-war years. Yquem, Coutet and Climens were delicious; and they were decidedly inexpensive.

1951 (9 OCTOBER)

This was the first year when chaptalization, or adding sugar to the must at the time of fermentation in order to increase the alcoholic content of the wine, was formally legalized. Since then each year it has been an *ad hoc* decision made by the Minister of Agriculture through the *préfet* of the department, shortly before the vintage. Originally intended only for bad years, there is little doubt that the practice has spread, and even in good years like 1966 and 1970 sugaring was permitted. Indeed it has been allowed every year since 1962. Some maintain this was a 'sell-out' of the essential qualities of Bordeaux, and a sign that the Gironde was going the way of the Côte d'Or. It is already being suggested that yearly approval should be dispensed with and the growers be allowed to use their own judgement – and buy their sugar in good time. This may well come about, but my view is that while it is legitimate to save a bad or indifferent wine by sugaring, to add sugar in a good year detracts from the quality; the avowed purpose in such years is to raise the alcoholic strength. A sugared wine tends to lack distinction: an over-sugared wine seems to produce an excess of glycerine, which results in the 'suave' taste associated with heavily-sugared Burgundy. But this decision in 1951 legalized but did not create the practice. There was one very fine '29 that in fact had been chaptalized, and it seems likely that Pomerols were often 'assisted' in the past.

Certainly 1951 was a year for such 'assistance'. It was miserably wet and the crop was very small. The only wines drinkable must have been well sugared. Even today those wines which have survived are deceptive, for some suggest the sweetness of a '47 or even '29, and of course have an 'old' colour. Among these are Cheval-Blanc, an agreeable but in appearance and flavour highly misleading glass of wine; and neither Latour nor Mouton needed to be apologized for on any table. The former was agreeable as late as 1975. Lafite, as might be expected, is more delicate and when I drank it last in 1967 it faded in the glass, no great condemnation sixteen years after a very bad vintage. I have enjoyed Bel-Air too, and earlier on I had some Gaffelière-Naudes which had cost me only 7s. a bottle from Harvey's, and was a bargain at the price.

1952 (17 SEPTEMBER)

The crop with *A C* was no larger than the previous year, but the wines were much better. I tasted many when first available in London in 1955, and at this early stage they seemed most attractive; but in fact the Médocs contained an excess of tannin which obscured the fruit and persisted. Thus they always lacked the charm of the succeeding '53s. Certainly they 'unbuttoned' as they grew older, and no one could say that they were poor wines, though disagreeably hard when young; and then when fifteen to twenty years old, though lighter, some had begun to lose their fruit. It is the old question of whether the fruit or the tannin will win, and usually but not always it seems to be the latter. One recalls '28, '34 and '37 – and there are some who already raise a query over the extolled '75s. Owing to their retarded development I tended to keep mine and drink the '53s. Also at that time I usually bought English bottlings, as they seemed notably less expensive. This is not to decry them, but if one is to make a serious assessment of a fine claret, I believe one must have the proprietor's own bottling.

Of the first-growth Médocs the Latour seemed to me the best but rather firm and hard, and even in the Christie tasting in 1977 (already referred to several times), although the bottle opened had plenty of colour and fruit it was a little bitter and short. So, much earlier, did the Lafite and Margaux, but examples in their time which gave me more pleasure than expected were Rausan-Ségla, Cantemerle and Angludet; but the last time I drank the first two, in the mid-seventies, they were losing fruit. They did better in the Graves. Haut-Brion had a lot of style, but the La Mission-Haut-Brion drunk with it had more fruit. Curiously enough the latter, opened in 1976 at the château alongside the '53 – normally an outstanding wine of that vintage – had more flavour than its junior. Two years earlier a bottle of Pape-Clément consumed in London was remarkably complete, with plenty behind it, but no hardness; the only time I have met it.

However, more welcoming wines were produced across the rivers, and although the St-Émilions and Pomerols show a hard streak, they have much more fruit and *rondeur*; until 1961 there was no vintage to equal them in quality, and the leading wines have some of the full, concentrated quality of the wines made in these districts during the later 1940s. Probably the Pétrus is today better than the Cheval-Blanc, and both have more flavour than the '53s. None are quite in the top class, and they too may be beginning to lose their fruit. However among Pomerols that have stood out for me are Vieux-Château-Certan, Lafleur-Pétrus, La Croix-de-Gay and Clos René, an excellent growth which I first met in this vintage. Some of the St-Émilions are more austere, not least Ausone, losing its fruit after twenty years, but Figeac, Gaffelière-Naudes and Bel-Air made firm but fruity wines. For Sauternes it was a less good year than 1950, and Yquem, for the second year in succession, produced no wine under the château label owing to frost or hail.

1953 (1 OCTOBER)

This may not be the greatest post-war vintage but probably among the most agreeable to date. Curiously enough it was a late vintage, starting only at the beginning of October, generally a bad omen, but following storms the weather combination just managed to turn out right; excellently balanced, soft wines were produced, which were already drinkable five years after they were made. The crop was reasonably large, 2·98 million hl. The wines were notable for lack of tannin and a natural sweetness which early made them most attractive. From about their tenth year there was always some uncertainty as to how well they would last, because although well-balanced many were light in body. Initially it was agreed that

Lafite led the field, and a very attractive wine it always was, with all the grace and aroma of a fine claret; I have scarcely ever had a poor bottle, though it showed rather brown in colour and a hint of age – as against a much more robust La Mission-Haut-Brion in 1977. I suspected that there was a reason for this, because for years I had been hearing accounts of Lafite's decline, and some averred Margaux to be the finer *premier cru* '53. However, partly owing to the fearsome frosts of February 1956, Lafite was bottling its '53 from December 1955 to June 1956, and it would be surprising if this did not entail some variation in the wine. I know this as I was at Lafite in June 1956, a week after they had finished. Lafite makes a great deal of wine and their bottling is often prolonged. Mouton, on the other hand, now employs a large number of bottlers and completes the job within a few weeks. In 1956 I went on to Latour, and they had bottled their '53s in three months. Nevertheless, although for a time Margaux seemed the finer wine, and I had one or two bottles that seemed more complete than the Lafite, more recent tastings – and one does not come across such wines very frequently – have awarded the palm to Lafite, a fine example of true, elegant claret with a delicious nose. Certainly a magnum at the château in October 1977 was as delicious and well-balanced a claret as one could wish for, without quite the body of the '49 but at the top of its form. I would not think that any '53 had more to give after about twenty years; some were going down and all should be enjoyed while so good.

Latour has remained consistently disappointing, and I cannot believe that even time, often the saviour of Latour, is going to turn it into a great wine; indeed it may already be in decline. At a dinner in Bordeaux in October 1972, a magnum showed very disappointingly alongside a magnum of Cantemerle and bottles of La Tour-de-Mons; but this last has always been one of the finest, best-balanced Médocs of the vintage, with the true elegance of Margaux (Soussans) wines.

The other great success among the leaders was Mouton-Rothschild, made in the centenary year of the Rothschild purchase. It was a big rich wine, completely different in style from its nearest neighbour, and wonderfully full and round with all the traditional concentration of aroma and flavour that one associates with Mouton, but not a wine for those who seek first for delicacy in claret. By 1977 it was as well to drink it. Haut-Brion seemed to take longer to come round than the others, and, although a fine wine, preserved a certain severity, whereas La Mission-Haut-Brion produced a very round fruity wine – one of those with a special reputation from the start. Pape-Clément also made a very agreeable '53, while Domaine de Chevalier, after so many disappointing post-war years, so far as the red wine was concerned, somewhat returned to form this year.

To enumerate the fine '53s is unnecessary, for it was a wonderful Médoc year, and a list of the successes would include a considerable slice of the classed growths, including Léoville-Barton (but not the other two Léovilles), Palmer, Grand-Puy-Lacoste, Lynch-Bages, Talbot, Gruaud-Larose, Langoa and Cantemerle already mentioned. Ronald Barton declared his Langoa '53 to be the best he had ever made. Some of the Pauillacs, like the two Pichons and Pontet-Canet, turned out a bit on the 'hefty' side, lacking the typical balance of the vintage. Other good *crus bourgeois* that I remember include Siran and Angludet.

The St-Émilions and the Pomerols on the whole did not come up to the Médocs and Graves. They seemed to lack the depth of flavour of the '52s, although they were perhaps better balanced. Cheval-Blanc '53 is an agreeable, well-made wine, but one is entitled to expect rather more than that, and the same might be said of the Pétrus and Vieux-Château-Certan too, although the former had more to it than Cheval-Blanc. However there were some particular successes in both *communes*, particularly Figeac, a splendidly deep-flavoured wine, in St-Émilion, and Clos René, L'Enclos and Certan in Pomerol. Clos René, bottled by Harvey's and retailed at 9s. a bottle, was one of my better buys. Until 1961, with few exceptions, neither district again produced such notable wines.

The '53 white Bordeaux were not so good as the '52s, nor so outstanding in their year as the reds; but nevertheless it was a fine vintage.

1954 (10 OCTOBER)

This was the worst year since '46, but better than '56. As in '51, skill and sugar saved the crop for some châteaux, but others may have suffered worse micro-weather at the vintage late in October. Not altogether surprisingly Latour and Mouton-Rothschild made very drinkable wines. They still were in the late seventies, which was remarkable for such an off-vintage. Latour in 1977 still had a big colour, rich nose and a surprising amount of fruit and body; once more a Latour that I would have guessed much younger. If this château's wines often turn up in these notes, particularly in the context of off-vintages, it is not so much because I have a penchant for such years, but owing to their unusual longevity which leads to their unexpected appearance on other claret *amateurs'* tables. For with a few exceptions I have not been an off-vintage buyer, having quite enough to do and to spend in keeping up with the probable, though not always eventual, successes of this vast *vignoble*. Further if certain châteaux's wines frequently figure, it is because I have tended to follow them, or I have had generously furnished opportunities to taste ranges of their wines, including off-vintages. Also some estates are notable for making long-lived wines, among them Latour, Mouton-Rothschild, several of the St-Estèphes and La Mission-Haut-Brion and La Tour-Haut-Brion. In general I would not include the Margaux wines in this class, and Rausan-Ségla '54, drunk in Bordeaux in October 1966, was already so brown and old-smelling that one might have guessed a 1920 in decline. Yet half-bottles of Ch. Margaux opened in London in February 1974 were surprisingly round and fruity for the year, if a little hard at the end. Another good Médoc when comparatively young was Léoville-Barton, if a bit 'short' in flavour. I remember being offered by Ronald Avery very cheaply, and slightly contemptuously rejecting Cheval-Blanc '54, when it was about three years old and not very attractive. In fact it turned out very pleasantly, but has now gone over, while Pétrus still drank surprisingly well in 1968, although by then distinctly pale in colour and two years later lacking the characteristic concentration. Very few '54s came to Britain. One that did was Yquem '54, which may not have had the lusciousness of a great year, but was not a wine to despise.

1955 (29 SEPTEMBER)

This was the first vintage when classed-growth prices began to rise markedly, a process accelerated by the two succeeding poor or short-crop years and continued in successful years until the slump in the seventies. The '55s, which were plentiful – up to then the largest *successful* vintage since the war, with 3·1 million hl and not to be surpassed in quantity until 1962 – were also highly praised. They seemed rather expensive at the time, but not of course dear by later standards (25s. a bottle for Lafite '55 compared with 20s. for the '53). Many, including myself, bought the St-Émilions and Pomerols because they were 'the last good vintage' before the frost devastation early in 1956.

The '55s were certainly good wines, but their fault was a certain lack of definition and a slight dull flatness arising from a shortage of acidity, or so they always seemed to me. There are those who still maintain that the finer wines will survive to produce splendid old bottles, but I doubt it, for if anything the wines are a bit 'short' in flavour. On the whole the best wines came from those estates making rather 'big' wines, including Latour, Mouton-Rothschild and Cos d'Estournel; whereas the Margaux were rather thin and disappointing, and some of them, including Ch. Margaux itself and Giscours, were losing fruit after about fifteen years; though bottles varied and I have drunk satisfactory if not exciting bottles of both when older than that. Some of the St-Juliens did well, and I would certainly place Léoville-Barton, Gruaud-Larose and Ducru-Beaucaillou among the successes, with the last-mentioned still full-tinted and strong, if a bit 'cart-horsey' when it was twenty years old. Another fairly full-flavoured if not very distinguished wine at that age was Mouton-Baron-Philippe. A little later still Lafite almost made up in elegance and flavour what it lacked in body. Many have regarded Cantemerle as one of the best wines of the vintage, and with that slightly 'steely' strike often to be found with this château, it lasted well.

Among the Graves, Haut-Brion has the typically Graves 'earthy' nose, and has not lacked body, but the wine has not been very distinguished for a first growth; La Mission appeared to have more acidity. However the most attractive red Graves was surely Pape-Clément, a very elegant wine, and its only fault was a rather short pontificate, in claret rather than clerical terms, for it thinned off. In 1976 in spite of a distinctly tawny tinge, a bottle was still fruity and well-balanced if light.

The trans-riverine wines suffered from the same dullness. Among the St-Émilions Cheval-Blanc and Figeac have stood out for their fruitiness, and, if anything, I have preferred the latter as having more flavour. It turned rather brown (Figeac has not usually been a deep-coloured wine), but it retained the sweet, concentrated flavour that, like Cheval-Blanc, makes it almost more of a Pomerol than a St-Émilion. Cheval-Blanc itself remained consistently fruity for over twenty years without ever aspiring to greatness. A neighbouring wine, La

Dominique, made a good '55. The finest Pomerol has always seemed to me to be Vieux-Château-Certan, one of the most attractive wines of the whole vintage, and better than Pétrus, which, good wine though it was, lacked the intensity of aroma and flavour that one looks for in a fine Pomerol. Two others that I formerly tasted frequently and liked were La Conseillante and La Grave-Trigant-de-Boisset; also Trotanoy.

It is a pity that the '55s did not achieve just a little more quality, for there is a big gap until the next fine year – 1959.

This was true also of the white wines. Among the dry wines I remember an excellent Haut-Brion Blanc and a very well-rounded Laville-Haut-Brion. Domaine de Chevalier was good but no more. The sweet wines were successful too without being outstanding.

1956 (14 OCTOBER)

A really terrible year, with production down to about one-third of the previous vintage. The February frosts, particularly damaging, as they occurred after a spell of unusually mild weather causing the sap to rise in the vines, ensured a small crop; and the summer was bad too. Even Latour could not pull out anything very attractive, and Mouton made a sharp, thin wine, though no worse than others. I drank the Latour in London in 1972. It still had a big colour, with a nose that was evident but not typical, and the flavour though not disagreeable was not altogether that of claret; there was also a hint of decay. It was passable for a '56, scarcely for a Latour. A Léoville-Barton, drunk at the château in 1970, was surprisingly fruity for the year, if already distinctly brown. I remember an acceptable Talbot, obtainable for a period on British railway restaurant cars, and a Margaux that survived to 1975 with fair nose and flavour but distinctly acid finish; but otherwise the vintage is best forgotten. It was said at the time that St-

Émilion and Pomerol would not recover their normal quality for at least ten years, owing to the number of vines killed. This proved exaggerated, as many vines put out shoots from the bottom, but above the graft. Nevertheless the next really good vintage for these districts was '61. The Médocs and Graves were less spectacularly damaged, but they suffered loss too. French wine-growers take their losses sadly, and it was commonly mourned as the worst disaster since the phylloxera. It was certainly a setback to those classed-growth proprietors who had been making reasonable profits only for the last few years, and for the often hard-pressed lesser growths. Things turned out not to be as bad as advertised, but at the time the more far-seeing (or credulous) went out and bought even more '52s, '53s and '55s. I was among them.

1957 (4 OCTOBER)

The amount of *AC* wine declared this year was scarcely greater than in '56. The later summer was poor and it was another October vintage. Not surprisingly the Bordelais put a brave face on the results which were well publicized, but the wines were hard indeed and lacking in charm. The only wines that have surprised me by their excellence are Haut-Brion – better balanced than most – a surprisingly fruity La Mission-Haut-Brion and Haut-Bailly, while Lynch-Bages, strong and fruity, was good but not very Médocain in style. Talbot gave me some pleasant drinking too. The vintage always had its adherents, who promised great things when the wines were about twenty years old. Had that been so, I should have been caught very short, for I scarcely bought a bottle and those that came my way were either dispatched prematurely or languished in isolation as the odd bottle of an unfavoured vintage can. Nevertheless, a bottle of Cos d'Estournel drunk in January 1978 had a surprising amount of colour, richness of bouquet and elegance of flavour, though it dried in the glass. An *amateur* of '57s present at the table declared with confidence that Cos made the best claret of the year.

1958 (10 OCTOBER)

Cos d'Estournel also made an agreeable wine this year, in which production was small in a mid-October vintage. Nearly all the wines were light, though with some successes in the context of the conditions. Latour had more personality than most, with the typical colour and big nose, and it drank very enjoyably through the sixties, but by the seventies the flavour, after starting well, fell away in the glass. At the 1977 Christie tasting it appeared very light, without much flavour. Mouton was not very impressive on the one or two occasions that I drank it*, but the Cantemerle was particularly firm and fruity for a time. Some of the wines were clearly heavily chaptalized and soon tasted more like old Burgundy than Bordeaux. However, the two leading red Graves were unexpectedly successful. If Haut-Brion was always light, it had style and it certainly held, though tawny-tinted and a little hard, when opened at the château in October 1977. Across the road, La Mission-Haut-Brion made a typically big, earthy wine, with lots of nose, body and fruit. Examples in my cellar were still drinking very well in the late seventies and showed no sign of declining. It might be claimed as the most successful wine of a vintage which has always had its supporters – with more justification than the preceding one. With the '59s hard on its heels, it was not much shipped to Britain, and perhaps I did not drink a wide enough range, while the St-Émilions and Pomerols were still licking their wounds or replanting their vineyards after '56; those '58s that I occasionally tasted all had a rather 'made', chaptalized flavour.

* Yet it did impress me at the château in July 1978. For it had a surprisingly big colour and good body for the vintage. There was some acidity, but after twenty years it remained an agreeable glass of claret.

1959 (20 SEPTEMBER)

It was not surprising, after three unsatisfactory years for quantity as well as quality, that 1959 was hailed somewhat extravagantly; a good vintage was on the order of the day. Moreover the summer was unexpectedly fine and hot even in Britain, and the not-so-initiated wine-drinking public equates a hot year with a fine vintage. In fact as 1921 and 1947 showed, this brings considerable problems. Too much sun means too little fixed acidity, and the danger of volatile acidity. However, before the grapes were gathered, '59 had been declared the Vintage of the Century (we have had four others since then: '61, '64, '70 and '75). Journalists have been blamed for this headline, but it certainly was not those who write regularly about wine, for they are commendably cautious. The crop of red and white *AC* wines was not in fact very large – 1·85 million hl and almost the same as the notoriously short '61; but the whites suffered more than the reds, and there seemed no initial lack of Médocs of quality.

It is now generally agreed that '59 was probably not such a fine year as originally thought, because there was a certain lack of acidity in many of the wines, so they turned out rather soft and lacked stamina; some are a little flabby. On the other hand the best wines were very good and had the true style of fine claret. All three Pauillac leaders made good wine, typical of their varying styles, but I have found Margaux disappointing on the one or two occasions tasted. However the adjoining Palmer was good. Léoville-Las-Cases had partly returned to form, but Léoville-Barton was exceptionally fine as was Ducru-Beaucaillou. Some bottles of the deliciously fruity Léoville seemed to me to turn exceptionally sweet in the mid-seventies, as if chaptalized, which of course they were not, and I had the confirmation of Ronald Barton for that. By that time the Ducru, though a typically elegant St-Julien, was showing signs of drying up; but Gruaud-Larose, with the fruitiness always well to the fore in Cordier-estate wines if sometimes at the expense of style, made a very agreeable wine; and the same on both counts was true of Lynch-Bages. Cantemerle, then in a very good period, was successful too.

Haut-Brion, after some years when it did not seem up to *premier-cru* standards, returned to form this vintage and had all the 'bricky' red Graves nose and elegant, slightly austere flavour typical of the best of them; but by the later seventies it did not promise long life. Pape-Clément was another typical Graves. The St-Émilions and Pomerols had by then recovered some but by no means all of their quality, and soon showed the brown colour of approaching old age. Among those that showed well in their time were Canon, L'Angélus and Figeac, particularly the last-named. Cheval-Blanc, in my limited experience, varied from bottle to bottle: some brown and tired, some still fruity. Ausone hung on until at least 1977, when I drank it at M. Moueix's table: fruity for vintage, easy-to-drink, but brown and requiring to be drunk up.

To some extent a vintage must be judged by its first growths, and it cannot be pretended that all turned out as well as predicted. That, however, is no reflection on the soothsayers, even if at times these might take a tip from the Oracle of Delphi and issue somewhat inscrutable forecasts of what in fact cannot be accurately gauged. However, one of the firsts scored an undoubted success: Lafite, as delicious and typical a fine Médoc as one could wish for. Typical Lafite at its best too, fruity, elegant, with lovely flowery nose and almost 'sweet' flavour. Maybe in the historical canon it will not figure as high as the '61, '53 or '49 of that château, but it was possibly the best wine of the vintage, and a magnum on the spot in October 1977 was *à point*. Unfortunately neither the Mouton-Rothschild nor the Latour were as successful, probably through slight lack of balance. I have excellent bottles of both, though not outstanding, and then distinctly disappointing ones, some of them showing acidity. Of Margaux I have no recent recollection, but I doubt whether any '59s will show much improvement, though one must not be ungrateful for many highly agreeable, accommodating wines of this vintage.

As might be expected in such a hot year, '59 was an excellent vintage for the Sauternes, and none of the well-known châteaux made as good a wine again until 1970. Yquem is splendidly luscious, though perhaps a slightly weighty wine, and perhaps was the exception, for its 1967 was very fine.

1960 (15 SEPTEMBER)

This vintage was at first treated in rather the same way as 1950, for the weather had been similarly wet, although this year the vintage was not late; yet now there was a shortage of wine in Bordeaux. Also chaptalization was permitted. The result was that some very drinkable wines were made in this fairly large vintage. Much depended, I suspect, on adroit use of sugar. Some put in too little, and the wines are thin, some too much and the wines were sweet enough to lose a good deal of their Bordeaux quality. Those however that had 'the mix' right did well. I would put Latour top of the list, Palmer second and Cantemerle third, but I do not claim to have drunk a great range. Grand-Puy-Lacoste was another attractive '60 and so certainly was Mouton-Rothschild, which had an affinity with Latour. Haut-Brion too proved much too sweet for my taste, and Léoville-Las-Cases a bit mawkish but easy-to-drink. Ausone made a very charming light wine, although its very brown colour after only six or seven years did not suggest long life. Cheval-Blanc was bigger and rather more acceptable, while Pétrus, in spite of the damage to its vineyard four years earlier, made a surprisingly full-flavoured wine. Clos Fourtet, however, was a thin, acid, despairing sort of wine. A great virtue of the '60s was that they were inexpensive and, provided one found the right wine, they were very good buys for the not so exceptional occasion. They were also a warning not to be put off too much by cries of 'off-vintage'. For it is surprising how the best of them have lasted. Pétrus I have drunk too seldom to know whether it kept up its surprisingly good quality when a dozen years old, but certainly Latour and Mouton-Rothschild continued to provide excellent bottles with all the varying quality and style expected of each of them. This was hardly a year for still-convalescent Pomerol, but bottles of both La Conseillante and Gazin were still *sui generis* if light in the mid-seventies. So was the La Mission-Haut-Brion as late as 1978: brown at the edges, with mature bouquet, and a light easy-to-drink wine.

1961 (22 SEPTEMBER)

This chapter is largely a summary of wines I have drunk rather than a vintage report. Although nowadays one cannot take as gospel the old Bordelais axiom that one should not drink fine claret until it is ten years old, the really distinguished wines have now become so expensive that there is a strong disincentive to open irreplaceable bottles before their time. This vintage was abnormally short, and, as we thought at the time, excessively dear. Only 550,000 hl of red wine was made – the smallest good vintage since the last war, and even shorter than '45. Perhaps the small crop and exceptional quality of both years are not without significance; but the weather in both years was particularly fine too, and 1961 had the driest summer of the fifties and sixties. That the opening prices seemed very high can be seen by reference to the first growths in Appendix D, but they were partly justified by the short crop. However, on the whole, British wine merchants, with plenty of '59s in their cellars, plus some '60s (in addition to older years), rather shied off buying these expensive '61s. To offer Lafite '61 at 50s. or so a bottle at opening prices seemed an extravagant exercise. In fact, such has been the progress of inflation and the advance of first-growth prices (followed by others) that the '61s now seem not to have been all that dear when first offered; but that always seems the case in an inflationary period, and there is no question but that they were expensive at the time. Since those days Lafite '66 opened retail at over 80s. and Latour '71 at not much short of £20. But by then the speculators had been at work for some years.

The fine quality of the '61s was soon not in doubt. The wines had plenty of fruit and lacked the tannin of the '45s. Today '61 is generally accepted as being the best vintage since '45 and possibly since 1929. Many might place it higher than '45, because of the hardness of the older year. Also the '61s seem more regular than the '45s, some of which must have been made under very difficult conditions, a few months after the end of the Second World War. The '61s were regrettably drinkable from quite early on, so it is hoped that enough have been preserved to be enjoyed when fully mature.

One of the first opportunities that I had for tasting a number of the leading '61s and comparing them with neighbouring vintages was at the Lebègue tasting in London in October 1967. This was one of the famous series of mammoth French wine tastings which Lebègue organized in their vast cellars below London Bridge railway station from 1949 onwards. Every professional and many amateur wine drinkers were in their debt for unparalleled opportunities to taste young and old clarets, burgundies, etc. Fortunately the rate of expectoration was high, though its level happily low, so guests after sampling their choice from nearly two hundred wines were still able to drink a special selection of the finest with the ensuing cold but lavish lunch.

At the 1967 session Guy Prince and his colleagues had arranged a tasting of the '66, '64, '62 and '61 vintages of Pétrus, Cheval-Blanc, Haut-Brion and Margaux. Certainly the '61s then showed their quality, and it was the only one of the four vintages in which I liked all the wines. I placed the elegant but very well-balanced Margaux first, and the Pétrus unhesitatingly second; a wonderfully rich, deep-coloured wine. I put Haut-Brion third as being a bit dumb, and the Cheval-Blanc last, although almost certainly the best wine of that estate from the late forties to the early seventies.

More recently, when the vintage was about ten years old, I had two opportunities of tasting the first growths including Mouton, and on one of these occasions Cheval-Blanc also. Each time Margaux emerged as the finest, most complete wine, with all the floweriness-of-nose and elegance that marks Margaux out in a great vintage. At the Ch. Margaux dinner in 1971, mentioned earlier in connection with nineteenth-century vintages, several of those present considered the '61 the finest wine of the evening. In the long run, Latour, generally judged second on the two occasions mentioned, may turn out the finest of the leaders; an enormously big, strong wine. Mouton-Rothschild, disappointing at the first of these two tastings, has since showed wonderfully well, with the seductive 'cedar-wood' nose often attributed to Mouton, and an overwhelming amount of flavour that made the wine seem even younger than its age. Haut-Brion is an excellently balanced wine, fairly forward like Margaux, but with plenty behind it, which perhaps might not be the case with the more elegant Margaux. Hitherto Lafite has disappointed me, as being rather dumb, even a shade dull for a first growth in such a vintage, but the wine may be taking its time. Both Cheval-Blanc and Pétrus have confirmed that 'welcoming' nose, extraordinary fruitiness and depth of flavour that make these wines exceptional. The latter was in exceptionally short supply – only $17\frac{1}{2}$ *tonneaux* – and is the most sought-after claret of the vintage. A bottle drunk by a wine-merchant friend at M. Moueix's table early in 1979 was reported as very fine but by no means ready.

In revising this book I have deliberately left untouched the preceding paragraphs dealing with the first growths and written in the early seventies; for that is how they appeared to me then, and I have also had the occasion to drink a fair number of lesser, but still fine growths. By the late seventies some of them have developed into at least mature wines and in some cases have shown signs of decline. If none of them could be described as goats, as in the metaphor, not all, to mix it, have turned out as swans.

The first growths, however, have continued to perform beautifully, though one or two unexciting bottles of Margaux made me wonder whether it would turn out a long-distance runner, as certainly the Latour, Mouton-Rothschild and Pétrus look like doing. The Haut-Brion has shown more forward but very typical and elegant, while the Cheval-Blanc is surely its best vintage since '47. Lafite seemed to have every indication of being a great wine with a good deal in reserve but everything in its favour.

Some of the second-rank Médocs were also big, full-bodied wines at this period, notably in my experience Cos d'Estournel, Gruaud-Larose and Pichon-Baron. Others seemed to vary, passing maybe through a phase, while a further number appeared already to have passed their peak, among them Léoville-Barton, Lascombes and Rausan-Ségla. At a lower level good *crus bourgeois* known to me were Chasse-Spleen, de Pez and Phélan-Ségur, and a remarkably fruity Bas-Médoc was the Loudenne, bottled in London in the days before all that château's wines were château-bottled.

Among the Graves La Mission-Haut-Brion was a very big, bold wine with lots behind it and plenty of future ahead, while the Haut-Bailly was characteristically lighter, more elegant and not a very big wine. Léognans tend to be lighter-flavoured wines than the Pessacs, and Pape-Clément, now embedded in the Bordeaux *banlieu*, was still a big but elegant wine in the late seventies. To generalize about the '61 St-Émilions is difficult, for some of them were not then making such good wine as their rank implies – including Ausone, Clos Fourtet and one or two other *premiers grand crus* – while others may not have recovered from the 1956 frosts. I have certainly had very poor bottles of La Gaffelière '61, but may have been unlucky, and was not too pleased with the one bottle of Magdelaine, drunk in 1976, although in the seventies this estate was producing fine, big-bodied wine*. At this period Figeac was not as robust as expected.

The Pomerols, however, seem to have been universally good, though they suffered no less in 1956. No proprietor in the commune is likely to feel flattered if his wine is described as burgundian, but such examples as the tremendously concentrated, rich Pétrus, Vieux-Ch.-Certan and Trotanoy have something of the wealth of flavour of a fine, albeit not over-sugared, Côte d'Or. Clos René was another delicious wine, with a strong blackcurrant nose and flavour, and so was the La Fleur-du-Gazin, a lesser growth. In so small a vintage the Pomerols were rare and expensive, and some of the leading growths were scarcely if at all shipped to Britain; I only secured a few bottles of the Pétrus myself owing to the generosity of M. Jean-Pierre Moueix, as it was not acquired by Avery's and Harvey's, previously the main importers of this wine, and Gilbey's, who held the British agency from the 1962 vintage, did not buy the '61. So my notes are fragmentary. Some Pomerols, however, seemed after about fifteen years to be showing their age, among them Gazin and a few lesser growths, particularly if they had been shipped in cask.

Two final comments should be made with reference to the much-admired '61s. First, in general they were never tannic wines like, for example, the '45s, and tannin is a preservative, so some of them may have a shorter term of life than has been

---

*This comment shows the dangers of judging a wine on a single bottle, although I admitted that the remark was based on this. For at a tasting held in London in December 1978, preparatory to a sale at Christie's in March 1979 of examples of thirteen vintages – from 1952 to 1975 – the '61 in half-bottles was a big, dark-coloured, rich wine, tasting almost like port; though easy to drink.

forecast. Second, suggestions that subsequent vintages such as '70 and '75 are 'like 1961' are almost certainly wide of the mark. For one thing it was the smallest red Bordeaux vintage in the thirty years following the Second World War; and, if other conditions are good, a small *récolte* is a positive pointer. For another the Gironde *vignoble* in 1961 had not been reconstituted, replanted or extended as it was in the sixties and early seventies. To take one example, the average production of Latour in the sixties was about 160 *tonneaux* (given as 250 *tonneaux* in the 1969 edition of Cocks et Féret), but the new British owners set out on the energetic programme of replanting, and the average is now nearer 200 *tonneaux*, although not all would be included in the *grand vin*. In the first edition of this book the output of Mouton-Rothschild was given as about 160 *tonneaux*; by the mid-seventies it was around 200. Similar examples could be given for other growths. This is not to imply that the wine is thereby less good; only that the average age of the vineyards was much older in 1961 than for vintages for the following twenty years, and that is a factor in overall quality. Also the yield per ha has increased.

The '61 white wines, though not outstanding, were among the best of a rather disappointing decade for the Sauternes; but Yquem was not one of the more successful, colouring rather early.

A curiosity of the '61s is that the *Commanderie du Bontemps du Médoc et des Graves* arranged to blend all the four first growths into a special *cuvée* and this was bottled by Barton & Guestier in Bordeaux, with numbered bottles.

The exceptional quality of the '61s, combined with the high prices they have been fetching at auction in the past couple of years, have inhibited the drawing of corks. In the decade '66 is the only other vintage with a broad range of wines likely to develop and improve over a fair period. As to prices, by the end of 1978 the first growths were fetching from £45 to almost £60 a bottle, while Palmer, now one of the most popular classed growths, had reached over £35 a bottle, and La Mission-Haut-Brion over £50. Such prices were based on a combination of repute, speculation and inflation. Owing perhaps to local difficulties some châteaux produced disappointing wine. La Lagune, with a vineyard newly replanted four years earlier, probably over-sugared the wine, as it has struck me as excessively sweet; and the same applies to Beychevelle, perhaps for the same reason. Lynch-Bages seems to have a slightly 'cooked' taste too.

1962 (9 OCTOBER)

This was the abundant vintage every Bordeaux grower and wine merchant had been praying for. Although it started well into October the grapes generally were sound and the wines well-balanced, though on the light side. The quantity of 3·74 million hl of *AC* wine was the largest since the war, and, for red wines, exceeded since only by 1967 and the increasingly large crops during the seventies; for white Bordeaux, 1962 remains the record harvest and is unlikely to be exceeded. There were no great wines, but they were real 'wine merchants' clarets', plentiful, inexpensive, quick-developing wines that could be drunk young. They had much of the charm and lightness of true claret, though they have tended to lack body and character, and, in my view, by the highest standards the Médocs have been over-praised – for the reasons given above. However, they and the Graves were usually superior to the Pomerols and St-Émilions.

Nevertheless on the whole all the superior wines lasted better than I predicted originally and demonstrate the point that clarets are often, like King Charles II, an unconscionable time dying, but to all but the most loyal supporters of the Stuarts, there may seem a good deal less need to excuse this in wine. For quite a number of the leading wines were still surprisingly fruity and well-balanced well past their first decade. The finest seemed to me Pétrus, with claims to be the finest wine of the year: deep-coloured, rich on nose and palate – the essence of Pomerol. Mouton-Rothschild perhaps came next, true to style but less concentrated than in the great years, followed by Latour, big but a bit shapeless and undistinguished. Yet Lafite at the château in 1977 revised earlier views of its being rather a dull wine, for though on the light side after fifteen years, it was still supple and well-balanced. Yet in a first-growth ten-years-after dinner early in 1973 it had generally been placed last, as having less character than Margaux. Mouton-Rothschild, then about to be promoted, was generally placed first, but Haut-Brion, a fine, elegant wine, had some support, and several years later it was still full in colour, aroma and body – an exceptionally well-balanced wine. (Pétrus and Cheval-Blanc were not included.)

What lowered the quality of many '62 Médocs was a lack of balance, leading to a touch of acidity in the finish; almost a mark of the year. For me unquestionably the best of the 'seconds' was Palmer (albeit officially a 'third'); a beautifully balanced wine, elegant yet fruity. Much bigger and bolder was Gruaud-Larose which remained surprisingly full in 'size' in the late seventies, although there was a little bitterness in the tail.

In the Graves Pape-Clément was the opposite number, as it were, to Palmer: a little lighter, but with the true Graves nose and flavour, and finely balanced. So too was the Domaine de Chevalier at the only time that I had the occasion to drink it, at the Académie du Vin in Bordeaux in October 1972, when I was admitted to that body of proud professionals and avid amateurs. La Mission-Haut-Brion seemed to vary from the powerful to the unbalanced. The Médocs and Graves, with certain exceptions, were more successful than the St-Émilions and Pomerols. Yet Ausone, usually so disappointing until the mid-seventies, was, in a magnum opened in 1974, deep in colour, nose and flavour. Cheval-Blanc was disappointingly uninteresting, and surpassed by Figeac, which was seductively fruity and rich for the year, but later tasted as if it had been over-chaptalized. The Pomerols encountered, Pétrus apart, were not very exciting; Vieux-Ch.-Certan was agreeable rather than distinguished, but an isolated bottle of Trotanoy in 1977 was a delicious bottle for early, easy drinking.

There were some very fine Sauternes made this year, the last until 1967. Among those that stand out in my memory are Yquem, Climens, Coutet and Rayne-Vigneau.

1963 (7 OCTOBER)

This vintage was another abundant one, but abundance that caused no joy, for the wines were very poor indeed after a bad summer and a cheerless October vintage. It is an arguable point as to whether '63 or '65 was the worse vintage, although the '63 may have won the unwelcome palm. Even sugaring could not save them. It is true that in Bordeaux I sampled one or two not undrinkable, very, very light wines. They were almost the colour of *vin rosé* when three or four years old. The only wine with any claim to quality I have come on is Latour, which did its best to maintain its off-vintage reputation and just succeeded; one can guess why it tasted sweet. It has been whispered that the new owners, the Cowdray family interests, were anxious to make a fine wine in their first year as the major proprietors. Nature did not favour them but, quite legally, some *vin de presse* of a superior vintage was added at the *assemblage*; certainly with good effect. Surprisingly this wine was still in good condition in 1978 and appeared to have absorbed some of the earlier sweetness.

This was a terrible year for the sweet white wines, and although Yquem actually bottled some '63, its dark colour suggested a wine old before it was young, and for a leading growth this was no credit.

1964 (28 SEPTEMBER)

Whoever was responsible for calling 1959 'the vintage of the century', there is no doubt that for '64 much of the responsibility can be pinned firmly on M. Édgard Pisani, the French Minister of Agriculture, who in August 1964 proclaimed a wonderful vintage. It was another of those misleadingly hot summers. Nevertheless conditions were good, in spite of some deficiency of rain. The vintage started in the last week of September, and those who picked at once generally made the best wine, but certain growths that often like to hang on to attain an alleged *surmaturité*, delayed or suspended picking. Then on 8 October the heavens opened and it rained for a fortnight. The late-pickers included Lafite, Mouton-Rothschild, Lynch-Bages and Calon-Ségur, and their wines were correspondingly light and disappointing. Those who finished their picking early included Latour, whose wine may yet turn out one of the best of the vintage, with a very large crop. Indeed it was a plentiful year for red Bordeaux, almost the equal of '62.

The St-Émilions and Pomerols were more fortunate than the Médocs, partly because their *vendange* usually takes place a few days earlier, and this applies to the Graves too. Certainly both Cheval-Blanc and Figeac made good wines, the latter for me among the most agreeable of the vintage, with the concentrated 'waxy' flavour associated with this estate's wines. Yet neither are likely to be long-livers. I have drunk other enjoyable, often not very well-known St-Émilions of this vintage. This applies also to the Pomerols, but Pétrus, usually so reliable, has seemed to me disappointing, owing to an excess of acidity. Superior this year was Vieux-Ch.-Certan, rich, concentrated and another of the plums of the vintage. L'Enclos, La Fleur-Pétrus, La Pointe, Clos René – I have enjoyed a number of bottles of each, and no doubt there are other wines equally good that I have not seen; but by the late seventies the vintage seemed at its peak.

This applies rather less to the Graves. There is a case for placing Haut-Brion at the top of the first-growth list in '64. Certainly it came out top in my ten-years-after dinner early in 1975: an exceptionally well-balanced, flavoury wine with the authentic Graves nose. La Mission-Haut-Brion was fruity enough too, a merit in this year, but a little on the coarse side at that point, whereas Haut-Bailly, much more elegant, was showing signs of age, but was a charming wine. So was Pape-Clément.

The Médocs were much more variable, and the difference cannot be entirely attributed to whether they picked early or late. It is true that those which finished really late, like the ones mentioned above, made very disappointing wine, but so did Palmer, where picking started on 21 September and finished on the first day of the downpour. Nor were Cantemerle and La Tour-de-Mons, both early pickers, successful; 'stringy' wines both of them. Certainly those 'first home' tended to do best, including Brane-Cantenac, which finished on the same day as Palmer, but began four days earlier. Among other early pickers that I have found well-balanced have been Grand-Puy-Lacoste, Beychevelle, Léoville-Las-Cases, St-Pierre and du Tertre. On the other hand one of the best Médocs that I have drunk was Gruaud-Larose, round and fruity; but they and Talbot, a little drier, both finished on 17 October, while Ducru-Beaucaillou, which was home and comparatively dry only on the preceding day, made a very acceptable '64. The record for lateness was held by Lynch-Bages, which did not start picking until 5 October and finished on the 24th.

All in all, in view of the early optimism, it must be said that 1964 was a disappointing vintage for red Bordeaux.

It was another disappointing year for Sauternes too, and I

believe that at Yquem no wine was sold under the château label, though Climens and Coutet did bottle some of their wine this year.

The prices obtained by the first growths were extremely – many would say excessively – high, in view of the uneven quality and the large crop. No doubt these prices were partly the result of the 'vintage of the century' aura. But the '66s were to be dearer still, and from the standpoint of the seventies the '64s appear modest indeed.

1965 (30 SEPTEMBER)

Following one of the wettest Septembers in the Gironde for many years, it is not surprising that the vintage, also partly carried out in the rain, was very poor indeed. Outside more than one *chai* some of the grapes could be seen in open cauldrons above fires, in an attempt to concentrate the must a little and add to the colour. Rot was widespread, and as the grape-loads were tipped into *fouloir-égrappoirs* it rose in a cloud of grey dust. As a result the '65s had little merit. Some growths by a process of ruthless selection made light clean wine; among these were La Mission-Haut-Brion and Cantemerle. Ch. Margaux, involved in its non-vintage blends, sold no wine with this vintage label. Both Latour and Mouton-Rothschild did, in my view, mistakenly as there was a taste of rot in the wine. One well-known growth, which I sampled when it was seven years old, smelled and tasted drinkable, if heavily sugared, when first opened, then slowly developed a most unpleasant odour of burnt rubber; the bottle could not be finished.

1966 (20 SEPTEMBER)

There is little doubt that after 1961, this is the best red Bordeaux vintage of the decade. The vintage generally began in the last week of September and the crop was medium in quantity. On the whole the opening prices were not high – apart from the first growths – and they only returned to something like the level of the '61s. The main reason why the '66s were not more enthusiastically received initially was that the expensive-seeming '64s had not risen substantially in price. However the reputation of the vintage gradually increased, and those who bought early from their wine merchants should have secured some bargains.

Writing in the late seventies, however, we are now reaching the point when many wines and some vintages have yet to show their real quality. Claret is a wayward wine, and that is part of its charm to those who like to discuss as well as to drink their wine. Whereas Burgundy pursues a fairly steady, smoother and quicker path to maturity, claret suffers from periods of what in humans would be called 'depressions'. The wines lack lustre and are dull and backward. This seemed to happen to many '66s when they were about ten years old, just when they might be expected to have blossomed. They could not be written off as poor, but they were not as 'welcoming' as might be expected from a vintage that earlier on had looked as if it would open out early. Lafite, Mouton-Roths-child, even Pétrus, seemed closed up and retarded. The same was true of several other Médocs, save Palmer, a deliciously rich, round wine, and Gruaud-Larose, though that had less distinction. Ch. Margaux, a bottle of which had tasted so well early in 1975, two years later seemed in recession and came last at my 'ten-year-old' dinner. At an interesting, enterprising tasting held by Harrods Wine Department in October 1978 the 1966 and 1971 Médoc first growths were shown. Of the former Latour, with a beautifully balanced flavour and long taste, seemed the best to me, and this appeared to be the general opinion. I put Margaux second for its balance, elegance and length, but it was lighter than expected. Other wines of distinction, such as Ducru-Beaucaillou, Brane-

Cantenac, Issan and Rausan-Ségla, appeared to lack a little backbone, though Giscours, Lascombes, Haut-Bages and Lynch-Bages were bigger.

As in 1964, the Graves seemed to score, with Haut-Brion again heading the *premier cru* list, though Lafite, a fine, aromatic but backward wine, ran it close. Haut-Bailly was light and elegant, Pape-Clément restrained, while La Mission-Haut-Brion was, as one might expect, a long way from being ready, but at the château in September 1978 showed great distinction and style, with a long taste – and future.

Across the two rivers, Cheval-Blanc showed well but did not seem as big a wine as Figeac, though this might alter. Vieux-Ch.-Certan had all the right Pomerol ingredients of rich nose and fruity body, but did not suggest a lot to give; Trotanoy, though backward, had plenty behind it.

It was a good year for the white Graves. Laville-Haut-Brion, when twelve years old, was a beautifully balanced, classic dry Graves.

All these comments, based entirely on wines that I have drunk from my own cellar or elsewhere, may well look absurd and outdated in a few years' time. At a time when there is a tendency even in Bordeaux to produce wines for early drinking, there is no reason to cavil at a slow-developer. The tannin has not been excessive, and if the fruit is sufficient the vintage should turn out well. Wait and see!

1967 (25 SEPTEMBER)

In red though not in white wine this was an even bigger vintage than 1962. Picking began at much the same time as the previous year, but conditions were more variable. The wines were on the light side in colour and body, and one might say that too much was produced to be of top quality; but then what about the much more prolific 1970s, so widely acclaimed? It is claimed that some growths made better wines in St-Émilion and Pomerol than in 1966, and of the leaders there both Cheval-Blanc and Pétrus are more developed, as well as being among the best wines of the vintage so far. At a blind tasting in October 1977, attended by the leading Bordeaux brokers in the cellars of Duclot, the shipping firm associated with the Libourne house of Moueix, Pétrus came out first – and Ausone, very brown and old-tasting, came last. Trotanoy '67, tasted alongside the '66, was very attractive and easier to drink, but had less body and fruit. Whether or not better than the '66s, it is not unlikely that the most successful clarets were made in those two districts rather than in the Médoc and Graves, where many of the wines, such as Palmer, Beychevelle, Haut-Bailly and Domaine de Chevalier, lacked body and fruit even when elegant. Some of the fruitier, rounded wines included Batailley and Haut-Batailley, Lynch-Bages and Giscours. Lafite was distinguished but rather attenuated after ten years, but Latour was much bigger if rather shapeless. Its second wine, Les Forts de Latour, was certainly more attractive at one time. The exceptionally deep-coloured La Mission-Haut-Brion may turn out one of the most long-lived and best.

Among the Sauternes Yquem is outstanding.

1968 (22 SEPTEMBER)

The third poor vintage of the sixties nevertheless produced some red wines at least better than the '63s and the '65s. The summer had been indifferent, with the vital month of August the wettest for many years. The result was wines lacking in body and fruit. The vintage was particularly unsuccessful in St-Émilion and Pomerol. In the former the status of a classified growth depends upon a tasting. If the wine is very bad then it may not even be called St-Émilion, but if it passes this test it may not be allowed to call itself *Premier Grand Cru Classé* or *Grand Cru Classé*. In 1968 the only estate allowed the full title was Figeac; Cheval-Blanc had to bottle its wine without the classification – a fine point unlikely to be noticed even by those familiar with the celebrated label. Certainly the Cheval-Blanc '68 was prematurely brown, and they might have done better to have decided against selling under its label; and the same applied to Lafite, a wine that was old and brown before it was ever young. On the other hand Figeac was reasonably fruity, and some Médocs were quite palatable, including Latour, Ducru-Beaucaillou and Cantemerle. However the '68 that attracted me most was Haut-Brion, light but true to character; the same also applied to La Mission-Haut-Brion. Another surprisingly attractive wine was Pétrus. Only a very small quantity was sold under the château label, and although brownish in tinge, even after ten years it was still surprisingly rich and fruity. However, most of the other wines were well on the way down before this – a vintage to be remembered only as a warning against the belief that Nature has been conquered in the Gironde. And it struck again the following year.

1969 (23 SEPTEMBER)

A good vintage had been prayed for this year, after the poor '68, which had followed the acceptable but not outstanding '67. Unfortunately after a good and at times very hot summer, the heavens opened in September, with a total rainfall only a fraction less than in the notorious 1965. This effectively spoiled the hopes of a fine vintage though October was very fine; but the quantity was small and the quality was somewhat talked up over the winter months. Moreover investment in wine was attracting wider circles of investors, so when the first growths issued their prices in the spring and early summer of 1970 they were two to three times higher than for the '67s; and they had no difficulty in selling their wines. Most of the other classed growths were content to advance their prices modestly, but Palmer and Pape-Clément rose fifty per cent or more, to 10,000 frs. per *tonneau*. Unfortunately the wines lacked colour and fruit, though they were healthy enough. In spite of some commercially inspired optimism, however, the wines lacked enough body to live on and turned out mean and 'ungenerous', often with a bitter taste at the finish. To be charitable, one could award points to Latour, Palmer, Haut-Brion, La Mission-Haut-Brion, La Tour-Haut-Brion, Pétrus and Cheval-Blanc; all of them agreeable 'introductory bottles' to something better, with Pétrus probably the most fruity, and, as tasted at the château in July 1978, the Mouton-Rothschild, though already brown-tinged, was fruitier and better balanced than expected. At a first-growth dinner in March 1979 Lafite and Pétrus showed the best. But it was a sad end to a decade that had started so well – particularly in view of the extravagantly high prices in relation to quality.

1970 (27 SEPTEMBER)

Prayers having largely miscarried over the 1969s, the Bordeaux trade was so desperate for a good, plentiful year that failing natural resources, it would almost have proved necessary to invent a successful 1970. Fortunately, after a very late spring, Nature provided. A fine summer was prolonged into a wonderful autumn. Little rain fell in the decisive months of August and September, and still less over the vintage period, which began in the last week of September. The harvest was brought in under ideal conditions. I have never seen healthier, rounder grapes without a hint of rot anywhere. Not surprisingly the crop was very large, much the biggest in the post-war epoch. The red wine at a little more than 2 million hl was more than half-a-million hl over the record 1967, but the white wine crop declared with *appellation contrôlée* was moderate only. However, in quality this was the finest year for Sauternes for a decade. The size of the red wine crop naturally raised some doubts as to whether the claims of outstanding quality were justified; not least because only those Bordeaux merchants who bought very early, before Christmas of that year for the most part, avoided paying the rapidly rising prices, two samples of which are given in the chapter on the Bordeaux wine trade. It was the châteaux that offered their wines first which soon increased them sharply. Estates such as Brane-Cantenac, Ducru-Beaucaillou, Lynch-Bages and Montrose which had started at 8,000 frs. a *tonneau* (plus about 15 per cent for keeping charges) soon jumped to 11,500 and 12,000 frs. Beychevelle opened at 10,000 frs. and rose to 12,000, which was Palmer's price and remained unaltered; but Pape-Clément which had opened at 11,000 frs. (including keeping charges) soon doubled its price, while Figeac and La Conseillante offered their wines at 16,000 frs. (keeping charges included). As mentioned in the chapter on the wine trade, the first-growth prices were initially comparatively moderate, except for Lafite, whose opening price of 59,000 frs. put the opening price on an English retail list of well over £10 a bottle, while the lower-priced Latour and Cheval-Blanc sold for £10·50 on one list. The second growths were around £3·50 a bottle, which did not look so cheap then as it did later; and of course these prices applied only to those who had bought early. However, those wine drinkers who delayed their purchases until the not-far-off slump that followed will have scored heavily.

What, after all this bourse atmosphere, are the wines really like? Certainly they are generally big fruity wines, but less forward than at one time they appeared to be. In fact, when seven or eight years old, many seemed determinedly closed up, though this is no bad sign for the future. Considering the size of the vintage they have a great deal of concentration. Most have a big colour too. They have more to them than the following '71s, although some claim superiority for the St-Émilions and Pomerols. Perhaps this is the best vintage of the seventies, though challenged by the '75s and '76s. The '70s definitely seem wines for which the ten-year rule of abstinence should be observed. Perhaps I have overmuch observed this rule of abstinence, as I have opened few of my own bottles, and those that I have shared have been at other tables. Certainly many have remained closed up, but the quality has shown. With the exception of La Mission-Haut-Brion, the Graves seem the most forward, including Haut-Brion, Pape-Clément and Haut-Bailly. Among the Médocs I have particularly admired Ducru-Beaucaillou and Léoville-Las-Cases, and found both Cos d'Estournel and Lynch-Bages typically big, fruity wines, by no means ready. Rausan-Ségla showed a good deal of style at the château as far back as 1976. Figeac, which I have drunk on a number of occasions, has been a charming wine, though less full and big than expected, and among the Pomerols Magdelaine has had more body. A fine, rich Pomerol is Trotanoy. This abstinence of course refers only to the leading wines; the wines of the *petits châteaux* for the most part have been making agreeable drinking for some time. With this vintage, nearly all those classed growths that had not already gone over to compulsory château-bottling now insisted on this, and they were followed by some of the better-known *crus bourgeois*.

1971 (27 SEPTEMBER)

This was the third Bordeaux vintage of passable quality in a row if '69 is just accepted; the most recent parallel being the last three vintages of the forties, although 1948 was largely overlooked at the time. With the greatly increased demand for claret there was no question of ignoring the '71s, in spite of the exceptionally high prices. After a poor flowering of the vine in June, which meant a small crop, and a moderate summer, once again the vintage period was very fine. As it was the Merlot which suffered most from the disappointing flowering, the proportion of Cabernet – producing rather harder, more tanniny wine – was greater; and the crop was particularly small in St-Émilion and Pomerol where the Merlot is so prominent. However the fine weather at the vintage ensured that the grapes were ripe, and those who delayed picking probably made the best wine. The quality was certainly less regular than the '70s and the wines much lighter. It is ironic, therefore, that in the hectic atmosphere of speculation that surrounded this vintage, prices opened at levels higher by two or three times or even more than for the first offers of the finer 1970 vintage. A few prices are recorded in the chapter on the Bordeaux wine trade, as well as those of the first growths in Appendix D. Then Lafite put out a second *tranche* at 130,000 frs. a *tonneau* (over £10 or $22 a bottle ex-château before brokerage, bottling, etc., which would probably lead to an opening retail price to the consumer not far short of double these initial figures). This price no doubt may be attributed to the fact that Mouton-Rothschild had trumped Lafite's opening 110,000 frs. by offering its own wine at 120,000 frs.! Some châteaux insisted on conditional sales, among them Léoville-Las-Cases, whose opening figure of 20,000 frs. a *tonneau* was available only to those who bought the wines of its associated (Bas-) Médoc property, Potensac, at 6,500 frs. It was a mad wine world in which the vital matter of quality was temporarily subordinated to considerations of investment and speculation. In the event, and taking into account early estimates of their quality, the wines seem rather disappointing; for they are nearly all unquestionably light, the *petits châteaux* markedly so. When four or five years old many, including Lafite and Mouton-Rothschild, were much more attractive to the taste than the reserved '70s, but thereafter showed a tinge of brown in their colour, which does not suggest longevity. Some appear to have more body than others, including Palmer and Ducru-Beaucaillou, and as already indicated, the St-Émilions and Pomerols have their supporters, mainly perhaps because the crop there was particularly small owing to severe *coulure* in May and June, affecting particularly the Merlot. This is not to suggest that this anything but a good vintage, but rather that early optimism does not seem to be borne out, with the wines not having a great deal more to give. It is, however, a little early to be too decisive about clarets that are charming to drink now. In the Harrods first-growth tasting in October 1978, already mentioned in respect of the '66s, of the '71s I placed Lafite and Latour first; the former for current consumption, the latter for keeping. The dry white Graves was excellent this year and Sauternes for the second year running was very successful, though probably not quite as good as the '70.

1972 (7 OCTOBER)

The summer was generally cool, and an exceptionally rainy August failed to produce the sun needed to ripen the grapes. By September the prospects of making even fair wine were poor, as the grapes were not ripe, and the acidity was high. However yet another fine vintage spell of weather saved the crop. A long run of warm days enabled the growers to delay the vintage until well into October, normally a very risky gamble. It turned out to be the latest vintage since the last war, and one of the latest of the century. Many leading châteaux did not begin picking until well into the second week of the month, and some did not start until the 14th. Once again those who waited almost certainly made the best wine, as the acidity declined. Nevertheless this must rank as one of the most unagreeable Bordeaux vintages ever offered at such high prices. First growths averaged 90,000 frs. a *tonneau*, and Lafite went to 100,000. With only a small mark-up ex-Bordeaux, this meant over £100 a dozen to British wine merchants, which with bottling charges, freight duty and VAT would probably mean, if bought at opening list prices, about £15 a bottle, for an inferior quality wine. The second growths averaged 35,000 frs. a *tonneau*, and some, whose identities may mercifully be forgotten, went even higher. Gloria, a *cru bourgeois*, offered its wine at 32,000 frs.! In the mad, speculative fever potential buyers were even refused tasting samples before being asked to place their orders. That many Bordeaux shippers did buy was owing to the exclusivity contracts that they had rushed in to sign a few years earlier, and which enabled growers in a rising market to name their own prices. The red wine crop was larger than in 1971, but some growers made less; the white wine harvest was not much bigger than the exceptionally small one the previous year. Once the wines became seriously tastable in the spring of 1973, the bubble burst, and this really heralded the end of the Bordeaux boom. When they were in bottle, the Institute of Masters of Wine, that august body of the best professional palates in the business, arranged a tasting in London late in 1975, and they were kind enough to ask a few outsiders such as myself. Among the forty-two château-bottled wines available nearly every famous château was represented, except Haut-Brion, but it was hard to say a kind word about more than half-a-dozen – headed by Cheval-Blanc, Léoville-Las-Cases, Branaire-Ducru and Giscours – and even about these the kind words were in decidedly short supply. Owing to the strong acidity of the wines, it was one of the most arduous tastings I ever remember attending. In a subsequent report a leading Master of Wine, David Peppercorn, formerly vintage wine buyer for the International Distillers and Vintners (Gilbey's) Group, put out a report in which he summed up his impressions thus: 'At the end of the tasting I was left with the feeling that if 1972 represented a high point as far as prices were concerned, it must surely represent one of the lowest in terms of quality. Certainly 1963 and 1965 were as bad or probably worse. But then no great claims were made for these years.' Nevertheless the '72s, or some of them, have had their defenders, and at much the same time as this London tasting, a distinguished, objectively-minded Médoc proprietor told me that he believed that they would be showing quite well by 1980, having discarded much of their acidity. There should be no lack of examples to try!

1973 (25 SEPTEMBER)

At one moment it looked as if this might become yet another 'vintage of the century'. Indeed a Paris agency message, published in an English Sunday paper on 16 September, quoted 'French wine experts' as predicting, after tasting the first samples of Beaujolais, that it might become the finest of the century, and a few days earlier in Bordeaux I was told of hopes of 'a great year'. Indeed the prospects had been good, with a plentiful *sortie* of grapes after the flowering, and a very hot August and first half of September, following a partly rainy July. But then at the last moment – on 15 September to be precise – storms set in, including hailstorms, rare at that time of year, damaging the crop at Haut-Brion and La Mission-Haut-Brion. The weather continued cold and wet during the first ten days of the vintage, which began on 25 September, but changed to beautifully fine weather for the remainder. However, as elsewhere throughout France which produced an unprecedentedly large vintage of 82·4 million hl, the heavy rain had swollen the grapes and reduced the sugar and acid content. The vintage in the Gironde was a record one, with a surplus of red Bordeaux *AC* of over 400,000 hl more than in the previous record year of 1970. Commercially this was not the type of vintage wanted at a time of growing recession, following the end of the investment/speculation boom that summer. So when the wines came to be offered early in 1974 there were not too many takers, even at prices something like one-third lower than for the '72s – and less still for the first growths, as may be seen in Appendix D. When the wines had had some bottle-age the better were seen to be agreeable light wines that would not make old bones, but could make pleasant drinking. Among the relatively few tasted since they were in bottle I would count Lafite, Haut-Brion, Giscours, Brane-Cantenac, Rausan-Ségla, Gruaud-Larose, Léoville-Las-Cases, Ducru-Beaucaillou and Boyd-Cantenac from the 'left bank', and Cheval-Blanc, Trotanoy, La Dominique and de Sales from the 'right bank'. Some wines, however, were obviously over-chaptalized to compensate for the dilution and consequent increase in output, and these have a distinctly sweetened flavour. Some too are excessively light in colour. The September rains meant a disappointing vintage in Sauternes.

1974 (26 SEPTEMBER)

If a small but fine vintage had been hoped for in 1973, it was imperative this year, but once again the Bordelais were cheated by cold wet weather that started in mid-September and continued right through a vintage that generally began in the last few days of September. Fine conditions in the summer were obliterated by the exceptionally poor vintage weather, although it was so unseasonably cold that there was said to be little rot. But the result was a crop second, so far as the red wines were concerned, only to 1973. By this time recession had become slump, and initially at any rate, this was a vintage that no one wanted; opening prices came out later than for a great many years. Indeed, almost the only *en primeur* offers came from the first growths in the course of the summer and autumn of 1975. As can be seen in Appendix D these were well down even on the '73s. Beychevelle, whose '73 had opened at 25,000 frs., made a deal with an American company to sell part of its crop at 11,500 and the general level of the seconds was not higher than 14,000 frs., though La Mission-Haut-Brion, always in an echelon on its own, secured 22,000. Although after a good summer '74 was no '65 or '68, the wines seemed very hard and unyielding when young, lacking much charm. La Mission-Haut-Brion seemed to have more character than most shortly after bottling. Among the few that have come my way and have appeared to be above average are Latour, less tannic than many, Mouton-Rothschild, less austere than expected, Ducru-Beaucaillou, Magdelaine and Figeac, fruity for the year. Yet most if not all lack 'length' and are unlikely to last long in an agreeable form. Some of the minor wines seemed particularly 'ungrateful', but the Bordeaux view, after preferring the '73s, seemed to swing round to believing the '74s the better. Certainly they have more body. They will probably take another three or four years before they can be truly judged. The white wines were undistinguished, particularly the washed-out Sauternes, which need a warm autumn.

1975 (22 SEPTEMBER)

This, at last, was the vintage needed by overstocked Bordeaux: fine in quality, small in quantity. After a hot summer, heavy storms in the pre-vintage weeks caused apprehension, but the vintage, in splendid weather, ran from 22 September to 11 October; later for the sweet white wines. Severe March frosts that damaged the early-budding Merlot and an uneven flowering led to a small crop. A widely publicized hailstorm during the vintage on 29 September devastated a narrow swathe of the central Haut-Médoc, passing through Moulis, Avensan, Arcins and Lamarque before crossing the Gironde and marginally affecting Bourg and Blaye. Passing through that belt a few days later I had never seen such an extent of brown, burnt-looking vines stretching as far as one could see in the direction of the estuary. It looked like the aftermath of a creeping forest fire. Part of the Moulis crop was saved but not much in the other communes, and the vineyards in many cases had to be replanted. Fortunately, however, neither

Margaux in the south nor St-Julien and Pauillac further north were damaged, as they certainly would have been if the storm had turned in either direction.

The red wine harvest of 1·77 million hl, though smaller than the three very large crops of '70, '73 and '74, was not as small as was made out in some quarters, and was larger than any in the sixties, though many château vineyards were now larger. The excellent white wine harvest was small, reflecting the gradual contraction of the white wine *vignoble*.

Naturally enough, the Bordeaux trade, after some years in travail, hailed this vintage with enthusiasm. Somewhat premature comparisons were made with '61, which for reasons given in the comments on that vintage seemed irrelevant. For, apart from the question of the age of the vines, whereas there was scarcely any rain in the hot summer of 1961, the rainfall in August and September 1975 actually exceeded the average, though happily confined to a few days.

Fortunately the growers kept their heads, obtaining from 54,000 frs. (Lafite) and 45,000 frs. (Latour) for the first growths, 16,000–18,000 frs. for the seconds, and moderate prices for the lesser names (Gloria at 12,500 frs.). A notable change also for the *crus classés*, as one result of the slump, was that all were now supplying 100 dozen per *tonneau*, compared with the 96 dozen usual previously. The excellent Sauternes were offered at 14,000–16,000 frs. However, after initial hesitation among foreign buyers, the word went around that this was 'a great year', and in the U.S.A., I believe, as 'the greatest since '61'. As a result, demand rose for relatively limited quantities, some speculation developed and by mid-1978 prices for leading growths had tripled. Indeed they were higher than for the now more assured as well as the obviously more mature 1970s.

Although the quality of the '75s is not in doubt, how they will turn out is unlikely to be determined for a number of years. For undoubtedly they are tannic wines, very hard when first bottled. Some think they could turn out like '52, while others compare them more pessimistically with '34; but one certain fact is that no two vintages are ever alike. From early tastings, I would guess that the St-Émilions and Pomerols might turn out particularly attractive.

1976 (13 SEPTEMBER)

A press-agency message from Bordeaux, published in the newspapers in the middle of the vintage, stated that owing to heavy rains early in September, '1976 will not after all be the vintage of the century'. For that relief much thanks, since in some quarters this had already been proclaimed for 1975! Even in such inflationary times as this vintage was picked in, we cannot do with too many vintages of a century in a row.

In fact the summer was extremely hot and dry, and the vine flowered early in June, so that the picking generally began exceptionally early on 13 September and was over by the end of the month. There were storms at the end of August, but on the whole they were beneficial, as some rain a few weeks before the vintage helps to swell the grapes; but the heavy rain in the third and fourth weeks of September did affect those growths whose picking was delayed, and this has caused a slight doubt as to future prospects. Certainly many of the *petits châteaux* produced wines light in colour and body, but most of the more important growths made charming, aromatic and fruity wines that the Bordelais would describe as *coulant* (i.e. flowing wines that 'slip down'). Indeed there are those who prefer the Médocs and Graves to the '75s on the grounds of the hardness of the earlier year. Is this another case of '52 versus '53? It is generally agreed, however, that in the early stages at least the St-Émilions and Pomerols lack the rich concentration of the '75s. The white wines, especially the Sauternes, are unlikely to be as good as in the previous year.

The quantity was much larger than in 1975, and within a whisker of exceeding the record '73. Although the growers were now saying that they had sold the '75s too cheaply, and they rose very sharply throughout 1977, this large vintage, the second fine one in succession, helped to keep opening prices at much the same level as for the previous year, in spite of inflation in France of about 10 per cent per annum. Since then, of course, they have risen, partly owing to the poor '77s and partly because they are likely to be drinkable before the '75s.

1977 (10 OCTOBER)

Bordeaux, like most of the rest of Europe, had a very poor summer unlike the two previous years, and this followed devastating spring frosts, one at the end of March, the other about ten days later, at Easter. There was even snow in Bordeaux on the second occasion. As usual on such occasions the early-budding Merlot was especially badly hit, and some growths in St-Émilion and Pomerol, predominantly Merlot, produced only about a quarter of their crop in 1976. The flowering was late and irregular, and cold wet weather persisted through the summer. The average daytime temperature was lower than in such notorious years as '56, '63, '65 and '72: 64·5° F. compared with 71·8° F. in 1976, with only one day in the three summer months achieving a temperature of 86° F. compared with 29 the previous year. The result was a great deal of mildew. At Latour, for example, they sprayed the vineyards seventeen times instead of the normal eight to ten. The growers therefore were prepared for one of the worst vintages in the previous decade, but they were saved by an unusually fine September and October. Such was the backwardness of the vines that the vintage was among the latest of recent years: it started on 10 October. Initially the wines were reported as distinctly acid, though it was suggested that this would decline substantially after the malo-lactic fermentation. As might be expected after the unusually severe spring frosts the vintage was very small indeed: 1,293,000 hl of *AC* red Bordeaux and 692,000 hl of white. The former was the smallest crop since 1971, the latter since 1945. In view of the previous two fine years, and the likely quality of the '77s this short-fall was perhaps just as well for red Bordeaux, and even for the whites, as the demand for this depressed sector of the Bordeaux trade would then improve. Indeed it did.

Although it is too early to come to any firm conclusions about the reds, they seem likely to be meagre wines, short and deficient in fruit; probably the worst vintage since 1972.

1978 (9 OCTOBER)

This proved one of the most extraordinary vintages in the Gironde for many years. After a cold spring the vital flowering took place two weeks late, and the summer weather was very poor until the middle of August. At this point no one expected any success in a vintage that must be late, and unlikely to take place in conditions even as good as in the preceding year. However, things turned out differently, and from that date fine weather prevailed, with a rainfall of only 53·2 mm. in the important pre-vintage months of August and September. As can be seen in Appendix E only 1961 had a lower total in the last quarter-century, although there was little more in 1962; and only 5·5 mm. fell in the whole of October when the picking took place in excellent conditions, with good sugar content and no rot.

Consequently, in a market little given to undue pessimism, optimism reigned and prices rose, stimulated by the early announced price of Gloria, which, having disposed of half its crop in a private deal with an American importer, offered the balance at 24 frs. a bottle, compared with 15 frs. for its 1976; and sold it at once. (There has been an increasing tendency for opening offers to be made in per-bottle terms. This has the advantage for the proprietor of being paid for the bottling long before he has to carry out the operation, whereas if the wine is offered on a *tonneau* basis, the buyer later pays extra for the château-bottling. The charge for this is fixed by the C.I.V.B. and at this time worked out at about 3,300 frs. a *tonneau*. So to convert per-bottle terms into the *tonneau* rate, one must multiply the former by 1,200 and subtract the bottling charge.) It was not surprising, therefore, that the classed-growth prices were more than 50 per cent up on the last good vintage, 1976. Beychevelle came out at 32 frs. a bottle (*c.* 34,000 frs. a *tonneau*, compared with 20,000 frs. for the '76) Léoville-Barton and Lynch-Bages at 26 frs., Branaire-Ducru at 28 frs., while among the châteaux offering in *tonneau* terms were Vieux-Château-Certan (38,000 frs.), Pichon-Lalande (29,500 frs.), Calon-Ségur (28,500 frs.), Duhart-Milon (26,000 frs.), Clerc-Milon (26,000 frs.), Gazin (25,000 frs.) and Phélan-Ségur (15,000 frs). The first growths offered their first *tranches* at 82,000 frs.

Early reports on the quality of the wine were enthusiastic, with colour deep, plenty of body and fruit, though it has been suggested that the poor summer had resulted in some lack of stamina, not least because the quantity had turned out unexpectedly large (2·25 million hl for *AC* red). The young wines had a good deal of tannin, and this was said to be very much of a Cabernet year, i.e. one that might take a good time to come round in the Médoc and Graves. Comparisons with earlier vintages are usually misleading, for two are never the same, but the most commonly quoted year was 1962. An accurate forecast of quality and when the clarets will be readily drinkable will not be possible for several years. Meanwhile, in view of the bad start to the active viticultural cycle, a little caution might be wise, with not too many berets basques being thrown in the air, nor too many bottles laid to rest in the cellar.

The white wine crop though disappointingly small was good in quality, but owing to lack of humidity the sweet wines might not be exceptional.

Appendix A: Table of Permitted Minimum Strengths and Basic Maximum Crops in Hectolitres Permitted under the Bordeaux *Appellations Contrôlées*

Since October 1974 the *Appellation Contrôlée* system has been made more flexible. By an official decree, formulated by the *I.N.A.O.*, the normal maximum yield per hectare, as listed below, is now called the *rendement de base*, or basic maximum permitted yield. This is susceptible to annual variation either up or down, on the proposition of the syndicate of growers of each *appellation* and is subject to the agreement of the *I.N.A.O.* This is known as the *rendement annuel*. On top of this annual permitted yield an additional percentage of that yield may be granted in the same way as the yearly one. The higher figure is known as the *plafond limité de classement* (*P.L.C.*). An increase in the *rendement de base* is granted, in the words of the official decree, 'only in an exceptional year when quality and quantity coincide'. The *P.L.C.* for all Bordeaux *appellations*, as for nearly all the rest of France, is 20 per cent above the annual figure, whether or not it is the normal basic one or a higher or lower permitted total. The annual yield figure is announced at about the vintage time, but before 1 December each year. For that is the latest date by which a grower, whose yield has exceeded the annual one, can apply to have all his crop, up to the level of the *P.L.C.*, granted the *appellation*. If his yield is even higher than the *P.L.C.* then at the time of his crop declaration he must agree to deliver the excess for distillation, the production of vinegar or of unfermented grape juice. If he does not do so he automatically loses the right to the *appellation* for all his production above the annual total. Moreover his submission to have his whole crop, up to the *P.L.C.*, given the *appellation* entails a chemical analysis and tasting by a committee, which has the power to turn down the whole of his crop. This has not worried the Bordelais growers, but the Burgundians by and large have refused to submit their wines to this additional test. It is the policy of the *I.N.A.O.* to insist on a tasting of all *AC* wines before what is generally known as the 'label' is granted, and in the 1974 decree this was due to come into force everywhere by 1979. This already applies in St-Émilion, where even the basic *AC* cannot be obtained without tasting, let alone the higher *appellations*, which are subject to further tests.

One result of these new regulations is that at the outset the grower has to state for which *appellation* he wishes to apply for his whole crop, and will thereafter be subject to the maximum yield for that *AC*, lower obviously for, say, Haut-Médoc than if he applies for Médoc or even for Bordeaux Supérieur. What, however, he would gain in possible yield he would certainly lose in price. Heretofore he has been able to operate what was known as the 'cascade' system, by which he could declare a certain quantity as, say, St-Julien, so much as Haut-Médoc and still more as Médoc or Bordeaux.

These regulations certainly introduced much-needed flexibility into a system that simply did not work honestly or efficiently. Not only are larger yields, the results of better cultivation methods, allowed for, but in bad years the *rendement* may be reduced. On the other hand, a good deal of scepticism may be allowed over the provision for an increase on the *rendement de base* only in years which are exceptionally good for quality and quantity. For the limits were immediately raised for the year of the regulations' inception – 1974!

Appellations		Degrees	Permitted basic maximum crop per hectare in hectolitres
Barsac	Blanc	13°	25
Blayais	Blanc ⎱	10°	45
	Rouge ⎰		50
Bordeaux	Rouge	10°	50
	Blanc	10·5°	50
Bordeaux clairet ou rosé		11°	50
Bordeaux-Côtes-de-Castillon	Rouge	11°	40
Bordeaux-Haut-Benauge	Blanc	11·5°	50
Bordeaux-Mousseaux	Blanc	10°	50
Bordeaux-Supérieur	Blanc	11·5°	40
	Rouge	10·5°	40
Bordeaux Supérieur Côtes de Francs	Blanc	11·5°	40
	Rouge	10·5°	40
Bourg, Bourgeais	Blanc	11°	50
Cadillac	Blanc	12°	40
Canon-Fronsac	Rouge	11°	42
Cérons	Blanc	12·5°	40
Côtes-de-Blaye	Blanc	11°	42
Côtes-de-Bourg	Rouge	10·5°	50
Côtes-de-Bx-St-Macaire	Blanc	11·5°	42
Côtes-de-Fronsac	Rouge	11°	42
Entre-Deux-Mers	Blanc	11·5°	50
Entre-Deux-Mers Haut-Benauge	Blanc	11·5°	50
Graves	Blanc	11°	40
	Rouge	10°	40
Graves-Supérieures	Blanc	12°	40
Graves de Vayres	Blanc ⎱	10·5°	43
	Rouge ⎰		40
Haut-Médoc	Rouge	10°	43
Lalande-de-Pomerol	Rouge	10·5°	40
Listrac	Rouge	10·5°	40
Loupiac	Blanc	13°	40
Lussac-St-Émilion	Rouge	11°	42
Margaux	Rouge	10·5°	40
Médoc	Rouge	10°	45
Montagne-St-Émilion	Rouge	11°	42
Moulis	Rouge	10·5°	40
Néac (merged with Lalande)	Rouge	10·5°	40
Parsac-St-Émilion	Rouge	11°	42
Pauillac	Rouge	10·5°	40
Pomerol	Rouge	10·5°	40

Appellations		Degrees	Permitted basic maximum crop per hectare in hectolitres
1ᵉ Côtes de Blaye	Rouge	10·5°	50
	Blanc	11°	42
1ᵉ Côtes de Bordeaux	Rouge	10·5°	40
	Blanc	12°	40
1ᵉ Côtes de Bordeaux followed by a commune name	Rouge	11·5°	40
	Blanc	13°	40
1ᵉ Côtes de Bordeaux–Cadillac	Blanc	12°	40
1ᵉ Côtes de Bordeaux–Gabarnac	Blanc	12°	40
Puisseguin-St-Émilion	Rouge	11°	42
Sables-St-Émilion	Rouge	10·5°	42
St-Émilion	Rouge	11°	42
St-Émilion grand cru	Rouge	11·5°	42
St-Émilion grand cru classé	Rouge	11·5°	42
St-Émilion 1ᵉ grand cru classé	Rouge	11·5°	42
St-Estèphe	Rouge	10·5°	40
St-Georges-St-Émilion	Rouge	11°	42
Ste-Croix-du-Mont	Blanc	13°	40
Ste-Foy-Bordeaux	Blanc	12°	45
	Rouge	10·5°	45
St-Julien	Rouge	10·5°	40
Sauternes	Blanc	13°	25

Appendix B: Red and White Bordeaux
Appellation Contrôlée Production 1945–1978

	Red	White
1945	586,934 hectolitres	681,787 hectolitres
1946	732,971	1,636,157
1947	1,209,389	1,462,088
1948	875,917	1,515,989
1949	733,976	1,501,332
1950	1,357,301	1,815,039
1951	732,221	1,204,337
1952	853,792	1,077,645
1953	1,225,909	1,758,145
1954	831,008	1,372,537
1955	1,285,095	1,831,202
1956	370,978	847,462
1957	456,806	831,315
1958	662,431	1,035,642
1959	705,501	1,153,104
1960	1,002,568	1,565,962
1961	550,106	1,281,639
1962	1,436,038	2,305,412
1963	1,236,689	1,737,828
1964	1,433,757	1,876,170
1965	1,131,641	1,486,028
1966	1,282,808	1,819,798
1967	1,512,596	1,846,369
1968	1,349,901	1,797,887
1969	913,662	1,315,684
1970	2,061,991	1,313,553
1971	1,222,340	912,853
1972	1,620,408	1,037,091
1973	2,484,723	1,290,373
1974	2,237,354	1,136,433
1975	1,769,658	987,528
1976	2,462,257	1,059,799
1977	1,291,700	685,800
1978	2,246,382	992,688

Appendix C: Representative Opening Prices
1831–1937

Below are two tables giving the opening prices of clarets. The first shows a representative selection of classed-growth Médocs, with Haut-Brion included, when the prices have been available, from 1831 to 1937, the last good vintage before the Second World War. The second concentrates on the *premiers crus* and Mouton from the officially fixed prices in that war up to 1978, the latest vintage produced when this edition went to press. The first list has been compiled from the incomparable records of Tastet & Lawton, the brokers; the omission of Haut-Brion, particularly in the early years, was because they did not deal in this red Graves, but I have been able to secure some figures from the château. To show a comparable *deuxième*, when possible I have included Léoville-Barton. With both lists it must be emphasized that while these were actual prices paid to the châteaux, such prices varied, not only according to the state of the market but also how long after the vintage the deal took place. This might mean a higher price than at first, or a lower one, as in the case of Mouton-Rothschild 1890, which, as noted below, passed through the brokers' hands in 1894 at a very low price compared with that given for the other leaders. Moreover there has long been established in Bordeaux the practice of a château selling its wines in two *tranches* (slices). The first is nearly always the larger, and where I have had figures for both I have given the earlier price. It is sometimes argued that opening prices are not always genuine, and either involved very small quantities to test the market or to try to establish a favourable price for the grower, or were on a returnable basis if the Bordeaux merchant could not sell all the wine. No doubt there is some substance in these objections, but by and large I have no doubt that the figures listed below did represent the opening prices of the various wines. It used to be the custom for a merchant or a group of merchants to make five- or ten-year contracts with the leading growths, guaranteeing to take all their crop over this period at a fixed price; who benefited most from this depended upon the run of the vintages. One celebrated

vintage in which the first growths certainly lost was 1920. All the
prices are given in francs per *tonneau*.

1831	Lafite	2,400	Latour	2,600
	Margaux (under contract)		Brane-Mouton	2,100
	Rausan-Ségla	2,500	Léoville-Barton	2,000
	Dauzac	1,250	Palmer	1,480

1834	Lafite	2,800–3,200	Latour	2,400
	Margaux	4,000	Brane-Mouton	2,100
	Léoville-Poyferré	2,100	Beychevelle	1,550

1841	Lafite	5,500	Latour (contract with Barton & Guestier)	1,800
	Margaux	2,500	Brane-Mouton	1,400
	Palmer (*en primeur*)	700	Dauzac	550–600

1847	Lafite (contract with Cruse)	1,025	Latour (contract with Barton & Guestier, 1844–53)	1,750
	Margaux (under contract 1844–52)	2,100	Brane-Mouton	800
	Pichon-Longueville	525	Dauzac	400

1848	Lafite	2,800	Latour (contract with Barton & Guestier)	1,750
	Margaux (under contract)	2,100		
	Léoville-Barton	850	Brane-Mouton	900–1,400
	Langoa	750	Gruaud-Larose	1,000

1854	Lafite (December 1854)	5,000	Latour	5,000
	Margaux (December 1855)	5,500	Mouton-Rothschild (December 1854)	5,000
	Rausan-Ségla (under contract)	1,200	Palmer	4,000

1858	Lafite	4,000	Latour	4,800
	Margaux	5,000	Haut-Brion	4,000
	Léoville-Poyferré	3,500	Mouton-Rothschild	4,000
	Léoville-Las-Cases	3,250	Léoville-Barton	3,000
	Palmer	2,400	Langoa	2,400
	Pontet-Canet	1,500	Lynch-Bages	1,500–2,000
	Dauzac	1,500	Cantemerle	1,500

1864	Lafite	5,000	Latour	4,500
	Margaux (under contract 1863–72)	4,200	Mouton-Rothschild	3,100
			Léoville-Poyferré	2,000
	Pichon-Longueville	2,400	Léoville-Barton	2,000
	Palmer	2,500–3,000	Lynch-Bages	1,200
	Dauzac	1,350	Batailley	1,200
	Le Tertre	1,350		

1865	Lafite (exclusive to six merchants)	5,600	Latour	5,600
			Mouton-Rothschild	3,500–4,000
	Margaux (under contract)	4,200	Léoville-Barton	2,400
	Palmer	2,250	Langoa	1,900
	Batailley	1,500	Cantemerle	1,400–1,500
	Grand-Puy-Ducasse	1,200		

1870	Lafite	4,500	Latour	3,000
	Margaux (under contract)	4,200	Mouton-Rothschild	3,000
	Pichon-Longueville	2,000	Léoville-Barton	1,000
	Palmer	1,000	Cantemerle	1,000
	Beychevelle	1,450		

1874	Lafite	5,500	Latour	5,000
	Margaux	3,200	Mouton-Rothschild	4,200
	Pichon-Longueville	2,400	Léoville-Barton	2,600
	Gruaud-Larose-Sarget	3,000	Pontet-Canet	1,400
	Gruaud-Larose-Faure	2,400	Lynch-Bages	1,000–1,400
	Mouton-d'Armailhacq	1,000–1,300	Cantemerle	1,100
	Batailley	1,200		

1875	Lafite	4,000	Latour	5,000
	Margaux	3,500	Mouton-Rothschild	3,000
	Rausan-Ségla	2,300	Léoville-Barton	2,000
	Pichon-Longueville	2,500	Brane-Cantenac	2,500
	Gruaud-Larose (both)	2,500	Palmer	1,600–1,800
	Beychevelle	950	Lynch-Bages	1,200–1,300
	Batailley	1,050	Lynch-Moussas	600
			Cantemerle	1,100

1878	Lafite	4,000	Mouton-Rothschild (November 1878)	2,800
	Margaux	4,000		
	Palmer	1,700–2,200	Léoville-Barton	2,200
	Latour	4,000	Langoa	1,600–1,700

1880	Lafite	3,600	Latour	3,800
	Margaux	3,800	Mouton-Rothschild	3,600
	Haut-Brion	3,200	Léoville-Barton	1,800
	Pontet-Canet	1,600		

1887	Lafite	3,800	Latour	3,250
	Margaux	3,800	Haut-Brion	3,200
	Léoville-Barton	3,400	Mouton-Rothschild	2,900

1890	Lafite	3,000	Latour	4,100
	Margaux	4,000	Haut-Brion	5,200
	Pichon-Longueville	1,600	Mouton-Rothschild (1894)	2,000
	Gruaud-Larose	3,100	Léoville-Barton	3,100
	Palmer	2,500	Giscours	2,500
	Beychevelle	2,100		

(In considering these prices in relation to current money terms, it is of interest that Pijassou in *Latour* (1974) estimated that they should be multiplied five times to be equivalent to prices in the early 1970s, since when inflation has probably increased the multiplier to six or even seven times. Even so this shows that classed-growth clarets were less expensive then than now, when demand is so much more widespread. Since prices moved little from 1870 to 1914 a similar multiplication factor might be applied to all vintages in this period.)

1891	Lafite	2,025	Latour	2,025
	Margaux	1,800	Mouton-Rothschild	1,800
	Haut-Brion	2,250	Cheval-Blanc	1,450
	Haut-Bailly	2,000	Pape-Clément	1,650
	La Mission-Haut-Brion	1,625		

(This was an indifferent vintage, but the prices are given because they include Graves, whose prices are less commonly available, as well as Cheval-Blanc, which obtained the same price as the second growths. At this time the Graves appear to have had a special *réclame*.)

1893	Lafite	2,000	Latour	1,750
	Margaux	1,750	Haut-Brion	2,500
	La Mission-Haut-Brion	1,500	Mouton-Rothschild	1,300
	Rausan-Ségla	1,500	Léoville-Barton	1,100
	Giscours	950	Langoa	950
	Cos d'Estournel	1,200		
	Palmer	1,050		

1899	Lafite	2,000	Latour	1,750
	Margaux	2,200	Haut-Brion	2,600
	Rausan-Ségla	1,400	Mouton-Rothschild	1,800
	Cos d'Estournel	1,000	Léoville-Barton	1,200
	Pichon (Baron)	850	Brane-Cantenac	1,400
	Pontet-Canet	850	Palmer	1,200
	Mouton d'Armailhacq	600	Cantemerle	900

(Owing to the immediate fame of the vintage many of these prices were paid in November 1899.)

1900	Lafite	1,200	Latour	1,150
	Margaux	1,150	Haut-Brion	1·50 frs. per bottle
	Rausan-Ségla	650	Mouton-Rothschild	950
	Brane-Cantenac	650	Léoville-Poyferré	600
	Pontet-Canet	600	Léoville-Barton	600
			Cantemerle	625

(These prices, much lower than for the preceding year, reflected both the existence of that vintage and the very large crop in 1900. Most of these prices were paid in the spring of 1901.)

1906	Lafite	2,100	Latour	1,650
	Margaux	2,100	Mouton-Rothschild	1,650
	Rausan-Ségla	1,400	(under contract to Calvet	
	Gruaud-Larose (both)	1,225	1902–13)	
	Palmer	1,200	Léoville-Barton	1,200
			Brane-Cantenac	1,500

1911	Lafite (under contract)	1,650	Latour	2,500
	Margaux (under contract)	1,650	Mouton-Rothschild	1,650
	Rausan-Ségla	1,800	(under contract)	
	Pontet-Canet	1,300	Palmer (under contract)	1,200
	Belgrave	850	Cantemerle	1,300

(Palmer had renewed this year from the previous one of 950 frs. Latour, just freed from a five-year agreement, secured its highest price for 20 years.)

1916	Lafite (under contract)	1,650	Latour	2,650
	Margaux (under contract)	1,650	Mouton-Rothschild	2,300
	Brane-Cantenac	1,500	Rausan-Ségla	1,400
	Léoville-Barton	1,200		

(For Lafite and Margaux, this was the last of a ten-year agreement. At a price equivalent to about 2,500 frs. *en primeur*, Latour did not sell until May 1917.)

1920	Lafite (under contract)	2,650	Latour (under contract)	2,650
	Margaux (under contract)	2,650	Mouton-Rothschild (1923)	
				8 frs. per bottle
	Rausan-Ségla	4,500	Léoville-Barton	4,500
	Gruaud-Larose-Sarget	3,000		

(The price of Mouton was equivalent to 7,680 frs per *tonneau*, but as it will have included bottling charges this is not a strictly comparable price, although but for contracts the leading prices might well have been about 7,000 frs.)

1924	Lafite	9,000–9,500	Latour	8,000
	Margaux	8,000	Mouton-Rothschild	9,000
	Rausan-Ségla	5,000	Léoville-Poyferré	5,000
	Pichon (Baron)	5,000	Léoville-Barton	5,000
	Cos d'Estournel	5,000	Gruaud-Larose-Faure	5,000
			Cantemerle	5,000

1926	Lafite	40,000	Latour	40,000
	Margaux	40,000	Haut-Brion	40,000
	Pichon (Baron)	15,000	Mouton-Rothschild	40,000
	Gruaud-Larose-Faure	22,000	Léoville-Poyferré	12,500
	Palmer	23,000	Léoville-Barton	12,500
	La Lagune	15,000	Cos d'Estournel	11,000
	Pontet-Canet	18,000	Mouton-d'Armailhacq	5,600

1928	Lafite	20,000	Latour	20,000
	Margaux	20,000	Haut-Brion	22,000
	Brane-Cantenac	7,500	Mouton-Rothschild	20,000
	Palmer	9,000	Léoville-Poyferré	9,000
	Talbot	6,500	Léoville-Barton	8,500
	d'Issan	10,000	Léoville-Las-Cases	7,500
	Calon-Ségur	7,000	Giscours	10,000
			Pontet-Canet	7,000

1929	Lafite	20,000	Latour	20,000
	Margaux	20,000	Mouton-Rothschild	20,000
	Rausan-Ségla	8,000	Léoville-Poyferré	11,000
	Cos d'Estournel	8,500	Léoville-Las-Cases	11,000
	Pontet-Canet	9,000	Cantemerle	9,000
	Grand-Puy-Lacoste	5,400		

1934	Lafite	10,000	Latour	10,000
	Margaux	10,000	Mouton-Rothschild	10,000
	Ducru-Beaucaillou	3,200	Cheval-Blanc	6,000
	Gruaud-Larose	3,100	Léoville-Barton	3,500

1937	Lafite	15,000	Latour	15,000★
	Margaux	12,000	Mouton-Rothschild	15,000
	Cheval-Blanc	7,000	Beychevelle	4,200
	Cantemerle	3,800		

★This figure is an estimate for a five-year contract was made with a Paris firm for the vintages 1935–9, with prices to be fixed according to the cost of living. It is probable that for the then highly-regarded 1937 the figure would not have been below that of Lafite and Mouton.

Appendix D: Opening Prices of First Growths and Mouton-Rothschild 1943–1978

In order to help the reader to understand the relation between the ex-cellars opening prices of the first growths and the various devaluations of the franc, the pound and the U.S. dollar the following table has been compiled. To give an early example, the opening price of Lafite 1949 worked out at £357 or $1,028 a *tonneau*. At the then accepted quantity of 96 dozen bottles per *tonneau* this represented an ex-cellars price of over 6s. and under 90 cents a bottle, although brokerage, bottling charges and the mark-up of the Bordeaux merchant who first purchased it had to be taken into account. Then there were the subsequent freight and import duty charges, and the profit of the importing merchant – in the U.S.A., importer, wholesaler and retailer,

STERLING AND DOLLAR FRANC EQUIVALENTS 1944–1979

	Francs in £s	in $s
1944	190	49·63
1945	480	119·63
1948 (January)	864	214·39
(October)	1257	312
1949	980*	350
1957	1225	437·5
1958	1485	530
1960	13·82†	4·79†
1967 (November)	11·83**	4·9
1969 (August)	13·20	5·5
1972	11·10***	5
1975 (October)	9	4·4
1978 (August)	8·40	4·3††
1979 (May)	9	4·4

* After devaluation of £ to equivalent of $2·80.
** After 14⅔ per cent devaluation of £.
*** After floating of £ in June 1972.
† After introduction on 1 January 1960 of new franc (100 old francs).
†† After floating of dollar in 1977.

in the U.K., generally only the retailer who imported direct. As, however, Lafite '49 was the most expensive wine of the whole 1949 Bordeaux vintage, it will be seen that the initial prices of lesser wines were small indeed. To take a more up-to-date example, when the 1977 first growths were first offered in the summer of 1978, with the £ standing at about 8·4 frs. and the $ at around 4·5, the opening price, ex-château, of Lafite and the other estates, which came out at 54,000 frs. per *tonneau*, was £4·50 and $10 a bottle: 15 times higher in sterling and 11 times more in dollars than 28 years previously – and for wine of much lesser quality. But in the immediate post-war epoch even the first growth proprietors made very little profit.

1943	Lafite	100,000	Haut-Brion	100,000
	Margaux	100,000	Mouton-Rothschild	100,000
	Latour	100,000		
1945	Lafite	225,000	Haut-Brion	225,000
	Margaux	225,000	Mouton-Rothschild	225,000
	Latour	225,000	Cheval-Blanc	100,000*
			Pétrus	100,000
1947	Lafite	200,000	Haut-Brion	200,000
	Margaux	130,000	Mouton-Rothschild	200,000
	Latour	130,000	Cheval-Blanc	100,000
			Pétrus	110,000
1949	Lafite	360,000	Haut-Brion	250,000
	Margaux	250,000	Mouton-Rothschild	350,000
	Latour	285,000	Cheval-Blanc	175,000–325,000
			Pétrus	225,000
1950	Lafite	300,000	Latour	325,000
	Margaux	250,000	Haut-Brion	250,000
			Mouton-Rothschild	300,000
1951	Lafite	300,000	Haut-Brion	300,000
	Margaux	300,000	Mouton-Rothschild	300,000
	Latour	275,000	Pétrus	200,000

*Up to and including the 1967 vintage Cheval-Blanc was offered plus keeping charges, which would add about 15 per cent to the price quoted. From 1968 onwards the whole crop was sold château-bottled with keeping charges included.

1952	Lafite	350,000	Haut-Brion	300,000
	Margaux	300,000	Mouton-Rothschild	375,000
	Latour	375,000	Cheval-Blanc	250,000
1953	Lafite	300,000	Haut-Brion	300,000
	Margaux	300,000	Mouton-Rothschild	350,000
	Latour	300,000	Cheval-Blanc	200,000–320,000
			Pétrus	370,000
1954	Lafite	300,000	Haut-Brion	300,000
	Margaux	300,000	Mouton-Rothschild	300,000
	Latour	300,000	Cheval-Blanc	225,000
1955	Lafite	500,000	Haut-Brion	500,000
	Margaux	300,000–400,000	Mouton-Rothschild	550,000
	Latour	300,000–400,000	Cheval-Blanc	325,000
1956	Lafite	400,000–500,000	Haut-Brion	450,000
	Margaux	380,000–450,000	Mouton-Rothschild	450,000
	Latour	400,000–450,000		
1957	Lafite	750,000	Haut-Brion	700,000
	Margaux	700,000	Mouton-Rothschild	780,000
	Latour	700,000	Cheval-Blanc	700,000
1958	Lafite	650,000	Haut-Brion	600,000
	Margaux	500,000–600,000	Mouton-Rothschild	525,000
	Latour	525,000	Cheval-Blanc	450,000
1959	Lafite	11,000	Haut-Brion	7,250
	Margaux	7,250	Mouton-Rothschild	9,500
	Latour	7,250	Cheval-Blanc	6,500

(On 1 January 1960 the New Franc was introduced, by which one New Franc represented 100 old francs. At this point £1 was equal to 13·82 frs. and $1 to 4·792 frs.)

1960	Lafite	14,000	Haut-Brion	12,000
	Margaux	8,500–11,810	Mouton-Rothschild	11,000
	Latour	10,000	Cheval-Blanc	7,750
			Pétrus	9,000
1961	Lafite	27,500	Haut-Brion	21,000
	Margaux	17,000	Mouton-Rothschild	22,750
	Latour	20,000	Cheval-Blanc	15,500
			Pétrus	27,000

(Some of the prices for Pétrus prior to 1961 are not available. Until 1961 Pétrus was sold subject to keeping charges of about 15 per cent extra.)

1962	Lafite	16,500	Haut-Brion (1964)	
				20 frs. per bottle
	Margaux	10,000–14,800	Mouton-Rothschild	15,000
	Latour	12,000–15,000	Cheval-Blanc	8,500
			Pétrus	24,000

(For four years Haut-Brion took to selling by the bottle some time after the vintage. Allowing 960 bottles to the *tonneau* this would give the price of the 1962 as 19,800 frs. including bottle charges. Although first growths and Mouton-Rothschild are sold without charges, the price of Haut-Brion in bottle in July 1964 would take into account interest charges, and the wine would not in fact be as expensive as the leaders.)

1963	Lafite	9,750	Haut-Brion	11 frs. per bottle
	Margaux	7,000	Mouton-Rothschild	10,000
	Latour	8,500	Cheval-Blanc	——†
			Pétrus	——†

1964	Lafite	13,000	Haut-Brion	18 frs. per bottle
	Margaux	15,000	Mouton-Rothschild	20,000
	Latour	18,000	Cheval-Blanc	13,000
			Pétrus	21,000

1965	Lafite	13,000	Haut-Brion	11 frs. per bottle
	Margaux – not sold		Mouton-Rothschild	13,000
	with vintage date		Cheval-Blanc	——†
	Latour	12,000	Pétrus	——†

1966	Lafite	27,000	Haut-Brion	20,000
	Margaux	19,000	Mouton-Rothschild	27,000
	Latour	24,000	Cheval-Blanc	16,500
			Pétrus	25,000

1967	Lafite	27,000	Haut-Brion	17,000
	Margaux	15,300	Mouton-Rothschild	27,000
	Latour	19,000	Cheval-Blanc	13,000
			Pétrus	20,000

1968	Lafite	20,000	Haut-Brion	18,000
	Margaux	19,000	Mouton-Rothschild	20,000
	Latour	18,000	Cheval-Blanc	10,000
			Pétrus	10,000†

† No Cheval-Blanc or Pétrus were sold under their labels in 1963 or 1965; in 1968 Cheval-Blanc was sold with the label, but this did not include its classification as *Premier Grand Cru*. A very small quantity (7 *tonneaux*) of Pétrus 1968 was sold in bottle but it was not generally offered on the market.

1969	Lafite	70,000	Haut-Brion	48,000
	Margaux	35,000	Mouton-Rothschild	75,000
	Latour	48,000	Cheval-Blanc	32,000
			Pétrus	48,000
1970	Lafite	59,000	Haut-Brion	44,000
	Margaux	44,000	Mouton-Rothschild	
	Latour	40,000		36,000–65,000
			Cheval-Blanc	40,000
			Pétrus	40,000

(The opening price for Mouton-Rothschild was abnormally low, owing to a special initiative of Baron Philippe de Rothschild to check the upward spiral of leading-growth prices. When Lafite failed to respond, the second *tranche* of Mouton, whose purchase was obligatory for buyers of the first one, was raised to 65,000 frs. Latour's low opening price was also influenced by Mouton.)

1971	Lafite	110,000	Haut-Brion	75,000
	Margaux	70,000	Mouton-Rothschild	120,000
	Latour	120,000	Cheval-Blanc	75,000
			Pétrus	120,000

(Ch. Margaux decided from the 1971 vintage onwards to sell its wine only in bottle, so the above price per *tonneau* is approximate; the price per bottle ex-château was 70 frs.)

1972	Lafite	100,000	Haut-Brion	90,000
	Margaux	75,000	Mouton-Rothschild	90,000
	Latour	90,000	Cheval-Blanc	90,000
			Pétrus	90,000

(The ex-château price of Ch. Margaux was 75 frs. a bottle.)

1973	Lafite	52,000	Haut-Brion	50,000
	Margaux	52,000	Mouton-Rothschild	52,000
	Latour	——*	Cheval-Blanc	50,000
			Pétrus	50,000

(Owing to the onset of the slump in Bordeaux prices the above figures are misleading because of special concessions given to purchasers. Lafite and Mouton-Rothschild gave two hogsheads of 1972 per *tonneau* of 1973 bought, provided that the purchasers had also acquired the 1972. Haut-Brion had no surplus 1972 so provided free bottling and supplied at the rate of 25 dozen per *barrique* instead of the normal 24 dozen. Cheval-Blanc, with a small production in 1972, gave some wine and returned some cash.)

* Latour did not offer its 1973 *en primeur*. (The ex-château price of Ch. Margaux was 45 frs. a bottle.)

1974	Lafite	32,000	Haut-Brion	25,000
	Margaux	39 frs. per bottle	Mouton-Rothschild	30,000
	Latour	25,000	Cheval-Blanc	25,000
			Pétrus	35,000
1975	Lafite	54,000	Haut-Brion	48,000
	Margaux	58,000*	Mouton-Rothschild	52,000
	Latour	45,000	Cheval-Blanc	48,000
			Pétrus	52–54,000

* Not offered *en primeur*, but first sold in 1977.

1976	Lafite	54,000	Haut-Brion	50,000
	Margaux	50,000	Mouton-Rothschild	54,000
	Latour	50,000	Cheval-Blanc	52,000
			Pétrus	54,000
1977	Lafite	54,000	Haut-Brion	54,000
	Margaux	52,000	Mouton-Rothschild	54,000
	Latour	52,000	Cheval-Blanc	53,000
			Pétrus	54,000
1978	Lafite	82,000	Haut-Brion	82,000
	Marguax	82,000	Mouton-Rothschild	82,000
	Latour	90,000*	Cheval-Blanc	82,000
			Pétrus	82,000

* First offered some weeks later than the other *premiers crus*.

Appendix E: Rainfall in the Gironde 1952–1978

The crucial annual factors affecting the success of a vintage are the rainfall and the amount of sunshine and temperature levels. Of these the rainfall is the most important, and so the annual totals and monthly averages are given below. The sunniest month on average is July with 247 hours, compared with 230 hours for June and 227 hours for August. But August is the warmest month with a maximum average of 79°F. (26·3°C.). December is the least sunny month with an average of 64 hours, but January is the coldest with a maximum average of 48·5°F. (9·3°C.) and a minimum of 35°F. (1·8°C.). For all the statistics I am indebted to M. Pierre Léglise from the *Centre de Recherches de Bordeaux de l'Institut National de la Recherche Agronomique*, Pont-de-la-Maye, Gironde.

ANNUAL RAINFALL IN MILLIMETRES

1952	1145·4	1957	746·1	1962	695·3	1967	711·3	1972	685·5
1953	577·0	1958	1047·6	1963	812·5	1968	820·6	1973	770·4
1954	807·3	1959	885·0	1964	836·1	1969	999·1	1974	805·3
1955	905·7	1960	1194·7	1965	1131·9	1970	676·5	1975	742·3
1956	740·4	1961	716·6	1966	1116·8	1971	882·0	1976	804·2
								1977	882·9
								1978	791·5

AVERAGE MONTHLY RAINFALL IN MILLIMETRES 1952–1978

January	85·9	April	54·2	July	52·4	October	77·0
February	75·2	May	65·0	August	62·5	November	89·8
March	59·7	June	55·6	September	78·8	December	95·1

One cannot equate fine vintages with dry years, although some of the best have had small rainfall. Among earlier years, for example, there were only 612·7 mm. of rain in 1929, and 650·4 mm. in 1945, but in 1928 there was 876·2 mm. Moreover although the heaviest rainfall since 1924 was in 1960 when the total was 1,194·7 mm., backed by 1,149·7 mm. in the disastrous year of 1930, these records were closely followed by the above-average 1952 when 1,145·4 mm. fell.

In fact more important than the total annual rainfall is that in the two months before and during the better vintages: August and September, as shown below from 1952–1978.

RAINFALL IN AUGUST AND SEPTEMBER 1952–1978 IN MILLIMETRES

1952	151·8	1957	105·5	1962	56·1	1967	100	1972	153·0
1953	86	1958	178·2	1963	167·4	1968	258·5	1973	151·4
1954	169·6	1959	132·2	1964	103·4	1969	236·7	1974	183·2
1955	70·8	1960	259·2	1965	255·7	1970	74·6	1975	216·0
1956	193·0	1961	36·1	1966	75	1971	118·3	1976	166·6
								1977	67·7
								1978	51·5

The most significant part of the rainfall year is from the vintage period to the near-end of winter at the end of February; an excess or deficit of winter rain will affect the wine roots and thereafter, perhaps, the productivity. A low winter rainfall is not generally a good sign.

In these 27 years the wettest August was in 1968 (161·2 mm.), with 1972 as the runner-up with 133·2 mm. The wettest September was in 1965 (212·8 mm.) which goes far to explain the failure of that vintage; but 206·7 mm. were recorded in September 1969, and that certainly put a query on this well-publicized year. Also to be noted is that on average October has been the fifth wettest month in the 27 years listed, but in 1969 the exceptionally wet September was followed by an almost rainless October (7·9 mm.). Nevertheless in most years the vintage continues well into that hazardous month, particularly in Sauternes. The celebrated variation in the 1964 wines, depending on whether the growers finished picking before or after the rain which began on 8 October is demonstrated in rainfall figures. In that year 231·5 mm. fell in the month, only being exceeded in the period by half a millimetre in 1960 when 232 mm. were recorded; well over twice the average. The driest summer of the period was certainly 1961 when only 69·7 mm. fell between June and August. It was also the finest vintage. It will be seen that the rainfall in August and September

ANNUAL RAINFALL TOTALS AND ABSTRACT FROM MID-SEPTEMBER
TO THE END OF FEBRUARY, 1924–1979

	Total	Totals from 15/9 to the end of February		Total	Totals from 15/9 to the end of February
	mm	mm		mm	mm
1924	709.0	341·5★	1949	700.9	463·4
1925	753·5	495·6	1950	847·7	665.4
1926	942·1	486·5	1951	1,089·3	513·1
1927	1,027·1	405·6	1952	1,145·4	689·3
1928	876·2	399·2	1953	577·0	352·4
1929	612·7	501·8	1954	807·3	504·7
1930	1,149·7	691.8	1955	905·7	380·0
1931	972·9	248·7	1956	740·4	332·6
1932	1,002·8	406·1	1957	746·1	358·9
1933	850·3	438·1	1958	1,047·6	341·1
1934	898·3	556.4	1959	885·0	657·1
1935	925·3	678·0	1960	1,194·7	830·2
1936	805·5	349·9	1961	716·6	496·4
1937	1,042·7	532.0	1962	695·3	383·8
1938	626·9	439·8	1963	812·5	285·7
1939	810·0	380·1	1964	836·1	531·1
1940	808·6	598·4	1965	1,131·9	800·0
1941	973.0	366·6	1966	1,116·8	536·2
1942	678·4	380·0? (war year)	1967	711·1	459·2
1943	752·9	348·9	1968	820·6	368·7
1944	738·0	538·2	1969	999·1	470·8
1945	650·4	285·2	1970	676·5	388·9
1946	692·5	540·9	1971	882·0	413·0
1947	843·4	483·1	1972	685·5	281·8
1948	590·6	187·7	1973	770·4	450·4
			1974	805·3	547·0
			1975	742·3	362·6
			1976	804·2	687·6
			1977	882·9	408·3
			1978	791·5	400·3

★The period extends from Sepetmber 1924 to February 1925, and thus in each year thereafter.

was exceptionally small in 1977 and 1978, and this saved the vintage in the former year and contributed considerably to its success in the latter, which had the lowest pre-vintage rainfall since 1961. In both 1977 and 1978 the October rainfall was much below average: only 50·3 and 10 mm. respectively; for the latter a record for many years.

This resulted in the *vendange* being completed in remarkably fine weather conditions. Since the prevailing wind in the Gironde is off the sea from the west and north-west, the highest incidence of rainfall is near the coast and in the Médoc, with a mean annual average of about 950 mm. In the east, in the Garonne Valley, it sinks to about 750 mm. The average annual isolation, i.e. hours of sunshine from 1946–75 was 2,071 hours, the maximum being in July with 276 hours, the minimum in December with 67 hours.

Appendix F: Wine Organizations

Bordeaux is full of organizations associated with wine and the wine trade. There are professional organizations of growers, brokers and merchants; and an *Union des Grands Crus Classés du Médoc*, founded in 1901. The Bordeaux Chamber of Commerce is naturally deeply concerned with the wine trade. However, such bodies are not of great interest to the general reader, while the publicity bodies associated with each district are referred to in their proper place.

However, the *Conseil Interprofessionnel du Vin de Bordeaux* (*C.I.V.B.*) is worthy of brief mention, and its headquarters are in the Maison du Vin, 1 Cours du XXX Juillet, on the corner of the Allées de Tourny facing the Théâtre. It began, like similar bodies in other French wine-growing districts, in the last war, in 1943. It was somewhat differently named and organized then, and its present form dates from 1948, with a further reorganization in November 1966. The role of this officially designated body is to regulate the trade and to see that the regulations made by the *Institut National des Appellations d'Origine des Vins et Eaux-de-Vie* (*I.N.A.O.*) appertaining to Bordeaux are carried out. The *C.I.V.B.* is also responsible for economic and statistical surveys, for seeing that there is permanent contact between growers and merchants; and finally for promoting the reputation of and demand for the *AC* wines of Bordeaux.

The composition of the *C.I.V.B.* is made up of 24 growers, 18 merchants, 2 brokers, 4 members nominated by the Ministry of Agriculture on the proposition of the Prefect of the Gironde department, including a consumers' representative, and 6 important local civil servants, among them the director of the Bordeaux Oenological Station, the *Administrateur du Centre de Recherches de Bordeaux de l'Institut National de la Recherche Agronomique* and the *Directeur de la Station de Recherches de Viticulture*. Also the regional delegates of the *I.N.A.O.* take part in the *Conseil*'s deliberations in an advisory capacity. The director of the *C.I.V.B.* is M. J. M. Courteau.

Within the *Centre de Recherches de Bordeaux de l'Institut National de la Recherche Agronomique* (*I.N.R.A.*) one finds several research stations working on viticulture.

There is the *Station de Recherches de Viticulture* whose work includes grape breeding and selection, grape physiology and applied virology. The *Station d'Agronomie* deals with vineyard soils, fertilization and mineral nutrition of the vine. The *Station de Pathologie Végétale* and of *Zoologie Agricole* investigate the fungal and animal parasites of the grape vine and their control. *C.R. Bordeaux* is one of the *Centres* of *I.N.R.A.*, the state-operated institute which covers all aspects of agricultural research in France. It operates seven research farms, among which two are devoted to viticulture: Domaine du Grand Parc in the Premières Côtes de Bordeaux and Château Couhins, cru classé de Graves.

What might be called a centralized propaganda organization is the *Académie du Vin de Bordeaux*. It has 100 members, some of them local, others nationally known. Periodical dinners, luncheons and other suitable celebrations are arranged.

Finally to be mentioned is the notable *Station Oenologique*, situated in the new University of Bordeaux buildings in Talence. It is associated with agronomy in the university, and the first director of the *Station Agronomique* was Professor A. Baudrimont (1806–80). He was succeeded by the celebrated Professor Ulysse Gayon (1845–1929), assistant and friend of Pasteur, who advised him in 1880 to take the vacant post in Bordeaux. He arrived at an unpropitious time as the phylloxera was starting and the mildew, with which he was greatly concerned, only a few years away. Although offered other important posts, including the directorship in 1904 of the Pasteur Institute in Paris, he preferred to remain at Bordeaux until 1920. He was succeeded by his son-in-law Professor Jean Ribereau-Gayon. His colleague was M. Emile Peynaud, the celebrated oenologist who has advised a great many of the estates, large and small. The work of the station consists of research and analysis. All wine exported is tested by chemical analysis to ensure that it is sound, and that there is adequate alcohol and acidity.

Bibliography

This is a list of the books and articles consulted in the course of writing this book, rather than an extensive bibliography on a vast subject. I hope it may prove helpful to others.

ALLEN, H. WARNER. *The Wines of France*, 1924. *Natural Red Wines*, 1951. *A History of Wine*, 1961.

BARENNES, J. *Viticulture et vinification en Bordelais au moyen âge*, 1912.

BERT, PIERRE. *In vino veritas: l'affaire des vins de Bordeaux*, 1975.

BERTALL. *La Vigne – voyages autour des vins de France*, 1878.

BOUTRUCHE, R. *La Crise d'une société: seigneurs et paysans du Bordelais pendant la Guerre de Cent Ans*, 1947.

BOWLEY, A. L. *Wages and Incomes in the United Kingdom*, 1935.

CAMPBELL, IAN M. *The Wayward Tendrils of the Vine*, 1947.

CARUS-WILSON, E. M. 'The Effects of the Acquisition and of the Loss of Gascony on the English Wine Trade', *Bulletin of the Institute of Historical Research*, 1947.

CASSAGNAC, PAUL DE. *French Wines*. Tr. Guy Knowles, 1930.

COCKS, CHARLES & FÉRET, ÉDOUARD. *Bordeaux et ses vins*, various editions, 1850–1969.

CRAWFORD, ANNE. *A History of the Vintners' Company*, 1977.

DANFLOU, ALFRED. *Les Grands Crus Bordelais*, 1867.

D'ARMAILHACQ, A. *De la culture des vignes dans le Médoc*, 1855, and subsequent editions to 1867.

DION, ROGER. *Histoire de la vigne et du vin en France des origines au XIXième siècle*, 1959.

DOYLE, WILLIAM. *The Parlement o, Bordeaux and the End of the Old Regime 1771–1790*, 1974.

DUIJKER, HUBRECHT. *The Great Wine Châteaux of Bordeaux*, 1975.

DUNHAM, A. L. *The Anglo-French Treaty of Commerce of 1860 and the Progress of the Industrial Revolution in France*, 1930.

FAITH, NICHOLAS. *The Winemakers*, 1978.

FÉRET, E. *St-Émilion et ses vins*, 1893.

FORSTER, ROBERT. 'The Noble Wine Producers of the Bordelais in the Eighteenth Century', *Economic History Review*, 1961.

FRANCK, WILHELM. *Traité sur les vins du Médoc et les autres vins rouges du Département de la Gironde*, 1824 and subsequent editions to 1868.

GINESTET, BERNARD. *La Bouillie Bordelaise*, 1975.

GUILLON, E. *Les Châteaux historiques et vignobles de la Gironde*, 1866.

HEALY, MAURICE. *Claret and the White Wines of Bordeaux*, 1934. *Stay Me With Flagons*, 1940.

HENDERSON, A. L. *The History of Ancient and Modern Wines*, 1824.

HIGOUNET, CHARLES. Ed. *Histoire de Bordeaux*, 1962–1969.

   1. *Bordeaux Antique*, par R. Étienne, etc., 1962.

   2. *Bordeaux pendant le haut moyen âge*, par Ch. Higounet, etc., 1964.

   3. *Bordeaux sous les rois d'Angleterre*, sous la direction de Y. Renouard, 1965.

   4. *Bordeaux 1453 à 1715*, sous la direction de R. Boutruche, 1966.

   5. *Bordeaux au XVIIIe siècle*, sous la direction de François-Georges Pariset, 1968.

   6. *Bordeaux au XIXe siècle*, 1969.

   Ed. *La Seigneurie et le vignoble de Château Latour*, 1974.

HYAMS, EDWARD. *Dionysus: a Social History of the Vine*, 1965.

JACOB, E. F. *The Fifteenth Century (Oxford History of England*, Vol. 6), 1961.

JAMES, MARJORY K. 'The Fluctuations of the Anglo–Gascon Wine Trade during the Fourteenth Century', *Economic History Review*, 1951.

JEFFERSON, THOMAS. *The Papers of Thomas Jefferson*. Edited J. L. Boyd. Vols. 9–15, 1956–8.

JOHNSON, HUGH. *The World Atlas of Wine*, revised edition, 1977.

JULLIAN, CAMILLE. *Histoire de Bordeaux depuis les origines jusqu'en 1895*, 1895.

JULLIEN, A. *Manuel de Sommelier*, 1826.

KIRBY, J. L. 'The Siege of Bourg', 1406. *History Today*, 1968.

KRESSMAN, JEAN. *Le Défi d'Édouard*, 1959.

LAFFORGUE, GERMAIN. *Le Vignoble Girondin*, 1947.

LICHINE, ALEXIS. *The Wines of France*, revised edition, 1969. *Encyclopaedia of Wines and Spirits*, revised edition, 1975.

LODGE, ELEANOR C. 'The Estates of the Archbishop and Chapters of St. André of Bordeaux under English Rule.' *Oxford Studies in Social and Legal History*, Vol. 3, 1912.

Gascony under English Rule, 1926.

LORBAC, CHARLES. *Les Richesses gastronomiques de la France: Les vins de Bordeaux*, 1867.

LYNCH, BERNADETTE. *Le Comte J.-B. Lynch Maire de Bordeaux, 1809–1815*, 1970.

MALVEZIN, FRANZ. *Histoire de la vigne et du vin en Aquitaine*, 1919.

MALVEZIN, T. *Histoire du commerce de Bordeaux*, 1892.

MALVEZIN, T. AND FÉRET, E. *Le Médoc et ses vins*, 1876.

MICHEL, FRANCISQUE. *Histoire du commerce et de la navigation à Bordeaux*, 1867.

ORDISH, GEORGE. *The Great Wine Blight*, 1972.

PENNING-ROWSELL, EDMUND and SUTTON, DENYS. *The Wine and Art of Mouton-Rothschild*, 1979.

PERRAUX, F. *Prise de vues sur la croissance de l'économie française 1780–1950*, 1950.

PERROUD, RÉGINE. *Eleanor of Aquitaine*. Tr. P. Wiles, 1967.

PIJASSOU, R. *Un Château du Médoc: Palmer*, 1964.

Lafite: trois siècles d'histoire viticole, N.D., (privately circulated).

PLUMB, J. H. *Men and Places*, 1963.

POWICKE, SIR F. M. *King Henry III and the Lord Edward*, 1947.

RAY, CYRIL. *Lafite: The Story of Château Lafite-Rothschild*, revised edition, 1978.

Mouton-Rothschild, 1974.

REDDING, CYRUS. *A History and Description of Modern Wines*, 1833,

RENOUARD, YVES. 'Bordeaux sous les rois d'Angleterre', *Economic History Review*, 1951.

RIBADIEU, HENRI. *L'Histoire des châteaux de la Gironde*, 1856.

Histoire de la conquête de la Guyenne par les Français, 1866.

RIOL, J. L. *Le Vignoble de Gaillac*, 1913.

ROGER, J.-R. *Les Vins de Bordeaux*, 1955 (translated into English, 1960).

SAINTSBURY, GEORGE. *Notes on a Cellar-Book*, 1920.

SALAVERT, JAN. *Le Commerce des vins de Bordeaux*, 1912.

SÉE, HENRI. *Histoire économique de la France: les temps modernes 1789–1914*, 1942.

SHAND, P. MORTON. *A Book of French Wines*, 1928 (revised edition, edited Cyril Ray, 1960; paperback edition, 1964).

SHAW, THOMAS GEORGE. *Wine, the Vine and the Cellar*, 1863.

SICHEL, ALLAN. *The Penguin Book of Wines*, 1965 (Revised, 1971 and 1972).

SIMON, ANDRÉ L. *History of the Wine Trade in England*, 1906–9.
Bottlescrew Days, 1926.
Vintagewise, 1945.

VIALLATE, A. *L'Activité économique en France de la fin du XVIIIe siècle à nos jours*, 1937.

YOUNGER, WILLIAM. *Gods, Men and Wine*, 1966.

General Index and Index of Wine Châteaux

General Index

Académie du Vin (Bordeaux), 628, *and* Appendix F
L'Activité économique en France de la fin du XVIIIe siècle à nos jours (Viallate), 150
d'Adhémar, Count, 118, 231, 318
Aguado family, 123, 319
alcohol, degrees in wine, 43; in 1840s, 535–6; *and see* Appendix A
d'Alesmes family, 103
Allied Breweries, 178, 212
altise (vine pest), 35
America, South, trade with, 161, 168
America, United States of, 185, 201
  economic difficulties with, 140, 153
  estates owned by Americans, *see* Bouscaut, Fourcas-Hosten, Haut-Brion, Malescasse, Le Prieuré, Nairac
  trade with, 138, 161, 175, 178
  vine-stocks from, 30, 34
Analyse chimique des grands vins de la Gironde (Faure), 253
Anglo-French Treaty of Commerce (1860), 144, 149, 151, 261
anthracnose (vine disease), 35
appellation contrôlée: legislation on (1935), 170
  I.N.A.O. regulations on *rendement de base, rendement annuel, P.L.C.* (1974), *see* Appendixes A and B
Arcins (commune), 355–7, 499
  co-operative, 356
d'Armailhacq, A., 20–21, 139, 224, 259–60, 278–9, 509
  family, 277–9
Arsac (commune), 342–3, 499

L'Art de faire, de gouverner et de perfectionner le vin (Chaptal), 43
assemblage, see vinification
Atkinson, Baldwin (firm), 190
d'Aulède, Marquis, 106, 111
Ausonius, 52, 397, 403
Aussel, Dr, 511
Avensan (commune), 355
Avery, Ronald, 222, 237, 406, 542, 551, 570; John, 557
Avery's of Bristol (firm), 408, 428, 433, 548, 560, 613

Baltic countries, exports to, 82, 136–7
Ban de Vendange, 53, 605
barrique bordelaise, 47, 55
Barsac (commune), 481–6, 504
  Office Viticole, 486
Barton family, 122, 192–7, 295–6, 500
Barton, Ronald, 196, 223, 258, 298, 305–6, 383
Barton & Guestier (firm), 122, 178, 192–7, 626
  trade links with England, 241, 267
Bas-Médoc, *see* Médoc
Bass-Charrington Vintners (firm), 178, 183, 217, 328
Bazas (communes), 495
Beaumont family, 251
Bégadan (commune), 363
Belgium, trade with, 161
La Bergerie (firm), 216, 278
Berkmann, Joseph, 549–51, 558, 571
Berland, Pey, Archbishop of Bordeaux, 77–9, 92
Berry Bros. & Rudd (firm), 172, 420, 445, 538, 585
Bert, Pierre, 184

Lawton family and firm, 147–8, 194, 203–4, 211, 239, 337
  see also Tastet & Lawton
Lebègue (firm), 242, 514; London tastings, 622
Lenz-Moser system, 492
Léognan (commune), 384–9, 503
Lesparre, 165, 362
Libourne, 60, 70
  as wine port, 64, 85, 89
  fighting over, 75–90
  merchants in, 204, 216–17, 396
Lichine, Alexis, 327, 341, 424, 520–21; firm, 177–8, 183, 191, 220, 317
liqueurs, distillation for, 63
Listrac (commune), 354–5, 499
Livre tournois (currency), value of, 56n.
Lodge, Eleanor, 72
Loeb, O. W. (firm), 590
London, wine auctions in, *see* Christie's, Restell's, Sotheby's
Longevity of wines, 34, 45, 580–81
Lorbac, Charles, 402, 405, 510
Lormont, early vineyards in, 57
Loubat, Mme, 427–8, 438
Louis, Victor (architect), 17, 122, 319, 447, 453, 465, 477
Loupiac (commune), 456, 486–7, 504
Ludon (commune), 351–2, 499
Lur Saluces family, 105, 461–6, 472, 478, 480, 482, 485
Lurton, Lucien, 326, 333, 482
Lussac (commune), 419
de Luze family and firm, 178, 210–11, 337, 347
Lynch family, 121, 192, 275, 345

Macau (commune), 348–51, 499
maceration, carbonic, 480, 493
madérisation, 392
Mähler-Besse (firm), 214, 339, 411
Malbec grape (Pressac), 20–21, 23
Malet-Roquefort, Comte de, 404, 407–8, 419

Malvezin, Franz, 114, 134, 499
Malvezin, Théophile, 29, 99, 370
Manoncourt, Thiérry, 415–16
Manuel du sommelier (Jullien), 198
marc, 46
Margaux (district), 317–32
Martillac (commune), 389–91
Martin, Henri, 312, 522
Médoc, the, 221–365
  area of vineyards, 32–3, 59, 224–5, *and see* Gironde
  classification of wines, 228, 496–527
  draining of marshes, 98
  expansion of estates, *see* Chapter 5
  grape varieties (*cépages*), 20–22, 24
  height above sea-level, 18
  rendement per hectare, 225–6 *and* Appendix A
  situation and soil, 223–4
Médoc, Bas-, 359–65
Médoc, Haut-, 221–359
Médoc, Fort de, 113, 364
Men and Places (Plumb), 112
Mentzelopoulos, M. and Mme, 320–21
merchants in Bordeaux, Chapter 6
  their modern role, 218
Merchant Wine Tonners of Gascony, 74
Merignac (commune), 81, 366, 503
Merlot grape, 20–23; Merlot-Blanc, 26
Merman (firm), 194, 211–12, 283, 510–11
Mestrezat family and firm, 205–6, 384, 514
Mestrezat-Preller (firm), 206, 273
Methuen Treaty, 132–3
Miailhe, Jean, 355, 358
Miailhe, William-Alain, 268, 339, 345–6
Michel, F., 258
mildew (vine disease), 31–2, 395, 648
millerandage (vine disease), 34, 38
Monprimblanc, 490

St-Lambert (St-Mambert) (commune), 499

St-Laurent (commune), 499

St-Laurent-des-Combes (commune), 419

St-Maixant, Cave-de-Bel-Air, 493-5

St-Michel-de-Fronsac (commune), 444

St-Pey-d'Armens (commune), 419, 504

St-Pierre-du-Mons (commune), 486-7

St-Sauveur (commune), 358

St-Seurin-de-Cadourne (commune), 358, 360

St-Sulpice-de-Faleyrens (commune), 419

St-Sulpice d'Ison, early vineyards in, 58

St-Yzans (commune), 360

Ste-Croix-du-Mont (commune), 456, 486-7, 504

Saintsbury, George, 424, 537, 541-2, 559

Saintsbury Club, 428, 599

Salavert, Jan, 161-2, 164

Saluces, *see* Lur Saluces

Sauternes (commune and village), 459, 471-3

Sauternes (wines), 456-86
  cépages and *rendement*, 456, 466
  classification, 463
  dry Sauternes, 467, 471-2, 480
  high prices, 181, 470
  the picking, 38, 461
  pourriture noble, 459-62
  sales difficulties, 457-8
  Sauternes/German wines compared, 463, 475
  vinification, 49-50, 466

Sauvignon, Petit-Sauvignon, grape, 25, *and see* Chapter 15

Scandinavia, *see* Baltic countries

Schröder & Constams (firm), 184

Schröder & Schÿler (firm), 156, 193, 202-3, 334, 514

Schÿler, Alfred (firm), 203

Schÿler, Guy, 202-3, 239

Scott, Sir Samuel, 142-3, 199, 233, 243, 286, 510, 536

Scott, T. G. D. (Consul), 511, 531

Seager Evans (firm), 329

Seagrams (firm), 178, 300

de Ségur family, 106, 114, 249, 288

de Ségur, Marquis, 110-11, 114, 119, 229, 232, 289, 366, 370

La Seigneurie et le vignoble de Château Latour (ed. Higounet), 13, 128, 155, 160, 247

Sémillon grape, 25, *and see* Chapter 15

Shand, P. Morton, 112, 422

share-cropping system (*agrières*), 102

Sichel family and firm, 183, 213-14, 339, 342, 469, 493

Sichel, Allan, 214, 339; Peter, 214, 340

Simon, André: his oldest bottle, 237; his ninetieth birthday wines, 257, 547
  Bottlescrew Days, 103, 498
  History of the Wine Trade in England, 84, 94-5, 98, 101
  Vintagewise, 149, 386, 428, 529, 537
  see also Chapter 18 for many comments on vintages

Société des Vins de France, 184

soil for wine growing: Graves, 367-8; Médoc, 224; Pomerol, 426-7; Sauternes, 456; St-Émilion, 397

Sotheby's, 429, 580

Soulac (commune), 362

Soussans (commune), 346-8, 499

soutirage (racking), 47

sparkling wine from the Médoc, 303, 345

speculation in wine, *see* investment

spider, red (vine pest), 35

Stay Me with Flagons (Healy), 221-2, 566

sulphur: used against oidium, 27, 34; used to stabilize wine, 368, 390, 392
  see also Bordeaux mixture

Index of Wine Châteaux

In complicated entries, bold type indicates most important references;
vintages years in brackets largely correspond to dated sections in Chapter 18.